ARCHITECTURE
THE WHOLE STORY

General Editor
Denna Jones

Foreword by
**Richard Rogers &
Philip Gumuchdjian**

ARCHITECTURE
THE WHOLE STORY

PRESTEL
Munich • London • New York

◀ Frank Lloyd Wright at a drafting
table at Taliesin East in December
1937, surrounded by members of
the Taliesin Fellowship.

First published in North America in 2014 by Prestel,
a member of Verlagsgruppe Random House GmbH

Prestel Publishing
900 Broadway, Suite 603
New York, NY 10003

Tel.: +1 212 995 2720

Fax: +1 212 995 2733

E-mail: sales@prestel-usa.com

www.prestel.com

© 2014 Quintessence Editions Ltd.

This book was designed and produced by
Quintessence Editions Ltd., London

Project Editor	Elspeth Beidas
Editors	Becky Gee, Fiona Plowman
Designers	Tom Howey, Isabel Eeles
Production Manager	Anna Pauletti
Proofreaders	Sarah Yates, Catherine Hooper
Editorial Director	Jane Laing
Publisher	Mark Fletcher

ISBN 978-3-7913-4915-2

Library of Congress Control Number: 2014937907

Printed in China

CONTENTS

FOREWORD

By 2025, almost 80 per cent of the population will live in urban settlements. The urban environment has now conclusively eclipsed the natural one as mankind's primary home. Given this, we will need to redouble our focus on designing buildings that create spaces in cities that energize, that inspire, that bring us together to interact, to share ideas, and to create just societies in real time and real space. Much recent work has gone into rethinking the city as a socially inclusive and environmentally positive place. Our future architecture will play the pivotal role in that quest for a fairer society and a healthier, more beautiful planet.

Architecture: The Whole Story challenges the reader to wonder about the type of architecture that will emerge from a modern society with broadly pluralistic, democratic, permissive, and environmental objectives. It forces us to consider what kind of buildings our new technologies will stimulate and what will be produced once we fully address the fact that unchecked appetites face triggering an environmental disaster of apocalyptic proportions. If climate change is the product of our activities, buildings and cities included, so buildings and cities must be part of the solution.

The book offers a staggering testament to the intellectual and material achievement of our past. From the earliest emergence of shelter in Mesopotamia to the present day, the book tracks the development of that skill into an art form that communicates the ideals, beliefs, and mores of human societies from ancient to modern. And it has done so while searching out beauty in every variety of form, in every climate, and on every terrain. Architecture from the barn to the palace is the product of our human spirit married to the astonishing mechanical power of the human brain. How quickly that art form became the instrument of religious, political, or economic purpose is unclear—maybe the two emerged together. This book offers as many insights as it provokes further questions.

We are reminded that architecture has been used as the primary tool to underpin the ambitions of the powerful and the visions of our visionaries. Architects have achieved this by creating and reworking symbolic forms and by energizing public spaces to inspire wonder and occasionally rival nature itself. It is architecture's power of promotion that has been sought out by leaders throughout the ages. Architecture is the king maker par excellence and has remained so, unrivalled perhaps until this day.

It is not surprising, therefore, that most of the iconic structures published here are the result of commissions by the few, rather than the expression of the many. Some of our greatest buildings represent the ideals of our most inspired leaders. In some cases, the buildings themselves have been catalysts for positive social change. But just as often, the sophisticated beauty of these structures masks the naked ambition of their patrons. Scratch the surface and the history of "civilized" mankind emerges, warts and all. Great buildings often catalog overstretched empires, cruel religions, dead-end social ambitions, and rampant economies. Architecture celebrates mankind, its humanism and barbarism alike.

But, ironically, the very greatest buildings tend to show longevity and now rub shoulders harmoniously with each other in the formidable living museum that is the modern city. A stadium for gladiators next to a temple for pacifists, a seat of omnipotent power next to an agora of open-minded thinking. Quality architecture has an ability to survive and be transformed by subsequent generations.

Each generation shows a constant willingness to reinterpret, to regroup, to pull itself together and pursue new utopias, new ideals. In this search, we connect to our origins and to our history, find inspiration from all our innovations and all expressions of harmony and beauty.

Architecture is surely one of the most optimistic of art forms. Our networked, pluralistic society will face up to our challenges with as yet unimaginable technologies, buildings, and cities.

RICHARD ROGERS &
PHILIP GUMUCHDJIAN

INTRODUCTION

Invited by David Chipperfield (b.1953), director of the 13th International Architecture Biennale, Venice, to provide an inspirational image for a display at the exhibition, Richard Rogers (b.1933) chose the 14th-century Guinigi Tower in Lucca, Italy. At the top of this square, red-brick and stone building, high above the city, grows a grove of oak trees. Breezes circulate through tall arcades near the summit, accessed by a multistory staircase. Short ladders terminate the climb and launch visitors through a trapdoorlike opening into an urban arcadia where oaks have grown for hundreds of years. Guinigi Tower embodies the familiar Vitruvian commandment to "build well," but it also represents architecture as a reflection of society, and a tool with which to change society. These are qualities that have been captured by each of the buildings featured in *Architecture: The Whole Story*, from the Persian Empire's ancient *qanat* water system to the humane cowsheds that Gion Caminada (b.1957) designed in 1999 in his native Vrin, Switzerland.

Architectural history and formal analysis—the visual structure and character of buildings—are the foundation of *Architecture: The Whole Story*, but they are not "the whole story." This book also attempts to counter a Western parochial bias and demonstrate how architecture has a long history of benefiting from cultural and religious cross-fertilization, such as the Kusheeite temples on the Island of Meroe, Sudan (8th century BC–AD 4th century), which show a heterogeneous mix of Pharaonic, Sahelian African, and Classic Greek and Roman architecture. Well-known buildings are highlighted and discussed

▼ Guinigi Tower (14th century) in Lucca, Italy, was built by the influential Guinigi family. The oak trees at the top were intended to be a symbol of rebirth.

◄ Fallingwater House (1939) was designed by Frank Lloyd Wright for Edgar and Liliane Kaufmann, whose son was studying with Wright at the Taliesin Fellowship. Wright chose to place the house on top of the waterfall in order to create a direct connection between the inhabitants and nature. The sound of breaking water can be heard throughout the house.

throughout, but so too are less familiar structures, such as the "mole-like" Olivetti Residence Hall (1971; see p.440) in Ivrea, Piedmont, Italy, by Roberto Gabetti (1925–2000) and Aimaro Isola (b.1928).

From the Neolithic settlements of hunter-gatherers in the Middle East, which reveal the early development of structured communities, through Neo-Palladianism, once seen as the purest form of architecture in Europe and the United States, to the shift toward digital architecture marked by buildings such as the Guggenheim Museum Bilbao, Spain (1997), by Frank Gehry (b.1929), *Architecture: The Whole Story* chronicles centuries of innovation in the history of architecture. Essays on vernacular buildings—the "good ordinary"—are found in each chapter. The influence of such architecture—not only its typically small scale, but also its reflection of local materials and building techniques—is a common thread throughout the book. Marc-Antoine Laugier's engraving of the "primitive hut" in the second edition of his *Essay on Architecture* (1755) was a major influence on modern architecture's pursuit of the simplicity and pureness represented by small, simple structures. It is an architectural Holy Grail that is still sought after today: the 21st-century mini-house movement in the United States is a product not only of economic downturn, but also of disillusionment with consumption and capitalism and a desire to return to basics. This same desire spurred designer William Morris (1834–96) in the 19th century, motivated Indian architect Laurie Baker (1917–2007) in the 20th century, and is an influence on the rising appreciation in 21st-century China of the values of Confucianism. "Simplify! Simplify!" Henry Thoreau admonished in the 19th century when he built his famed cabin on Walden Pond, Massachusetts.

Frank Lloyd Wright (1867–1959) reinterpreted elements of the vernacular in his masterpiece Fallingwater House in Pennsylvania (1939), which incorporated

▲ The brise soleil on Le Corbusier's Palace of Assembly (1963) in Chandigarh was designed according to his Modulor system of proportion, which was based on the golden ratio.

▼ *Mashrabiya* screens such as this one at the Alhambra (begun 1238) in Granada, Spain, have been used in Islamic architecture for centuries. As well as providing privacy, they also enable cool air to be distributed around the building's interior.

elements of Japanese architecture to create a feeling of harmony between the inhabitants and nature. A similar sense of space was produced in his Usonian houses, such as Pope-Leighey House (1940) in Virginia, which has an open, interconnecting plan, where Wright differentiated between use and meaning via room heights. Low ceilings created a sense of shelter (as did his ubiquitous hearth and fireplace), whereas higher ceilings created the illusion of greater space and of "sky." Antecedents for the careful crafting of space include Blackhouses in Scotland and Norse-era longhouses in Iceland. The latter feature a small, wood-lined "closet bed" tucked to the side of the main open hall, with an interior bolt mechanism to help ensure security.

Le Corbusier (1887–1965)—arguably the 20th century's most influential architect—was not alone in being influenced by the "good ordinary." He may have believed that old buildings were "worn out tackle," but that did not prevent him from being influenced by them. In *Le Corbusier: The Noble Savage* (1999), Adolf Max Vogt postulated Corbusier's debt to Neolithic pile houses on Swiss lakes. He also made the case that 18th- and 19th-century stilt houses, admired by Corbusier as he sailed the Turkish Bosphorus, influenced his pilotis in the "Five Points of a New Architecture." Others cite the influence of North African and South American sunscreens on Corbusier's development of the brise soleil, as used in his Palace of Assembly in Chandigarh, India (1963). The monumental yet human-scale buildings of Louis Kahn (1901–74), such as the Indian Institute of Management, Ahmedabad, Gujarat, India (1974), also contributed to the revival of vernacular traditions. Paul Rudolph (1918–87) furthered this changing attitude in his criticism of Modernism's failure to consider the context of buildings—a result, perhaps, of over-idealization of the isolated hut.

The atavistic desire to "revolve back to a better future," coupled with what architecture critic Martin Pawley described as Modernism's "magnificent mutiny" against Historicism, Revivalism, and (incorrectly) the vernacular, is evidence of Friedrich Nietzsche's "eternal hourglass of existence" rather than a linear, progressive theory of history. The hourglass of vernacular traditions continues to increase in importance in the 21st century. Resiliency is a watchword for 21st-century architecture and signifies a growing concern to design and program buildings to be responsive to natural disasters and custodians of finite natural resources. Resurgent interest in parts of Europe and North America for self-build, timber-frame (post and beam construction) homes may be due in part to ideas of Resiliency and self-sufficiency, but is also reflective of concerns for healthy buildings. In South Korea there is a growing re-evaluation of traditional underfloor-heated, mud-brick and thatched houses as potentially curative for chronic illnesses such as asthma and eczema. The ascendancy of vernacular building traditions—particularly when reassessed by architects such as Gion Caminada—is in inverse proportion to the declining popularity of solutions such as the "Molecular Engineered House (For the Year 2020)" (2003) by John Johansen (1916–2012), in which buildings were intended to be coded and grown from vats of chemicals.

Architecture: The Whole Story represents the resurgence of history and formal analysis of architecture after decades dominated by the primacy of theory. In 2012, The Architectural Review introduced the theory of Integral Architecture. Despite itself introducing a new theory, the editorial acknowledged the detrimental effect on architecture of hijacking architectural theory from literary or philosophical treatises. This practice proliferated throughout the 20th century, giving rise to movements such as Deconstructivism, which influenced Frank Gehry's (b.1929) design for the Walt Disney Concert Hall (2003) in Los Angeles. The editorial concluded by saying that over-reliance on theory "must now be regarded as woefully misguided, as

▼ The fragmented, sail-like form of the Walt Disney Concert Hall (2003) in Los Angeles is a prime example of Deconstructivist architecture. Architect Frank Gehry originally planned to clad the building in stone, but was urged to make the exterior metal after the success of his titanium design for the Guggenheim Museum Bilbao (1997).

► Herman Hertzberger designed Centraal Beheer (1972) in Apeldoorn, the Netherlands, so that the building's occupants "would have the feeling of being part of a working community without being lost in the crowd."

it disconnects architecture from historical, cultural, and experiential reality." Architecture critic Edwin Heathcote is one of many who decry "barely readable academic jargon," in which he probably includes *The Autopoiesis of Architecture* (2010), the generative theory manifesto for computational architecture by Patrik Schumacher (b.1961), director of Zaha Hadid Architects. Schumacher is a proponent of the style known as parametricism, in which digital models use variable factors such as daylight or material costs to decide a building's form. Examples of parametric buildings include the sweeping Heydar Aliyev Center (2012) in Baku, Azerbaijan, by Zaha Hadid (b.1950). However, many of the essays in *Architecture: The Whole Story* offer contrasting views to Schumacher's belief that "only theoretically informed building design constitutes architecture," and his assertion that "architecture advances as a progression of styles."

Although "the whole story" must use images to support the history, *Architecture: The Whole Story* seeks to avoid what Joseph Grima of *Domus* magazine criticized in 2011 as the "nonstop stream of 'pornographic' form-led images of architecture." The "good ordinary" buildings that are featured in this book temper what critic Christopher Hawthorne deems over-reliance on "supremely photogenic" architecture. In 2014, *The Architect's Newspaper* published "A Manifesto from the Architecture Lobby," in which architects declared that they no longer wanted to be known only for design; rather, the media must showcase them as "keepers of sustainable spatial intelligence." It demanded that architects write a letter of protest for "every article in every journal and newspaper discussing only form." Although it is undeniable that the media focuses on form, it is equally true that programming—a building's ability to function well for its users—is not always seen as a priority. This is a result, says Mohsen Mostafavi, dean of Harvard Graduate School of Design, of programming being viewed as non-glamorous work.

However, Centraal Beheer (1972; see p.480) in Apeldoorn, the Netherlands, is an exception. It is a leading example of what can be achieved when architects prioritize what the vessel holds (programming) over the form of the vessel. Rejecting sculptural expression and the primacy of the exterior to focus instead on reciprocity of form and function, the Centraal Beheer office building by Herman Hertzberger (b.1932) became a beloved "city" and "workshop" where employees fulfilled Hertzberger's dream of "a world in which architects make neutral things that inspire the people who use them to do something with them." Archive footage confirms that employees used the building as Hertzberger hoped. It is tempting to wonder if Steve Jobs knew of Hertzberger's

► Zaha Hadid used the fluid form of the Heydar Aliyev Center (2012), Baku, Azerbaijan, to establish a relationship between the building's interior and the surrounding plaza. The shape of the building's curves was inspired by Islamic calligraphy.

◄ Building 20 (1943) at the Massachusetts Institute of Technology was said to have been designed in a single day. It comprised six wings, which were built out of wood due to the scarcity of steel at the time of its construction. The building was adapted frequently by its residents to meet the demands of their research projects.

human-scale workers' village when he lobbied for Apple's headquarters to be designed to encourage serendipitous encounters and casual, rather than mandated, intellectual exchange. Or whether the designers of the "communal environments" and "spaces for social exchange" prioritized in headquarters for social media companies such as Google in London and Weebly in San Francisco realize their debt not only to Centraal Beheer, but also to structures such as Building 20 (1943) at the Massachusetts Institute of Technology.

Built cheaply and quickly during World War II as a low-slung temporary structure, Building 20 was notorious for leaks, poor ventilation, inferior insulation, and cheap materials. But it became well known during its fifty-year life span as a crucible for innovation and one of the most consistently creative spaces in the world, quantifiable by the patents, inventions, theories, and awards accumulated by its residents. Although designed by an architect, Building 20 behaved like a vernacular, adaptable building. As at Centraal Beheer, residents were allowed to treat Building 20 like home. It was laid out on a horizontal plan, referred to by U.S. writer Stewart Brand as a "low road" structure, which unlike narrow, tall towers had more research variety on each floor and thus greater opportunities for the chance encounters that led to creative breakthroughs for its multidisciplinary residents. The Council on Tall Buildings and Urban Habitat reports that the popularity of tall towers among developers is undiminished in the 21st century—particularly in Asia and the Middle East—despite widespread knowledge that low-rise "groundscrapers" are less expensive to build. Low-rise buildings also provide more rentable space because less of their area is taken up by lift shafts and their floor space is not reduced by the tapered form that is often employed in contemporary skyscrapers, such as the Al Hamra Tower (2004) in Kuwait City, Kuwait. Yet, despite growing reappreciation for Hertzberger's Centraal Beheer, the clamor for space in urban centres will mean more, not fewer, skyscrapers.

Architecture: The Whole Story is a prompt to learn more, to visit the buildings discussed in its pages and to discover those that are not, such as St. Petri Church (1966) by Sigurd Lewerentz (1885–1975) in Klippan, Sweden, where water drips from the baptismal font into an irregular hole in the floor. Its dark pool looks limitless, as though a visitor could stand on its edge and dive into eternity. In his Royal Institute of British Architects Gold Medal speech in 2012, Herman Hertzberger called for architects to make the ordinary special. The diverse selections in *Architecture: The Whole Story* highlight the extraordinary and the ordinary, and demonstrate the limitless potentials of architecture.

◄ The Al Hamra Tower (2004) in Kuwait City, Kuwait, was designed by Skidmore, Owings, & Merrill LLP, a company renowned for its glass and steel skyscrapers. The building is among the world's tallest, with a height of 1,354 feet (413 m).

1 | NEOLITHIC—900

NEOLITHIC

1 Carved stone pillar (c.8500 BCE)
  Architect unknown
  Gobekli Tepe, Turkey

2 Remains of a communal store
  (c.9000 BCE)
  Architect unknown
  Dhra', Jordan

3 Reconstructed wooden house
  (5000–4500 BCE)
  Architect unknown
  Hemudu, China

Architectural advances are an important part of the Neolithic period (10,000–2000 BCE), during which some of the major innovations of human history occurred. The domestication of plants and animals, for example, led to both new economies and a new relationship between people and the world, an increase in community size and permanence, a massive development of material culture, and new social and ritual solutions to enable people to live together in these communities. New styles of individual structures and their combination into settlements provided the buildings required for the new lifestyle and economy, and were also an essential element of change.

The earliest and most closely researched expression of the Neolithic took place in the Middle East. The first settlements were composed of structures that differed substantially from earlier shelters constructed by hunter-gatherers. There was a focus on the community rather than individual family or household units, as indicated by the discovery in 2009 of Structure O75 (c.9600 BCE; see p.20) in Wadi Faynan, southern Jordan. As the economy became increasingly dependent on a limited number of harvests and the community wished to stay in one place, secure storage of food between harvests became essential. The produce from the harvests was kept in communal stores, such as those found at Dhra' in Jordan (see image 2), which were often designed with raised floors to minimize damage from pests such as mice. Processing of cereals also grew in importance, and some buildings appear to have been designed primarily for this task, with one or two stone mortars built into the plaster floors at the center of the structures. Some of these workshops were

KEY EVENTS

c.10,000 BCE	c.9600 BCE	c.8500 BCE	c.8000 BCE	7400 BCE	7000 BCE
The earliest identified Neolithic settlements arise in the Middle East out of increasingly sophisticated hunter-gatherer societies.	The rapid development of purpose-made structures includes buildings for communal storage, reflecting agricultural production cycles.	Spectacular carved stone pillars are set into circular structures at Gobekli Tepe in Turkey, probably built during ceremonial gatherings.	Multistory buildings are built as populations grow and settlements become more dense. Basements begin to serve as private storage areas.	Catalhöyük in Turkey grows to be a large but isolated settlement. Good archaeological preservation shows a lifestyle rich in symbolism.	A settlement process starts in China, characterized by the growth of communities there.

built with substantial floors but insubstantial wattle and daub screen walls, with a ring of wooden posts supporting a light roof. Other, more solid roofs appear to have been built with a series of timbers, placed at right angles to one another, that supported brushwood and reeds on which insulating mud layers were placed. In some cases stones appear to have been placed around the edges of the roofs, presumably to stop water run-off eroding the mud.

Other, more dramatic buildings were erected as part of the need to restructure human society to enable habitation in increasingly big groups. A large stone tower was built at Jericho in Palestine (c.9500–8500 BCE), inside the wall that was constructed around part of the settlement and possibly protected it from floods. The tower appears not to have had any defensive function, but as a monumental and highly visible construction served a communal ceremonial role. The site of Gobekli Tepe in Turkey (begun c.8500 BCE) consists of a series of circles of stone pillars, many covered with animal carvings (see image 1). The pillars themselves appear to have represented people. Gobekli Tepe was probably a regional center where groups from different areas came together.

As populations rose and the processes of domestication took hold, there was a shift to greater privacy, growing evidence for the idea of ownership, and a focus on the household. Multiroomed structures appeared, with storage hidden within the houses. Settlements became densely packed, with rectangular architecture replacing circular and elliptical buildings, and multistory buildings became common. Even ritual activities became more private, or at least restricted in who could participate, as the shrines of the later Neolithic were smaller than the large open spaces that preceded them.

Development did not take place at the same time around the world. In some places, such as the Middle East, China, and Mesoamerica, the Neolithic was an entirely local innovation with its own distinctive history. Areas where the Neolithic arrived ready-made from outside, such as Europe, show a very different sequence that begins not with development but replacement. This was followed by local modification that gradually transformed the Neolithic into something adapted to local conditions, such as at Skara Brae in Scotland (3200–2200 BCE; see p.22), where cellular architecture is protected by thick layers of sand and refuse.

Architectural traditions vary enormously. Good preservation produced by waterlogged conditions demonstrates that in some areas wood construction was important. Rapidly accumulating evidence from China shows that sophisticated carpentry techniques were used to build extensive wooden buildings above lakes, such as at Hemudu (see image 3). Similar levels of preservation have been encountered at sites in Switzerland, where buildings were erected on piles over the edge of lakes, and in the Western Isles of Scotland, where artificial islands, or crannogs, were created. From wood, through cobb and mud-brick, back to wood, almost every vernacular architectural technique has a Neolithic origin. **BF**

6500 BCE	5500 BCE	4400 BCE	4000 BCE	c.3000 BCE	c.2500 BCE
Pottery, an important Neolithic technology, is adopted in the Middle East, although it had appeared much earlier in China and Japan.	The Neolithic starts to spread across Western Europe, characterized by settlements of wooden long-houses.	The Neolithic comes to an end in the Middle East as innovations in copperworking commence.	The Neolithic reaches the British Isles, spreading fairly rapidly up to Orkney.	Plants in North America are domesticated, well after the independent appearance of agriculture in Mesoamerica and South America.	The working of bronze becomes established at the end of the European Neolithic.

Structure O75 *c.*9600 BCE
ARCHITECT UNKNOWN

Structure O75,
Wadi Faynan, Jordan

⬥ **NAVIGATOR**

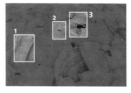

A surprising aspect of the architecture in the earliest Neolithic settlements is the presence of community structures. In southern Jordan, a small site called WF16 has provided a very early example. An elliptical structure named O75 is composed of a large central mud-plastered area bordered by benches. The building technique is similar to the way in which the other structures on site were made, regardless of their size or function. A pit was excavated into the underlying deposits made up of the remains of older buildings and refuse. A stone foundation was laid around the vertical faces of the pit, and a wet mud mixture was used to build the walls lining the face. This mud was mixed with a plant temper made of chaff, possibly from the wild barley that had recently begun to be cultivated. Some collapsed sections suggest that parts of walls above ground were built around a core of sun-dried mud bricks. In contrast to the idea that early architecture is largely about shelter from the elements, this structure served an important public role, possibly bringing together a community for tasks that required combined labor, such as the harvest. It also represents a substantial project in terms of construction and maintenance. **BF**

1 BENCHES

The central space is bordered by two tiers of benches, each about 3 feet (1 m) deep and 1½ feet (0.5 m) high, well preserved on one side and badly eroded on the other. Their form suggests that they provided a place for people to watch the activity being performed in the central area.

2 CHANNELS

The herringbone pattern of channels looks as if it should drain liquid to the center. However, the curvature would not have allowed the channels to act as drains. They all have holes where wooden posts have been removed, and it seems likely that they divided the floor space.

3 GRINDING STONES

The presence of two symmetrically placed grinding stones, embedded in slightly raised platforms at one end of the structure, suggests that food processing was the focus of the public activity. The harvest of new cereal crops would have been an important occasion in the community.

▲ The faces of some of the benches are decorated with a pattern of lines. The mud plaster is neither hard-wearing nor weather-proof, and these faces have been repeatedly replastered, suggesting regular maintenance.

NEOLITHIC RITUAL

Archaeologists often categorize buildings as either ritual or domestic. Such a division is inappropriate in the early Neolithic, when it is unlikely that people divided the world in such a manner and when many buildings incorporated ritual space, frequently in the form of underfloor burials that were later reopened for modification (such as skull removal). At the same time that lime plaster was introduced as a construction material for floors, it was also used to create plaster faces on skulls for display (right). The incorporation of items such as pairs of horns within walls, and their repeated replastering, suggests that the building process itself was often imbued with meaning and ritual.

Skara Brae 3200–2200 BCE
ARCHITECT UNKNOWN

Skara Brae,
Mainland, Orkney,
Scotland

⚙ NAVIGATOR

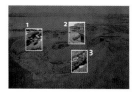

Skara Brae, on the west coast of the Scottish island Mainland, Orkney, represents a settlement lying at the extreme edge of the spread of the Neolithic from the Middle East across Europe. By the time the Neolithic had become established in Orkney, it had already ended in the Middle East. The village settlement at Skara Brae was well adapted to its local environment and building conditions. This tradition of Neolithic architecture is distinctively Orcadian, and similar sites have been found near to Skara Brae, including settlements at Barnshouse village and at the Ness of Brodgar. Association with the nearby stone circle of the Ring of Brodgar, the standing stones at Stenness, and the impressive burial mound of Maes Howe, with its corbeled ceiling, is linked to an increasing appreciation that some of the buildings in the settlements may have had ritual functions. For example, Structure 8 at Barnshouse has an entrance that is aligned with midsummer sunrise, and there is a massive, apparently symbolic, wall that isolates the Ness of Brodgar site on its peninsula. These suggest that the settlement was constructed within an extraordinary built landscape, highly charged with symbolic meaning. **BF**

1 FLOOR COMPARTMENTS

Full advantage was taken of the local sandstone to create internal floor compartments. It was also used to construct beds, dressers, hearths, a drainage system below the floors, and stone boxes, which may have been used to store bait for fishing.

2 CELLULAR STRUCTURE

The buildings at Skara Brae are clustered together like cells, insulated by thick layers of material full of refuse. The soft piles of waste and sand would have been easy to dig in, and placing structures within this would have made them stronger and more sheltered.

3 CORRIDORS

Although the site is made up of a series of well-defined separate cellular structures, these are all interlinked by covered corridors. This connectivity suggests a tightly linked community, and one with a low requirement for privacy.

◄ The most striking internal features are the impressive dressers. These are thought to have displayed some of the well-made material goods present on the site and also to have provided storage space.

NEOLITHIC STYLES

The amazing levels of preservation at Skara Brae result from a lucky combination of the circumstances of burial and the use of the local flat stone slabs. Inevitably, such well-preserved sites have become iconic representations, when in reality they may have been exceptional. Architectural styles varied widely through the Neolithic in Scotland—patterns of post holes in the ground suggest long timber houses in the east (right), while in the Hebrides there were timber sub-rectangular houses—yet none is as well known as the Skara Brae architecture. The interior structures at Skara Brae, the dressers and beds, look just like stone versions of wooden objects, but whether similar furniture was made of wood elsewhere is unknown.

ANCIENT EGYPT

Modern imaginings of ancient Egypt are heavily influenced by the surviving traces of monumental architecture. Many formal styles and motifs were established at the dawn of the pharaonic state, around 3100 BCE. The inspiration for many of these styles lay in the organic elements used in early buildings made from perishable materials. While the original structures are almost totally unknown, stylized motifs of plants continued to be replicated and adapted well into the Roman period. The endurance of forms over such a long period means that pharaonic architecture is easily recognizable today, and has been widely imitated by architects in modern times.

An important material in Egyptian architecture is the humble brick, made from unfired Nile mud. Mud bricks were used in construction throughout the pharaonic period, but were employed on a vast scale during the Early Dynastic period (c.3100–2600 BCE). Large funerary enclosures of this period display a niched "palace facade" design probably derived from neighboring Mesopotamia, where the large-scale building of cities was already well established. Yet, the Egyptians manipulated mud-brick architecture to create their own distinctive styles, and even the term "adobe" derives from the ancient Egyptian word *djebet*, meaning "brick."

The dominance of stone in Egypt arrived with the Step Pyramid complex of King Djoser at Saqqara (2667–2648 BCE), which heralded the beginning of

KEY EVENTS

2667–2648 BCE	c.2589–2566 BCE	2375–2345 BCE	2055–2004 BCE	1870 BCE	c.1473–1458 BCE
The Step Pyramid of King Djoser at Saqqara (see p.28) signals the beginning of major stone architecture worldwide.	King Khufu builds the Great Pyramid of Giza—Egypt's largest pyramid, and the last surviving wonder of the ancient world.	The Pyramid of King Unas at Saqqara is the first to contain extensive hieroglyphic inscriptions.	King Mentuhotep II builds an innovative terraced temple-tomb at Deir el-Bahri.	King Senwosret II is the first to build a pyramid constructed from unfired mud brick at Lahun.	The graceful terraced Temple of Queen Hatshepsut is built at Deir el-Bahri.

the Old Kingdom or "Pyramid Age" (c.2686–2125 BCE). The first smooth-sided pyramid was built by King Sneferu, who ruled from c.2613 to 2589 BCE. This was an important leap toward an abstract geometrical shape—perhaps representing the mound of creation—as opposed to an obviously organic form. Huge amounts of limestone were extracted from quarries relatively close to the sites of the pyramids. Granite from Aswan, more than 373 miles (600 km) to the south, was often used to line burial chambers. One of Sneferu's pyramids is one of the few identifiable architectural failures from ancient Egypt—the so-called "Bent Pyramid." Structural problems necessitated a reduction in the angle of the slope, creating a bent appearance.

Sneferu's son Khufu reigned from 2589 to 2566 BCE and built the Great Pyramid of Giza (see image 1), the last surviving wonder of the ancient world. At 456 feet (139 m) tall, it is the largest pyramid in Egypt. The most spectacular internal feature is the high corbeled Grand Gallery (see image 2). As with non-royal tombs of this period, the style is spare, almost minimalist, and with an absence of text and image inside, the religious function of the architecture is not made explicit. After the Fourth Dynasty (Old Kingdom), a shift in priorities occurred. There was a sharp decrease in the size of pyramids, and an increase in the scale and decoration of surrounding temples. This coincided with the first appearance of extensive hieroglyphic inscriptions inside the pyramids during the Fifth and Sixth Dynasties (both Old Kingdom), which may reflect a change in the religious interpretation of the royal afterlife.

By the end of the Old Kingdom, the cavetto cornice (concave molding) had been introduced. This decorative element would go on to accentuate the top of almost every formal pharaonic building. Also at this time, those who might be recognized as architects—Overseers of the King's Works—tended to be members of the royal family. No formal plans or pattern books survive, and the question of exactly how the pyramids were built continues to provoke debate.

The scale and ambition of royal tombs depended on political circumstances. At times of decentralized government, such as during the First Intermediate Period (c.2160–2055 BCE), provincial governors appropriated and adapted styles in royal funerary architecture. For instance, King Mentuhotep II, who began his reign in c.2055 BCE, built his innovative temple-tomb at Deir el-Bahri as a terraced edifice with veranda-style walkways. The pyramidal tomb reappeared later in the Middle Kingdom (c.2055–1650 BCE), although the pyramids were often built of limestone-clad mud brick rather than solid stone.

By the New Kingdom (c.1550–1069 BCE), security concerns led to a separation between a temple for the celebration of the king's memory and a hidden, subterranean tomb. Thus, the Valley of the Kings (with a naturally pyramid-shaped mountain above it) became the royal cemetery with deep, elaborately decorated passageways leading to a pillared burial chamber. A special settlement, now known as Deir el-Medina, was created in the desert

1 **Great Pyramid of Giza (c.2589–2566 BCE)**
Hemiunu
El Giza, Egypt

2 **Grand Gallery (c.2589–2566 BCE)**
Hemiunu
El Giza, Egypt

1390–1352 BCE	1279–1213 BCE	c.1184–1153 BCE	700 BCE	380–342 BCE	332–30 BCE
The architect Amenhotep, son of Hapu, becomes one of the few ordinary people to be worshipped at his own palace.	The rock-cut temples of Abu Simbel are inaugurated for the worship of King Ramesses II and Queen Nefertari.	The innovative Syrian-inspired "Migdol" gate is built by Ramesses III at his memorial temple, Medinet Habu.	High official Petamenope commissions the largest Egyptian non-royal tomb at the Assasif in western Thebes.	The last native pharaohs, Nectanebo I and II, undertake a major temple-building program in the Nile Delta.	Macedonian Ptolemaic kings sponsor extensive religious constructions throughout the Nile Valley.

near the valley to house the workers and artisans who built the tombs. Later, royal sepulchres are less well known, but tended to be more modest in size and were located within temple enclosures to protect the rich burial goods inside.

While monumental royal tombs varied in scale, temple architecture seems to have consistently gained in scale and ambition with time. Religious structures of the Predynastic period (5500–3100 BCE) and Old Kingdom appear to have been made of perishable materials. During the Middle Kingdom, there was a "petrification" of temples, which saw most religious structures rendered in stone. A standard temple plan was fully developed by the New Kingdom. The basic function of an Egyptian temple was to act as the dwelling place of the god. The temple represented a "cosmos" in stone, a copy of the original mound of creation on which the god could rejuvenate himself and the world. It was fronted by a massive twin gateway (pylon), such as that at Karnak (see image 4), symbolizing the hills of the horizon, and had columned halls symbolizing a primeval papyrus thicket. From the entrance courtyard through a series of hallways of decreasing size, the floor level rose steadily and ceiling heights became lower until the sanctuary was reached, where the god's cult statue was kept. Carved wall scenes emphasize the ritual maintenance of the universe by the king. Chaotic elements were kept safely outside, with scenes of battle restricted to exterior walls. Many later temples were fortified with undulating brick enclosure walls that were both defensive and represented the waves of the primordial ocean from which the island of creation (the temple) emerged.

The temple complex of Karnak is one of the largest religious sites in the world and best illustrates the desire of successive kings to expand structures with the addition of courtyards, shrines, statuary, and obelisks. Reuse of older building material was common, and many structures deliberately evoked or included elements of much older features. Kings who built extensively—and whose buildings survive—thus dominate the historical record. King Seti I and his son Ramesses II, who reigned consecutively from c.1294 to 1213 BCE, were responsible for the Hypostyle Hall (see image 3), which covers 59,201 square feet (5,500 sq m) and is the largest of its kind in Egyptian architecture. The hall roof rests on 124 columns, each in the shape of a stylized papyrus stalk, up to 69 feet (21 m) in height, with a raised nave and light provided by clerestory windows. Smaller hypostyle halls were common in temples from the New

Kingdom onward. All temples would have been brightly painted, and texts survive describing fixtures and fittings of precious metals and inlays.

A notable experiment in sacred architecture is the crenellated Migdol gate of Ramesses III, ruler from c.1184 to 1153 BCE, at his memorial temple at Medinet Habu; the gate imitates Syrian fortified towers encountered by the Egyptians on military campaigns. Other innovations combined traditional motifs. One of the most graceful is the memorial temple of the female pharaoh Hatshepsut (c.1473–1458 BCE) at Deir el-Bahri. The temple rises in elegant terraces, rather than successive courtyards, fronted by colonnades—likely inspired by the much earlier temple of Mentuhotep II nearby. Hatshepsut's colonnades, like those of other temples, integrate sculptures of the pharaoh against pillars (see image 5), although the statues themselves are not load-bearing, like Greek caryatids. In comparison to this temple's elegant proportions, later Ramesside memorial temples adopt a more Baroque style (see p.222), with columns and engaged statues of a more squat appearance.

A surge in temple building occurred with the last native Egyptian pharaohs, Nectanebo I and II, who ruled successively from 380 to 342 BCE. Despite being made of granite and basalt, those temples built in the delta to the north have been almost entirely destroyed. Ptolemaic and Roman temples in the Nile Valley, such as Philae Temple (380 BCE–CE 117; see p.30), are much better preserved. They continued to employ traditional pharaonic components, with subtle embellishments such as an increased range of column capital designs. Religious architecture had a strong political dimension, with the aim of presenting a non-Egyptian ruler as maintaining divine order in time-honored pharaonic fashion. Many of the earlier motifs are preserved only in these Graeco-Roman versions and these in turn have inspired modern, Egyptianizing designs.

While monumental structures loom large in our impression of ancient Egypt, domestic architecture survives in only the rarest circumstances. Exceptions include workers' settlements located on the desert edge that were abandoned rather than destroyed or built on. Tomb scenes and three-dimensional funerary models give some idea of the upper stories of homes of the elite (see image 6). More is known about palaces, which were, in general, built of mud brick. Notable preserved examples include the palace built for the jubilee celebrations of Amenhotep III (c.1390–1352 BCE) at Malkata, Thebes, which included an artificial lake and a stage for rituals. Surviving paint shows how vibrant the interiors must have been. **CP**

3 **Hypostyle Hall** (*c.*1294–1213 BCE)
Architect unknown
Karnak Temple Complex, Luxor, Egypt

4 **Khonsu Temple Pylon** (*c.*1184–1153 BCE)
Architect unknown
Karnak Temple Complex, Luxor, Egypt

5 **Temple of Hatshepsut** (*c.*1473–1458 BCE)
Architect unknown
Deir el-Bahri, Egypt

6 **Funerary model of a house** (*c.*1900 BCE)
Egypt

Step Pyramid 2667–2648 BCE
IMHOTEP c.2650–2600 BCE

Step Pyramid,
Saqqara, Egypt

❖ NAVIGATOR

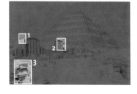

The Step Pyramid at Saqqara has a good claim to be the first monumental stone building ever constructed. Built as a tomb for King Djoser of the Third Dynasty (c.2667–2648 BCE), it was conceived as a single flat *mastaba* (eternal house) structure. Six such structures were layered one on top of another to reach the impressive height of 196⅞ feet (60 m). A large vertical shaft under the pyramid leads to a granite-lined, subterranean burial chamber. A warren of tunnels leads to other burial apartments, including an underground "palace." The pyramid itself is surrounded by a complex of other structures and courtyards. Religious buildings that had been made out of perishable materials were rendered for the first time in limestone, their organic details designed to last for eternity. Thirty chapels of at least three different types reflect varying local traditions. All are of solid masonry and could only be entered by the king's spirit after death. Later non-royal tombs (c.750–100 BCE) in the area imitate the arrangement of a paneled enclosure and deep burial shaft, the latter being a key security feature. Most of the standing structures, including the one gateway to the complex, are actually modern reconstructions by French architect Jean-Philippe Lauer (1902–2001). **CP**

◉ FOCAL POINTS

1 TORUS MOLDING

Djoser's complex includes the first preserved instance of this typical pharaonic motif. Torus molding most likely originated in the corner posts of early structures built of brick or matting. In later structures, it is often paired with a cavetto cornice, probably representing a stylized frieze of palm fronds.

2 ENGAGED COLUMNS

Several forms of engaged columns feature in Djoser's complex, before three-dimensional versions became functional, load-bearing elements in architecture. Djoser's elegant examples imitate stylized papyrus stalks and the original bundles of reeds that would once have supported roofs of structures.

3 ENCLOSURE WALL

The entire Step Pyramid complex is surrounded by a 908¾ x 1,784¾ foot (277 x 544 m) rectangular enclosure wall, with one true gate and fourteen false ones. A recessed niche design (imitating the elaborately decorated facade of the royal palace) was carved into previously laid courses of stone.

◄ The underground burial apartments of the pyramid complex were covered with vibrant blue-green faience tiles, in imitation of bundles of reed matting.

IMHOTEP

The innovative Step Pyramid complex at Saqqara is more closely associated with one creative talent than any other building from ancient Egypt. That genius was a man called Imhotep (right), who is the first recognized architect and engineer in history. Very little is known about him from contemporary sources, but the chance find of a statue base belonging to his master, King Djoser, records Imhotep's titles as "high priest," "sculptor," and "carpenter"—terms that qualify him well as the mastermind behind Djoser's complex. However, graffiti written more than a millennium after the Step Pyramid was built records the wonder of passing visitors to the monument, and credit King Djoser (rather than his well-known architect) as the "opener of stone." Some sources cite Imhotep as being the first to use columns to support the structure of a building. Centuries after his death, Imhotep (whose name means "the one who comes in peace, is with peace") was still revered, before being deified as the god of healing and wisdom in the first millennium BCE. He was worshipped throughout Egypt into the Roman period as the son of the god of craftsmen, Ptah, born to a human mother named Khereduankh.

Philae Temple 380 BCE – CE 117
PTOLEMAIC KINGS AND ROMAN EMPERORS

Philae Temple, Agilkia Island,
Lake Nasser, Aswan, Egypt

NAVIGATOR

The temple complex of Philae is among the best preserved from ancient Egypt. The main structures are dedicated to the worship of the goddess Isis, and were embellished and enlarged by several Ptolemaic kings and Roman emperors between c.380 BCE and CE 128. Expansions had to take account of the island's limited space, resulting in a more irregular layout than is seen in other temple complexes. Standard elements, such as the forecourt, pronaos (inner area of the portico), and hypostyle hall, were reoriented, the light proportions of the hall's columns suggesting Hellenistic influence. What can be seen today is a mixture of styles and influences. The temple's main features are classically Egyptian: fronted by pylon gateways and decorated with traditional scenes of the pharaoh. Philae boasts perhaps the most beautiful "birth house" in Egypt, dating to the reign of Ptolemy VIII (170 to 116 BCE). The columned structure may be intended to evoke papyrus thicket, in which Isis supposedly reared her son, Horus, hidden from his evil uncle, Seth. As is typical in Greco-Roman temple architecture, intercolumnar walls provide decorative space and screen the rituals inside from view. Philae's most iconic structure is Trajan's Kiosk; called "Pharaoh's bed," it was the entrance to the island from the river. With its picturesque ruins and traces of wall paint, Philae contributed greatly to the romantic image of Egypt in the Western imagination. **CP**

1 WINGED DISK

The sun disk with feathered wings represents a form of the falcon god Horus, son of Isis, triumphant over his enemies. The image was also a common protective device over temple entrances. Winged disks are a popular motif in modern Egyptianizing architecture.

2 PYLON GATEWAY

Two massive towers, flanking a central gateway, form a stylized representation of the horizon. Philae is one of the few temples in Egypt to preserve both pylons to their full height. Recesses in the facade would have held tall wooden flag staffs to fly colorful pennants.

3 EASTERN COLONNADE

This Roman addition to the approach to the Temple of Isis has sixteen columns, each with a different capital design. This abandons the pharaonic preference for regular patterns and symmetry. Some capitals are unfinished, showing the stages before final carving.

◀ The temple complex of Philae was moved to higher ground, on neighboring Agilkia Island, in the 1960s. This was to avoid flooding by the waters of Lake Nasser caused by the construction of the Aswan High Dam.

EGYPTIAN REVIVAL

Ancient Egyptian architecture continues to exert a hold over popular imagination. Revivals in the 19th and 20th centuries often led to corrupted pastiches, but a uniquely original modernist concrete complex, centered on a grand Egyptian-style slanted pylon, was built in Valinhos, Brazil, between 1929 and 1938. The Fazenda Capuava (right) was designed and built by Flávio De Carvalho (1899–1973). Trained as a civil engineer and employed as a concrete engineer, De Carvalho evolved into a multidisciplinary artist and theatrical personality, which may explain his choice of an Egyptian pylon—a monumental gateway— as the focal point of his complex. In an adaptation of the original Egyptian design, De Carvalho built two verandas on either side of the central room that spread like the wings of the Egyptian falcon god Horus from the main pylon body.

ANCIENT GREECE

1 **Temple of Segesta (fifth century BCE)**
Architect unknown
Calatafimi-Segesta, Trapani province,
Sicily, Italy

2 **Porch of the Maidens at Erechtheum**
(421–405 BCE)
Architect unknown
Athens, Greece

3 **Plan of a peripteral temple**

From the tenth century BCE, monumental structures rarely seen since the corbeled vaults of tholos (dome-shaped) tombs, palaces, and megalithic fortifications of the Bronze Age began to re-emerge. Early structures, such as the vast apsidal hall at Lefkandi on the island of Euboea, sought monumentality through sheer length. Surrounded by a colonnade of wooden posts supporting a thatched roof, the hall was of uncertain function; however, it was seen as the source of Greek peripteral temple design, which features a single row of columns on each side (see image 3). In the seventh century BCE, the introduction of cut stone—worked with chisels, perhaps under Egyptian influence—and tiled roofs transformed architecture. Around 630 BCE, figural decoration brought a dazzling polychromy to Archaic temples: painted wooden panels on walls and sculpted terracotta images on the upper part of the building (entablature) and roofs communicated heroic genealogies. In the sixth century BCE, stone cornices were painted with red and blue palmettes. The contemplation of this spectacle of temple images was as much part of the ritual of the early Greek sanctuary as the processions, sacrifices, games, and dress.

The Doric order (see image 5) was established by the first quarter of the sixth century BCE. All recognizable elements, such as fluted columns, Doric capitals, triglyph and metope frieze, cornices with projecting blocks (mutules) on the underside of eaves, and sculpted pediments, are present in the Temple of Artemis at Corfu (c.580 BCE), which presents the familiar *opisthodomos* (rear false porch) and a *cella* (inner area) roofed on two rows of columns.

KEY EVENTS

c.580 BCE	c.550 BCE	480 BCE	447 BCE	429 BCE	405 BCE
A long-distance aqueduct is built to supply fresh water to Samos. It includes a mountain tunnel designed by Eupalinus of Megara.	Croesus, the last king of Lydia, dedicates the columns in the third Temple of Artemis at Ephesus.	Xerxes I, king of Persia, leads his troops in the sack of Athens, in which many buildings of the Agora are destroyed.	Construction of the Temple of Athena Parthenos, or Parthenon, begins. The structure is intended to show the wealth and power of Athens.	The "age of Pericles" comes to an end when the great statesman, orator, and general of Athens dies from the plague.	The Erechtheum in Athens is completed. The caryatids on the southern portico are one of its most striking features.

The largest projects, however, were in Asia Minor and the Greek colonies of southern Italy and Sicily. The huge Doric structures begun at the end of the sixth century BCE at Selinus and Acragas, Sicily, were never roofed satisfactorily and were left incomplete. It was there, too, that relationships in ground plan and elevation were developed through experiments with geometry.

The Ionic order (see image 5) seen at Didyma, Ionia, and the Greek island of Samos differed sharply from the Doric structures in southern Italy. Doric temples are low, ship-like structures almost sculpted into the landscape, their *cella* walls ringed by a single *peripteros*, whereas Ionic temples are higher, spacious structures, in which the *cella* is surrounded by a forest of columns. Ionic columns and entablature present a greater depth of architectural ornament: column drums at the third Temple of Artemis at Ephesus (*c.*550 BCE), sculpted with figures in relief, probably stood just below the capital, rather than at the base, and the entablature moldings consisted of abstract forms painted for greater visibility. In the western Greek colonies, these elements were also inserted into the Doric order: at Poseidonia (Paestum), the floral ornament on the neck of Doric capitals of the first Temple of Hera (*c.*550–520 BCE; see p.36) was followed by the Ionic-like division of the entablature in the Temple of Athena (sixth century BC). Columns were sometimes replaced by anthropomorphic images, telamons (male figures) or caryatids (female figures; see image 2).

From the second quarter of the fifth century BCE, standardization was evident in mainland Greece and the West. Many Doric temples were designed according to modular principles, based on the width of the triglyph as a determinant of the width of the bays between columns; accordingly, the design of the Doric temple was driven by the facade instead of the plan. At the unfinished Temple of Segesta in Sicily (see image 1), the design process can be reconstructed: the lifting bosses were left on the blocks of the *peripteros*, but the foundations of the *cella* walls had not yet been laid, thereby suggesting that it was normal practice to build the *peripteros* before the *cella*, although several examples suggest the reverse procedure. Modular design also encouraged refinements, such as curvature of the stylobate (continuous base that supports the columns), to prevent the appearance of sagging; entasis or swelling of the profile of columns; and tapering or inclination of columns and entablatures. These refinements reached their apogee at the Acropolis, Athens, in the Temple of Athena Parthenos (447 BCE) and the Propylaea (437–432 BCE; see p.38), where the adjustments are extremely minimal yet contribute to the impact of the architectural setting. In both buildings, the refined modular Doric was combined with an Ionic order. The smaller Temple of Athena Nike overlooked the new entrance to the Acropolis on a bastion of the older fortification. It was rebuilt in *c.*424 BCE as an amphiprostyle temple, a form that has a portico at each end. The style occurs several times in Athens around this time and also fifty years later at the Phoenician Sanctuary of Eshmun in Sidon.

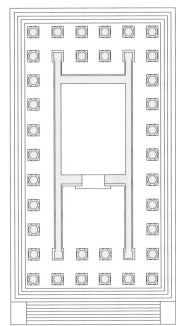

c.380 BCE	c.357 BCE	c.353 BCE	323 BCE	c.300–100 BCE	c.170 BCE
Architect Theodoros of Phocaea writes his treatise on the Doric tholos at Delphi. The monument was the only peripteral tholos of its time.	A series of colonnaded courts containing altars and temples and offering far-reaching views of the sea is built at the Sanctuary of Asclepius at Cos.	Mausolus, Persian satrap of Caria, dies. He is best known for his tomb, the Mausoleum (353–351 BCE), one of the seven wonders of the world.	The death of Alexander the Great marks the beginning of the Hellenistic kingdoms in southwest Asia and northeast Africa.	The Theater of Epidaurus (see p.40) is built. The design of the auditorium is renowned for its excellent acoustics.	Work begins on the frieze at the Altar of Pergamon. The classicizing sculptures of Telephos contrast with the flamboyance of the exterior decoration.

The final part of this project, the Erechtheum, reorganized the site of the old Temple of Athena, resolving the uneven terrain through three separate porches on different levels. The best known, the Porch of the Maidens, saw its caryatids successively copied at the Forum of Augustus in Rome, at Hadrian's Villa in Tivoli and, centuries later, in twin versions at the church of St. Pancras in London (1819–22; see p.282). Even more influential was the anthemion frieze of alternating palmette and lotus, replicated in Augustus's Forum and subsequently a ubiquitous emblem of the Greek Revival (see p.280).

The architect of the Parthenon, Ictinus, also designed the more elongated Temple of Apollo Epikourios at Bassae (c.420 BCE). The interior was ringed by three-quarter columns and, opposite the entrance, there was a single column with a Corinthian capital (see image 5), which supported two mythological friezes. This new order, more embellished than Doric or Ionic with a double volute and acanthus leaves, developed in Athens, where it supported Phidias's statue of Athena Parthenos (438 BCE) in the Parthenon. During the fourth century BCE, the order decorated the interiors of the Temple of Athena Alea and the tholos at Epidaurus as a particularly sacred form, but found no exterior use before the Lysicrates Monument, where it was built into the blind walls of the tholos and supported a Dionysiac frieze. The decorated monumental simplicity of this design, roofed by rounded tiles diminishing in size toward the conical summit, crowned by a finial, was reproduced during the Greek Revival, seen in the open colonnade on Edinburgh's Calton Hill (1830–31) and the crowning of St. John's Church in Chichester, West Sussex (1812).

From the fourth century BCE, the Ionic order was the dominant mode of monumental temple design. The Temple of Athena Polias at Priene (see image 4) was, with a highly decorative entablature and cornice, the product of a geometrical scheme by the architect Pytheos: its six-by-eleven *peripteros* was established in plan by a grid of squares with sides of 12 Attic feet. To this plan, the architect Hermogenes added a high substructure and deep frontal stair in the Temple of Dionysus at Teos (second century BCE). His Temple of Artemis at Magnesia (c.150–130 BCE) was more original. Its eight frontal columns by fifteen along the flanks provided a spacious peristasis (porch or hall). Facing west like other Artemis temples, the front pediment was pierced by three rectangular openings intended for the appearance of cult statues on festivals, and through the main door the gilded statue of the *cella* was illuminated at the full moon. Hermogenes also prescribed a set of proportional relationships for temple intercolumniations, which formalized aesthetic awareness of the height and spacing of temple porticoes.

Greek architectural accomplishments were not confined to temple architecture. In mainland Greece, civic architecture is little attested before the late sixth century BCE, and only then in buildings of rudimentary design. Yet, some parts of the Greek world saw precocious innovation. At the Greek colony of Metapontum in southeast Italy, the second phase of the monumental building northeast of the agora (public space for meetings, etc.), dateable to the middle of the sixth century BCE, consisted of two banks of seats on either side of a rectangular space forming all together an almost perfectly circular assembly building (*ekklesiasterion*). This conception provides an architectural correlate of early philosophical thinking about the disc-shaped cosmos.

No less evocative, tholos structures grounded in earth had held associations with the underworld since the Mycenaean period (c.1600–1100 BCE). The tholos of the Sanctuary of Athena Pronaia at Delphi (see image 6) is thought to have been connected with chthonic (underworld) cults. Probably designed by architect Theodoros of Phocaea, its raised floor rested on a three-stepped podium and supported an outer ring of twenty Doric columns, a circular *cella* wall and an inner ring of ten Corinthian columns standing on a

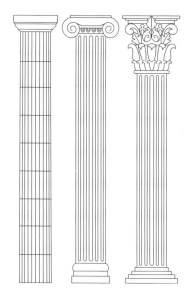

bench-like socle of black limestone. The *cella* was paved with slabs of the same stone, apart from a circle of sparkling white Pentelic marble in the center, which contributed to a multicolored effect. The tholos of the Sanctuary of Asclepius at Epidaurus (third century BCE) had twenty-six outer Doric and fourteen inner Corinthian columns as well as a pavement of alternate black and white limestone diamond-shaped stones around a central opening to a sacred pit.

The tholos form was adapted for memorial structures of the Macedonian kings in the Philippeum at Olympia (*c.*339–300 BCE) and Arsinoeum at Samothrace (288–250 BCE). At the latter site, the Propylon of Ptolemy II (*c.*282 BCE), built over a tunnel that is one of the earliest examples of vaulted stone architecture, gave the Corinthian capital a new structural use in the facade. An inscription in squared lettering was displayed on the architrave; previously, such dedications had been placed low down on the stylobate. The sacred aspect of Corinthian architecture was suggested by a common hierarchical use of the orders in Hellenistic architecture. In the *temenos* (sacred enclosure) of the ruler cult at Pergamon, for example, a Doric courtyard led through an Ionic colonnade to a Corinthian shrine. Even more influential on later architecture was the stoa form. Although this simple open portico, with a single row of supports to hold a wooden truss roof and a rear wall, had a long history of use along the edges of sanctuaries and civic spaces since the Archaic period (650–480 BCE), its potential as an interior space was realized in the long Stoa of Attalus at Athens (see image 7), reconstructed in the twentieth century. This spacious construction also extended the potential for monumental inscriptions, now in larger letters across the architrave.

Monumental Greek architecture was predominantly based upon squared stone construction, perfected through techniques such as dressing the edges of the stone's outer face and anathyrosis on the sides of blocks to enable them to fit closely together. However, the common assumption that mortar was not used until the Roman period (146 BCE–CE 330) is incorrect. Although mortars were not used in Greek architecture for bonding squared stone masonry, where instead iron clamps were employed, they found an application as rendering on interior surfaces. In hydraulic structures, water-resistant mortars made from lime, sand, and volcanic materials were used from the Archaic period to coat cisterns and, later, to bond walls in harbor structures. Mortars were even used to bond walls of rubble in houses from the early Hellenistic period (323–30 BCE). **EVT**

4 **Temple of Athena Polias (fourth century BCE)**
Pytheos
Priene, Aydin province, Turkey

5 **Left to right: Doric, Ionic, and Corinthian orders**

6 **Tholos of the Sanctuary of Athena Pronaia (380–360 BCE)**
Theodoros of Phocaea
Delphi, Greece

7 **Stoa of Attalus (*c.*150 BCE)**
Architect unknown
Athens, Greece

Temples of Hera c.550–c.460 BCE
ARCHITECT UNKNOWN

Temple of Hera I,
Paestum, Italy

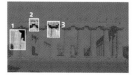
NAVIGATOR

T
wo adjacent limestone temples dedicated to the goddess Hera face east at the southern end of the Greek colony of Poseidonia (Paestum). The more southerly was built in c.550 to 520 BCE. Although some of its decorative forms are similar to those of temples in mainland Greece, it was not a derivative colonial product, but a strongly independent work. Planned with a rear porch (*opisthodomos*), it was built instead with an innovative rear inner shrine that became typical of the western Greek colonies. A single row of columns formed a central spine in an archaic manner in the raised *cella*. Two doors into the *cella* and the *adyton* (restricted area) beyond may have accommodated ritual processions or served a double cult. The second temple, built some sixty years later, is larger but more compact. Its *opisthodomos* and steps to a *cella* show the influence of mainland Greece. It is thought to be the purest surviving Doric temple, with refinements that include a slight curvature at the center of the stylobate, to correct the optical illusion of sagging, inward inclination of the columns and angle contraction with the corner intercolumniations of fronts and flanks reduced to center the triglyphs over the columns. The columns were stuccoed to make the travertine look like marble. **EVT**

 FOCAL POINTS

1 COLUMN SHAFT

The bulge in the column shafts was known as entasis (tension), which metaphorically expressed a column's load-bearing function. Ancient architects honed this visual refinement into the much less pronounced swelling of the second Hera temple and the very delicate curves of the Erechtheum and other buildings of classical Athens.

2 ARCHITRAVE

The architrave was separated from the frieze by a sandstone string course, originally decorated with leaf-like patterns. The ends of the backing blocks preserve the large cut "U"-shapes used to hold rope to lift the blocks into place. These blocks are all that remain of the frieze. No metopes or triglyphs of the frieze survive.

3 CAPITAL AT WEST END

The necks of the capitals are decorated with carved floral patterns offering parallels with northwest Greece. At the rear of the temple, some capitals have further decoration, composed variously of lotus flowers, rosettes, tendrils, and palmettes. Originally more prominent through the use of paint, they may represent the work of different sculptors.

FRAGMENT OF CARVED AND PAINTED TERRACOTTA REVETMENT

The roofline of the temples was decorated in conventional style with architectural terracottas. Nothing is left above the frieze course, but numerous painted terracotta antefixes (upright ornaments) from the eaves of the roof have been found. This fragment (right), dating from c.520 BCE, comes from one of the long sides of the roof of the first Temple of Hera. It consists of a *sima* (upturned roof edge that serves as a gutter) decorated with palmettes and lotus flowers, with fantastical lion's head water spouts.

ANCIENT GREECE 37

Propylaea 437–432 BCE
MNESICLES

Propylaea,
Athens, Greece

Mnesicles's design repeated the main elements of the previous entrance to the Acropolis in Athens—a gate structure to receive processions, with spaces on either side—but turned the gatehouse into a unified complex, reoriented to face the ramp ascending to the sanctuary. On the inner side, this had the effect of offering a three-quarter view of the Parthenon's north and west faces. In order to accommodate extensive processions, the passageway was almost doubled in breadth: the central intercolumniation of the new six-column facade was widened with three metopes and two triglyphs, instead of the two metopes and single triglyph typical of the Doric order. From here, the Athenian procession filed through an inner court, with a ceiling supported by two rows of Ionic columns. The outer dining room was situated perpendicular to the gatehouse and hung with paintings. Its columnar front was repeated opposite; crowning statues of horsemen emphasized these western projections flanking the deep-set center in a stage-like arrangement. On the northern side, an inner wing with a columned hall added depth. This formula of a central building flanked by wings was recycled for monumental entrances from the Roman period onward. **EVT**

✦ NAVIGATOR

⊙ FOCAL POINTS

1 STYLOBATE

To serve the higher order of the central building, yet maintain the unity of the complex, a fourth step was added below the usual three of the stylobate. The lowest step was distinguished by dark Eleusian stone instead of the white Pentelic marble of the others.

2 INNER IONIC ORDER

The inner hall is supported on the west side by a huge Ionic order: two rows of columns flanking the processional passageway. It had a symbolic function, mirrored in the back room of the Parthenon temple, proclaiming Athens's Ionian identity against Dorian Sparta.

3 IONIC ARCHITRAVE

The architraves are reinforced with iron bars. Unlike the use of steel reinforcement in modern concrete beams, this was not done to exploit the material's tensile strength, but to prevent the marble ceiling beams falling directly on the central part of the architrave.

◄ In the southwest wing, perhaps for the first time in Greek architecture, a narrow rectangular pillar was used instead of the familiar circular column. It supported an architrave and frieze, which, unusually, lacked triglyphs. This variant of the Doric order also facilitated access to the small Athena Nike Sanctuary.

MNESICLES

The Propylaea is Mnesicles's only certain work, although he has also been credited with the Erechtheum (421–405 BCE; right) and the Stoa of Zeus (c.425–410 BCE) in the ancient Agora. He used innovative expedients to reshape the Doric order, interweaving it with the Ionic, or introducing Ionic elements such as the bed molding of the Doric cornice, to produce a unified entrance complex on a site where the Acropolis rock was still rising toward the summit. Some argue that he intended a fully symmetrical structure with the northern wing matched by corresponding structures on the south, but Mnesicles's genius was to conceal the asymmetry of the arrangement by the symmetrical impression of the entrance court.

Theater of Epidaurus Third century BCE
ARCHITECT UNKNOWN

Theater of Epidaurus,
Epidaurus, Greece

⚙ **NAVIGATOR**

In the second century CE, traveler and geographer Pausanias considered this theater in the Sanctuary of Asclepius to be the finest in Greece, attributing it to the architect Polykleitos the Younger, who lived in the middle of the fourth century BCE. However, the discovery of reused blocks in the foundations of the lower part of the auditorium and in the ramps leading to the stage have led to a redating of the theater to the third century BCE, with the auditorium extended and the stage widened in the second century BCE. Nevertheless, the building took several decades to construct and was probably not completed until the third century BCE at the earliest. Its gradual development is belied by the structure's unified appearance. It consists of a steep curved auditorium, extending more than a semicircle around the orchestra, with rows of stone seats symmetrically arranged up the hillside. The lowest rows formed the seats of honor, for magistrates and state visitors. The stage, or scene building, is set on a tangent to the orchestra; a later Hellenistic innovation was the raised stage (proscenium) added along the facade, adapted to the direct engagement between actors and audience. The building's influence on theatrical space and identity has been felt abroad, notably at the National Theatre in London, designed by Denys Lasdun (1914–2001). This building houses three venues, based on different historical models, and the Olivier (opened in 1976) derived its open stage and fan-shaped auditorium from the model of Epidaurus. **EVT**

◉ FOCAL POINTS

1 SEATING

The wedge-shaped blocks of seating are separated by stairways; above the horizontal gangway, the stairways occur twice as frequently, and the steeper slope produces taller seats, making cushions necessary for comfort. Estimates have suggested an original capacity of more than 12,000.

2 ORCHESTRA

This circular space traditionally commemorated the dithyrambic dance in honor of Dionysus. Its paradigm was the dance platform at Knossos, Crete, designed by architect Daedalus. Defined by a circle of white stone, with a stone altar at the center, it follows five-sixths of the curve of the lowest benches.

3 ENTRANCE GATEWAYS

Gateways on either side of the stage not only funneled spectators into the theater, but also helped to overcome the lack of connection between the seating blocks and scene building. The wider entrance to the left admitted spectators, while the narrower opening gave access to a ramp leading to the stage.

ACOUSTICS

In the belief that the human voice was diffracted in circles like ripples but also rose vertically, Vitruvius suggested that the ascending rows of seats in Greek theaters were designed to receive the actors' voices harmoniously using mathematical rules and musical methods. When Peter Hall directed the *Oresteia* by Aeschylus at Epidaurus in 1982, he explained the architecture of the theater there as an embodiment of Aristotle's principle of catharsis, because treating the soul contributes to more general bodily therapy. The acoustics, he claimed, were imperfect because the human body was not perfectly symmetrical. The ancient architect had wanted his theater to feel human, not geometrically perfect, in keeping with the healing sanctuary where ailing bodies were in a state of disharmony. The superb acoustics at the Olivier Theatre, London (right), can present a challenge to directors because they pick up the slightest sound.

ACHAEMENID

1 Tomb of Cyrus the Great (540–530 BCE)
Architect unknown
Pasargadae, Iran

2 Bas-relief figures from the Persepolis complex (sixth–fifth century BCE)
Architect unknown
Persepolis, Iran

3 Frieze from the palace complex of Darius I (c.510 BCE)
Architect unknown
Susa, Iran

W hat is called "Achaemenid" architecture is a distinctive repertoire of architectural sculpture and structural types that is visible in the limited remains of palatial complexes, most of which lie in the territory of what is now Iran. The buildings were constructed between the sixth and fourth centuries BCE, and their definitive form was reached during the reign of Darius I, who ruled from 522 to 486 BCE. In the second half of the sixth century, the founder of the Achaemenian Empire, Cyrus II (also known as Cyrus the Great), who ruled from 559 to 530 BCE, created a new kind of complex of columned halls, porticoes, and structures, set separately around gardens below a fortified hill at Pasargadae in the modern province of Fars, Iran. Partial columns, lower segments of door jambs, foundations, and the niched facade of a mysterious tower building survive. Assyrianizing fragmentary bas-relief figures appear in some doorways, and an outlying gate structure preserves a hybrid winged figure wearing an Egyptian crown. The structure known as the Tomb of Cyrus the Great is the best preserved (see image 1); a stone "house" on a monumental stepped base, it is reminiscent of models from the ruler's westernmost territorial conquests in Asia Minor.

Columned structures began to rise in the plain of Marv Dasht by the last quarter of the sixth century, but the terrace of Persepolis was most intensively developed from the reign of Darius I onward. Darius I also undertook the physical transformation of the ancient city of Susa, west of the Zagros Mountains. Persepolis and Susa show different but parallel repertoires of structure and decoration on impressive, artificially elevated sites. Both featured grand stairways giving access to open space on a platform beyond detached gateways, in front of a monumental hypostyle hall (an interior space in which the roof rests on pillars or columns) known as the *apadana*. The main complex at Susa was built on gravel foundations around internal courtyards faced with glazed brick wall decoration (see image 3), reminiscent of earlier neo-Babylonian architecture. At Persepolis, a series of buildings built on an irregular rock platform clusters behind two massive columned halls, all adorned with dense lines of orderly and static sculptural figures. The *Apadana* and smaller structures at Persepolis (see p.44) consisted of a raised central hall surrounded by smaller chambers that were reached by shallow stairs lined with sculpted bas-relief figures of guards, attendants, or imperial subjects (see image 2). At Babylon, an Achaemenid-style columned portico was grafted onto the older neo-Babylonian palace by the end of the fifth century BCE.

The unified, subtly varied set of forms and decorative motifs linked directly to the creation and adherence to an Achaemenid dynastic identity following a period of turbulence and rebellion after the death of Cyrus II's son, Cambyses II, in 522 BCE. Key decorative elements—zoomorphic column capitals, bell-shaped bases, engraved pacing lions and bulls, ranks of guards, and winged disks—were frequently reproduced in small artifacts such as tableware, jewelry, and textiles, suggesting that the dynastic environment was replicable beyond stone monuments. The motifs were highly mobile and appeared in elite environments across the empire. The landscape around the royal centers was also annexable; small stone-built "pavilions" excavated at various sites in Fars show some of the palatial architectural elements in miniature.

Because of its limited accessibility and relative incomprehensibility as an architectural canon until the late nineteenth century, Achaemenid architecture had limited modern imitators. At the height of the Qajar period (1794–1921), the aristocratic elite of Shiraz created villas faced with imitation Persepolitan reliefs. In 1925, U.S. art historian Arthur Upham Pope advocated a revival of historic Persian architecture following the takeover of the monarchy by Reza Shah Pahlavi. A blend of "heritage" styles, such as Achaemenid-style faux columns, featured in the creation of new civic structures and monuments in Iran, including the National Bank (1935), the Police Building and Ministry of Foreign Affairs (1939), and the rebuilt mausoleum of Ferdowsi in Tus (1934). The excavation of Persepolis between 1931 and 1939 was described as a "restoration" on behalf of the government by the Oriental Institute of Chicago and part of the complex was restored as a dig house and museum. **LA**

491–490 BCE	480–479 BCE	C.440 BCE	405–359 BCE	338–336 BCE	331–330 BCE
Darius I sends a punitive expedition to the Greek mainland in response to support of a revolt in Asia Minor. The Greeks win a decisive victory at Marathon.	In 486 BCE, Xerxes I, having succeeded his father, Darius I, emulates his predecessor in both his architectural projects and frontier campaigning.	Greek historian Herodotus publishes *Histories*. The ill-fated invasion of the Greek mainland by Xerxes I forms one of the main stories.	Artaxerxes II, son of Darius II, embarks on a building program in Susa, restoring the *Apadana* of Darius I and creating a new riverside structure.	Turmoil in the royal court leads to the murder of the king, Arses; he is succeeded by Artashata, who is not in the direct line of succession.	After overcoming the Persian army at Gaugamela, Alexander the Great takes over the cities of Babylon and Susa.

Apadana, Persepolis Sixth–fifth century BCE
DARIUS I 522–486 BCE

Apadana, Persepolis (modern Takht-e-Jamshid), near Shiraz, Fars province, Iran

⬖ NAVIGATOR

The Achaemenid complexes at Susa and Persepolis were dominated by monumental columned halls (*apadanas*) that dominated areas of open space on their elevated sites. The facades of stairways on the north and east sides of the Persepolis structure feature carved rows of bas-relief figures representing courtiers, subjects, and soldiers of the Persian king. The original decoration included a central relief showing the king in audience with a subject. Buried under opposite corners of the foundations were stone boxes containing silver- and gold-inscribed tablets proclaiming in the voice of Darius I, "this is the kingdom which I hold, from the Scythians, who are beyond Sogdiana, thence unto Ethiopia; from Sind, thence unto Sardis." Such foundation texts encapsulated in a single building the vast geographical extent of the king's territory. The stone figures facing the king are thought to mirror the multiethnic subjects who aspired to a real audience among the giant columns. The name *apadana* occurs not in the founder's building inscriptions adorning the halls at Persepolis and Susa, but in texts left by his successors Darius II and Artaxerxes II, who undertook repair work at Susa. Their records of this endeavor embodied the genealogical descent underpinning their legitimacy. **LA**

⊙ FOCAL POINTS

1 BULL AND LIONS

Bull and lions are pictured in the stairway reliefs, and were also used in the design of the capitals that once sat atop the columns. The two animals appear as a recurring motif at Persepolis, and may have been a symbol of royal strength.

2 COLUMNS

The *Apadana* originally featured a total of seventy-two columns, but only thirteen remain standing today. The royal audience hall that they encapsulate is 272 feet (83 m) square, and could possibly have accommodated thousands of people.

3 BAS-RELIEF

The bas-relief on the north and east stairways depict courtiers, guards, and representatives of twenty-three ethnicities who were subject to the Achaemenid king. The imperial wealth that they display includes jewelry, vases, weapons, and fabrics.

▲ The Palace of Darius lies immediately south of the *Apadana*. Built on a 10-foot (3 m) high podium, it housed a twelve-columned central hall.

CONTEMPORARY ACHAEMENID

In 21st-century Iranian architecture, Achaemenid elements appear as disarticulated pieces that echo Persepolis as a ruin, rather than as a whole structure. Achaemenid-style columns and other fragmentary pastiches feature in the external landscaping and internal decoration of the Dariush Grand Hotel on Kish Island (2003). The facade of Shiraz train station (2011; right) evokes the clustered forms of the door and window frames of the Palace of Darius as viewed from the south (above right). Like an Achaemenid monumental gate, modern Persepolitan miniatures serve as transitional gateways. Outside Iran, images of Achaemenid-style sculpture and architecture have been important since the late 20th century as nationalist symbols for the Iranian diaspora.

ROMAN REPUBLIC AND EARLY EMPIRE

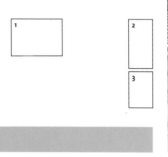

1 Ancient Theater of Orange
(first century CE)
Architect unknown
Orange, France

2 Plan of a pseudoperipteral temple

3 La Conocchia (first century BCE)
Architect unknown
Capua, Naples, Italy

The architecture of ancient Rome has been one of the most influential in the world. Its legacy is evident throughout the medieval and early modern periods, and Roman buildings continue to be reused in the modern era in both traditionalist and Postmodern emulations. Yet Roman architecture encompasses an exceptionally diverse range of styles and historical periods. While the most important works are to found in Italy, Roman builders also found creative outlets in the western and eastern provinces—the best examples preserved are in modern-day North Africa, Turkey, Syria, and Jordan.

The ambition of Rome's builders was already apparent at the end of the sixth century BCE in the Temple of Jupiter on the Capitoline Hill, and the dedication of the temple in 509 BCE traditionally marked the start of the Roman Republic. Raised on a high terraced platform, with walls of massive blocks of the local volcanic tuff, the temple was fronted by a portico with columns set widely apart and a roof with overhanging eaves and terracotta decoration, producing an appearance that, according to Vitruvius five centuries later, looked ungainly and old-fashioned. Yet the temple's emphasis on frontal dignity and its imposingly elevated setting not only remained a feature of Roman architecture into the later empire, but also became a substantial influence on building design in subsequent periods.

Roman architecture was particularly influenced by Greek and Etruscan styles. A range of temple types was developed during the republican years (509–27 BCE), modified from Greek and Etruscan prototypes. Of these the pseudoperipteral temple form (see image 2), with free-standing columns in the front porch, but

509 BCE	390 BCE	211 BCE	c.200–c.100 BCE	146–43 BCE	27 BCE
The Capitoline Temple of Jupiter Optimus Maximus is said to have been dedicated by the first consuls of the Roman Republic.	The sack of Rome by the Gauls destroys much of the earlier city; new city walls are constructed.	The sack of the wealthy Greek city of Syracuse by M. Claudius Marcellus brings vast quantities of marble statues to Rome.	The scenic Temple of Jupiter Anxur (see p.50) is built at Terracina, on the cliff of Monte Sant' Angelo.	The Temple of Jupiter Stator in the Portico of Metellus in Rome, by architect Hermodorus of Salamis, is reported as the first building in Rome made of marble.	Vitruvius presents his treatise "On Architecture," which from the Renaissance onward becomes an arbiter of architectural design.

half-columns built into the walls behind, giving the illusion of a fully peripteral temple, became typical not only in the West, but also in North Africa and the Levant. The full integration of columns into a continuous wall became a hallmark of later classicism, as in Todmorden Town Hall, Yorkshire (1875), where the half-columns wrapped around the building take the form of a Giant Order, but the debt to the Roman pseudoperipteral podium temple remains evident.

Between the fourth and first centuries BCE, Italian cities also exploited Hellenistic Greek developments in fortification architecture. The voussoir (tapered stone) arch adopted for gate structures in the formerly Greek cities of Poseidonia (Paestum) and Velia (Elea) in southern Italy and in the northern Italian cities of Falerii and Cosa became a hallmark of the Roman city. The walls of Telesia in northern Campania epitomize the sophistication of late republican city walls, with re-entrant curving wall segments between round and polygonal towers. In these structures, the use of a rubble concrete consisting of lime mortar with a stone aggregate—varying from flint to lightweight volcanic pumice from the area of Pozzuoli—illustrated the most decisive contribution of Roman architecture in giving rise to new ideas of volume and space. Developed in utilitarian structures, such as the Porticus Aemilia in Rome (193 BCE), it facilitated the volumetric spaciousness of the barrel-vaulted hall at Ferentinum, built in c.100 BCE against the hillside below the citadel and flanked by barrel-vaulted rooms in a formula that reached greater sophistication in the main hall of Trajan's Markets in Rome (c.CE 100–110). The use of concrete also encouraged inventiveness in monumental tomb architecture. The three-tier tomb near Capua known as La Conocchia (see image 3) consists of a tholos (dome-shaped tomb) perched on a reverse-curve pavilionlike form over a podium that prefigures church designs by Francesco Borromini (1599–1667).

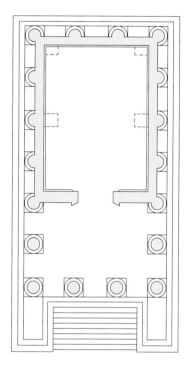

Roman architecture was transformed by the use of Greek marble from the second century BCE. Temples in white marble of the Ionic and Corinthian orders challenged the old terracotta forms, and by the first century BCE colored marbles from Greece, Asia, and North Africa embellished the stage fronts of temporary theaters and the interiors of basilicas, culminating in the Basilica Aemilia in Rome (CE 14) with polychrome marbles and caryatidlike support figures. Porticoes of white marble were built to enclose public spaces. The Corinthian order, showcased in Augustus's marble temples and the Forum Augustum (2 BCE), became a model for provincial centers, of which the Maison Carrée in Nîmes remains an exceptional example. Theaters were provided with permanent stage buildings adorned with columns of polychrome marble, which derived from the Roman tradition of temporary stage buildings in the final decades of the republic. The Theater of Pompey (55 BCE) was the first permanent theater in Rome, and its layout influenced provincial versions. In the theater at Arausio (now Orange) in southern Gaul (see image 1), the stage building was adorned with three tiers of columns framing statues in niches.

2 BCE	CE 21–23	64	80	c.123	135
The dedication of Emperor Augustus's Forum inaugurates a new kind of public space much replicated in the provinces.	Castra Praetoria in Rome, headquarters of the Praetorian Guard, is the first building in the new style of brick-faced concrete.	The Great Fire of Rome offers the opportunity for Nero's new plan for the city, including his Golden House with innovative room designs.	The dedication of the Flavian Amphitheater (nicknamed the "Colosseum") on the site of Nero's lake is celebrated by animal shows and events.	The Pantheon (see p.52) is completed in Rome, construction having begun in 114 under Emperor Trajan.	The Temple of Venus and Rome is consecrated. It is a large peripteral temple with cellas for the two goddesses.

4 **Golden House of Nero** (*c*.64–68)
Severus and Celer
Rome, Italy

5 **Colosseum** (70–80)
Architect unknown
Rome, Italy

6 **Library of Celsus** (*c*.112–120)
Architect unknown
Ephesus, Turkey

In Rome the use of concrete contributed gradually to a standardization of practice. The scale of building was transformed by the use of fired brick, first seen in the Castra Praetoria in CE 20. However, its potential was not fully realized until almost a century later when it was used as a facing for apartment buildings and warehouses in Rome and its expanded port of Ostia in a building boom under emperors Trajan and Hadrian. The great fire of CE 64, which provided the opportunity to create a unified scheme using the new vaulted architecture, accelerated what some have called the "Roman architectural revolution." In the surviving Oppian wing of Nero's Golden House, groups of high rooms with concave ceilings were centered on dominant central volumes, most notably the octagonal room (see image 4), which with eight broad openings was roofed by a domical vault with a central oculus (round opening), the first surviving attempt to build in Rome a dome like the pavilions at Baiae in Campania. Two decades later, in Domitian's Palace, the same principle was developed to break away from the traditional pattern of the Roman house of atrium (open hall) and *tablinum* (open living room). On the upper level were suites of rooms with wide halls for public reception, laid out around two courts, and on the lower level were other rooms for private use. The modern concept of a palace was born.

The Colosseum (see image 5) used technology more conservatively. Its ersatz, modern replica—the Vancouver Public Library, Canada (1995), which architect Moshe Safdie (b.1938) alleged emerged subconsciously—repeats the elliptical form and the exterior tiers of paired columns in a sandstone-colored concrete, but replaces the mass of concrete vaulting and access corridors in the original with a sleek glass-fronted interior with visible air ducts and pipes. The dynamic of the ancient building lay in its conservative exterior facade of travertine masonry, consisting of superimposed arcades framed by columnar orders. These visible elements concealed an elliptical interior comprising an arena framed by banks of seating, covered by overhead canvas.

The Roman architectural revolution was not only a revolution in spatial forms: it also saw a growth of new rhetorical fashions. City gateways were embellished to appear like triumphal arches with *ressauts* (projections) and console keystones. Similar modes in facadism resembling the early modern Baroque style (see p.222) were adopted in fountain buildings and libraries in Roman Asia Minor in the later first and second centuries CE. The Library of Celsus at Ephesus

(see image 6) presented a syncopated arrangement of pedimented niches in its two stories, marked by composite capitals below and Corinthian ones above and framing allegorical statues of the virtues of the former governor whom the building honored. Elsewhere, fluted columns and conches above the niches enlivened the aedicular architecture favored since the later republican period.

In Rome, the central area of the city was expanded under Emperor Trajan by architect Apollodorus of Damascus (fl. second century CE) in his contrasting Forum and markets. The rectilinear Forum culminated in the Basilica Ulpia, Trajan's Column, and a temple to Trajan, while the markets used concrete to create a series of simple but bold vaulted spaces on different levels of the cutaway hillside of which the highest was the central Aula. The barrel vault of the Aula gained extra height from the clerestory arches springing from stumpy piers that appear to be unique in Western architecture.

The fullest phase of the Roman architectural revolution was achieved in Hadrian's Villa in Tivoli (CE 117), which contains several spaces inventively conceived by the emperor architect. Two deserving of mention are the Piazza d'Oro (golden square) and the Maritime Theater. In the former, an octagonal vestibule with transverse windows and semicircular niches on the diagonals, roofed by a dome of eight scalloplike gores rising to an oculus, led to a broad court with long water features, which carried forward the scheme of Domitian's Palace in Rome (CE 81). The court, in turn, led toward a reverse-curve nymphaeum with six fountains and interconnecting suites. The dome of the vestibule was replicated on a larger scale in the garden dining area, known as the *serapeum*, and was probably designed by Hadrian himself (and derided by Apollodorus as "pumpkins"). The Maritime Theater consisted of an island with concave and convex colonnaded screens, reached only by wooden drawbridges and situated within a concentric outer circular court. Hadrian further challenged the conventional language of Classical architecture with the use of an arched lintel for the central span of the portico facade of the reservoir structure for his new aqueduct in Athens, a design anticipated in two buildings dedicated to the emperor at Ephesus. Even more radically, the Temple of Hadrian in Rome (CE 145), completed under Antoninus Pius, was roofed by an inner barrel vault, a form only rarely used for religious architecture. **EVT**

Temple of Jupiter Anxur Second–first century BCE
ARCHITECT UNKNOWN

Temple of Jupiter Anxur,
Monte Sant' Angelo,
Terracina, Italy

⚙ NAVIGATOR

Seven terraced sanctuaries on the margins of the Roman *suburbium*, some oracular in function, appeared in the second and first centuries BCE. They share spectacular scenography, and all were built for impact in the landscape, to be seen as unities from a distance; once entered, though, they offered a sequence of more or less disconnected parts. Many were placed to confront travelers on important road routes, and the most striking ones are at Terracina, Praeneste, Tibur, and Nemi. However, their problematic and overlapping chronologies make it impossible to establish which sanctuary was built first or how they influenced one another.

The Sanctuary at Terracina is the farthest from Rome and occupies the most audacious position, on the cliff of Monte Sant' Angelo, 745 feet (227 m) above the Tyrrhenian Sea. On one side was a small temple terrace; on a different orientation stood a courtyard on heavy foundation walls, an internal colonnade, and possibly arches opening onto a central court. In front and below stretched the main temple terrace. The pseudoperipteral temple, built of a concrete core with front columns of local stone, was oriented obliquely toward the morning sun in the east, whereas the oracle, on a different alignment, was set within a rectangular enclosure with the same orientation as the temple. The traditional ascription to Jupiter Anxur rests on very little evidence. **EVT**

FOCAL POINTS

1 TEMPLE STRUCTURE

The structure of the Temple of Jupiter Anxur was built using Roman concrete for both the *cella* wall and the engaged columns, while the six front columns and three columns on either side were constructed using local stone. The temple structure consists of a concrete core built on a stone podium.

2 ARCADED FRONT

The terrace facade, arcaded on three sides, gives the sanctuary a unified appearance, but lacks an applied order: its arches spring from impost blocks that resemble Tuscan capitals. The concrete on the rest of the structure was covered by a coarse facing known to the Romans as *opus incertum* (an irregular masonry technique).

3 CLIFF FACE

The natural slope of Monte Sant' Angelo was heavily cut back to make way for the terrace and to provide a stable foundation for the substructures. Given the steep slopes of the cliff, the extent of the terraces was limited, with just a single portico behind the main temple serving the adjacent oracle.

▲ A barrel-vaulted cryptoportico, accessed from a stairway leading down from the temple terrace, ran behind and parallel to the barrel-vaulted compartments of the terrace facade.

ROMAN CONCRETE

Roman concrete, described by Vitruvius and first attested in structures of the 2nd century BC, is a variety of mortared rubble made up of large pieces of rough broken stones, and later broken brick, each laid separately and contained by wooden centering until the mortar set. The addition of a local volcanic material called *pozzolana* gave Roman mortar greater strength than the pure lime mortar used in Greek architecture, as well as hydraulic properties that allowed the mortar to set underwater. Scientists at the University of California, Berkeley, sampled Roman concrete and discovered that it is more durable and more "green" than modern concrete. The Romans added aluminum and decreased the silicon content, which increased longevity. Less lime in the mix meant it could be heated to 1,652°F (900°C) rather than at the 2,642°F (1,450°C) needed for modern concrete.

Pantheon 114–c.123
ARCHITECT UNKNOWN

Pantheon,
Rome, Italy

A ll that remains of Roman statesman Agrippa's original Pantheon are the circular foundations. The present building, consisting of a rotunda, transitional block with staircases, and portico with columns and a pediment, was completed in *c.*123, after a fire in 80 destroyed the original. The new building was allegedly planned by Emperor Domitian, but construction began in 114 under Emperor Trajan and was completed under Emperor Hadrian. The high rectilinear portico introduces the vast domed interior: a "cosmic space" illuminated by sunlight radiating through the oculus at the top of the concrete dome faced with a gradation of materials (lightest at the top). The dome rests on a wide cylindrical drum on a deep concrete foundation. The interior of the dome, attic, lower story, and marble floor are organized on their own logic, avoiding a unified interior. The floor comprises circles of red and gray Egyptian granite in squares of *giallo antico* (ornamental marble), alternating with red granite squares on a background of white and purple Phrygian marble. Side walls are interrupted by seven exedrae (rooms for conversation, with benches), alternately rectangular and curvilinear, with columnar screens. The wider rear exedra is fronted by free-standing columns. Opposite, the sanctity of the entrance is marked by a threshold block of African marble and an arched lintel. **EVT**

👁 FOCAL POINTS

1 COFFERS

Usually square or rectangular in shape, coffers are sunken panels used as ceiling decoration. However, the purpose of the stone coffers in the cupola of the Pantheon are not purely decorative. They serve to lighten the weight of the dome. The coffers are distributed in five horizontal rows, diminishing in size.

2 ATTIC

The attic story was reworked in stucco in the 1740s by architect Paolo Posi (1708–76). Niches were embellished with a pediment and large square frames set between them; the original marble capitals were dispersed. In the 1930s, a small part of the original attic scheme was restored from earlier architectural drawings.

3 PEDIMENTED SHRINES

Between the exedra columns are small aedicules with triangular or segmental pediments, restored in the Renaissance with columns of yellow Numidian marble, granite, or red porphyry. Now reused for Christian statues, they must originally have sheltered images of the many deities that gave the building its name.

APOLLODORUS OF DAMASCUS

The architect of the Pantheon is unknown, but its construction date of 114–*c.*123 and its similarities of style and design with Trajan's Forum (below) make Apollodorus of Damascus a leading candidate. Apollodorus accompanied Emperor Trajan on his Dacian campaigns and in 103–05 designed a great wooden bridge extending around 3,724 feet (1,135 m) across the Danube on twenty stone piers.

▼ The portico appears unduly squat. This may be because the granite columns were reduced in size as a result of supply problems.

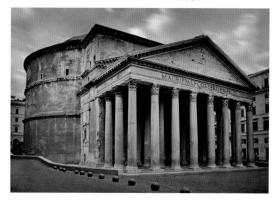

CHINA: SACRED

What is recognized today as Chinese culture has its roots in the Neolithic period (10,000–2000 BCE), covering the cultural sites of Yangshao, Longshan, and Liangchu in central China, around the middle portion of the Yellow River and the lower reaches of the Yangtze River. Sections of present-day, northeast China also contain sites of the Neolithic Hongshan culture that manifested aspects of proto-Chinese culture. Evidence of ritual activities abounds at these sites and indicates that they took place either on open ground at the center of the settlements or in large subterranean buildings. Pounded earth structures were used for ritual purposes.

Native Chinese belief systems included naturalistic, animistic, and hero worship. Knowledge of early Chinese religions, understood more as general belief systems than organized religious activities, is gleaned from early texts such as oracle bone inscriptions (c.2000–1000 BCE), and texts from around the first century BCE. In general, open-air platforms (*tan*, or altar) were used for worshipping naturalistic deities, such as the gods of wind and earth, whereas formal buildings (*miao*, or temple) were for heroes and deceased ancestors. Examples can be seen at sites in Fengchu, Anyang, and Panlongcheng.

Pictorial evidence of early religious architecture is found in engravings in the tomb chambers of eastern China. Those discovered from the Wu Liang (Wuliangci) Shrine (see image 2) in Jiaxiang, Shandong province, are some of

KEY EVENTS

507 BCE	CE 67	151	534	574	582
Lu Ban is born. He becomes an ingenious carpenter and is later worshipped as the patron saint of craftsmen and builders.	Buddhism is transmitted into China. Baima Monastery near Luoyang in central China is the first Buddhist temple established there.	Confucian official Wu Liang dies. His shrine is embellished with an extraordinary series of bas-relief decoration.	The wooden pagoda of Yongning Monastery, built in 519 in Luoyang, is destroyed. It is said to have exceeded 330 feet (100 m) in height.	Emperor Wu of Northern Zhou leads the destruction of Buddhist monasteries.	A new capital is founded at Changan (modern Xian). A state Buddhist monastery and Daoist temple are located centrally in the city.

the most vivid images of early Chinese religious structures. Dated to around CE 151, Wu Liang depicts the story of Confucius and daily life. Images of a number of the buildings illustrate the essential features of a Chinese building style prominent until the end of the imperial era, including the structural system, construction method and choice of building materials.

Most early buildings in China were timber structures. Columns on the face of the buildings, mostly in even numbers, made the central intercolumnal space the largest interior opening. The top of the columns connected to the transverse beam through a simple set of brackets composed of small blocks and extended arms. Developments saw the bracket set become very complicated, with many layers and large projections from the building. These bracket sets allowed for flexibility in the structure for protection against earthquakes. Larger eave projections served to shield the timber column from rain in addition to being an aesthetic statement. Heavily tiled roofs sat squarely on the timber building with walls constructed in brick or pounded earth. Similar structures can be seen in early pictorial illustrations, suggesting that this typology was prevalent at the time despite the fact that no timber building from earlier than the eighth century CE has survived.

The transmission of Buddhism into China around the first century CE ushered in a new era of religious practice. The earlier form of worship did not differ from those of indigenous religions. Buildings housing images for worship were adapted from secular architecture, such as palatial or government buildings. These had no interior division and were similar in design, whether secular or sacred. Two new building forms came about with the growth of Buddhism in the third to fourth centuries: cave temples and pagodas.

Primitive Buddhism in India before the advent of Mahayana Buddhism centered on individual practice. However, small communities of practitioners began to emerge around hill sites in central and northwest India, giving rise to places of worship in the form of cave temples, such as those found in Karle, Ajanta, or Ellora. These caves were originally for both living and cultivation of the mind. When Mahayana Buddhism became prevalent, they were used by monastic communities for worshipping the Buddha presented in a human form. This practice was transmitted to China and resulted in many Chinese cave temples, particularly in areas close to capital cities that attracted imperial patronage. Some of those remaining have a temple front modeled after the form of a timber hall such as at the Xiangtangshan cave temples (see image 1). Most of these temples are three or five bays across with four or six columns, and with bracket sets atop the columns, occasionally decorated with a roof ridge and finials. The interiors of these rock-cut temples are fully decorated with large sculpted images and wall-relief sculpture or paintings depicting the life of the Buddha or Buddha's Pure Land (the celestial realm). The main Buddha halls at the time would have had the same interiors.

1 South Xiangtangshan Cave Temple, Cave 7 (565)
Architect unknown
Fengfeng, Handan, Hebei, China

2 Wu Liang Shrine (151)
Architect unknown
Jiaxiang, Shandong province, China

627	667	782	840–45	857	960
Xuanzhuan, the most revered monk of the Tang, introduces a new pagoda form from the Western Regions.	Buddhist monk Daoxuan promotes an ordination platform and also writes an essay on the construction of an ideal Buddhist temple.	The main hall of Nanchan Monastery is completed. It is the earliest surviving wooden building in China housing Buddhist images.	Emperor Wu of the Tang dynasty leads a persecution of Buddhism with the destruction of Buddhist buildings.	The Great East Hall of Foguang Temple (see p.60), a well-preserved building of high specifications, is completed.	The Song dynasty is founded. Longxing Monastery in Zhengding is built; it is the best-preserved monastery of the Song period.

Another new building type introduced with Buddhism was the Chinese form of the stupa (*ta*) or pagoda. In India, stupas were erected to commemorate well-known people or teachers; consequently, the Buddhist tradition adapted the structure to remember the great teacher, the Buddha. In Mahayana Buddhism, Buddha was worshipped as a deity and his image appeared as a stand-alone sculpture on the face of the stupa. The Chinese pagoda shared a similar symbolism with the Indian stupa and was built with sponsorship mainly from imperial patrons who hoped to gain earthly merits for the next life. The form of the Chinese pagoda, however, is rather different from that of a stupa. It is usually a tall structure on a square or polygonal plan. The building consists of a lower level with an inner chamber housing the image of the Buddha, and multiple stories or roof eaves. The pagoda first appeared around the third century and gained popularity in the sixth century. Masonry pagodas in stone or brick were usually lower than wooden ones. Since the sixth century, pagodas have invariably featured an odd number of stories. It was believed that odd (*yang*) numbers were suitable for buildings in the *yin-yang* schema.

The form of the Chinese pagoda, with its polygonal shapes, multiple roof eaves, and tapering tower, was a new creation corresponding to the *chatravalli*—the cone-shaped pillar of multiple disks—of an Indian stupa. The earliest surviving pagoda is Songyue Monastery (523; see p.58) in central China, built by Emperor Xiaoming. Its high status is demonstrated in its fifteen levels of eaves. It is also the only extant pagoda in China with a twelve-sided plan, approximating a full circle as in Indian stupas. Until 1000, most pagodas were square and built of timber. Records suggest that many pagodas commissioned by imperial households were made of wood and reached great heights, some as tall as 330 feet (100 m). Wooden pagodas were prone to catch fire and the earliest surviving example is Fogong Monastery pagoda (1056) in Yingxian, Shanxi province.

Buddhism reached its peak from the sixth to the eighth centuries when there was an unprecedented number of monasteries throughout China. More

3 Main hall, Nanchan Monastery
(renovated in 782)
Architect unknown
Wutai, Xinzhou, Shanxi province, China

4 Guanyin Pavilion (984)
Architect unknown
Dule Monastery, Jixian, Ji County,
Tianjin, China

than 4,600 official and 40,000 unofficial monasteries were built. They varied in size by the number of cloisters they contained, ranging from six to 120. Each cloister consisted of a main building—a hall, pagoda, or pavilion—and was surrounded by a covered corridor in a rectangular compound served by a gate building. Each cloister had a different purpose, ranging from the worship of a deity to a functional use, as illustrated on the building of Jetavana monastery ordination platform in India. The way the monastery was described by Daoxuan in 667 suggests that it was an adaptation of the Chinese monastic layout.

The form of a Buddha hall was similar to that of a hall in a secular or imperial setting. Its size was determined by the sumptuary law governing the scale of building to the position of the patron in the social hierarchy. The size was measured by the number of bays framing intercolumnal space. The three-bay minimum was for common buildings and eleven bays were reserved for the emperor, or the Buddha halls he sponsored. Each bay was on average 16 3⁄8 feet (5 m) wide. There are only two surviving buildings from the Tang dynasty (618–907) because of the massive destruction of Buddhist structures that took place from 840 to 845. The smaller of the two existing halls is Nanchan Monastery (see image 3). The main cloister consists of a gate building leading into a courtyard enclosed by a perimeter wall. The main hall is built at the northern end of the courtyard with the main facade facing the gate. The hall's construction is simple, reflecting the status of the monastery. Writings on a main beam suggest that the building was renovated or rebuilt in 782 by a monk called Faxian. There are three bays in the frontal elevation, with simple brackets to support the roof. The interior is taken up by a low dais on which there are seventeen images including the central Buddha figure and other deities.

Another popular building type was the two-story pavilion, such as that for the bodhisattva of mercy, Guanyin, in Dule Monastery, Jixian (see image 4). The basic materials and form of construction of this pavilion are no different from those of a main hall, although the technology to erect a hall of this height was quite advanced—it is difficult to build a three-story timber building without mechanical fasteners or nails. A small opening in the center of the interior allows the colossal image to rise all the way up to the ceiling. This building type exemplified the monumentality of the deity. **PPH**

Pagoda of Songyue Monastery 523
ARCHITECT UNKNOWN

Pagoda of Songyue Monastery,
Mount Song, Henan province, China

Songyue Monastery was built during the Northern Wei dynasty (386–534), next to the emperor's palace. At this time, pagodas were usually sponsored by the imperial family or by aristocrats and were three or five stories high. The pagoda of Songyue Monastery is unique for its grand scale, comprising fifteen layers of eaves, and for its plan of twelve sides. It is the only building extant from the Northern Wei and is therefore important for understanding the building construction of that time. Built entirely of bricks, except for the precious vase of the finial, the structure has two initial tall stories: the first has a plain exterior and the second has four doors in the cardinal directions and eight faces, each carved with a window. At the corners of two faces are columns with flame decoration at the capital; this was common in cave temples at the time and indicates the influence of Central Asia. The interior is an octagonal chamber rising all the way to the top, changing into a square shape at the upper level. The soaring height of the pagoda must have been very impressive in the landscape, thereby signifying the level of patronage that the monastery received and the majesty of the Buddhist faith. **PPH**

FOCAL POINTS

1 EAVES

The main tower of the pagoda is constructed in the form of projected roof eaves or cornices in fifteen layers. Each layer has a height of around 5 feet (1.5 m) with projected brickwork. Under the eaves, in each of the twelve facets of the body, is a carving of a door and two windows, of no more than 20 inches (50 cm) high. The composition of this brick pagoda seems to imitate timber constructions, a pattern seen in later brick pagodas.

2 ARCHED OPENING

The lower body of the pagoda contains four arched openings that rise up two stories at the four cardinal directions. These tall openings allow access to the interior. Above the openings are flamelike door heads, a common feature seen on cave temples and stele of this period.

3 SECOND STORY

The second story features a series of rectangular projections with openings carved in the center. Each one is set between two columns, complete with a lotus capital and a base. There are panels of decorative floral or lion motifs both above and below the openings.

4 FINIAL

The stone finial crowning the top of the pagoda, also known as the precious vase or precious pearl, rests on an inverted lotus base. It is an oblong vase shaped with horizontal rings. The prototype for the rings is probably the parasol-like structure of the Indian stupa. The pearl or vase atop the finial connotes the achievement of an enlightened mind. The rings of the vase also symbolize the many layers of Buddhist heaven.

▲ The pagoda of the monastery forms a stark contrast with the massive rocky mountain range, covered with vegetation.

Great East Hall, Foguang Monastery 857
ARCHITECT UNKNOWN

Great East Hall, Foguang
Monastery, Mount Wutai,
Shanxi province, China

⚙ NAVIGATOR

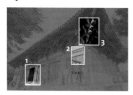

Foguang is a large monastery on Mount Wutai, the sacred mountain in Shanxi province, and its main hall replaced buildings that were destroyed during the persecution of Buddhism between 840 and 845. The building has seven bays in the front elevation, five of which, in the center, feature doors. Windows with vertical grilles are located at the end bays of the front and side elevations. The pitched roof has a pronounced ridge ending with gigantic finials. These features indicate that the building was constructed according to the highest standard of sumptuary law in imperial construction. The interior of the hall is a large undivided space with a platform located toward the center of the hall, measuring five bays wide. On the platform are three images of Buddha and other minor deities. Behind the images is a screen wall, leaving the space of one bay around the altar for circumambulation. There is an area for worship at the front of the platform, which was a standard arrangement for the interior of important Buddha halls. Remnants of paint have been found between the brackets, indicating that the interior walls must have been painted. The combination of wall painting and the images on the altar created a sacred environment for devotees of Buddha. **PPH**

1 DOORS

There are five doors on the facade of the building, with an almost 1:1 proportion of the height of columns and the span between two columns. The panel doors are constructed of solid timber planks tied together with horizontal battens on the inside face.

2 WINDOWS

The bays at either end of the building facade contain windows in a style that was typical of the period. Each is constructed with fifteen vertical posts and a central horizontal rail. Paper would have been pasted on the inside of the window to keep the interior dry and warm.

3 ROOF BRACKET

The corner of the roof is supported by a massive bracket set with seven layers, conforming to imperial building standards. The modular system for different parts of the building is based on the size of the wooden block situated immediately above the column.

◄ The Great East Hall is located on a high platform, possibly due to the terrain and the unusual east-facing orientation of the site.

BUDDHA IMAGES

The image platform inside the Great East Hall (right) occupies five bays of the seven-bay building. On the platform are five groups of images, with the three central groups each focusing on a Buddha with accompanying bodhisattvas and attendants. The two end groups each center on a major bodhisattva, who serves as an intermediary to help the sentient being enter Buddhahood. Most of the time, the Great East Hall would have been used for paying personal homage to each of the images and for circumambulation of the platform. On occasions of major ritual, however, the hall would be occupied predominantly by monks, and most devotees would stand or kneel outside the building.

JAPAN

1 Mausoleum of Emperor Nintoku
(forth century)
Sakai, Osaka, Japan

2 Grand Shrine of Ise (late fifth century)
Ise-Shima National Park, Ise,
Mie prefecture, Japan

3 Pagoda at Horyu-ji (607)
Ikaruga, Nara prefecture, Japan

The Jomon period (*c.*14,000–*c.*800 BCE) refers to Japan's prehistoric hunter-gatherer culture, and it was followed by the wet-rice agricultural Yayoi culture (*c.*800 BCE–*c.*CE 250), influenced by China. The state-level Kofun, or Old Mound, period (*c.*CE250–552) is characterized by Megalithic keyhole tumuli (see image 1), common to Kyushu and the western part of Honshu, with late examples found in South Korea. However, pit dwellings are the most common type of architectural remains indicative of everyday life from the Jomon to the Kofun periods. In 1949, early modernist architect Sutemi Horiguchi (1895–1984) was the first to reconstruct a Jomon-era pit dwelling at the Yosukeone site in Nagano prefecture. Referencing the much later pre-modern vernacular *irimoya-zukuri* genre of *minka* (farmhouse), Horiguchi included a thatched hip-and-gable roof. Shortly afterward, two other reconstructions were made at the Kofun-period Hiraide site, also in Nagano prefecture, and at the Yayoi-period Toro site in Shizuoka prefecture, both of which also adopted thatched hip-and-gable roofs.

Until the 1990s, almost all Jomon, Yayoi, and Kofun pit dwelling adaptations incorporated *minka*-style thatched roofs, constructed using the stems of silver grass, sedge, or other grasses. The excavation of four pit dwellings in 1986 to 1987 at the Kofun-period Nakasuji site in Gunma prefecture indicated that houses of this era probably had sod, rather than grass, roofs. The

KEY EVENTS

*c.*300 BCE	*c.*CE 250	*c.*250	574	587	Early seventh century
Slow, wheel-thrown Yayoi pottery appears, contrasting with older Jomon examples. The latter is named after its place of discovery near Tokyo in 1884.	Yamato clan rulers, claiming descent from goddess Amaterasu Omikami, found the present-day imperial dynasty leading to a unified regional state.	The Kofun period (*c.*250–552) sees the introduction of *haniwa*, terracotta cylinders and hollow sculptures, arranged around tombs.	Prince Regent Shotoku Taishi, semi-legendary father of the sinicized Japanese state and the first great patron of Buddhism, is born.	Having vowed to build a temple for the adoration of Buddhist images, probably to cure his illness, the ailing Emperor Yomei dies.	The West Precinct of Horyu-ji (Temple of the Flourishing Law) has the world's oldest wooden structures and replicates the destroyed temple in Ikaruga.

excavation of the northern Goshono Site (c.2500 BCE; see p.64) in 1996 in Iwate prefecture convinced scholars that the sod house might have been a common type of Jomon dwelling, especially in snowy areas. Interpreting Jomon pit dwellings as sod houses has led to deciphering prehistoric Japanese ways of life in comparison with those of Native American and other indigenous peoples.

Mainstream organized religion was an import to Japan. However, Japanese Shinto, or Way of the Gods, dates to antiquity, with animistic origins similar to other northeast Asian religions. By convention, latter-day Shinto constructions are referred to as "shrines," as opposed to "temples." Whereas a rock, tree, or mountain was often the focus, or site, of the descent of *kami* (the omnipresent godhead), a demountable altar surrounded by a fenced enclosure (*kekkai*) was also used to construct a sacred zone, or *himorogi*, to attract *kami*. Initially this consisted of a swath of sacred land surrounded by evergreens, but it was later symbolized by a decorated *sakaki* branch (a flowering evergreen) on an eight-legged table within a precinct designated by a rope of twisted rice straw (*shimenawa*) and embellished with plaited paper streamer talismans, representing the brilliance of the sun. The Kaguraden at Izumo-taisha (1776), one of Japan's most venerable Shinto shrines, features the largest *shimenawa* in Japan.

Ubiquitous Shinto-style buildings (shrines) are believed to derive from the perpetual early necessity in a rice-growing culture to offer prayers for harvest bounty. They appear to derive from the raised granary (a form found in multiple global cultures), as seen at the Grand Shrine of Ise (see image 2). Situated west of Nagoya, it is a unique imperial variant of the *shinmei-zukuri* architectural style, dating to the Kofun era. The Shikinen Sengu system of rebuilding the two primary Grand Shrine buildings—Kotaijingu (Naiku, or inner shrine) and Toyouke Daijingu (Geku, or outer shrine)—now occurs every twenty years. The old (occupied) and new (reserved) sites are adjacent, equally sized plots. Fourteen nearby smaller shrines and Naiku's Uji Bridge are also rebuilt at the same interval. Ceremonies in honor of the rebuilding include Mito-sai for the keyhole in the sacred door, a motif used for the landform of the earlier imperial keyhole tumulus. Dismantled timber is distributed to shrines throughout Japan for reuse, with emphasis placed on disaster zones: in 1993, wood from the shrine aided reconstruction in Hokkaido after the earthquake.

The core doctrines of Buddhism were imported to Japan in the mid-sixth century, via the neighboring Korean kingdom of Paekche, having previously reached the Chinese mainland from India. By the century's end, Japan was constructing Continental-style monasteries, notably the temple, now known as Horyu-ji (see image 3), in Ikaruga, Nara prefecture. Its five-story pagoda (*goju-no-to*), main hall (*kondo*), inner gate (*chumon*), and much of the surrounding cloister (*kairo*) are the oldest surviving timber constructions in the world, far more ancient than anything found on the Chinese mainland. **JH/DBS**

607	645	710	739	760	794
Empress Suiko and her nephew, Shotoku, complete their predecessor's temple construction in Ikaruga, but it succumbs to fire in 670.	Prince Kotoku promotes Taika reforms, while Chinese-style bureaucracy and imperial hegemony encourage legal and religious changes.	The Imperial court shifts its capital to Heijo-kyo, modeled on Changan in Tang China, with eventual adoption of Buddhism as the state religion.	The East Precinct of Horyu-ji is rebuilt and includes the octagonal Yumedono (Hall of Dreams) on the site of Shotoku's former palace in Ikaruga.	The original Great Buddha Hall and Lecture Hall at Todaiji (Nara) are erected as part of the great center of state Buddhism.	The new capital at Heian-kyo sustains the Chinese-style plan and initiates the Heian era, emulating the Tang dynasty of China (618–907) until 1185.

Goshono Jomon Site c.2500 BCE
ARCHITECT UNKNOWN

Goshono Jomon Site,
Ichinohe Town,
Iwate prefecture, Japan

✦ NAVIGATOR

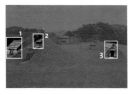

Dated to the second half of the Middle Jomon period (*c.*2500 BCE), Goshono in Ichinohe Town is a large settlement site associated with pit dwellings and clusters of ceremonial stone features. The excavation at Goshono started in 1989, and a few years later in 1993 it was designated as a Special National Historical Site. Excavation of the site in 1996 revealed multiple pit dwellings that showed evidence of fire. Charred beams, posts, and other architectural remains were identified in each of these pit dwellings, but curiously there was no evidence of thatched roofs. Tightly packed clumps of sod found inside these pit dwellings led architect Shigeo Asakawa to suggest that these were sod houses, not thatched-roof houses. In 1997, Kazunori Takeda, the chief archaeologist of the Board of Education of Ichinohe Town, started to reconstruct one of these dwellings as a sod house. This was a radical departure from the conventional assumption that most of the Jomon pit dwellings and other structures must have had thatched roofs, as did farmhouses during and after the Edo period (CE 1600–1868). Today, multiple reconstructed sod houses are among the features that attract visitors to the Goshono site in far northern Japan. **JH**

1 RAISED FLOOR

A post mold is evidence of a post hole. Accordingly, a set of six wooden posts, placed in a rectangular plan, has been used to reconstruct a small raised-floor building. Such a building may have functioned as a store house or perhaps a summer house.

2 AIR VENT

Stratigraphic observations in pit dwellings at Goshono show that an air vent may have been placed on top of the hearth. Even with a vent, the inside of a sod house must have been very humid, which suggests that sod houses were occupied only in the winter.

3 CHESTNUT

Archaeobotanical studies of charred wood excavated from Goshono pit dwellings indicate that chestnut was the most commonly used wood for house construction. Following these results, chestnut posts and beams were used in this reconstruction.

◀ Charred architectural materials were found inside a large pit dwelling at Goshono. The charred architectural remains were covered with tightly packed sod clumps with the exception of the hearth area, above which an air vent may have been placed.

REVERTING TO SOD

From the 1950s to 1990s, many pit dwellings—the most common type of architectural remains from the Jomon to Kofun period (c.14,000 BCE–CE 552)—were reconstructed in Japan with *minka*-style (farmhouse) thatched roofs (right). An excavation in 1986 at the Nakasuji site in Gunma prefecture showed that in fact these houses probably had sod roofs. The excavation at Goshono in 1996 persuaded many scholars that sod houses were the most common type of Jomon dwelling, especially in snowy areas. By reconstructing Jomon pit dwellings as sod houses, scholars have begun to reconstruct the Jomon lifestyle using ethnographic examples of Native Americans and other indigenous peoples, who also built sod houses.

PRE-COLUMBIAN CENTRAL AMERICA

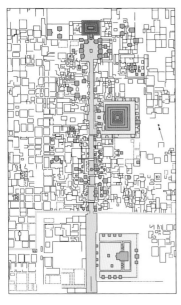

Public architecture in Mesoamerica (Mexico and northwest Central America) evolved alongside social and political complexity. Early Neolithic (to c.3600 BCE) small, thatched-roof, wattle-and-daub dwellings and household shrines progressively developed into multiroomed palaces and temples on tall platforms. Distinctive regional traditions coalesced late in the first millennium BCE. The two most elaborate—Teotihuacan in the Valley of Mexico and Maya in the lowlands of Guatemala and Yucatán—represent distinct western and eastern urban and architectural traditions. In the Valley of Mexico, Teotihuacan became a truly urban community, arranged on a grid with dense residential groups surrounding clusters of temple-pyramids (see image 2). The most distinctive feature of Teotihuacan architecture is the *talud-tablero* style of constructing platforms. The retaining walls of each terrace have lower batters (backward slopes; *talud*) topped by vertical segments, usually with projecting rectangular frames (*tablero*). Maya cities were less densely occupied than Teotihuacan and their layouts were adapted to local topographies. Residences were progressively more widely spaced away from civic cores. Tall temple-pyramids and palaces often had elaborate exterior decoration in modeled plaster with painted details, and interior walls sometimes had murals. These two great foci of architectural innovation established patterns that shaped the architectural history of most of pre-Columbian Mesoamerica.

KEY EVENTS

200 BCE	C.100 BCE	C.150	C.250	C.250	C.400
By this time, distinctive regional civilizations have developed in western Mexico, central Mexico, Puebla, Oaxaca, and the Maya lowlands.	Teotihuacan emerges as a powerful urban political center.	Construction begins on the Pyramid of the Feathered Serpent (see p.70) on the main thoroughfare of Teotihuacan.	Teotihuacan is transformed when exterior architectural decoration disappears and apartment compounds subsume all domestic life.	Lowland Maya centers take on their classic form with the appearance of stelae glorifying kings.	*Talud-tablero* and foreign craft styles reflect Teotihuacan involvement in royal succession at Tikal and Copán in the Maya lowlands.

By CE 200, Teotihuacan covered approximately 7 ¾ square miles (20 sq km) and housed a population approaching 100,000. The Avenue of the Dead (see image 1), lined by the largest temple-pyramids and grandest palace complexes, formed the axis of the urban grid and extended for at least 3 miles (5 km) south-southwest from the Pyramid of the Moon (c.200–450). Near its midpoint, the avenue ran between the Ciudadela complex and a second, slightly smaller compound. The city's largest structure, the Pyramid of the Sun (c.100–200), stood about halfway along the avenue, to one side.

The elaborate Pyramid of the Feathered Serpent (c.150–200; see p.70) and its temple formed the original focus of the Ciudadela. A series of flanking, multiroom buildings may have been a royal palace complex. State complexes are hard to discriminate from other elite building groups, perhaps because architecture was not intended to mark political function, but the Ciudadela is a strong candidate for the residential and administrative space of the city's early rulers. Another possibility is a huge, partly walled cluster of buildings, platforms, and plazas that straddled the Avenue of the Dead between the Ciudadela and the Pyramid of the Sun.

A radical organizational transformation in the third century slowed the pace of urban growth but did not bring it to an end. The Pyramid of the Feathered Serpent and its temple were destroyed and partly covered over by a simpler construction. Multiroom apartment compounds with plain exterior walls and few entrances replaced individual domestic buildings around courtyards. By CE 400, more than 2,000 compounds in Teotihuacan housed a population in excess of 100,000. Apartment compounds, like palaces (see image 3), had flat roofs of beam and mortar construction. The most elegant were decorated with murals and with relief carving, coated with plaster and painted, sometimes with insets of obsidian or other stones. Rigid adherence to a grid and uniformity of apartments suggest centralized political control, but there are no monumental royal portraits and, apart from prominent figures in a few interior murals, nothing that suggests political themes. The city of Teotihuacan clearly had a political and social order that was very different from that of other Mesoamerican societies.

Teotihuacan dominated the Valley of Mexico and it must have cast a large political and economic shadow over the surrounding region. The city also maintained close connections with distant regions, from Jalisco in the northwest to Guatemala in the southeast. These links, and their accompanying influence, are most clearly marked by local adoptions of variants of the *talud-tablero* construction style. The degree of Teotihuacan control in these areas—as distinct from local emulation of a prestigious connection—is debated, but Teotihuacan strongly affected dynastic politics in some Maya cities. Teotihuacan itself was a cosmopolitan city, attracting residents from throughout Mesoamerica.

1 **Avenue of the Dead (CE 1–600)**
Architect unknown
Teotihuacan, Mexico

2 **Plan of Teotihuacan**
Mexico

3 **Courtyard of Quetzalpapalotl Palace (c.250)**
Architect unknown
Teotihuacan, Mexico

c.550–600	c.750–850	c. 750–850	800	c.900–950	c.1100
Public buildings at Teotihuacan are destroyed and the city's power fades, triggering a long period of unsettled economic and political conditions.	Regional states flourish at Xochicalco, Teotenango, El Tajín, Cholula, and elsewhere in western Mesoamerica.	Political and economic dislocation spreads to the east; southern lowland Maya states begin to fail.	The construction of the Nunnery Quadrangle, Uxmal, begins. It comprises four buildings, seventy-four individual rooms, and a ball court.	With their capital at Tula, the Toltecs emerge as the dominant power in central Mexico, with hegemonic influence extending well beyond.	The collapse of Tula ushers in a period of instability and population shifts, setting the stage for the emergence of the Triple Alliance (Aztec Empire).

Teotihuacan's architecture and urban design defined a distinctive western Mesoamerican tradition. City layouts involved directional orientation, single-story, flat-roofed buildings were typical, and terraced platforms were built in styles derived from the Teotihuacan *talud-tablero*. During the sixth century, Teotihuacan's involvement with distant areas diminished, and the ensuing process of decline ended the city's regional dominance. This triggered a period of sociopolitical disruption and population dislocation that affected much of Mesoamerica. Many buildings along the Avenue of the Dead were burned, suggesting that either foreign attack or internal revolt played a role in the city's decline. The environmental impact of Teotihuacan's continued demand for wood for cooking, heating, and construction, as well as for burning limestone to make the plaster needed for resurfacing buildings and plazas, was also a causal factor. In the late first millennium, city-states competed for power after the decline of Teotihuacan. Xochicalco, south of the Valley of Mexico, Tula to the north, Teotenango to the west, and El Tajín on the Gulf Coast all reflect the legacy of Teotihuacan, most obviously in variations of *talud-tablero* terraces.

Maya architecture contrasts with the western Mesoamerican tradition in urban planning, building design, and construction technique. Maya cities do not exhibit strong directional orientations, although individual groups of buildings do. Furthermore, the cities generally had smaller populations and were less clearly bounded, with residential density diminishing gradually away from central public precincts. Civic buildings were often decorated, and moldings, cornices, and inset corners added visual interest to terrace retaining walls. Elaborate modeled and painted plaster decoration was especially common on early terraces and building facades. The use of corbels (a type of structural bracket) for vaults was a defining construction feature that created relatively tall structures, but the need to counterbalance lateral thrust limited the size of interior spaces. Interiors were typically very plain, although many had built-in benches. Doors were open but often had perforations in the jambs for cords that held textile or animal-hide curtains.

Some palace buildings had multiple stories, usually achieved by setting higher levels back over solid fill. Direct superposition was much less common and less successful because of the limited load-bearing capacity of corbeled vaulting. Palaces were organized around interior courtyards, as were ordinary

residences. Temple-pyramid (see image 5) construction emphasized height, both in the proportions of terraces and the steepness of stairways. Multiple-terrace construction leaves little space at platform summits, so temples had only a few small rooms. Temple buildings often carried "roof combs": structures placed atop the roof to enhance the building's height and to provide an additional field for decoration. Many Maya temple-pyramids were mortuary monuments and contained royal tombs.

Architectural decoration and monumental sculpture featured political themes. Stelae (free-standing tabular monuments carved in relief) bore portraits of rulers adorned with emblems of legitimacy and hieroglyphic texts celebrating their ancestries and achievements. These were often placed in plazas, venues for state ceremonies defined by palace complexes and temple-pyramids. Stelae that now appear unadorned were probably plastered and painted with similar motifs. Many structures aligned with celestial phenomena. The most distinctive of these are the so-called E-groups: complexes featuring an observation point, usually on a pyramid without a superstructure, and a series of three buildings placed so as to mark sunrise on the solstices and equinoxes.

Architectural facilities for the ball game, which had symbolic, ritual, and political associations, were fixtures of Maya cities. The core feature of ball courts was a long and narrow playing alley defined by two parallel platforms. Their sizes varied, presumably in relation to the venues and the sizes of the teams appropriate to them. Sweat baths, venues for birth, and "life" rituals that established local identity, were also fixtures of domestic architecture throughout Mesoamerica. Elaborate sweat baths were built in public spaces, especially in Maya cities. The potential political advantage of affirming a local identity through public ritual would not have been lost on rulers, especially if their local credentials were suspect.

During the fourth and fifth centuries, Teotihuacan stylistic features appeared in the art and architecture of Maya cities. Hieroglyphic texts and political art at Tikal and Copán suggest that social groups who identified with Teotihuacan had important political roles in those cities at least. *Talud-tablero* terrace construction in Maya buildings built after the decline of Teotihuacan may be, in part, an archaism reflecting the lingering mystique of the ancient city. Use of the same *talud-tablero* variants in post-Teotihuacan central Mexico, however, points to the possibility of ongoing interaction with Teotihuacan's successors.

From the ninth century, most Maya city-states in the southern lowlands began to fail. Environmental stresses caused by intensified farming, ever-increasing demands for wood, and in some regions, droughts, were important causal factors. Exchange networks, political alliances and social relationships among Maya polities were being transformed, largely due to pressures from the West, and were in the final stage of a domino-effect process of disruption and population dislocation triggered by the decline of Teotihuacan.

The transformation process was slower to affect the northern lowlands. Cities in the Puuc region of northwest Yucatán only peaked in the ninth and tenth centuries. The heyday of Chichén Itzá, in the north-central part of the peninsula, came even later. The Puuc architectural style, most flamboyantly expressed at Uxmal, Kabah, and Labná, involved elegant stone dressing, with veneers facing rubble-cored walls (see image 4). Vaults were constructed with "boot-shaped" stones anchored in solid fill with tenons; carefully dressed flat sides form the vault. Elaborate mosaic decoration on upper facades included geometric designs, house elevations, and representational elements, most distinctively masks of long projecting noses (see image 6). These creatures are usually identified with Chac, the rain god, but other long-nosed deities are equally plausible interpretations for many examples. **JSH/KMH**

4 **Governor's Palace (800–1000)**
Architect unknown
Uxmal, Yucatán, Mexico

5 **Temple of the Great Jaguar (*c.732*)**
Architect unknown
Tikal National Park, Guatemala

6 **Nunnery Quadrangle (800–1000)**
Architect unknown
Uxmal, Yucatán, Mexico

Pyramid of the Feathered Serpent c.150–200

ARCHITECT UNKNOWN

Pyramid of the Feathered
Serpent, Avenue of the Dead,
Teotihuacan, Mexico

 NAVIGATOR

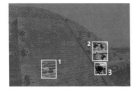

With four platforms, two major palaces, and an elaborately decorated temple-pyramid, the Ciudadela is among Teotihuacan's premier architectural complexes. In the original second-century design, the Pyramid of the Feathered Serpent was the visual focus of the complex. Feathered serpents, notably the Aztec god Quetzalcoatl, were prominent in later Mesoamerican belief systems, but the degree to which Teotihuacanos shared their meanings is a matter for debate. A large tomb chamber beneath the pyramid suggests that one of its functions was a mortuary, but its contents were looted in pre-Columbian times. Dedicatory activities included the interment of sacrificed warriors around the perimeter. A radical restructuring of Teotihuacan's urban organization in the third century transformed the Ciudadela. The Pyramid of the Feathered Serpent was burned and its temple was razed. Debris from the destroyed buildings was incorporated into the fill of a new platform (the Adosada), which covered the front of the old pyramid. Like all later platforms, it was simply plastered and painted—never again did Teotihuacan create anything comparable to the exterior ornamentation of the Pyramid of the Feathered Serpent. **JSH/KMH**

1 STEPS

The front of the temple was previously covered by the Adosada platform (below); the facade is visible again because archaeologists left it exposed after excavation. The extent of the ancient destruction of the original facings of the pyramid can be seen in the damage to the steps.

2 HEADS

The goggle-eyed heads that are located near the rattlesnakes' midsections bear some resemblance to Tlaloc, the Aztec god of rain, with whom they are often identified. However, they appear to be dependent emblems that are attached to the rattlesnakes.

3 SERPENTS

Repeated images of feathered serpents decorate the *talud* and *tablero* of the platform terraces. The heads set into the stair balustrades represent the same creature. Spaces formed by the undulating serpent bodies are filled with seashells carved in stone, with details in painted plaster.

◄ The Adosada platform that covered the front of the Pyramid of the Feathered Serpent reflects the typical form and proportion of Teotihuacan *talud-tablero* terraces.

ATETELCO PATIO SHRINE

The transformation marked by the destruction of the Pyramid of the Feathered Serpent included a radical shift in residential patterns, and large apartment compounds housed virtually all of the city's inhabitants. These compounds consist of several suites of rooms organized around small patios. Many patios are unroofed, serving as light wells, and some have central shrines (right). Apartment compounds range from grand palaces along the Avenue of the Dead to very plain complexes with many cramped rooms far from the city center. In Atetelco, an elegant compound near the Avenue of the Dead, elaborate murals decorate the walls of sizeable rooms and miniature temples function as shrines in spacious patios.

LATE ROMAN EMPIRE

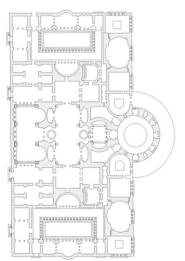

From a technological point of view, Roman architecture reached its height by the second century CE. Although in the outer precinct of the Baths of Caracalla in Rome two octagonal interiors within outer squares may show early instances of the spherical pendentive later developed at Hagia Sophia, Constantinople (537), subsequent changes were mainly in form, materials, and ornamentation. Fused Western and Eastern technologies promoted fluid ideas and motifs, which allowed Roman architecture's potential for spectacle and display to be realized in a focus on facades and a dramatic articulation of interior space.

The plain exterior of the Baths of Caracalla offered no hint of the inner bathing halls (see image 2): free-standing columns projecting from huge concrete piers appeared to support the cross-vaulted concrete ceiling of the frigidarium (cold pool). From there, scenic vistas looked in one direction toward tiers of statuary in columned niches behind the swimming bath and in the other toward the domed caldarium (the hottest room in the baths). Yet grand facades were designed: the coastal frontage of the Antonine Baths (157–161) and harbor at Carthage; the vast terraced structures of the Severan (193–235) extension to the Palatine palace in Rome; the sprawling villa at Nennig, Germany (third century); and the Propylon of the Sanctuary of Jupiter at Baalbek (third century), with a huge arched lintel at the center of a long colonnade.

KEY EVENTS

193	203	203–211	c.212–220	216	284
The accession of Septimius Severus marks the beginning of the Severan dynasty (193–235).	The Septizodium of Severus is dedicated at the southeastern entrance to the Palatine in Rome.	Severus's large marble map of Rome, known as *Forma Urbis Romae*, is created.	A monumental arch (see p.76) is constructed over the principal street of Palmyra.	The Severan Basilica (see p.78), started by Severus, is completed by his son, Caracalla.	Emperor Diocletian establishes the tetrarchy, a system of government in which the power is divided between four rulers.

The influx of extravagant styles from the East encouraged grand conceptions in the West. The Piliers de Tutelle in Bordeaux, Gaul, (third century) consisted of a platform enclosed by a rectangle of twenty-four Corinthian columns supporting an architrave with *ressauts* (projections), which carried an arcade of pilasters embellished with female figures and vases in relief. Uniquely, voussoirs (tapered stones) were inserted in the architrave, one between each intercolumniation, a feature suggesting that this building was the source for the great colonnade (1667–70) of the Louvre in Paris by Claude Perrault (1613–88). The colonnade was also thought to be inspired by the Propylon at Baalbek, drawings of which were already known by the 1660s, and the attics over the end pavilions of the east and south colonnades also echo the design at Baalbek.

Honorific arches demonstrated extravagant design: Severus's arch at Lepcis Magna (216; see p.79) has broken pediments on all sides, and the four-way Arch of Caracalla, Thebeste (*c*.214), has paired columns on all sides, projecting entablatures, and medallions with divine busts. The center of the passage is roofed by a domical vault, and the upper part consists of four kiosklike columnar forms. In Asia Minor, colored marble was employed to embellish public buildings: at Perge in Pamphylia two early third-century fountain buildings were decorated with spirally fluted columns of brecciated marble. Later, the canonical Western style of architectural ornament was gradually abandoned, and a new balance was established between East and West; local workshops set up away from the main foci of cultural exchange innovated according to need, combining Western-imposed norms with older local models. In Emperor Philip's colony of Philippopolis (Shahba) in Hauran, Syria, which was orthogonally planned like a Western city, the South Baths (see image 1) were vaulted with light volcanic materials, including a domed room with an oculus, but the city gates were decorated with Nabataean "horn capitals." The basilica, a large, timber-roofed hall with large windows and an apse roofed by a concrete half-dome, anticipates the forms of the later four tetrarchic capitals.

In Italy, economic pressures obliged substantial recycling of architectural materials. Although the practice was first seen in the Pantheon-lookalike round temple at Ostia (second century), the best-known example is the reused reliefs of the arches of emperors Diocletian and Constantine in the early fourth century. Built from recycled materials in brick-faced concrete with stone gateways, Rome's Aurelian Walls (271–275) presented clinical functionalism. The circular structure of Emperor Aurelian's Temple of the Sun (*c*.273), recycling the ideas of Emperor Trajan's Forum in the inner courtyard with columnar *exedrae* and broken pediments supported by half-columns, boasted eight porphyry columns, later taken by Emperor Justinian to Hagia Sophia.

Diocletian's notorious "lust for building" exploited the fire of 283 to execute grand schemes that reinstated old forms dressed in grandiose material. The Senate House (284–305) followed "Vitruvian" principles of proportion, but

1 **South Baths (244–249)**
Architect unknown
Shahba, Hauran, Syria

2 **Plan of the Caracalla Baths of Rome**
Italy

3 **Frigidarium of the Baths of Diocletian/ Church of St. Mary of the Angels (299–306 and 1561–66)**
Diocletian and Michelangelo
Rome, Italy

295	305	312	315	326	327
Work begins on the Palace of Diocletian (295–305; see p.80) in Spalato.	The Baths of Diocletian are dedicated. Emperors Diocletian and Maximian abdicate and Diocletian retires to Spalato.	Emperor Maxentius is defeated by Emperor Constantine at Milvian Bridge in northern Rome.	The Arch of Constantine, built to commemorate Constantine's victory at Milvian Bridge, is dedicated in Rome.	Work on the Old St. Peter's Basilica begins in Rome.	Constantine commissions the building of the Church of the Nativity, Bethlehem.

its inner walls and floors, enriched with porphyry and polychrome marble, were illuminated by three large semicircular "thermal" windows; the exterior was merely stuccoed to mimic masonry. A monument with five monolithic columns, one for each tetrarch and a fifth for Jupiter, was erected in the Forum. Diocletian's tax reforms, allowing payment in kind, encouraged the revival of local pumice and tuff in concrete structures. This facilitated the construction of the Baths of Diocletian, dedicated with his co-regent Maximian in 305 to 306. As in the Baths of Trajan and Caracalla, the central bathing structures were surrounded by an outer enclosure wall; instead of the domed caldarium of Caracalla's baths, a cross-vaulted hall projected outward from the facade with three round apses, and domed rotundas stood at the outer corners of the enclosure on the southwest side. The cross-vaulted frigidarium (see image 3), high with a Giant Order of projecting free-standing columns and well-lit by thermal windows, was transformed by Michelangelo (1475–1564) into the Church of St. Mary of the Angels, and became the inspiration for large railway halls of the modern era, such as (the original) Penn Station in New York (1910), its voluminous space now steel-framed, and Paris's Gare du Nord (1846), with enlarged thermal windows and outer caryatids.

Emperor Maxentius replicated Diocletian's regal tastes. The Temple of Venus and Rome (135) was remodeled with two large vaulted apses, back to back, replacing the Hadrianic rectilinear wall between the cult rooms of the two goddesses, and veneered with porphyry and polychrome marble. A new basilica (see image 5) facing it had three high naves like the frigidarium of Diocletian's baths, with thermal windows in the groin vaults and a central axial apse; a transverse apse was added opposite a new entrance from the Forum side.

From 284, Rome was no longer the only imperial capital. Of the emerging imperial palaces and cities at Milan, Trier, Thessaloniki, Nicomedia, and Antioch, most buildings were covered by their modern successors, but common features included huge bath buildings and palaces with apsidal halls, well-lit by arched windows. The best preserved are at Thessaloniki, Greece, and Trier, Germany, the latter with a flat coffered ceiling, two tiers of round-headed windows, and solid brick walls in the Eastern style (see image 4). Also typical of these tetrarchic palaces were domed octagons and rotundas, lit by huge windows in the drum; forms are found in Rome in the imperial mausolea of Helena and Constantia and the later Basilica St. Stefano. At Thessaloniki, the Mausoleum (or Rotunda) of Galerius (see image 6) had eight barrel-vaulted recesses on two levels, the upper ring with large windows, enclosed in an exterior octagon. Its walls of mortared rubble, interspersed with brick bands, and brick

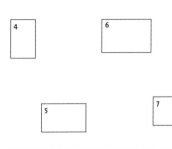

arches and vaults, were laid not just radially, but "pitched" in the tradition of Mesopotamian mud-brick architecture, like earlier examples at Argos and Aspendus, an independent development of the Western tradition found subsequently in the Great Palace of Constantinople (330). In Rome, the Tor de'Schiavi on the Via Praenestina, a domed rotunda with a pedimented porch dated to 305 to 309, differed from its model the Pantheon (c.114–123; see p.52) in the four circular windows in the dome and the porch roofed with concrete cross vaults. This fenestrated version was followed in the replica Pantheon at Monticello, in the United States, by Thomas Jefferson (1743–1826). Similarly, the fourth-century Temple of Minerva Medica was a decagonal domed structure, a dining room in the former Horti Liciniani gardens whose dome was decorated in glass mosaic and interior walls revetted with marble. The amphorae embedded in its concrete vaulting reveal a construction practice, first attested in the second century, which was common under Maxentius and Constantine and probably intended not to lighten the vaults as often supposed, but to save on materials (*pozzolana*, lime, tuff) and manpower. Similar expedients adopted elsewhere include the use of vaulting tubes in North Africa and hollow box tiles at Chester, England. In the East, architectural techniques combined local with Western traditions. In Jerash, domes in the West Baths (*c.* second century) were set on squinches of cut stone, but the nymphaeum had a semi-dome of mortared rubble. The Western tradition of stone-faced rubble walls with intermittent brick bonding was common from southeast Europe to the city of Dura-Europus, and vaults of mortared rubble occur throughout the Near East.

Emperor Galerius's villa Felix Romuliana (*c.*298) at the Gamzigrad complex in Serbia was fortified by a wall with twenty large polygonal towers. Inside were two podium temples, baths, and an apsidal hall lit by tall arched windows. However, there were also two lobed buildings, a triconch (with apses on three sides) and a tetraconch (with apses on four sides). The triconch is already found at Hadrian's Villa at Tivoli, and in the later fourth century, the Peirene Fountain (see image 7) at Corinth, Greece, was remodeled into a triconch court. The form became common in Early Byzantine palatial architecture (see p.82). Constantine's Old St. Peter's Basilica, Rome (*c.*326–360), set a new pattern for later Christian church design, with its timber-trussed roof and three aisles separated by reused columns. Almost as far-reaching was its centrally placed screen of twelve decorated spiral columns around the tomb of the apostle. Invented as a new order by Giacomo Barozzi da Vignola (1507–73), this device was disseminated in Jesuit churches from Mexico to Macao as an emblem of Solomon's Temple. **EVT**

4 **Basilica of Constantine (*c.*306–12)**
Architect unknown
Trier, Germany

5 **Basilica of Maxentius and Constantine (312)**
Architect unknown
Rome, Italy

6 **Mausoleum (or Rotunda) of Galerius (*c.*300–11)**
Architect unknown
Thessaloniki, Greece

7 **Peirene Fountain (rebuilt *c.*380–410)**
Architect unknown
Corinth, Peloponnese, Greece

Palmyra Arch _c.212–220_
ARCHITECT UNKNOWN

Palmyra Arch,
Palmyra, Syria

✦ NAVIGATOR

In the second century, the principal street of Palmyra was laid out with a central thoroughfare, flanked by porticoes. Such colonnaded streets are a striking feature of eastern Roman cities, with well-preserved examples at Apamea and Jerash. As the main street's orientation differed from the access route to the precinct of the Temple of Bel (32), a three-bay arch was built around 212 to 220 to join the two streets. This represented the culmination of a series of monumental gateways across the empire, which marked the juncture between city districts. The eastern street leading to the sanctuary was never completed. The central piers of the west side are aligned with the colonnade of the city street; on the opposite side, the outer piers correspond to the colonnades on either side of the temple approach. Within the gateway, a sophisticated hingelike design presented two lateral arches on the outer side of the bend in the direction of the street, and one on the inner side of the gateway. The decoration is typically exuberant. Pedimented niches above the side gateways are framed by Corinthian pilasters with relief decoration of foliage and plant scrolls; the undersides of the arches are decorated with rosettes and the fronts with palmettes; the sides are embellished with rich foliate designs and spirals. **EVT**

1 THE "HINGE"

The twin arches unfolding from the central hinge are embellished with Eastern decoration. Circulated through pattern books, the design of four ovals within a circle around a rosette on the underside of each arch also appears on textiles found at Palmyra.

2 TRANSVERSE ARCHES

The central and side passageways of the arch are linked by smaller arches, with Western laurel forms around the archivolt and richly decorated latticelike coffering. This highly textured ornamentation contributes to the stagelike effect of the arch.

3 ROSETTES

The use of classical decorative motifs, such as rosettes, within an interlocking tendril design is common in the architectural ornament of Italy and Asia Minor. Textile fragments from a tomb at Palmyra show similar flowers within squares set on the diagonals.

◄ The two inner shrines of the temple, accessed by stairways, have highly decorative ceilings. The ceiling of the north *adyton* (left) represented a central sun surrounded by octagons, while the south *adyton* had at its center a shallow dome ringed by a frieze of signs of the zodiac.

ROBERT ADAM

The ruins of Palmyra were disseminated among 18th-century architects by the publication of Robert Wood's *The Ruins of Palmyra* in 1753. Scottish architect Robert Adam (1728–92) found the decorative patterns of Palmyrene relief sculpture a particular source of inspiration. The drawing room ceiling of Osterley Park, London (1780; right), draws its composition from the ceiling of the north *adyton* of the Temple of Bel and recycles its central motif—core flower and overlapping petals and leaves—and the outer pattern of octagons enclosing shell-like motifs. Another Palmyrene design by Adam was for the dining room of Bowood House, Wiltshire (1770), which was moved in 1986 into the Lloyd's Building, London (see p.486), by Richard Rogers (b.1933).

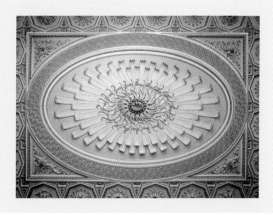

Severan Basilica 216
ARCHITECT UNKNOWN

👁 FOCAL POINTS

1 PILASTER WITH RELIEF
The apses are framed on each side by decorative pilasters that correspond to elaborately carved pilasters on the short walls of the colonnades. They are carved with scrolls covered by interlocking vine and acanthus leaves, the work of sculptors from Aphrodisias.

2 FREE-STANDING COLUMNS
The two levels of superimposed orders are interrupted by two colossal columns on octagonal pedestals, accentuating the long axis. The emphasis on this axis was hard to reconcile with the familiar judicial and administrative hierarchies of Roman basilicas.

3 HERCULES AND BACCHUS
On the northwest side, scenes from the labors of Hercules are carved within scrolls. Either side of the southeast apse, figures associated with Bacchus emerge from the foliage. Hercules and Bacchus were the Roman correlates of the Punic deities Melqart and Shadrapa.

4 APSE WALL WITH NICHES
Each apse was originally ringed by two superimposed orders of free-standing white marble columns on pedestals, above which statues appeared to support the dome of the apse. These were later stripped, leaving two levels of arched niches for statuary.

◆ NAVIGATOR

Begun by Septimius Severus and completed by his son, Caracalla, the basilica was integrated into the forum complex consisting of an existing open space to the west of the basilica and perhaps a second equally extensive space on the east. Here, a passageway lined by free-standing columns on pedestals connected the old city with the new building. Two arched colonnades, with columns of red Egyptian granite and bases and capitals of Proconnesian marble (from Marmara Island) divide the interior into a nave and two side aisles, and carried an upper order overlooking galleries above the side aisles. Almost 245 feet (75 m) long, the building was modeled on the Basilica Ulpia (c.CE 112) in Rome and likewise included an apse at each end. Whereas the outer walls of the Basilica Ulpia followed the curves of the two apses, here the apses are enclosed within the outer wall. The strongly orthogonal design, forced onto an irregular site, betrays the influence of military camps. Furthermore, although each apse of the basilica in Rome was separated by a screen of columns, those at Lepcis were directly connected to the nave. A dedicatory inscription runs the full length of the building and is the first attested use of interior space for monumental writing. The side walls are of yellow limestone ashlar, quarried locally for Severus's building program, and the apses are concrete-faced with brick or alternating bands of brick and small stone blocks. Both were covered with colored marble revetment. The floor was paved with white Proconnesian marble, which was also used for the architectural ornament. In the sixth century, the building was converted to a church with the apse at the southeast end used for the altar. **EVT**

Severan Basilica,
Lepcis Magna,
Libya

LEPCIS MAGNA

Septimius Severus commissioned an extensive building scheme at Lepcis Magna, which in addition to the forum and basilica included a colossal nymphaeum, an arch with split pediments (right) and the rebuilding or expansion of a bath complex. The last was comparable in size and symmetrical arrangement to the imperial baths of Rome, with a similarly projecting vaulted hot room and an enormous *palaestra* (sports arena) with two apses. These were linked by a colonnaded street, like those in cities of the Roman Near East. Severus perhaps intended to use these grand architectural schemes to elevate the city of his birth to a status comparable with that of Rome, where his Septizodium was located. A nymphaeum with two orders of niches framed by free-standing columns of colored marble, the Septizodium celebrated Severus's North African heritage and was explicitly designed to meet those arriving in Rome from Africa.

Palace of Diocletian 295–305
ARCHITECT UNKNOWN

Palace of Diocletian,
Split, Croatia

Located on the shore at Spalato, the extensive fortified villa now known as the Palace of Diocletian was modeled to give those arriving by sea the impression of a traditional Western Roman building, fashioned in the severe aesthetic of the tetrarchy. The two tiers of the wall on the seaward side were intended to be viewed from a distance: an upper arcade with an engaged order, like earlier Roman buildings, but with larger triple openings covered by arched lintels at the center and the ends. Below was a wall that was bare apart from its unornamented central door. The northern entrance, the Golden Gate, was quite different, and its sources were Eastern. Its decoration highlighted the gate's ceremonial purpose as the main land entrance to the palace: richly decorated brackets supported detached columns on two levels. The *ressauts* (projections) of the upper level carried a row of arched niches, enlivened by the acanthus and spiral foliage of the column capitals. Below, two niches with arched lintels framed a broad open arch above the straight lintel of the gate, in a formula apparently drawn from facades in the Roman Near East. The interior decoration of polychrome mosaic, marble veneer, and *opus sectile* has been mostly stripped: the palace was plundered in the seventh century. **ET**

 NAVIGATOR

FOCAL POINTS

1 CORNER COLUMN
On each side of the peristyle, the arcade is supported by four columns of red granite, from the Mons Claudianus quarry in Egypt, and two of *cipollino* marble, all carrying reused marble Corinthian capitals. The four columns of the porch, also of Egyptian red granite, stand on plinths.

2 ARCUATED LINTEL
At the center of the pediment, the entablature breaks into an arch. This "Syrian pediment," recalling Babylonian forms, is used on the Missorium of Theodosius I (388) to frame the emperor on his throne. Found in the tetrarchic hall of the imperial cult at Luxor, it seems to be a ceremonial marker.

3 ENTRANCE TO VESTIBULE
Seven steps lead up from the peristyle to a *prothyron*, the raised porch at the front of the private rooms of the palace. The intercolumniations were originally filled by high stone *transennae* (openwork screens); in the sixteenth century two chapels were inserted between the columns and a wall added to support the arch. Ornate doors lead into the domed rotunda, which formed the vestibule.

▲ The plan of the modern city of Split still shows how the "palace" was laid out like a military camp.

MAUSOLEUM
Two carved ceremonial structures stood on either side of the peristyle. To the west was a rectangular building, now the baptistery, vaulted in cut stone. Identified as the Temple of Jupiter, it was one of the last Roman pagan temples built. The structure to the east is octagonal on the exterior. Now the cathedral, it served as the Mausoleum of Diocletian (below).

EARLY BYZANTINE

The adoption of Christianity as the official religion of the Roman Empire (27 BCE–CE 476) in CE 313 and the transfer of the imperial capital from Rome to Constantinople in 330 mark the beginning of one of the most influential epochs in Western architecture. From its fourth-century origins to its apogee two centuries later, and from its seventh-century "dark phase" to its ninth-century renaissance, Early Byzantine architecture flourished in areas of Italy, Greece, Asia Minor, and Syria. The most important manifestations of the style are found in churches. With domed masonry or timber roofs, and centralized or longitudinal plans, Byzantine churches reflect the central role of religion in the organization of the Roman state from the fourth century onward.

The early development of Byzantine architecture was distinguished by the emergence of the timber-roofed basilica. Frequently encountered in Constantinople, Thessaloniki, Ephesus, Rome, Ravenna, and Milan, this type dominated church construction in coastal eastern Mediterranean settlements from the fourth to the sixth centuries. The standard basilica was an introverted building: an atrium (open hall) filtered access from the street, and plain facades concealed an ornate interior, sheathed in variegated marble and mosaic. The Basilica of St. Sabina in Rome (see image 1) is typical of this order. Oriented on an east–west axis and preceded by a transverse vestibule, the congregational space is divided into a nave and two side aisles. Wider than the aisles, and illuminated on each side by thirteen large clerestory arched windows, the double-height nave terminates in the apse focal point. In most

KEY EVENTS

313	392	476	527	532	c.536
Constantine's recognition of Christianity calls for a new architecture, expressing the Church's power within the Roman Empire.	Theodosius I outlaws pagan worship and authorizes the demolition of pagan shrines, which are looted as sources of building material.	The abdication of Romulus Augustulus, the last Western Roman emperor, marks the loss of Italy and reorients the Byzantine sphere of influence eastward.	Justinian becomes emperor. His patronage of monumental architecture goes on to generate some of the most influential Byzantine structures.	The construction of Hagia Sophia at Constantinople begins. The church marks the apogee of Byzantine vaulted architecture.	Sts. Sergius and Bacchus Church (see p.86) is built in Constantinople, featuring a complex octagonal interior.

basilicas, the area in front of the apse was a sanctuary demarcated by a low parapet or colonnade. Sanctuaries included an altar, which was often sheltered by a light structure called a ciborium, and an ambo (raised pulpit). A *synthronon*, a series of amphitheatrical benches for the clergy, was often fitted into the apse. This type had many variants. In the Church of St. Demetrius in Thessaloniki, Greece, built in the late fifth century, the congregational space has a nave and four side aisles. In Greece and Asia Minor, many basilicas had galleries over the aisles. In the major Constantinian basilicas, such as St. Peter's in Rome (c.360), transept arms were placed at right angles to the direction of the nave, giving the church a cruciform shape.

For all its inventiveness, the architecture of the Christian basilica did not break entirely with the past. Its ground plan developed within the framework of secular Roman assembly halls, such as the Basilica of Constantine in Trier, Germany (fourth century). Its internal colonnades featured sculptural, marble, and mosaic decoration, but their elements often referred back to the classical orders. Roman influences are also detected in martyries, the centralized Early Christian shrines of martyrs, and in octagonal baptisteries, which were inspired by Roman mausolea, such as the octagonal tomb of Diocletian in Spalato.

Christian basilicas were functional and practical. Their strong directional axes responded to an important aspect of Early Christian liturgy: the offertory procession of the faithful. Their internal files of slender columns supporting architraves or arches demarcated spaces without blocking views. Basilicas were also cost-effective. Their column shafts, bases, and capitals were either the standardized product of imperial quarries or heterogeneous *spolia* taken from previous buildings, as with the Roman Corinthian columns of the Basilica of St. Sabina. Their simple design could be easily adapted to the frame of a previous structure. For example, the first church of St. Mary at Ephesus (fourth century) was adapted to the remains of a Hadrianic stoa (colonnade), and the Cathedral of Aphrodisias (c.500) reused the structure of a pagan temple. Even without recourse to *spolia*, Christian basilicas were easy to build. Their timber trusses and load-bearing walls—often made of alternating layers of brick and rubble masonry—did not present major constructional challenges, but they were not always durable. Indeed, some of the finest basilicas were destroyed by fire less than a century after their construction. When rebuilding took place in the sixth century, building practices were changing, and increasingly the model of the timber-roofed basilica was abandoned in favor of vaulted church architecture.

The churches that emerged in the sixth century in Constantinople and west Asia Minor recaptured the magnificence of Roman vaulted architecture. However, three elements distinguish Byzantine vaulting from its Roman precedents: the use of fired bricks instead of concrete, construction without formwork (molds), and the invention of the pendentive. Shaped as triangular segments of a sphere, pendentives carried the weight of a dome and ensured

1 **Basilica of St. Sabina (422–432)**
Architect unknown
Aventine Hill, Rome, Italy

2 **Church of St. Eirene (sixth century)**
Architect unknown
Topkapi Palace, Istanbul, Turkey

549	605	720	880	961	c.1050
The Basilica of St. Apollinare in Classe (see p.88) in Ravenna is completed, nine years after the Byzantines recaptured the city from the Goths.	The war with Persia begins. It is followed by Arab invasions, during which Palestine, Syria, and Egypt are lost by the Byzantine Empire.	Emperor Leo III's edict against the veneration of icons generates the first iconoclastic period and modifies the themes of church decoration.	Nea Church in Constantinople, commissioned by Basil I, is completed. It is probably the first example of the cross-in-square church type.	The Byzantines reconquer Crete. It is one of several military successes during a period of political and cultural resurgence.	Kapnikarea church (see p.90) is constructed in Athens, featuring brickwork and masonry details typical of the "Greek school" of church architecture.

that the transition from the dome's circular base to the arches was upheld by massive stone piers. The idea of employing arches and vaults as means of abutment and support was one of the hallmarks of the new style.

The serial, repetitive use of vaulted compounds provided new approaches to the design of the basilica. In the sixth-century Church of St. Eirene in Constantinople (see image 2), the nave was articulated in two bays flanked by aisles and galleries. The bay adjacent to the apse was covered by a full dome on pendentives, and the western bay was crowned by a barrel vault. This barrel vault was later replaced by a pendentive dome, a shallow spherical vault in which the pendentives are co-spherical with the crown. West Asia Minor played a major role in this development. In the great vaulted basilicas of Anatolia, plural bays covered with spherical vaults iterated in modular designs. In the sixth-century Basilica of St. John the Theologian at Ephesus (see image 3), five domed bays formed a cruciform space enveloped by aisles and galleries. The combination of pendentive domes over the cross arms and a full dome on pendentives over the crossing made the latter the climax of the design, and also highlighted the location of the tomb of St. John. The same design was employed in Justinian's Church of the Holy Apostles in Constantinople (c.550). It was also imitated several centuries later in the churches of St. Mark in Venice and St. Front in Périgueux in southwest France.

Notwithstanding architectural advances in Asia Minor, the greatest achievement of Byzantine vaulted architecture is found in Constantinople and the church of Hagia Sophia, commissioned by Emperor Justinian. The architects were Anthemius of Tralles (c.474–c.558) and Isidore of Miletus. Built in only five years, and consecrated in 537, Hagia Sophia brought the type of the domed basilica to an unprecedented perfection (see images 4 and 5). At the center of the design lies a square bay covered by an enormous dome on pendentives. East and west, the dome is buttressed by massive semi-domes covering large niches. Each of these niches opens into two diagonal exedrae and a central rectangular niche, which, in the east side, gives access to the apse. The soaring perspective distracts the eye from the massive corner piers and the broad arches that abut the dome on the north and south sides. The colonnades that screen off aisles and galleries diminish the visual impact of the piers. The latter dissolve into a cluster of corner supports, sheltering inner chambers

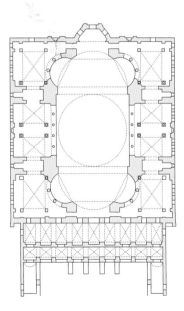

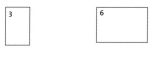

that form part of the aisles and galleries. The same desire to avoid heaviness is encountered in the dome: the closely spaced windows piercing its base create the illusion that the giant shell is suspended in the sky.

Hagia Sophia influenced architectural traditions centuries after its construction, including the early Ottoman mosques of architect Mimar Sinan (c.1489–1588). The domes and minarets of his Süleymaniye Mosque (1558) are influenced by Hagia Sophia. However, the architectural apogee of Hagia Sophia was never repeated by Byzantine architects. Poor economic administration combined with plague and war during the seventh and eighth centuries prevented large-scale monumental construction. Nevertheless, the emergence of the new type of cross-domed basilica during that time confirms that architectural experimentation survived these unfavorable conditions. The Hagia Sophia church in Thessaloniki (see image 6) is one of the few surviving examples of the cross-domed type. What distinguished this building from previous domed basilicas was the cruciform shape of the nave, which, enfolded in a system of aisles and galleries, is inscribed into a rectangular outline. The structural mass of the piers is exposed in a way that disrupts views from one space to the other. It is uncertain whether Byzantine architects were conscious of this problem, but they soon abandoned the formula in favor of a new church type in which transparency played a major role.

Having emerged in the ninth century, the typology of the cross-in-square church was common in Greece and Asia Minor for more than five centuries. One of the earliest examples is found at the Church of the Theotokos at the Monastery of Hosios Loukas, Greece (946–955). Here, the arches carrying the small central dome rest on four slender columns. Most of the work of abutting the dome is entrusted to four barrel vaults that expand along the main axes, reaching the rectangular outline of the building. Four vaulted corner bays and three eastern apses complete the design of the interior. Unlike earlier typologies, in these churches both internal and external appearances mattered. The concern about external articulation is reflected in elements such as blind arches, decorative brick patterns, and the grouping of windows.

Cross-in-square churches were small. Their reduced size made possible a graceful fusion of all the elements that architects had struggled previously to combine in much larger structures. Everything is included in this humble formula: the transparency of the basilica, the vertical accent of the dome, and the symbolism of the cross. There could be no better architectural testament to the inventiveness and continuity of Byzantine architecture. **NK**

3 Basilica of St. John the Theologian (sixth century)
Selcuk, Izmir province, Turkey

4 Plan of Hagia Sophia
Istanbul, Turkey

5 Interior of Hagia Sophia (537)
Anthemius of Tralles and
Isidore of Miletus
Istanbul, Turkey

6 Hagia Sophia (eighth century)
Thessaloniki, Greece

Sts. Sergius and Bacchus Church c.536
ARCHITECT UNKNOWN

Sts. Sergius and Bacchus
Church (now Little Hagia
Sophia), Istanbul, Turkey

⚙ NAVIGATOR

The vaulted church of Sts. Sergius and Bacchus consists of an internal octagonal core covered by a dome and enveloped by a lower, two-story ambulatory. The interior is complex: eight piers define the octagonal nave and the openings between the piers are occupied by rectangular niches, alternating with semicircular recessed exedrae reminiscent of Hagia Sophia. In seven sides of the octagon, niches, and exedrae are closed with two-story triple arcades. This theme is interrupted in the east side, where the central, octagonal nave merges with the sanctuary. Rectangular niches are covered by barrel vaults, and semi-domes cover each of the exedra. Barrel vaults and semi-domes mark the transition from the composite perimeter of the ground plan to the octagonal base of the dome. The building is a blend of contrasting influences, combining the directional axis of the basilica with the vertical emphasis of a centralized church. Arcades with slender columns typical of the basilica are set next to huge pillars typical of vaulted buildings. The architectural detailing juxtaposes trabeated and arcuated colonnades. These architectural blends confirm the architect's aim to create a building in which different styles are unified. **NK**

1 GALLERY COLUMNS

In the pseudo-Ionic impost capitals employed in the galleries, the Ionic element has been reduced to four crudely carved volutes. These are surmounted by finely decorated imposts shaped to ensure the transition of loads from the springing surface of the arches to the significantly smaller top surface of the columns.

2 DOME

The internal surface of the building's umbrella dome consists of alternating concave and flat parts. The transition from dome to octagonal system of supports is not well resolved. The concave compartments are set back and disjointed from the corners of the octagonal plan of the supports.

3 ENTABLATURE

The upper part of the entablature consists of a pillow-shaped frieze with acanthus leaves; an inscription honoring St. Sergius, Emperor Justinian (who commissioned the church), and his wife, Theodora; and a modillion cornice. The lower screens have columns with deeply undercut "melon" capitals.

VAULTED CONSTRUCTION

The main types of vaults used by the Byzantines were barrel, groin, and spherical. The material was usually fired brick, set on thick mortar beds. Byzantine builders combined these materials with a "free-hand" method of construction often limiting the need for a temporary formwork. This was achieved by setting the bricks to form self-supporting units. For example, barrel vaults sometimes consisted of pitched brick courses. After each course was completed, the bricks stayed in position thanks to their adhesion with the mortar. The most distinctive element of Byzantine vaulted construction was the spherical dome on pendentives (above). Made of horizontal brick courses, pendentives helped in building domes over rectangular plans. Ribbed or plane, shallow or hemispherical, Byzantine domes had various structures. The most common pattern consisted of circumferential brick courses with a gradually increasing inclination.

◄ Systems of external buttresses counteract the lateral thrusts of the dome and distribute its loads evenly. These buttresses are found directly behind the concave compartments of the interior. Below the dome, the apse has a polygonal external outline and the ambulatory ensured the transition from the nave to the rectangular external envelope.

Basilica of St. Apollinare in Classe 549
ARCHITECT UNKNOWN

Basilica of St. Apollinare in
Classe
Ravenna, Italy

NAVIGATOR

The construction of the Basilica of St. Apollinare in Classe was begun during the period of Ostrogothic rule, and was completed in 549, nine years after the Roman reconquest of the city. Having all the attributes of a building traditionally associated with imperial patronage, this basilica must have become one of the strongest symbols of the recovered status of Ravenna as a Roman city. However, the dedication of the basilica to the first Bishop of Ravenna, and the fact that it was built on the site of a cemetery, make it possible that the building was intended as a funerary shrine. The plan of the church follows the traditional division between nave and aisles, separated by arcades, and its dimensions are related to one another through simple numerical ratios. The sense of proportion is combined with a sense of refinement. This is reflected in the uniformity of the marble columns, imported from the imperial quarries of Proconnesus (Marmara Island). The columns rest on ornate pedestals, an unusual feature in this context. Everywhere, elements are well matched. The wind-blown leaves of the composite capitals interact harmoniously with the veins of the marble shafts. The nave terminates in an apse that is flanked by side chambers, in a layout that echoes the fifth-century church of St. John the Evangelist in Ravenna. On the exterior, the windows are inscribed in a blind arcade, which articulates the facades in a way that mirrors the rhythm of the internal colonnades. **NK**

1 COMPOSITE CAPITALS

The columns are crowned by composite capitals with wind-blown acanthus leaves. The capitals have been deeply undercut with a drill to create stark contrasts between relief surface and ground. Crude by comparison, the impost blocks over the columns are employed as arch supports.

2 APSE

Facing the main entrance, the apse semi-dome is covered by a mosaic representing the Transfiguration of Jesus in Mount Tabor in the presence of Moses, Elijah, and the disciples. The composition is dominated by a floating cross below which stands St. Apollinare, greeting the visitor.

3 CLERESTORY WINDOWS

The height difference between the aisles and the nave made it possible to introduce light into the nave through a series of closely spaced, large clerestory windows. Ample light floods the interior through these windows, which follow the rhythm of the arcade below.

◀ The basilica was originally accessed from the west through a narthex vestibule flanked by towers to the north and south. Most of this fabric became derelict over time. The present narthex and its adjoining tower were rebuilt, restoring the aesthetic unity of the monument.

THE BASILICA IN CONTEXT

The sites of the first Christian basilicas were carefully chosen. Appearing in cities that maintained strong pagan institutions, they were often erected on the outskirts. This is reflected in the peripheral location of Constantine's basilicas in Rome. Many 4th-century basilicas were built over the graves of martyrs, in Roman extramural cemeteries. For example, Church EA in Sardis, Asia Minor, occupied part of the Roman necropolis outside the city walls. The proximity of this church to a Christian residential quarter shows that urban dynamics were considered when choosing a location. From the 5th century, basilicas played a more prominent role in urban life and many were built at the heart of cities, such as Justiniana Prima (right) in Serbia, which had ten basilicas, including one whose form has similarities with that of St. Apollinare in Classe.

Kapnikarea c.1050

ARCHITECT UNKNOWN

👁 FOCAL POINTS

1 DOME

Raised on a tall drum, the dome is a major element of the church's silhouette. Its corners are decorated with marble capitals supporting arched cornices with a chamfered profile. The friezes below and the recessed arch rings generate interesting light contrasts.

2 GABLES

A chamfered marble cornice at the level of the window sill lies beneath a tall, two-light window with a marble colonette at the axis. This is surrounded by a typical dog-tooth frieze and flanked by cloisonné masonry consisting of small stone blocks framed with bricks.

3 CRUCIFORM MASONRY

At the base of the external walls, a series of large, reused limestone blocks form contiguous crosses in the masonry. This structure, known from Roman times as "Opus Africanum," was particularly strong and was ideal for the church podium.

4 ENTRANCE PORCH

An external entrance vestibule (exonarthex) with a south porch was added long after the completion of the main church. Two columns made of reused elements (note the mismatch between shafts and capitals) support a semicircular arch with elevated springs.

◆ NAVIGATOR

B uilt around the middle of the eleventh century, the Kapnikarea church is a typical example of the four-column, cross-in-square type favored during the Byzantine period. Certain features of this church, such as its cloisonné brick and stone masonry, have been recognized as elements of the "Greek school" of church architecture. The church forms the oldest part of a complex that included two other components—the north Chapel of St. Barbara and the esonarthex (inner narthex)—both added in the twelfth century. The conditions in which the church was constructed are uncertain. Its peculiar nickname has been interpreted as an indication that its patron was the collector of the tax on hearths known as *kapnikon*. The small congregational space is dominated by four columns, which consist of reused material. These carry small arches that support, in their turn, the four barrel vaults that surround the central square bay. Four pendentives establish the transition from this square outline to the circular base of a fenestrated drum that supports a small dome. An apse in the east termination of the main axis and its two side chapels complete the design. This spatial articulation is also readable from the outside, thanks to the height differentiation of spaces. Heights increase from the corner chambers to the arms of the cross and from there to the tall dome. The same attention to detail on the church's external appearance is reflected in the rich decoration of the elevations. This is seen in the ornamental use of exposed stone blocks and bricks, following cloisonné and cruciform patterns and the sophistication of the octagonal drum of the dome. **NK**

Kapnikarea (Church of the Virgin), Athens, Greece

PSEUDO-KUFIC DECORATION

In several Byzantine churches in Greece, cloisonné masonry is combined with an ornamental use of small, broken pieces of brick set in curvilinear, playful patterns. These occupy limited areas in the elevation, typically a number of isolated vertical joints, the spandrels of an arcade or a decorative band. It is commonly accepted that these decorative patterns constitute imitations of Arabic "Kufic" script and illustrate the attempt of Byzantine builders to emulate its angular and curvilinear strokes. Numerous examples of pseudo-Kufic brick decoration are known in Byzantine church architecture in Greece, for example in the Church of Theotokos of the Monastery of Hosios Loukas at Stiri (right). Here, pseudo-Kufic decoration is mainly employed in a decorative band below the cornice. The fact that Byzantine builders were aware of the aesthetic potential of Arabic script indicates the strong cross-cultural influences between Byzantium and Islam at the end of the first millennium.

EARLY ISLAM

After the Prophet Muhammad returned to Mecca in the Arabian Peninsula in 630, he removed all animistic idols from the Kaaba (Sacred House) and established the Mosque of al-Haram, or Masjid al-Haram (c.630; see p.98), that surrounds it. The Prophet's Mosque, or Masjid al-Nabawi (622; see p.96), in the city of Medina had been founded shortly before. The four Rashidun caliphs (Abu Bakr, Umar, Uthman ibn Affan, and Ali) were aware of the significance of the freshly created legacy entrusted to them. Uthman enlarged and preserved the Kaaba, and the Prophet's Mosque, which millions of pilgrims continue to visit today. In less than three decades, the four Rashidun caliphs advanced the new faith, which spread across the Red Sea to the west and the Arabian Gulf to the east. By 644, Umar had displaced the Sassanid Empire and threatened Byzantine territory. Uthman conquered a majority of what is now Iran and in 650 sent a delegation to Changan (Xian), China, the capital of the Tang dynasty (618–907). The Great Mosque of Xian (see image 2) was founded in 742, and legend associates its later expansion with the well-known Muslim navigator Zheng He, who served the third Yongle emperor of the Ming dynasty (1368–1644). Xian resembles a Buddhist temple. Its axis

KEY EVENTS

622	c.630	632	632–61	661	750
The Prophet Muhammad leaves Mecca for Yathrib to escape assassination. The year 622 becomes the first of the Islamic calendar.	The Mosque of al-Haram is founded and the Kaaba (cube) is rebuilt. The Kaaba represents the house of Abraham, at the center of the mosque.	Muhammad makes the first Islamic pilgrimage to Mecca, and it remains the model for the hajj to the present day. Muhammad dies on June 8.	The first four Rashidun caliphs establish architectural precedents that are reinterpreted in each region they conquer.	Based in Damascus, the Umayyad dynasty is established by Muawiya ibn Abi Sufyan. The Great Mosque typifies its architectural style.	Relatives of Abbas ibn Abd al-Muttalib, an uncle of Muhammad, found the Abbasid caliphate. They move their capital eastward to Baghdad.

links five successive courtyards, each prefaced by elaborately carved portal roofs and screens, with a central pagoda-like minaret. The axis was shifted to conform to the *qibla* (the direction of Mecca), and ends at the prayer hall, with a huge roof that contrasts with the delicate screens and mihrab (to indicate the direction of Mecca) inside. Carved with Chinese motifs and calligraphy verses from the Koran, their design reflects local influence. The Great Mosque of Xian illustrates the ability of Muslim architects to assimilate local building traditions—they had no qualms about adopting local vernacular styles. This pragmatic approach was undoubtedly a significant factor in conversion. Muslim architects were also tolerant of mixing sacred and secular uses, such as having commercial activity directly adjacent to mosque walls, as seen in Xian.

In 651, Uthman occupied most of Khorasan. More territory meant increased power and prosperity, and the Rashidun caliphs—as empires often have—used architecture to establish their legitimacy. A primary way of achieving this was to construct a *masjid* (mosque), and thousands were built throughout Uthman's rapidly expanding empire. These generally followed the pattern established by the house and mosque of the Prophet Muhammad in Mecca: an elongated, rectangular boundary wall, a large internal courtyard that occupied about half of the space and a covered hypostyle room at one end.

The Umayyad (Second Islamic) caliphate was based in Damascus, Syria. The Great Mosque of Damascus (see image 1), commissioned by Caliph al-Walid, conveys the power of the domestic source of the first prototypical mosque, since it has a courtyard and a relative distribution of interior and exterior space, as well as a hypostyle structure. It also demonstrates assimilation, since it occupies the site of a Christian basilica dedicated to John

1 Great Mosque of Damascus (706)
Caliph al-Walid
Damascus, Syria

2 Great Mosque of Xian (742)
Emperor Hongwu
Xian, Shaanxi province, China

775	851	972	1071	1171	1258
Ukhaider Palace, one of the earliest Abbasid palaces, is constructed near Kerbala, Iraq.	Abbasid Caliph al-Mutawakkil orders the construction of the Great Mosque of Samarra, well known for its massive, spiraling minaret.	Fatimid Caliph al-Muizz conquers Egypt and builds a new capital, al-Qahirah (now Cairo). He commissions Al-Azhar Mosque the following year.	Seljuq Turks defeat the Byzantines at Manzikert, weakening the empire and paving the way for the later Ottoman conquest of Constantinople in 1453.	Salah ad-Din (Saladin) takes over Cairo and founds the Ayyubid dynasty. He moves his citadel outside the walls and opens up the city to the public.	Mongols destroy the Abbasid capital of Baghdad, and attack Cairo in 1260. They initiate a building campaign of staggering scope and creativity.

the Baptist, and contains relics associated with him. It is a rare example of the use of naturalistic mosaics, indicating the lush vegetation in the city when the Abbasids occupied it, before the disapproval of such decoration.

The Dome of the Rock (see image 3), completed during the reign of the fifth Umayyad caliph, Abd al-Malik, is the best example of the Muslim appropriation of architectural forms and significant sites to establish power. Located directly on top of the Temple Mount in Jerusalem, it adopts the Christian Martyrium form. This was first used at the Rotunda of the Holy Sepulchre nearby, which also inspired the centralized church typology introduced by the Byzantine Emperor Justinian. Early examples, such as Sts. Sergius and Bacchus Church (c.536; see p.86), the Hagia Sophia (537), and Church of St. Eirene (sixth century), convey Justinian's resolve to replace the basilica, which had pagan associations, with a new type of church that would allow him to reunite the Roman Empire. The rock in the Umayyad structure, which usually occupies the central position dedicated to a martyr, commemorates the night flight of the Prophet Muhammad into Heaven. Blue and white tile with Arabic calligraphy, quoting verses from the Koran, is used very effectively as a datum for the dome above it. The site is also believed to be where Abraham offered his son Isaac as a sacrifice, and is therefore of great significance to Jews and Christians, as well.

The Umayyads continued to expand the Islamic Empire until they were conquered by the Abbasids in 750. One faction escaped across North Africa, occupied the Maghreb and moved on to Spain, establishing the caliphate of Cordoba (al-Andalus), which lasted until 1031. The Abbasid (Third Islamic) caliphate was founded in Kufa, Iraq, in 750 by descendants of the Prophet Muhammad. The second Abbasid caliph, al-Mansur, commissioned a new capital at Baghdad after expelling the Umayyads from all territory except al-Andalus, the Maghreb, and Ifriqiya. Neither did they control the Fatimids. Originally based in Tunis, the Fatimids eventually ruled from Cairo, which they founded in 969. The Fatimid Shiite regime was supplanted by the legendary leader Salah ad-Din Yusuf ibn Ayyab (Saladin), who moved the Fatimid palace complex to a citadel outside the walls. Salah ad-Din introduced *madrassas* (educational centers) into the city to solidify Sunni traditions. After he died,

Ayyubid power waned and ended with the death of Sultan Salih Najm al-Din. The Mamluks—mercenaries that Salah ad-Din had recruited—seized power.

Ghazi warriors advanced the faith during the tenuous early phase of Islamic expansion. They established front-line desert fortresses, such as the Ukhaider Palace (see image 4) near Kerbala, Iraq, built by Isa ibn Musa, the nephew of the Abbasid caliph as-Saffah. It is notable for having a *beit* (house) for each of Isa's four wives, placed around a central courtyard within the rectilinear fortress. Each of these have a set of T-shaped *iwan* (covered rooms) that are enclosed on three sides, with a fourth side open to a square central courtyard, which became the basis for the Qaa typology. The Great Mosques at Samarra, Iraq (see image 5), and Kairouan, Tunisia, are two important examples of the early fortress and mosque typology. The mosque in Samarra was commissioned by Caliph al-Mutawakkil and is best known for its massive, spiraling minaret, which was the inspiration for the Ibn Tulun Mosque in Cairo (879). The Kairouan (al-Qayrawan) Mosque, with its forbidding circuit wall and dominant minaret at one end, was built by Caliph Muawiya in 661.

The conquest of the Byzantine Empire by a sequence of Turkish tribes ended the final phase of this early period of Islam and its varied architectural precedents. The Seljuqs of Rum (eastern Rome) conquered most of it and controlled it from their capital in Konya from 1097 to 1243. Their architecture, typified by the Great Mosque and Hospital in Divrigi (1228–29), is bold and innovative, adapting Persian elements, such as the *pishtaq* (formal gateway), in a distinctively primal way. Turkish tribes known as the Ghazi Emirates displaced the Seljuqs and the Osmanlis, becoming known as the Ottoman Turks. They would eventually lay siege to Constantinople, bringing an end in 1453 to the 1,000-year-old Roman Empire in the East. **JMS**

3 **The Dome of the Rock (691)**
Caliph Abd al-Malik
Jerusalem, Israel

4 **Ukhaider Palace (775)**
Isa ibn Musa
Kerbala, Iraq

5 **Great Mosque of Samarra (c.851)**
Caliph al-Mutawakkil
Samarra, Iraq

Prophet's Mosque 622
FOUNDED BY THE PROPHET MUHAMMAD

👁 FOCAL POINTS

1 PLAZA

The mosque is surrounded by a large marble plaza that can hold more than 500,000 worshippers. This is part of a new marble extension that wraps around the older section and adds to the architectural texture of the building.

2 DOME

The green dome sits on the southeast corner of the mosque. Built in 1279, it marks the location of the house of Muhammad's wife, Aishah. It has been rebuilt several times since then, but was first painted green in the nineteenth century.

3 MINARET

This is one of four minarets around the oldest part of the mosque where the green dome is located, two of which frame the elevation that projects on to the plaza. There are a further six minarets on the new perimeter walls of the building.

4 PARASOLS

In 2011, SL-Rasch in Stuttgart designed computer-controlled, PTFE-membrane parasols to provide shade for two interior courtyards. They open when temperature levels rise and close after sunset to allow the heat in the building to escape.

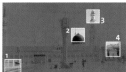

The Prophet's Mosque is the second most important mosque in Islam (after the Mosque of al-Haram, Mecca) since it is located next to the original site of the house of the Prophet. Muhammad also helped to build it and is buried there, together with the caliphs Abu Bakr and Umar. It has the same courtyard typology used at the house of the Prophet itself, and served as the model for many of the early mosques built after it. The green dome on the southeast corner of the mosque is a familiar symbol to Muslims around the world, and it also inspired the color of the national flag of the Kingdom of Saudi Arabia. The minaret, which along with a dome has come to symbolically represent a mosque in popular perception, came much later. The minaret was adapted from the light towers that were once used to mark the path between the sacred sites for pilgrims, and became the tower from which a muezzin gave the five daily calls to prayer (azan). The Umayyads, Abbasids, and Mamluks have renovated the mosque many times over the centuries, as well as the Ottomans prior to the foundation of the kingdom in 1932. To the east of the mosque is Jannat al-Baqi Cemetery, an important historical and architectural site containing the graves of the successors of Muhammad. **JMS**

Prophet's Mosque
(Masjid al-Nabawi),
Medina, Saudi Arabia

▼ The Prophet's Mosque began as a simple 98 by 115 foot (30 x 35 m) mud-brick enclosure. Today the mosque is more than one hundred times the size of the original building.

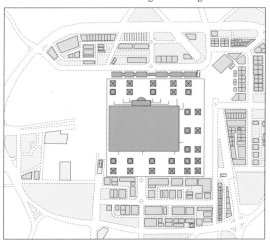

▲ The interior arched limestone colonnade provided smaller and more intimate areas for worship. The white marble columns are topped by brass capitals that support slightly pointed arches.

Mosque of al-Haram c.630
FOUNDED BY THE PROPHET MUHAMMAD

Mosque of al-Haram
(Masjid al-Haram),
Mecca, Saudi Arabia

The Mosque of al-Haram and the Kaaba it shelters are the holiest sites in Islam. Changes to the original precinct began in 634, when Caliph Omar ibn al-Khattab cleared the area around the Kaaba to make room for pilgrims. Between 644 and 656, Caliph Uthman ibn Affran enlarged the prayer area and covered it with a roof supported by a wooden arcade. In 692, the Umayyad caliph, Abd al-Malik, further enlarged the complex. The Abbasid caliph, Abu Jafar al-Mansur, doubled the size of the northern and western wings in 754, and erected the Bab al-Umrah minaret. Caliph al-Mahdi made major changes due to the growing number of pilgrims. The mosque was replaced, the enclosure enlarged, and the Bab al-Salam, Bab Ali, and Bab al-Wadi minarets added. After a fire in 1399, the mosque was rebuilt, followed by extensive renovations in 1571 by Mimar Sinan. Several building campaigns followed the 1932 foundation of Saudi Arabia: the first (1955–72) involved the Mas'a gallery, which was heightened to two stories, and four minarets were added. The second campaign (1982–88) saw a two-story wing added to the southeast of the mosque, and a new gate placed on axis with it. The outer capacity of the Haram al-Sharif has more recently been increased to 1.2 million worshippers. **JMS**

⬡ NAVIGATOR

👁 FOCAL POINTS

1 BAB AL-SALAM

It is traditional for those visiting the mosque for the first time during the pilgrimage period to enter through the Bab al-Salam (Gate of Peace). Those arriving at other times use the Bab al-Umrah, although there is no specific requirement to do this.

2 MAS'A GALLERY

The Mas'a gallery encloses the al-Safa and al-Marwah hills and a pathway between them. It is divided into two sides like a road. Pilgrims follow this route when they perform the devotional act of walking back and forth seven times between the two hills, known as Saie.

3 KING FAHD GATE

The gate, named after the late Saudi king, was completed in 2007. It has three elongated, black-and-white arches and delicate, white marble carving. It is flanked by two minarets designed to match those built before it, with an encircling roofed porch above the gate.

◀ The Arabic word *kaaba* means "cube," although the dimensions of the granite structure that marks the site of Abraham's house are not equal. The Kaaba is the focal point of all Muslim prayers. Hajj pilgrims are required to walk counter-clockwise around it seven times.

🕐 ARCHITECT PROFILE

1489–1537

Koca Mimar Sinan Aga, best known as the architect and engineer Mimar Sinan, was born near Kayseri, Turkey. He joined the elite Janissary corps in 1512 and moved to Constantinople (now Istanbul), where he converted from Christianity to Islam. He fought in several important military campaigns, but his engineering skills were recognized when he produced designs for bridges that could be built quickly and resulted in Ottoman victories.

1538–57

Sinan was appointed architect of Dar-Usaadet (Abode of Felicity) in 1538 and held the post until his death fifty years later. During his career, he designed or supervised the construction of more than 300 buildings and other structures, and in the process was able to achieve a seamless synthesis between Ottoman Islamic architecture and its Christian Byzantine antecedents (see p.82), primarily seen in his numerous mosque designs.

1558–88

Sinan's most important work includes the Suleymaniye Mosque in Istanbul, commissioned by Sultan Suleyman and finished in 1558, and the Selimiye Mosque in Edirne, completed in 1574. The Suleymaniye complex follows the kulliye model of Sinan's other mosques: it not only serves a religious function, but also has other buildings, including a hospital, schools, and community facilities surrounding the mosque. In Selimiye Mosque, Sinan achieved the internal unity he was searching for in his earlier mosques, by covering the octagonal prayer hall with one large dome and placing the mihrab in a niche to make it less obtrusive.

REGIONAL VERNACULAR

1 **Water Cistern (date unknown)**
Architect unknown
Kawkaban, Yemen

2 **Shellfish Mounds (date unknown)**
Architect unknown
Saloum Delta, Senegal

3 **Chand Baori (800–900)**
Architect unknown
Abhaneri, Rajasthan, India

The ingenuity of early human survival preceded formal architecture and prioritized the engineering of natural resources. Access to water is a critical human requirement, but permanent proximity to a water supply is not. Water was sourced from mountains, aquifers (underground water-bearing rocks), and vaporous air. Impluvian courtyards channeled rain. Stone *aflaj* (irrigation systems) delivered mountain water to deserts. Sunken *qanat* (well-like shafts) provided water from Armenia to China. "Windcatcher" towers exploited Earth's hydrologic cycle to redirect "reservoirs" of cool air to building interiors in arid regions. Reeds provided foundations and building materials. Lakeshore pile dwellings and pile-footed crannogs (fortified dwellings) provided access to fish stock. Stilt dwellings high above water, floods, or jungle are native to multiple regions. While historian Karl August Wittfogel defined "hydraulic" civilizations as those, such as ancient Egypt, in which the control of floods and irrigation was a tenet of power, despotic control of water in early human civilization was not an absolute.

Water influenced early building typology. Sabaens and Shiites, known as Marsh Arabs, occupied the Mesopotamian marshes in southern Iraq for 5,000 years. An Assyrian stone relief sequence in the British Museum, London, shows the army of King Sennacherib, who reigned from 705 to 681 BCE, hunting marsh

KEY EVENTS

c.750,000 BCE	c.8000 BCE	c.7000–c.2500 BCE	c.5000–500 BCE	c.3400 BCE	c.3000 BCE
There is evidence of a Paleolithic troglodyte human settlement at Matera, Italy. Later buildings show continual habitation into the 20th century.	Sun-dried mud bricks, a common earth-based material, are used. Rectangular bricks are also common, and cone-shaped ones are known in Africa.	The mud-brick village of Mehrgarh, Kacchi Plain, Balochistan, Pakistan, is one of the earliest sites with evidence of farming.	Pile dwellings (stilt houses) are built in Alpine areas on or near lakes, rivers, and wetlands. Similar dwellings include Celtic crannogs.	There is evidence of the use of sun-dried bricks during the pre-palatial Minoan culture at Knossos, Crete, Greece.	Reed structures first appear in Mesopotamian marshes. Grasses, bamboo, and palm are used for housing in other cultures.

dwellers concealed in their camouflaged patchwork of aquatic villages. Reed and mud-brick houses were built atop both natural and artificial islands. A "litter layer" of Phragmite reeds provided a foundation for artificial islands. Multiple layers of woven reed mats and mud were placed on this layer until the water table was exceeded. The Marsh Arabs built barrel vault reed *mudhifs* (see p.104), or guest houses, *saraif* (reed huts), and five-arched *raba* (high-status dwellings). Villages had single-cell houses built of compressed mud, alongside mud-brick compounds. Corrals were built with a reed palisade buried in the "bed," their plume spikes bunched and tied to create a conical roof. Evidence suggests that the Puebloans of Cliff Palace in Mesa Verde, Arizona, used a related concept in which trees were grown and shaped to provide living roof beams.

Where reeds enabled land reclamation in marshes, so too did shellfish in the Saloum Delta, Senegal, West Africa. The cultivation of shellfish enabled regional trade and the 2,000-year-old practice of man-made shell islands (see image 2) with shell causeways to the mainland where shells were used in structural builds. Shell tumuli landscaped with baobab trees formed funerary sites. Found in Africa, Madagascar, and Australia, the baobab's capacity to store water for drought relief is allied to its bulbous hollow trunk, which encouraged ad hoc use as human habitation. Premodern civilizations often traded over wide areas, for example at Alpine pile-dwelling sites and in the Native American Hopewell culture (200 BCE–CE 500) of eastern North America.

The Arabian Peninsula is mostly desert, and present-day Oman's network of more than 3,000 *aflaj* water channels, some of which date to at least the second century BCE, bring underground mountain water sourced from a man-made mother well (*umm*) to desert villages and date fields via gravity, stone canals, and sub-surface channels. *Aflaj* represent a continuous, unbroken record of crop irrigation and settlement, and their network of visible channels shapes the landscape (see p.102). In contrast to hydraulic civilizations, *aflaj* traditionally allows an equitable allocation of water within communities. In the twenty-first century, allocation is via an *aflaj* agent, who determines the timing and volume of water to fields and gardens via regulated sluice gates. Fortified settlements like those in the Hajar region, spanning Oman and the United Arab Emirates, include two-story mud-brick and stone watchtowers near *falaj* oasis entry points. Access was via rope and toeholds on the mud-brick exterior, like those found on similarly dated regional conical icehouses.

The invention of *aflaj* accelerated the development of Omani communities beyond the common single-well system, found for example in Yemen, where a mosque and a cistern anchored communities (see image 1), or the fifth- to nineteenth-century stepwells of the Indian subcontinent, such as at Chand Baori (see image 3). *Aflaj* removed much of the uncertainty of access to water and makes this Iron Age infrastructure of predictable, reliable, large-scale irrigation one of the first enduring modern structures. **DJ**

c.1500 BCE	c.1200 BCE	c.1000 BCE	c.800 BCE–c.CE 350	CE 700	800–1400
Hunter-gatherer sea nomads, the Moken of the Mergui Archipelago, Burma, live on *kabang* boats and only use land-based dwellings in monsoons.	Rammed-earth (*pisé de terre*) structures are recorded in China but possibly date to much earlier.	The Persian Empire invents the hydraulic *qanat* system of water collection and distribution. The technology spreads globally.	Meroe island, Sudan, trades with India and China, leading to an architectural mix of pharaonic Egypt, Greek, Roman, and Kush elements.	Square lava stone houses in Pantelleria, Italy, known as *dammusi*, feature Arabic-style white domed roofs as rainwater cisterns.	A settlement of some 120 mounds with buildings atop the mounds at Cahokia, North America is established.

Falaj Al-Malki Date unknown
ARCHITECT UNKNOWN

Falaj al-Malki,
Izki, Oman

⬡ NAVIGATOR

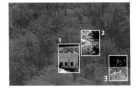

Oman's ancient *aflaj* network of stone *falaj* (singular) channels mountain or aquifer water to the desert from a mother well (*umm*) via gravity, an engineered surface, and underground canals and aqueducts. Vertical shafts are dug sequentially downslope from the *umm*. Collection shafts, the deepest, are nearest the *umm*, followed by the conveyance section (both open canals and underground shafts of decreasing depth), ending at the usage and agriculture points. Borehole shafts in the conveyance section are left open for cleaning and repair. Simpler *falaj* include spring-water capture and damming cyclically dry and wet riverbed *wadi* (channels) to capture seasonal rainfall. The use of *aflaj* means a division into equal shares for the communities who built a *falaj* and use is hierarchical: drinking, ritual washing, bathing, cleaning, animals, and irrigation. *Aflaj* use continues in the twenty-first century, with the alternative government-piped water supply seen as prohibitively costly by many. New farms can rent *falaj* water or potentially become shareholders. Ancient security required fortifications along *falaj* routes, and round or rectangular watchtowers were sited near strategic entry points. Five Omani *aflaj* are inscribed by UNESCO as World Heritage Sites. **DJ**

1 AQUEDUCT

Stone aqueducts span topographic depressions such as *wadi* to move water from one side to the other. Aqueducts must span at the same level as each end to ensure even water flow. Lush growth indicates location in or near a *wadi*.

2 STONE CANAL

Canals to channel water were engineered out of stone slabs, and used the natural gradient of the land to direct the flow of water. The open design of the canals left *aflaj* vulnerable to water piracy and enemy attacks on the water supply network.

3 FLOW OF WATER

The channel next to the aqueduct acts as a reservoir. Rainwater is the chief source of *aflaj* water and because the *falaj* system is always flowing there is potential for wastage during heavy rainfall. Conversely, flow decreases in hot months.

◀ *Falaj* networks travel from the mother well to "shareholder" destinations, which include oases, agricultural fields, and verdant villages with date plantations, such as Misfat al Abreyeen, Oman.

TUNNEL VENTILATION

Hazardous *aflaj* excavation conditions led to nicknames, such as "the murderer," which referred to Iran's similar *qanat* system. The Bridge and Tunnel Commissions of New Jersey and New York collaborated on the underwater Hudson River Vehicular Tunnel (1927). Pairs of ventilation shafts on the New York and New Jersey riverbanks (right) each have eighty-four fans to exchange air every ninety seconds. The underwater Blackwall Tunnel in London links the north and south sides of the Thames River. Terry Farrell (b.1938) designed the second bore's ventilation towers (1962) as tapered ellipses—an intake funnel 40 feet (12 m) high and exhaust funnel 89 feet (27 m) high. The roof of the Millennium Dome (1999) was designed around Farrell's southern pair; a huge monocle opening allows headroom for the historically significant funnels.

Mudhif Date unknown
ARCHITECT UNKNOWN

Mudhif, Chobaish
Marshes, Iraq

⬡ **NAVIGATOR**

Sponsored by the community's sheikh, *mudhifs* have been the focal point in Sabaen and Shiite villages in the Mesopotamian marshes of southern Iraq for thousands of years. Built on artificial islands created from reed beds, the robustness of *mudhifs* relies on two key elements—"leathered" reeds recycled from older buildings to form the "steel" core of each arch bundle and the self-supporting catenary arch considered by mathematicians as the ideal arch shape. Arches are overlaid with horizontal rows of tightly bound reed bundles over which reed mats and latticework are fixed. On the interior, the lower third of the curve is revealed, while the same area is covered on the exterior. Ventilated latticework is installed between each arch on the lower third of the *mudhif*. Western visitors entranced by *mudhifs* include English writer Gertrude Bell, who had a central role in the creation of the Iraqi nation. On a visit in 1916 she reported: "[Sheikh Ibadi al Husain] invited us to his *mudhif*, his guest house. . .a huge, perfectly regular and exquisitely constructed yellow tunnel 50 yards long. In the middle is the coffee hearth, with great logs of willow burning. On either side. . .a row of brocade-covered cushions. . .the whole lighted by the fire and a couple of small lamps, and the end of the *mudhif* fading away into a golden gloom." Drained in the twentieth century under the dictatorship of Saddam Hussein, Nature Iraq is leading the twenty-first-century recovery and reflooding of the marshes to allow for resettlement and rebuilding. **DJ**

1 REED COLUMNS

Built from the native marsh *Phragmite* reed, which grows to a height of 26 feet (8 m)—approximately four to five times the average human height—fasces-like vertical bundles create a pair of reed columns at the entrance. A further four rise above the slope of the barrel roof at the *mudhif*'s four corners.

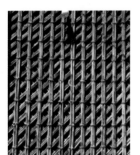

2 VENTILATION

Variously sized sophisticated reed weaves are both decorative and functional. Main ventilation is confined to the lower third of both sides of the building where occupants sit on floor-based cushions. Cross ventilation is enhanced with entry points at either end. Flush roof vents flank the roof's reed ridgepole.

3 ENTRANCE

The tripartite latticework entrance is an enduring template found elsewhere in the Islamic world, for example in the entrance of Kolahduzan house, Yazd, Iran. Its division into a central window with two side lights is not dissimilar to that of windows found in the east end of many Christian churches.

▲ *Mudhifs* were built atop the dead "litter layer" of reed beds of *Phragmite*. The litter layer was fortified with alternating layers of woven reed mats and mud until the water table was exceeded and a stable "island" created. Multiple natural and artificial islands form a village with the sheikh's *mudhif* as the focal point.

REED ARCHITECTURE

Ancient Sumerian stone carvings depict cattle standing next to corrals with reeds spiked into the ground, their tops bunched and tied to create a "roof" with plume spikes bursting from the crown. An Assyrian stone relief (705–681 BCE) in the British Museum and the Nile mosaic of Palestrina (1st century BCE) depict reed boats and barrel-shaped reed huts that are similar to *mudhifs*. *Hunting on the Lagoon* (*c.*1490; right), by Italian painter Vittore Carpaccio, is the background panel to his foreground painting *Two Venetian Ladies* (*c.*1490). In the latter work, the women sit at a window awaiting the return of their princely sportsmen, who stand in reed boats on the Venetian lagoon enjoying a fishing expedition aided by servants and trained cormorants. An island-based trio of mud, wood, and reed huts have hipped (or pyramid-hipped) roofs shingled in thatch with a central smoke vent. Reed mat rolls lean against the main hut, while reed fences corral fish and a single wooden outhouse stands at the edge of the island.

2 | 900–1400

PRE-COLUMBIAN CENTRAL AMERICA

Mesoamerican architecture remained a vibrant tradition during the last centuries of the pre-Columbian era. Urban plans, building designs, and styles incorporated a host of innovations alongside the legacy of Teotihuacan, the dominant city of the alliance that comprised the Aztec Empire, and the Maya civilization. During the tenth century, the Toltec state, with its capital at Tula just north of the Valley of Mexico, became the first polity since Teotihuacan to achieve broad political and economic control. Later city-states viewed the Toltecs as the inventors of civilization and flaunted claims—some architectural—to a Toltec heritage.

The main palace complex at Tula (see image 1), although not an enclosed apartment compound, was organized around unroofed patios that are reminiscent of Teotihuacan. The use of round columns to carry the roofs of surrounding rooms may reflect connections with western Mexico, where similar column construction was common and probably earlier. A building with columns at Chetro Ketl in Chaco Canyon has been taken as evidence for a Toltec presence in the southwest, but western Mexico is a more likely focus of the interaction. Pyramid B (c.900–1200) is Tula's most elaborate temple platform and it has a variant of *talud-tablero* style, with relief decoration in framed panels. The temple building shares features with the Temple of the Warriors (c.900–1200; see p.112) at Chichén Itzá in the Maya world. The similarity is striking and clearly indicates interaction between Chichén Itzá and western Mesoamerica, but it does not constitute strong evidence for the frequent

KEY EVENTS

c.900	c.1100–1200	c.1200–50	c.1250	c.1300–50	c.1400–50
The Mayas abandon Chichén Itzá. It is resettled a century later and is the major political and economic force in the northern Maya lowlands.	Tula and the Toltec state collapse, initiating a period of intense competition among central Mexican city-states.	Chichén Itzá's political and economic sphere disintegrates.	Mayapán emerges as the most powerful city in northern Yucatán.	The Mexica found the city-state of Tenochtitlan. In its heyday, it is the largest city in the pre-Columbian Americas.	Q'umarkaj Utatlán emerges as the center of an expansionist Ki'che state in the Guatemalan highlands.

interpretation that Toltec immigrants dominated Chichén Itzá. Several features of central Tula became hallmarks of a Toltec architectural style that was adopted by later city-states hoping to clothe themselves in political legitimacy through affiliation with the legendary Toltecs. A *coatepantli* (a free-standing wall with snakes in relief bounding the central civic precinct; see image 2) and a *tzompantli* (a low platform that supported a wooden frame for displaying the heads of sacrificed warriors) are the prototypes for features found in Aztec city centers.

The city of Tenochtitlan reflects both the legacy of the Toltecs and the particular history of its Aztec founders, who referred to themselves as "Mexica." It was built on an island in the lake system that occupied much of the Valley of Mexico. A complex of temples formed the focus of the city, with royal palaces and the main market clustered around the enclosing *coatepantli*. Main streets radiated from the sacred precinct, connecting to causeways that linked the city with the mainland. Traffic within the city was primarily by canoe on canals parallel to the streets. Each quarter of the city had its own temple and administrative palace, as did the constituent neighborhoods.

The main temple-pyramid, at the east edge of the sacred precinct, was the conceptual focus of the Aztec world. It had twin shrines to the principal state deities at the summit and hosted a variety of ceremonies, most notably the sacrifice of captured foreign warriors. Its symbolism was a seamless blend of religious, political, mythic, and historical themes revolving around the relationship of the Mexica with Huitzilopochtli, the deity embodying their identity and political legitimacy. The creation of a glorious (fictitious) history for the Mexica, by linking them to the legendary past, was a major theme of architectural decoration and of offerings interred during construction and

1 **Palacio Quemado** (*c.*1000)
Architect unknown
Tula, Mexico

2 *Coatepantli* (*c.*900–1200)
Architect unknown
Tula, Mexico

c.1425	c.1450	c.1450–1520	c.1475	1519	1521
Tenochtitlan, Texcoco, and Tlacopan defeat the Tepanecs, marking the birth of the Triple Alliance (Aztec Empire).	Civil war brings an end to Mayapán's hegemony.	The Triple Alliance secures control of the Valley of Mexico and establishes tribute provinces in central Mexico.	Kaqchikel lords break away from K'iche control and establish a new capital at Iximché.	The Spanish invasion of mainland Mexico and Central America begins with Hernán Cortés landing on the Gulf Coast and the founding of Veracruz.	Spaniards and their Tlaxcalan allies destroy Tenochtitlan and take over the Aztec Empire.

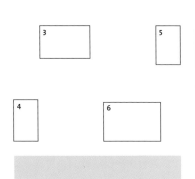

3 **Bench in sacred precinct (c.1325)**
Architect unknown
Tenochtitlan, Mexico

4 **Plan of Chichén Itzá**
Yucatán, Mexico

5 **North Terrace Ball Court (c.900–1200)**
Architect unknown
Chichén Itzá, Yucatán, Mexico

6 **Plaza A (1450–1525)**
Architect unknown
Iximché, Kaqchikel, Guatemala

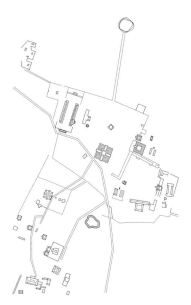

remodeling. An adjacent building featured benches (see image 3) with painted reliefs of warriors that were so similar to those in a small room at the base of Pyramid B at Tula as to suggest self-conscious emulation.

Chichén Itzá (see image 4) had emerged as a political and economic center in the northern Maya lowlands in the ninth century, when the town of Uxmal and its neighbors flourished in the Puuc region to the west. At its peak, in the eleventh century, Chichén Itzá dominated the northern and western part of Yucatán, and its architecture has a hybrid quality, reflecting strong interactions with central Mexico as well as with other Maya cities in Yucatán. Many buildings are in the Puuc style, which suggests an early connection with Uxmal. Some share design features and decoration with central Mexico, especially with Tula; others combine elements of these styles.

The North Terrace, a cluster of grand structures built on a massive platform and enclosed by a bounding wall, forms Chichén Itzá's civic core. El Castillo (c.800–1200)—also called the Pyramid of Kukulcán (the Yucatec Maya feathered-serpent deity) because of its decoration—is the most imposing temple. The Temple of the Warriors, the counterpart of Tula's main pyramid, stands nearby. Its Toltec elements are striking, but it also incorporates Puuc characteristics, notably long-nosed deity masks. The main North Terrace Ball Court (see image 5) is the largest at Chichén Itzá and one of the largest in all of Mesoamerica. Like most late ball courts, it has end courts bracketing the main playing alley and vertical rings in the side walls for scoring points. The placement of these rings, more than 23 feet (7 m) above the playing surface, and the sheer size of the court may indicate that it was also used as a venue for other public events. An elaborate masonry sweat bath stood adjacent to a smaller ball court. Colonnaded buildings with benches may have been council chambers and low platforms without superstructures were stages for ceremonies and other public performances. An elevated causeway leads from the North Terrace to the Sacred Cenote, the largest of several sinkholes within the city. Offerings and human sacrifices were cast into the cenote, which was still a focus of pilgrimages and was sacred to the rain god in the colonial period.

Central Mexican features are concentrated on the North Terrace. Most of the Puuc-style buildings and all of the hieroglyphic texts are found in somewhat less imposing complexes to the south. The chronology of Chichén Itzá's public architecture has not been established precisely, but most evidence suggests that the contrast between the North Terrace complex and building groups to the south resulted more from variations in building function and social differences within the city than from change through time.

Chichén Itzá's central Mexican features have been attributed to influence from Tula, or to the presence of Toltecs, sometimes thought to have been politically dominant in the city. However, Chichén Itzá's civic core is far grander than Tula's, making one-way influence emanating from Tula seem unlikely. By the mid-twelfth century, Chichén Itzá's power was beginning to fade and, a century later, Mayapán emerged as the dominant center in the northern lowlands. The city of Mayapán has an unusual layout, with all of its civic structures and elite residences packed densely within a city wall. Much of Mayapán's civic architecture echoes that of Chichén Itzá, but on a smaller scale and with less elegant masonry. The serpent jambs of the main temple, inspired by El Castillo, typify the contrast; they are roughly executed in plaster rather than finely carved in stone.

Many of Mayapán's civic structures were decorated with painted murals in a variant of the widely shared Mixteca-Puebla style, indicating that Mayapán, like Chichén Itzá, maintained links with western Mesoamerica. Puuc-style mosaic masks of long-nosed deities adorn at least one platform and are probably another example of archaism rather than a survival of the style. The independent city-states that succeeded Mayapán shared its preference for small buildings with heavy plaster over coarse masonry. Continuing use of the Mixteca-Puebla style for murals indicates that interaction with western Mesoamerica persisted through the final century of the pre-Columbian era.

In 1519, Spanish invaders found highland Maya societies organized into regional states. The largest was K'iche (Quiché) state, with its capital at Q'umarkaj (Utatlán) in the central highlands of Guatemala. The political structures of these states were built on the framework of lineages, the key feature of highland Maya social organization. Kingship was dual; heads of the two highest-ranking lineages were senior and junior rulers, and state offices were occupied by officials of the dominant lineages. The layout and architecture of late highland political centers, especially Iximché, capital of the Kaqchikel state, reflect this political structure. Lineage compounds comprise the civic core of the site. Plaza A (see image 6), the compound of the highest-ranking lineage, is dominated by a pair of temples dedicated to the lineage's patron deities. Iximché was founded shortly before the arrival of the Spaniards when the Kaqchikel rebelled against K'iche, but it was not occupied long enough for architectural remodeling and urban growth to obscure the basic plan. **JSH/KMH**

Temple of the Warriors c.900–1200
ARCHITECT UNKNOWN

Temple of the Warriors,
Chichén Itzá,
Yucatán, Mexico

The Temple of the Warriors in Chichén Itzá embodies a central issue in late Maya prehistory: the nature of the relationship with the Toltecs of central Mexico. Many features of design and decoration are shared with Pyramid B, the main temple at the Toltec capital of Tula, and the costumes of the warriors are distinctly Toltec in style. Other features, notably the vaulted roof, once supported by a frontal colonnade, and the Puuc-style masks that adorn the facade, are part of the Maya architectural tradition. Painted reliefs of warriors and animals fill framed panels on the terrace bodies, which are constructed in a variant of the central Mexican *talud-tablero* style. Serpent heads adorn the tops of the balustrades and small figures with outstretched hands seem designed to hold banners. A *chacmool*, an altar in the form of a reclining figure with an offering plate on its stomach, stands in front of the door. Twin feathered serpents form the door jambs; square columns support the vaulted roof. A table-like altar occupies most of the interior space. The concentration of features shared with central Mexico does indicate that a Toltec connection was an important dimension of Chichén Itzá's power structure, but there is no unequivocal evidence for Toltec political control. **JSH/KMH**

✣ NAVIGATOR

1 FEATHERED SERPENTS

The feathers adorning the bodies of the serpents whose rattled tails supported the lintel over the main temple door represent the widely venerated Mesoamerican feathered serpent deity. This deity was called Quetzalcoatl in central Mexico and Kukulkan in Yucatán.

2 MASKS

Mosaic masks in the style of Puuc cities of northwestern Yucatán flank the temple door and decorate the building's corners. The long-nosed images, usually identified as Chaak, the rain god, could be representations of Ah Bolon Dzakab, the supernatural patron of royalty.

3 *TABLEROS*

The *tableros* of the terrace bodies frame painted reliefs of human figures in central Mexican warrior garb, carrying shields and spear throwers. The accompanying figures of eagles and pumas (or jaguars), associated with warrior groups in ancient Mesoamerica, continue the warfare theme.

◄ A mural from the interior room of the temple depicts a fleet of armed warriors arriving by sea to attack a village.

PYRAMID B IN TULA

Pyramid B (*c*.900–1200; right), the most elaborate temple platform in the civic center of Tula, is certainly related to the Temple of the Warriors at Chichén Itzá, but it is not obvious that Pyramid B was the inspiration for the temple, as is often assumed. Although both temples share a concentration of features, unfortunately the relationship of the two buildings has been confused by the reconstruction of Pyramid B. There is no archaeological evidence for most of the colonnade in front of the building or for the columns part way up the stair. They were restored entirely on the basis of features at Chichén Itzá, on the assumption that the Temple of the Warriors was designed as the twin of Pyramid B.

INDIA: SACRED

1 **Kandariya Mahadeva Temple**
(c.1030)
Architect unknown
Khajuraho, Madhya Pradesh, India

2 **Vamana Temple (mid-eleventh century)**
Architect unknown
Khajuraho, Madhya Pradesh, India

3 **Lingaraja Temple (c.1060)**
Architect unknown
Bhubaneshwar, Orissa, India

The early centuries of the second millennium saw a period of intense building activity and creativity on the Indian subcontinent, fueled by the emergence of new political powers. Moved by a desire to establish their dynasty as a superpower amid a climate of emulation and rivalry, kings made large donations to Hindu deities and launched vast programs of temple building. Impressive structures demonstrated the prestige of the dynasty, and a few of the temples reached truly monumental proportions.

Indian temple architecture is conceived in terms of aediculae: miniature reproductions of buildings combined and embedded in one another to form a full-scale building. The analogy between the parts and the whole gives the impression that Indian temple architecture is fractal. These building shapes are perpetually in renewal: shrine types, once developed, were used as compositional elements in new temple types. By the seventh century, two architectural traditions had been formed: Nagara in north India and Dravida in south India, and they spread throughout the Indian subcontinent. Coming out of a common architectural stratum, they proposed different interpretations, not only in the selection of the architectural components but also in the ways in which they were combined.

In north India, three general types of monumental shrines were discernible: Valabhi, Phamsana, and Latina. The barrel-roofed Valabhi type fell out of use for full-scale edifices by the ninth century, except in eastern

KEY EVENTS

c.954	c.1010	c.1026	c.1030	c.1060	c.1060
Chandela ruler Yashovarman constructs Lakshmana Temple in Khajuraho, India. The complex is built on a high platform.	Brihadeshvara—a monumental edifice with a shrine 217 feet (66 m) high—is erected in Tanjavur, Tamil Nadu, during the reign of the Chola king, Rajaraja.	The Sun Temple in Modhera, Gujarat, is completed during the reign of Bhimadeva I. The pavilion overlooks a stepped tank adorned with small shrines.	Kandariya Mahadeva, an archetypal complex of Sekhari design at Khajuraho, Madhya Pradesh, is built under the rule of Vidyadhara, the Chandela king.	Lingaraja Temple is built at Bhubaneshwar. The 180-foot-high (55 m) shrine is the first of several huge Orissan temples.	The Shiva Temple, Ambarnath, Maharashtra—the prime achievement of the Silahara dynasty—combines Dravida and Nagara features.

India, where Valabhi shrines continued to be built until the thirteenth century. However, Valabhi aediculae were integrated into other types of temple in western and central India, as cardinal projections, wall niches, and most significantly, as antefixae to the main shrine. Similarly, Phamsana structures with pyramidal roofs made of horizontal slabs were used mainly for halls and porches. In western India they evolved into the Samvarana type, the roof of which comprises bands of bell-topped pavilions with axial horseshoe gables and small bells at the corners, as seen in the hall in front of Mahanaleshvara Temple (late eleventh century) in Menal, Rajasthan.

Latina temples dominated the early landscape of north India and enjoyed a certain popularity in Deccan. A Latina temple is characterized by a curved spire, with a central spine decorated with intricate horseshoe dormers, and superimposed corner pavilions topped by ribbed cushions. The main variations occur in the number of projections and stories. Projections often resembled pilasters, as seen at Ghateshvara Temple (tenth century) in Baroli, Rajasthan. The twenty-one-story Vamana Temple (see image 2) at Khajuraho in Madhya Pradesh is an example of how the features also became increasingly compressed. From the tenth century onward, full-scale Latina temples fell out of favor, but Latina aediculae were used to form new designs. In Orissa, a regional version of the Latina temple blossomed at a comparatively late date, as demonstrated by the impressive Lingaraja (see image 3) and Ananta Vasudeva Temples (thirteenth century), both at Bhubaneshwar.

The tenth century brought the start of a period marked by a profound architectural renewal. From the Latina sprang the Sekhari and Bhumija types. Characterized by a composite appearance, they featured similar architectural components but differed in their arrangement. A Sekhari shrine is characterized by multiple Latina spires embedded in one another, along with components resembling pillars crowned by miniature towers. Multispired temples appeared in central and western India around the same time and were later adopted in Orissa and Karnataka. The half-embedded projections along the cardinal axes seem to emerge from the core, while other architectural components proliferate between. This burgeoning process generated dynamic compositions and favored experimentation, as testified by the site of Khajuraho in Madhya Pradesh, where the numerous Sekhari temples erected by the Chandela dynasty, during its rule from the tenth to the thirteenth centuries, such as the Lakshmana (c.954) and the Vishvanatha (c.999), offer an insight into possible permutations of the type. Complexity in these designs increased over time. The adoption of a stepped diamond plan and the addition of re-entrant projections and quarter spires led to particularly dense compositions, such as Kandariya Mahadeva Temple (see image 1).

Bhumija shrines, also fully articulated, are made of vertical chains of aediculae resembling pillars crowned by miniature superstructures, flowing

c.1080	c.1100–1150	c.1100–1200	c.1112	c.1213	c.1240–60
Udayeshvara Temple (see p.118) is consecrated at Udayapur, Madhya Pradesh, under the reign of the Paramara king, Udayaditya.	The so-called Surya Temple in Jhalrapatan, Rajasthan, is constructed. Its hybrid shrine combines Sekhari and Bhumija features.	Nataraja Temple in Chidambaram, Tamil Nadu, is built with multiple enclosures, *gopuras*, a Devi shrine, dance hall, pillared hall, and tank.	Features from north and south Indian traditions are combined to create the Mahadeva temple in Ittagi, northern Karnataka.	Ramappa Temple in Palampet, Andhra Pradesh, is founded by a general of the Kakatiya king Ganapatideva.	Surya Temple in Konarak is founded by the Ganga king Narasimha I, marking the peak of Orissan architecture.

downward between cardinal spines like those of a Latina temple, made up of intricate dormers. Bhumija temples were erected over a vast territory between the eleventh and thirteenth centuries, and variations occur mostly in the type of plan—orthogonal or stellate—and the number of projections and stories. The Paramaras, who ruled western Madhya Pradesh from the eleventh century to the end of the thirteenth century, favored the Bhumija type. Udayeshvara Temple (eleventh century; see p.118) in Udayapur is one of their greatest achievements. It shows an awareness of different architectural traditions through the use of Dravida components in this predominantly Nagara structure. Bhumija temples were also erected in Maharashtra, where the finest example is the Gondeshvara (twelfth century) in Sinnar, and in distant southern territories in Andhra Pradesh and Karnataka, where notable examples include Chennakeshava Temple (twelfth century) at Belur.

In south Indian temple architecture, a basic shrine has a pyramidal outline and is crowned by a domed or barrel-roofed aedicula. More complex temples are formed by the integration of one structure with another, typically with one becoming the superstructure of the other. Lower tiers are commonly composed of square-domed aediculae at the corners and rectangular barrel-roofed aediculae in the center. From this basic principle, two main traditions emerged, centered in Karnataka and Tamil Nadu. The main differences occur in the type of plan, the type of crowning, the number of projections, and the number of types of aedicula used.

In the Tamil tradition, although the architectural components are embedded in the structure they are clearly distinct, and in early temples the number of projections was often reduced from story to story. From the eighth century onward, two-story aediculae were introduced. With the rise of the Chola dynasty (848–1279) in the ninth century, the pace of construction increased. Temples were endowed with a greater number of stories and projections, without disturbing the continuity of the earlier tradition. Brihadeshvara Temple (see image 4) in Tanjavur reaches 217 feet (66 m) over its fourteen stories, in a vast enclosure that is entered via the first monumental axial barrel-roofed gateway (*gopura*), a feature that is typical of the later southern temple complexes. The shrine's composition lacks clarity, however, due to the use of multistoried aediculae and the fluctuating number and types of aediculae composing the tiers. Clarity and symmetry would govern later designs such as those of Brihadeshvara Temple (mid-eleventh century) at

Gangaikondacholapuram and Airavateshvara Temple (mid-twelfth century) at Darasuram, in which tiers comprise a uniform number of aediculae.

In Karnataka, the architectural tradition is characterized by experimentation, with the components becoming increasingly interpenetrating. The tendency to preserve an odd number of aediculae, generally identical, reinforces the radial continuity, the epitome being the uniform stellate Doddabasappa Temple (late eleventh century) in Dambal. From the tenth century onward, the variety of aediculae increased through the combination of existing types and the use of both Nagara and Dravida designs. The Dravida structure of Kashivishveshvara Temple (see image 5) in Lakkundi, for example, is adorned with Sekhari and Bhumija forms. Aediculae also seem to burst apart during this period; staggered, they bring rhythm and dynamism to the surface. Stellate plans became popular during the eleventh century, particularly in southern Karnataka. From the twelfth to the fourteenth centuries under the Hoysala dynasty (1026–1343), highly decorated stellate temples with whole galleries of deities were raised on high platforms, as seen at Hoysaleshvara Temple, Halebid (twelfth century), and Keshava Temple (see image 6), Somanathapura.

With the establishment of the Delhi sultanate in the thirteenth century and the Mughal Empire in the sixteenth, Hindu architectural traditions were disrupted in north India. In south India, under the Vijayanagara Empire in the fourteenth to the sixteenth centuries, vast urban centers and large religious complexes developed. Earlier sanctuaries were enlarged, for example by adding concentric enclosure walls and *gopuras*, increasing in size toward the periphery. Such designs would culminate in the creation of temple cities in Tamil Nadu, such as the seventeenth-century Minakshi-Sundareshvara complex in Madurai.

Indian culture had a great impact on the political and cultural development of Southeast Asia as a result of trade links that developed from the first centuries CE. Hinduism spread beyond India, and Hindu temples were erected in Southeast Asia, conceived as the deity's heavenly abode on earth like their Indian counterparts. In Cambodia, stone architecture seems to have been equally thought of in terms of aediculae, and governed by similar dynamics. From the ninth century to the twelfth century, most of the Khmer kings founded temple mountains to mark the center of their kingdom. Symmetry and concentric hierarchic organization were pushed further than in Indian architectural counterparts. The monumental complex of Angkor Wat (twelfth century) represents the macrocosm, with its main shrine surrounded by sub-shrines, rising above a stepped pyramid enclosed by concentric galleries and a moat. **DT**

4 **Brihadeshvara Temple
(early eleventh century)**
Architect unknown
Tanjavur, Tamil Nadu, India

5 **Kashivishveshvara Temple
(mid-eleventh century)**
Architect unknown
Lakkundi, Karnataka, India

6 **Keshava Temple (mid-thirteenth
century)**
Architect unknown
Somanathapura, Karnataka, India

Udayeshvara Temple   Eleventh century
ARCHITECT UNKNOWN

Udayeshvara Temple,
Udayapur, Madhya
Pradesh, India

⬧ NAVIGATOR

The Udayeshvara Temple is an exquisite example of Bhumija architecture. Consecrated to the god Shiva in 1080, during the reign of the Paramara king Udayaditya (1070–93), the red sandstone edifice is composed of a seven-story shrine built on a twenty-eight-point star plan and a closed, stepped-diamond-plan hall with three porches. The shrine has a curved spire topped by a ribbed cushion that is characteristic of Nagara temples. The cardinal axes are formed by spines made of interlaced horseshoe dormer designs like those of a Latina temple. Between them, five chains of seven pillarlike components cascade downward. A dynamic composition is created through the repetition of identical expanding forms at every level. The pyramidal shape of the roof of the hall offers a gentle transition toward the tower of the shrine. Its sloping bands are punctuated by small pavilions typical of a Samvarana structure. The temple rests on two sets of base moldings, and is composed of pillarlike aediculae crowned by miniature reproductions of the superstructure; the shafts of those in the first story form the external walls. As is characteristic of Bhumija temples, this predominantly Nagara structure features elements deriving from the Dravida tradition, testifying to an awareness of temple forms from other regions in central India. **DT**

1 AEDICULAE

Pillarlike aediculae emerge from the nucleus of the structure. The lower part of their shafts is occupied by a standing deity that is framed by two pilasters crowned by Dravida pavilions receiving a vegetal arch. This creates a ring of deities around the temple.

2 DRAVIDA ELEMENTS

The finials of the cardinal projections of the shrine are composed of Dravida elements. The first is an onion-shaped medallion made of foliage; the second a stepped pyramidal pavilion hidden by a niche defined by pilasters, the capitals of which receive vegetal scrolls.

3 CAPITALS

The temple is composed of images of temples; the capitals of the pillarlike aediculae of the shrine are orthogonal Bhumija spires. The central spine is composed of horseshoe dormers framed by two vertical rows of five miniature Dravida components.

◀ The hall has a highly decorated corbeled ceiling. From a single hollow circular lotus, half-lotus lobes emanate in concentric rings, reinforcing the analogy between the whole and the parts. Multiple miniature domes comprise the larger dome. The radiating proliferation of miniature domes creates a striking effect.

"SAMARANGANASUTRADHARA"

The "Samaranganasutradhara" is a treatise on architecture attributed to the Paramara king Bhoja (c.1010–55), to whom is also attributed the Shiva temple at Bhojpur, Madhya Pradesh (right). However, the monumental treatise of almost 7,500 Sanskrit verses actually emanates from different sources and was probably not finalized until the 15th century. Like similar Indian treatises, it is governed by typological classifications. Thirteen chapters focus on temple architecture and reveal four broad categories of temple type: Nagara, Dravida, Bhumija, and Vavata. Designs are hierarchically arranged within their categories, and plans, components, and elevations, as well as patronage, reward, and gods' preference for a particular type of temple, are discussed in detail.

CALIPHATE AND CATHEDRAL

1 **Complex of Sultan Qalawun (1285)**
Amr Sangar
Cairo, Egypt

2 **Mosaics in the Palatine Chapel (1132–89)**
Architect unknown
Palermo, Sicily, Italy

3 **Court of the Lions, Alhambra (1362–91)**
Muhammad V
Granada, Spain

The beginning of the second millennium was one of the most creative periods in history. In Europe and the Middle East, architecture defined two diametrically opposed civilizations and formal iconography was a powerful weapon in this struggle. The golden age of the Abbasid caliphate (750–1258) reached its apogee some two centuries after a papal mission from Rome to England established the See of Canterbury in 597. Iconic and idiomatic examples of formal architecture were built by both European and Middle Eastern cultures, but the architecture of Islam and Christianity had, at times, mutual regard and produced, for example, Mudéjar, a hybrid of Moorish, Gothic, and Romanesque architecture. The Great Mosque of Cordoba (c.953–1523; see p.124) in Spain is an idiomatic as well as an iconic example of enforced heterogeneity between Christianity and Islam. But while Cordoba is an extreme, other architecture of the period merged Crusader and Islamic influence, and Christian exemplars such as Durham Cathedral (1093–1133), England, employed identifiable caliphate architectural motifs.

Al-Azhar Mosque (972; see p.126) in Cairo was founded in the tenth century by Caliph al-Muizz and is the most venerated university in the Islamic world. Its two Koranic schools bracket a large hypostyle (many-columned) mosque with a courtyard arcade of cross-tied triangular Fatimid keel-shaped arches.

KEY EVENTS

969	987	1104	1132	1144	1258
The Fatimids establish the city of Cairo as their capital and commission the prominent Islamic institution al-Azhar the following year.	Additions to the Great Mosque of Cordoba (see p.124) by the ruler of al-Andalus, Almanzor, include the ablutions courtyard known as "Patio de los Naranjos."	The Basilica of St. Mary Magdalene at Vézelay, France, is dedicated. Its sculpture becomes the subject of great interest.	Work begins on the Palatine Chapel inside the palace of Roger II, the Norman king of Sicily.	Abbot Suger finishes his conversion of the Romanesque Abbey of St.-Denis (see p.152). It is the first Gothic cathedral.	Mongol armies destroy the Abbasid capital of Baghdad and the House of Wisdom, which had fueled the golden age of Islam.

The fourth Islamic caliphate, the Fatimids ruled from 909 to 1171 and introduced a plan that reconciled the street-facing mosque with multidirectional street plans, and the *qibla* (the direction of Mecca) with a bent-axis plan to create an angular entrance to the prayer hall. The Mamluks, who ruled form 1250 to 1517, imposed their own personality on Cairo, balancing military prowess with a visceral understanding of urban planning, as demonstrated by the *madrassa* (educational center), hospital, and mausoleum complex of Sultan Qalawun (see image 1), which stretches along Sharia al-Muizz.

Qalawun's articulated street facade has Syrian (Crusader and Islamic) arrangements with niches framing double-arched windows, similar to the intersecting arch pairings at Durham Cathedral, and to the Palatine Chapel, Palermo, Sicily, begun in 1132 and built for Roger II, King of Sicily. The chapel (see image 2) is a mix of Christian and Islamic Fatimid palace architecture, including a Byzantine dome, Islamic arches, classical columns, and a carved timber *muqarnas* (polycellular, three-dimensional, stalactitelike device) ceiling, in which Islamic rotated squares are quadrupled to form Greek crosses. Qalawun's mausoleum dome and adjacent minaret reinforce the iconic power of these two Islamic symbols, although the minaret was more frequently built during the Abbasid caliphate and is less frequent in Fatimid architecture. Inside, the bent-axis torques from the street, toward the *qibla*, and a long corridor leads from the *madrassa* into the mausoleum. The tomb is hidden behind a *mashrabiya* (latticed window), within a colonnade that supports the octagonal drum of the dome.

The Alhambra in Granada, begun in 1238, and the Great Mosque of Cordoba are overt examples of both the clash and the assimilation of cultures. The Alhambra (al-Hamra, or "red house") was built under the rule of the Nasrids (1238–1492), the last Arab–Muslim–Spanish dynasty. The palace sits on a plateau above the Darra River and began to coalesce when Yusuf I built the Tower of Justice in 1348, initiating a sequence from public to private zones. The Hall of the Ambassadors in the Comares Tower, the northern anchor of the axial plan, was located near the escarpment to capture cool river air rushing up the cliff. This public zone houses the throne room, the administrative offices, and a small mosque. The Court of the Myrtles (1354–91) stretches southward from the official zone to the residential quarter, which includes the harem and baths. Muhammad V built the Court of the Lions (see image 3) at a right angle to his father's palace to set it apart. The refined fragility of the Alhambra, conveyed through exquisite detailing, is a cumulative, unlikely combination of local traditions and materials, and it reinvented Islamic conventions, such as tall, polylobe (scalloped) arches, colorful tilework, plasterwork, and improbably delicate *muqarnas*. As part of the Christian reconquest of Spain, the Catholic Frederick III took Cordoba in 1236 and Seville in 1248, leaving Granada as the final Muslim city, until it capitulated in 1492 to King Ferdinand II of Aragon and Queen Isabella I of Castile.

1260	1285	1312	1492	1523	1532
Chartres Cathedral in northwest France, built between 1194 and 1250, is consecrated by King Louis IX.	Mamluk Sultan Qalawun builds a religious school, hospital, and mausoleum in Cairo. It is one of the first hospitals in its region.	Ibn Idhari writes his important text "Al Bayan al-Mughrib" (*The Amazing Story*), documenting the history of the Maghreb.	The Alhambra, a Nasrid palace in Granada, Spain, and the last Islamic bastion in al-Andalus, is captured by King Ferdinand II and Queen Isabella I.	Holy Roman Emperor Charles V orders a Gothic cathedral to be built in the middle of the Great Mosque of Cordoba.	Charles V commissions a massive palace in the middle of the Alhambra, but thankfully does not raze the Alhambra.

The beginning of the second millennium had eschatological significance for Christians. The description in the Book of Revelation in the New Testament described a heaven-sent building—a "New Jerusalem"—which influenced the design of the first Gothic cathedral: Abbot Suger's rebuilding of the Abbey of St.-Denis, Paris, into a basilica (c.1135–44; see image 4). It also fueled the Crusader conviction that the Christian version of the Apocalypse had arrived. Suger borrowed Durham Cathedral's quadripartite rib system—a bay divided into four quadrants by diagonal and transverse ribs, which enables pointed arches—to replace heavy, Romanesque barrel vaults, and to achieve what architectural historian John Fitchen called the "maximum height and maximum light" of French Gothic architecture.

The horseshoe-shaped, double-arched, red-and-white hypostyle interior of the Great Mosque of Cordoba defines the Moorish style. The structure was originally built by Caliph Abd al-Rahman I on the site of a Visigoth chapel, which was atop a ruined Roman temple, and Abd al-Rahman II built a second prayer hall in c.836 parallel to the original. Al-Hakam II built a third in 961. Ibn Idhari's medieval text "Al Bayan al-Mughrib" (*The Amazing Story*; 1312) records that Muslim conquerors typically converted only half of the physical space of churches to mosques, leaving the rest for the original congregation. Catholic appropriation of the mosque initially seemed to follow a similar precept. The mosque was reconsecrated as the Cathedral of the Assumption of the Virgin, and a chapel was inserted in 1275. In 1371, the Royal Chapel was built in Mudéjar style. However, the insertion of a Gothic cathedral into the geometric center of the mosque in 1523 was far more destructive. Bishop Alonso Manrique de Lara's plan was opposed by the city council, which objected to the loss of the mosque's "perfection." The Holy Roman Emperor and King of Spain, Charles V, agreed the plan, and the cathedral was inserted, marooned within the mosque complex. The tenth-century square stone minaret—the model for other minarets, including the Hassan Tower, Rabat, Morocco (1199), and the Giralda minaret in Seville (1184)—was entombed inside a Catholic bell tower.

Durham Cathedral acknowledges architectural inspiration from the fourth-century Old St. Peter's Basilica in Vatican City, including its spiral incised "Solomonic" columns in the shrine of St. Cuthbert. Intriguingly, the cathedral also suggests Andalusian inspiration from Aljafería Palace (see image 5) and the Great Mosque of Cordoba. Aljafería—a *taifa*, or autonomous Islamic emirate or kingdom—was a Hudid fortification in Zaragoza, northern Spain.

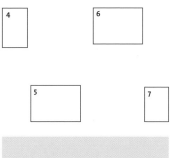

4 **Choir, Basilica of St.-Denis (c.1135–44)**
Abbot Suger
Paris, France

5 **Aljafería Palace (ninth–eleventh century)**
Ahmad I (b. Sulayman, Sayf al-Dawla
'Imad al-Dawla al- Muqtadir)
Zaragoza, Aragon, Spain

6 **Wells Cathedral scissor arch (1338–48)**
William Joy
Wells, Somerset, UK

7 **Replica horse sculpture (twentieth century)**
Based on an original fourth-century
quadriga by Lysippos
St. Mark's Basilica, Venice, Italy

Known as Qasr al-Surur (Palace of Joy), the palace was an Islamic frontier post influenced by the design of the tenth-century Madinat az-Zahra near Cordoba, commissioned by Abd-al-Rahman III, which served as an administrative center of al-Andalus for the Umayyad caliphs. Only a small part has been excavated, but several colonnades amid the ruins are clearly the less elegant antecedents of those in the Great Mosque of Cordoba. Exterior elevations at Aljafería include plain and interlaced blind arcades. The palace was further fortified in the sixteenth century with a moat and five circular bastions.

Aljafería became the residence of Christian rulers, who made a series of alterations from the twelfth to the fourteenth centuries, including in the courtyard, where double-register, interlaced, polylobe arches are supported on slender columns. The elaborate arch perforations—as though an engineer has effortlessly cut then unfurled a folded stack of paper into a *papel picado*, or perforated paper decoration—create a series of figure eights similar to those seen in the scissor arch (1338–48) at Wells Cathedral (see image 6), the first English cathedral begun as a Gothic enterprise. The instability of the cathedral's tower created the circumstances for master mason William Joy's internal scissor-arch support, which succeeds where buttressing failed. Enabled by the palace's patrons, Aljafería's master craftsmen, including Faraig de Gali, ensured that Mudéjar spread beyond the Aragon region. But did clerical visitors or the diaspora of craftsmen inspire elements of Wells and Durham cathedrals? The intersecting arcades in Durham Cathedral's nave closely mimic those of Aljafería and Mudéjar buildings in Zaragoza, including La Seo Cathedral (1119–1520), which replaced the mosque captured during an assault in 1118. In addition, the cellular eight-point decorated tracery of the upper third register of Wells Cathedral's Lady Chapel windows has visual similarities to the cascade effect and cellular construction of *muqarnas*.

The Crusader siege of Constantinople in 1204 is both an epitaph for and an example of the tangle of influences between Islamic and Christian architecture. The fourth-century BCE Greek four-horse quadriga sculpture was looted from Constantinople, and Enrico Dandolo, doge of Venice, had it installed on the terrace facade of St. Mark's Basilica (1071). Napoleon Bonaparte looted it again in 1797, and the sculpture was repatriated to Venice in 1815. It was replaced in the twentieth century by a replica (see image 7), which now adorns the basilica whose Byzantine architectural style recalls the civilization that Venice betrayed. **JMS**

Great Mosque of Cordoba c.953–1523
VARIOUS ARCHITECTS

Great Mosque of Cordoba,
Cordoba, Andalusia, Spain

C aliph Abd al-Rahman I built the first section of the mosque in 784, on the site of a Visigoth church that he removed. Abd al-Rahman II added another prayer hall parallel to the first one and Al-Hakam II, the son of Abd al-Rahman III, added a third. This included a *mihrab*, which is unusual in being an entire room rather than just a niche, and in being off-center, because of the proximity of the Guadalquivir River and caliph's palace. Al-Mansur bi-llah added the final segment, placing it across the bottom of the first three, to make a square hypostyle whole. An open walled courtyard planted with orange trees was then placed at one end. When the King of Castile, Ferdinand III, conquered Cordoba in 1236, he converted the mosque into a cathedral and it was used as such for more than 300 years. Very few changes were made to the original structure, but as time went by, a faction inside the Church favored the construction of a nave, choir, and altar, which required the demolition of the center of the mosque. Alonso Manrique de Lara was Bishop of Cordoba from 1516 to 1523, when this new cathedral inside the mosque was planned. Had it not been for the opposition of the Mayor of Corboda and many townspeople, the entire mosque would have been leveled. **JMS**

 NAVIGATOR

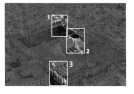

1 FORECOURT
The walled forecourt, added to the four-staged, square plan that finally emerged, had a sophisticated irrigation system that was used to water a grove of orange trees inside it. This hydraulic system, and the trees it supported, must have perfumed the air as visitors entered the mosque.

2 CATHEDRAL
The Gothic cathedral that was built in the middle of the mosque is hardly visible from the outside (except for the nearby bell tower, which was converted from the original carefully detailed minaret that remains inside it). Otherwise, the building fits seamlessly into the streetscape.

3 MOSQUE EXTERIOR
The exterior of the mosque is characteristically plain, as was customary for Islamic public buildings in the past. The only suggestion of the spectacle that awaits the visitor inside is a single, red-and-white striped, horseshoe arch over the main entrance from the street.

◄ The 856 double-arched columns, partially made from Roman remnants, such as capitals and shafts, support arches with red and white voussoirs (wedge-shaped blocks). The top arch is semicircular and the bottom arch has the rounded horseshoe shape that defines the Moorish style.

THE POINTED ARCH

The pointed arch—one of the most distinctive features of Islamic architecture—evolved quickly as the faith spread, and adapted to local building traditions. It first appears in modest form in 629, in the Jawatha Mosque in al-Kilabiyah, near Hofuf, which is the oldest surviving mosque in Saudi Arabia, after the Mosque of al-Haram, Mecca (c.630; see p.98) and the Prophet's Mosque, Medina (622; see p.96). By the time Umayyad Caliph Abd al-Malik and his son, al-Walid, built Al-Aqsa Mosque (right) in Jerusalem in 705, Muslim architects were comfortable using pointed arches in arcades. By 775, when Isa ibn Musa, the nephew of the first Abbasid caliph, built Ukhaider Palace, near Karbala in Iraq, they had completely assimilated the concept of iterative rhythm.

Al-Azhar Mosque 972
JAWHAR IBN ABDALLAH (AL-SIQILLI)

Al-Azhar Mosque,
Cairo, Egypt

The Fatimids were Berbers, who ruled from Tunis before marching across North Africa to found al-Qahirah (modern Cairo) in Egypt in 969. During their move east, they saw several Roman cities that were based on a grid, with a north–south-oriented street (*cardo maximus*) and an east–west-oriented street (*decumanus*). When Berber general Jawhar al-Siqili laid out Cairo, he also used a grid as it allowed the city to be built quickly. By making the main street narrow and placing it on a north–south axis, he was able to ensure that it would always have shade. A sequence of courtyards, scaled from large institutional *maidans* (squares) near the main street, named Sharia al-Muizz after the founding caliph, to smaller residential equivalents, ensured that convective currents would keep the city cool. When the Fatimids established al-Azhar, soon after they founded Cairo, they located it near Sharia al-Muizz and organized the university around a large, marble-paved *sahn* (court) for this reason. That court is lined with an arcade of characteristically flat, cross-tied Fatimid keel arches to accelerate the flow of cool air into the hypostyle mosque that surrounds it. Two *madrassas* bracket the mosque and these buildings contribute to the overall convective strategy. The Fatimids were Shia and they placed great importance on education. Al-Azhar, which is one of the few surviving reminders of Fatimid Cairo, has retained its reputation as the most venerable educational institution in the Islamic world. **JMS**

✤ NAVIGATOR

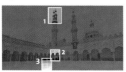

FOCAL POINTS

1 MINARET

The minarets of al-Azhar established the elegantly stacked profile that is now associated with Egyptian mosque architecture. Until recently, a muezzin would climb the internal stairway to the balcony around the top segment five times a day to deliver the call to prayer, which is now recorded.

2 KEEL ARCH

The keel arches used by the Fatimids are as distinctive as their minarets. Unlike the horseshoe-shaped Moorish arch or the rounder, fuller, Mamluk variation, they are straighter on the side, with a shallow curve at the top, and require a cross-tie to provide full structural strength to the span.

3 MARBLE COURTYARD

The exterior of al-Azhar belies the magnificent marble courtyard in the middle of the university. This is consistent with a past general principle of Islamic architecture in which a modest facade was presented to the outside world and any show of luxury was restricted to the interior of the building.

◄ The hypostyle hall used at al-Azhar Mosque is well suited to accommodating rows of people kneeling in prayer. Worshippers face the *mihrab* (prayer niche), which is located on the *qibla* wall that points toward Mecca.

INDO-ISLAMIC

Indo-Islamic architecture began with the invasion of the Sindh by the Caliph Umar in 643, and the absorption of this region of India into the Umayyad caliphate by 712. As Islam spread beyond Arabia, the architectural conventions established in the formative years of the faith mutated in order to conform to the cultures encountered. In addition to their functional purpose, these conventions conveyed highly charged, deeply symbolic, sociopolitical meanings and a prescient, idealized vision of the status that the nascent empire would achieve. Muslim armies invaded Egypt, Syria, Palestine, Mesopotamia, North Africa, and parts of the Persian and Byzantine empires little more than a decade after the Hijrah—Muhammad's migration from Mecca to Medina—in 622. The incremental assimilation that followed shows how Arabian architectural archetypes, and those of the Muslim surrogates that supplanted them, were reciprocally absorbed by their Indian colonies.

As the Islamic empire expanded, its Arab identity weakened due to sheer size. After the conquest of the Sindh, the impetus shifted to other Muslims in northern India such as the Ghaznavids (977–1186) and the Ghurids (1148–1215). The monotheistic Muslim ontology, which prohibits effigies, fundamentally

KEY EVENTS

977	1192	1206	1231	1290	c.1303
Sebuktigin founds the Ghaznavid dynasty.	While serving the sultan of the Ghurid Empire, Muhammad Ghori, Aibak commissions the Qutb Minar to commemorate a victory over the king of Rajput.	Aibak seizes power and establishes Mamluk rule in northwest India, becoming the first sultan of Delhi.	The first Islamic mausoleum, Sultan Ghari, is built for Prince Nasirud-Din Mahmud, the eldest son of the Mamluk ruler Iltumish.	Mamluk rule in Delhi ends following the death of the tenth sultan, Muiz ud din Qaiqabad.	Siri Fort in Delhi is built during the reign of Ala al-Din Khalji. It includes the Hauz Khas reservoir for supplying water to the inhabitants.

128 900–1400

differed from the more diverse, generally polytheistic Indian cultures. Islam is ethereal, revealed to a primarily nomadic people within the context of a pure, harsh, arid environment. Hinduism originated in one of the earliest urban cultures in the world, the Indus River valley, and spread throughout a mostly humid, subtropical and tropical subcontinent. The structural consequence of these two extremes was that Muslim builders substituted the implied supernatural verticality of the arch and the dome for the horizontal, earth-oriented corbeling (a structural type of bracket) preferred by Indian builders.

Mosque arches establish lines of prayer, allow room for a large congregation and provide selected views toward the mihrab, which implies a divine presence in an empty niche as well as the direction of Mecca. By contrast, massive Hindu temples have a small interior chamber to embody one or several divine presences, whose identities are reaffirmed by a multitude of statues around and inside it, and to represent universal cardinal directions.

Indo-Islamic identity advanced during the Delhi sultanate founded by Qutb-al-Din Aibak, whose Mamluk dynasty ruled from 1206 to 1290. When Aibak took power he made Delhi a safe haven from the Mongols. This act, along with Delhi's strategic location as the hub of several trade routes across northern India, helped to consolidate its Indo-Islamic identity.

Prodigious builders and warriors, the Mamluks left an impressive, if still largely unappreciated, legacy from Cairo to Levant, Jerusalem, Tripoli, Lebanon, and India. The Qutb complex in Delhi, inaugurated by Aibak in 1192, is characteristically Mamluk in its monumentality. Three progressively smaller open-air rectangles built against a linear backdrop of now ruined tombs are fronted by rudimentary *pishtaq*, or gateways, of various sizes. The domed Alai Darwaza (see image 1), which is the only surviving example of another series of gates along the outer rectilinear perimeter, is an important precedent for the Indo-Islamic tomb typology that followed, but the Qutb Minar (see image 2) is the showpiece of the ensemble. Six distinct stages, each marked by an exquisite band of calligraphy, taper upward from its base. An extant symbol of Delhi, the sandstone and marble tower is inscribed with verses from the Koran and Brahmic Nagari script. Its bundled shafts are interspersed with circular balconies supported by corbeled *muqarnas* (stalactitelike decorations).

The Mamluk dynasty was followed by the Khalji (1290–1320); Tughlaq (1320–1414); Sayyid (1414–51); and Lodi (1451–1526) dynasties. The end of the Lodi dynasty saw the end of the Delhi sultanate, ushering in the start of the Mughal Empire (1526–1707) and the peak period of Indo-Islamic building design. The Delhi sultanate has not received the same level of attention as its more glamorous successor, but was an important stage in the development of Islamic architecture in the region. During the relatively brief period that its five dynasties held sway, a blending of Muslim and Hindu culture took place that set the stage for the Mughal renaissance that followed. **JMS**

1 **Alai Darwaza (1311)**
Ala al-Din Khalji
Delhi, India

2 **Qutb Minar (c.1202)**
Qutb al-Din Aibak
Delhi, India

1316	1320–24	1354	1375	1444	1451
Ala al-Din Khalji builds a madrassa in the southwestern area of the Qutb complex.	The Mausoleum-Shrine of Rukn-i-Alam (see p.130) is constructed in Multan, in the Punjab region of Pakistan.	Feroz Shah Tughlaq establishes the fortified city of Ferozabad as the new capital of the Delhi sultanate.	Khirki Masjid is built by Khan-i-Jahan Junan Shah, prime minister under Feroz Shah Tughlaq.	The tomb of the Sayyid ruler Muhammad Shah is built in Lodi Gardens by Ala-ud-Din Alam Shah.	Ala-ud-Din Alam Shah voluntarily abdicates the throne of the Delhi sultanate in favor of Bahlul Khan Lodi, thus ending the Sayyid dynasty.

Mausoleum-Shrine of Rukn-i-Alam 1320–24
ARCHITECT UNKNOWN

Mausoleum-Shrine of Rukn-i-Alam,
Multan, Pakistan

The Mausoleum-Shrine of Rukn-i-Alam (pillar of the world) is located in Multan, the Punjab region of Pakistan. Due to its large white dome and its prominent location on the southwest side of the plateau of the Multan fort, it is the most visible of the numerous Sufi shrines that can be found in the city. There are two theories about the mausoleum's origin. The first is that it was built by the Delhi sultan Ghiyas ud-Din Tughlaq (who ruled from 1320 to 1325) for himself, but was later appropriated for Rukn-i-Alam by Feroz Shah Tughlaq during his reign from 1351 to 1388, who moved Rukn-i-Alam from the tomb that he shared with his grandfather. A second, more recent theory is that Rukn-i-Alam designed the mausoleum for himself but died before it could be completed and so was temporarily buried alongside his grandfather until it was finished. In spite of the great age of the mausoleum, the raised and covered sarcophagus inside—which is protected by brightly colored beaded curtains and is frequently covered with fresh flowers—looks as if it was prepared recently. Major conservation work to the building was started in 1971 and took six years to complete. Renovations included strengthening the foundations, rebuilding the brick walls of the first story, remaking and replacing damaged or missing tiles, and repairing the woodwork. **JMS**

✦ NAVIGATOR

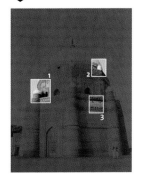

◉ FOCAL POINTS

1 BALCONY

The second level is 26 feet (8 m) wide, and features a narrow balcony from where a muezzin can give the call to prayer. The first level is 52 feet (16 m) wide, with walls that are 41 feet (12 m) high and 13 feet (4 m) thick. They are supported at each corner by sloping, cupola-capped buttresses.

2 DOME

The white dome at the top of the building is 58 feet (18 m) in diameter. The entire structure is 100 feet (30 m) high, and because the fort is already 50 feet (15 m) above the surrounding town, the shrine dominates the skyline. The stark white color of the dome is a symbol of purity and ascension.

3 MATERIALS

The mausoleum has red-brick walls, with glazed blue and white tiles that stand proud of the flat surface of the brick wall and cast shadows on it. The sparing use of tiles in strategic locations makes their decorative effect even brighter and more impressive when contrasted with the relative roughness of the brick.

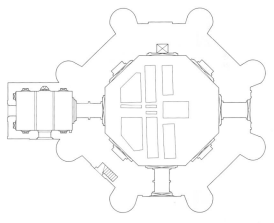

▲ The mausoleum is octagonal, with battered (backward-sloping) walls. Openings at ground level are on the east, south, and north faces; the west face has a mihrab, indicating the direction of Mecca.

▲ As part of the restorations, a training program was established to teach local masons the techniques of Multan tile work. Their efforts were recognized with an Aga Khan Award in 1983.

ROMANESQUE

The term "Romanesque" is rooted in the nineteenth century, when it was coined to describe medieval churches built from the tenth to twelfth centuries, before the rise of steeply pointed arches, flying buttresses, and other Gothic (see p.148) elements. For nineteenth-century critics, the Romanesque reflected the architecture of stonemasons who evidently admired the heavy barrel vaults and intricate carved capitals of the ancient Romans, but whose own architecture was considered derivative and degenerate, lacking the sophistication of their classical models.

Scholars in the twenty-first century are less inclined to understand the architecture of this period as a "failure" to reproduce the achievements of the past, and are far more likely to recognize its profusion of experimental forms as a series of creative new inventions. At the same time, however, research has questioned the value of Romanesque as a stylistic term. On the surface, it provides a convenient designation for buildings that share a common vocabulary of rounded arches and thick stone masonry, and appear in between the Carolingian revival of classical antiquity in the ninth century and the swift evolution of Gothic architecture after the second half of the twelfth. One

KEY EVENTS

1010	1013–20	1049	1066	1095	1098
Bernward of Hildesheim, a powerful bishop of the Holy Roman Empire, orders the construction of St. Michael's Church in Germany (see p.136).	Bernard of Angers writes *The Book of Sainte Foy*, recording miracles and encouraging pilgrimage to Conques in southern France (see p.138).	Hugh of Semur begins his sixty-year tenure as Abbot of Cluny, leading the abbey through an era of rapid expansion.	The Battle of Hastings is won by William, Duke of Normandy, resulting in cultural and political changes in Britain.	Pope Urban II preaches at the Council of Clermont, inspiring the First Crusade and the capture of Jerusalem in 1099.	A small band of Burgundian monks, reacting against the excessive wealth and luxurious lifestyle of Cluny, founds the Cistercian order.

problem, however, is that the term encompasses a broad array of regional variations, some with closer links to Rome than others. It should also be noted that the distinction between Romanesque architecture and its immediate predecessors and followers is not at all clear. For example, although the Carolingian gatehouse at Lorsch Abbey, Germany (764) was built in the eighth century, it shows the same rounded arches and engaged columns that could be considered hallmarks of the Romanesque style. In France, the western facade of Chartres Cathedral (c.1144–50) is often cited as a key example of Gothic art, while its counterpart at Conques (1120–35) is viewed as a paradigm of the Romanesque. Yet, their well-known sculpted portals were constructed within two decades of one another, and their similarities are arguably greater than their differences. There is little evidence that medieval viewers were concerned with the stylistic distinctions that we observe today, making the slow evolution of medieval architecture difficult to separate into neat chronological categories. Nevertheless, Romanesque remains a useful word despite its limitations, because it reflects a period of intensive building activity that maintained some continuity with the classical past, but freely reinterpreted ancient forms in a new and distinctive manner.

In the United Kingdom, structures from this period are sometimes described as Norman rather than Romanesque in reference to the major buildings produced in the century immediately following the Norman Conquest (1066). Surviving examples include the cathedrals of Ely (1083–1375) and Durham. The interior of Durham Cathedral (see image 1) is richly carved with ornamental diamonds and zigzags, but beneath these dazzling surface patterns are many of the same structural features that define Romanesque architecture in Normandy. The connection to Normandy is visible in the ruins of the Abbey Church of Notre-Dame at Jumièges (see image 2) with its three-story elevation composed of thick columns and rounded arches. Much like Durham, the second-story gallery level features smaller arches nested within larger ones, as well as engaged column shafts that rise from the floor and reach almost to the base of the third-story clerestory windows. These parallels suggest the invading Normans brought knowledge of their architectural style with them to Britain, where local architects fused continental forms with local innovations in craftsmanship. It is essential to recognize, however, that Norman architecture in Britain remained distinct from the buildings made for Norman patrons in other regions. Conquered by Normans in 1061, Sicily saw the flourishing in the twelfth century of a unique blend of northern and Mediterranean traditions, bringing Romanesque architecture to the southern frontier of Europe.

A striking number of Romanesque churches were built along a network of roads associated with pilgrimage. Medieval pilgrims traveled great distances to visit the shrines of Christian saints, whose relics were understood as sites of heavenly power. Jerusalem and Rome had attracted pilgrims since the early

1 Durham Cathedral (1093–1133)
Architect unknown
Durham, England

2 Abbey Church of Notre-Dame (1040–67)
Architect unknown
Jumièges, Normandy, France

1115	1130	1135–44	1146	c.1150	1192
A new Cistercian monastery is founded at Clairvaux, France, and rapidly becomes well known for its austerity under Abbot Bernard.	Roger II is crowned King of Sicily and unites the Norman territories in southern Italy before his death in 1154.	The Basilica of St.-Denis (see p.152), the burial church of French kings, is rebuilt with innovative vaults under the guidance of Abbot Suger.	Bernard of Clairvaux preaches at Vézelay, inspiring King Louis VII and his wife, Eleanor of Aquitaine, to join the Second Crusade.	The oldest surviving manuscript of the "pilgrim's guide" to Santiago de Compostela, known today as the Codex Calixtinus, is written.	Bernward of Hildesheim is recognized as a saint, sparking a series of renovations to his burial site at St. Michael's, Germany.

3 **Tympanum detail from Autun Cathedral (1120–32)**
Gislebertus
Autun, Burgundy, France

4 **Notre-Dame of Paray-le-Monial (1092–1109)**
Architect unknown
Burgundy, France

5 **Abbey Church of Fontenay (1147)**
Architect unknown
Montbard, Burgundy, France

Middle Ages, but the eleventh and twelfth centuries also saw vast numbers of devout Christians trekking to Santiago de Compostela, located in the northwest corner of the Iberian peninsula. The tomb of St. James (Sant'lago), one of the twelve apostles, had been miraculously discovered at this site in the early ninth century, attracting the patronage of Alfonso II, King of the Asturias from 791 until 842. A growing series of legends linked James with the ongoing wars against Islam, dubbing him "the Moor-slayer" (Matamoros) and giving him a prominent place among the pantheon of medieval saints. Medieval travel books, including a twelfth-century manuscript called the *Codex Calixtinus* that still survives at Santiago, recorded useful advice about paths to follow and dangers to avoid. They also describe additional churches and shrines that pilgrims could see along the way, each one competing to attract the attention and veneration of visitors. Pilgrims who had received (or hoped to receive) protection, healing, and grace from saints would offer votive gifts at their shrines; these gifts could be used to finance the construction of larger and more lavish buildings, attracting more pilgrims and more donations in turn.

The results of this spiritual economy are visible in the profusion of Romanesque churches constructed along the road to Santiago in the eleventh and twelfth centuries. Some of the most lavish were constructed in Burgundy, where pilgrims could visit the shrines of major saints, including Mary Magdalene at Vezelay (after 1120) and Lazarus at Autun. A typical feature of these churches was a round tympanum set above their portals, richly carved with narrative sculptures to inspire devotion. The expressive Romanesque sculptures at Autun are the work of French sculptor Gislebertus, whose decoration of doorways, tympanums, and capitals represents some of the most imaginative work of the period. The tympanum at Autun also bears an imposing image of Christ at the Last Judgment, together with angels and demons who weigh the souls of humankind and separate the saved from the damned. Tiny figures lined up on the lintel wait to receive judgment; one carries a bag decorated with a cockleshell, the emblem of St. James, and gazes up hopefully at Christ (see image 3). The shells evoked Santiago and its location close to the sea; the little figure is thus marked as a pilgrim, and his position on the lintel reminded travelers that their efforts would be rewarded with successful entry into heaven.

Many of the same churches that attracted pilgrims were attached to monasteries. Following the Rule of St. Benedict, a guide for proper behavior written in the sixth century, monasteries housed monks who were expected to follow a life defined by humility, chastity, and prayer. Wealthy aristocrats sometimes donated large gifts of land and precious artwork to monasteries, with the understanding that these endowments would be rewarded with perpetual prayers for the souls of deceased donors. One of the key beneficiaries of this system was the monastery of Cluny in Burgundy, which was among the wealthiest and most powerful institutions of the twelfth century. Not unlike a modern corporation, Cluny controlled a vast empire of smaller monasteries spread across Western Europe, all of which were under the direct protection of the mother house in Burgundy, that in turn answered directly to the Pope and enjoyed immunity from local politics. The spectacular wealth of Cluny is evident in the vast scale and lavish decoration of its main church, which was the largest building in Europe at the time of its third expansion (dubbed "Cluny III" by modern scholars) in the twelfth century. Cluny was largely destroyed during the French Revolution, with only one lone transept arm surviving today. A glimpse of what has been lost is still visible, however, in Paray-le-Monial (see image 4), a Cluniac church that was built as a smaller architectural copy of the mother house. Despite the ideal of poverty set down in the Rule of St. Benedict, many Cluniac monasteries were elaborately decorated with wall paintings and sculpture. The sumptuous effect of these buildings can still be observed today in the sculpted cloister of Moissac (c.1100) in southwest France, and the lavish wall paintings of Clayton (twelfth century) in Sussex, England.

The lush decoration of Cluniac architecture was not always viewed favorably by contemporaries, many of whom felt that monks should live in austere surroundings, without the distractions of material wealth. The Cistercian order, founded in 1098 at Cîteaux by Robert de Molesme, was in many ways a reaction against Cluny. Its ideals of poverty, silence, and manual labor were reflected in the simplicity of its buildings, and their lack of narrative sculptures and paintings. The minimalism of Cistercian architecture, however, should not be confused with a lack of quality. At the Abbey Church of Fontenay (see image 5), for example, the smooth capitals of the nave are shaped into remarkably sophisticated forms, and the gently pointed arches of the arcade are constructed with perfect blocks of high-quality stone. The effect of Cistercian austerity was an emphasis on refined craftsmanship and elegant design, producing aesthetics of sobriety and restraint that soon gained popularity across much of northern Europe, particularly in France and Germany.

Pointed arches can be found in Romanesque buildings such as Fontenay and Durham, but they are the exception rather than the rule. In the middle of the twelfth century, architects began experimenting with this form, raising the angle of these arches to produce taller, more imposing vaults. Around the same time, the development of the flying buttress allowed for thinner, lighter walls pierced by larger windows, creating a new style that made Romanesque churches seem heavy and dark in comparison. In the modern world, however, the Romanesque style has continued to attract admiration, sparking revivals such as the Richardsonian Romanesque in the 1870s and 1880s, and inspiring new generations of pilgrims to travel the road to Santiago de Compostela, stopping to admire the many architectural gems that still stand along the way. **SF**

St. Michael's Church 1010–31
ARCHITECT UNKNOWN

St. Michael's
Church,
Hildesheim,
Germany

S t. Michael's Church was begun in 1010 under the patronage of Bernward, a bishop whose creativity and ambition left a lasting impact on artistic activity in Hildesheim. Constructed in the time of the last Ottonian rulers of the Holy Roman Empire, St. Michael's continues the double-apse design that had been a hallmark of Carolingian and Ottonian architecture, and exemplifies the conservatism and historicism of the Romanesque style. A low-ceiling crypt, set beneath the raised floor of the western apse, served as the site of Bernward's burial. In the main space of the church, tall transverse arches rise above the transepts almost to the level of the painted ceiling, adding a series of rounded forms that harmonize with the decorated nave arcade and the high clerestory windows. The symmetrical design of the church is apparent from the exterior, where six turrets—two heavy, square towers set over the nave crossings, flanked by four delicate round spires—can be seen rising above the twin transepts. The round arches and structure of the nave find antecedents in earlier buildings, but they are also repeated in the later eleventh and twelfth centuries. Although St. Michael's was destroyed by Allied bombs in 1945, a faithful reconstruction was completed in 1957, and incorporates many original elements that were hidden away and saved from the brutality of war. **SF**

FOCAL POINTS

1 CAPITALS

The finely detailed capitals of the nave are carved from massive blocks of stone. No two are exactly alike, and yet they all share the same proportions, and many feature similar plant motifs. The result is a series of playful variations on the ancient design of the Corinthian capital.

2 CEILING

The painted ceiling (c.1230) is one of only a handful of surviving wooden ceilings from the Middle Ages. It depicts the genealogy of Christ as the Tree of Jesse, tracing his lineage back to Adam and Eve through a series of Old Testament kings. This asserted Christ's ancestry while also positioning him as the Messiah of Jewish prophecy.

3 NAVE ARCADE

The nave arcade is marked with square piers that alternate with pairs of columns topped by delicately carved capitals. This creates a complex geometric pattern that is unified by the regular round arches linking the columns and piers together, and echoes the simple clerestory windows set above a massive wall.

BERNWARD OF HILDESHEIM

Bishops attained remarkable degrees of status and luxury in the medieval Holy Roman Empire, and none has left a more dazzling legacy as a patron of the arts than Bernward of Hildesheim. As personal tutor to the young Emperor Otto III, Bernward had access to the best artists and richest treasuries of Europe. As well as building St. Michael's, he acquired an extraordinary array of art objects, including massive bronze doors, intricate silver candlesticks, Byzantine ivories, and illuminated manuscripts. Not all of these treasures were intended for St. Michael's: Bernward is known to have given rich gifts to Hildesheim Cathedral and to have donated a large wooden crucifix (below) to the Convent of Ringelheim in the Harz Mountains, where his sister Judith served as abbess.

St. Foy 1087–1107
ARCHITECT UNKNOWN

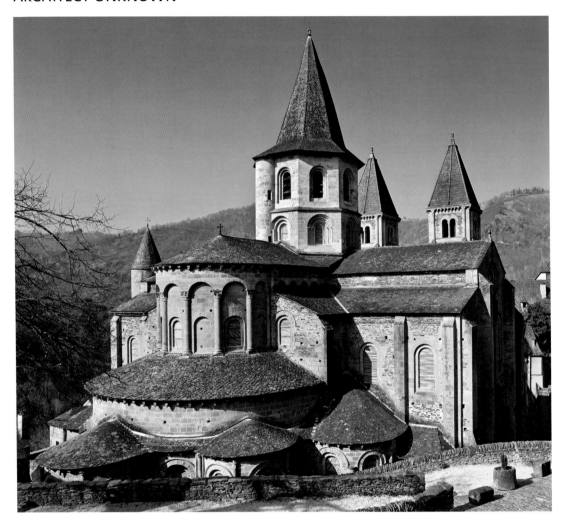

St. Foy, Conques, France

✦ NAVIGATOR

Despite its small size and remote location in the mountains of the Midi-Pyrénées region, Conques attracted many visitors from the tenth to the twelfth centuries as a major stopping point along the pilgrimage routes that flowed westward to Santiago de Compostela. Pilgrims were drawn to Conques because of the relics of St. Foy, a young girl who was martyred in the early Middle Ages. The relics came to Conques in the ninth century, when they were stolen from a nearby church by a zealous monk. The arrival of the holy bones of the young martyr meant newfound wealth and prominence, thanks to a steady stream of pilgrims eager to show their piety with precious votive gifts. By the end of the eleventh century, Conques had become wealthy enough to construct a new abbey church. The resulting structure is not overly large, its scale limited by the steep hillside upon which Conques is situated, but it reflects the key innovations of Romanesque architecture from the decades around 1100. This includes a cross-shaped basilica floor plan, with a barrel-vaulted nave flanked by groin-vaulted side aisles that lead visitors to the ambulatory, an added passageway that lines the semicircular apse. This type of ambulatory with radiating chapels became an essential feature of pilgrimage churches, and it was particularly well-suited to give visitors access to sacred spaces. **SF**

⊙ FOCAL POINTS

1 APSE

The eastern end of the church terminates in a round apse, which is elegantly embellished with a series of engaged columns connected by round arches. This blind arcade, which echoes the ancient Roman Doric and Corinthian orders, creates an illusion of delicacy, despite the thickness of the wall and the small size of its clerestory windows.

2 TOWERS

The massive west facade of the church is structured by two tall, symmetrical square towers. Between them, the shallow arch over the doors shelters a richly carved tympanum. This space represents the Last Judgment through images and inscriptions, reminding visitors of the rewards of heaven and the tortures of hell.

3 RADIATING CHAPELS

The apse is pierced by a number of small radiating chapels that are connected by a vaulted interior aisle known as an ambulatory. This feature was probably developed to accommodate the pilgrimages to relics and altars inside the church without intruding into the special spaces that were reserved for quiet monastic prayer.

RELIQUARY OF ST. FOY

St. Foy is embodied by her reliquary (below), a golden statue that developed over the course of centuries to contain the bones (or relics) of the saint. It seems that the original object was a simple wooden container constructed at the end of the ninth century, which was gradually refashioned as an enthroned statue of Foy by the beginning of the eleventh century. Many of the gems that decorate the surface are carved with ancient Roman images, and were already considered precious antiques when they were applied to the medieval statue. The reliquary inspired Bernard of Angers, an avid devotee writing in the years 1013–20, to record a series of miracle stories associated with St. Foy. Many of these tales read as almost amusing anecdotes of the mischievous young saint playing small tricks on members of the local community, sometimes harassing stingy or impious men and women until they gave generous donations of gold and gemstones to the church at Conques. If the sumptuous materials that encrust the medieval statue are any indication, later pilgrims were inspired by such stories to continue offering lavish gifts in praise of St. Foy.

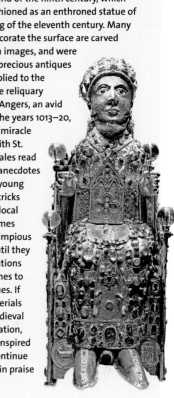

◄ Christ sits in majesty at the center of the tympanum. Hell is shown as utter chaos on the right, contrasting with the calm, structured space of heaven on the left. Although much of the paint has weathered away, traces of blue and red give hints of its formerly bright colors.

CHINA: SACRED

1 **Hall of Three Purities (1262)**
Architect unknown
Yongle Palace, Ruicheng,
Shanxi province, China

2 **Buddha Pagoda (1056)**
Architect unknown
Fogong Monastery, Yingxian,
Shanxi province, China

The Tang dynasty (618–907) marked the height of cultural development in China, but the 400 years that followed witnessed territorial division: into north China, governed by successive non-Chinese dynasties, and south China, which continued the cultural refinement. Although the Mongols had united the country by 1279 and ruled with an iron fist, they were overthrown in 1368 by the Ming dynasty, which reigned until 1644. Architecture in China between 1000 and 1400 followed the particular regional style and ethnic characteristics in both the north and the south. The few extant buildings from this period are mainly religious structures built in wood.

One of the most monumental structures from the Liao dynasty (907–1125) is the main hall of Fengguo Monastery in Yixian, Liaoning province, completed in 1020. It was sponsored by a retired official, Jiao Xiyun, with works supervised by a monk named Qinghui. The main hall is majestic: it has nine bays on the front and five bays on the side. Measuring 183 by 85 feet (56 x 26 m), it is one of the largest and most important timber halls extant in China. The uninterrupted interior has few columns and brings clarity of space. Toward the north is a long dais where seven large sculptures of Buddha are set in individual bays. The gigantic scale of the hall architecture, the sculptures, and the timber pieces are in keeping with the spirit of the northern nomadic tribes.

Another spectacular building from the period is the earliest extant wooden pagoda in China: Fogong Monastery in Yingxian (see image 2). Completed in 1056, this gigantic pagoda exemplifies the monumentality of Buddhism. The octagonal structure consists of five stories inside and out, to a total height of

KEY EVENTS

1013	1020	1052	1056	1062	1102
The main hall of Baoguo Monastery in Ningbo is completed. It is the earliest extant wooden building in south China.	The building of the main hall of Fengguo Monastery in Yixian is finished. It is the one of the largest wooden halls in China.	The Sakyamuni Hall of Longxing Monastery in Zhengding is built (see p.142). Its unique building form has been preserved to this day.	The completion of the pagoda at Fogong Monastery in Yingxian makes it the tallest wooden pagoda in existence.	Huayan Monastery in Datong is built as both a Buddhist establishment and a hall for housing images of deceased emperors.	The Jinci temple complex is rebuilt. The Hall of the Holy Mother is of a standard close to the official manual, *Yingzao Fashi*.

220 feet (67 m), making it the tallest surviving wooden pagoda in East Asia. Between each story is another, hidden, story, added to increase the perception of height. Different deities are placed in the middle of each of the five stories, beginning with a large image of Buddha on the first floor. On the upper floors, accessible via a perimeter stair, the deities are positioned in the middle of the floor following a circumambulatory path. On the exterior of the pagoda, a ring of balconies forms another pathway. There are fifty-four bracket sets used in the pagoda, differentiated by location and the extent of the projection.

In 1103, during the Northern Song dynasty (960–1127), the construction manual *Yingzao Fashi* was compiled by the imperial Minister for Works, Li Jie, and promulgated by the court, detailing the method, specification and materials for the construction of imperial buildings. The manual outlines an eight-grade system of building, applied according to the scale of the building and the dimensions of the bracket block at the top of the column. In a modular system specific to the grade of building, the dimensions of every component are determined by the dimensions of the block. However, none of the extant buildings from this period conforms to the modular dimensions entirely.

The main hall of Baoguo Monastery, Ningbo, Zhejiang province, dated to 1013, is the earliest and best preserved timber building in south China. This five-bay building demonstrates a more delicate southern style, with the dimension of the bracket blocks corresponding to a fifth-grade standard in the *Yingzao Fashi*. Two prominent features are the columns with a distinctive petal cross-section, a form described in the *Yingzao Fashi* but rarely seen, and the three cupola ceilings constructed with timber members. The hall's delicate proportions and its roof with exaggerated upturned corners are indicative of the southern style.

During the Yuan dynasty (1271–1368), Daoism also received imperial patronage. The tradition centered on the worship of indigenous deities organized in a hierarchy similar to that of Buddhism. The most complete Daoist temple of the Yuan dynasty is Yongle Palace. Located in Ruicheng, Shanxi province, it has a long central axis on which five buildings now stand. It was built between 1247 and 1262, but the other four buildings are dated to the Yuan dynasty, including the inner gate and three halls dedicated to different Daoist deities. The four Yuan dynasty buildings manifest the characteristics of the period, including a facade without a clear column grid, a massive roof with a shallow pitch but a large projection of the eaves, and tall, dragon-shaped ceramic finials at either end of the main ridge. The main hall (see image 1) is the largest building in the temple, and the deities of the Three Purities (highest gods of Taoism) are placed on an altar to the north of the interior. Most impressive are the wall paintings that have survived in this and other Yuan dynasty buildings of the palace. In the main hall, the paintings illustrate different deities congregating to worship the Three Purities. **PPH**

1103	1129	1176	1241–53	1279	1368
Yingzao Fashi is published. It contains specifications for imperial building works and is the best means of understanding the modular system.	The Song dynasty retreats to south China. The capital city is moved to Hangzhou, with new religious structures to serve Buddhism or Daoism.	The rebuilding of Shanhua Monastery takes place in Datong, the western capital of the Jin dynasty (1115–1234).	A hierarchy of state monasteries of the Chan School with similar architectural forms is established as "Five Mountains and Ten Monasteries."	The unification of the territory of China takes place and the capital is located in Beijing. New monasteries are established.	The Ming dynasty is established with its capital in Nanjing. Major monasteries are built in the city and surrounding hill sites.

Sakyamuni Hall, Longxing Monastery 1052
ARCHITECT UNKNOWN

Sakyamuni Hall,
Longxing Monastery,
Zhengding,
Hebei province, China

 **NAVIGATOR**

Longxing Monastery is one of a remarkable group of buildings from the Northern Song dynasty. Although first built in 586, it was the imperial patronage bestowed by the first emperor of Northern Song that gave it the grand scale seen today. The building exemplifies the rich architecture of Buddhist monasteries and is representative of the layout and composition of the era, with two cloisters from south to north along the central axis. The southern axis begins with the Hall of Heavenly Kings, which now serves as the main gate. It is built on a timber structure but without external columns, except for the robust sets of brackets above the masonry wall. The second building along the axis is the largest in the monastery and dates to the thirteenth century; it has seven bays and a marble image platform. The last building is the cross-shaped, double-eaved Sakyamuni Hall, which houses the altar for the Buddha. The northern cloister has five buildings, the main one being the Hall of Great Compassion (960). Inside the replica seen today is the original bronze statute of the Bodhisattva. Farther to the south on either side of the central axis are two pavilions from the twelfth century, one for *sutra* (Buddhist scripture) storage and one housing the image of Maitreya. **PPH**

1 DRAGON HEAD

The ridge of the building is terminated at either end by a massive finial known as the Dragon Kiss, shown as a giant dragon head biting the end of the ridge. The finial is made of glazed ceramic pieces dating to c.16 century. The dragon finial symbolizes protection of the building from fire.

2 EAVES

The corner of the upper eaves of the roof is supported by a complex wooden bracket set with three layers allowing the eaves to project away from the body of the building. The diagonal struts of the bracket set penetrate into the building interior, supporting a beam in the upper part of the roof.

3 WALL

The wall of the building is not load-bearing and is constructed using pounded earth built over a low brick wall. There are no windows and only four main doors. The doors are formed of six panels, with lattices on the upper part and full panels below.

◄ The bronze statue in the Hall of Great Compassion, the last building along the monastery's central axis, is the Thousand-armed Bodhisattva of Great Compassion (Guanyin). Cast in 971, it is one of the earliest colossal statues in China.

YINGZAO FASHI

The most comprehensive and well-illustrated Chinese building manual, *Yingzao Fashi*, was written in the early 12th century by the imperial Minister for Works, Li Jie. The manual defines different construction processes in materials including timber, stone, brick, and stucco, as well as the construction method and measurement of labor. It aimed to create a standardized method of determining materials and labor, thus leading to effective cost-control. Accompanying the text are 218 drawings (right) that illustrate the standard of construction and decorative motifs of the era. The manual also describes the modular system of timber construction for imperial buildings, divided into eight grades, with the parts of each grade of building explained.

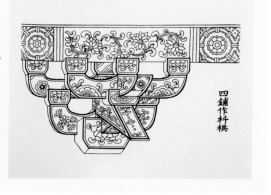

JAPAN

1 Great South Gate, Todaiji Temple (1199)
Shunjobo Chogen
Nara, Japan

2 Temple of the Golden Pavilion (1398)
Architect unknown
Kitayama, Kyoto, Japan

The stereotypical Japanese second-millennial building style, characterized by meandering low-slung pavilions with reed thatches, mat flooring, and paper-screened walls—surrounded by a spare and imaginative form of gardening—grew from aristocratic *shinden* residential codes of the late eighth century. This palatial form of architecture was taken over from the hereditary aristocracy and adapted during the early Middle Ages to suit a status-conscious warrior class; it was further modified by the philosophical and aesthetic influence of tea masters and subsequently survived the later period of national isolation into the early modern age.

With notable input from diverse but ubiquitous Japanese vernacular styles of building, the noble residence morphed into a generic upper-middle-class style. However, despite an increasing sense of intimacy, it retained a strong degree of formality throughout. Meanwhile, a native tradition of Shinto shrine building continued to evolve alongside sophisticated Buddhist temple construction methods imported to Japan from China via Korea. These three modes are completely separate in terms of purpose, function, and style. There was also an emphasis on both structure and woodcraft that was far more related to Greek *techne* (the term both for a practical skill and for the systematic knowledge or experience that underlies it) than is common in latter-day Western architecture. Moreover, until the sixteenth century at the earliest, little real claim can be made for Japanese buildings as containers of interior space: the common view of architecture throughout the West from the mid-Renaissance through to twentieth-century international modernism.

KEY EVENTS

1052	1077	1180	1185	1187	1192
Fujiwara no Yorimichi converts his father's villa near Kyoto into a Buddhist temple; it becomes Byodoin Temple, with Phoenix Hall (1053; see p.146).	Emperor Shirakawa's Hoshoji temple in Kyoto initiates a temple-building upsurge over the next seventy-five years, especially among Pure Land adherents.	Fire destroys the two great eighth-century temples of Todaiji and Kofukuji at Nara, setting the scene for their rebuilding.	The destruction of the last Kyoto warrior clan and the end of the Heian period lead to the establishment of the Kamakura shogunate.	The monk Myoan Eisai visits China for the second time. He returns to Japan a few years later to establish the Japanese Rinzai sect of Zen.	Samurai jurisdiction removes the government to Kamakura, initiating a feudal military reign away from Kyoto until 1333.

For all these reasons, the history of all middle-period Japanese architecture is intimately concerned with the articulation of structural detail as expressive of a certain evolving decorum.

Until the establishment of the Kamakura shogunate in 1192 in eastern Japan, after the Heian period (794–1185), most significant building activity remained in the Sino-Japanese cultural homeland, namely present-day Kyoto (the former Heian capital) and the earlier capital of Nara. The government-sponsored enterprise of official temple building was long past and, with other sects of Buddhism increasingly hedged by political intrigue, the gentler Pure Land (Jodo) sect emphasized personal salvation. It flourished in Japan from the mid-tenth century and its temples became increasingly aristocratic and private, if hardly small, affairs. The temples were centered on a hall dedicated to the worship of the Amida Buddha, Lord of the Western Paradise.

Although uncharacteristically plain in its architectural detail, the main hall (1107) of the remote, austere Joruriji temple in Kyoto (an ancient temple rebuilt in 1047) is the sole surviving Amida Hall, with nine images of the Buddha, out of some thirty others in Japan built by the end of the Heian period. The key to Buddhist temple construction was the imposing roof with its deep overhang sometimes composed of successive eaves, which were supported, in all cases, by cantilevered rafters on purlins, themselves supported over increasingly differentiated and complex bracket-arm systems. Although whole styles may be defined by such distinctions, the early surviving Amida Hall at Joruri-ji comprises supports of so-called boat-shaped profile at the corners, and these are among the most basic. It is also a frontal, eleven-bay structure, housing nine images, that faces a lotus pond. Moreover, this hall employs a typical hidden- or double-roof construction, unique to Japan, that was first developed in the tenth century.

The reconstruction of the war-ravaged principal Great South Gate at Todaiji in Nara (see image 1) was completed in 1199 in a style imported directly from Song dynasty China by the great prelate builder Shunjobo Chogen (1121–1206). The radical so-called Great Buddha style is severe, rational, modular, and magnificent, with its multilevel tiers of bracketing keyed visibly into the massive pillars and, quite exceptionally for Japan, articulated spatially. It also marks the beginning of Japan's feudal period. Chogen has been compared to Filippo Brunelleschi (1377–1446), one of the leading architects of the Italian Renaissance, but his influence was lamentably brief, lasting only a generation. After Kamakura, a new shogunate was founded in 1338, spanning more than two centuries. The third Ashikaga shogun, Yoshimitsu, constructed a villa for himself in Kyoto's northern hills. The gold-leafed principal three-story edifice (see image 2) is superbly eclectic, combining the *shinden* residential style with deep verandas on the first floor, a so-called Japanese-style Buddha hall above and the Cupola of the Ultimate in designated Zen style at its apex. **DBS**

1195	1212	1243	1338	1339	1398
Todaiji's Great Buddha Hall at Nara is reconstructed, followed by Chogen's rebuilding of its Great South Gate in 1199.	Rooted in Buddhist thought, Kamo no Chomei's essay "The Ten Foot Square Hut" details his deep mountain retreat from Kyoto's vicissitudes.	The monk Dogen founds Eiheiji Temple in mountainous Fukui as a center of Soto Zen teaching brought back from China.	The new Muromachi age (Ashikaga shogunate) begins. It eventually brings in revised standards of modular design.	The monastic scholar-poet Muso Soseki is reputedly called to restore Saihoji's exemplary Zen-style garden.	The Kitayama culture flourishes. It takes its name from Kyoto's northern hills, where Yoshimitsu's Temple of the Golden Pavilion is sited.

Phoenix Hall 1053
ARCHITECT UNKNOWN

Phoenix Hall,
Byodoin Temple, Uji,
Kyoto prefecture, Japan

NAVIGATOR

Apart from the survival of the early twelfth-century Amida Hall at Joruriji, atypical in its quiet austerity, Phoenix Hall at Byodoin Temple best illustrates the resurgence of color and sensuality accompanying the new intensification of elite Buddhist patronage. This was paralleled in secularly oriented vernacular literature, including the celebrated *Tale of Genji* written by Murasaki Shikibu in the early eleventh century. Both works, in which the religious and secular are inextricably intertwined in a rich yet otherworldly mood, typify the so-called Fujiwara-era (*c.*794–1185) cultural flowering of delicate and essentially new Japanese taste. By the year 1000, Fujiwara no Michinaga, the greatest of the Fujiwara patrons, is said to have been able to create or depose emperors at will, the clan members having assumed a hereditary role as imperial regents. His son, Fujiwara no Yorimichi, decided to transform a private domain in the *shinden* style into a temple of the Pure Land (Jodo) sect as a sumptuous place of family worship. The inclusion of garden and pond are essential to the illusion of the Western Paradise of the Amida; the surviving Phoenix Hall is just one of many Buddhist projects undertaken by the clan in the Kyoto region. At Uji, the main hall was dedicated in 1053, widely believed by Buddhist orthodoxy, including the Heian aristocracy, to mark the start of a catastrophic era of decline in piety and prosperity, from which only the Lord of the Western Paradise could save humankind. **DBS**

◉ FOCAL POINTS

1 WINGS

Two L-shaped wings are elegantly set above the first level, with added turrets. They complete a composition deriving from the mandala (a circular figure representing the universe) scheme of the Jodo Western Paradise and echoed at the time by the Great Hall of State at Heian-kyo (no longer standing in present-day Kyoto).

2 RAFTERS

Circular base rafters with square flying rafters are combined with triple-stepped bracket complexes in the tradition of Nara period construction, but with the corner brackets here thought to achieve a new perfection of structure. Phoenix Hall may be named after the bronze birds on the central roof ridge.

3 CENTRAL CORE

A high-ceilinged, three-by-two bay enclosure houses a nearly 10 foot (3 m) high image of Lord Amida (Buddha), with gracefully interpolated pent-roof skirting to suggest increased exterior height. Overall, the Phoenix Hall achieves a consummate elegance and lightness through attention to detail.

◄ A suspended, meticulously gilded, wooden filigree canopy above and multiple-lotus dais below serve to demarcate the Buddha platform. Behind is a tall, swirling gilt mandorla.

GOTHIC

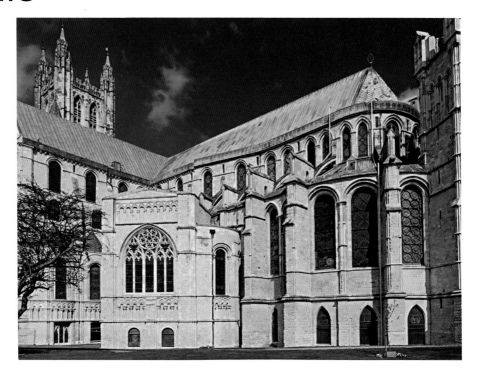

Gothic architecture began with a series of experiments, which were conducted to fulfill specific requests by patrons and to accommodate the ever-growing numbers of pilgrims visiting sites that housed precious relics. Pilgrims in the high Middle Ages increasingly traveled to well-known pilgrimage sites, but also to local sites where local and national saints were reputed to have performed miracles. The churches and monasteries housing important relics therefore wanted to heighten the popularity of their respective saints and build appropriate shrines for them. These shrines were not merely gem-encrusted reliquaries, but more importantly took the form of powerful architectural settings characterized by colored light emitting from the large areas of stained glass. The use of stained glass, however, is not the defining element of Gothic and neither are the pointed arch, the ribbed vault, the rose window, or the flying buttress, as many of these elements were used in one way or another in preceding architectural traditions. It was rather the combination and constant refinement of these elements, along with the quick response to the rapidly changing building techniques of the time, that fueled the Gothic movement in architecture.

KEY EVENTS

c.1135	1163	1170	1174	1194	1209
Abbot Suger begins to rebuild the choir and west end of the Basilica of St.-Denis in Paris, France.	Work begins on Notre-Dame in Paris. On its completion, the cathedral will stand as one of the tallest in Europe at the time.	The flying buttresses of the Abbey of St. Remi in Reims are built. Today they represent the earliest example of surviving exposed flying buttresses.	A fire destroys the choir of Canterbury Cathedral, and the monastery decides to rebuild the east end in the new French Gothic fashion.	Work begins on Chartres Cathedral, the first truly High Gothic building, by simplifying its architecture to emphasize height.	After Archbishop Albrecht II von Kefernburg travels in France, work begins on Magdeburg Cathedral, Germany, in the Gothic style.

Consequently, it is difficult to point to one element or the exact place where Gothic first emerged; however, it is traditional to initiate a discussion of Gothic architecture with the Basilica of St.-Denis (c.1135–44; see p.152) and its patron, Abbot Suger, who began to rebuild the west front and the choir of the church. As he wrote in his *De Administratione*, the old building could no longer accommodate the large volumes of pilgrims who were coming to venerate the relics of St. Denis, and the solution for this was twofold: a west facade with three large portals and the innovative new choir, which combined an ambulatory with radiating chapels that were unique as they were not separated by walls. Instead a row of slim columns was inserted between the chapels and the choir arcade to support the rib vaults. The result enabled visitors to circulate around the altar and come within reach of the relics without actually disrupting the altar space, while also experiencing the large stained glass windows within the chapels. As confirmed by Suger, the desire for more stained glass was not necessarily to bring more daylight into the building but rather to fill the space with a continuous ray of colorful light, rather like mosaics or precious stones, which would make the wall vanish. The demand for ever more stained-glass windows and the search for techniques that would support them are constant throughout the development of Gothic architecture, as is evident in the writings of Suger, who was fascinated by the mystical quality of such lighting.

England, with its direct links to France, was probably the first place where early Gothic traveled, and the best example is Canterbury Cathedral (see image 1), which was built after 1174 by French architect William of Sens (d.1180). By the time Canterbury Cathedral was begun, the town was already the location of a quickly growing cult around the body of Thomas Becket, the former Archbishop of Canterbury, who was canonized as a saint only a year before the old choir burned down in 1174. The chosen architect was almost certainly familiar with the rapidly advancing new French architecture in churches such as St.-Denis and the Notre-Dame cathedral (see image 2) in Paris. As a result the latest French style was applied to better accommodate the growing numbers of visitors and to honor the saint's body. Similarly to St.-Denis, an ambulatory with large stained-glass windows was built around the shrine of the saint, called the Trinity Chapel, which was raised on a platform. Other French elements, such as detached shafts, ribbed vaults, pointed arches, and flying buttresses, were also employed. Yet Gothic architecture in England, as in other European countries, quickly took on its own individual character and although many similar developments occurred, the English were more fascinated by decorative elements in stone and the length of their churches than by accentuating verticality and elegance.

French emphasis on verticality is especially evident in the inner elevation of the bays of French High Gothic churches, which usually consist of an

1 **Choir and Trinity Chapel, Canterbury Cathedral (c. 1174–84)**
William of Sens
Kent, UK

2 **Notre-Dame Cathedral (begun 1163)**
Various architects
Paris, France

1211	c.1245	1248	1272	1281	1356
Work on Reims Cathedral (see p.154) begins, using a new type of clerestory window with bar tracery, a development of the Rayonnant style.	Work begins on the nave of Strasbourg Cathedral. The building is widely held to be one of the best examples of High Gothic.	Work begins on Cologne Cathedral, Germany, directly after the St. Chapelle, Paris, is finished.	The Beauvais Cathedral choir is consecrated. When it collapses just twelve years after its completion, it will mark the end of High Gothic in France.	The new nave of the Basilica of St.-Denis is completed in the Rayonnant style; it employs a glazed triforium.	German architect Peter Parler (c.1330–99) is brought to Prague. The next year he begins work on the Old Town Bridge Tower (1357–c.1388; see p.156).

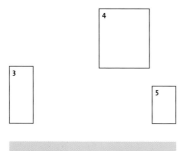

3 **Chartres Cathedral (1194–c.1220)**
Architect unknown
Chartres, France

4 **Amiens Cathedral (1220–c.1270)**
Robert de Luzarches and
Thomas de Cormont
Amiens, France

5 **Choir, Cologne Cathedral (1248–1322)**
Master Gerhard
Cologne, Germany

arcade supported by piers on the ground level, a triforium (gallery) on the first level and a clerestory above. The refinement of this elevation played a very important role in Gothic church building as architects experimented to create a more skeletal appearance in the architecture, to emphasize the height of their buildings, and to find ways to support larger stained-glass windows. An important step in this development—distinguishing the High Gothic church elevation from the Romanesque (see p.132) or early Gothic—is the absence of a gallery in the first level and the enlargement of the clerestory windows above. This development was also assisted by the application of the flying buttress, which supported the weight of the building without appearing thick and bulky, and by replicating the skeletal impression of the inside on the outside of the building. Notably, one of the first churches to combine these new techniques successfully is Chartres Cathedral, which was begun in 1194. Its elevation set a new standard for architecture in France at the time. The arcade on the first level is composed of circular pillars surrounded by four shafts, which connect to the shafts above them to draw the eye upward and create a sense of continuity. The second level consists of a simple arcaded triforium and the top level employs large clerestory windows composed of two lancets and an oculus framed by plate tracery. The features of this building all combine to emphasize not only the vast amount of stained glass (see image 3) but also the tremendous height, which is interpreted today as one of the defining elements of the High Gothic. The stained-glass panels shown here depict St. Laumer being visited by the Bishop of Chartres (left), St. Mary of Egypt (right), and an unidentified abbot saint (top).

Chartres was the first in a line of High Gothic cathedrals that were constructed in the same tradition at about the same time in Bourges, Reims (see p.154), Amiens, and Beauvais. This small group of buildings clearly drew on one another and created an architectural rivalry, with each being taller and more sophisticated than the last. Hence, Bourges was built taller than Chartres, Reims taller than Bourges, and Amiens taller than Reims. This "competition" ended with Beauvais Cathedral, begun in 1225, and which at some time during its forty-seven-year-long building process set out to be the tallest Gothic church in Europe. Its glazed triforium, incredibly wide bays, narrow buttresses and extreme height caused the building to collapse only twelve years after the choir was finished. In the more successful Amiens Cathedral (see image 4), begun in 1220, the height was also emphasized by the clustered pillars and shafts, which continue from the floor to the vaulting even more elegantly than in Chartres Cathedral. Additionally, the triforium became much more elaborate here, as did the clerestory, which employs bar tracery instead of plate tracery and is composed of windows with two lancets and an oculus inside bigger lancets that repeat the pattern. Although Amiens is still classed as a High Gothic building, its evolving window design and tracery marked the advancement toward yet another division of Gothic architecture, known as Rayonnant Gothic.

The Rayonnant style is often misunderstood as marking the end of High Gothic architecture in France even though it should rather be interpreted as a shift in focus toward lighting the walls further by using intricate blind tracery, as well as by the addition of more stained glass. An example of this is the choir of Cologne Cathedral (see image 5), begun in 1248, the upper parts of which have often been described as a copy of the influential St. Chapelle in Paris. The choir is characterized by the elegance of its stone architecture, which visually disappears between the vast amounts of stained glass in its clerestory and glazed triforium. The complexity of patterns in Rayonnant buildings has frequently been associated with the birth of architectural drawings, which started to appear at this time either as sketchbooks or full-blown plans, for

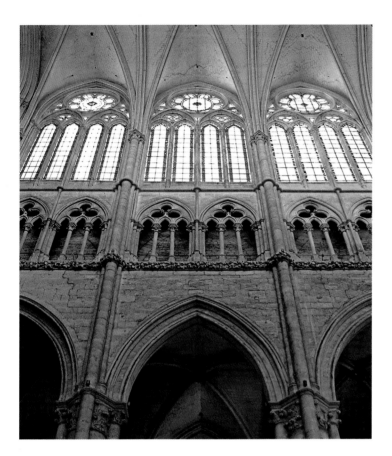

example the well-known Plan F of the Cologne Cathedral facade, and it may be
due to such drawings that Rayonnant architectural elements can be found
more readily outside France.

Accordingly, by the thirteenth century, the architecture of England,
Italy, Spain, Germany, and central Europe also boasted a Gothic character,
although this developed with its own priorities and traditions. It was not only
in churches, however, that Gothic elements could be spotted by this time,
as blind tracery, pinnacles, micro-architectural niches, clustered columns,
pointed arches and rib vaulting also found their way into secular architecture.
Still, as the function of secular architecture—namely castles, gates, and
towers—was primarily defensive, Gothic architecture could not quite reach
the same level of elegance in secular as it did in sacred buildings. Nevertheless,
what these buildings may have lacked in elegance, they compensated for
in adornment as their facades were often covered with complex sculptural
programs surrounded by micro-architectural settings. One example of this is
the facade of the Old Town Hall of Aachen, Germany, built in c.1267, which is
today composed of two rows of pointed arches above a gateway—the first
row decorating windows and the top row containing figures. Other examples,
whether simple or complex, are found throughout secular buildings in Europe
from the thirteenth and fourteenth centuries as their patrons and architects
adapted the new Gothic vocabulary to fit them. All things considered, the
elegance and power of Gothic architecture never really disappeared after the
fourteenth century, because it evolved in different forms into the sixteenth
century as Late Gothic and then began to be reused again in the eighteenth
century as Gothic Revival (see p.284). **JG**

Basilica of St.-Denis c.1135–44

ABBOT SUGER c.1081–1151

Basilica of St.-Denis,
Paris, France

⬡ NAVIGATOR

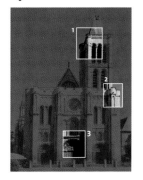

When Abbot Suger rebuilt parts of St.-Denis in the twelfth century he created the first truly Gothic building. He started by demolishing the western facade of the abbey, replacing it with a new extension with three doors and two towers. He added a choir and side aisles in 1144. He was inspired by the Book of Revelation to replicate the idea of heaven on earth, using allegory, symbolism, transparency, and light to reflect universal order, and to recreate his church in the image of the New Jerusalem. He replaced heavy, Romanesque barrel vaults with quadripartite ribs, which spring from columns rather than a load-bearing wall, similar to the design of pointed arches in Islamic architecture. These were introduced in the nave vaults of Durham Cathedral in 1093, but Suger took full advantage of the fact that the load-bearing wall between the columns could be replaced with non-load-bearing stained glass. His allegorical vision continued with statuary in the tympana above the doors and niches throughout the cathedral, which he used to relate biblical stories and morality tales to a largely illiterate medieval audience. In retrospect, it is remarkable how quickly this new style spread, and evolved, mostly because it allowed for the construction of the wider naves needed to accommodate the growing number of pilgrims moving between cities. **JMS**

◉ FOCAL POINTS

1 TOWER

St.-Denis now has only one tower although it originally had two. As is the case with many other Gothic cathedrals, such as Chartres, fires and other disasters have altered its external appearance over time. This requires the viewer to imagine what it must have looked like when it was first completed.

2 FLYING BUTTRESSES

The flying buttresses at St.-Denis are less prominent than those on later cathedrals, which had increasingly higher and thinner walls that required buttresses with a more angular design. Flying buttresses, which first appeared at Notre-Dame in Paris, are today considered synonymous with the Gothic style.

3 ENTRANCE

Abbot Suger constructed the entrance of St.-Denis first, and its cubelike shape reflects the influence that the description of the New Jerusalem in the biblical Book of Revelation had on him. This imagery also permeates the rest of the building, and also directed its proportional relationships.

▲ Suger's amendments to St.-Denis more than doubled the size of the previous abbey church. Rebuilding of the nave was carried out after his death, in the Rayonnant Gothic style.

▲ Most of the kings and queens of France are buried at St.-Denis and are realistically portrayed in sculptures on top of their tombs.

Reims Cathedral 1211–75
VARIOUS ARCHITECTS

Reims Cathedral,
Reims, France

Reims Cathedral was begun in 1211 on the site where Clovis, the first king of the united Franks, was baptized and where French kings were crowned. It is obvious that the architecture of Reims Cathedral owes a debt to the architecture of another great church—Chartres Cathedral. In many ways, the master mason of Reims set out to build a more advanced version of Chartres by creating a greater sense of continuity and by further reducing the surface areas of the walls. The use of bar tracery was first introduced in the clerestory here, which allowed for a more elegant impression than the plate tracery used in Chartres. The new Gothic church also employed flying buttresses to bear the weight of the building as its large stained-glass windows would not have been adequately supported by the dwindling amount of wall between them. In addition, a new west facade was built in the Gothic style with three large sculpted portals, a rose window, a row of figures in niches above the rose, and two flanking towers that were never finished. A Coronation of the Virgin scene crowns the central portal of the facade and slender Gothic jamb sculptures of saints come alive as they turn toward each other. This west front is often quoted as the perfect rendition of a Gothic facade. **JG**

FOCAL POINTS

1 FLYING BUTTRESSES

The system of exposed flying buttresses, supporting the building and its vast amount of glass, is one of the most recognizable features of the High Gothic style. The flyers are not hidden as they were in early Gothic structures, but are visible even on the facade here as they peek out from behind the sheer towers.

2 BAR TRACERY

The rose window of Reims employs bar tracery that differs from the plate tracery of Chartres Cathedral. It consists of very narrow pieces of stone, held together by metal rods, rather than thick pieces of stone, connected to the wall. This allows for a more delicate appearance of patterns.

3 PORTAL

The portals of Reims are distinctive not only for their quality but also for the amount of sculpture, which covers the jambs, archivolts, gable, lintel, and trumeau between the doors. The tympana in the portals are decorated by stained glass, adding to the richness of these thresholds and their Gothic character.

▲ Although the elevation of Reims appears to resemble Chartres Cathedral, it uses more sophisticated technology, such as bar tracery.

DE HONNECOURT SKETCHBOOK

Villard de Honnecourt traveled from northern France to Hungary in the first half of the 13th century, sketching sculpture and architecture. His drawing of the choir of Reims Cathedral (below) is probably copied from an original architectural sketch. Even though it is unlikely that de Honnecourt was an architect, his sketchbook emphasizes how architectural drawings may have been circulated at this time and how the design of tracery, for example, traveled long distances.

Old Town Bridge Tower 1357–c.1388

PETER PARLER C.1330 – 99

Old Town Bridge Tower,
Prague, Czech Republic

Old Town Bridge Tower was begun in 1357 as a gate tower to the new Gothic bridge in Prague. Crowned by a steep roof, the tower is the best surviving example of a Gothic bridge tower in Europe and its facade illustrates the way in which Gothic elements were used in secular buildings at this time. The architect behind the bridge has been disputed, but it is clear that the Bridge Tower owes its most interesting features to Peter Parler. The foundation stone of the bridge was laid by Emperor Charles IV, who was determined to turn Prague into the capital of the Holy Roman Empire after his coronation in Rome in 1355. On account of the bridge's position in the heart of medieval Prague, the sculptural program on the east facade of the tower represented the most public display of urban propaganda surviving from the time of Charles IV. It is decorated by blind tracery that resembles a cross section of an upper part of a Gothic church. Enthroned figures of Charles IV and his son, Wenceslas IV, sit surrounded by this tracery, flanking a model of the bridge, upon which a figure of St. Vitus stands. In the upper register, Sts. Adalbert and Sigismund are also portrayed. In addition to the sculpture on the east facade, a net vault decorates the first level of the gate and the royal character of this building is reflected in the central boss of the vault, which is a sculpted image of a Bohemian crown. **JG**

NAVIGATOR

FOCAL POINTS

1 ROOF
The steep Gothic roof was constructed between 1380 and 1388 as a crown to the Old Town Bridge Tower and composed of a complex pattern of original fourteenth-century wooden beams that are hidden underneath the slates. This roof was copied in the nineteenth century as a model for neo-Gothic buildings.

2 PINNACLE
Pinnacles were often used in Gothic churches to top the buttress pillars, as a way of decorating the flying buttresses rather than hiding them. Here, the pinnacle is used as a part of the blind tracery, which helps hide the thickness of the wall behind it but also forms an abstract image of a church with flying buttresses.

3 COATS OF ARMS
Coats of arms and personal emblems often decorated facades of secular buildings in the High Middle Ages. The coats of arms on the Old Town Bridge Tower represent the lands that were under the influence of Emperor Charles IV during this time and were arranged according to their significance.

ARCHITECT PROFILE

c.1330–56
Peter Parler was born in Germany, the son of Heinrich Parler, a master mason who was active in Schwäbisch Gmünd and Cologne. In c.1356 the young Parler was called to Prague by Emperor Charles IV to take over the building of the new cathedral because its first builder, Matthias of Arras, had died in 1352. Parler was in his early twenties at the time, which underlined the apparent talent that the emperor must have recognized in him.

1357–99
The architectural style of Parler was almost certainly influenced by the intimate involvement of Charles IV, whose demands often required Parler to alter his designs. It was his own innovative vaults, hanging bosses, and use of tracery, however, that marked the transition between High Gothic and Late Gothic. Parler is credited with the building of the new Gothic bridge in Prague in an inscription under his bust in the triforium of St. Vitus's Cathedral. On Parler's death, his son, Wenceslas, continued the work on St. Vitus's Cathedral.

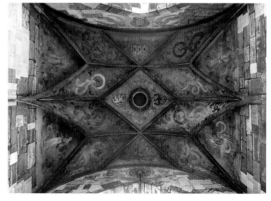

▲ The Bohemian crown that forms the central boss may refer to the procession that would pass through here before a coronation.

REGIONAL VERNACULAR

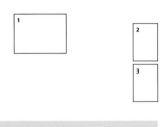

1 **Icehouse (date unknown)**
Architect unknown
Meybod, Iran

2 **Icehouse (date unknown)**
Architect unknown
Tramuntana Mountains,
Mallorca, Spain

3 **Beehive House (date unknown)**
Architect unknown
Pouss, Cameroon

S now was a commodity in fifth-century Athenian markets and the Chinese harvested and stored ice for emperors. However, it was the Persian Empire that excelled at water-cistern (*ab anbar*) and icehouse (*yakhchal*) engineering, such as at Meybod in Iran (see image 1). Built in hot climates from perishable mud brick and with little incentive to preserve rather than replace industrial buildings, extant early icehouses are difficult to date, but medieval versions on the Mediterranean island of Mallorca indicate icehouse knowledge was exported and influenced icehouse design in the West for centuries.

Mallorca's hydraulic infrastructure during Islamic rule (ninth–thirteenth centuries) included underground *qanat*, which transported water to terraced fields, and icehouses (*case de neu*) in the Tramuntana Mountains (see image 2). Built at high altitudes, these icehouses exploited existing crevasses, which were enlarged conically to withstand the volumetric thrust of the ice pack, lined in stone, and roofed. Snow was shoveled through windows; doors at either end allowed access to tamp the snow and create block ice, and reeds were layered on the ice for insulation. Once the icehouse was full, its doors and windows were sealed until spring. A similar early, possibly late-medieval, icehouse in Amagno Strozza near Milan, is bottle-shaped, its mass buried beneath the street. Snow was dropped through the ground level "bottle mouth." Tunnel access to the midsection from an adjacent building allowed the snow to be tamped, after which doors were sealed and the mouth "corked" until spring.

Dependent on proximity to mountain ice, early Iranian icehouses were either for storage only or for both ice-making and storage. Dirt excavated on site became sun-dried mud bricks, which were stacked, mortared, and cantilevered layer by layer until they met at the center to form a dome. Domes prevailed as icehouse shapes because they wick heat upward away from the ice stored in the subterranean inverted cone pit that pulls ice blocks inward to minimize melt and funnel meltwater to a drain. The dome's oculus allowed air to circulate to disrupt heat radiation. Mud brick's thermal mass restricts heat ingress during the day and radiates heat outward at night. Icehouses too far from mountains for ice transfer were built with adjacent shallow pools where water from *qanats* enabled on-site, winter ice manufacture. Icehouses had north-facing entrances and south-facing shade walls.

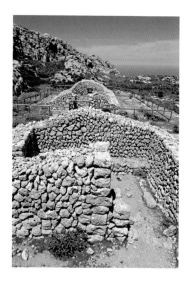

Dependent on location and climate, icehouses might also require temperature control via the integral wind towers (*bad gir*) more commonly associated with water cisterns, whose high humidity required flanking wind towers and *ajor ab anbari* (water reservoir bricks) mortared with *srooj*—mud, ash, goat hair, clay, sand, lime, and egg whites. Region-specific top-vented wind towers exploit prevailing winds and pressure differentials to exchange hot air for cool. Iranian *qanat* technology includes subterranean water mills, such as one in Nain, Isfahan province, Iran (see p.160). Accessed by a deep corridor, a *qanat* channel fills a water tank; when the water is released its kinetic force rotates the turbine. The shapes, materials, and thermal properties of cisterns and icehouses were also used for dwellings. Householders in Yazd without courtyard pools to further cool internal temperatures from air circulating across the water, placed damp straw over wind tower vents to cool air through evaporation. Similarly shaped earthen houses called beehives (but distinct from beehive tholoi tombs such as the Treasury of Atreus, Mycenae, Greece, c.1350–1250 BCE) are found in northern Syria and Cameroon. Both types are corbeled mud-brick builds with an oculus for air circulation. The domed earthen houses (*cases obos*) of the Musgum people in northern Cameroon have grooved exteriors to expedite drainage during rainstorms (see image 3).

The influence of Islamic icehouse building techniques spread to Europe and the United States. The eighteenth-century brick icehouse in Capability Brown's landscape at Croome Park, England, has a *pishtaq*-like projecting portal and thatched dome similar in typology to an early Iranian icehouse on the road to Shiraz. Dormer roof ventilation on many nineteenth-century Western icehouses mirrors the form of wind towers. The octagonal brick icehouse at Castle Brolio, Chianti, Italy, is similar in size and shape to the sunken, domed, double-walled icehouse (1781) in Philadelphia by Robert Morris (1734–1806). A false ceiling between ice and dome was packed with straw for insulation, and a gravel base provided drainage. So successful was Morris's structure that George Washington sought his advice for his icehouse at Mount Vernon. **DJ**

12th century	c.1180–c.1250	1271–1368	c.early 14th century	14th century	14th century
"New Jerusalem" monolithic Christian churches are hewn and chiseled from solid rock at Lalibela, Ethiopia.	Borgund Stave Church, Borgund, Lærdal, Norway, is built. Vertical wooden staves with side notches and grooves interlock to form walls.	In the Yuan dynasty, east–west aligned Beijing *hutong* (narrow street) communities include Siheyuan-style houses (traditional courtyard).	At Leigh Court Barn, Leigh, Worcestershire, England, a cruck frame capitalizes on a natural tree shape with wattle and daub infill panels covered in mud.	Timurid icehouses are constructed in Turkmenistan. The mud-brick structures are built with concave floors.	Vicars' Close, Wells, Somerset, England, is built—the oldest surviving, intact, planned and purely residential street in Europe.

Nain Cistern and Wind Tower Date unknown
ARCHITECT UNKNOWN

Nain Cistern and Wind Tower,
Nain, Isfahan province, Iran

NAVIGATOR

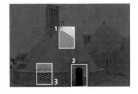

Domed subterranean reservoirs or cisterns (*ab anbar*) are reliant on rainwater or aquifer-fed *qanat* as their water supply. This cistern is in Nain, a city famed for its *qanat* system, which features a subterranean water mill. The high volumetric heat capacity of water requires large domes. A varying number of multidirectional wind towers (*bad gir*) with top vents exploit wind and pressure differentials to keep the water chilled through passive evaporative air exchange. There are five wind tower vent patterns: unidirectional, bidirectional, quad-directional (sometimes with false "vents" on two opposite sides), and octagonal with two vents on each of the eight faces. Earth is excavated on site to create flat, square, sun-dried water reservoir bricks (*ajor ab anbari*). Wind towers are also used for civic, domestic and religious buildings. Cities in the Iranian desert plateau are renowned for their *bad gir*. Despite the redundancy of many cisterns, including Haj Ali Mohammad in Meybod, which was converted in 1998 to host Iran's first ceramics museum, twin *ab anbar* modeled on traditional types in Yazd were built in 1992 to supply water for crop irrigation in the Portuguese Valley, Queshm Island, Iran. **DJ**

1 DOME

Catenary domes with low rise-to-span ratios are typical in Iran. The brickwork is similar to the Seljuk-style domes at nearby Jameh Mosque. Catenary arches require brick layers using highly compressed bricks. Low domes have greater outward thrust contained by a brick "belt."

2 ENTRANCE

The public entrance is generally through a *pishtaq* or *bad gir* and down a ventilated staircase to water taps. Other doors are for maintenance; there is no public access to the main body of water to ensure that the water remains clean. Water tanks are below ground.

3 RESERVOIR BRICKS

Square bricks reduce dome weight and provide greater strength. The *bad gir*, which serves two cisterns, is built of bricks, mortared on their edges in a decorative pattern. The number, vents, and orientation of *bad gir* are decided by wind direction and temperature.

◄ Located in the city of Abar Kooh, in Yazd province, Iran, this icehouse (*yakhchal*) features a telescoping cone shape with an oculus to release heat that is wicked upward by its deliberate shape. The ice is stored in a subterranean inverted cone-shaped pit.

CATENARY ARCH

The self-supporting catenary arch is ubiquitous in Iran, such as those at Shahid Bahonar University of Kerman (right). It is modeled on the inversion of the drape of a chain hanging from its ends, and the line of the thrust was calculated by Robert Hooke (1635–1703) in 1675. The catenary is ideal for icehouses and brick kilns where the arch expands during firing and retracts during cooling without structural damage or the need for metal supports. In the West, architects such as Antoni Gaudí (1852–1926) and Eero Saarinen (1910–61) used catenaries for Casa Milà, Barcelona (1905), and the Gateway Arch, St. Louis, Missouri (1963), respectively. The spherical dome of St. Paul's Cathedral, London (begun 1675), is a false dome supported by a hidden, brick catenary arch.

3 | 1400–1700

LATE GOTHIC

1 **Vault of St Barbara's Church (1511)**
Benedikt Ried
Kutná Hora, Bohemian region,
Czech Republic

2 **Chapel of Henry VII, Westminster Abbey (1503–09)**
Robert Janyns (attributed)
London, UK

3 **Royal Mausoleum (1437–c.1500)**
Huguet, Mateus Fernandes and Diogo Boytac
Batalha, Portugal

The term "Late Gothic" not only describes a well-defined stylistic culmination of one of the grandest epochs of medieval architecture, but also refers, on a more general level, to a period of transition between two major eras in world history: the Middle Ages and the Early Modern Age. As such, Late Gothic stands for continuity and an organic development of its architecture to match the requirements of a dynamically changing time.

From the second half of the fourteenth century, a true building boom occurred in many areas. Not only were churches and castles erected, but also ambitious public buildings such as town halls and guild houses. As in previous periods, major projects were initiated by royalty, the nobility, or the high clergy; however, the role of rich merchants as patrons also became more important. Simultaneously, builders emerged from the anonymity of previous centuries. The mobility of these architects, as well as their strong will to share experiences and to make use of up-to-date ideas for their own projects, caused a rapid spread of newly developed designs. However, the regional developments throughout Europe differed profoundly. Common features of the Late Gothic period are the tendency to reduce the structural complexity (elevation, support system) and the emphasis of the decorative character of former structural elements, such as vault ribs. Due to a preference for organic forms, these often underline a dynamic expression of the architecture.

One of the most prolific areas of Late Gothic architecture was the center of the Holy Roman Empire, where important developments were triggered

KEY EVENTS

1401	1408	1420	1425	1437	1443–52
Committees of French, Italian, and German architects conclude their consultation in Milan to discuss the cathedral project.	Hans von Burghausen (c.1350–1432) plans the choir for the Franciscan church in Salzburg, Austria, with an innovative, continuous rib vault.	Filippo Brunelleschi (1377–1446) is selected to design the dome for the Cathedral of St. Maria del Fiore in Florence (see p.166).	Italian mason Matteo Raverti (a.1398–1436) begins his designs for Ca D'Oro in Venice (see p.168).	Work begins on St. Maclou in Rouen, France, a central monument of the French Flamboyant style.	Leon Battista Alberti (1404–72) writes the first Renaissance treatise on architecture; it is based on Vitruvius's *De architectura (On Architecture)*.

by the Parler architect family. The style originated in southern Germany, where the erection of vast hall churches such as Heilig-Kreuz-Münster in Schwäbisch Gmünd (choir, 1351–1410) set the course for further development— by the fifteenth century, the region was covered with sites for new churches, predominantly parish churches of the wealthy bourgeoisie. Master masons frequently traveled between sites, planning and surveying large projects that often had to be finished by their children or pupils. In the second half of the fourteenth century, members of the Parler family moved to the royal residence in Prague, where Peter Parler (1330–99) became the architect of Emperor Charles IV. In numerous buildings in Bohemia, the architects of the Parler family developed an enormous "static, spatial, and decorative potential," which was taken on and refined about 1500 by Bohemian architect Benedikt Ried (c.1454–c.1534). His masterpieces are the Vladislav Hall in Prague Castle (1493–1510) and the completion of St. Barbara's Church in Kutná Hora (see image 1), which had been begun by Johann Parler (c.1359–c.1405). Both of these buildings show a new type of vault, the loop vault, which in Kutná Hora covers all three naves, thus suppressing the old concept of separated bays. The strong horizontal division of the elevation and the use of window frames in the Vladislav Hall show an awareness of Early Renaissance architecture (see p.172).

In Italy, a strong polemic against the Gothic style and the simultaneous rediscovery of classical architecture had been virulent since the 1420s. This restricted the Italian Late Gothic to independent areas such as Venice and to singular buildings such as the cathedral in Milan, begun in 1386. This ambitious building was erected by Italian, German, and French architects; however, little is visible of the floral qualities that were promoted in France from the late fourteenth century onward by the Flamboyant style, named after the flamelike shape of its tracery. The ideals of this curvilinear style are opposed to the Perpendicular style, simultaneously developed in England, in which the tracery also defines the main characteristic of the architecture. Windows contain numerous vertical mullions, which rise to the top of each arch and are cut across by horizontal strips of tracery. The most important monument of this style is the Chapel of Henry VII in Westminster Abbey, London (see image 2), which also features a unique pendant fan vault.

The Iberian Peninsula also developed its own strongly independent Late Gothic styles—the Isabelline Gothic in Spain and the Manueline Gothic in Portugal—which were named after the respective sovereigns. The latter style is defined by its exuberant sculptural decorations, containing nautical and botanic forms, the use of twisted ropes as columns, polylobed arches deriving from Moorish models, and the integration of Renaissance elements such as round arches and shell niches. Among the most notable examples are the unfinished Royal Mausoleum in Batalha (see image 3) and the Jerónimos Monastery of Belém (1501–80). **TK**

1446	1459–62	1471	1477	1501	1503–09
Work begins on King's College Chapel, Cambridge, England. It is a fine example of the Perpendicular style.	On the orders of Pope Pius II, the cathedral of Pienza, Italy, receives an interior that echoes the Late Gothic style of southern German hall churches.	The construction of Palace Chapel in Meisenheim, Germany, (see p.170) begins. It is attributed to Philipp von Gemünd (d.1523).	King Ferdinand II of Aragon and Queen Isabella I of Castile commission the Monastery of St. John of the Kings, Toledo, Spain.	The construction of Jerónimos Monastery of Belém, the key work of Manueline Gothic architecture, begins under architect Diogo Boytac (1490–1525).	The Lady Chapel of Westminster Abbey is renewed in the Late Perpendicular style as a burial place for King Henry VII.

Cathedral of St. Maria del Fiore 1296–1436
ARNOLFO DI CAMBIO, FRANCESCO TALENTI, FILIPPO BRUNELLESCHI

Cathedral of St.
Maria del Fiore,
Florence, Italy

Shortly before 1300, the city council of Florence decided that the modest Church of St. Reparata did not meet the demands of the rapidly developing city and would be replaced by a new cathedral. Arnolfo di Cambio (c.1240–1310) made the first design, which determined the unusual typology of a three-aisled basilica with a large domed octagon surrounded by radial chapels as a choir. However, after decades of little progress, Francesco Talenti (c.1300–70) enlarged the octagon, and with it the dome above. In 1367, after a popular vote and a commission of experts reconfirmed the project, the work accelerated. By 1417, the cathedral was completed with the exception of the dome; with a width of 144 ⅜ feet (44 m), its size was unprecedented and no plans for the actual construction had been made. In two competitions in 1418 and 1420, Filippo Brunelleschi (1377–1446) was chosen over his lifelong rival Lorenzo Ghiberti (1378–1455). Brunelleschi's dome is one of the most remarkable achievements of late medieval engineering. Early on in the planning, the idea of visible buttresses had been abandoned, which made the structural stability of the dome one of the main issues. To solve this problem, Brunelleschi developed a double-shell dome with four stiff horizontal stone and iron rings, holding the masonry, mainly consisting of light bricks, in place. With Brunelleschi's realization of di Cambio's project, the dome became a conspicuous sign of the city's power and wealth, and influenced countless buildings of later ages. **TK**

◉ FOCAL POINTS

1 UNFINISHED GALLERY
When Brunelleschi died, the planned double gallery between the drum and the dome had not begun. In 1508, Baccio d'Agnolo (1462–1543) designed a gallery to finish this part of the cathedral, but after the southeastern section was completed, his project was abandoned as unsuitable.

2 INCRUSTATION
The incrustation with black and white stone slabs creates a distinctive geometric pattern, which is a prominent feature of Florentine churches. This tradition, which began with eleventh-century buildings such as the Baptistery, was believed to be of Roman origin for centuries.

3 WINDOWS
The windows in the lower stories reveal the medieval origins of the cathedral. They are adorned with rich tracery, consisting of cusped, pointed lancets and polylobed oculi. Initially, similar windows were planned for the clerestory instead of the large circular openings that are visible today.

▲ The interior shows how the building connects Gothic traditions and Early Renaissance (see p.172) ideals. While the nave is covered with pointed rib vaults and divided by large composite piers, the heavy horizontal galleries and friezes, as well as the proportions and windows of the octagon, derive from a new repertoire of forms.

Ca D'Oro 1425–c.1440
MATTEO RAVERTI fl.1398–1436 AND GIOVANNI BON 1355–1443

Ca D'Oro, Venice, Italy

NAVIGATOR

The erection of Ca D'Oro (Golden House), or Palazzo St. Sofia—the most impressive medieval palace in Venice—was initiated by aristocrat Marin Contarini in about 1420. The site was previously occupied by the Palazzo Zen, which Contarini acquired through his marriage to Soramador Zen and subsequently demolished. Unusually for the time, the patron acted as his own clerk of the works by employing several autonomous masons. The structure of the building is typical for Venice: access was possible through a court on the land side and via an open hall from the water side. Behind the unique, colonnaded loggias (galleries with one or more open sides) were the large hall and two *porteghi* (long halls), while the living rooms were in the less open, towerlike part of the building flanking the loggias. The principal facade of the Ca D'Oro faces the Grand Canal. Made of marble, it screens the brick structure behind and is an impressive decorative example of the Venetian Late Gothic. It was designed between 1425 and 1431 by Milanese master mason Matteo Raverti, who was probably responsible for the rich tracery, and by the Venetian stonemason Giovanni Bon. The decoration merges elements from the Byzantine tradition, such as the marble incrustation with a color pattern, with delicate Gothic tracery, seen on the balconies of the two upper stories. **TK**

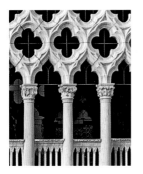

1 SCREENED LOGGIA
The design of the lacelike arcade, which screens the loggia, is comparable to the model of the Doge's Palace (1424), which also makes use of a row of uniform columns connected by a balustrade. However, the tracery is enriched by truncated quatrefoils, creating the impression of a continuous pattern.

2 SPOLIA
The palace facade makes use of several *spolia*, decorative elements of the older Palazzo Zen that stood on the same site until 1420. The practice was common, and this interest in visualizing the history of the palace most probably goes back to the ideas of the patron, Marin Contarini, who had a strong influence on the design of the waterside facade.

3 INCRUSTATION
The incrustation on the facade, with white and red marble and other stones, is typical of the Byzantine (see p.82) tradition that persisted until the Gothic period in Venice. This tradition is also illustrated by the use of chess-pattern friezes and inlaid medallions, which derive from the facade of the Cathedral of St. Mark, remodeled in the twelfth to thirteenth centuries.

VENETIAN GOTHIC

Although Renaissance architecture (see p.172) flourished in other areas of Italy from c.1420, Venetian Gothic reached its heyday only in the fifteenth century, when Venice had risen to previously unknown power in the Mediterranean. It is remarkable that the doges chose to retain the traditional Gothic style of the older south wing of their palace when the west wing was renewed between 1424 and 1438. About 1400, the Romanesque (see p.132) facade of the Cathedral of St. Mark had already been decorated with Late Gothic tabernacles and ogee arches as gables, thereby creating a prominent example for the merging of colorful marble incrustation of Byzantine style (see p.82) with Gothic tracery and pinnacles. The picturesque appearance of the buildings inspired writer John Ruskin to base his principles for good architecture on the Venetian Late Gothic in the three volumes of *The Stones of Venice* (1851–53), which deeply influenced Gothic revival architecture in the nineteenth century.

◄ The main room on the first floor is the large columnar hall. It opens into a small courtyard with a staircase to the upper stories. Toward the loggia next to the canal is a large window with rich tracery. The floor is covered with geometric marble inlays of the opus sectile type.

Palace Chapel, Meisenheim 1471–1504
ATTRIBUTED TO PHILIPP VON GEMÜND d.1523

Palace Chapel,
Meisenheim,
Rheinland Pfalz,
Germany

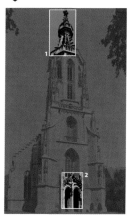

The small Palace Chapel in Meisenheim was erected between 1471 and 1504 on behalf of Ludwig the Black, Count Palatine of Zweibrücken, who retired to the town in 1479. The chapel is not only remarkable for its sophisticated architecture, but also for its multiple uses: it was owned by the local commandery of the Order of St. John, served as an oratory and mausoleum for the count, and was the parish church for the townspeople. This situation is reflected in the ground plan and the choice of decoration. The hall nave with simple star and net vaults was the space for the townspeople, while the first bay of the choir, with a complex star vault, belonged to the Order. This bay was flanked by the count's private oratory to the north, and his funerary chapel to the south. The vault of the latter represents a culmination of Late Gothic design principles and innovative technical solutions, by combining figures of loop and net vaults and making use of detached ribs. The sanctuary has a remarkable, centralized shape formed by seven sides of a ten-sided polygon. The star vault with a tracery rose around the keystone marks the place where an octagonal model of the Holy Sepulchre once stood. While the architectural forms of the church, which was probably planned by Philipp von Gemünd, are typical of the Frankfurt School, the shape of the choir is certainly inspired by the Gothic enlargement of the Palatine Chapel in Aachen (fourteenth–fifteenth centuries)—a highly symbolic statement, made by an ambitious count. **TK**

FOCAL POINTS

1 TOWER AND SPIRE
The octagonal tower, surrounded by a multitude of pinnacles, and the high openwork spire that crowns it, emphasize the ambition of the count for his palace chapel to rank among the much larger cathedral buildings of the Rhine region. This type of tower belongs to a tradition established in the fourteenth century with buildings such as Freiburg im Breisgau and perpetuated in the fifteenth century by cathedrals such as Strasbourg.

2 CRUCIFIXION GROUP
The tympanum (triangular space) of the porch is filled with a monumental Crucifixion group that visitors had to pass beneath in order to enter the church. The sculptures are merged with the architecture in a typical Late Gothic manner, with the cross beam emerging directly from the trumeau (pillar between two openings). The portal is framed with a polylobe ogee arch, a common element in buildings of the Frankfurt School.

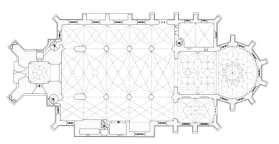

▲ The ground plan of the church shows its highly systematic composition. The tower defines the width of the nave with rectangular bays; the aisles are half as wide and have square bays.

FRANKFURT SCHOOL

The term "Frankfurt School" groups together about ten builders who were active in the Middle Rhine region in the fifteenth and early sixteenth centuries. All were pupils of or had been influenced by architect Madern Gerthener (c.1360–1430). His most important building is the tower of Frankfurt Cathedral (right), which shows an innovative use of tracery vaults and hanging tracery forms that became typical of Gerthener's work.

EARLY RENAISSANCE

The passage from Gothic (see p.148) to the Renaissance entailed an adoption of forms and aesthetic principles that were copied from—and, to some extent, aspired to revive—Roman antiquity. The more recent Romanesque (see p.132) and Gothic of Tuscany had a part to play, too. These turned out to be not a regression, but transitions from medieval to proto-modern. Broader developments in the structure and culture of Florentine society had made it sympathetic toward a brief sequence of architectural projects in Florence in the early 1420s. Filippo Brunelleschi (1377–1446), while working on the Gothic dome of Florence Cathedral, St. Maria del Fiore (1296–1436; see p.166), introduced the Renaissance style in two smaller works, both within a few hundred feet of the cathedral, and both begun about 1421: the Hospital of the Innocents (see image 1) and the Sacristy of St. Lawrence (see image 2).

The Hospital of the Innocents was the first orphanage in Europe, commissioned by a silk guild at a time when charity was becoming common practice in secular society, even though the material wealth of Florence had begun to decrease. Brunelleschi was perhaps more conscious of introducing a new style than had been Abbot Suger, the so-called inventor of Gothic, three centuries earlier. Yet, in both cases, all the components existed already. The real innovation lay in the arrangements and combinations of these elements to create a new overall effect. The hospital's facade was symmetrical with nine bays. Rhythm was established by the columns, emphasized by the pedimented

KEY EVENTS

1402	1419	c.1420	1426	1434	1436
Filippo Brunelleschi, having lost the competition for the doors of the Florence Baptistery, travels to Rome to study Roman buildings.	The building of St. Lawrence begins. The basilica will become host to the Sacristy by Brunelleschi and the New Sacristy (1524) by Michelangelo.	Brunelleschi's public demonstration of the use of linear perspective in drawing becomes a watershed in the Renaissance conquest of spatial expression.	Ciriaco de' Pizzicoli, an Italian merchant, returns from Greece and Constantinople with drawings and written records of ruins and epigraphs.	Cosimo de' Medici returns from exile and resumes the exertion of political power as well as patronage of the arts.	At St. Spirito, Brunelleschi fuses classical details (Corinthian columns) and proportions into the design of a Romanesque basilica.

windows (which corresponded to the bays), and punctuated by the *tondi* (roundels). These were blank until the late fifteenth century, when Luca della Robbia populated them with swaddled babies in terracotta. The most prominent feature is the colonnade with its semicircular arches. These were of ancient Roman origin, as were the Corinthian columns and the proportionately correct architrave. Yet the Romans would not have rested such wide arches on such slender columns, normally used for interiors. This ancient form appeared in Brunelleschi's time and the architect incorporated it in a colonnade facing the street. The result was a bright loggia expressive of the Renaissance desire for a public life with a clarity of purpose.

The Sacristy of St. Lawrence was originally devoid of ornament. The fluted pilasters with Corinthian capitals, and the originally empty roundels inscribed in the pendentives were conceived not as decorative embellishments, but as architectural references. Brunelleschi complained about subsequent interventions in the Sacristy, by Donatello (*c*.1386–1466) and others, and with good reason in some cases: the small roundels along the frieze weakened the effect of *pietra serena* (Italian sandstone) set off by the off-white color of the walls. As much as Brunelleschi's mental image of pure architecture may appeal to modern sensibilities, it did not necessarily correspond to ancient realities; he conjured it from the sight of ruins during his trip to Rome in 1402, where frescoes had worn off, interiors had been sacked, and the paint or gilt on facades had been removed or replaced with overgrown vegetation.

In any case, such objections would have made no sense during the Gothic era—they would have seemed absurdly egotistical. But from the Renaissance period onward, the tendency arose for artists and architects to be seen as

1 Hospital of the Innocents (1421–45)
Filippo Brunelleschi
Florence, Tuscany, Italy

2 Sacristy of St. Lawrence (1421–40)
Filippo Brunelleschi
Florence, Tuscany, Italy

1452	c.1455	1460	1462	1464	1476
Leon Battista Alberti publishes *De Re Aedificatoria* (*On the Art of Building*), the first architectural treatise since ancient times.	Piero de la Francesca's *Flagellation of Christ* uses architecturally constructed and radically fragmented space in its composition.	Alberti turns the facade of St. Maria Novella into a classical composition with scrolls, a pediment, a round window, and framing columns.	Bernardo Rossellino redesigns the square at Pienza, adding the Piccolomini Palace. The modest scale does not conflict with the old city fabric.	The erection of the new cathedral in Urbino (designed by Francesco di Giorgio Martini) triggers a new phase of changes in the palace layout.	Andrea Mantegna builds his cubical house in Mantua with a cylindrical courtyard in its center, an intuitive elaboration on Albertian theory.

noteworthy individuals, even heroes. Their names were emphasized and their works were studied in the context of their careers, later covered at length by critics and biographers. There also existed a mutual sympathy between these intellectual circles and the patrons: the powerful banking and merchant families of Florence—the Medici (see p.176), the Strozzi, the Rucellai—whose businesses operated offices abroad. It was in that spirit of internationalism that architecture sought expression through a universal language that would abrogate the regional boundaries of the Romanesque and Gothic periods.

The Library of St. Mark in Florence (see image 3), built by Michelozzo di Bartolomeo Michelozzi (1396–1472) as an adjunct to the convent, was the first public library in Europe. Its high ceiling, with groin vaults over the side aisles and a barrel vault over the central aisle, creates a light and airy space. Michelangelo's Laurentian Library, built a century later, imagined learning as a form of intense introspection and knowledge as directed toward God. In contrast, the wide arches and the elegant Ionic columns of the Library of St. Mark embodied the vision of a modern, civilized life that revolved around the study of the humanities.

Leon Battista Alberti (1404–72) studied ancient architecture in real life as well as through texts; he understood its fundamental principles in a way that his contemporaries did not. In his treatise, *De Re Aedificatoria* (*On the Art of Building*), he referred to architecture as a purely mental product, or as a scientific application not separate from optics or philosophy. Imitation of natural beauty—seen as divine expression—was still the aim, but the prescribed method was different to anything that had preceded it.

People with an active interest in construction were intimidated by this new way of thinking about buildings, but Alberti's intellect appealed to patrons. Some of the most important commissions he received involved renovations of existing buildings. In 1446, he was asked by Sigismondo Malatesta, the Lord of Rimini, to remodel the ruined Church of St. Francesco—renamed Tempio Malatestiano (see image 4) after its patron; later, Giovanni Rucellai hired Alberti to alter the facade of St. Maria Novella in Florence (1460–67). Both works presented the challenge of applying Renaissance language to church architecture with historical depth. Until then, that language was manifest in palaces and interiors predominantly, while the facades of St. Spirito and St. Lawrence had been left untreated by Brunelleschi. Alberti used the Roman triumphal arch for the facade as a reference to the facade of St. Francesco.

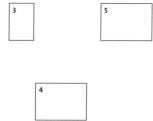

The Arch of Constantine offered a suitable template for a facade with three bays, while several details, such as the low base and the columns half-sunken into the wall were copied from the nearby Arch of Augustus. On the south face of the church, Alberti applied classical composition—heavy piers arching over niches—to the otherwise Gothic tradition of having sarcophagi placed inside the niches. An imposing dome was planned for the east side, but the church was left unfinished after Malatesta's fortunes declined. Alberti was an idealist; he famously maintained that a building should be composed in such a way that nothing could be added or removed without spoiling its perfection. There is a suitable irony in the fact that many of his works, conceived as finite, remained incomplete.

The Ducal Palace of Urbino (see image 5) was built in stages during the rule of Federico da Montefeltro, Duke of Urbino, and lacks that perfectly controlled order exercised by Brunelleschi and Michelozzo in Florence. It shows different faces to the town and surroundings: its northeast side, which faces the main street and the piazza with the medieval and Renaissance monuments, is mundane; the west side is magnificent, with two towers turned toward Rome. This side saw the most radical development of the complex when, in the mid-1460s, the steep slope was turned to a formal prospect. The terrace of the Mercatale was erected to reduce the vertical distance between the palace and the valley below. Stables and a tower with a staircase provided the final connection. It gave the impression that the palace extended beyond the city walls—an analogue of Duke Federico himself, who wandered out every morning to survey his duchy.

The interior courtyard of the palace (built in the early 1470s, possibly by Luciano Laurana, c.1420–79) reflects the calculation found in Florentine architecture of the time. The Roman inscription on the entablature can be read as a desire to model life on that of ancient Romans but, ultimately, the bright arcades and pale colors of the courtyard were not more antique in their expression than Brunelleschi's works in Florence. In this fact, one recognizes the most important pattern in Early Renaissance architecture: a constant modulation, deliberate or intuitive, between imitation and innovation. Put into perspective, Early Renaissance works were uncommon in the fabric of Florence, and even scarcer in other cities, but they prepared the ground for the High Renaissance (see p.196) of Donato Bramante and the radical transformation of Rome during the following two centuries. **EA**

3 **Library of St. Mark (1437–51)**
Michelozzo di Bartolomeo Michelozzi
Florence, Tuscany, Italy

4 **Tempio Malatestiano (1446–68)**
Leon Battista Alberti
Rimini, Italy

5 **Ducal Palace of Urbino (1470–75)**
Luciano Laurana
Urbino, Italy

Palazzo Medici 1445–68
MICHELOZZO DI BARTOLOMEO MICHELOZZI 1396–1472

Palazzo Medici,
Florence, Italy

NAVIGATOR

The size and appearance of the Palazzo Medici was deliberately modest for political reasons: Cosimo de' Medici, who commissioned Michelozzo di Bartolomeo Michelozzi to build it, had been exiled previously and wanted to keep a low profile and to avoid ostentation. Originally square in plan, the palace featured a loggia opening to the street at ground level. Although the loggia was subsequently walled up, the projecting stone benches for passers-by recall the palace's inviting civic character during its first politically untroubled phase. The three-story facade of graduated design—rough-hewn rustication on the first floor, smooth on the *piano nobile* (main floor), and absent on the third floor, the floors separated by bold protruding bands—became the prototype for other palaces in Florence, such as the Strozzi (begun 1489) and the Pitti (1458). In the interior courtyard, epigraphs and relief fragments of ancient masonry hang on the walls, arranged in Baroque frames. These date from the ownership of the Riccardi family in the early eighteenth century and were a later addition to the rich collections inside the palace—assembled from the Renaissance onward—of statues, frescoes, paintings, and furniture, all proclaiming a changed attitude toward the classical past. A number of erudite visitors have left behind letters after their stay at the palace, praising its treasures and the owners' refined taste. These testimonies are now archived in the palace's library, along with photographs that are accessible online through the Mediateca. **EA**

FOCAL POINTS

1 ENTABLATURE

A series of classical motifs is concentrated underneath the heavy protruding cornice of the entablature. In ascending order, these include a dentil band; a band with egg-and-dart ovoli (convex molding); rosetta-bearing coffers, separated by volute-shaped modillions (brackets); and a fluted band.

2 MULLIONED WINDOWS

A mullion is a vertical element—originally of stone and usually structural—that divides the window into two. Its progenitor may have been Islamic, but mullions of this thinness are seen from Gothic architecture (see p.148) onward. In Gothic, the mullion is used to separate lancets, whereas here it ends at semicircular arches.

3 ROCK-FACED RUSTICATION

The stone—*pietra forte* in this case—is chiseled so that its projected surface appears rougher. The desired effect is to make the first floor appear more primitive in comparison to the refined *piano nobile*—a contrast perhaps seen as analogous to that between nature and architecture.

◄ The interior courtyard by Michelozzo is a typical Renaissance colonnade, with wide arches and columns with Corinthian capitals. The architrave has festoons, set off by *pietra serena*, and connecting medallions with coats of arms or mythological themes.

CHINA: MING

1 **Dacheng Hall, Confucius Temple (1499)**
Architect unknown
Qufu, Shandong province, China

2 **Pagoda of the Da Bao'en Monastery (1412–28)**
Architect unknown
Nanjing, Jiangsu province, China

3 **Ancestral Hall of Luo Dongshu (c.1539–1616)**
Architect unknown
Chengkan, Huangshan, Anhui province, China

The Ming dynasty (1368–1644) was characterized by a stable but rather insular regime. Economic development gained pace and exports to Southeast Asia and the West flourished. However, the political climate was stale and architecture remained conservative with little innovation.

Of surviving building compounds from this period, many are considerably intact. One notable example is the Confucius Temple in Qufu, Shandong province. As the birthplace of Confucius, Qufu has been a center of worship since Confucianism was adopted as the state ideology in the second century BCE. A temple to the philosopher was first erected after he died in 478 BCE, and a major rebuilding took place in 1499 after destruction by fire. The current form and scale of the temple can be traced to this golden age of Confucian worship. The extensive central axis of the Confucius Temple consists of no fewer than nine buildings from south to north, organized in three cloisters. The outer cloister is composed mainly of gate buildings, whereas the second cloister terminates in the tall Kuiwen Pavilion, first erected in the Song dynasty (960–1279) and rebuilt in 1499 as a seven-bay, two-story structure. The first floor is an open space for ritual practices and the upper story is a library. This is an unusual arrangement. The last cloister contains the Dacheng Hall (see image 1) of the temple in which Confucius was worshipped. A perimeter corridor surrounds this cloister, following a practice seen in the Tang dynasty (618–907). In front of the hall is a large platform used for ritual dance, similar to that found in the

KEY EVENTS

1412	1416	1417–21	1430	1456	1499
Construction of the porcelain Pagoda of Da Bao'en Monastery in Nanjing begins; it is the most prominent pagoda in China.	The Golden Hall is built by imperial order on Wudang Mountain, Hubei province; it is the earliest building covered with bronze sheets imitating wood.	The Yongle emperor moves the capital to Beijing and orders a large-scale construction project for the city and imperial palace.	The Jingjue Mosque in Nanjing is rebuilt; it is the first mosque to be built in the former capital and one of five major mosques in China.	The main hall of Lu Family Mansion in Zhejiang province (see p.180) is built. The mansion eventually comprises more than twenty-five buildings.	The Confucius Temple in Qufu is rebuilt following imperial construction standards; it is the largest building complex in the empire.

imperial palace. Like the main hall of the imperial palace, the Dacheng Hall has a frontal elevation with nine bays. The carved dragon stone columns along the front are unusual in official architecture, and the bracket sets are much smaller in proportion than those from the Tang or Song dynasties.

Religious architecture continued to flourish during the Ming dynasty. A significant example from the south is the main hall of Kaiyuan Monastery in Quanzhou, Fujian province. The earliest surviving buildings are the two stone pagodas to either side of the main axis, dating from the Song dynasty. The main hall was based on Song foundations and a surrounding corridor was added at about the end of the fourteenth century. The hall's squarish plan is most unusual for a Buddhist hall. As is common to buildings in south China, the roof pitch is very shallow. Although the bracket sets are of larger proportion than Ming dynasty brackets, the most interesting features are the interior brackets with a stacked design, seen in Song dynasty building manuals, and the use of flying deities as decoration in the interior brackets, showing influences from Silk Route art.

Another unusual building was the pagoda of the Da Bao'en Monastery in Nanjing, Jiangsu province, which was entirely clad in porcelain tiles of various designs (see image 2). The nine-story octagonal pagoda was completed in 1428 and stood at 256 feet (78 m) high. When the monastery was constructed, Nanjing was the capital city of the Ming and the construction therefore received unsurpassed imperial patronage. The exterior of the pagoda was tiled with white porcelain bricks, and five-colored decorative tiles surrounded the windows and doors. Glazed-bricked pagodas gained popularity in the Ming dynasty due to technical advances and the easy availability of glazed porcelain. The Nanjing pagoda was so impressive that it was recorded by travel writer Johan Nieuhof when he visited China in the mid-seventeenth century. Although the structure was destroyed in 1856 during the Taiping Rebellion (1850–64), many glazed pieces found their way into Western and Chinese museums, such as the Victoria & Albert Museum, London, and Nanjing Municipal Museum.

During the Ming dynasty there was an increase in the popularity of organized clan communities in the villages. The centers of these villages were usually occupied by ancestral halls, which brought the villagers together. Most ancestral halls were three bays wide, as stipulated by Ming sumptuary laws, and there was usually a minimum of three buildings along the central axis. However, the ancestral hall of Luo Dongshu (see image 3) in Chengkan village, Huangshan city, Anhui province, has four buildings along the axis. The first is a wooden fence gate structure, the second is the gate building, the third is the main hall of five bays, and the fourth is the two-story tablets hall of three sections of three bays. The ancestral hall is characterized by the large dimensions of the columns, extremely decorative wood carvings and painted timber members in the roof structure. **PPH**

1513	1559	1566	1616	1644	1693
The Zhuozheng Yuan Garden in Suzhou is completed; it contains many scenic zones, a planning method that is adopted in later garden design.	Plans for the Yu Garden in Shanghai are conceived; it is a typical garden designed for merchant families.	Tianyi Pavilion, a private library in Ningbo, is completed. The two-story building is the oldest extant library in China.	Construction of the ancestral hall for Luo Dongshu in Chengkan is finished; it is the most representative example of regional ancestral halls.	The Manchurian army overthrows the Ming dynasty and continues to locate the capital city in Beijing.	The Red Palace of Potala Palace, Lhasa, Tibet, is completed. Together with the White Palace (1653), it serves as the residence of the Dalai Lama.

Lu Family Mansion 1456
ARCHITECT UNKNOWN

Lu Family Mansion,
Dongyang, Jinhua city,
Zhejiang province, China

NAVIGATOR

Most of the few remaining houses from the Ming dynasty are located in south China in regions rich in culture. The Lu Family Mansion consists of more than ten house compounds for members of the large and prosperous family who settled in the area after the Song dynasty. A bell-shaped canal runs through three sides of the settlement, with hills to the rear. It was believed that the auspicious feng shui of the site contributed to more than 150 members of the extended family becoming high officials in the imperial government. This achievement is attested in the many ceremonial gates erected in front of the site, representing the imperial graduates from the family. The center of the main house is Suyong Hall, a five-bay building for worshipping ancestors, and for weddings, funerals, and other family affairs. To the rear of the main hall are the inner quarters, where a wall separates the outer compound, used for receiving guests, from the inner compound, used as the main residence. The interior timber elements of the hall were sumptuously decorated with color paintings and ornate sculptures. The Dongyang area is well known for its wooden sculpture, and the examples found around the house are some of the best that the region has to offer. **PPH**

◉ FOCAL POINTS

1 CENTRAL BAY

The central compartment of the three-bay opening to the hall is wider than the two side bays, which has the effect of accentuating the centrality of the architecture. The hall is open to the courtyard at all times, allowing an unobstructed connection with external air and light.

2 ROOF

The roof tiles of the main hall of the mansion are gray, because colored glazed tiles were not permitted in the construction of buildings of commoners. The bracket sets are very regular and of a small proportion, indicating that the building dates to the mid-fifteenth century.

3 DOORS

The folding doors are typical of Chinese vernacular architecture. They are usually divided into equal panels with a lattice opening over the base panel. The design of the lattice that has been used in this building is very simple, consisting of fine members in a grid pattern.

◄ Two ceremonial gateways line the approach to the mansion. Their construction was approved by the emperor to either commend members of the Lu family for good deeds or commemorate their high social status.

FENG SHUI

Feng shui is the reading of the natural landscape and its effect on the fortunes of people within that landscape. The idea that the siting of a tomb might attract good or bad fortune for the descendants of the deceased has a history of more than 2,000 years in China. It stems from the belief that the spirit of the deceased and the natural environment have the power to influence the well-being of the living. Feng shui masters are hired to site and orientate tombs and houses, known as *yin* dwellings and *yang* dwellings, respectively. The effect of feng shui reading on architecture is seen in the positioning of houses in the landscape and the orientation of the building. The Ming dynasty tomb complex in Beijing (right) was laid out according to these principles.

ISLAMIC

I n 1370, Timur, founder of the Timurid dynasty (c.1370–1507), made Samarkand the de facto capital of Persia. He was a member of a Turko-Mongol tribe from Transoxiana (roughly corresponding to present-day Uzbekistan), and his military conquests included all of Central Asia, greater Iran and Iraq, as well as parts of southern Russia and the Indian subcontinent. Timur had a keen interest in architecture and introduced a fusion of Seljuk and Persian styles, with large *pishtaqs* (gateways), ribbed domes, *muqarnas* (stalactite-like decorations) crestings, colored tilework, and white calligraphy.

Timur's architectural legacy was continued by his grandson, Ulugh Beg (1409–49), who commissioned the Ulugh Beg Madrassa (1417–20) in Registan Square, Samarkand. This was later joined by the Shir Dar Madrassa (1619–36), which equals the 167-foot (51 m) length of the Ulugh Beg Madrassa, and the Tilla Kari Madrassa (1646–60; see p.184), which is longer and features an off-axis dome and arched *aivan* (covered gallery), creating a ventilated connection to the square. These two later buildings also employ a range of architectural features that are typical of the Timurid style, demonstrating its enduring appeal beyond the end of the dynasty in 1507.

Timurid influence can also be seen at the Shah-i-Zinda necropolis (ninth–nineteenth century) in Samarkand. The complex consists of more than forty tombs spread over three levels on the slope of Afrasiab Hill; they are generally square, with a dome and an elaborately tiled *pishtaq*, and the grave below. The middle cluster includes many Timurid-style domes (see image 1) as well as the large Dargah Abd al-Aziz gatehouse at the southern end of the necropolis, in honor of the deceased son of its sponsor, Ulugh Beg. The collapse of the Timurid dynasty gave rise to the Safavids, who ruled Iran from 1501 to 1722 from Ardabil and paved the way for a modern, unified, national identity. Shah Abbas, who ruled from 1588 to 1629, transferred the Persian capital to Isfahan in 1597 to 1598. There he built a new city alongside the old one. Shah Abbas was a great patron of the arts and commissioned many notable buildings, including the Shah Mosque (1611–c.1630), and the Qaysariyya Bazaar (1617–19).

The main rivals to the Safavids during this period were the Ottomans, whose empire expanded dramatically following the capture of Constantinople by Mehmed II in 1453. Proclaiming the city the new capital of his empire, Mehmed II ordered the construction of Topkapi Palace in 1459. Damaged by earthquakes and fires, it became a work in progress over several centuries. Mehmed II's Topkapi was a city in microcosm, partitioned into a sequential series of four telescoping courtyards. The first of these, near Hagia Sophia (532–537), was public, leading to smaller private, residential quarters at the end of the peninsula. The Gate of Salutations, which introduces this sequence, was also used for executions as a public display of Ottoman justice. The elite Janissary guard were reviewed in the first courtyard and fed from the nearby domed kitchens, redesigned by Mimar Sinan (c.1489–1588) in 1574 after they were destroyed by fire. Mehmed II received foreign ambassadors and supplicants while seated under a raised pavilion between the second and third courtyards. His harem spans the second and third court, stretching along the western cliff. A closed system under the strict supervision of the sultan's mother, her private quarters, including the rooms for the concubines below, are the largest in the harem. Like other hierarchies within Topkapi, the levels of the harem are clearly reflected in the apartments, pools, and gardens of the Courtyard of the Favorites. The sultan received officials, friends, and family on his appropriately named, dome-covered imperial Sofa. He retreated from the pleasures of the harem into the pavilions and mosque of the final private court, the Baghdad Kiosk (see image 2). Built by Murad IV in 1638, it has a Mamluk-style portico and Iznik tile interior. Topkapi Palace served Ottoman sultans for 400 years, but lacked modern amenities. In 1856, Sultan Abdul Mecid I moved his court to his European-style Dolmabahçe Palace on the Bosphorus in Istanbul. The Tanzimet-era residence was designed in a fusion of Baroque (see p.222), Rococo (see p.238), and Ottoman styles by imperial architects Garabet Balyan (1800–66) and his son, Nigogayos (1826–58). **JMS**

1 **Mausoleum Domes at Shah-i-Zinda (c.1420)**
Architect unknown
Samarkand, Uzbekistan

2 **Baghdad Kiosk (1638)**
Murad IV
Topkapi Palace, Istanbul, Turkey

1550	1574	1597–98	1603	1619	c.1630
Suleyman the Magnificent commissions Mimar Sinan to build Suleymaniye Mosque and its surrounding complex.	Selimiye Mosque in Edirne, designed by Mimar Sinan, is completed.	Shah Abbas moves the Safavid capital to Isfahan and begins the construction of Ali Qapu royal palace.	Sheikh Lotfallah Mosque, Isfahan, is commissioned by Shah Abbas.	Work begins on Shir Dar Madrassa in Registan Square, Samarkand.	Shah Mosque in Isfahan is finished. A masterpiece of Persian architecture, it is Shah Abbas's largest architectural monument.

Tilla Kari Madrassa 1646–60
ARCHITECT UNKNOWN

Tilla Kari Madrassa,
Registan Square, Samarkand,
Uzbekistan

❖ NAVIGATOR

Registan Square is the urban heart of Samarkand and comprises three madrassas—Ulugh Beg (1417–20), Shir Dar (1619–36), and Tilla Kari—as well as the Chor-Su domed market, built in the eighteenth century. The Shir Dar and Tilla Kari madrassas were both commissioned by General Alchin Yalantush Bahadur. After the Bibi Khanum (1404) and Alikeh Kukeltash (c.1440) mosques fell into disuse, the function of Tilla Kari Madrassa expanded from being a theological school to including a mosque. The impressive facade of Tilla Kari, which is almost 395 feet (120 m) long, acts as a backdrop to the open side of the square. The apparent symmetry of its large *pishtaq*, repetitive array of arched openings, geometrically patterned tiles, and domed corner towers visually pulls together the disparate facades on either side. On closer inspection, however, its appeal is more complex and subtle, because it is bi-axial. In order to offset the apparent frontal symmetry, there is a separate external entrance into the mosque on the northwest side of the site, covered by a large turquoise dome. Domed prayer halls project outward on either side of the central entrance below this dome, maintaining the spatial integrity of the mosque. The central chamber is faced with intricate, blue and gold mosaic tile inlay, with an unusually high and deep arched frame around the minbar. Richly polychrome *muqarnas* take up more than a third of this opening, creating a majestic roof over the alcove. At certain times of the day, the entire recess has a golden glow. **JMS**

⊙ FOCAL POINTS

1 DOME

The exaggerated height of the turquoise-tiled dome over the main prayer hall of the mosque effectively counterbalances the axial symmetry of the madrassa. Tilla Kari's single dome is smooth, contrasting with the twin ribbed domes of Shir Dar Madrassa, which are more commonly associated with the Timurid style.

2 *PISHTAQ*

The lavishly decorated arch of the monumental *pishtaq* is typically Timurid. The recessed niche that it frames has five sides, a design that may have been influenced by the typology of sixteenth- and seventeenth-century madrassas in Bukhara. The *pishtaq* is framed by calligraphic inscriptions from the Koran.

3 TILEWORK

Tilla Kari means "golden," a characteristic that is manifest in its tile decoration. The blue and gold color scheme of Tilla Kari's exterior continues the theme established by the other two madrassas on the square. It is also employed on its interior in the form of richly embellished gilt ornamentation.

◄ The spectacular interior of Tilla Kari Mosque demonstrates the virtuosity of the local tileworkers and their ability to achieve complex effects.

PRE-COLUMBIAN LATIN AMERICA

D uring the colonization of Latin America from the late fifteenth century, the Spanish and Portuguese demolished many indigenous settlements in order to construct a new urban system connecting towns and cities across the continent. Although the Spanish built new cities over the existing indigenous capitals, such as Lima and Mexico City, a few of the latter remain today, particularly those remotely located, such as Cuzco (see images 1 and 2), the historic capital of the Inca Empire in Peru.

Although pre-Columbian Latin America appears to be a homogenous territory, major permanent settlements with cultural differences have been identified in Mexico, Caribbean Central America in the Gulf of Mexico, and a strip of land between the Andes and the Pacific coast in South America, stretching from Ecuador to Chile. Although these areas comprised only around five percent of Latin America, a high percentage of the pre-Columbian population was concentrated in them, in urban settlements that responded to the expansion and retraction of the Aztec (1428–1521), Maya (900–1500), and Inca (1438–1533) empires. Recent studies have also revealed complex societies existing in what are now Colombia, Ecuador, Bolivia, and the Amazonas, the origins of which date from c.3000 BCE.

Planned pre-Columbian cities were political, administrative, religious, cultural, and military centers. Each had a high population density and division of labor, and also acted as a center of production, services, and commerce for the wider region, as it was dependent on trade and taxes. These cities emerged

KEY EVENTS

1430	1438	1440s	1450s	1520	1532
The Incas control the valleys around Cuzco, a hilly territory between the Apurimac Canyon and the valley of the Urubamba River.	The Incas are victorious over the Chanca tribe under the leadership of Pachacuti, the last Inca emperor before the Spanish Conquest.	Coricancha, the central religious site in Cuzco known as the "Golden Enclosure" due to its elaborate, gold-covered decoration, is rebuilt.	Work on the building of the "royal estate" of Machu Picchu begins (see p.190).	The Spanish begin to explore the Pacific Coast of South America, which leads to clashes with tribes in Colombia, Bolivia, and Chile.	Spanish conquistador Francisco Pizarro captures Inca Emperor Atahualpa on his *usnu* (ceremonial platform) at Cajamarca.

from complex societies with significant political and cultural influence within the wider region, and developed through careful planning and organization of labor, materials, and human resources. Moreover, when the first ceremonial centers, such as Teotihuacan, Tenochtitlan, Tikal, and Cuzco, were planned and constructed, previously developed political and organizational structures for decision-making were firmly in place. As a result, such centers and related monuments were later overbuilt and incorporated into existing historic settlements. Across the region, however, each power group with political and social control over the land would decide (with the intention of establishing a complex network of settlements) the type, function, and characteristics of the group of buildings in accordance with the specific features and stage of evolution in each location.

Stone was the main construction material; in some places it was also used for ornamentation, with distinctive regional characteristics. In each city, it is possible to identify standards and systems used in the composition of the plans, such as modules and axes that may have been culturally transmitted through generations and across different cultures. For example, the watchtowers in Ollantaytambo (see image 3), one of the last cities built during the Inca Empire, were constructed of large-scale blocks of red porphyry, and employ a historic technique of infilling the joints with smaller pieces of the same stone material. With this method, the separation between stone blocks was minimized to achieve a smooth finish when very large stone pieces—some reaching almost 6 ½ feet (2 m) in length and height—were used. This, together with ornamental elements, such as the stepped design of the tower blocks, may express the survival of the Tiahuanacan tradition (c.CE 500–800).

By about CE 1000 several new states had emerged on the coast of Peru, the most significant of which was Chanchan. The largest city in ancient Peru, it consisted of eleven citadels and intermediate spaces, and covered an area of 7 ½ square miles (20 sq km). Little is known about the function of these citadels and their high perimeter walls, or even how the spaces around them were used, although it is possible they were constructed to allow for subdivisions and groupings of the population within the city. The grouping of buildings in the citadels, which housed several rooms connected by open corridors and courtyards, inspired later building compounds. However, these structures were probably better suited to the mild temperatures and dry weather of the coastal villages than to the more extreme conditions of the highlands.

From its capital in Cuzco, the Inca Empire expanded in South America during the fifteenth century. The great conqueror Pachacuti, and his son Topa Inca Yupanqui, led vast programs of city planning and colonization, and built complex road networks. Expansion works led by Pachacuti included the transformation of Cuzco from a clay and straw village into a planned capital city. There, new construction techniques, such as those achieving a high-quality

1 **Street in Cuzco (1400–1600)**
Architect unknown
Cuzco, Peru

2 **Plan of Incan Cuzco**
Cuzco, Peru

3 **Watchtower at Ollantaytambo (c.1450)**
Architect unknown
Ollantaytambo, Peru

1535	1542	1609	1651	1821	1911
The Incas attempt to reclaim the city of Cuzco from the Spanish, leading to a large fire that destroys wooden structures and thatched roofs.	The Spanish Crown establishes the Viceroyalty of Peru. It marks the beginning of a reorganization of the area based on silver mining.	Garcilaso de la Vega (El Inca) writes *Comentarios Reales de los Incas*—a historical chronicle of the Incas and the Conquistadors.	The construction of the Catholic Church of the Society of Jesus is led by the Jesuits in Cuzco.	After remaining loyal to the Spanish Crown longer than other Latin American countries, Peru wins its independence.	Professor Hiram Bingham of Yale University discovers Machu Picchu on July 24.

stone finish, and new spatial concepts, such as *kancha* compounds—a walled rectangular block enclosing groups of one- and two-room buildings—were tested. Cuzco's architecture and urban layout probably provided the model for new towns and cities throughout the empire as it expanded.

Despite its political power in the Inca Empire, Cuzco lacked the commercial activity of Tenochtitlan, the monumentality of Teotihuacan, and the architectural detail and expression of Tikal. Nevertheless, Cuzco's city plan was harmonious and fitted in naturally with the surrounding topography. Historians estimate that around 200,000 Indians were living in Cuzco and its suburbs by the time the Spanish arrived.

The simplest dwelling in Inca architecture consisted of a single, rectangular room, with the perimeter walls varying in design. In warmer regions, one of the long walls was replaced by a wooden beam upon which the roof slope rested. This type of house, in which the top of the roof frame rested on a central wall, has been called a *masma* (see image 4), or "double" *masma*. More complex dwellings included the walled, rectangular *kancha* that may have been inspired by architecture in the coastal villages. *Pirca* was the main construction method for stonework, in which shaped fieldstones (limestone, granite, or mica) were set in clay mortar. Blocks of stone were cut, shaped, and polished until their surfaces interlocked with absolute precision.

The Incas believed that they had descended from the Sun (Inti); their ideology was significantly linked to the cosmos and their rituals involved complex astronomical studies. The Temple of the Sun (or Qorikancha, which in Quechua means "enclosure of gold") guarded the treasures of the Inca people; the main chapel was located on the upper platform and the chapels of the Stars, Moon, Thunder, Lightning, and the Rainbow were oriented around a central courtyard (see image 6). Priests' rooms, administration, and gardens were on the lower floors and the building also had a conical tower crafted from stone. Although the Spanish demolished the temple in 1559 and built the Church and Convent of St. Domingo on its foundations, remains of the temple's circular wall (see image 5) testify to the original structure's masterful stonework.

In general, Inca cities were not as perfectly sculpted as other pre-Columbian examples, such as those in the Maya culture. However, during the Inca Empire new architectural concepts were developed, such as the use of small polished blocks of stone for construction. Inca architecture was

4 Masma House (1450–70)
Architect unknown
Machu Picchu, Peru

5 Circular Wall, Temple of the Sun/Church and Convent of St. Domingo (1440s)
Architect unknown
Cuzco, Peru

6 Plan of the Temple of the Sun
Cuzco, Peru

7 Trapezoidal Doorway (1450–70)
Architect unknown
Machu Picchu, Peru

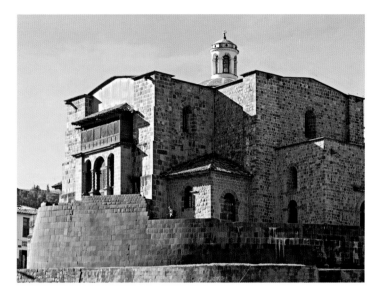

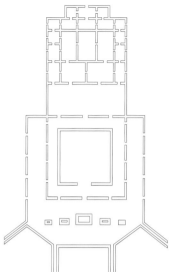

functional, with ornament minimal and carefully designed; it was logically expressed through calm geometrical forms, dimensional accuracy, perfect detailing, and the use of compact volumes. The repetitive character of Inca architecture was particularly significant, and the use of pattern and the application of a broadly recognized technique gave buildings a sense of formal unity. Stone was not only used for building; it was also crafted to form thrones and altars (*usnu*), which were found in plazas and temples as well as on open sites.

Cities in the Inca Empire were not usually fortified, although small fortresses were sometimes built in surrounding areas. A common element to all Inca cities, however, was the plaza or square. Usually large in dimension and regular in shape, the space had varying functions—as the location for public festivities and commercial exchange, or even for the administration of justice. Plazas were usually crossed by the Inca Road (Camino del Inca), which connected all the principal cities in the empire.

There are clear differences between urban architecture in Central and Latin America. Teotihuacan and Tenochtitlan in Mexico, for example, demonstrate high urban density with rows of houses aligned along streets, whereas Tikal in Guatemala represents a low urban density and a more organic structure linked with natural factors. The Inca region appears to have been formed of small urban centers, connected by a complex road network, which do not seem to follow the same urban pattern, although architecture and landscape were often beautifully integrated. Architecture in the Inca Empire evolved out of a desire to simplify technology and perfect detailing, rather than out of a search for new formal and spatial expressions. The state directed its building work through the application of widely used construction techniques; the trapezoidal doorway (see image 7), niche, and alcove, for example, are the most common elements across all Inca buildings. The most striking aspect of their construction, however, was the shaping and fitting of stones to a dimensionally tight tolerance.

During the colonization of Latin America in the sixteenth and seventeenth centuries, a fusion of cultures can be identified. Although colonial urbanism was based on a set of clear rules laid down by the Spanish Crown, the influence of native art, architecture, and urbanism is recognizable in the location, buildings, and plans of the first colonial cities. **SGF**

Machu Picchu 1450–70
ARCHITECT UNKNOWN

Machu Picchu,
Cordillera de Vilcabamba,
near Cuzco, Peru

NAVIGATOR

In 1911, Hiram Bingham of Yale University discovered Machu Picchu, a unique city integrated into the landscape, 60 miles (96 km) from Cuzco. Machu Picchu (Old City) is difficult to characterize in terms of the urban and architectural ideas of the Incas. In particular, its location, on a narrow promontory 1,310 feet (400 m) above the Urubamba River, suggests that it was peripheral to the Inca Empire. Inca ideology is encoded within the architecture of Machu Picchu, and it is unsurprising that many of its buildings are designed to allow solar, lunar, and stellar observations, which were central to Inca culture. The function of the city remains unclear, but scholars agree that it was a "royal estate," built by the Inca king for relaxation and entertainment. There are about 200 rooms in the city, but it is probable that the only permanent residents were caretakers and servants, and that elite households were occupied for short periods. Most probably, the topography of the city was used not only to organize dwellings hierarchically but also as a means for capturing a variety of viewpoints and connections to the surrounding landscape. When the Inca Empire collapsed, royal estates like this failed to continue, and larger cities closer to Cuzco became simple villages, integrated into the emerging colonial economic system. **SGF**

1 STREETS

Most of the urban elements follow the contours of the landscape in which the city was constructed. Short streets define the urban pattern, and a number of stairways, which meet streets perpendicularly, offer magnificent perspectives of the surrounding mountains.

2 COMPOUND HOUSES

To the east of the central plaza are a number of compound houses, probably occupied by the Inca elite. Each compound (developed from the *kancha* typology) is unique in shape and has distinctive features. The largest is known as "Ingenuity Group."

3 CHANNELS AND FOUNTAINS

A series of channels and sixteen ritual fountains supplied water from a perennial spring located north of the city. The first fountain was adjacent to the royal compound and allowed the Inca ruler to take a ceremonial bath in private.

◀ A key feature of Inca architecture is rooted in the accurate formation of stone walls with very tight tolerance, as seen in the Temple of the Sun, Machu Picchu.

STONE TOLERANCE

The Incas are renowned for the extremely tight tolerance of their stone walls, and the watchtowers in Machu Picchu are astounding examples of this skill. Perfection in construction detailing when using stone has been explored by modern architect Richard Neutra, and by Eric Parry whose stone-block-built 30 Finsbury Square, London (2002; right), achieves 0.04 inches (1 mm) tolerance where the 21st-century industry norm is closer to 0.24 inches (6 mm). Stone is a fascinating and timeless material. It is at the same time beautiful and utilitarian. From the ancient world to the present day, stone has been crafted for creating and shaping architectural space, in which qualities of cultural continuity and cultural context, as well as solidity and mass, are embedded.

JAPAN: SENGOKU

1 **Himeji Castle (1609)**
Architect unknown
Himeji, Hyogo prefecture, Japan

2 **Silver Pavilion (1490)**
Architect unknown
Kyoto, Kyoto prefecture, Japan

3 **Nikko Toshogu (1617)**
Architect unknown
Nikko, Tochigi prefecture, Japan

The influence of the austere ethos of fifteenth-century Higashiyama culture outlasted the Sengoku or Warring States period (1467–1605), and spread throughout Japan from its epicenter at Silver Pavilion (Ginkakuji Temple; see image 2), Kyoto. The Noh theater, tea ceremony connoisseurship, evolving *shoin-* (audience hall) style buildings, and stylized gardens constituted the elitist experimental aesthetic of Ashikaga Yoshimasa, the eighth shogun of the Ashikaga shogunate, who reigned from 1449 to 1473. By the end of the Sengoku era, the dais-based tatami reception-room style (*shoin-zukuri*) had been generalized as the *kiwarijutsu* modular design system. It was adopted by the warrior class to replace the open-plan *shinden-zukuri* architecture, which flourished during the Heian period (794–1185). This had used expansive outdoor corridors to join essentially unfurnished pavilions, whose broad outer-facing verandas had to be either open or closed. *Shoin-zukuri* architecture introduced *fusuma* and *shoji* vertical sliding panels to create divisible space.

The two-story Silver Pavilion was completed in 1490 by Ashikaga Yoshimasa as a counterpart to the Golden Pavilion (Kinkakuji) built by his grandfather, Ashikaga Yoshimitsu, in Kyoto in *c.*1400. Both of these are eclectic architecturally. The first floor of Silver Pavilion is in the *shoin* residential style, and its second-floor windows are cusped or flame-headed, which is endemic to Zen Buddhism. Golden Pavilion's first floor is in the earlier aristocratic *shinden-zukuri* style, and the second floor is a Buddha hall. Both pavilions feature a "Sound of Waves" tower; each of these is Zen in style and architecturally unrelated to the substructure.

KEY EVENTS

1467	1484	1522	1534	1543	1549
The beginning of Japan's ten-year Onin War initiates the so-called Warring States period culminating in Japanese unification 150 years later.	The former Ashikaga shogun Yoshimasa begins his Silver Pavilion mansion and garden, thus initiating the so-called Higashiyama (Eastern Hills) culture.	Japan's great connoisseur of the *wabi* (rustic simplicity) tea ceremony, Sen no Rikyu, is born in the merchant port of Sakai.	Oda Nobunaga, major Warring States *daimyo* and first among the "three great unifiers of Japan," is born at Nagoya Castle.	Blown off course by a storm, Portuguese traders are shipwrecked near Tangeshima, an island off the southern coast of Japan.	Francis Xavier establishes Japan's first Christian mission at Kagoshima, Kyushu, succeeded a generation later by a church at Kyoto itself.

The ultimate sixteenth-century development of the *sukiya-zukuri* teahouse, described by Japanese architect Arata Isozaki (b.1931) as "anti-urban, and even anti-authoritarian," promoted the diversity and asymmetry of latter-day tea ceremony spaces. Unique are the linked late-sixteenth-century Umbrella Pavilion (Kasa-tei) and Drizzling Rain Pavilion (Shigure-tei), Kyoto, in which slender, canted sapling pillars uphold the rustic, deep-eaved, thatched teahouses, one with an umbrella roof of radiating interlaced bamboo and logs.

During the Sengoku era, provincial castle towns grew in a labyrinthine pattern around the fortifications of local *daimyo* warlords, as a foil against attack. However, the oldest extant donjon, Maruoka Castle in central Japan, dates from only 1576. The massive fortress of Himeji Castle (see image 1), west of Osaka, belongs to the "flatland-mountain" (*hirayamajiro*) and "multiple-donjon" (*renritsushiki tenshu*) types. Finished in white stucco, the compound's four separate keeps are interconnected by corridors, broadly surrounded by a maze of walls, gates, and turrets, and encircled by subsidiary compounds and a great moat. A pair of massive columns supports the structure's six stories, parts of which are outfitted as a siege residence. The castle was built as a defence against enemies of the Tokugawa, and today remains Japan's best and most intact example of feudal architecture.

In contrast to both fortification and town-style palaces, the *sukiya-shoin* style of Katsura Imperial Villa (seventeenth century; see p.194) was a rarified residential form, which paradoxically influenced twentieth-century Western architecture. Katsura's three main post-and-beam buildings are arranged in a staggered line. The villa's celebrated link between interior and exterior is the open-air, moon-viewing platform (*tsukimi-dai*) attached to the Old Shoin veranda and projecting into the landscape. Made of yellow bamboo culms, it stands out from the wooden veranda and creates an effect opposite to the egress of the landscape into built space seen in Katsura's Shoi-ken teahouse.

In 1603, Tokugawa Ieyasu assumed the title of shogun and installed his eldest son at Edo Castle (finished in 1636). The site of present-day Tokyo went on to become the commercial and administrative node of an ultimately unified Japan and the world's largest pre-modern city. After Ieyasu's death in 1616, his remains were entombed in a severe bronze stupa pagoda, reached via a stunningly ornate, gated Shinto shrine complex. The mausoleum was set in deep mountainous terrain and today is known as Nikko Toshogu (see image 3). Its gates and outbuildings are of an almost Hindu profusion, later becoming the watchword for Japanese architecture after the opening up of Japan to the West. The entire structure was renovated and embellished, in colorfully executed raised and gilt lacquerwork, by Ieyasu's grandson, Iemitsu, who is commemorated by a second shrine set alongside the first. The complex lost its reputation as a style setter to its exact contemporary and polar opposite, Katsura Imperial Villa, in modern times. **DBS**

1571	1575	1590	1603	1609	1635
Oda Nobunaga destroys the Buddhist monastery of Mount Hiei near Kyoto, whose warrior monks he considers as subversive of Japanese unity.	Battle of Nagashino, near Nagoya, illustrates Nobunaga's sophisticated use of firearms to defeat skilled cavalry from behind stockades.	Toyotomi Hideyoshi, a peasant rising to generalship under Nobunaga, unifies Japan in defeating his Hojo rivals at Odawara Castle.	Tokugawa Ieyasu extends Nobunaga's iron-clad, warrior class codification and founds the Tokugawa shogunate.	Himeji Castle, today Japan's most complete surviving feudal period work of defence, incorporates materials from Hideyoshi's former donjon.	The "Closed Country Edict" forbids all travel abroad, confirms Hideyoshi's anti-Christian policies, and further restricts foreign commerce.

Katsura Imperial Villa Seventeenth century with later modifications
ARCHITECT UNKNOWN

Katsura Imperial Villa,
Kyoto, Japan

⬡ NAVIGATOR

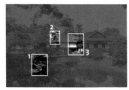

K atsura Imperial Villa in the western suburbs of Kyoto was built by Imperial Prince Toshihito and his son Toshitada in the early Edo period (1603–1867), but nothing is known of its designer. Constituting about 743,000 square feet (69,000 sq m) of exquisite grounds, the eclectic, finely balanced surroundings consist of a stroll garden (diminutive, stylized landscapes) around an irregular pond. The main building deploys linked *shoin* and a room for musical instruments in staggered, or "flying geese," formation. The estate, gardens, and five separate teahouses were built and added to over time; the Old Shoin built by Toshihito may date from 1616 and Toshitada's Middle Shoin is thought to date from 1641. Katsura perfectly illustrates the *sukiya-zukuri* style, which was influenced by the greater informality of the tea ceremony in the sixteenth and seventeenth centuries. Nonetheless, the Middle Shoin is more formal than the Old Shoin, while the refinement of the New Palace suggests an imperial suite. In 1933, German architect Bruno Taut (1880–1938) visited Katsura and described it as a pure expression of the imperial style. In the prevailing political climate, his remarks were used to promote modernism, which in prewar Japan was largely excluded from building competitions. **DBS**

⊙ FOCAL POINTS

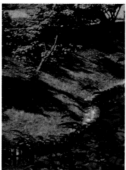

1 GARDENS

The gardens of Katsura are no less well known than the villa itself, and continue the building's diagonal alignment. Next to a river in the midst of agricultural terrain, the villa faces a man-made lake, islands, and peninsulas that are linked by ten bridges. It is a world in itself.

2 ROOF

A non-unified roof system reflects tea-style convention, which does not restrict itself to a traditional modular gridded floor plan. This comparative freedom in placing vertical supports creates a new lightheartedness and economy of overall structure.

3 STAGGERED LAYOUT

The linkage between *shoins* exemplifies the *sukiya-zukuri* layout of the complex, where a stepwise floor plan supplies a rule of thumb. Katsura Imperial Villa is one of the most complete surviving expressions of such a grouping, along with the Rinshun-kaku Villa, now in Yokohama City.

◀ The oldest and largest of Katsura's outlying informal teahouses, Pine Lute Pavilion is rustic on the exterior but more sophisticated within. A main room was used for poetry and musical recitals, and is equipped with a veranda for light cooking.

THE SOAN

The grass teahouse (*soan*) is a key achievement of Japanese architecture. Tea tasting expressed an entire approach to life and came from China to Japan, where it developed during the Kamakura (1185–1333), Muromachi (c.1337–1573), and Momoyama (1573–1615) periods, well into the Edo era. Tea gatherings reached their climax in the 16th century, when tea drinking was an upper-class pastime, but retained some religious overtones. The *sukiya-zukuri* architectural style derives from the ritual tea ceremony and its aesthetic taste. The wabi (rustic simplicity) tea ceremony reached its peak in the hands of the Japanese tea master, Sen no Rikyu. He stripped back the ceremony, reducing the area of tea preparation and serving to a few tatami mats and a sunken hearth. The Taian (right) at Yamazaki, south of Kyoto, is the sole surviving *soan* teahouse by Rikyu.

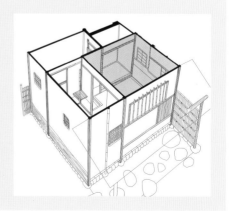

HIGH RENAISSANCE

1 **Courtyard, St. Maria della Pace (1504)**
Donato Bramante
Rome, Italy

2 **Hall of Perspectives, Villa Farnesina (1505–10)**
Baldassare Peruzzi
Rome, Italy

3 **Villa Madama (1518–25)**
Raphael of Urbino
Rome, Italy

In the last decades of the fifteenth century, artists and architects began to visit Rome to study the ruins in earnest. They left behind precious records of their studies in the form of drawings. While humanist interest in Rome had been building over more than a century (dating back at least to Petrarch in the fourteenth century), antiquarian considerations of monuments had focused on literary, epigraphic, and historical information rather than on the physical remains. Although some artists and architects, such as Filippo Brunelleschi (1377–1446), Donatello (c.1386–1466), and Leon Battista Alberti (1404–72), are reported to have made studies of Roman sculpture and ruins, almost no direct evidence of this work survives. By the 1480s, prominent architects, such as Francesco di Giorgio (1439–1502) and Giuliano da Sangallo (c.1445–1516), were making numerous studies of the ancient monuments, undertaken in ways that demonstrated that the process of transforming the model into a new design had already begun. In many cases, drawing ruins in their fragmentary state necessitated a leap of the imagination, as Francesco himself readily admitted in his annotation to his reconstruction of the Campidoglio, noting: "largely imagined by me, since very little can be understood from the ruins."

This intensive study bore immediate fruit, inspiring a series of increasingly bold attempts to match the scale, ambition, and sheer achievement of the ancient works. The most dramatic demonstration of this new attitude toward the antique—which aimed not just for imitation and emulation but for

KEY EVENTS

1480	1485	1485	1492	1497	1503–13
Donato Bramante begins work on his illusionistic perspective chapel at St. Satiro (1486) in Milan.	Leon Battista Alberti's treatise, *De Re Aedificatoria* (*On the Art of Building*), is published in Florence.	Giuliano da Sangallo begins work on Villa Medici at Poggio a Caiano (see p.200).	Lorenzo de Medici dies; Columbus arrives in the New World; and Ferdinand and Isabella conquer Granada, ending the last Muslim dynasty in Spain.	The Carthusian monastery and complex of Certosa di Pavia is completed in Lombardy, Italy.	Pope Julius II commissions the Belvedere Courtyard, the Sistine Chapel ceiling, and the new St. Peter's in Rome.

rivalry—occurred in the work of Donato Bramante (c.1444–1514), an architect who first trained as a painter in Milan.

Bramante's earliest commission in Rome was the courtyard of St. Maria della Pace (see image 1), built for Cardinal Oliviero Carafa. Based on a close study of the Colosseum, it included a subtle reprisal of the hierarchical arrangement of the orders, with the Doric on the first level and the Ionic above. While not obvious to the casual observer, this was a major conceptual shift in the use of the orders, introducing a compositional principle that would be regularly followed from that point onward. His next work in Rome was the Tempietto (1502; see p.202), which although small in size achieved a monumental effect. Marking the site of St. Peter's crucifixion, it was immediately recognized as similar to the status of an ancient monument.

Bramante's early success brought him to the attention of Pope Julius II, who employed him first for the massive Belvedere Courtyard, built to house his collection of ancient sculptures, then, in what would be one of the most ambitious and significant building projects of the sixteenth century, the construction of the new St. Peter's. Although Bramante's centralized plan was never fully realized, later architects, such as Michelangelo (1475–1564), admired and emulated its clarity and monumentality. The sheer size and complexity of St. Peter's, as well as its expense, meant that it was destined to remain incomplete for decades, and subject to the changing agendas of successive popes and architects.

Two other architects first trained as painters, Baldassare Peruzzi (1481–1536) from Siena and Raphael of Urbino (1483–1520), emulated Bramante's deep engagement with ancient Roman architecture in their own distinctive ways. Peruzzi, an avid draftsman, perspectivist, and student of Vitruvius (c.80–c.15 BCE), arrived at a new typology of the suburban villa in the Villa Farnesina (1505–10), built in Rome for Agostino Chigi, the banker to Pope Julius II. Almost entirely frescoed on the interior with illusionistic landscapes and architecture, culminating in the spectacular Hall of Perspectives (see image 2), it was modeled on literary descriptions of ancient villas. In form and location, it was a cross between an urban palace and a country villa, built with an open loggia and a generous garden in a part of the city typically occupied only by orchards and vineyards. The villa became well known for its extravagant parties, in which Chigi would encourage his guests to toss their expensive silver into the Tiber River following their meal—only to retrieve it later from the nets he had carefully put in place.

Analogous to Peruzzi's inspiration from Roman literary sources, Villa Madama (see image 3), built by Raphael for the Medici popes Leo X and Clement VII and begun in 1518, was based on Pliny the Younger's descriptions of his villas, and even prompted Raphael's composition of a letter about his villa. It included a circular courtyard, fish pond, garden, theater, and specific area for

1508	1511	1513–21	1518–25	1526	1527
The Marquis de Mendoza brings the *Codex Escurialensis* to Spain, beginning their Renaissance.	Architect Fra Giocondo (1433–1515) publishes the first illustrated edition by Vitruvius, allowing architects to understand the classical orders.	Pope Leo X (son of Lorenzo de' Medici) commissions the facade of St. Lawrence and the Medici Chapel, starting Michelangelo's architectural career.	Raphael builds the Villa Madama and composes his letters on the villa and on the destruction and preservation of Rome.	Spanish architect Diego de Sagredo (c.1490–1528) publishes *Medidas del Romano* (*Roman Measures*) in Toledo, Spain.	Rome is sacked by the armies of Holy Roman Emperor Charles V. Artists and architects flee, dispersing across Italy and Europe.

walking and talking. The interior included spectacular stuccoes and paintings by Giovanni da Udine, Raphael's frequent collaborator, based on the discovery of ancient paintings in Nero's Domus Aurea. While Raphael's letter describes the villa as a place for contemplation and quiet conversation, its position as a natural stopping place on the road to Rome also gave it an important political role, as a semi-official location where the pope could entertain visiting foreign dignitaries.

In contrast to the tradition of painter-architects, Antonio da Sangallo the Younger (1484–1546) emerged from a family of established architects and was trained as a professional. Antonio's reputation has suffered by comparison to that of Michelangelo, who he preceded both at Palazzo Farnese (begun 1517) and at St. Peter's, and next to whom he assumes the role of the orthodox conservative. Projects such as the unusual concave facade of the papal Mint demonstrate that Antonio was not only an ardent student of Vitruvius, but also an imaginative, resourceful architect who sought to transform ancient models such as the triumphal arch into bold new compositions.

Scholars tend to describe Rome as a center from which all good ideas flowed, but many other Italian cities followed paths more connected to their own local histories and building traditions than with any sense of competition with Rome. In Florence, the aftershock of Dominican friar Girolamo Savonarola and his bonfires of the vanities (the burning of art, books, etc.) incited anxiety about displays of wealth, and resulted in a conservative approach to building that lasted through to the end of the fifteenth century. Giuliano da Sangallo modeled his Palazzo Strozzi (begun 1489) and Palazzo Gondi (begun 1490) on Palazzo Medici (1445–68; see p.176), built by Michelozzo di Bartolomeo Michelozzi (1396–1472) for Cosimo de' Medici. Against this backdrop, Michelangelo's formation as an architect in Florence is all the more remarkable. His first works forged a dialogue with the Florentine tradition and specifically with the legacy of Brunelleschi and Giuliano da Sangallo. The Medici Chapel, begun in 1521, housing the tombs of St. Lawrence (see image 4) and Giuliano de' Medici within the church complex of St. Lawrence, began with the footprint, material palette and columnar grid of Brunelleschi's Old Sacristy. These served as Michelangelo's point of departure for his own transformation of the marble tomb in both its figural and architectural elements.

Venetians prided themselves on their peaceful, egalitarian society, but when it came to architecture they had no scruples about conspicuous wealth. A prime example is the material richness on display in the Church of St. Maria dei Miracoli (see image 5), designed by renowned architect and marble sculptor Pietro Lombardo (1435–1515). Melding specifically Venetian references to St. Mark's in the use of marble panels and porphyry roundels with *all'antica* (antique-style) vocabulary and details, he encased all four sides of the church with luxurious, polychrome marble, and continued the same pattern seamlessly on the interior. The effect is a startling coherence between interior and exterior, a rare occurrence in Renaissance buildings.

Rome's cultural dominance came to an abrupt end when it was sacked in 1527 by troops under Holy Roman Emperor Charles V. Rome's loss became Italy and Europe's gain, as the artists and architects fleeing the city brought their spirit of experimentation and innovation with them. This dramatic event effectively transformed the insularity of regional building traditions through the infusion of new ideas. While architects in Rome were intensely focused on negotiating a relationship with the ancient past, in other parts of Europe ambitious rulers and elite patrons employed architecture as a means of articulating their own agendas. In Spain, the reconquest of Granada by the Catholic monarchs Ferdinand of Aragon and Isabella of Castile, brought with it the question of how to build in a land so distinguished by its Islamic architectural tradition. Spanish noblemen traveled frequently to Italy, and a consequence of one of these trips was the construction of an exceptionally ambitious new palace, La Calahorra (1512), within the outer walls of a Moorish fort. The patron, Don Rodrigo, Marquis de Mendoza, imported materials and workmen from Genoa, and employed a book of drawings of ancient Roman monuments and sculpture (*Codex Escurialensis*) he had acquired in Rome. By building an Italianate courtyard in this utterly unexpected site, Mendoza provided a new idiom for the Catholic elite. Despite its physical isolation, the building was widely imitated in palaces such as the early sixteenth-century Vélez Blanco Patio (now located in the Metropolitan Museum of Art, New York).

Across the Mediterranean, in Istanbul, Sultan Mehmed II had been educated in Greek and Latin classics, and his artistic and architectural patronage reflected his enthusiasm for European art. Scholars have suggested that his Topkapi Palace (see image 6), a well-ordered series of residential structures, audience halls, and barracks, built around courtyards and gardens, may have been shaped in part by the gridlike organization of the community hospital Ospedale Maggiore, Milan (begun 1456), by Florentine architect Filarete (c.1400–69). While there is no direct evidence that Filarete traveled to Mehmed's court, other artists such as Giovanni Bellini did. Artists thus served both as cultural ambassadors and as agents in the transmission of aesthetic information.

Another well-documented invitation to court came from Francis I, King of France, who enticed Leonardo da Vinci (1452–1519) to reside close to his chateau at Amboise from 1516 until his death. Francis I's interests inspired him to incorporate Italian elements into the construction of his new chateau at Chambord (begun 1519), and to invite more Italian artists to take part in the construction and decoration of the gallery at Fontainebleau.

Some Italian forms and ideas reached very far indeed: the Palazzo dei Diamanti, Ferrara (begun 1493), finds close echoes in the pointed rustication of Crichton Castle, Scotland (c.1580). Furthermore, the idea of the pediment as a marker of distinction for a villa was taken up by Andrea Palladio (1508–80), passed to England in country houses such as Chiswick House, London (1727; see p.250), and took on new life in the recently formed republic of the United States, where Thomas Jefferson (1743–1826) used it as the crowning feature of his villa at Monticello in Virginia. **CB**

Villa Medici at Poggio a Caiano Begun 1485
GIULIANO DA SANGALLO c.1445–1516

Villa Medici at
Poggio a Caiano,
Tuscany, Italy

NAVIGATOR

Fear of the plague, anxiety about extravagant spending, and inspiration from classical texts by Pliny the Younger combined to generate the conditions for a new type of humanist villa in the late fifteenth century. Prominent among these was Villa Medici at Poggio a Caiano, built by Giuliano da Sangallo for Lorenzo de' Medici. Lorenzo harbored a special enthusiasm for architecture and is reported to have read the first edition of Alberti's treatise on the subject as it came off the press in 1485. Compared to the earlier Medici villas, Poggio a Caiano was exceptional in its grandeur: elevated on a podium on a hilltop site, it commanded a view over the countryside. On the exterior, its most imitated and innovative architectural feature was its pediment, an element typically associated with ancient temples. The pediment is adorned by an elaborate terracotta frieze by the della Robbia brothers. The interior includes a broad barrel vault, coffered with gold symbols of the Medici dynasty; it was the first of its scale built since antiquity. Radical and extravagant in its time, this Villa Medici became the model—in the rational, symmetry of its plan and in its pedimented, porticoed facade—for the villas of Andrea Palladio, and thenceforth the international model for aristocratic rural luxury and sophistication. **CB**

1 STAIRS

The stairs were originally straight, but Giuliano made a decision to replace them with a double set of monumental exterior stairs. The idea probably came from his studies of the Temple of Serapis for his book on Roman monuments, the *Codex Barberini*.

2 PEDIMENT

Probably inspired by the ancient Temple of Serapis on Quirinal Hill, Rome, this was the first use of a temple pediment on a domestic house. The exquisite terracotta frieze depicts an allegory of time's cyclical return, and refers to the Medici family.

3 PODIUM

The podium elevated the living spaces to take further advantage of the view, and also allowed a separation of agricultural functions on the first level. Among these were a dairy farm—an innovative feature Lorenzo imported from Lombardy—and a silk farm.

◀ Villa Medici boasted the first large-scale, coffered, barrel-vaulted ceiling since antiquity. It imitated ancient vaults such as those of the ancient Roman Basilica of Maxentius and Constantine.

DRAWING ROME

Architects developed their vocabulary of ancient Roman architecture through drawing. Surviving drawings can give insight into the process whereby architects used their studies as the basis for new designs. Giuliano da Sangallo produced two books of drawings, which encapsulated his years of study of ancient Roman ruins, such as his plan and elevation of the Colosseum (right), and gave him a large compendium from which to draw for his own designs. Bernardo della Volpaia (c.1475–1525), a member of Sangallo's circle, took a more systematic approach and meticulously classified his drawings of ancient details and monuments. It was this book that Michelangelo used as a means of developing his own competence in architectural detail.

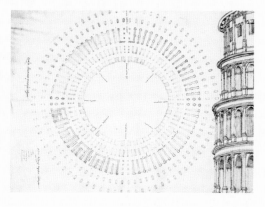

Tempietto 1502
DONATO BRAMANTE   C.1444–1514

Tempietto, San Pietro in Montorio
Rome, Italy

The Tempietto, which marks the site of St. Peter's martyrdom, has attained an architectural significance disproportionate to its size. Commissioned by King Ferdinand and Queen Isabella and enclosed within the complex of San Pietro in Montorio, it was one of the first Roman works of Donato Bramante. Contemporaries recognized it almost immediately as a re-creation of an ancient temple. Bramante combined the models of Roman tombs along the Appian Way, ancient round temples at Tivoli and along the Tiber River, and the form of the Christian reliquary. While these examples often inspired architects to design round structures, the Tempietto is one of the few actually built. Its aura of "antiquity" derived not only from its overall form, but also from its use of the Doric order, including columns with entasis and a "correct" Doric frieze—alternating metopes and triglyphs—and its inclusion of a geometric floor mosaic, recalling early Christian churches. The lower chapel (crypt) contains the relics of St. Peter's martyrdom and the foundation stone. The original design included a circular courtyard enclosing the Tempietto itself. It achieves an extraordinary impression of monumentality despite its size. The building soon gained canonical status and was included in compendiums of ancient monuments almost as if it were one of them. **CB**

◉ FOCAL POINTS

1 BALUSTRADE

The exterior feature that stands out as belonging to the Renaissance rather than antiquity is the balustrade— a form employed by Donatello and perfected by Giuliano da Sangallo. It is an example of the way in which Bramante combined ancient and contemporary models into a new, authoritative form.

2 FRIEZE

Bramante was among the first to understand and correctly replicate the Doric frieze, with its alternative metopes and triglyphs. However, he playfully replaced the pagan symbols of the ox skull with Christian liturgical instruments. He probably modeled the frieze on Filippino Lippi's painted version at the Carafa Chapel.

3 COLUMNS

The columns struck contemporaries as forcefully ancient with their proportions, entasis, and profiles of their capitals and bases. The granite column shafts further reinforce this impression; since granite had not been quarried since antiquity, its use identified the shafts as reused materials (*spolia*).

▲ The mosaic floor with geometric decorative inlay was probably included to emphasize the connection of St. Peter to the early Church.

VITRUVIUS IN PRINT

Vitruvius wrote in a language that was notoriously difficult to understand. The first illustrated edition by Fra Giocondo (1511) had the most impact in that his lucid woodcuts allowed architects to see, in many cases for the first time, exactly what Vitruvius meant when he described the elements and proportions of the Doric, Ionic, and Corinthian orders (below).

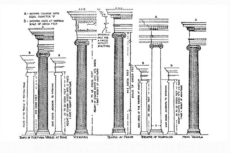

MANNERISM

According to Giorgio Vasari (1511–74) and other contemporary sources, sixteenth-century Italy was artistically superior to that of the fifteenth century. The evolution of art between these periods lay, they thought, in the more direct pursuit of *maniera* (meaning "style" or "manner"), which created new freedom for artists and architects. In Palazzo Massimo alle Colonne in Rome (see image 1) by Baldassare Peruzzi (1481–1536), this heroic spirit is embodied in the top cornice, whose dynamic line emphasizes the outward curve of the site, and so departs from the perfect squares of the Renaissance. The rest of the facade verges toward abstraction: the traditional hierarchy among windows is absent. Also absent is the prominence of the second level (*piano nobile*). This lack of differentiation draws attention to the monotonous, rusticated wall as the unifying element. It seems that during the later stage of his career, Peruzzi arrived at a new understanding of the facade as a device that conceals the private realm. At the palace's ground level there is no

KEY EVENTS

1517	1520	1527	1527	1530	1535
The Reformation begins in northern Europe. In the climate of political and economic uncertainty, artistic activity ceases in Rome.	Michelangelo begins the New Sacristy of St. Lawrence in Florence, the first Mannerist interior.	The sacking of Rome by imperial troops marks the official end of the Roman Renaissance.	Michele Sanmicheli (1484–1559) alters the look of Verona with the design of three new palaces and two city gates, all Mannerist.	A center of Mannerism is established at Fontainebleau, France, by King Francis I of France.	The design of Palazzo Massimo alle Colonne, Rome, by Baldassare Peruzzi, indicates the architect's shift toward Mannerism.

strict physical barrier. Instead, a short row of single and paired columns marks the entrance: a passage through a dark loggia that neither invites nor rebuffs the visitor.

The subtlety of works such as Palazzo Massimo eluded the art critics of the eighteenth and nineteenth centuries, who saw Mannerism as the effete conclusion of the Renaissance. From the 1920s, a gradual shift in opinion led to a positive re-evaluation of the period and eventually to another view: that the germ of modern art can be traced back to "mannered" poetics, such as excess, artificiality, and introversion; in short, to the first overwhelming signs of self-consciousness in art. It is now generally accepted that Mannerism was a reaction fueled by discontent or anxiety, because the work of its boldest exponents marked an undeniable break from the architectural textbooks of the Renaissance. Peruzzi took cautious steps away from the established grammar, Giulio Romano (c.1499–1546) engaged in exercises of anti-orthography in Palazzo del Te in Mantua (1534; see p.206), and Michelangelo (1475–1564) rearranged the vocabulary of architecture into a new, highly personal language that would inspire but also trap his contemporaries and successors.

1 **Palazzo Massimo alle Colonne (begun 1535)**
Baldassare Peruzzi
Navona, Rome, Italy

2 **Vestibule of the Laurentian Library, (1534)**
Michelangelo
Florence, Italy

The vestibule of the Laurentian Library (see image 2) by Michelangelo consists of inverted facade walls, as seen in the number and depth of the extrusions and recessions, in gabled niches with alternating triangular and segmental pediments, and by the height of the paired columns that sink into the walls like bone in flesh—all bringing a new, abstract plasticity to architecture. Large, dynamic volutes hang freely on the walls, hinting at column support where there is none. Michelangelo's plan to omit windows and light the room from the top would have created a powerful metaphor for introspection for visitors entering the library, but was discarded. Bartolomeo Ammannati (1511–92) executed the overscaled, dramatic staircase from a clay model that Michelangelo had left behind before going to Rome. The staircase was without precedent and maintains an enigmatic aura.

Sebastiano Serlio (1475–c.1554) taught Mannerism in Fontainebleau, France. However, Vitruvian correctness meant little in France, Spain, and Eastern Europe, so outside Italy the reactionary nature of Mannerism diminished. The imported *maniera* afforded architects merely a richer palette of designs with an Italian pedigree. Even in Italy, Giacomo da Vignola (1507–73), Vasari and others could not carry Michelangelo's innovations further. His architectural heirs are found in other centuries. Francesco Borromini (1599–1667) rightfully saw himself as a follower; in England, Nicholas Hawksmoor (1661–1736) developed a personal style in which study of the past was intuitive. Charles Holden (1875–1960) elaborated on Michelangelo's vocabulary in his extension of the Library of the Law Society in London (1906). Tension is compacted into small areas, like the surrounds and crowning of the miniature windows on the sides. Their composition is mannered and obsolete, a shibboleth from a distant century. **EA**

1536	1537	1537	1543	1550	c.1550
Michelangelo is commissioned to carry out improvement works on the Capitoline Hill, Rome, where he introduces a novel giant order.	Jacopo Sansovino (1486–1570) begins the Library of St. Mark, a prime example of Venetian Mannerism.	Sebastiano Serlio publishes his treatise on architecture in Bologna and subsequently teaches the Mannerist style in Fontainebleau, France.	The publication of Nicolaus Copernicus's *On the Revolutions of the Celestial Spheres* significantly alters human perception of the universe.	Giorgio Vasari publishes his encyclopedia of biographies, which celebrates artists as heroes.	Andrea Palladio (1508–80) comes to prominence. His relatively serene style will eventually become the most influential in Europe.

Palazzo del Te 1534
GIULIO ROMANO 1499–1546

Palazzo del Te,
Mantua, Italy

Giulio Romano had been a pupil of Raphael but showed no interest in being part of the Bramante-Raphael circle, or in building within that tradition. His most radical departure from it is represented in the inner courtyard of Palazzo del Te, a fairly inconspicuous space within the palace grounds and, for that reason, ideal for bold experimentation. Rustication should provide enough differentiation between stones, but stone sizes are irregular, and the odd stone sticks out here and there. In the entablature, parts of the frieze drop out of place, columns placed uncomfortably close together hem in niches, and the proportionately gigantic keystone of the gate breaks into the pediment from underneath. These are examples of the architect's impatience with architectural grammar, petrified in these courtyards, which overwhelm the visitor who has studied or practiced the classical language. The resulting enterprise is a confident articulation of doubt, but it remains arguable whether Romano, having undermined the old grammar, seeks to replace it with a new one.

The palace contains plenty of calmer spaces, but the inner courtyard and the Chamber of the Giants have given history ample material for sketching out Romano's caricature portrait: he appears as the impudent Mannerist who sets out to question Vitruvian ideals and to mock his predecessors' notions of architecture as part of a supposed cosmic harmony. **EA**

✦ NAVIGATOR

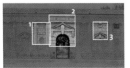

 FOCAL POINTS

1 IRREGULAR SPACING

The columns are placed at irregular distances. In the narrower bays, the niches lack frames and pediments. Further up, ambiguous rectangular niches are found. The most irrational, anti-architectural elements are the triglyphs that drop out of position, below the line of the frieze, at the mid-point of each bay.

2 PEDIMENT

A true classical pediment should rest on a frame, but in this instance it appears to float on the wall, with only a pair of volutes supposedly supporting it on each side. The gigantic keystone breaks into the pediment and fills up the vertical space. Normally, the two elements are not combined.

3 RUSTICATION

The stones are consistent in roughness but their sizes vary. It is usual for variation to occur over different stories to emphasize the hierarchy (rougher surfaces at ground level, flatter and more elegant in the *piano nobile*). Distances between the stones are exaggerated grotesquely by especially wide joints of mortar.

◄ The east side of the Palazzo del Te is home to two fishponds and an arcaded loggia. Here, Romano eschewed the rusticated surfaces used elsewhere on the building in favor of a more polished facade, creating a harmonious symmetry out of its irregular details.

INDO-ISLAMIC

1 Humayun's Tomb (1569–70)
Mirak Mirza Ghiyath
Nizamuddin East, Delhi, India

2 Stone carvings at Sidi Saiyyed Mosque (1573)
Built by Sidi Saiyyed
Ahmedabad, India

3 Marble *pietra dura* panels at the Red Fort (1648)
Ustad Ahmad Lahauri
Delhi, India

The Delhi sultanate set the stage for the Mughal Empire (1526–1707), the most glorious period of Indo-Islamic aesthetic synthesis. The dynasty had a tenuous start. Its founder, Babur, defeated Ibrahim Lodi, the last of the Delhi sultans, in 1526, and the Rajput princes the following year. Babur's son, Humayun, was defeated by the Pashtun leader Sher Shah Suri and exiled to Afghanistan in 1530; Humayun returned in 1555 to reoccupy most of northern India. His son, Akbar, embarked on a remarkable building campaign, prefaced by the construction of his father's tomb in 1569–70, near the Purana Qila (1538), or Old Fort, in Delhi, built by Sher Shah Suri. Designed by Persian architect Mirak Mirza Ghiyath, Humayun's Tomb (see image 1) incorporates the advances made in the Alai Darwaza gateway, such as the use of a podium base, bilateral symmetry, central dome, and naturalistic motifs, but notably deviates from the prevailing trabeated, or post and lintel, system (favored by Hindu builders) to Persian arch and vault or arcuate construction introduced to India by the Turks. This combination of local architectural elements, including corbel brackets, balconies, and pendentives, became the distinctive Mughal style.

The tomb also set a precedent for the future architectural image of the dynasty, not only because it commemorates the life of a person, which is forbidden in Sunni Muslim doctrine, but also because it expands on the use of natural, floral motifs, which are abhorred as a presumptuous attempt to reproduce anything divinely created. The Humayun Tomb has more red

KEY EVENTS

1526	1530	1556	1556	1571	1571–81
Zahir ad-Din Muhammad, or Babur, whose lineage includes Genghis Khan and Timur, establishes Mughal rule in Delhi and Agra.	Babur dies and is succeeded by his son Humayun.	Humayun dies. Fourteen years later his wife and son, Akbar, commission his tomb, in Delhi. Its design sets a Mughal precedent.	Akbar establishes the Mughal dynasty in northern India.	Akbar commissions the construction of his new capital, Fatehpur Sikri.	The tomb of Salim Chishti is built inside the Friday Mosque complex at Fatehpur Sikri, marking the rising influence of Sufism in India.

sandstone than Alai Darwaza and an impressive *pishtaq*, or portal, previously found in Iraq and Iran. The *pishtaq* takes the arch of Alai Darwaza into a third dimension, making the gateway into a space of its own. Over time, Mughal architects added more stories and arches to the sides of the *pishtaq*, and a larger, flat, framelike front. The tomb also has *chhatri*, or raised pavilions, on the roof, which became another predominant feature of Mughal architecture. With these new architectural features, it became the patriarchal symbol of the Mughal dynasty, and was expanded to include the graves of other Mughal rulers.

By 1569, Akbar had secured Mughal control over most of northern and central India, and in 1571 commissioned a new capital city on a high ridge west of Agra. The new city was originally called Fathehabad, but became Fatehpur Sikri after Akbar's victories over the Chittor and Ranthambore Forts during the Mughal–Rajput war (1558–78). The axial, northeast–southwest orientation of the ridge determined the planning of the walled city and its reservoir at one end, and the red sandstone for the city's construction was also quarried on the ridge. The first, roughly square, sacred compound, introduced by the magnificent Buland Darwaza Gate (1576), is located on the highest, southwest end of the ridge. The Jami Masjid (mosque, 1571) occupies an entire wall of the square and the tomb of Salim Chishti (1571–81) is set apart, like a jewel, on its northern edge. It is delicately detailed and built of white marble instead of the red sandstone used elsewhere, in order to highlight its sacred status.

The second royal compound, built on a lower elevation to the northeast, includes the semipublic and private parts of the city. It is set apart from the sacred square and consists of stacked, interlocking courts. The Diwan-i-Am and Diwan-i-Khas are the most significant, along with the Panch Mahal (*c*.1569–75; see p.210). The Panch Mahal housed the emperor's harem, hidden behind now disintegrated wooden *jaali*, or pierced screens. Stone variants of a similar age that have survived elsewhere, such as at Sidi Saiyyed Mosque (see image 2) in Ahmedabad, convey an impression of how exquisite the wooden Panch Mahal screens might have been. The Hawa Mahal (1799) in Jaipur is a more complex Rajput-style example of architectural purdah. This palace also used stone *jaali* for the large and small covered balconies, which has ensured their preservation.

Akbar's grandson, Shah Jahan, reinforced the power and prosperity that Akbar had secured for the Mughal dynasty. Although he is best known for the Taj Mahal (*c*.1649; see p.212), Shah Jahan first consolidated his power by building the fortress-palace called the Red Fort, or Lal Qil'ah, Delhi, in 1648. The citadel exterior is a twin-gated irregular red sandstone octagon that contains marble palaces within, whose marble *pietra dura* panels (see image 3) are attributed to a Florentine artisan. The Taj, or "crown," that Shah Jahan commissioned in 1632 in memory of his third wife, Mumtaz Mahal, represents an extraordinary aesthetic achievement perhaps best appreciated in comparison to other contemporary monuments. **JMS**

1601	1632	1648	1659	1660	1707
The Buland Darwaza, or high gate, is commissioned by Akbar to commemorate military victories in Gujarat and Uttar Pradesh.	Shah Jahan commissions the Taj Mahal as a resting place for his third wife, who died in childbirth. It is a supreme example of a Mughal garden tomb.	The construction of Shah Jahan's new capital, Shahjahanabad, is completed in Delhi. It is now known as Old Delhi.	The Adil Shahi dynasty creates a variation on the Indo-Islamic style with the Gol Gumbaz mausoleum in Bijapur. The diameter of its dome is 144 feet (44 m).	Emperor Aurangzeb builds the white marble Pearl Mosque inside the Red Fort in Delhi for his own use.	The death of Aurangzeb ends the most glorious period of Mughal rule.

Diwan-i-Khas and Panch Mahal Complex *c.*1569–75
ARCHITECT UNKNOWN

Diwan-i-Khas and
Panch Mahal Complex,
Fatehpur Sikri, India

The proximity of Diwan-i-Khas and Panch Mahal—two spatially interrelated, but distinctly different, public and private institutions—provides an insight into the daily life of the Mughal emperor, who saw little difference between his public and private personas. Diwan-i-Khas was used by Akbar to hold private audiences with courtiers and important visitors. Its four-square, rather utilitarian exterior conceals one of the most remarkable spaces in the canon of Mughal architecture. The cube-shaped, two-story building has corner *chhatri* on the roof that denote a stairway below. Guards were posted at the bottom and top of the staircases, which each correspond to a bridge leading to a dais in the middle of the room. The platform is supported by a pillar with an elaborate pendulous decorated capital. The location of the dais and the *muqarnas*-shaped roof above it were designed to scramble conversations acoustically.

The Panch Mahal and a small pool nearby mark the beginning of the *zenana*: the city's family section. Panch Mahal means "five floors," and refers to the stacking of successively smaller levels. This elegant columnar pavilion once housed the royal harem, which was hidden from view behind delicately carved wooden *jaali* (pierced screens), which are no longer extant. It is not difficult to imagine how much softer and more appealing this rather puzzling, edgy structure would have been with the wooden *jaali* inserted between the columns and the multicolored curtains blowing in the wind, as described by chroniclers. Far from being the erotic seraglio of public imagination, this harem, which may have housed several thousand women, operated more like one large, extended family, headed by the mother of the emperor. **JMS**

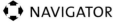
◆ NAVIGATOR

FOCAL POINTS

1 CUPOLA

The five-story Panch Mahal, is topped by a square *chhatri* with a cupola roof. This dome is the only arched element on the building; the rest of the structure is composed of horizontal beams. The design of the Panch Mahal may have been inspired by Persian *bad gir*, or wind towers.

2 SANDSTONE

Red sandstone is widely available in the region and is relatively soft, making it easy to carve into the intricate patterns favored by Mughal builders. However, the area is prone to high winds and sandstorms, so the sandstone has eroded over time and is difficult to preserve.

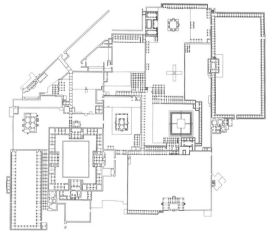

▲ The Diwan-i-Khas and Panch Mahal are part of Akbar's Fatehpur Sikri palace complex, which is formed by a series of linked spaces that included up to sixty buildings (forty of which still exist).

Taj Mahal *c.*1649

SHAH JAHAN, WITH USTAD AHMAD LAHAURI AND MIR ABD-UL KARIM

Taj Mahal, Agra,
Uttar Pradesh, India

The "crown" of Mahal continues the Mughal tradition of the *charbagh* (four gardens) tomb but refines it in significant ways. The use of white marble instead of red sandstone makes the tomb seem pure, like the tomb of Salim Chishti in Fatehpur Sikri. This religious association is reinforced by the raised mausoleum, which sits on a simplified plinth free from the arched distractions seen on the Humayun Tomb. Large minarets on each chamfered corner frame the dome. The Ottomans used this same device when they converted Hagia Sophia in Constantinople (537) to a mosque in 1453, raising a minaret at each corner.

The Taj Mahal took thousands of builders twenty-one years to complete and its cost threatened to bankrupt the Mughal Empire. The dome and *pishtaq* assemblage on the Taj differs from previous Mughal monuments in the use of stacked archways between a monumental gateway at each cardinal point. In addition to the spires on top, these add to the sense of verticality implied by the minaret frame. The dome above the tomb is the final, defining distillation of Mughal convention, since its entire curvaceous form is more prominent than in previous examples. Framed by four smaller *chhatri* (dome-shaped pavilions), it is capped by a lotus design and finial that accentuate its verticality. The extent of the influence of this innovation is best seen on the roof of the Pearl Mosque (Moti Masjid; 1660), inside the Red Fort complex in Delhi. **JMS**

◈ NAVIGATOR

👁 FOCAL POINTS

1 DOME FINIAL
Similar to the hierarchical use of domes, the finials also establish a comprehensive verticality, so that the entire ensemble seems to soar. On the four *chhatri*, and the main dome itself, each finial is encircled by a lotuslike crown; this highlights their importance.

2 MINARETS
Mughal minarets are distinctive in their use of a segmented shaft and an octagonal, domed top. Those at the Taj Mahal are echoed by the cupolas that flank the *chhatris* beside the main dome, providing a unifying theme that was unprecedented in the Mughal canon prior to this.

3 *PISHTAQ*
The mausoleum has four nearly identical facades, each of which contain a large central *pishtaq*—a deep, recessed gate, with a high, intricately decorated, flat facade. Framed by carved inscriptions from the Koran, each *pishtaq* reaches 108 feet (33 m) in height.

4 REFLECTING POOL
The reflecting pool in front of the mausoleum forms part of a cross-axial watercourse that divides the garden into quadrants, providing a striking approach. The Mughal tradition of combining gardens and water was inspired by Persian gardens, which were designed to symbolize Paradise.

▼ The inner layer of the dome is designed to strike a balance between intimacy and grandeur. The chamfered corners and double level of arched windows contribute to this impression, as do the delicacy of the inlay and the use of gemstones such as lapis lazuli, jade, crystal, turquoise, and amethyst.

LATE RENAISSANCE

1 **Library of St. Mark (1537–88)**
Jacopo Sansovino
St. Mark's Square, Venice, Italy

2 **Palazzo dei Conservatori (1563–84)**
Michelangelo
Rome, Italy

3 **Il Gesù (1568–84)**
Giacoma Barozzi da Vignola
Rome, Italy

With the sack of Rome by Holy Roman Emperor Charles V in 1527 and the subsequent stagnation of all papal projects, artists and architects left the city and spread across Italy. Among them, Jacopo Sansovino (1486–1570), a pupil of Giuliano da Sangallo (c.1445–1516), moved to Venice, where he became the official architect of the Republic. Sansovino was charged with the design of all public buildings facing St Mark's Square: the restoration of the basilica, the completion of the Procuratie project and the new design for the Library of St. Mark (see image 1), and the Mint (begun 1537), across from the Gothic Doges' Palace (1424). The ground level of the library consists of a classicizing loggia, designed to host bankers and goldsmiths' workshops, blending the traditional functions of the medieval square with the grandeur of the Roman forum. The marble facade is organized by a sequence of engaged half-columns supporting a full entablature on both stories, crowned by a balustrade. Each bay has a minor order supporting arches and decorated spandrels. Sansovino's library was the first structure in Venice to follow the Renaissance canons, with the correct juxtaposition of architectural orders. The interior is one of the most lavishly decorated spaces in Venice, hosting paintings by Titian, Tintoretto, and Paolo Veronese.

Another example of the renovation of public space was the vast program that transformed the center of Florence, as commissioned by Cosimo de'

KEY EVENTS

1527	1537	1541	1560	1562	1563
After the sack of Rome, Italian architects abandon the city and spread the architectural language of the High Renaissance throughout and beyond Italy.	Jacopo Sansovino begins the Library of St Mark and the Mint, the first rigorous Renaissance buildings in Venice.	Philibert Delorme (c. 1514–70) begins the chateau at St Maur-des-Fossés, an influential prototype of Renaissance architecture in France.	Giorgio Vasari commences construction of the Uffizi in Florence, part of the renewal of the city under Cosimo de' Medici.	Jacopo Barozzi da Vignola publishes *Regola delli cinque ordini d'architettura*, with limited text but extensive illustrations of the five orders.	Juan Bautista de Toledo and Juan de Herrera begin the monumental convent and court retreat of El Escorial for Philip II, King of Spain.

Medici, with Giorgio Vasari (1511–74) as architect. Vasari is best known as the author of what could be considered the first work of art history: *Lives of the Most Eminent Painters, Sculptors, and Architects* (1550). Architecturally speaking, his most ambitious project was the construction of a new administrative building for the reorganized state bureaucracy: the Uffizi (1560–81). On the first floor, a portico connects the entrances to the different offices and provides a protected waiting area. The facade is organized in modules consisting of three bays, which renders the sequence less repetitive; only the first floor employs a full architectural order, but Vasari's clever design of the two upper levels maintains the overall classicizing appearance of the structure.

After his first architectural works in Florence for the Medici family, Michelangelo (1475–1564) returned to Rome and was entrusted by Pope Paul III with the completion of important projects that had been left unfinished by Antonio da Sangallo the Younger (1484–1546), such as Palazzo Farnese (1534–46) and St. Peter's Basilica (1539–46). In addition, Michelangelo was commissioned to reshape the Capitoline Hill, on which the city government buildings stood. He altered the facades of the medieval palaces and designed the pattern of the square to enhance the ancient bronze statue of Marcus Aurelius (175). The facade of Palazzo dei Conservatori (see image 2) was organized around the first secular use of the giant order (an architectural order spanning more than one floor), a solution that was influential in later palatial architecture. The Corinthian giant order frames the smaller Ionic order of the first-floor portico, respecting the classical tradition of the juxtaposition of architectural orders. Michelangelo specifically designed the Ionic columns to be encased in the wall of the portico, increasing the *chiaroscuro* effect and further emphasizing the column's form. Every bay of the portico is imagined as a separate entity, with four columns supporting an imaginary baldachin that provides a grandiose entrance to the different city offices.

Jacopo Barozzi da Vignola (1507–73) was one of the leading architects in mid-sixteenth-century Rome, put in charge of completing all buildings left unfinished by Michelangelo. Vignola did not share the creative mind of his predecessor; instead, he followed the traditional style of Sangallo. Vignola was the author of *Regola delli cinque ordini d'architettura* (*Canon of the Five Orders of Architecture*), published in 1562. This was not a treatise, but rather a pictorial handbook for the construction of the architectural orders, and it was widely used by architects of the seventeenth and eighteenth centuries. The Farnese family commissioned Vignola to design a suburban villa in Rome (Villa Giulia; 1553) and a fortified palace-villa at Caprarola (1559–73; see p.220). One of his last projects was the mother church for the newly founded Jesuit Order in Rome: Il Gesù (see image 3). The plan of this church represents the first attempt to adopt new directives on ecclesiastical architecture that emerged during the Council of Trent (1545–63), which was organized by the Roman Catholic Church

1568	1570	1571	1580	1593	1605
The construction of Il Gesù, mother church of the Jesuit Order, begins in Rome. It is considered the archetype of Counter-Reformation churches.	Andrea Palladio publishes his architectural treatise, *The Four Books of Architecture*, in Venice.	The Holy League fleet defeats the Turks at the Battle of Lepanto, halting the expansion of the Ottoman Empire.	Robert Smythson starts to build Wollaton Hall, one of the first houses in England with classical architectural elements.	The Venetian Republic founds the star-shaped ideal city of Palmanova, designed by Vincenzo Scamozzi using the latest military innovations.	Henri IV, King of France, begins the construction of the first of three 'royal squares' in Paris, archetypes of modern urban planning.

as a response to the Lutheran Protestant Reformation. Without free-standing columns forming lateral aisles, the unobstructed nave covered with a barrel vault focuses attention on the high altar. The simple and clear configuration of this design made it greatly successful, and it was repeated numerous times beyond the borders of Europe as a symbol of a renewed Catholicism.

Andrea Palladio (1508–80) was the most influential Renaissance architect, due to the clarity of his design and the immense popularity of his architectural treatise—*The Four Books of Architecture* (1570)—in which he published many of his own works alongside buildings from antiquity. His first major public project, known as the Basilica Palladiana (1546–1614; see p.218), contributed to the architect's fame; shortly thereafter, the local nobility entrusted him to build their palaces and villas in the new classical style. Part of his success was due to the fact that he reduced the time and money needed for each project, through the use of very cheap construction materials—brick, wood, and stucco—with a few blocks of stone for the bases and capitals of columns. Unlike Roman and Florentine examples, many of Palladio's villas were also designed as functioning estates, and he always included all service buildings used for the daily activities of a farm. In contrast, Villa Almerico Capra (or La Rotonda; see image 4) features four temple facades projecting outward from a cubic central block, surmounted by a dome. The carefully planned relationship between the villa and the surrounding landscape facilitates the understanding of the success of Palladian architecture in England in the seventeenth and eighteenth centuries. During the last period of his career, Palladio was commissioned to build four important churches in Venice, and these projects demonstrate different solutions for the problem of covering the facade with two interlocking temple fronts. The Church of St. Giorgio Maggiore (1566–1610), built on an island across from the Doges' Palace, visually completed the public square initiated by Sansovino.

Due to the frequent exchanges of architects and the circulation of treatises, France was the first country outside Italy to adopt a personal Renaissance style. At the beginning of the seventeenth century, Henry IV promoted the modernization of Paris, planning three royal squares of different shapes: square, triangular, and semicircular. Place Royale (now Place des Vosges; see image 5) is a square 460 feet (140 m) in diameter, with all the facades unified by a similar design. Place Dauphine (1609) makes remarkable use of the

triangular shape at the end of Ile de la Cité, with one of its corners placed at the middle of Pont Neuf.

In Spain, the austere convent at El Escorial (see image 6) was the most ambitious project built during the reign of Philip II, from 1556 to 1598. The three functions of the building—a Jeronymite convent, a mausoleum for Philip's father, Charles V, and a residence for the court—were accommodated by architects Juan Bautista de Toledo (*c*.1515–67) and Juan de Herrera (*c*.1530–97) in a large, organized plan influenced by Diocletian's Palace at Split (295–305; see p.80) and by Milan's Ospedale Maggiore (*c*.1456), designed by Antonio Filarete (*c*.1400–69). With its merging of medieval and Renaissance traditions, Spanish architecture of the sixteenth century was quickly exported across the ocean to its colonies.

In England, Robert Smythson (1536–1614) was one of the architects of "prodigy houses," built to house the queen, Elizabeth I, and her court. His masterpiece, Wollaton Hall, has a nearly square plan, symmetrical on both axes, very similar to drawings by Sebastiano Serlio (1475–*c*.1554) for the palace at Poggio Reale in Naples (1487–90). The plan and details such as the disposition of the fireplaces and the use of the architectural orders are clear proof of the success achieved by Serlio's treatise in northern Europe. Inigo Jones (1573–1652) was the first English architect to travel to Italy and to be extensively trained in the new classical language of architecture. He is credited with the introduction in England of the three Renaissance secular typologies: the private villa, the city palace, and the public square. As the king's Surveyor of Works, he built a house for Queen Anne in Greenwich (begun in 1616), considered the first rigorous classical building in England. The plan resembles that of Sangallo's Villa Medici at Poggio a Caiano, near Florence (begun 1485; see p.200), but the spatial organization is completely Palladian, featuring an Ionic entrance loggia and a cubic hall with a gallery.

Finally, there is an aspect of Renaissance architecture that did not involve ancient prototypes but was instead associated with the latest scientific discoveries: military architecture. The improved design of cannons made medieval fortifications obsolete in one generation, and the sixteenth century was a period of constant innovation. The response to heavy artillery was the construction of triangular bastions and star-shaped fortresses, with wide ramparts to absorb the cannon balls and to protect the defenders' artillery. Entire new cities were founded as military outposts: Francesco Laparelli (1521–70) designed the new city of Valletta, Malta (*c*.1566), and Vincenzo Scamozzi (1552–1616) the Venetian stronghold of Palmanova, founded in 1593. **LV**

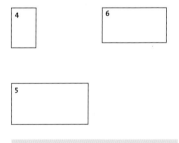

4 **Villa Almerico Capra (1556–67)**
Andrea Palladio
Near Vicenza, Italy

5 **Place Royale (1605–12)**
Architect unknown
Paris, France

6 **El Escorial (1563–67)**
Juan Bautista de Toledo
and Juan de Herrera
Madrid, Spain

Basilica Palladiana 1546–1614
ANDREA PALLADIO 1508–80

Basilica Palladiana,
Piazza dei Signori,
Vicenza, Italy

◆ NAVIGATOR

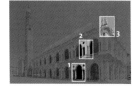

At the end of the fifteenth century, the 300-year-old Palazzo della Ragione in Vicenza partially collapsed, prompting the Vicentine citizens to consult the best available architects, including Jacopo Sansovino and Sebastiano Serlio, to submit a restoration plan. The nobles of the city campaigned instead for a local architect, and in 1546 Andrea Palladio was commissioned to update the old Gothic structure by replacing the double portico with a double classical colonnade. Palladio's main challenge was to align the new openings with the irregular pre-existing medieval passageways on the first floor and with the windows of the main hall on the upper floor without compromising the regular rhythm of the new classical portico. Although influenced by Sansovino's facade for the Library of St. Mark in Venice, Palladio's design was innovative due to his creative use of the serliana: a classical architectural element consisting of a central arch flanked by two rectangular openings framed by columns and crowned with an entablature. By changing the width of the side openings of each serliana, Palladio adapted the new double portico to the irregular medieval layout. The use of solid stone for the orders on both levels of the colonnade—Doric below, Ionic above—greatly strengthened the structure. **LV**

1 FUNCTIONAL BASE

The smaller Doric order has a cylinder as a base, instead of the expected plinth. This helps to withstand the heavy traffic flowing through the first floor of the basilica (probably after the second-century BCE Temple of Hercules Victor in the Forum Boarium in Rome).

2 SERLIANA

The eye is attracted to the central arch of each serliana and not to the variable size of the side openings (the one on the corner is much narrower). Palladio may have got the idea from the Abbey of St. Benedetto in Polirone (1544) by Giulio Romano (c.1492–1546).

3 CORNER SOLUTION

The corner is enhanced visually and structurally by the double Doric and Ionic semi-columns. This design was inspired by sketches made by Renaissance architects of the ruined facade of the ancient Basilica Aemilia in Rome (179 BCE), which no longer existed in Palladio's time.

◄ From beneath the colonnades, Palladio's intent is evident: the irregular Gothic structure of the old palace is enveloped within a Renaissance portico. The brick walls to the right contrast with the more regular rhythm of the white marble columns.

THE SERLIANA

One of the most recognizable elements in classical architecture, the serliana is a triple opening where the central opening is arched and taller than the two flat-topped openings at the sides. It was first employed in ancient Roman architecture to break the monotony of a colonnade or to emphasize an entrance. It was named after Sebastiano Serlio, who first described it in his treatise in 1537 with accompanying illustrations. The first Renaissance architect to employ the serliana was Filippo Brunelleschi (1377–1446), who interrupted the continuity of an entablature through the insertion of an arch. Donato Bramante was the first to use the serliana as an opening element, later seen at Rocca Pisani, Lonigo (1578; right) by Vincenzo Scamozzi. Because of its success in Neoclassical architecture after Palladio, the serliana can also be called a Venetian or Palladian window.

Palazzo Farnese 1559–73
JACOPO BAROZZI DA VIGNOLA 1507–73

Palazzo Farnese,
Caprarola, Italy

 NAVIGATOR

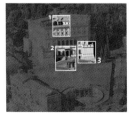

During his early years as a cardinal, Pope Paul III began to renovate the Farnese family estate at Caprarola, creating a pentagonal fortress. The structure's shape conditioned Jacopo Barozzi da Vignola's project for a palace that was to be built on top of the fortress itself. The palace is organized around a circular courtyard with two superimposed porticoes of ten bays each, built with peperino, a local volcanic gray stone. The lower portico is fully rusticated, with niches on the piers supporting the arched openings; the upper level features a flat finishing with paired Ionic half-columns supporting a full entablature and a crowning balustrade. Each bay corresponds to a door alternatively leading to a room or a staircase. In addition to the monumental spiral staircase, Vignola built five smaller ones leading from the basement to the quarters of knights and footmen under the roof, providing a great deal of mobility. The plan of each floor is symmetrical and consists of two apartments: one to be used during the summer (facing north) and one during the winter (furnished with additional fireplaces). Taddeo and Federico Zuccari lavishly decorated almost all the rooms of the palace, while Antonio Tempesta painted the vaults of the stairs and the porticoes of the courtyard. From two sides of the bastions, drawbridges link the palace to the vast park, organized in two symmetrical Italian gardens with fountains, grottos, and a casino (small house or pavilion). **LV**

👁 FOCAL POINTS

1 INTERNAL COURTYARD
Similar to the Palace of Charles V in Granada (1527), the external shape of the palace masks the inner circular courtyard. This design was taken from the study of ancient Roman baths and Hadrian's Villa. Raphael (1483–1520) planned a similar central space in Villa Madama (1525) in Rome, but it was never completed.

2 DIFFERENTIATED ACCESS
The upper pedestrian entrance to the palace and the lower archway for carriages serve to separate arriving traffic. Important visitors could access the living quarters directly from the basement, ascending the inner staircase, while the carriages continued in a turnaround space constructed beneath the circular courtyard.

3 FORTRESS
When designing the palace, Vignola had to make certain compromises, adapting his plan to the pentagonal shape of the pre-existing fortress that had been begun by Antonio da Sangallo the Younger. At the basement level, Vignola hid functional spaces such as kitchens, warehouses, water cisterns, and a grinding mill.

▲ Thirty Doric columns and corresponding pilasters support a full entablature that spirals upward, culminating in a dome. Italian painter Antonio Tempesta decorated both the walls and the dome.

RUSTICATED FACADES

The medieval tradition of public city halls coupled with the misidentification of the rusticated wall behind the Temple of Mars the Avenger, Rome (20–2 BCE) as the Palace of Caesar led to the extensive use of rustication on palace facades during the Renaissance. Donato Bramante (c.1444–1514) was the first to use feigned rustication manufactured with stucco, a cheap and widely available type of decoration. Starting with Palazzo dei Diamanti (1503) in Ferrara, by Biagio Rossetti (c.1447–1516), pointed rustication became one of the most luxurious decorative choices for a palace and spread across Europe, from the Palace of the Facets in Moscow's Kremlin (1492) by Marco Ruffo and Pietro Solario (c.1445–93), and the Casa dos Bicos in Lisbon (1523; right), to the addition to Crichton Castle, Scotland (c.1580) by Francis Stewart (c.1562–1612).

BAROQUE

Europe was slow to catch up with the political realism and artistic spirit of fifteenth-century Florence. During the Renaissance, classical architecture was overshadowed by the Gothic tradition that endured in most of northern Europe. Then, born in the spirit of Roman Catholicism, the Baroque spread from Rome and became the definitive style of seventeenth-century Europe, reaching as far afield as the colonized Americas in the West and the Philippines in the East. St. Peter's Piazza (see image 1), which was designed by Gian Lorenzo Bernini (1598–1680), was the most significant development on this site after the conception of the new basilica by Pope Julius II in the early sixteenth century. It amplified the scale of the edifice, matching the ambitions and expansionism of the Roman Catholic Church at the time. Its foremost section, comprising two colonnades drawn as segments of an oval, was

KEY EVENTS

1568	1603	1603	1624	1648	1660
Giacoma Barozzi da Vignola (1507–73) begins the Church of the Gesù in Rome. Its facade is considered a precursor to Baroque.	Carlo Maderno's St. Susanna in Rome introduces a novel plasticity to church facade design.	Inigo Jones returns to England after a five-year trip to Italy, during which he studied the Italian manner.	Bernini designs the baldachino (a large sculpted bronze canopy) in St. Peter's and becomes Supervisor of Works at the new basilica.	The end of the Thirty Years' War marks the end of the Counter-Reformation, in the spirit of which Roman Baroque was born.	Borromini completes his most personal work, St. Ivo alla Sapienza in Rome, which epitomizes radical invention on a constricted scale.

conceived as an extended embrace reaching out to the masses of the faithful who had kept the Church alive and its predominance intact throughout the Protestant Reformation.

The words "theatricality" and "expansiveness" are often associated with the Baroque. Bernini, as the pope's favored supervisor of works, appeared at ease with these concepts. He set the stage for a larger-than-life theater of human concerns, and conducted the activities and emotions of the people with architectural gestures that were sweeping and yet relaxed. Strictly speaking, the piazza is not architecture but urban development, and Bernini chose sober, muscular Doric columns over more ornate orders. The first link with the basilica was established with the balustrade of the colonnade, which perpetuates the parade of statues begun in the facade designed by Carlo Maderno (1556–1629). The final addition to the site was a trapezoidal outdoor corridor that joins the piazza to the building. For a person heading to the basilica, the narrowing of space implies a transition from collective joy toward sacredness.

In the climate of Counter-Reformation, the persuasiveness of music was not lost on the Catholic Church. The Oratorian Order, founded by Filippo Neri, was informal and anti-elitist; the intention of its teachings was to use sound and music to heighten religious emotion. Francesco Borromini (1599–1667) was brought into the project of the Oratory of the Filippini (1650) as he was about to begin work on his first commission, the Church of St. Charles at the Four Fountains (1638–77; see p.226). The oratory was the more prestigious project, but also presented numerous limitations, not least a demand that its facade would not compete with that of the adjacent New Church. Borromini made a brilliant career out of responding to such problems; in this instance, the overall effect is softened by the subtle deviations of the facade.

French Baroque appears severe and more detached by comparison, pre-empting Neoclassicism (see p.272) and the architecture of the Enlightenment. In France, the sixteenth and seventeenth centuries were so conflict-ridden that architecture reverted to more stable forms. This is reflected in a type of building important to the story of Baroque, the country house. In that tradition, the Louvre had facades constructed over various stages by prominent architects, such as Pierre Lescot (1510–78), for the court facade, begun in 1546, and Claude Perrault (1613–88), for the east wing (1665). But even religious buildings avoided the intense spatial drama one finds in the work of Borromini. Begun in 1632, the Temple of Marais (see image 2) was a relatively small commission for which an idealist architect, François Mansart (1598–1666), established links with other epochs. Some of these are drawn knowingly, yet seem fanciful or, at least, interrupted: the centralized plan points to ancient rotundas and early Christian mausolea in Rome and Ravenna. It was apparently modeled on the Pantheon in Rome (see p.52), but the buttresses that turn up around the drum lead the mind away from classical decor, promoting structural integrity instead. It is

1 **St. Peter's Piazza (1666)**
Gian Lorenzo Bernini
Rome, Italy

2 **Temple of Marais (c.1632)**
François Mansart
Paris, France

1661	1667	1670	c.1690	1729	1737
Andre Le Nôtre (1613–1700) begins work on the gardens at Versailles, France, the most heroic and idealized landscape design of the Baroque.	Christopher Wren begins work on the new St. Paul's and on the rebuilding of fifty-two churches in London after the Great Fire of 1666.	Claude Perrault's east facade of the Louvre envisages a national style that is serene yet assured.	Johann Fischer von Erlach (1656–1723) and Johann Lukas von Hildebrandt (1668–1745) begin a forty-year period of Baroque in Austria and Germany.	Chiswick House, London, by the Earl of Burlington (1694–1753), reinstates Palladian architecture, while lending it unprecedented vigor.	Joseph Fischer von Erlach (1693–1742) completes Karlskirche, Vienna (see p.230). It had been begun by his father in 1715.

perhaps other connections that now strike the viewer as more concrete: the clear, elemental geometry of the dome and the arched entrance is not far removed from the secular classicism of eighteenth-century visionary Claude Ledoux (1736–1806). Although small, interconnecting oval chapels embellish the plan, they are overpowered by the circular dome and ultimately subordinated.

Baroque quickly became established in Central Europe—which had been unified for centuries under the Holy Roman Empire—and reached Eastern Europe. The plan of the small Polish town of Zamosc, conceived by Bernardo Morando (1540–1600) in 1578, is based on Renaissance ideas of urban geometry and predetermined movement. In the main square, the City Hall (see image 3) owes its peculiarity to the various stages of embellishment. When first erected, it was an even more dynamic structure, with only a first floor and tower. In the mid-seventeenth century, three more stories were added, with heavy, protruding cornices establishing a horizontal rhythm until interrupted by the tower's gargantuan buttresses. The open, exposed space of the square and the layout of the town should have an overbearing effect on the visitor, but the next century saw the square as a theater set and a projected fan-shaped staircase was added in front of the building, in line with earlier Roman developments such as the Spanish Steps (1725) and the Piazza Sant'Ignazio, designed by Filippo Raguzzini (1690–1771) in 1728.

Meanwhile, in England, as far as the climate of the period is concerned, the century-old independence of the Anglican Church meant that most buildings did not seek to promote one dogma over another, or to denote their architects' religious zeal. The Great Fire of London in 1666 provided opportunities for the new architectural language to blossom, although these proved fewer than initially thought. Christopher Wren (1632–1723) was commissioned to rebuild fifty-two churches in London, but his plan for a new Baroque layout of the city

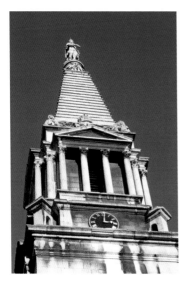

never came close to realization. Wren was, however, responsible for additions at Hampton Court Palace between 1689 and 1700, and was the surveyor at Greenwich Royal Naval Hospital from 1696 onward. John Vanbrugh (1664–1726), a successful dramatist with no architectural training, continued and enriched the tradition of the English country house with Castle Howard (1699–c.1799; see p.228) and Blenheim Palace (1705–24).

The Renaissance reached England through a version of Andrea Palladio's *Four Books of Architecture* (1570) acquired by architect and imaginative stage and costume designer Inigo Jones (1573–1652). The Roman style arrived in the form of sketches drawn by affluent Englishmen while exploring the cultural legacy of classical antiquity on the Grand Tour of Europe. Wren happened to be in Paris in 1665, just before his career developed, and was impressed to discover its architectural school and culture. He was at the Louvre during the competition for the eastern facade, in which Bernini took part, and probably had the opportunity to glance at Bernini's submitted drawing. These long and obscure routes through which classical language found its way to England led to some of the most exciting derivatives of continental Baroque, most notably in the work of Wren's apprentice, Nicholas Hawksmoor (1661–1736).

St. George's in Bloomsbury (see image 4) is the last built of Hawksmoor's six London churches, most of which were in peripheral locations. The northern facade features unusually large keystones, one of his trademark eccentricities. Inside, the arches are drawn as sharp oval segments, somewhat less ceremonious than round or pointed arches. Typically for Hawksmoor, the richest play occurs away from the main body of the building, in the tower, which is visible in the background as if it is another distant building. Hawksmoor's practical education was purportedly complemented by his perusal of a book of engravings of fictional buildings, such as the Temple of Solomon. The tower of St. George's, therefore, is not a compendium of precedents in the sense of a comprehensive summary, but more like a liberal mixture of languages derived from both real and mythical architectures. The stepped pyramid is modeled on the non-extant Mausoleum of Halikarnassos. It sits atop textbook types in miniature form, such as the Roman triumphal arch and the Palladian quadruple of Ionic porticoes—a contrast to the church's portico, which is executed in the Corinthian order. Further narratives are embodied in statues of a lion and a unicorn, and of King George I.

From as early as the sixteenth century, Christian brotherhoods and orders of monks had founded towns in colonial South America. By the time of Bernini's death in 1680, churches executed in the Baroque style were already populating the towns of Brazil and Mexico, as well as the villages and plateaus of Guatemala, Peru, and Bolivia. The first Church of El Carmen in Antigua, Guatemala, was built around then, but was destroyed by an earthquake. The current ruins are of a second version, erected in 1728 (see image 5). In earthquake-ridden regions of South America, the later and lighter Rococo (see p.238) treatment was delayed or altogether prevented; the height of churches remained constrained and masonry grew heavier. At El Carmen, columns were multiplied to an unusual extent resulting in a forest of them masking the bulkiness of the walls. The most interesting elaboration here is the split central pediment over the entrance. In the upper tier, Ionic capitals, still paired, are decorated with intricate, stuccoed mesh, and elaborations on Vitruvian scrolls run along the architrave. In places, the stucco has fallen off to reveal brick masonry, and some of the capitals' volutes have long since disappeared. Photographs from the 1940s show a statue of the Virgin in front of the choir-light, encircled by a wreath on the wall. The remains of El Carmen speak of a moment when local craftsmanship and imagination obscured the Baroque ideal that had been transported from the other side of the world. **EA**

3 **City Hall (1578)**
Bernardo Morando
Zamosc, Poland

4 **St. George's, Bloomsbury (1730)**
Nicholas Hawksmoor
London, UK

5 **Church of El Carmen (1728)**
Architect unknown
Antigua, Guatemala

Church of St. Charles at the Four Fountains 1638–77

FRANCESCO BORROMINI 1599–1667

Church of St. Charles at the Four Fountains (San Carlo alle Quattro Fontane), Rome, Italy

◆ NAVIGATOR

The Church of St. Charles at the Four Fountains was Francesco Borromini's first independent commission after working under Gian Lorenzo Bernini. The facade was completed long after Borromini's death, but drawings confirm it was executed according to his designs, with the exception of the medallion at the top and the arch that crowns it. These drawings also reveal Borromini's reworkings of the facade and his preoccupation with deviating from walls designed along parallel planes. The double "S" curve of the facade is formed by two concave bays on the sides and a convex one in the middle. Borromini made the rhythm more idiosyncratic with a concave central bay on the upper story. However, an elegant oval aedicule bulges outward, in contrast to the niche in the Oratory of the Filippini, where he had used a similar rhythm. Each bay is marked by a large order of columns and contains a niche flanked by smaller columns. Borromini traced the plan of the church over tangent ovals, circles, semicircles, and triangles, so inside the effect is expressive of the Baroque dream of movement. In three-dimensional space it is impossible for the viewer to mentally disentangle one shape from another, and white stucco provides further camouflage. Above the cornice, trapezoidal pendentives support the oval, coffered dome, and natural light brightens what are clearer shapes and volumes. **EA**

FOCAL POINTS

1 PLANES

The walls of the side bays are not built along parallel planes. They slope toward the middle bay, in contrast to Renaissance principles. Numerous adjustments were required so that they would correspond to the interior, up to and including the niches on the upper story, but above that level the facade is free-standing.

2 UNDULATION

The bay of the entrance is the only convex bay of the facade. It introduces a complex rhythm and completes the undulating effect. The aedicule on the upper story is the only corresponding element. It also lends the entablature its form, a double "S" in plan. This is the most prominently curved Baroque facade.

3 GIANT ORDER

Two sets of columns of different sizes create an interesting variant of giant order—without pilasters (as was the case in Michelangelo's palaces on the Capitoline Hill). The lack of a stronger differentiation has led to the reasonable theory that this was not executed according to Borromini's design.

MARIO BOTTA

The wooden life-size section of Borromini's church by Mario Botta (b.1943) had a short lifespan for a monument. It stood on a platform in Lake Lugano, Switzerland, for a mere four years (1999–2003). Rather than commemorating the building it represented, it was erected to celebrate the 400 years since Borromini's birth in the region. In essence, it was as close to an essay as to architecture or sculpture because it proposed a theory, more explicitly than monuments normally do: it linked the treasured cultural artifact to its creator's early life, to the lake and the mountains he looked at as a child. This link may be fanciful or non-existent, but the choice of surroundings is probably owed to the growing appreciation of Borromini as the purest architect of Roman Baroque. Botta's model also shared with Borromini's works a process of intense calculation, whose outcome was nevertheless wild and unexpected.

◄ The columns provide strong support, but are slightly sunken into the walls in a sculptural manner, so they become a part of the flow of the walls rather than interrupting them. The columns are of the composite order, but some have volutes that face inward.

Castle Howard 1699–c.1799

JOHN VANBRUGH 1664–1726

Castle Howard,
Near York, North Yorkshire,
UK

Castle Howard in North Yorkshire epitomizes the idea of a "stately home" and is one of the largest private homes ever built in England, with 145 rooms. When the third Earl of Carlisle decided that he wanted to replace the existing structure on the site, he appointed John Vanbrugh to design a new building in 1699. This was a surprising choice because Vanbrugh had no training or experience in architecture, but instead was well known as a dramatist and political activist. However, Vanbrugh had the good sense to employ architect Nicholas Hawksmoor to work with him and drew up a design for an imposing Baroque building, symmetrically arranged with two long wings on either side of the central north–south axis. Contrary to expectations, the center part of the building was not built first; in fact, construction started with the east wing and moved westward. The result is a certain asymmetry. Castle Howard was not completed for nearly one hundred years, well after Vanbrugh's death in 1726. The west wing, designed by Sir Thomas Robinson (1703–77), uses a more austere Palladian style than the exuberant Baroque of Vanbrugh's design. Although the wing is elegant in its own right, it does not sit comfortably with the earlier work. Much of Castle Howard was destroyed in a fire in 1940. There has been considerable reconstruction work, including of the dome in 1960, but the east wing remains a shell although it has been restored externally. Castle Howard was built to impress and still manages to do so, despite its vicissitudes. **RSI**

✪ NAVIGATOR

1 DOME

The imposing dome at the center of the building above the entrance hall is unique to Castle Howard. Although it was common to have a shallow cupola or a small lantern in this position, no previous architect had attempted a dome of such ambition, and nobody chose to imitate it afterward.

2 DECORATION

Baroque architecture is not understated, and Castle Howard is adorned with coronets, cherubs, urns, and cyphers (carved capital letters). There are Doric pilasters on the north front and Corinthian on the south. When challenged about this design, Vanbrugh said that the two were never seen together.

3 SETTING

The Palladian wing is far plainer than the rest of the building, completed after England's short-lived love affair with the Baroque was over. It is slightly discordant, but provides a reminder that even the greatest of houses were unlikely to be completed in a short enough period to use the same style throughout.

◄ The main hall is a magnificent space, defined by the dome that sits above it. Four great arches support the dome and are essentially free-standing so that there is a central dramatic space. The original paintings by Antonio Pellegrini on the dome roof were recreated after the fire in 1940.

Karlskirche 1715–37

JOHANN FISCHER VON ERLACH 1656–1723

Karlskirche,
Vienna, Austria

◆ NAVIGATOR

After a period in which architectural creativity in northern Europe had lain dormant, post-Counter-Reformation stability gave Austrian and German architects of the late seventeenth century the assurance to innovate once again. The brief but happy Baroque period in Austria revolved mainly around the rivalry between Johann Fischer von Erlach and Johann Lukas von Hildebrandt. Fischer von Erlach's intellect convinced patrons to trust him with major projects. His erudition also allowed him to carry out works such as Karlskirche with the confidence to which they owe their exoticism. Karlskirche is a symbol of imperial grandeur, but it lacks the fluency of buildings by Gian Lorenzo Bernini in Rome. The imagination is captured by isolated narratives on the exterior—the imitations of Trajan's Column (CE 106–113), the Baroque dome, and oval arches—then it is abruptly fragmented and set loose again by the next derivation. So the mental distances between these elements become as important as the elements themselves. Fischer von Erlach's architecture and, more broadly, Austrian and German Baroque attempted to unite architecture with sculpture and painting, and to integrate them in the fabric of the city. This was a reflection of how the seventeenth and eighteenth centuries perceived architecture's place in society, but the short lifetime of the Baroque in these regions attests that these art forms grew further apart thereafter. **EA**

 FOCAL POINTS

1 COLUMNS

The positioning of the columns was probably derived from the Temple of Jerusalem (957 BCE), but the figures in spiral relief and the gigantic pedestals imitate Trajan's Column in Rome. The column depicts scenes from the life of reformer Carlo Borromeo. The walls behind curve inward to accommodate the columns.

2 DOME

The drum is distinctly Baroque, with slender columns and graduated protrusions that continue on the entablature. A clever transition from the entablature to the dome takes place via a sculptural program above the cornice: it includes figures, finials, and elongated (slightly oval) oculi, which are pierced into the dome.

3 TOWERS

The upper section confirms the progression from clear to more complex forms, with windows reminiscent of Baroque furniture shapes. Oval arches crown the mid-section. The lower section of the side towers is modeled on the triumphal arch, but with pairs of pilasters flanking the archway on either side.

⏱ ARCHITECT PROFILE

1656–89

Johann Fischer von Erlach was born in Austria and studied in Rome under Bernini. In about 1687, he returned to Vienna, where he became widely recognized and successful.

1690–1711

Commissions for several palaces and some temporary arches in Vienna were crowned with Fischer von Erlach's appointment as Imperial Court Architect. A multitude of travels in Europe further enriched his architectural palette, with influences from Mansart and Palladian architecture.

1712–23

Fischer von Erlach's late period began with the writing of the first history of architecture, *Entwurf einer Historishen Architektur* (*Outline of a History of Architecture*; 1721), in which he included engravings of his own buildings.

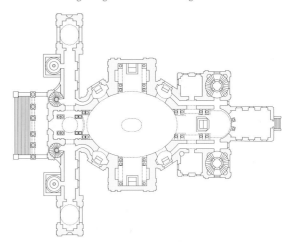

▲ The broad facade of Karlskirche masks the building's long, slim plan. The interior features an oval nave sandwiched between two rectangular chapels, with oval chapels on the diagonals, and a long choir housing the altar that terminates in a screen of columns.

◀ An Italianate sculptural program and the heavy stucco decoration do not set the interior in motion because it was not conceived as fluid space. Instead, it is the static continuation of the exterior's unconnected narratives.

REGIONAL VERNACULAR

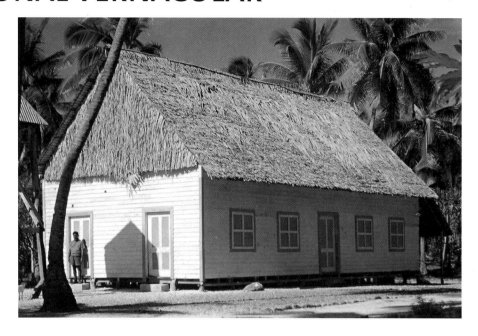

Ubiquitous, prosaic, and common to hundreds of countries, varieties of grasses, palmlike *pandanus* (screw pine), reeds, straw, and leaves of the Ti plant have thatched roofs for millennia. Despite thatch being banned in colonial Boston due to its flammability, and English thatch bans made in the fifteenth century, the use of wood and thatch continued in England in part due to low cost, but also because it was widespread and emblematic. Although the thatched roof of the Shakespeare's Globe Theatre in London was set alight by a cannon fire in Act I of *Henry VIII* in 1613, the conflagration did not deter London's use of roof thatch. It took the mother of all conflagrations, the Great Fire of London in 1666, before thatched roofs were banned once again. One of the few buildings spared was Staple Inn (*c.*1586). In grateful hindsight, its owners stuccoed fire retardant lime plaster on its Holborn facade. When the new Globe Theatre opened in 1997, it was granted the first thatched roof London licence since the Great Fire.

In Korea, thatched roofs were made from rice straw bundled into rolls with flat brush ends. It was the most popular material for roofs, and only a minority favored tiles. Seattle Asian Art Museum's Korean house exhibition in 1999 noted that thatched-roof houses of commoners were smaller and had fewer rooms than tile-roof houses. Thatch was part of the garden, with plants such as pumpkins ripening on the roof. Hahoe, in southeast South Korea, has

KEY EVENTS

*c.*15th century	15th century	15th century	15th century	16th century	*c.*1557
The Neolithic Korean underfloor heating system *ondol* is widely adopted. It is superior to the Japanese system of heating air with a brazier.	Iranian arch and dome engineering includes pendentives, which ensure a smooth flow between a square room and a spherical dome above.	The Chuxi Tulou cluster, China, is built, comprising five defensive circular and ten rectangular multiresidential soil buildings.	The Dogon villages of Bandiagara, Mali, West Africa, are characterized by mud-brick Togu Na (communal buildings) with thatched roofs.	The Fishermen Net Huts are built in Hastings, England. Their wooden clinker weather-boarding typology remains consistent into the 21st century.	The circular stone windmill used to grind bread flour in Orbetello Lagoon, Tuscany, Italy, becomes a legacy of the Spanish naval occupation.

functioned as a clan village of the Pungsan Ryu family since the fourteenth to fifteenth centuries (see p.234). The village preserves the Confucian layout of the Joseon dynasty (1392–1910) with three districts to reflect productivity, residential and spiritual. The few large tile-roof houses sit in the village center encircled by many smaller thatched houses.

Roofs in temperate or tropical climates need fewer leaves or fronds. Thatch houses in Hawaii (see image 1) were often finished at the eaves and roof-ridges with "an edge of fern, the rich brown color of which forms an agreeable contrast with the grayer and paler color of the ordinary thatching." Ki-leaf on the sides and ends of a house was paired with cane-leaf on the roof. Countries with snow, however, including Korea, Japan, the UK, and Denmark, required bundled thatch in thick layers or rolls. A correspondent for *The New York Times* in 1959 noted that the deep thatched roof on his North Jylland cottage provided insulation in winter and coolness in summer, but that after centuries of use most new Danish builds were roofed in red tile because insurance premiums on thatch was nearly triple. His defence of a thatched roof included a fuel bill far lower than it would be with a tile roof.

In the United Kingdom, frequent fires notwithstanding, timber-frame (cruck and box) houses maintained popularity. Despite chimneys replacing open hearths, their variable quality, use, and maintenance meant that fire remained a perennial problem. Authorities in the fifteenth and seventeenth centuries introduced by-laws prohibiting thatch and requiring existing houses to be re-roofed in slate or tile, but prohibition and enforcement were patchy, and owners of thatched houses in Oxfordshire flouted the law (see image 2). During the English Civil War (1642–51) Royalist troops in Weymouth used "small Iron Sluggs heated in a Forge, which they shot out of their Muskets, set fire on a Thatcht-House." Winter battles, such as at Nantwich, Cheshire, meant that damp thatch was less likely to burn. Postwar rebuilding saw regulations relaxed to encourage replacement housing, which resulted in yet more thatched roofs.

The Atlas of Vernacular Architecture of the World (2007) records thatched roofs in Asia, Latin America, Sub-Saharan Africa, and Europe, but notes that they are remarkably absent in North America. However, fires such as those in Boston in 1631 were not uncommon in colonial America. Governor John Winthrop banned thatched roofs and wooden chimneys the same year, and Benjamin Franklin organized the Union Fire Company of Philadelphia (1736), a volunteer fire brigade. The mood in colonial America reflected resiliency and new rules. Thatch was flammable and using it was a vote against logic. Perhaps it was also no coincidence that Franklin was one of several North Americans who assembled at the Thatched House Tavern, London, in 1774, prior to delivering their petition to Parliament to protest Crown punishment following the Boston Tea Party (1773). Thatch represented more than the illogic of building with a highly flammable material: it was the past best left behind. **DJ**

1 Thatched-roof house (date unknown)
Architect unknown
Honolulu, Hawaii, USA

2 Thatched-roof cottage (date unknown)
Architect unknown
South Hinksey, Oxfordshire, UK

c.1570–c.1700	16th–17th centuries	16th–19th centuries	1666	18th century	1799
A period of "Great Rebuilding" occurs in England; houses with chimneys, staircases, glazed windows, and private rooms replace open halls.	St. Stepanos Monastery, East Azerbaijan, Iran, is rebuilt. It includes a round, fluted roof, with Byzantine, Orthodox, and Persian influences.	Sixteen wooden *tserkvas* (churches) of horizontal log construction are built in the Carpathian Region, Poland and Ukraine.	A ban on thatched roofs is introduced in London after the Great Fire of London.	A distinct *mestizo* Baroque vernacular emerges in Arequipa, a geographically isolated city in Peru.	The Russian–American Company, chartered by Czar Paul I, competes for territory with Hudson's Bay Company. Alaska and California are two of their chief trade areas.

Thatched and Tiled Houses, Hahoe Date unknown
ARCHITECT UNKNOWN

Thatched and tiled houses, Hahoe, Andong, Gyeongsangbuk-do province, South Korea

⬖ NAVIGATOR

Founded in the late fourteenth century, the walled clan village of Hahoe reflects *pungsu-jiri* (feng shui) principles that include its orientation on a meander in the Nakdong River with its back to the mountains, and Joseon dynasty social distinctions based on Confucian teachings. The main house types—*yangban* tiled roof (*waga*, above right) for the aristocracy and thatched roof (*choga*, above left) for commoners—reveal Joseon dynasty social distinctions. Both roof types are well insulated, with deep eaves. *Yangban* compounds include a varying number of houses with separate quarters for men and women, receptions and teaching halls with *choga*-style servant quarters, storage and grain stores. *Yangban* compounds surround the main village courtyard, and in turn are surrounded by single-story commoner houses, with combined living and service areas. Scholar-diplomat Ryu Seong-ryong's house has the typical *yangban* hip-and-gable concave and convex tiled (*kiwa*) roof. On Yangjin house, the hip-and-gable tiled roof features twin eaves. Village houses have underfloor heating (*ondol*) from a kitchen stove (the only room in the house not raised) at one end of the house. Heat circulates beneath a thin stone floor supported on stone piers. Heat escapes via a courtyard ceramic chimney or tile vents. Confucian lecture halls isolate warm, *ondol* rooms from wooden-floor rooms. *Hanji* paper is oiled and plastered onto stone floors and fixed to the wooden window, sliding screens, and walls. **DJ**

1 THATCH

The four sloped sides of the hipped roof are easy to thatch. Rice thatch is secured with cords tied to bamboo poles fixed to the post-and-beam frame beneath extended eave roof poles. The proximity of the two different house types indicates that the thatched *choga* is part of the *waga* service compound.

2 ROOF TILES

The hip-and-gable roof is covered in terracotta clay tiles that reflect the color and texture of their source material. Tile size and angle vary in the complex roof pattern. Half-barrel tiles form long curved or straight loglike main areas. Tile-roof design may differ regionally, depending on the climate.

3 FOUNDATIONS

With the exception of ground-based kitchens, stone-block platform foundations support both house types. Each type has timber-framed, lime-rendered earth walls, sliding screens, and latticed windows with oiled paper panes and wooden doors. Wooden floors circulate the air beneath for added ventilation.

HEBRIDEAN BLACKHOUSES

Extant "blackhouses" of the Outer Hebrides, Scotland (right), probably date to the 19th century, but the design is much older. Low, twin dry-stone walls are filled with earth in the center void for insulation. The elliptical houses are faced into the wind to reduce wind resistance. Wooden rafters support the thatched roof, which covers the house above the twin wall stone platform. As there was no chimney, smoke wafted through spaces intentionally left between peat slabs layered under the thatch. Icelandic turf houses are similar: turf-covered, gable-roof wooden frames are slotted between stone walls and fixed to stone footings. Turf squares are stacked on top of the walls against the roof. Inside, the post-and-beam structure rests on stones. Pillars carry the roof weight as the walls are non-load-bearing. Conjugate rafter beams make good use of the island's scarce timber and driftwood.

4 | 1700–1870

ROCOCO

1 **Queluz National Palace (1752)**
Mateus Vicente de Oliveira
Lisbon, Portugal

2 **Pilgrimage Church of Wies (1754)**
Dominikus and Johann Baptist
Zimmermann
Wies, Steingaden, Bavaria, Germany

3 **Interior of Claydon House (1775)**
Luke Lightfoot
Middle Claydon, Buckinghamshire, UK

Rococo originated in France in about 1700, principally as an interior style for the aristocracy. Its importance lies in what architect and critic Peter Collins described in 1965 as "artificial parallax"—a mid-eighteenth-century shift to devices (often mirrors or interior classical colonnades) that created a palpable illusion of architectural and physical displacement, and encouraged a vogue for the aesthetic potential of parallax. Collins differentiates between *trompe l'oeil*—seen in the Chamber of the Giants at the Palazzo del Te (1534; see p.206), Mantua, Italy—a static trope that does not adapt to the viewer's movement, and the mid-eighteenth-century Rococo salon, where a visitor experienced "not enclosing walls, but a series of open arcades through which architectural spaces extended in an infinite parallactic sequence beyond the confines of the room."

Creative impetus came from Pierre Lepautre (1648–1716), a designer in the French Royal Works. His designs for rooms at Versailles and the Château de Marly in the 1690s developed out of decoration by Jean Bérain (1637–1711) during the height of Louis XIV's reign, when architectural orders were attenuated and formal geometric paneling gave way to a non-monumental style of interior more suited to personal apartments and informality. Lepautre made the all-important transition from Bérain's flat decoration to decoration in relief and, with the Grand Trianon (1703), he developed this into a coherent scheme. Narrow, ceiling-height panels decorated with carved scrolls, ribbonwork, curves, rosettes, tendrils, and arabesques drift across panel surfaces, and alternate with the windows, doors, fire surrounds, mirrors, and

KEY EVENTS

1702–03	1711–13	1716–20	1717	1730–35	1735
Pierre Lepautre develops Bérain's flat designs into a high-relief, elaborately decorative style at the Grand Trianon.	An exodus of the court from Versailles to Paris takes place. The building of a number of private townhouses helps to disseminate the new style.	François-Antoine Vassé and Gilles-Marie Oppenord emphasize verticality and introduce a freer use of arabesque and asymmetry.	Work begins on a sumptuous palace at Mafra, Portugal. Its Rococo library, built by Manuel Caetano de Sousa (1738–1802), is one of its highlights.	Nicolas Pineau and Juste-Aurèle Meissonnier carry the style to a flamboyant and extreme phase, subsequently known as Genre Pittoresque.	Germain Boffrand begins work on the Salon de la Princesse, Paris (see p.240). He employs Rococo painter François Boucher to supply works of art.

paintings, to give vertical emphasis and create a rhythmical whole. The resulting Régence style developed rapidly, particularly after 1712 in the reception rooms of the new private townhouses springing up in the fashionable districts of Paris. Decorative sculptor François-Antoine Vassé (1681–1736) and Gilles-Marie Oppenord (1672–1742) carried forward Lepautre's style. Both emphasized height by linear surface treatment and adopted a freer use of arabesque and a certain degree of asymmetry, as seen in Vassé's Hôtel de Toulouse and Galerie Dorée (1719), and Oppenord's remodeling of the Palais Royale (1720) in Paris.

A second phase, subsequently called Genre Pittoresque, evolved from c.1730 to 1735. Nicolas Pineau (1684–1754), a carver and ornamental designer, and Juste-Aurèle Meissonnier (1695–1750), an architect, goldsmith, sculptor, and designer, carried the style to a flamboyant and extreme phase. Meissonnier's influence was largely through his metalwork and engravings of ornament, but they both experimented with asymmetrical elements, rocaille (rockwork) and exotic motifs, such as chinoiserie. Eventually, straight lines tended to be avoided altogether. Germain Boffrand (1667–1754) made further significant contributions. His blurring of structure and use of curves made the relationship of the wall/ceiling junctions ambiguous, as seen in his suite of interiors at Hôtel de Soubise (1740; see p.240). Reaction against the extravagance of the style was becoming more vocal, however; in 1737, the architectural theorist Jacques-François Blondel, himself trained under Oppenord, criticized the excesses as a "ridiculous jumble of shells, dragons, reeds, palm trees, and plants." Although Rococo continued in a more conservative and stiffer manner following Pineau's death, by the 1750s the first Neoclassical (see p.272) manifestos were beginning to appear in Paris and within twenty years Rococo had all but disappeared.

Between 1740 and 1760, Rococo spread to most of Europe, disseminated by publications of ornamental engravings and French artists working abroad. Its adoption varied and was usually influenced by national character. Except in the north, Rococo exerted little influence in Italy, although to some extent it was anticipated by the work of Borromini. Rococo enjoyed success in Portugal where building on a grand scale included the Queluz National Palace (see image 1) by Mateus Vicente de Oliveira (1706–86). In Germany, Rococo was enthusiastically taken up by competing principalities and the Church, particularly in the Catholic south, where it merged with the still active and freer local Baroque style (see p.222) to form less disciplined and unconstrained works of the highest invention. A principal example is the interior of the Pilgrimage Church of Wies (see image 2) by Dominikus Zimmermann (1685–1766) and his brother Johann Baptist.

In England, the style never really became established. In architecture, it remained essentially a veneer on traditional Neo-Palladian (see p.246) structures such as Claydon House (see image 3)—where interiors include elaborate wood carving by Luke Lightfoot and stucco decoration by Joseph Rose—and in the "Rococo Gothick" interior of Shobdon Chapel (1756) in Herefordshire. **RS**

1739	1750s	1752	1754	1756	1756
The Amalienburg hunting lodge at Nymphenburg Palace, Munich, is built by François de Cuvilliés (1695–1768).	The first Neoclassical manifestos begin to appear in Paris. Within twenty years the Rococo style disappears from fashionable French interiors.	Queluz National Palace is completed. Rococo arrives late in Portugal, where the wealth derived from Brazilian gold allows building on a grand scale.	The Pilgrimage Church of Wies is completed. South Germany produces unconstrained works of the highest invention.	Bartolomeo Francesco Rastrelli (1700–71) builds Catherine I of Russia's summer palace at Tsarskoye Selo in a flamboyant Rococo style.	Shobdon Chapel is rebuilt in the ruins of a Romanesque church in Herefordshire, England. Its interior is a unique blend of Rococo and Gothic.

Salon de la Princesse 1740

GERMAIN BOFFRAND 1667–1754

Salon de la Princesse,
Hôtel de Soubise,
Paris, France

✦ NAVIGATOR

In 1735, Germain Boffrand began a suite of rooms in the garden wing of Hôtel de Soubise in the form of a two-story pavilion housing two oval salons. The upper room, Salon de la Princesse, is the more elaborate and epitomizes French Rococo style. Such rooms emerged out of the general exodus of the royal court from Versailles to Paris about 1711 to 1713, and the subsequent desire for a non-monumental style of interior, more suited to informality. Originally, the rooms would have contained elegant furniture, sculpture, wall paintings, ceramics, silver, and possibly decorative tapestries, all designed to complement and echo the design motifs of the architectural setting. This room is faceted with eight principal arches, framing doors, windows, and mirrors, alternating with smaller painted boiseries (wood panels decorated with gilded shallow-relief arabesques). Gilded putti recline on the upper curves of these panels and support irregularly shaped canvas pendentives painted with mythological scenes. In this room, the architectural boundary between wall and ceiling becomes ambiguous, with architecture, painting, and sculpture uniting to form a single ensemble bathed in natural and reflected light. **RS**

1 PENDENTIVE PANELS

The pendentive panels were painted by Charles-Joseph Natoire and depict the legend of Cupid and Psyche. Extending over the arches, they unite the room horizontally and create ambivalence in the wall/ceiling relationship in a plastic blend of architecture, sculptural decoration, and painting.

2 CEILING

Pendentives are surmounted by gilded stucco foliage cartouches that not only form part of a sinuous horizontal frieze, but also merge with delicate gilded filigree scrollwork extending symmetrically across the pale-blue ceiling and terminating at the elongated central rosette.

3 BOISERIES

Originating as flat painted panels, boiseries rapidly developed into intricate shallow-relief decoration with scrolls, tendrils and arabesques flowing across surfaces, often asymmetrically. Boffrand's panels, although restrained and symmetrical, exhibit lightness and lively plasticity.

◄ Boffrand's pavilion adjoins Pierre-Alexis Delamair's principal wing (1705–07). By 1735, Delamair's architecture, firmly rooted in the late seventeenth century, was viewed as old-fashioned. It forms a striking contrast with Boffrand's Rococo interior, where straight lines give way to an obscuring of architectural structure and use of arabesque.

⏱ ARCHITECT PROFILE

1667–99

French architect and interior decorator Germain Boffrand was born in Nantes. In 1681, he went to Paris, where, after a period studying sculpture under François Girardon, he entered the Royal Works under Jules Hardouin-Mansart (1646–1708). He participated in a number of projects, including the Orangerie at the Palace of Versailles (1686) and initial designs for the Place Vendôme (1699).

1700–34

Throughout the early decades of the eighteenth century, Boffrand worked independently in Paris, Lorraine, Bavaria, and the Low Countries, designing, building, and remodeling private houses, chateaux, and small palaces. In the process he made a number of the most significant contributions to the

further development of the Rococo style. Crucial stages were his designs for the salons of the Petite Luxembourg (1709–16) in Paris and La Malgrange (1711–15), near Nancy, where his use of convex and concave curves, rounding of corners, and softening of structural lines created ambiguity in the relationship between wall and ceiling planes.

1735–54

In 1735, Boffrand took on the design of the suite of interiors at Hôtel de Soubise in Paris, his last and finest work as well as one that for many represents the high point of the domestic Rococo style. In addition to his architecture, Boffrand's publication *Livre d'architecture* (*Book of Architecture*; 1745) was instrumental in disseminating French taste and the Rococo style across much of eighteenth-century Europe.

CHINA: IMPERIAL

1 **Purple Forbidden City (1420–1911)**
Architect unknown
Beijing, China

2 **Hall of Prayer for Good Harvests, Temple of Heaven (1545; rebuilt 1890)**
Architect unknown
Purple Forbidden City, Beijing, China

3 **Summer Palace (1703–90)**
Architect unknown
Chengde, Hebei province, China

Throughout the centuries, the most important and lavish buildings in imperial China were those in palace compounds. Textual records describe the main hall of the palace of the first emperor as having a raised platform large enough to accommodate 10,000 people. The palaces of emperors during peaceful and prosperous reigns were particularly majestic, such as those in the Tang dynasty (608–917). The only palace spared destruction by warfare in the subsequent eras was the Forbidden City (see image 1) in Beijing, the capital of Ming China (1368–1644), due to the uncertainty of the Manchu conquerors over whether they would retain power. The succeeding Qing dynasty (1644–1911/12) inherited the palace from the Ming and did not make changes to the layout or the positioning of the buildings.

The full title given to the Beijing palace—Purple Forbidden City—made reference to the constellation of that name, which was said to be the abode of the heavenly emperor. The palace compound had first been constructed in 1420, when the second emperor of the Ming dynasty moved the capital city from Nanjing to Beijing. However, due to destruction by fire, or on the wishes of individual emperors, many buildings in the palace were rebuilt or renovated multiple times (see p.244). Almost all extant buildings date to and maintain characteristics from the Qing dynasty, being much more regulated and with less innovation. The complex can be divided into two halves: the southern half

(see p.244)

KEY EVENTS

1703	1703	1725	1729	1730	1734
The Jesuit North Church and South Church in Beijing mark the beginning of Western-style church building in an inner city of China.	Work begins on the Summer Palace in Chengde, Hebei province. It is used as a summer retreat for half the year by many Qing emperors.	Yuanming Imperial Garden is begun. By its completion in 1772, the garden had grown into the largest garden in the world.	Lei Jinyu (b.1659) dies. He was the first of many generations of the Lei family serving as the official in charge of the imperial Ministry of Works.	Planning and construction begins of the Western Mausoleums for Qing dynasty emperors and empresses.	The Qing Imperial Construction Manual is promulgated, detailing specifications, materials, and construction methods for imperial buildings.

for audience, and the northern half for residential chambers for the consorts and maids. There are three halls along the central axis in the southern half, the first of which is a large nine-bay building containing the throne. Two additional bays on either side are now enclosed and have become part of the interior. There are also three buildings in the northern half of the palace. These were used as sleeping chambers by the emperor and empress. On the side of the central axis are cloisters for housing the consorts and other concubines. There are also a variety of other buildings in the palace that served different functions, such as Buddha Halls, theaters, and gardens.

Most of the imperial buildings were constructed following a code of practice promulgated by the Ministry of Works in 1734. The code stipulated every detail of a building's construction, material, structure, proportion, decorative pattern, and color. A modular system was also detailed for eleven grades of building. The code served as specifications for works, both for quality assurance and budget control.

There were two types of structure for the practice of the state religion: enclosed buildings for worshipping imperial ancestors, and open-air altars for worshipping natural deities such as the gods of heaven, earth, sun, and moon. The Imperial Ancestral Temple is located just outside the southeast corner of the Forbidden City. There are three main halls housing ancestral tablets of deceased emperors. The first hall, constructed in 1541, is one of the very few imperial buildings barely altered since the Ming dynasty.

Of the imperial altars, the most impressive is the Altar of Heaven compound, first built in 1530 and later reconstructed in 1749–51. The compound consists of three groups of buildings: the Abstinence Palace, the building for praying for good harvest, and the altar for praying to heaven. During the winter solstice, the emperor would ascend the three-level open-air circular altar to offer a ritual to renew his mandate to rule. The Hall of Prayer for Good Harvests (see image 2) is a circular building (because heaven is considered round) and has a three-tier roof. The roof tiles are glazed blue, the color of heaven.

Imperial gardens, such as the Yuanming Garden, the Summer Palace in west Beijing or the Summer Palace in Chengde (see image 3), were all planned along the principles of garden design from southern China, with winding paths and scenic cells. Yuanming Garden, known also as the Garden of Gardens, had seventy-two scenes; the Summer Palace in Chengde had thirty-six scenes. However, the buildings in these imperial gardens had to be constructed according to the imperial codes, and thus are more formal than southern architectural forms, which are poetic and free spirited. Imperial gardens were additionally imbued with political overtone, such as the reproduction of famous southern scenes in the Summer Palace in Chengde for the demonstration of political hegemony, or the scenes in Yuanming Garden extolling social harmony. **PPH**

1756	1760	1774	1818	1844	1860
A representative defensive manor of the illustrious Qiao family is built in Qixian county, Shanxi province.	Western-style palaces are constructed in Changchun Garden, designed by Italian missionaries Giuseppe Castiglione and others, with fountains.	Imperial libraries are built in the Purple Forbidden City and six other locations.	Salt merchant Huang Yingtai completes Ge Garden in Yangzhou, Jiangsu province. It is an important example of a private-merchant garden.	Western trading houses occupy a stretch of land along Huangpu River, Shanghai, in the British Concession, known later as the Bund.	British and French military forces almost completely destroy Yuanming Imperial Garden. A section is rebuilt in 1880 as the Summer Palace.

Taihe Hall 1698
ARCHITECT UNKNOWN

Taihe Hall,
Beijing, China

The throne hall of a palace was a symbol of power for the ruler of the vast empire of China, and the architecture of the hall reinforced that sense of power. Taihe Hall (Hall of Supreme Harmony) was first built in 1420, during the early Ming dynasty (1368–1644), and the building was larger than the present one, which was rebuilt in 1698 during the Qing dynasty (1644–1912) after the first hall was destroyed in a fire. The smaller size might be attributed to different practices between the two dynasties. The throne hall has nine bays across the front elevation and five along the side. There are two additional bays, serving as corridors on either side of the building, which were enclosed within the interior at a later time. Measuring 197 by 109 feet (60 x 33 m), the hall is the largest building in the imperial palace. The single-story structure has a large glazed tile roof, sitting on a three-tier platform. At a height of 92 feet (28 m), Taihe Hall is also the highest building in the palace. The bracket sets are much smaller, in proportion to the height of the column, than those from the early Ming dynasty. This indicates the gradual reduction of the functionality of bracket sets, from being a structural element to a decorative feature. In the central bay, there are eight intermediate bracket sets, and the height of the bracket set is about one-seventh of the height of the exterior column. The inside of the hall is dominated by a throne on a three-level platform. Despite being a large space, during daily audience the throne hall was occupied by the emperor only, with no more than ten officials. Hundreds of officials would occupy the large courtyard outside. The power and central status of the emperor were presented in no uncertain terms. **PPH**

⬕ NAVIGATOR

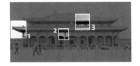

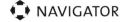

FOCAL POINTS

1 EAVES

The roof is double-eaved, which indicates that it is of the highest order of construction. The finials at either end of the roof ridge are in the shape of a dragon, 11 feet (3.4 m) in height. At the end of the diagonal ridge are ten sculpted animal figures, which are also an indication of high status.

2 BRACKET SETS

Bracket sets allowed the eaves of a building to project out a considerable distance, thus providing protection for the structure below. The bracket sets used in Taihe Hall are more decorative than those seen in earlier buildings, such as the main hall of Foguang Monastery (857; see p.60).

3 HIERARCHY

The bright yellow roof tiles and decorative schema on the wooden members of the building (the dragon and phoenix), are two clear indications of hierarchy. Imperial architecture of the Qing dynasty follows a standard that can be used to reveal the hierarchy of the buildings.

LEI FAMILY

The design of imperial constructions in the Qing dynasty was undertaken by the design office of the Ministry of Works under the Imperial Household Department. In the early Qing dynasty, Lei Fada (1619–93) became the head of the office due to his skillful interpretation of the requirements of the imperial family. After his death, members of the Lei family continued as chief designers of imperial buildings for more than 200 years. They designed all major projects, including imperial palaces in Beijing and Chengde (right), imperial parks and gardens, religious structures, and mausoleums. The sites for construction were surveyed before a sketch design was produced. The design was presented in various scaled plans, elevations, perspectives, detailed patterns, and designs, as well as 1:100 models in paper. These would be presented to the emperor for approval. Perspective used in the presentation was orthogonal projection, thus allowing both plan and elevations to be seen at the same time.

NEO-PALLADIANISM

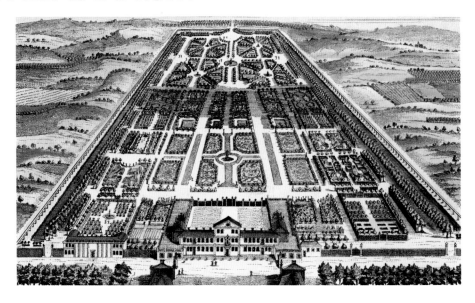

During the first half of the eighteenth century in England, the simple, rational Neo-Palladian style was thought to be the purest form of architecture and the best reflection of ancient classical architecture since antiquity. Its flourishing was an almost inevitable response to three key factors: a growing disdain for the perceived licentiousness of the Baroque style (see p.222) that had dominated architecture in the late seventeenth century; the cult of antiquity that gripped England; and the rising certainty that Elector George of Hanover would become the next King of England, as George I. This last factor helped define the precise aesthetic of the style now known as Neo-Palladianism.

George was from the Brunswick-Lünebergs, a branch of the Guelphs, one of the oldest aristocratic houses of the Holy Roman Empire. He sought visible ways to strengthen the family name and hence his claims to be both elector and, later, monarch of England. One way was to adopt the same classical architecture as had his Guelph ancestors, thus re-establishing an ancient family connection. George often traveled to Italy, and promoted the villa as a building type, drawing on Italian Renaissance forms (see p.196) and the Venetian legacy of Andrea Palladio (1508–80). He favored simple symmetrical solutions, a restrained use of the orders, a lack of external adornment, tripartite elevations and a predilection for using the cube as a measure of space. These were all common features in designs emanating from Hanover at this time, typified by the late seventeenth-century royal palace at Herrenhausen (see image 1), which was rebuilt to a classical design in 1821.

KEY EVENTS

1708	1714	1715	1718	1719	1721
William Benson builds the seminal Wilbury House in Wiltshire, based on Amesbury Abbey (1660), by John Webb, a pupil of Inigo Jones.	Elector George of Hanover is crowned King of England. His preferred architectural style takes shape as English Neo-Palladianism.	Colen Campbell publishes the first edition of *Vitruvius Britannicus*, which aids in disseminating the early style throughout England.	Benson becomes Surveyor of the King's Works, ousting Sir Christopher Wren (1632–1723) and signaling the death of the Baroque.	Lord Burlington returns from the Grand Tour and commences his passionate quest to establish Neo-Palladianism as the nation's style.	Campbell designs Stourhead, Wiltshire, for banker Henry Hoare. Its proportions reflect Palladio's fascination with proportionate room sizes.

It was the German interpretation of Palladio's style (and those elements that Palladio himself had borrowed from contemporaries and forebears) that dominated English architecture for five decades. After the Act of Settlement in 1701, English visitors flocked to the court in Hanover to curry favor with the next king. They saw Hanoverian architecture first-hand and transported the style back to England. Aristocrats looking for opportunities under George's reign could see that Hanoverian Palladianism was linked closely with the Palladio-inspired architecture of Charles I and his court architect Inigo Jones (1573–1652). English Neo-Palladianism, therefore, became a mixture of Palladio's original works, filtered by a Hanoverian interpretation, coupled with Jones's seventeenth-century interpretation of Palladio's compositions. George was crowned King of England in 1714 and from this time forward the style disseminated rapidly, later spreading to North America.

The first Neo-Palladian villa to be built in England was Wilbury House (1708) in Wiltshire, designed by "gentleman architect" and nefarious con merchant William Benson (1682–1754). Benson saw Palladian style first-hand in Hanover, and his seminal villa relies heavily on nearby Amesbury Abbey (1660), which Benson knew was designed by John Webb (1611–72), a pupil of Inigo Jones and therefore of the highest pedigree. Wilbury incorporates a tripartite elevation and the innovative use of two grand reception rooms, each a cube and a half, flanked by two cube apartments. After Wilbury, and probably with the help of architect Colen Campbell (1676–1729), Benson pressed on in his campaign to establish Neo-Palladianism as the new national style. Benson went on to obtain the influential position of Surveyor of the King's Works in 1718 and he employed advocates of the new style, including Campbell as his deputy.

Campbell published *Vitruvius Britannicus* in 1715 and this book, together with its subsequent editions of 1717 and 1725, became a key vehicle in disseminating the style. Campbell worked hard to promote Neo-Palladianism, carrying out commissions including the enormous house at Wanstead, Middlesex, for Sir Richard Child in 1713 and other, more idiomatically unresolved interpretations of Neo-Palladianism in the villas of New Hotham for Sir Charles Hotham (1714), Newby for Sir William Robinson (1718), and Ebberston Lodge for William Thompson (1718), all in Yorkshire.

Campbell quickly matured as a Neo-Palladian architect and, as early as 1721, he was designing Stourhead (see image 2), Wiltshire, for Benson's brother-in-law, banker Henry Hoare. Not being an aristocrat, Hoare hoped that Stourhead would win him acceptance with the landed gentry. Stourhead's design reflects Palladio's belief that simple mathematical relationships and correct proportions could achieve beauty and harmony. The entrance hall is a 30-foot (9 m) cube with the flanking cabinet and music rooms each measuring 30 by 20 feet (9 x 6 m). Throughout Campbell's original house at Stourhead, the dimensions of the rooms all carefully related to one another.

1 **Eighteenth-century drawing of Herrenhausen (1698)**
Georg Ludwig Friedrich Laves
Hanover, Germany

2 **Stourhead (1721–25)**
Colen Campbell and Nathaniel Ireson
Stourton, Wiltshire, UK

1738	1740	c.1750	1755	1759	1773
Neo-Palladian Drayton Hall is built in South Carolina, borrowing from Palladio and Campbell's Whitehall Villa.	Batty Langley's *Treasury of Designs* is published and helps to establish the Neo-Palladian style in provincial England and colonial America.	With his two pattern books, Robert Morris (1703–54) is the first to define exactly what constitutes a Neo-Palladian villa.	The restrained Harleyford Manor, near Marlow in Buckinghamshire, by Robert Taylor (1714–88), is built and owes much to Robert Morris.	The building of the Neoclassical Kedleston Hall in Derbyshire signals the end of Neo-Palladianism's dominance in 18th-century England.	Neo-Palladianism continues to thrive in colonial America as George Washington rebuilds his villa at Mount Vernon.

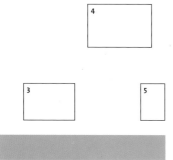

3 **Marble Hill House** (1729)
Roger Morris
London, UK

4 **Monticello** (1772)
Thomas Jefferson
Charlottesville, Virginia, USA

5 **Redwood Library and Athenaeum** (1750)
Peter Harrison
Newport, Rhode Island, USA

No assessment of English Neo-Palladian style is complete without discussing Richard Boyle, 3rd Earl of Burlington (1694–1753). Although Neo-Palladianism was well established before his involvement, Burlington drove the style into the 1730s and beyond with the aid of his protégé William Kent (c.1685–1748). As long as Neo-Palladianism prevailed, Burlington was as content in the company of the lowliest joiner as he was with the greatest aristocrats. Consulted by his fellow peers in all matters architectural, Burlington was frequently seen with the intelligentsia of the day at Marble Hill House (see image 3), a Neo-Palladian villa designed by little-known London craftsman Roger Morris (1695–1749) for George II's mistress Henrietta Howard. Its form set the pattern for Morris's signature, simple, cubic villa style with its plain, restrained elevations. By the mid-1720s, Burlington was accepted as the leading authority on architectural style, and as a great proponent of Neo-Palladianism he also sought to build in the style himself, including his small villa at Chiswick (1727; see p.250). Chiswick is overrun with classical references, many of which seem to have conflicting messages that are difficult to disentangle at a distance of nearly 300 years.

The ease with which Neo-Palladianism could be adapted by careful selection of architectural "quotes" to reflect multiple visual messages explains its long-lasting popularity. Compendiums of features, motifs, and other classical references allowed, for example, Sir Robert Walpole to cleverly select the restrained Neo-Palladian elements at Houghton Hall—designed by Campbell, Kent, and James Gibbs (1682–1754)—to support his privileged Whig politics and broadcast his rationalism and virtue. Viscount Cobham blanketed the landscape at Stowe, Buckinghamshire, with his version of Neo-Palladianism to protest Walpole's aggrandizement and political self-advancement. Staunch Jacobite and Tory Lord Bolingbroke used Neo-Palladianism at his home in Dawley, Middlesex, to challenge his political exile and create a haven for intellectual and sensual pleasures, thus emulating one of the original purposes behind Palladio's Renaissance villas in the Veneto.

Architectural pattern books of the 1740s and 1750s aided the dissemination of the style's popularity in North America. Gibbs's *A Book of Architecture* (1728) and Abraham Swan's *The British Architect* (1745) were key to transporting the style beyond England. English architect Robert Morris had considerable influence on the style in the British colonies. George Washington's house at Mount Vernon was built in stages (1757–78), and used many architectural details and motifs from pattern books, thus re-creating what was considered

to be quintessentially English Neo-Palladianism. Colonial America's Neo-Palladianism was at its most defined fifty years after the death of Burlington, largely through renowned architect and politician Thomas Jefferson (1743–1826), who relied heavily on Morris's pattern book *Select Architecture* (1755; previously published as *Rural Architecture* in 1750). Jefferson was inspired by the more restrained English Neo-Palladian architects, such as James Paine (1717–89) and Robert Taylor, when he designed his famous Monticello villa near Charlottesville, Virginia (see image 4). Monticello is fundamental Neo-Palladian architecture at its best and adheres closely to the tenets of the early eighteenth-century style as built in England.

Peter Harrison (1716–75) was another key exponent of the style. Adapted closely from Palladio's *I quattro libri dell'architettura* (*The Four Books of Architecture*; 1570), Harrison's Georgian-Palladian design for the Redwood Library and Athenaeum (see image 5) in Newport, Rhode Island, was the first in the country to include a classical portico (in this case in the Doric style). Wood for the exterior was cut in a manner to feign rusticated stonework. This proved popular in the eighteenth century as a method to mimic Palladian stonework, and both Monticello and Mount Vernon have feigned rustication. Although diffused, diluted, and in some cases diminished, Neo-Palladianism never lost its allure. Early twentieth-century U.S. Colonial Revival style references Neo-Palladianism, and the resurgent popularity of Palladian-inspired architectural pattern books in the twenty-first century in the United States is seen by many as a direct result of the influence of adherents of the urban design movement known as New Urbanism.

The demand for Neo-Palladian compositions continues in twenty-first-century Britain, met by architects such as Quinlan Terry (b.1937) and Julian Bicknell (b.1945). Terry's Ferne Park (2001) in Donhead St. Andrew, Wiltshire, is a prime contemporary example. The heirs apparent—dubbed the "Young Athenians" by *RIBA Journal*—Francis Terry (b.1969), George Saumarez-Smith (b.1973), and Ben Pentreath (who, without an architecture degree, embodies the concept of a modern-day "gentleman architect") continue to promulgate the style. Although Neo-Palladianism is not as absolutist or widely popular as it was in the eighteenth century, it nevertheless persists. **CF**

Chiswick House 1727
VARIOUS ARCHITECTS

Chiswick House,
Chiswick, London, UK

⚜ NAVIGATOR

By the mid-1720s, Richard Boyle, 3rd Earl of Burlington, was the accepted authority on architectural style in Britain. Expounding on the subject was not enough, however; he also sought to build in the style, starting with Chiswick House in 1727. Although Burlington did live there, this could not have been his original intention due to its size. Lord Hervey once famously exclaimed, "House! Do you call it a house? Why! It is too little to live in, and too large to hang on one's watch." Its diminutive size made it inconvenient as an eighteenth-century house and its service functions had to be accommodated outside the villa. A central room makes little sense in a house, and it is more likely that the villa, with its perfect cuboid proportions, was designed to be a showpiece Neo-Palladian composition. One theory is that Burlington intended Chiswick as a venue for entertaining small groups and for housing his art collection. Chiswick's designer is a mystery. James Gibbs (1682–1754) was first employed at Chiswick to assist Burlington, but he was sacked on the advice of Colen Campbell (1676–1729), who then replaced Gibbs as Burlington's adviser. William Kent (c.1685–1748) was at the same time a protégé of Burlington's, and it is likely that Chiswick's final design is in fact a culmination of the ideas of all four men. **CF**

👁 FOCAL POINTS

1 PORTICO

The front elevation features an elegant portico with six Corinthian columns on the *piano nobile*, surmounted by a dome. Burlington's Roman villa design was partly inspired by Palladio's Villa Rotunda, in Vicenza. The beauty of the house lies in its simplicity.

2 DOME

The shallow, stepped dome is derived from the Pantheon (see p.52) in Rome, which is still the largest unreinforced concrete dome of its kind. Chiswick's octagonal shape and shallow drum are taken directly from Villa Pisani by Vincenzo Scamozzi (1548–1616).

3 OBELISKS

Obelisks are cleverly used to disguise chimney stacks. The British climate was unsuited to Italian architecture and practical building solutions had to be found to overcome this. Obelisks were one way of incorporating chimneys without affecting the classical roofline.

▲ The rear facade has three Serlian windows, a style that Palladio popularized. It consists of a large window divided into three with the central, arched window being the largest. Although first illustrated by Sebastiano Serlio (1475–c.1545) in 1537, it derives from earlier Roman sources, such as the triumphal arch.

THE ARCHITECT EARL

Burlington was devoted to establishing Neo-Palladianism. With the help of architects and artists, he was responsible for many Neo-Palladian designs including London's Burlington House and the Assembly Rooms in York. By securing posts for his protégés in the Office of Works he influenced public architecture and his hand can be seen in the designs for the Treasury Buildings and Horse Guards, London (right). His political tendencies remain unclear; he did incorporate Jacobite symbols into the Chiswick interior, which has questioned his loyalty to the Hanoverians. Was Burlington's obsession with Neo-Palladianism an attempt to emulate George I's style or was it a desire to reinstate the architecture of Inigo Jones and the Stuart kings?

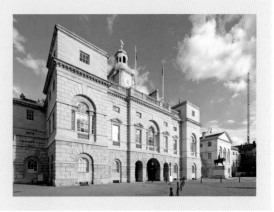

GEORGIAN: BUILDERS' CLASSICISM

Georgian architecture—a stylistic label derived from the reigns of Britain's Kings George I to IV (1714–1830)—had great reach. However, this architecture owed more to builders than to kings. Britain grew mighty during this period, through naval supremacy, seaborne trade, industrialization, and a consequent empire. Its artisan-capitalist builders constructed a brick, timber, and later stucco-covered vernacular classicism. These men may have styled themselves as architects, but building was their forte—and design was a preliminary necessity. Their work manifested itself in proliferations of row houses, suburban villas, warehouses, mills, and institutional buildings. An architecture of handsome proportionality sprang up across the world, from Baltimore to Bengal.

London's spectacular growth—it tripled in size in the seventeenth century to become Western Europe's largest city—generated a shift in building practice. The role of speculative development was not new, but its scale and sophistication were. Intricate financing and capital collaborations spread from entrepreneurs, such as Nicholas Barbon who was obliged to write *An Apology for the Builder* (1685), to carpenters and bricklayers. Rapid urban expansion for a prospering bourgeois market resulted. Streets were lined with houses of increasingly standardized form, generally brick-built rather than timber, unified and ornamented by classical elements.

KEY EVENTS

1714	1724	1727	1729	1757	1762
The end of the War of the Spanish Succession sparks a building boom in London's West End. Hanover, Cavendish, and Grosvenor squares follow.	A new London Building Act tries to control fire losses through limiting the use of timber, with specifications about details such as cornices and window frames.	John Wood the Elder returns to Bath to promulgate rebuilding plans; Ralph Allen acquires Combe Down quarries; and the Avon Navigation begins.	The town of Baltimore is founded and 60 acres (24 ha) are speculatively laid out on a simple grid, as happened in Philadelphia from 1682.	Dublin's Wide Streets Commissioners are appointed. The Battle of Plassey leads to the East India Company's dominance of Bengal from Calcutta.	The Westminster Paving Act creates a new legal framework for orderly urban streets and tidy public spaces that is to be much imitated.

The eighteenth-century house-building world has been understood as a time of classical orthodoxy, but old or vernacular outlooks, practices, and materials endured. Humble builders and craft skills prevailed. Ireland Row on the Mile End Road in east London (see image 2), designed and built in 1717 by Anthony Ireland, epitomized the new flat regularity. Graceful carved door-hood brackets provide depth and ornament. East London was dependent on the sea and the trading connections it brought. So were many prosperous provincial British towns, from dockyard and depot towns in Kent—Woolwich, Chatham, and Deal—up the east coast to Whitby and Newcastle, and west to the slave-trade ports of Bristol and Liverpool.

Emigrants to North America included many artisans who knew how to build. There, in a different climate, architectural forms were modified with a familiar vocabulary: in brick, especially in urban contexts such as Philadelphia or Baltimore, and in timber, as in New England.

From about the mid-eighteenth century, the Industrial Revolution promoted technological innovation alongside improved methods of production. No one exploited industrialization and greater capitalization in the century's later decades more than Adam & Company. Robert Adam (1728–92) is remembered as a great Neoclassical (see p.272) architect, but his success would not have been possible without the underpinning of the family building firm, established with his two brothers. The Adams deployed workforces of an unprecedented scale with material from their own timber wharves and quarries. They undertook grand speculations in London's West End of a kind none had previously dared, such as at the Adelphi (1768–72, demolished 1936), a huge riverside block of dwellings. Contemporary developments of note occurred in Edinburgh (New Town) and Dublin, and many other architects, including, Sir John Soane (1753–1837), emerged from building-trade origins.

Adam & Company was instrumental in the building from 1800 of East London's West India Docks, a gargantuan state-backed project to protect the interests of merchants and slave-owning planters. These and other huge enclosed docks, such as Liverpool's Albert Dock (1847; see p.254), were lined with parades of plain and minimally classical brick warehouses for high-value imports. John Nash (1752–1835) was a speculative builder who gained sufficient favor to be given the chance to reshape central London after 1810. His "Metropolitan Improvements," a great linear thrust that included Regent Street and Regent's Park (see image 1), were lined with stucco-faced buildings. Nash's Park Villages of the 1820s and 1830s were a new and influential kind of villa suburb. The free-standing villa had developed as a classical house type through the eighteenth century, from London's environs to the Lake District and the growing empire, as in Calcutta, a "City of Palaces" where the profits of East India Company trade made possible the construction of numerous great stuccoed classical houses. **PG**

1 **Chester Terrace, Regent's Park (1825)**
John Nash
London, UK

2 **Ireland Row, Mile End Road (1717)**
Anthony Ireland
London, UK

1767	1775	1793	1800	1811	1838
James Craig wins a competition to design Edinburgh New Town. His symmetrical grid layout leads to the transformation of Scotland's capital.	Designed by John Wood the Younger, the Royal Crescent (see p.256) at Bath is completed.	The Anglo-French Wars start and lead to a financial crisis that has a huge impact on Britain's building world.	London's enclosed wet-dock building program begins at the West India and London Docks, to be followed by the East India Docks and others.	New York City's (Commissioners) grid plan for Manhattan is adopted.	John Nash's Park Villages are completed to the north of Regent's Park. The project establishes a suburban picturesque idiom.

Albert Dock 1847
JESSE HARTLEY 1780–1860

Albert Dock,
Liverpool, UK

⚓ NAVIGATOR

A t the beginning of the Georgian period, Liverpool was a small settlement, but it grew rapidly to become a major port. It was only after 1841 that closed docks with secure warehouses for the storage of high-value bonded goods became possible. Drawing on the precedent of St. Katharine Docks in London, Jesse Hartley prepared ingenious plans. Hartley began his working life as a mason and had served as civil engineer to Liverpool's Dock Estate since 1824. Combining assiduity and flair, he produced a perfectly integrated dock-warehouse complex on a Herculean scale. The complex comprises five big, but unequal, five-story warehouse stacks that are distinguished by their austere classicism. The functional approach does not neglect aesthetics. Hartley saw to every detail, down to the placement and variations in the characteristically rough but elegant granite dressings. Dereliction followed the dock's closure in 1972, but conversions from the 1980s into museums, hotels, shops, bars, offices, and apartments have led to the Albert Dock becoming Liverpool's principal architectural draw. **PG**

👁 FOCAL POINTS

1 DOCK WALLS

Hartley insisted on granite to make the dock walls strong. The irregular construction is known as Cyclopean because of the Greek myth that only Cyclops had the strength to move the boulders used in ancient dry-stone walls. Here huge bonding header stones are bound together with rubble, all topped with great coping stones.

2 ARCHES

The Greek Doric colonnade along the quay is made up of columns of hollow cast iron filled with masonry. The covered quay, for unloading and transit, is opened up by the arches that allow for the swing of quay cranes, creating the impression of an arcade. These warehouses were the world's first to be fitted with hydraulic cranes.

3 PROPORTIONAL ELEVATIONS

The loading or loophole doors directly above the arches articulate the functional rhythm of the warehouse elevations. Flanking cast-iron-framed windows in the bare brick walls are spaced according to the dictates of use, not aesthetics. Yet the elevations as a whole retain harmonious, if not strictly classical, proportions.

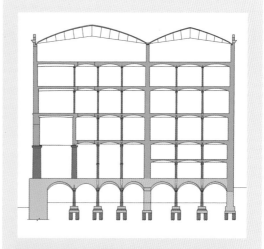

"FIREPROOF" CONSTRUCTION

Earlier dock warehouses had timber floors, often supported by timber piers. Fire prevention was not the priority that it was in textile mills, but devastating fires in other warehouses made comparatively costly fireproof construction seem an imperative at Albert Dock. Hartley designed load-bearing brick walls (above, pink) around a modular cast-iron frame (blue) that drew on precedents in mills. There are stone vaults (gray) below brick jack-arch floors and an inventive, lightweight, stressed-skin roof—wrought-iron framed and covered with galvanized plates. Such structures are not strictly fireproof, yet these innovative buildings were significant constructional forerunners of the concrete and steel that appeared at the end of the 19th century.

▼ Liverpool does not hide its industrial buildings. The Albert Dock is close to the city center on the Mersey River and within easy reach of the great office blocks of Pier Head. It does them no architectural disservice. The layout of the dock is generous, leaving room for the warehouses to be appreciated in long views.

Royal Crescent 1754–75
JOHN WOOD THE YOUNGER 1728–81

Royal Crescent,
Bath, UK

⚙ NAVIGATOR

John Wood (1704–54) and his son, also John, gave the fashionable resort of Bath the beginnings of a stylish new town through speculative development. Their highly original array of houses was inventively classical. Laid out with panache, it had great influence. The elder Wood had worked in London's West End as a joiner and, although young, was already an experienced developer when in 1727 he returned to his birthplace of Bath. Significantly, that same year a local entrepreneur, Ralph Allen, set about improving the accessibility of Bath's stone quarries. Beginning at Queen's Square (1728–36), Wood headed north and uphill, laying the foundations for the Circus in 1754, the year of his death. The younger Wood oversaw completion there in 1767, and broke away westward for the hilltop Royal Crescent (1767–75). Overall, the complex combines coherent planning and regularity with picturesque informality that is both a reflection of the project's gestation through time and an embrace of its natural setting. It is also self-consciously classical. The Royal Crescent is strictly a half ellipse, and may have been intended as a "demi-Colosseum" to invoke antique Roman precedent. In the absence of another half, it presents a serendipitous open composition that was widely imitated in later urban developments. **PG**

◎ FOCAL POINTS

1 IONIC ORDER

The facade is regularly proportional, unified by the simple classicism of a giant Ionic order above a high plain podium. Bath's honey-colored, durable stone is a great asset; through craftsmanship, it is rendered into finely calibrated classical architecture.

2 LAYOUT OF HOUSES

Party walls rising above the slate-covered roofs define each of the thirty-three houses. The chimneys indicate the typical side-wall fireplace layout of Georgian terrace row houses. Doors are in the outer bays of the three-window fronts— a pragmatic asymmetry.

3 TERRACES

Terraces (row houses) were so-called because they involved tiered ground levels. Basements were excavated and the spoil was used to build up raised side walks in front of railed areas. On the Crescent's high ground the existing landscape offered open prospects.

◀ From the air the geometry of the Woods' Circus and Crescent sequence is apparent. At the same time, glimpses of irregularity at the backs reveal the superficial nature of classicism in the context of commercial speculative development. Adaptation and customization of the houses was expected.

PRIMITIVISM

Classicism can be a kind of primitivism, a romantic search for legitimacy in the old (antique) perceived as pure. The elder Wood took this further than most. At the Circus, Bath, his intention may have been to invert and miniaturize Rome's Colosseum. It is rigorously classical, with three superimposed orders, the lower frieze of which is embellished with 525 emblems (detail, left). Wood wanted to root his classicism in ancient Britain—the Circus was scaled to match the "divinely" proportioned Stonehenge in Wiltshire. Yet it is as closed as the Royal Crescent is open. Here, in the words of historian Sir John Summerson, "the treatment of a row of ordinary townhouses as a monumental unity [is]. . .as if some simple-minded community had taken over an antique monument and neatly adapted it as a residence."

ISLAMIC

By the beginning of the eighteenth century, the three most prominent empires of the Islamic world—Turkey, India, and Iran—started to fragment. This was accompanied by a paradoxical, inversely proportional dissemination of shared institutions. Both public and private conventions consolidated: public squares, mosques and minarets, caravanserais (commercial inns), covered markets, palaces, and private houses became the ubiquitous symbols of Islamic society. The Industrial Revolution brought new stylistic models from the West. The colonialism that came with it differed from Islamic imperial expansion in being dependent on naval power, rather than armies, and this led to misguided architectural hybrids.

In spite of Ottoman military setbacks, Istanbul entered a tranquil era known as the Tulip period (*Lale Devri*) in 1718, as an obsession with Europe prevailed among the upper classes. This halcyon age, which ended when Sultan Ahmed III was deposed in 1730, was accompanied by a playful, easily recognizable architectural style, merging classical Islamic with European Baroque motifs (see p.222), and resulting in relatively flat roofs with wide scalloped overhangs, angular cupolas, and arched masonry bases. Built in 1728, the Fountain Kiosk of Sultan Ahmed III in front of the main Topkapi Palace gate epitomizes the Tulip period. It is a square-plan fountain with five small domes, and the mihrab-shaped niches on each of the facades contain drinking fountains.

KEY EVENTS

1718–30	1744	1755	1798	1807–76	1824
The Tulip period of Ottoman architecture marks the point when Turkey begins to assimilate European styles.	Abd al-Rahman Katkhuda builds the Sabil-Kuttab of Katkhuda in Cairo. A *sabil* provides fresh water for passers-by and a *kuttab* is a type of school.	The European-influenced Ottoman Baroque style sweeps Istanbul, typified by the Nuruosmaniye Mosque built in this year.	Napoleon Bonaparte defeats Mamluk forces at the Battle of the Pyramids, marking the beginning of the end of Mamluk rule in Egypt.	During the Tanzimat period of the Ottoman Empire, modernization is institutionalized through secular reform.	The Anglo-Dutch Treaty trades British interests in Indonesia for Dutch control of Malaya (Singapore), resulting in a Mughal architectural legacy.

The house form advanced in Ottoman Cairo. The best surviving domestic complex is Bayt al-Suhaymi, built by Abdel Wahab el Tablawy in 1648, and bought in 1796 by Sheikh Ahmed as-Suhaymi, who enlarged it by incorporating neighboring houses. The complex includes buidings spanning three centuries: the Sabil Kutab Qitas (1630), the Mustafa Gaafar (1713), and the nineteenth-century El Kharazati (1881). The compound stretches along the Darb al-Asfar, with a street-facing facade and an indirect *skifa* (bayonet) entrance into the first of two courtyards, which are arranged to circulate cool air during each diurnal cycle. The front courtyard is paved, and the second courtyard is planted so that vegetation traps the cooler desert night air. When the front courtyard heats up at midday, convection pulls stored, cool air forward. The main, private rooms of the house are organized around this court in order to take full advantage of this cooling cycle. The room used for the midday meal is built of masonry and Iznik tiles, to slow heat gain, and is suspended like a bridge over an opening between the two courtyards to catch the breeze. A covered second-floor room on the street side of the front paved courtyard has a porchlike open front. It faces the prevailing northwest evening breeze and was used as a dining room. Reception rooms, divided between male and female visitors, had a small, covered central courtyard and a fountain, flanked by *iwans* (alcoves) on each side, cooled by a pair of *malqaf* (windtowers), with one oriented toward the prevailing breeze to direct it into the interior, and another above the fountain, which expelled hot air. A series of *mashrabiya*—pierced wooden window screens—redistribute cool air while providing occupants with a discreet view of the courtyard or street.

Although the sixteenth-century Wikala al-Ghuri in Cairo is one of the best known Islamic caravanserai, the Wikala Nafisa al-Bayda (see image 1) is one of the more unusual—its curved facade, with upper-story *mashrabiya*, was built by a woman. Adjacent to al-Bayda's Wikala is her Sabil-Kuttab, which like hundreds of other sabil-kuttab in Cairo, offered free water (an act of charity in an arid environment) and classes for reading and writing. The Sabil-Kuttab of Katkhuda (see image 2) is one of the treasures of Ottoman architecture. Built by Abd al Rahman Katkhuda in a mix of Ottoman Mamluk and Islamic styles, the two-story building is on a triangular site, open on three sides; the first floor has a public fountain and the second story is a tiered, arcaded pavilion. The Sabil-Kuttab built by Sultan Mustafa III in Cairo in 1760 is a mix of Turkish style with Cairene rounded marble arches, half screened in the upper register, and an interior covered in hundreds of Dutch Delft blue wall tiles.

In Khiva, Uzbekistan, Muhammad Amin Khan commissioned a madrassa (1851–55; see p.260). Although its Kalta Minar minaret was unfinished, the design confirms that the Timurid style remained vital in Central Asia for centuries after his death. The inscription above the entrance reads, "This beautiful building will stand to please the descendants forever." **JMS**

1 **Wikala Nafisa al-Bayda (1796)**
Nafisa al-Bayda
Cairo, Egypt

2 **Sabil-Kuttab of Katkhuda (1744)**
Abd al Rahman Katkhuda
Cairo, Egypt

1849	1851	1851	1857	1878	1911
The Ottoman ruler of Egypt, Muhammad Ali, dies. He made medieval Cairo more European in plan and destroyed its environmental effectiveness.	The Ottoman court moves from Topkapi to the Dolmabahçe Palace, Istanbul, built by father and son architects Garabet and Nigoğayos Balyan.	Muhammad Amin Khan commissions a madrassa in Khiva, Uzbekistan (see p.260), but dies before it can be completed.	The British seize Delhi, ending 332 years of Mughal rule and 1,000 years of Muslim dominance in India.	The Ottoman Empire ends under Sultan Abdul Hamid II with the Treaty of Berlin in 1878, whereby it loses most of its territory in Eastern Europe.	The new imperial capital of Delhi is established under colonialism. It fosters an indigenous reaction in architecture and the arts.

Muhammad Amin Khan Madrassa 1851–55
ARCHITECT UNKNOWN

Muhammad Amin
Khan Madrassa,
Khiva, Uzbekistan

By the middle of the nineteenth century, the Uzbek khanates of Central Asia were under pressure from tribal leaders to relinquish their power. In an attempt to use architecture and urban initiatives to strengthen his position, Muhammad Amin Khan commissioned a madrassa in Khiva, which bears his name. It was built near the Ata Darvaza gate into the Ichan-Kala, or inner fortress, and was the largest religious school in the city at the time. Part of Muhammad Amin's grand plan was to tear down the old city walls and to build the tallest minaret in the region, to be attached to his madrassa, but he was killed in a battle with the Teke Turkmen tribe in 1855 before he could complete it. The Timurid heritage of the madrassa is clear in its large *pishtaq* (portal), which leads into a central courtyard that provides light and air for all of the student rooms. It also has towers at each of its four corners, and four *iwans* dedicated to each of the schools of Islamic jurisprudence. There is a wooden bridge, from one of the arched openings that frame the exterior windows of the students' rooms, connecting the second floor of the madrassa to the unfinished minaret next to it. Although the Kalta Minar minaret is more than 86 feet (26 m) high and 46 feet (14 m) wide, the Friday Mosque in Khiva (1788; above right) stands at 105 feet (32 m) high and provides a vivid image of what Muhammad Amin's minaret would have looked like had it been completed. The Kalta Minar, however, would have been fully glazed. **JMS**

⟐ NAVIGATOR

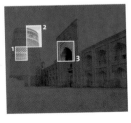

👁 FOCAL POINTS

1 GLAZED TILES

Colored tiles and calligraphy are used to transform the surface of the Kalta Minar into a three-dimensional work of art. This decorative combination of multicolored, majolicalike glazed tiles and intricately detailed brickwork is only found on minarets in Central Asia.

2 MINARET

The Kalta Minar minaret was intended to be about 262 feet (80 m) tall, which would have made it the tallest in Central Asia. Local legend holds that when Muhammad Amin learned of a minaret of similar size being built in Bukhara, he suspected that his architect had designed it and threw him from the top of the Kalta Minar.

3 *PISHTAQ*

The *pishtaq* that forms the entranceway into the courtyard of the madrassa is decorated with bands of colored tiles and capped with calligraphy. The truncated shape of the unfinished minaret complements the scale of the *pishtaq* and the other buildings of the old city around it.

▲ The Friday Mosque in Khiva is made of beige clay brick, relieved by bands of glazed tile, leading up to a fully tiled and domed enclosure for the muezzin to offer the call to prayer, at the top.

TIMURID STYLE

Muhammad Amin Khan led the Qungrats (1717–1920), who were one of three Uzbek groups that claimed descent from Genghis Khan and divided control of the Amu Darya and Syr Darya river basins in the eighteenth century. By adopting the Timurid style for his monuments, Muhammad Amin also invoked the authority of the most powerful khan in the past. Timur sought to restore the glory of the Mongol Empire (1206–1368) and used Islamic symbolism, interwoven in glazed tilework, to legitimize his claim. Examples of this artform include the Ak Serai Palace in Shakhrisabz (1379–1410; right). By the time the Kalta Minar minaret appeared, the rapidly oxidizing lead glazes used by Timur's artisans had been replaced by colored or pigmented oxides, which produced more durable glazes, and this advance, along with the use of single-color tiles, produced a more glistening and vibrant appearance.

EARLY ECLECTICISM

1 **Royal Pavilion (1787–1823)**
John Nash
Brighton, UK

2 **Chinese Tea House (1757)**
Johann Gottfried Büring
Sanssouci Park, Potsdam, Germany

3 **United States Capitol (1793–1800)**
William Thornton, Benjamin Henry
Latrobe, and Charles Bulfinch
Washington, D.C., USA

E clecticism and Revivalism dominated Western architecture in the eighteenth and nineteenth centuries. "Idealists" (deemed zealots by some) pursued "revivals" or the reintroduction of a single "archaeological" style (Greek, Gothic, etc.). Their pursuit of purity was complicated by practitioners who saw all styles as equal. Use was therefore dictated by the client, mood, or commercial circumstances. However, Eclecticism merged two or more styles (its subgenre "Syncretism" involved indiscriminate merger) in a crucible in which heterogeneous styles might become homogenous. The ultimate objective was a new modern style, fueled by an increasingly defensive desire to repel uncertain times. Syncretism was a novelty, but Eclecticism was pragmatic, harmonious—an antidote, wrote Julie Buckler in 2005, "to unreflective revivalism, and not an example of it."

Eclecticism in architecture evolved from the philosophy of Denis Diderot's *Encyclopédie* (1751–72). Diderot's eclectic metaphor was the city. "Uniformity of the buildings," he wrote, "would give to the whole city a sad and tiring appearance." Evidence, experience, and reason allow the "eclectic scholar" to create "a philosophy of his own." Diderot correctly predicted that Eclecticism would spread beyond philosophy, but he warned against reckless extremes. Legatees included Sir John Soane (1753–1837) and his protégé Joseph Michael Gandy (1771–1843), who railed against imitation architecture and advocated drawing on all sources. Soane and Gandy's Freemasons' Hall in London (1828) manifested their interest in the Eclecticism of universal symbolism.

KEY EVENTS

1727	1751–72	1779–95	1780s	1784	c.1790
Batty Langley's *The Builder's Chest Book; or A Complete Key to the Five Orders of Columns in Architecture*, a book of Masonic elements, is published.	Denis Diderot's *Encyclopédie* (*Encyclopedia*) distinguishes Eclecticism as superior to Syncretism.	The Schloss Garten Mosque (see p.264) is one of several Eclectic buildings constructed in the garden of Schwetzingen Palace, Germany.	Claude-Nicolas Ledoux designs an Eclectic collection of private houses with unusual layouts and elevations, and Doric architectural features.	Philosopher Johann Gottfried Herder portrays history as a heterogeneous garden of healthy choice, which Nietzsche later refutes.	Richard Payne Knight advocates for Eclecticism combining the picturesque and the Gothic.

Eclecticism could also include the astylistic vernacular. Marie Antoinette's Hameau de la Reine (Queen's Hamlet; 1783) at Versailles allowed her to experience a "peasant" lifestyle in a simple vernacular village. Yet it was the vogue for "slight" structures that encouraged eclectic experimentation. Writer Ciaran Murray has demonstrated that "Chinese" and "Indian" were blanket terms to describe designs from a vast geographic area. King of Prussia, Frederick II's Chinese Tea House (see image 2) at Sanssouci Park was in a "Sharawadgi" or Chinese landscape. Sir William Temple's *Upon the Gardens of Epicurus* (1692) contrasted Western symmetry with Oriental asymmetry, and introduced the term Sharawadgi, a corrupted Japanese term that Temple learned from naturalist Engelbert Kaempfer, who had visited Kyoto's gardens with the Dutch East India Company. Asymmetry paired well with Eclecticism. Books such as *Rural Architecture in the Chinese Taste* (1755) by William and John Halfpenny, with plans for pavilions, temples, and summerhouses, fueled a vogue that led to structures such as Sezincote (1805) in Gloucestershire, which inspired the Prince Regent (later George IV) to adapt plans for his Royal Pavilion at Brighton (see image 1).

Eclectic architecture became associated with what Claude-Nicolas Ledoux (1736–1806) described as "proper character"—the symbols of politics, morals, science, literature, economy, and commerce. The unrealized design by Jean-Jacques Lequeu (1757–1825) for a royal bovine stable featured a monumental cow wearing a howdahlike urn. These visions, in which the building's function is expressed through its form, anticipated the "duck" of twentieth-century Postmodernism (see p.502). Jacques-Francois Blondel (1705–74) lobbied for pragmatic symbolism: Tuscan for the military; Doric for sacred; Ionic for country houses; Corinthian for kings; Composite for the public. Simple symbolism evolved into interchangeable symbolism. Eclecticism encouraged form and meaning—the social readings of buildings—to enter the modern era. Borrowing from old styles, art collector Thomas Hope believed, would birth "a new, truly national architecture." The idea of a "modern" style was a concept that suited the nascent United States. Greek Revival (see p.280) was favored as an adaptable, Eclectic form. *The Beauties of Modern Architecture* (1839) by Minard Lafever (1798–1854) advocated Eclecticism to create new classical capitals, such as the magnolia, tobacco, and corn capitals designed by Benjamin Henry Latrobe (1764–1820) for the Neoclassical United States Capitol (see image 3).

Eclecticism surged in the nineteenth century, but its demise was alluded to by George Aitchison (1825–1910) in his lecture at the Royal Institute of British Architects in 1864. Eclectic ornament was either advertising, he said, or pandered to the vulgar. Absence of ornament, purity of outline, and elegance of proportion would create architecture of the age, and so it did, in what critic Martin Pawley called in 1998 a "magnificent mutiny against historicism, revivalism, and the vernacular." **DJ**

1805	1821	1835	1835	1864	1874
Hegel views eclecticism as a denial of integrative philosophy.	Sir John Soane is commissioned to design an extension to Freemasons' Hall, London. He adds a gallery and later designs a new hall.	Thomas Hope's *Historical Essay on Architecture* calls for composite styles taken from the past but to suit national climate, culture, and topography.	Nikolai Gogol's essay "On the Architecture of the Present Day," champions Eclectic cityscapes as a balance between choice and tradition.	George Aitchinson decries Eclectic ornament as either "advertising" or "vulgar."	Nietzsche condemns the "curious tourist" who plunders the history "garden" turning "plants" into "weeds," leading to Modernism's hostility to Historicism.

Schloss Garten Mosque 1779–95
NICOLAS DE PIGAGE 1723–96

Schloss Garten Mosque,
Schwetzingen, Germany

The mosque at the summer residence of the Prince-elector of the Palatinate in Schwetzingen is the only surviving example of an eighteenth-century European garden mosque. Its substantial scale and unique design contributed to its survival. Part of an Eclectic ensemble, including a Chinese bridge and Roman water tower, the cloisterlike, colonnaded quadrangle, pavilions, and mosque were built alongside a "Turkish" garden. Historian Nebahat Avcioglu describes its "high drum punctured with arched windows, lofty cupola topped by a lantern, and the neoclassical portico," and mentions that it was the only garden mosque of the period to attract criticism because "it looked convincingly genuine." The Eclectic result, however, lacks the essential mihrab to indicate Mecca's direction and there is no provision for ablutions before prayers. Although the mosque has similarities with images of Mecca's holy places published by Johann Bernhard Fischer von Erlach (1656–1723) in 1721, it was more likely modeled on Ottoman Baroque architecture of the period. Others suggest similarities to the mosque built by William Chambers (1723–96) in 1761 at Kew Gardens, London, but Chambers's now-lost design was pure, playful folly; its minarets more closely resemble Arthurian-style towers with victory pennants flying than the Islamic Eclectic homage at Schwetzingen. **DJ**

◉ NAVIGATOR

◉ FOCAL POINTS

1 MINARET

The two minarets, connected to the central building by quarter-circle walls, are based on Turkish models, but are capped with onion domes, rather than tapering to a point. The classical portico, attic, tambour, dome, and cuboid lateral extensions to the mosque are similar to those found in Christian churches.

2 PORTICO

Gilded Islamic inscriptions appear on the gray marble set into the central gable of the portico and the four blue painted plaques on either side of the portico. Other motifs, such as the five-pointed blazing star carved in sandstone above the entrance, have been suggested as links to Freemasonry.

3 WALLS

The garden mosque is constructed from locally quarried sandstone, which can be seen in the portico steps. The rendered walls are painted in tones of pink that are amplified by the setting sun and its reflection in the lake, which was created later to provide a more formal setting for the mosque.

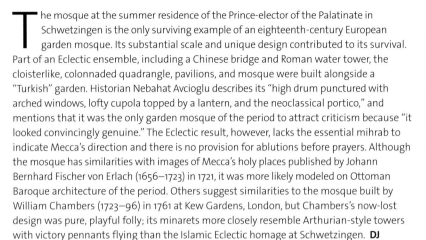

▲ The inscribed plaques on the interior of the cupola extol virtues and warn against vices.

NURUOSMANIYE MOSQUE

An eighteenth-century Western traveler described the Nuruosmaniye Mosque in Istanbul (1755; below) as reflecting the desire of Sultan Mahmoud to have a mosque "in the most modern taste." Its lack of an ablution fountain (as at Schloss Garten) is atypical and perhaps contributed to opposition to the initial plan, which was decried as resembling a Christian temple.

SCIENCE REVOLUTION

In the eighteenth and nineteenth centuries temporary and permanent architecture provided settings for scientists, architects, and engineers to pursue environmental design experimentation. Four buildings in London— the Palm House at Kew (see image 1); the Great Exhibition Building at Hyde Park (1851), which was rebuilt and enlarged to become Crystal Palace at Sydenham (see image 2); and the Palace of Westminster (1840–70; see p.270)—provided infrastructure for the empirical testing and refining of technical solutions to environmental problems, and for evaluating the effect on human physiology of closed-space surroundings. Experimentation was driven by unprecedented challenges during Europe's Industrial Revolution. The imperative to protect workers from noxious fumes or extreme temperatures, and the need to create pleasant environments in public buildings and eradicate the transmission of fatal diseases in crowded spaces, drove research in respiration and ventilation. The *British Medical Journal* and *Scientific Monthly* reported on ventilation experiments as part of the effort to lower institutional mortality rates.

Horticulture was also an impetus for environmental experimentation and the emergence of glasshouse (greenhouse) architecture. The aspiration to grow fruit and vegetables out of season and to cultivate nonnative plants drove horticulturists to design glass enclosures that would receive maximum daylight with passive microclimates (thermal storage, external shading, insulating shutters) or mechanical climates (fermenting dung, hot air, steam and hot-water central heating). Scientific methods were introduced

KEY EVENTS

1727	1816	1833	1836	1840	1848
Stephen Hales's *Vegetable Staticks* discusses the value of empirical observation in understanding ventilation and disease transmission.	John Loudon publishes *Remark on the Construction of Hothouses*, which explores bioclimatic principles underlying glasshouse design.	David Boswell Reid builds a chemistry laboratory in Edinburgh, deploying a chimney-driven forced ventilation system to manage fumes.	Reid erects a model chamber in Edinburgh and remodels the temporary House of Commons to test his proposed stack ventilation system.	Reid develops first plans for stack ventilation to be integrated into Charles Barry's design for the Palace of Westminster.	The Palm House at Kew's Royal Botanic Gardens, designed to create ideal light and climate conditions for tropical plants, is completed.

into building design but, unlike civil engineers, glasshouse designers were concerned with environmental properties, not the building's structural dimension. External appearance was secondary to environmental performance.

The design of the Palm House at Kew was a collaborative and cross-disciplinary effort, led by ironmaster Richard Turner (1798–1881) and architect Decimus Burton (1800–81), who collaborated with botanists William Hooker, John Lindley, John Smith, and experimental chemist and photographer Robert Hunt. An expansive transparent envelope was achieved with a slim profile wrought-iron structure and curved-pane glazing system. A powerful mechanical heating and humidification system maintained the tropical climate. The team's botanists requested glazing that would protect the more light-sensitive tropical plants from solar radiation, but would not interfere with growth. Hunt's treatise of 1841 on photography and the chemical agency of light, combined with Kew-specific experiments from 1845 to 1847, resulted in glazing based on the composition and thermal, photochemical, and optical properties of natural light, and plant growth differential when sunlight is filtered through panes of differently colored glass. Hunt verified the performance of his glazing from optical, chemical, and plant physiological perspectives.

Despite efforts to exploit the most advanced environmental technology and scientific understanding of the time, reports showed that maintaining the high humidity and temperature required to sustain tropical plants during British winters posed practical technical challenges. On several occasions valuable plants were lost. The internal environment was studied, and heating and humidification arrangements were modified based on observations of convection currents, stratification of hot and cold air, and the impact of condensation, heat loss, and solar gains.

Critical insights from the Palm House's post-occupancy history were disseminated in specialist literature—a common practice that formed an integral part of an empirical design approach used to advance glasshouse technology. Building performance studies were not only used to critically review the effectiveness of technical solutions, but also to provide the insights required to refine them. Glasshouse performance studies included ad hoc technical experiments, the monitoring and recording of the internal climate with scientific instruments, and day-to-day observations of the indoor environment and its impact on the growth and vigor of the plants.

The potential of glasshouse technology for human, non-horticultural purposes was explored in various hypothetical proposals, including a public Winter Park (1852), a glass exercise hall for the London Chest Hospital (1851), and Joseph Paxton's glass-arcaded Great Victorian Way (1856). Paxton demonstrated how glasshouse technology could be exploited to create new types of urban spaces, providing a year-round healthy and comfortable artificial atmosphere, as well as protection from the pollution of industrial London.

1 **Palm House (1848)**
Richard Turner and Decimus Burton
Royal Botanic Gardens, Kew,
London, UK

2 **Plan and elevation for Crystal Palace (1854)**
Joseph Paxton
Sydenham, London, UK

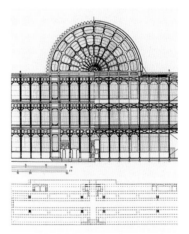

1850	1851	1852	1921	1941	1944
Joseph Paxton completes Victoria Regia House at Chatsworth. It provides the conditions required to grow tropical water lilies in England.	Joseph Paxton's Great Exhibition Building becomes the subject of an environmental post-occupancy evaluation by the Royal Engineers.	The Great Exhibition Building is moved to Sydenham, where the original ventilation system is modified and a heating system is introduced.	The National Physical Laboratory uses physical models and experiments in the debating chamber at Westminster to study air currents.	The original Westminster debating chamber with the Victorian stack ventilation system is destroyed during German air raids.	A new House of Commons chamber is erected by Giles Gilbert Scott (1880–1960). It is equipped with mechanical ventilation and air conditioning.

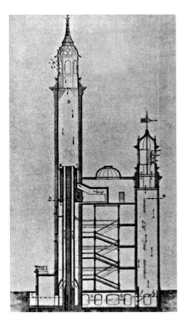

3 Section of new ward block at Guy's Hospital (1850s)
Rhode Hawkins and John Sylvester
London, UK

4 South Kensington Museum (1857)
Captain Francis Fowke
London, UK

5 Newgate Prison (1782)
George Dance
London, UK

Although none of these proposals was realized, the Great Exhibition Building and the Crystal Palace at Sydenham provided Paxton with the opportunity to test the feasibility of adopting glasshouses as spaces of mass congregation. Various critics, including members of the Royal Commission, publicly questioned the feasibility of Paxton's plan from an environmental perspective, arguing that it was a risky experiment, a charge that Paxton admitted. He argued, however, that the experience and knowledge that he had gained as a glasshouse designer enabled him to produce the environmental conditions required for the exhibition.

Similar to the Palm House, the Great Exhibition Building posed a range of technical challenges that required collaboration to resolve. Paxton adopted a passive environmental strategy, which combined natural ventilation with evaporative cooling and shading. Under the direction of the Royal Engineers, the indoor temperatures were monitored and recorded from May to October 1851, and the state of the atmosphere and its effect on the physical and mental conditions of visitors and staff were monitored. In the journal *Healthy Respiration* (1855) the physician Stephen Ward reported that the exhibition provided a laboratory setting in which the effect of ventilation in crowded spaces could be directly observed.

Both the Palm House and the Great Exhibition Building demonstrated the effect that the internal environment had on the occupants' state of health, whether they were plants or human beings. This criterion continued to be used to evaluate building performance. The Great Exhibition's passive environmental strategy was not always successful in preventing overheating during the summer of 1851, and several modifications were made to its ventilation, including the temporary removal of a number of vertical glazing units, which resulted in some improvements in temperature and air quality. A more permanent arrangement of auxiliary ventilators was subsequently adopted. The findings of the post-occupancy evaluation, summarized in the First Report of the Commissioners for the Exhibition of 1851, provided insights into the technical difficulties, which informed several proposals for improving Paxton's original environmental strategy. These plans were unrealized, but the cross-section was altered and ventilators rearranged and enlarged to boost the natural stack ventilation. A glass vault equipped with a system of ventilators to exhaust hot, consumed air was installed over the transept and nave.

The Great Exhibition Building and Crystal Palace can be understood as two consecutive experiments in which Paxton explored how the environmental principles and technologies of the glasshouse could be applied to the design of large public buildings. The designs at Hyde Park and Sydenham were based entirely on experience and empirical observations. There is no evidence that mathematical calculation and other methods of predicting the behavior of his designs were used. The use of full-scale structures for testing and developing environmental solutions was not limited to horticulture and exhibition halls, but was a common method in the eighteenth and nineteenth centuries, most notably in hospitals, such as Guy's (see image 3) and St. Thomas's in London; prisons, including Newgate in London (see image 5) and Perth General; museums; and law courts. It was an integral part of an iterative process, in which proposals were tested and refined through experimental structures or studies inside real buildings. In *Vegetable Staticks* (1727) and *Treatise on Ventilators* (1738) Stephen Hales reported on the importance of an empirical approach to understand the relationship between disease transmission and ventilation in hospitals, prisons, and ships. Another example is the Sheepshanks Gallery (1858), designed by engineers Francis Fowke (1823–65) and Goldsworthy Gurney (1793–1875) as a model picture gallery for what later became the South Kensington Museum (see image 4), now known as the Victoria & Albert Museum.

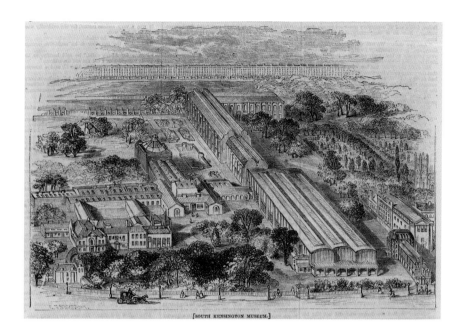

[SOUTH KENSINGTON MUSEUM.]

Extensive experimental research on the ventilation of crowded spaces was conducted inside the British Houses of Parliament from the seventeenth century onward under the direction of leading scientists including Humphry Davy and John Desaguliers. After the fire of 1834, chemist and physician David Boswell Reid developed a debating chamber from first principles, addressing questions of acoustics, ventilation, and lighting. The debating chamber of the permanent House of Commons (1852) was designed from the findings of three temporary debating chambers, which were used for ventilation research conducted in parallel to the design of the actual Palace of Westminster between 1835 and 1851. An experimental debating chamber was constructed in Edinburgh to verify and optimize the ventilation strategy underlying plans for an ideal debating chamber, which was followed by the remodeling of the temporary House of Commons in London according to environmental principles. Occupied between 1836 and 1851, it enabled testing of the ventilation system at full scale and under real-life conditions. In 1839, it was extended to include the temporary House of Lords. A sophisticated environmental monitoring and management regime was introduced, combining measurements with user feedback on air quality and thermal comfort. The air temperature in the chamber was continuously recorded during sittings, complemented by ad hoc measurements of air speed, carbon dioxide concentration, and relative humidity, and detailed observational studies. As part of the routine monitoring procedures, Members of Parliament were tasked with providing feedback.

In the permanent House of Commons, environmental studies continued into the twentieth century, following on from scientific understanding of the system's behavior and the internal atmosphere developed between 1852 and 1936 as new methods of chemical and bacteriological analysis became available. The House of Commons continued as the subject of various scientific and technical studies, which included chemical and microbiological analyses of the internal atmosphere (1904) and a study of the air flow by the National Physical Laboratory (1921–24), which highlighted how scientists and engineers relied on late-nineteenth-century technical and scientific building studies to fully understand the actual performance of Victorian ventilation systems from a technical, environmental, and physiological perspective. **HS**

Palace of Westminster 1840–70

SIR CHARLES BARRY 1795–1860,   AUGUSTUS PUGIN 1812–52

👁 FOCAL POINTS

1 VICTORIA TOWER

Proposed as a high-level air inlet for the palace, in 1847 the Victoria Tower was adopted as the main air supply for Barry's House of Lords. In 1854, it was converted by the resident engineer into the House's principal air discharge.

2 RIVERFRONT TURRET

This is one of three ventilating turrets that were introduced in the mid-1840s by David Boswell Reid as local air and smoke discharges for the rooms on the riverfront side of the palace, including the Committee rooms.

3 CENTRAL TOWER

The tower has been significantly reduced in height, compared to original plans from the early 1840s. It never functioned as the central discharge tower for the entire building, for which it had originally been introduced.

4 CLOCK TOWER

A feature in the original scheme, the tower was later adopted by Reid as one of the principal air inlet towers. After 1852, the resident engineer made it into a ventilating chimney to drive consumed air out of the Commons chamber.

⊕ NAVIGATOR

The Palace of Westminster is based on a scheme by Sir Charles Barry and Augustus Pugin, procured through competition in 1835. After 1840, their Gothic Revival plan was modified to include the towers of a stack-driven ventilation system introduced by David Boswell Reid. The competition brief outlined ventilation as a key functional design criterion. A model debating chamber proposed by Reid had been recommended by the Select Committee on Ventilation, and in 1836 an experimental chamber was erected inside Reid's laboratory in Edinburgh to verify the feasibility of his proposal. This was followed by the remodeling of the temporary House of Commons (1836) and Lords (1839) according to the principles of his model chamber. After five years of experimentation, Reid developed the ventilation system, although it was not implemented in its entirety. The original scheme comprised a tall central tower by which the vitiated air and smoke from fireplaces were to be drawn out of the palace. The Victoria and Clock Towers were intended as primary inlets for the supply of fresh air. Following problems with the complex process of techno-architectural integration and Reid's personal conflicts with Barry, the original plan was abandoned. A decentralized ventilation strategy, involving a system of local discharge turrets each serving a section of the building, was introduced. **HS**

Palace of Westminster,
London, UK

▼ The temporary House of Commons was designed by Robert Smirke (1780–1867) in 1834, and remodeled in 1836 by Reid according to principles outlined in his model debating chamber, first presented to the Select Committee on Ventilation in 1835.

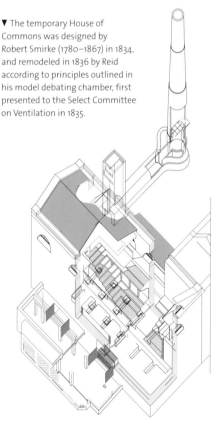

▲ The historic House of Commons chamber shows the perforated cast-iron floor, which admitted fresh air. The vitiated air escaped through apertures in the moldings of the paneled ceiling.

NEOCLASSICISM

Neoclassicism—the classical revival of the mid-eighteenth to mid-nineteenth centuries—differed from earlier forms of Classicism. It was not only an aesthetic prototype but also a moral imperative. Underpinned by a rigorous body of theory, it linked with the rational, scientific spirit of the Enlightenment. The style was supported by a new mood in Western society—aspirational, moralizing, and based on rational principles traceable to antiquity. Linking to an idealized past, it was believed, would lead to a new rational society. For architecture to provide the paradigm and setting for this new society, it needed to reject the frivolity and decadence of Rococo (see p.238). The Petit Trianon at Versailles (see image 1) exemplifies early Neoclassicism and displays an informed knowledge of the Roman Corinthian order. There is an overall sense of harmony combined with a mathematical restraint and minimal forward breaks in the wall planes, and the concealment of the pitched roof behind the balustrade enhances the sense of formal geometry. Structural purity is shown by the columns, which even though they do not entirely support the entablature give the illusion of doing so. The surface has minimal decoration—the building's Classicism is conveyed largely through proportion and chaste surfaces.

Survey, recording, and dissemination of knowledge about ancient buildings lies at the heart of Neoclassical architecture. The syntax and vocabulary of the

KEY EVENTS

1745	1752	1755	1771–77	1774–84	1780
Piranesi publishes *Le Vedute di Roma*. These and other prints of Roman antiquity generate a Romantic sensibility in the age of Neoclassicism.	Construction begins on one of the last great set-piece European palaces—at Caserta for Charles II of Naples—designed by Luigi Vanvitelli (1700–73).	After a devastating earthquake, Lisbon is rebuilt. The new city is the first planned according to Neoclassical geometry and rational planning.	*Cours d'architecture* (*Course of Architecture*) by Jacques-François Blondel (1705–74) is published.	An exotic landscape garden built at Désert de Retz, Chambourcy, includes a summer house inside a ruined column and an Egyptian pyramid.	The Grand Theater of Bordeaux by Victor Louis (1731–1800) sets a new standard for theater design and for civic buildings in Europe.

272 1700–1870

new style were collectively provided by French architect Julien-David Le Roy (1724–1803), who wrote *Ruines des plus beaux monuments de la Grèce* (*Ruins of the Most Beautiful Monuments of Greece*; 1758); British architects James Stuart (1713–88) and Nicholas Revett (1720–1804), authors of *The Antiquities of Athens and Other Monuments of Greece* (1762); the excavations at Herculaneum and Pompeii; and Johann Winckelmann's pioneering classification of ancient Greek sculpture.

Ancient Roman architecture was championed by artist Giambattista Piranesi, whose detailed surveys of ancient ruins were rendered in immaculate but melodramatic engravings. Piranesi argued that the Romans adapted and developed new building types, such as the amphitheater, basilica, arch, and concrete construction, in order to enable a range of architecture adapted to their imperial expansion. Following his return to England from Rome in 1758, Robert Adam (1728–92) introduced a fresh, practical, and elegant form of Neoclassicism. However, Adam's major rival for commissions, William Chambers (1723–96), had the advantage of having studied in Paris, the hotbed of Neoclassicism, as well as a rare knowledge of Chinese buildings from his voyages to the Orient. Chambers was commissioned to build Somerset House in 1776, a large complex of government offices on the bank of the Thames in London. Its style was Neoclassical but it was also Palladian in its restrained harmony. Chambers's success was probably a factor in the declining financial well-being of Robert Adam and his brother James (1732–94); his encroachment on Adam's home city of Edinburgh must have been particularly galling, as seen in his mansion for Lawrence Dundas on St. Andrew Square in the New Town.

Adam's reputation as a scholar-architect capable of producing tasteful, domestic interior designs of refined elegance, as well as exteriors that incorporated unexpected quotations from ancient architecture in bold new configurations, brought him commissions for the renovation of aristocratic country houses. At Syon in west London, Adam designed a magnificent anteroom resembling the chamber of an ancient Roman imperial palace. At Kedleston Hall (1759–92) in Derbyshire he adapted the Arch of Constantine and the dome of the Pantheon to create a Neoclassical facade of considerable monumental power. As a decorator Adam was unrivaled—the Adam style is characterized by rooms shaped as rectangles or cubes, apsidal dining rooms with screens of columns to subdivide the space, and walls rhythmically subdivided by arched recesses set against flat astylar walls. Color was highly important in creating atmosphere: cool monochrome entrance halls, pastel for libraries and ladies' rooms, and rich polychromy for public rooms. Adam was not entirely a Roman revivalist; he used a restrained delicate Greek style for the library at Mellestain (1768) in the Scottish Borders, for example. Adam's home town also provided opportunities for his ambition. He advised on the completion for the plan of the New Town, designed the Register House

1 **Petit Trianon (1764)**
Ange-Jacques Gabriel
Versailles, France

2 **Old College, University of Edinburgh (1789–93)**
Robert Adam
Edinburgh, Scotland

1790	1803	1806	1823	1841	1858
The Panthéon (see p.276), by Jacques-Germain Soufflot (1713–80) and Jean-Baptiste Rondelet (1743–1829), is completed in Paris.	Benjamin Henry Latrobe (1764–1820) is appointed Surveyor of Public Buildings for the United States.	Gallery of Architecture opens in Rue de Seine, Paris. Its purpose is to educate the people in the role of architecture in forming the new French state.	George Gordon Noel, sixth Baron Byron (1788–1824), joins the movement for Greek independence from the Ottoman Empire.	Harvey Londsdale Elmes (1813–47) designs St. George's Hall in Liverpool. It exemplifies the emotive power and austere authority of Neoclassicism.	Auguste de Montferrand (1786–1858) completes St. Isaac's Cathedral (see p.278) in St. Petersburg, Russia.

(1774–89), and planned and designed the elevations of Charlotte Square, as well as a new building to replace the Old College (see image 2) of the University of Edinburgh. Although both remained unfinished at his death they constitute the best surviving examples of Adam's contributions to cityscapes in Britain.

Adam also developed the Adam castle style. This was a creative reinvention of Norman, late Roman imperial, Scottish tower house architecture, and other castellated forms. The Romantic silhouette was devised, as Adam wrote, to give "the rise and fall, the advance and recess. . .convexity and concavity. . .to produce an agreeable and diversified contour, that. . .creates a variety of light and shade, which gives great spirit, beauty and effect to the composition." The style, which is almost entirely free of ornamental detailing and with plans developed from simple but idiosyncratic geometries, recalls the plans of French visionary architects. Adam's castles are among the most ingenious abstract compositions ever realized, two of the best being Culzean Castle in Ayrshire (1772–90) and Seton Castle in East Lothian (1789).

Unlike the settled political climate of Britain in the eighteenth century, France experienced social and cultural upheaval culminating in the Revolution in 1789. Even before the collapse of academicism in 1793 there had been evidence of political tension in the work of French architects. The logic of structure, first explored by theorist Abbé Carlo Lodoli in Italy, was integrated into French academic theory. Abbé Marc-Antoine Laugier, a theorist and tutor, argued in the second edition of his *Essay on Architecture* (1755) that architecture should return to its origins in the primitive hut and dispense with superfluous ornament in favor of structural necessity alone. Claude-Nicolas Ledoux (1736–1806) and others were committed to a return to an architecture founded on basic principles. Their buildings were formal reductions of Platonic solids. For his unbuilt (and unbuildable) funerary monument to the English physicist Isaac Newton—a hero of the new empirical and scientific age—Etienne-Louis Boullée (1728–99) invented a spherical planetarium to represent Newton's intellectual achievement (see image 3). Ornament was banished in favor of imagery that embodied the literal or symbolic function of the building. For example, in Ledoux's plans for the Royal Saltworks at Arc-et-Senans—a utopian project intended to provide for every possible need of its citizens—the planning and distribution of the buildings were hierarchical and expressive. The house of the works' manager and the schoolhouse were overscaled with panopticonlike

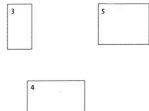

rooftop observatories. Such calculated social control was in fact benign and was intended to create a new kind of public-spirited, even heroic citizen.

The political foundations of the United States were equally inspired by a vision of a democratic society based on liberty and equality, and embodied in Neoclassical architecture. President and political theorist Thomas Jefferson (1743–1826) planned an ideal community—an "academical village" with parallel ranks of pavilions—at the University of Virginia, Charlottesville. The Rotunda library (see image 4) , which stood at the head of a lawn surrounded by pavilions, quoted the dome of the Roman Pantheon but in a mood that is domestic and informal. When fire destroyed the wooden dome and gutted the library in 1895, McKim, Mead & White, who held Jefferson's architecture in high esteem, were commissioned to rebuild (externally) to Jefferson's original design but with the addition of a north portico to echo the original south portico facing Jefferson's lawn. Although there is a distinctive tendency in Neoclassical architecture to quote accurately from antiquity this was rarely done slavishly, and most Neoclassical buildings are inventive adaptations of antique forms.

In other contexts, Neoclassicism was a fashion. During his military campaigns, Napoleon Bonaparte took the opportunity offered by his occupation of Italy and Egypt to plunder valuable antiquities that were later installed in the Louvre, Paris. This influx of rare and exotic objects resulted in the Empire style in France. Charles Percier (1764–1838) and Pierre Fontaine (1762–1853) designed and renovated suites of rooms for Napoleon and the Empress Josephine at Chateau de Malmaison (see image 5), and the style spread to include dress, hairstyles, crockery, textiles, and furniture. By the turn of the nineteenth century, architectural education in France, as elsewhere, was directed toward the practical demands of increasingly complex public institutions for the industrial economies and empires. In order to meet this demand, Neoclassicism, which previously was employed for single monumental structures, was adapted for commerce, government, hospitals, and universities. In France, Jean-Nicolas-Louis Durand (1760–1834), a tutor at Ecole Polytechnique in Paris, published the *Précis des leçons d'architecture données à l'École royale polytechnique* (1809). This book formalized architectural plans and building types, and provided patterns that enabled nineteenth-century architects to tackle large complex institutional buildings. **MS**

3 **Monument to Isaac Newton (1784)**
Etienne-Louis Boullée

4 **The Rotunda (1826)**
Thomas Jefferson
University of Virginia,
Charlottesville, Virginia, USA

5 **Empress Josephine's Bedroom (1800–02)**
Charles Percier and Pierre Fontaine
Chateau de Malmaison,
Rueil-Malmaison, France

Panthéon 1758–90

J-G SOUFFLOT 1713–80,   J-B RONDELET 1743–1829

Panthéon,
Paris, France

❖ NAVIGATOR

Founded as a church, the Panthéon was built by Louis XV in thanksgiving for his recovery from a serious illness in 1744. The task of overseeing its construction was given to the Marquis de Marigny, and in 1755 he commissioned Jacques-Germain Soufflot as architect. The church was planned as a vast Greek cross—360⅞ feet (110 m) long and 278⅞ feet (85 m) wide—and with a dome 272¼ feet (83 m) off the ground. Covering the enormous spans posed structural challenges that impacted on the design and prolonged its construction from 1758 to 1790. It was completed ten years after Soufflot's death, by his pupil, Jean-Baptiste Rondelet. The giant Roman Corinthian order of the portico was also used for the interior colonnades that support a continuous entablature binding together the entire interior space. The dome over the crossing is constructed of three shells: the lower shell is coffered in the Roman fashion, with an oculus to the second shell; the exterior dome is (unusually) built on stone masonry secured with iron clamps and covered with lead. The church is one of the first professionally engineered buildings. Gothic structures were studied, stones tested for structural strength, and steel pinning introduced following careful mathematical calculations for the vaulting system. **MS**

1 CAPITAL

The fine acanthus leaf capitals exemplify the expenditure lavished on this building by the last two kings of the *ancient regime*. The accurate interpretation of the Corinthian order, confers an Antique authority to this modern building.

2 PEDIMENT

The pediment sculpture (1830–37) by Pierre-Jean David depicts St. Geneviève, patron saint of Paris. In 1790, the church became a national mausoleum for the heroic French dead. The inscription on the pediment reads: "To great men, their grateful country."

3 COLUMNS

The six columns at the front of the building form a hexastyle portico. The church was secularized and renamed after the Pantheon of Rome in 1790, and the portico is the only part of the Panthéon that resembles its Roman namesake.

◄ The structural innovations devised by Soufflot and his team of engineers enable the lofty interior to be filled with light and a sense of weightlessness. This is the first example of the idea that a building's final image could be obtained from engineering rather than simply from the repetition of traditional architectural forms.

🕐 ARCHITECT PROFILE

1713–37

Jacques-Germain Soufflot was born at Irancy, in Auxerre, France. In 1731, he studied in Italy, including a period at the Royal Academy in Rome, where he developed his knowledge of Andrea Palladio (1508–80) and surveyed St. Peter's in Rome, Milan Cathedral, and the Greek temples at Paestum.

1738–63

On his return to France in 1738, he settled in Lyon, where he became a member of the Académie Royale, and was soon employed to alter several important civic buildings. His reputation as a scholar-architect who was familiar with Italy and the Neoclassical style of his work attracted the attention of Louis XV's mistress, Madame de Pompadour. In 1750, she asked Soufflot to accompany her young brother on a study tour of Italy in advance of his appointment as Director General

of Royal Buildings for Louis XV. On his return, Soufflot designed the Théâtre du Quartier St. Clair in Lyon, which opened in 1756. In 1755, Marigny appointed him architect of the Panthéon in Paris. At the Panthéon, Soufflot uniquely combined Gothic construction with ancient classical architecture thereby demonstrating new structural possibilities.

1764–80

Soufflot published *Suite de plans de trois temples à Péstum* (*Plans of Three Temples at Paestum*) in 1764. The Panthéon dominated the rest of his career but he executed other works, including Chateau de Menars (1764) on the bank of the Loire and Hôtel Marigny (1771) in Paris. In later years he became skilled at designing nymphaeums (1774–77), or grottoes, including one for Marigny and another for Monsieur Bertin, a minister of state, at Chatou, near Paris.

St. Isaac's Cathedral 1818–58
AUGUSTE DE MONTFERRAND 1786–1858

St. Isaac's Cathedral
(Isaakievskiy Sobor),
St. Petersburg, Russia

⟡ NAVIGATOR

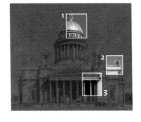

St. Isaac's is one of the tallest cathedrals ever built and one of the few Orthodox churches built in a Westernized Neoclassical style. Its vast structure took forty years to complete at great cost to human life and to the government of Czar Alexander I, who commissioned it. St. Isaac's was the life's work of its French architect, Auguste de Montferrand. Although his design was criticized by the czar's commissioners, it was the one preferred by Alexander I. The design reflects Montferrand's French Neoclassical training (he had studied under Charles Percier in Paris) and his particular knowledge of the Panthéon (1790; see p.276) in Paris. There are also strong echoes of the Palladian church in the central Russian town of Nevyansk. The cruciform plan has four octastyle pedimented porticoes with Corinthian capitals of red granite. Montferrand carefully scaled the enormous height of the central dome, and as a result the high drum and golden dome rise majestically over the cityscape. Although the cathedral is self-evidently Neoclassical in scale, form, and detailing, the Greek cross plan, the extremely high central dome over the central crossing, four subsidiary domes on the south and north roofs, the polychromy of the exterior, and its opulent interior place it firmly within the Orthodox tradition. During the Soviet period the church became the Museum of Atheism. Although still officially a museum, it was renovated and restored to the Orthodox Church after the fall of the Soviet Union and services have resumed. **MS**

⊙ FOCAL POINTS

1 DOME

The central dome is plated in pure gold and is 333 feet (101.5 m) high. William Handyside (1793–1850), the cathedral's Scottish engineer, gilded the dome with liquid gold in a mercury solvent. He also designed a cast-iron structural frame comprising three hemispherical shells to support the dome.

2 SCULPTURE

On the attic level are pairs of angels that were sculpted by Ivan Petrovich Vitali. Their Baroque forms disclose Vitali's Italian heritage from his father, Pietro Vitali, a naturalized Russian sculptor. Fitted with gas burners, the torches held by the angels were traditionally lit at Easter time.

3 COLUMNS

The monolithic columns in the cathedral's porticoes and domes are made of polished red granite. Each column weighs up to 114 tons. The engineer William Handyside solved considerable problems of building on this scale, including the special lifting frames he devised for placing each of the 112 columns.

▲ The interior is decorated with sculpture, carving, gilding, and colored marble, including green malachite for the giant order columns and deep blue lazurite for the subsidiary columns.

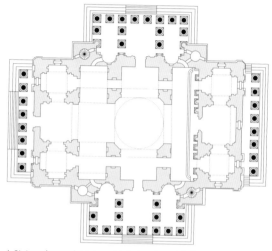

▲ St. Isaac's cruciform layout is in keeping with the traditional Greek cross plan used for all Orthodox churches.

RUSSIAN CHURCH DESIGN

Church building in Russia began with the Christian conversion in 988. Early churches had cross-in-square plans embellished with gilded domes, polychromy (derived from the Byzantine tradition), and typical roofscapes comprising tiers of tiara-shaped gables and onion domes. This was all derived from carpentry construction. Foreign influences had a notable impact, but local tendencies were never entirely obliterated. Hence, the "tented" roof of stone cathedrals such as St. Basil's (1561; right) in Moscow, the extravagant ornamentation of the Naryshkin Baroque of the 1690s, and the richly colored stucco walls and jewel-like interiors of the 18th-century St. Petersburg palaces all represent Russian taste. For 18th-century Rome-trained architects such as Charles Cameron (1745–1812), Russia provided opportunities to experiment with luxurious decor on a scale unavailable to most other Neoclassical architects in the West.

GREEK REVIVAL

1 **Bank of England (1826)**
Sir John Soane
London, UK

2 **Tower of the Winds (1764)**
James Stuart
Shugborough Hall, Staffordshire, UK

3 **Brandenburg Gate (1788–91)**
Carl Gotthard Langhans
Berlin, Germany

P art of the Ottoman Empire from the mid-fifteenth century, Greece was
largely inaccessible to the Western visitor, although incursions by British
and French travelers with antiquarian interests occurred throughout the
sixteenth and seventeenth centuries. In 1699, following defeat by the Holy
League in the Great Turkish War, the Ottomans agreed peace under the Treaty
of Karlowitz, which included ceding extensive territories. Spasmodic conflict
persisted, but relative peace created safer conditions for culturally adventurous
travelers. By the 1750s, southern Europe and Asia Minor (modern Turkey) were
on the itinerary of the Grand Tour. Direct exposure to Hellenic sites further
stimulated a general intellectual enthusiasm for ancient Greece and the Antique.

Early travelers were mainly English and included James Stuart (1713–88)
and Nicholas Revett (1720–1804). In 1751, they embarked on detailed studies
of the major monuments; their four-volume series *The Antiquities of Athens*
(1762–1816) was designed as accurate archaeological description and architectural
treatise. From 1800, a profusion of British, including William Wilkins (1778–1839)
and Robert Smirke (1780–1867), traveled to Greece and were followed in the
next decade by many architects of the succeeding generation. The result was
a plethora of scholarly architectural and archaeological publications amply
illustrated with measured drawings taken directly from original sources.

The Greek Revival was not solely about superficial emulation of historic
style, however. As the culminating phase of Neoclassicism (see p.272), it aimed
for a new approach to composition and demanded classical orders be used

KEY EVENTS

1751	1758	1762	1788	1798	1800–10
Funded by the Society of Dilettanti, James Stuart and Nicholas Revett travel to Greece, excavating, measuring, and recording Grecian antiquities.	Stuart builds the Doric landscape temple at Hagley Park, Staffordshire. Greek Revivalism is launched with the earliest use of Grecian Doric.	Stuart and Revett publish the first volume of *The Antiquities of Athens*, an archaeological record and architectural treatise of Grecian taste.	Carl Gotthard Langhans begins work on the Brandenburg Gate in Berlin. Modeled on the Propylaea, it is the earliest Greek Revival structure in Germany.	Napoleon Bonaparte's invasion of Egypt results in a Western enthusiasm for ancient Egyptian art, history, and culture.	A flood of English tourists and architects to Greece results in a plethora of illustrated architectural and archaeological publications.

honestly rather than as decoration. Aspects of the Picturesque were also embraced with an emphasis on disparity, asymmetry and variety. Up to the turn of the nineteenth century, the main figures of the Greek Revival, and those most associated with the earliest use of the Greek Doric order, were Stuart, Revett, Joseph Bonomi (1739–1808), and Benjamin Henry Latrobe (1764–1820), best known as the architect of the White House and Capitol in Washington, D.C. Key early works include Stuart's temple and Tower of the Winds at Shugborough Hall (see image 2), Revett's portico at Standlynch, Wiltshire (1766), and Latrobe's Paestum portico at Hammerwood House, Sussex (1793).

Development in the early years proved slow, partly due to opposition from "anti-Greek" architects, including Sir William Chambers (1723–96) and Robert Adam (1728–92); however, the first decade of the nineteenth century proved a turning point. In 1806, the highly influential, remodeled Stratton Park, Hampshire, by George Dance (1741–1825) combined austere geometry with a Paestum-derived Doric portico, and in 1809 Smirke's Doric Covent Garden Theatre in London found widespread favor. After 1810, the Grecian style became the dominant architectural style in burgeoning cities, such as Liverpool, Manchester, and Bristol. Public buildings were eminently appropriate to the style, as exemplified in the Bank of England (see image 1) by Sir John Soane (1753–1837) and Smirke's British Museum, London (1823–47).

Greek primacy, however, was short lived in England, and by the 1840s Gothic (see p.148) and Italianate styles were in the ascendant. Greek Revival remained in favor in Scotland as late as the 1870s. St. Vincent Street Church (1859) in Glasgow, by Alexander "Greek" Thomson (1817–75), sits on massive plinths on a steep site. Greek and Egyptian Revival are evident, but Thomson was said to have taken inspiration from the Temple of Solomon, considered "divine" architecture by Freemasons and the font of Vitruvian ideas, as well as the Corinthian, Doric, and Ionic orders of classical architecture. Greek Revivalism was less popular in France, and in Germany it centered on Munich and Berlin, where it was heavily patronized by the courts of Ludwig I and Frederick William II. The latter commissioned Berlin's Brandenburg Gate (see image 3), based on the Propylaea (437–432 BCE; see p.38), the gateway to the Acropolis in Athens, and designed by Carl Gotthard Langhans (1732–1808). German Greek Revival reached its zenith with the Glyptothek (1816–30) and Walhalla (1816–42) by Leo von Klenze (1784–1864), and in Berlin with the Neue Wache (1818) and Altes Museum (1823–30) by Karl Friedrich Schinkel (1781–1841).

Latrobe emigrated to the United States in 1796 and shortly afterward was appointed Surveyor of Public Building by Thomas Jefferson (1743–1826). His works in Washington and Philadelphia, and subsequent influence on pupils and followers, such as William Strickland (1788–1854), Thomas Walter (1804–87), and Robert Mills (1781–1855), effectively made Greek Revival the national style of the nascent United States. **RS**

1804	1821–33	1822	1830	1830	1848
An Ionic design by William Wilkins defeats James Wyatt's Doric design in the competition for Downing College, Cambridge.	The Greek War of Independence occurs. Hellenism and Grecian style reign supreme in the West and are a major influence across all the arts.	William and Henry Inwood build the St. Pancras New Church (see p.282). Nearly thirty London Greek Revival churches are built in this period.	Karl Friedrich Schinkel finishes the Altes Museum in Berlin, marking the high point of his career.	Greek Revival reaches its apogee in England. It is followed by a strong Victorian reaction to Regency Greek.	Thomas Walter finishes Girard College for Orphans in Philadelphia, one of the last expressions of Greek Revival style.

St. Pancras New Church 1822

WILLIAM INWOOD c. 1771–1843, HENRY INWOOD 1794–1843

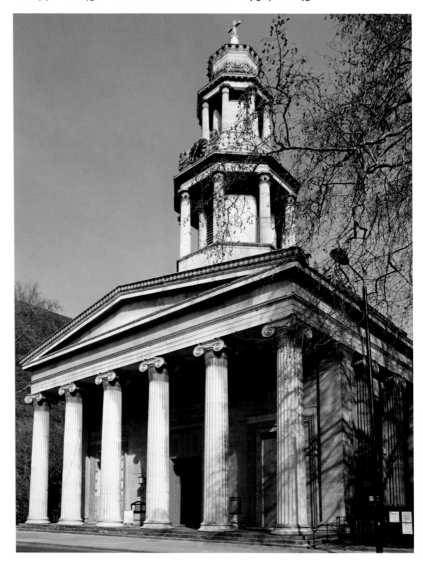

St Pancras New Church,
London, UK

✦ NAVIGATOR

L ocal architect William Inwood won an open competition with his son, Henry, to
design St. Pancras New Church, one of the first to be built in the Greek Revival style.
The brick base is faced with Portland stone, the ubiquitous building stone of London.
The west end follows the steeple/portico pattern of Anglican preaching church design,
established by James Gibbs (1682–1754) at St. Martin-in-the-Fields (1724) and paraphrased
from classical Greek prototypes. Henry's tour to Greece followed the competition win, so
initial inspiration may have included engravings and the lantern circle of Greek-inspired
Coade stone caryatids in the Bank of England Stock Office (1792) by Sir John Soane.
Caryatid porches flank the north and south sides of the east end apse. The hollow
caryatids, with internal cast iron to support the weight of the entablature, function as
columns in female form (the male version is an atlante). Although the north porch is a
bold feature on London's Euston Road, the church was not universally praised at the time.
The *London Magazine* decried "the tawdry prodigality of the heathen temple at Pancras." **RS**

FOCAL POINTS

1 TOWER

The triple-staged octagonal tower is an interpretation of the first-century BCE Tower of the Winds in Athens. The lower two stages have fluted columns and sit on Portland stone ashlar drums. The tower terminates in an octagonal drum with anthemion banding, corbelled entablature and finial bearing a cross.

2 PORTICO

The full-width hexastyle Ionic portico, raised on a platform of three steps, is directly based upon the east portico of the Erechtheum on the Acropolis (fifth century BCE). The capitals feature a deep ornamental band, decorated with anthemion and palmette motifs, terminating the fluted shafts below the volutes.

3 ENTRANCE DOORS

Three trapezoidal openings, with heavily paneled timber doors, give access to the interior. Their richly molded architraves consist of alternating bands of rosettes, bead-and-reel astragals, guilloche, and variants of waterleaf and dart decoration, based upon plaster casts taken from the Erechtheum.

▲ The caryatids differ from the Greek originals because they hold a lowered torch and a water ewer, symbolizing mortality and their role as guardians over the entrance to the burial vaults.

COADE STONE

Ruth Siddall of University College London Department of Earth Sciences made a report in 2013 of the materials used in St. Pancras New Church; they include several that contribute to a convincing three-dimensional *trompe l'oeil* effect. The entrance porch doorway moldings and motifs are fake Portland stone, molded from crushed limestone and cement. The female caryatids are not stone, but an architectural stoneware ceramic made of "grog" (waste ceramic), quartz sand, and flint, based on an original recipe from Coade's Artificial Stone Manufactory, London. Founder Eleanor Coade refined the original recipe to make Coade stone the most successful "fake stone" in Britain. Her products were used in country houses, at the Royal Pavilion, Brighton (1823), and by William Frederick Woodington to sculpt the Coade Lion (1837; right) on Westminster Bridge.

GOTHIC REVIVAL

1 **Strawberry Hill (1760–90)**
Horace Walpole
Twickenham, UK

2 **Fonthill Abbey (1796–1809)**
James Wyatt
Fonthill Gifford, Wiltshire, UK

3 **Hadlow Tower (1840)**
Sir Walter Barton May
Hadlow Castle, Hadlow, Kent, UK

T hree key components—decay, dogma, and decline—mark the timeline of Gothic Revival, the architectural style that began with Horace Walpole's residence at Strawberry Hill, Twickenham (see image 1), and continues into the twenty-first century with Whitman College, Princeton University, New Jersey (2007) by Demetri Porphyrios (b.1949). Britain was the font of the revival, but style exemplars occurred in continental Europe, Ireland, Russia, and colonial outposts. Many of Gothic Revival's highest highs and lowest lows were mooted and built in the United States, but in Britain it became in effect the quasi-official style creating a unique epoch in British architectural history.

The revival style that emerged in the late eighteenth century was influenced directly by the Gothic style that began in northern France in the early twelfth century (see p.148) and continued into the seventeenth century as Gothic Survival. Its re-emergence is credited to the literary genre of Gothic novels, incuding Walpole's *The Castle of Otranto* (1764). Tropes from the novel are reflected in Strawberry Hill, where he incorporated medieval architectural fragments, anticipating the nineteenth-century popularity of mixing myriad satellite styles that fall within the Gothic rubric. Walpole's studied decay—inaccuracy, antiquarianism, and theatricality—became widely influential.

Fonthill Abbey (see image 2) epitomizes the elements of "unreality" that were prevalent in early Gothic Revival before Augustus Pugin used Gothic

KEY EVENTS

1764	1824	1836	1838	1843	1846
The "crumbling castle" theme of Horace Walpole's novel *The Castle of Otranto* sets the tone for the early stages of Gothic Revival.	Sir Walter Scott (1771–1832) transforms a medieval ruin into Abbotsford House. It inspires the Scottish Gothic Revival.	Augustus Pugin publishes *Contrasts*, which argues for a revival of medieval Gothic architecture.	Alexander Jackson Davis designs Lyndhurst mansion in Tarrytown, New York. He becomes one of the United States's prime exponents of the Gothic Revival.	James Renwick (1818–95) wins the competition to design Grace Church, New York City. It references York and Beverly Minsters in England.	Richard Upjohn (1802–78) designs Trinity Church in Manhattan and diffuses ecclesiological influence along the United States's eastern seaboard.

Revival as an expressive and realistic response to functional building problems. Designed by James Wyatt (1746–1813), Fonthill was a constructed "medieval relic," but Wyatt raised the bar with his use of asymmetry and the careful placement of towers and spires to create shadows and intense atmosphere. Considered a grotesquerie that mirrored its eccentric commissioner, William Beckford (1760–1844), the building's failure was fueled by Beckford's interference, abetted by speculative or insufficiently tested materials. Sections routinely failed, often in dramatic fashion. The main tower collapsed in 1825, probably caused by Beckford's insatiable desire for increasing the tower's height. Despite Fonthill's notorious collapse, Sir Walter Barton May modeled his octagonal tower (see image 3) at Hadlow Castle, Kent, on Fonthill.

The early period was not all shortcuts and sham. The Russian Orthodox square-plan Gothic Chapel (1834) in St. Petersburg was inspired by antiquarianism and theatricality, supported by sound engineering. Architect and set designer Karl Friedrich Schinkel (1781–1841) designed it as a domestic chapel for the Romanov family. His bijou may resemble one of his stage sets, but his study of original Gothic cathedrals and his insistence on engineering accuracy enabled the chapel to survive multiple wars.

By the mid-nineteenth century, Gothic Revival was notable for dogma, diametrical opposition, and extremes of style. The revival reached its zenith with the Palace of Westminster (1840–70; see p.270) in London by Sir Charles Barry (1795–1860) and Augustus Pugin (1812–52), while the Oxbridge Ecclesiologists and Tractarians championed Gothic as the only style of architecture appropriate for the parish churches that were being built to accommodate the growing population. Pugin embraced the medieval ethos and Gothic as the only Christian form of architecture. Although the Houses of Parliament is his best-known work, his Roman Catholic church, St. Giles in Cheadle (see image 5), inspired a generation. Equally influential was All Saints Church in Fitzrovia, London (see image 4): an unconventional masterpiece designed by William Butterfield (1814–1900). An interpretation of the exuberant "Holy Zebra" style of brickwork, All Saints's exterior—with horizontal bands of black and red bricks bracing an upper register of brickwork crockets—is a mix of English, Byzantine, and Flemish influences.

The amateur antiquarianism of Walpole led indirectly to a desire to preserve and renew the original Gothic buildings that had inspired the revival. Frenchman Eugène Emmanuel Viollet-le-Duc (1814–79) and Englishman John Ruskin (1819–1900) led the movement, but their methods differed. Whereas Ruskin advocated an architectural version of the medical dictum *Primum non nocere* (First, do no harm), Viollet-le-Duc insisted that the "patient" should not only be saved but also should live as an improved version, using engineering and materials that would have been unknown to medieval craftsmen. Although his methods are now largely abandoned, Viollet-le-Duc's

1859	1859	1861	1862	1868	1878
The publication of the anonymous tract "A Word to the Goths" highlights the divisiveness of hardcore adherents to "pure" Gothic Revival.	The Gothic Revival precinct at Parliament Hill, Ottawa, Canada, is begun. It dismisses the United States's Neoclassical style for government buildings.	The beginning of the American Civil War marks the rise of the military Gothic Revival: a profusion of armories, arsenals, prisons, and asylums.	The "Battle of the Styles" in Britain and the United States exposes the ideological underpinnings of Neoclassicism (see p.272) vs. Gothic Revival.	The construction of St. Pancras Station and Midland Grand Hotel, London, by George Gilbert Scott, begins (see p.290).	Harvard University Memorial Hall is completed in Collegiate Gothic Style. By this date, Gothic Revival is seen as reactionary rather than revolutionary.

influence lives on in the popularity of architecture as entertainment, as seen in twentieth-century projects such as Disneyland, California (1955). Ruskin's influence made architecture part of a discussion of culture, and his belief that restoration equals destruction continues to influence contemporary academic practice and guides the principles of modern preservation. The decaying glory of Venice was Ruskin's *vade mecum*, his map and guide to understanding medieval architecture, and his highly influential books *The Stones of Venice* (1851–53) and *The Seven Lamps of Architecture* (1849) inspired architects to value the craftsman but "do no harm."

Competitions were increasingly popular ways to attract architect submissions for new buildings without the expense of speculative commissioning. However, the practice was widely condemned. U.S. architects believed that the majority of competitions were rigged (the outcome known in advance), cribbed (commissioners would not declare a winner so they could steal submissions and build on the cheap), showy (style over substance in presentation drawings), and shameful (the entire process was wicked). When George Gilbert Scott (1811–78) competed to design the government offices at Whitehall, London (1861–75), political chicanery skewed the outcome. His Gothic design (with a prominent external helical staircase inspired by the Chateau de Chambord, France, 1519–47) did not rank first. Nevertheless, Scott was appointed. When the Conservative government was routed, the prime minister, Lord Palmerston, demanded a new outcome. The merits of Classical versus Gothic were debated in Parliament and reported in the press. Which was better, "the rounded arch or the pointed spire, the horizontal line or the perpendicular, the flat cornice or the broken gable, Pagan symmetry or Christian symbolism, Greek Gods or Gothic gargoyles?" Underlying notions of nationhood provoked Palmerston to question whether the Gothic style was national enough. Scott swiftly jettisoned his Gothic submission in favor of a Byzantine then a classical design. Palmerston prevailed and Scott's Classical Revival offices were built.

In the United States, Gothic Revival was considered a choice for the many, whereas Greek Revival (see p.280) was a style for the few. The idea that Gothic

4 **All Saints Church (1859)**
William Butterfield
Fitzrovia, London, UK

5 **St. Giles Church (1841–46)**
Augustus Pugin
Cheadle, Staffordshire, UK

6 **St. Elizabeths Hospital (1855)**
Thomas Walter
Washington, D.C., USA

belonged to everyone made it a popular option in the United States, where the democratization of pattern books led to a profusion of Gothic Revival cottages as championed by Andrew Jackson Downing (1815–52) and Alexander Jackson Davis (1803–92). Simple timber iterations called "Carpenter Gothic" (see p.288) came to be viewed as uniquely American, immortalized in Grant Woods's painting *American Gothic* (1930), in which a stoic farmer and his daughter stand in front of their Carpenter Gothic homestead. The most exemplary and joyous U.S. rural "cottage villa" is Roseland Cottage in Woodstock, Connecticut. Roseland has survived almost wholly intact inside and out, and retains its Downing-inspired landscape. Built in 1846 for Henry Chandler Bowen by Joseph Collins Wells (1814–60), a founder of the American Institute of Architects, Roseland is a textbook example of Gothic Revival. Its board-and-batten exterior is painted in the original pink with red and forest-green trim. Details are quintessentially Gothic Revival: quatrefoil bargeboards, crockets, and finials.

Within the Gothic Revival, there was one area of architectural design that was both championed and vilified: "mongrel" builds, which combined various revival styles. In 1877, the *New York Times* fulminated against professional architects whom they held responsible for creating rules that only they could break. Many architects were either incapable of successfully mixing styles or did so at the insistence of a commissioner. The riotous, unchecked mishmash of buildings designed by the moderately gifted for the enormously wealthy was one of the primary reasons for the decline of Gothic Revival.

By the end of the nineteenth century, Gothic Revival was out of favor as an academic style. It splintered into three architectural ciphers: conservative (castellated complexes to house militia headquarters, armories, prisons, and asylums), nostalgic (universities and colleges), and eccentric (The Great Mausoleum at Forest Lawn Cemetery, Glendale, California, 1906). Historian Kenneth Clark summed up the opinion of many when he wrote in 1928, that Gothic Revival "produced so little on which our eyes can rest without pain."

Despite Clark's comment, Gothic Revival survived the twentieth century, to emerge in the twenty-first as increasingly representative of conservative values. St. Elizabeths Hospital (see image 6), Washington, D.C., was designed by Thomas Walter (1804–87) in Italianate Gothic Revival style. Opened in 1855 as "The Government Hospital for the Insane," it was used as a military hospital during the American Civil War (1861–65). The vast historic campus, with its listed Center Building, has been deeded to "The Department of Homeland Security," the U.S. Government agency created in 2001 the wake of 9/11. In one of the largest U.S. government development projects since the Pentagon (1943), and not scheduled for completion until 2026, the once wildly popular, universally democratic Gothic Revival style has been enlisted to fight the war on terror. **DJ**

St. Andrew's Church 1853–54
ATTRIBUTED TO PETER LEE AND JOE GLASGOW

St. Andrew's Church, Prairieville, Hale County (formerly Macon, Marengo County) Alabama, USA

⬧ NAVIGATOR

St. Andrew's Church is an exquisite example of Carpenter Gothic, a uniquely American diffusion of Gothic Revival. It is also a lesson in how ecclesiological dogma can be translated, with limited means and simple materials, into an architectural example that illuminates the doctrine of divine simplicity. The church's fortunes were bolstered by Henry Augustine Tayloe, scion of wealthy Virginia slaveholders, and two of his master carpenter slaves—Peter Lee and Joe Glasgow—are credited with building St. Andrew's Church. The design is probably copied from Richard Upjohn's *Rural Architecture: Designs, Working Drawings, and Specifications for a Wooden Church, and other Rural Structures* (1852). On a raised foundation to avoid problems with expansive clay, St. Andrew's is a simple frame clad in board and batten. A dormer with lancet window projects from the steep pitch shingle roof. Stepped vertical buttresses provide decoration, with clasping buttresses holding the corners. Single and twinned lancet windows illuminate the nave, and a trinity of lancets highlights the east chancel. The open-beam ceiling is braced with carved quatrefoil bolection molding, and the southeast entrance has a lancet door. The church was consecrated in 1858 when a lien on the church was repaid. **DJ**

1 FOUNDATION AND BUTTRESSES

Sham, non-supporting buttresses are a deviation from Upjohn's pattern-book plan. Their functional role is to bridge the visual gap between the pier and beam raised foundation and the ground, and to add visual rhythm to the red-brick pier footings.

2 SIDING

Board-and-batten siding is a distinct feature of Carpenter Gothic. Wide planks are fixed vertically to the wooden frame with joins hidden by narrow vertical battens. Vertical boards, lancet windows and steeply pitched gables signpost the godliness of "Upjohn Gothic."

3 FRETWORK

Curvilinear bargeboard made with a hand fret-saw decorates the two sides of the gable entrance porch and the small dormer window on the opposite elevation. The addition of pierced decorative trim is a common feature of Carpenter Gothic style.

◄ Hand-carved pews, quatrefoil molding, the altar rail, and other furniture in the interior of St. Andrew's are attributed to Peter Lee. Upjohn specified that church furniture be "made in strict accordance with the plans and well put together'."

ARCHITECTURE PATTERN BOOKS

Before there were professional architects, architecture books were used to realize buildings. Pattern books (right), such as James Gibbs's *A Book of Architecture* (1728), were expensive publications prized for *à la mode* designs and classical precedents, whereas handbooks were aimed at the average man. Asher Benjamin wrote the first United States handbook, *The Country Builder's Assistant* (1797). His subsequent books were necessary, he said, because few European handbooks were useful to United States builders. Handbooks were usually classed as "tools" and therefore exempt assets in the event of bankruptcy. Plan books evolved from pattern books and replaced handbooks after architects became professionalized.

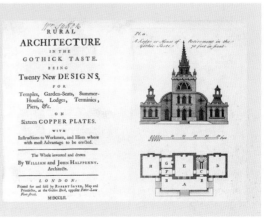

St. Pancras Station and Midland Grand Hotel 1868–76

GEORGE GILBERT SCOTT 1811–78

St. Pancras Station and
Midland Grand Hotel,
Euston Road, London, UK

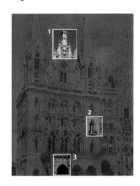
Fierce competition and a desire to overshadow the Neoclassical King's Cross Station (1851–52) and Great Northern Hotel (1854), designed by Lewis Cubitt (1799–1883), were the impetus for George Gilbert Scott's magnum opus: St. Pancras Station and Midland Grand Hotel. Midland Railway rented "running rights" from the Great Northern Railway, whose London terminus was King's Cross. However, congested tracks meant delays for Midland's trains and so the company countered by building a dedicated four-track railroad and terminus next door to King's Cross. In the shadow of Scott's Gothic Revival colossus, Great Northern's station and hotel were demoted to bit-player status. Midland's triumphant architectural message was further underscored by a statue of centurion-clad Britannia staring down triumphantly at King's Cross.

St. Pancras Station's polychromatic, Venetian-inspired facade dominates Euston Road. The most impressive interior element is the double grand staircase, a feature of Neo-Renaissance architecture. Few would disagree with railway historian Christian Wolmar's assessment of St. Pancras: "No doubt the grandest and most famous station in Britain." Some might argue it is the grandest in Europe. **DJ**

◉ FOCAL POINTS

1 FLEMISH GABLES

Pitched-roof gables are faced with flat, Flemish gables, featuring "crow step" pediments. They are decorated with foliate crockets, rising to a chimneylike column. Gable faces are built with low-fired silica bricks, known as "rubbers," which can be carved for a superior fit and flush gable face.

2 WINDOWS

Mansfield Red sandstone— "one of the best building stones in the kingdom," according to Scott—is used to frame the windows. Mansfield Red columns support banded brick and stone voussoir arches with recessed trefoil arches. Some single windows have narrow-profile Juliet balconies supported by corbel tables.

3 ARCHES

"Light–dark" banded Neo-Byzantine arches reflect what John Ruskin termed "constructional polychromy." This lively element reflects the building's principal Venetian Gothic Revival style, which incorporates both Byzantine and Moorish influences. Gothic style was admired by Scott during his trip to Venice in 1851.

⏱ ARCHITECT PROFILE

1811–53

George Gilbert Scott was born in Buckinghamshire the son of a clergyman. Having studied architecture under James Edmeston (1791–1867), he worked for several architects before setting up his own practice when his father died. Inspired by the writings of Augustus Pugin, Scott restored many Gothic churches in keeping with the trend for preserving and "improving" medieval church architecture.

1854–78

The architect's career was at its peak from the mid-1850s to late 1860s, and he exerted a strong influence on the development of Gothic Revival style. His prolific output included the Albert Memorial, Kensington Gardens, London (1864–76). Scott's success continued toward the end of his career, but he was criticized for his overzealous church restorations. He was knighted in 1872 and died of heart failure in 1878.

▲ Scott's sweeping dual staircase is the hotel's focal point and frames a nineteenth-century mural of a scene from the illuminated manuscript *Roman de la Rose* (c.1500).

BEAUX ARTS

No art or architecture school has garnered more accolades and attracted more criticism than the Ecole des Beaux-Arts in Paris. From its official inception in 1819 to World War I, this state-sponsored, independently run institution trained an international roster of painters, sculptors, and architects, and its architecture section was the most populated.

In the nineteenth century, when office apprenticeship prevailed in most countries, the Ecole offered an unmatched framework to master the art, if not the science, of designing buildings. All scientific requirements were catered for in the second class, whereas the first class was dedicated to refining compositional and artistic skills. The ultimate goal was winning the Rome Prize, administered by the Institute of France. Students below the thirty-year age limit remained registered at the Ecole as long as they submitted two designs or took two examinations each year. Any admitted student could claim the official title of *ancien élève* (former student), even without earning a single credit, as did Charles McKim (1847–1909). The term "Ecole graduate" was restricted to recipients of the *diplôme*, a final project for those who had fulfilled requirements in both classes.

Attendance at lecture courses was not mandated and studies were governed by two tenets: the social and physical locus of the atelier and the

KEY EVENTS

1795	1819	1863–64	1867	1888	1898
The Institute of France is created in Paris, replacing the five Academies.	Royal edict institutionalizes the Ecole des Beaux-Arts, which moves to its current premises on the site of the Museum of French Monuments.	Authorities fail to impose the reforms of Eugène Viollet-le-Duc (1814–79) to update the Ecole curriculum and to limit the age of students to twenty-five.	The first *diplôme* is granted at the Ecole. This terminal professional degree is decried by promoters of architecture as an art form.	Students are allowed to select topics for the *diplôme*, yielding opportunities for socially and practically minded projects.	Julia Morgan (1872–1957) from California becomes the first female officially admitted to study architecture at the Ecole des Beaux-Arts.

292 1700–1870

medium of design competitions. The Ecole's precinct hosted three official architecture ateliers headed by government appointees. However, most students congregated in "outside" ateliers, headed by the critic of their choice—one of the most popular around 1900 was Victor Laloux (1850–1937), architect of the Gare d'Orsay (see image 1). Studio heads—Rome Prize winners and members of the Institute of France—trained selected students to enter competitions endowed with great prestige but commanding low success rates. One of them was the Prix Chenavard, open to Frenchmen only, which provided five students with a stipend and prize money to work on an ambitious topic of their choice. Paul Cret (1876–1945) was awarded second prize for his study of a commemorative monument at the Paris Panthéon (1903; see image 2).

The Ecole inherited its monthly core of competitions from the pre-revolutionary training offered by the Académie d'Architecture in Paris. These included twelve-hour sketch problems and projects lasting from three weeks to three months. Many competitions endowed by private donors and contests sponsored by the Institute of France were added over the course of the nineteenth century. Their various agendas, from interior detailing to master planning, offered opportunities to excel according to individual talent. Competitions followed a quasi-immutable ritual. Working in isolation and without aids, students were given a program and prepared a comprehensive sketch: they would be disqualified if their final project diverged too much from this sketch. Projects were developed in the atelier and transported by hand-held cart to the jury room. Submitted drawings had to be self-explanatory because their authors were barred from the jury room. Evaluation entailed a gradation of credits, from mentions to medals. The finale was a public display, enabling student work to be discussed in professional journals. Premiated drawings were reproduced in commercial portfolios and the Ecole retained the submissions awarded the highest marks in construction and first-class design.

Although the privately run Ecole Spéciale d'Architecture opened in Paris in 1864 and regional schools of fine art were authorized to confer *diplômes* after 1904, the Paris Ecole des Beaux-Arts maintained its monopoly on France's architectural education. Its principal mandate was to replenish the pool of designers that France and its colonies needed in order to modernize their infrastructure of administrative, educational, cultural, and penitentiary buildings. The most prestigious of these commissions went to Rome Prize winners.

The Ecole was bound to play an international role because only in Paris could aspiring architects find a comprehensive alternative to the engineering-oriented curriculum offered by German polytechnic schools. While its French alumni started teaching and practicing in places as far afield as Brazil, the Ecole welcomed European students, especially from Switzerland and Romania. The British contingent, albeit modest, included Royal Academy Professor Richard Phené Spiers (1838–1916), Royal Gold Medalist John Burnet (1814–1901)

1 Gare d'Orsay (1900)
Victor Laloux
Paris, France

2 Concours Chenavard: A commemorative monument at the Paris Panthéon (1903)
Paul Cret

1898–99	1910	1913	1915–17	1968	1975
Won by a Frenchman, the competition for the UC-Berkeley Campus is symptomatic of the international prestige of Ecole-trained architects.	Paul Cret completes the Organization of American States in Washington, D.C. (see p.298).	The first French woman is admitted to study architecture at the Ecole des Beaux-Arts.	The Ecole des Beaux-Arts closes its doors as the bloodshed of World War I greatly affects its current and recent students.	Student unrest triggers the dismantling of the Ecole into smaller and highly differentiated architecture programs.	In the wake of postmodern Classicism, New York's Museum of Modern Art displays competition drawings from the Ecole des Beaux-Arts.

3

4

5

3 **Singer Building (1908)**
Ernest Flagg
New York, USA

4 **National Museum "George Enescu"**
(1901–03)
Ioan D. Berindei
Bucharest, Romania

5 **Petit Palais (1900)**
Charles Girault
Paris, France

and Louis de Soissons (1890–1962), the designer of Welwyn Garden City in Hertfordshire (1920). In addition to the free tuition and critical mass of overachieving classmates, foreigners were attracted by the authentically Parisian mix of grandeur and charm of the Ecole's Left Bank precinct and by its unique folklore, epitomized by the boisterous Bal des Catz'Arts.

By 1900, when an annual admission cap of ninety Frenchmen and thirty foreigners was enforced, the architecture section attracted "South Americans, Spaniards, Portuguese, Persians—anything but Prussians," according to John Mead Howells (1868–1959), one of 102 United States citizens awarded a *diplôme* between 1895 and 1914. New York City, where Howells practiced, boasted the highest concentration of Paris-trained architects outside France. Indeed, nowhere was the architectural impact of the Ecole des Beaux-Arts more determinant than in the United States, which offered no formal academic training in architecture until the late 1860s. This snowball phenomenon began with the admission of Richard Morris Hunt (1827–95) in 1846, gathered momentum after Henry Hobson Richardson (1838–86) attended the Ecole in the 1860s, and acquired national significance in 1893 with the creation of the Society of Beaux-Arts Architects in New York City. World's Fairs held in Chicago in 1893, Paris in 1889 and 1900, Buffalo in 1901, and St. Louis in 1904 were major stimuli.

A belated and abbreviated Ecole tenure did not prevent Ernest Flagg (1857–1947), designer of the Singer Building (see image 3)—the world's tallest skyscraper upon its completion in 1908—from absorbing Ecole methods and from becoming one of its major champions in the United States. Lesser known but equally significant is the role of former Swiss and Romanian students returning home. For example, Ioan D. Berindei (1871–1928) studied under Honoré Daumet (1826–1911) and Charles Girault (1851–1932), who designed the new castle at Chantilly (1875–82) and Petit Palais (see image 5), respectively. For Romania's elite, Berindei produced the National Museum "George Enescu" in Cantacuzino Palace, Bucharest (see image 4), and homes reflecting either Belle Epoque cosmopolitanism or a simpler national style.

As foreigners flocked to Parisian ateliers and Frenchmen were called abroad to practice or teach, members of the French diaspora and indigenous Beaux-Arts lobbies played significant roles in enhancing architectural professionalism, education, and journalism. The Ecole regimen of preliminary non-negotiable sketches, swift rendering, and a closed-door jury led to success in professional competitions of national or international stature. Today, from Bucharest to Buenos Aires and from San Francisco to Brussels, the Beaux-Arts stamp survives in opera houses, civic structures, university campuses, and commemorative monuments as well as in luxury hotels and townhouses. Monumental flights of steps, colonnades, high-pitched and crested roofs, projecting pavilions, and overscaled swags echo those seen in Parisian landmarks. They prove that, despite its elite status, the production of Paris-trained architects was suited to accommodate rituals of democracy.

This international aesthetic, which Americans of the Gilded Age baptized "Modern French," finds its origin in the Paris Opéra House (1860–75; see p.296), designed by Charles Garnier (1825–98), at once bombastic and eminently "functional" for its festive purpose. The supervising office of the Opéra, where the hard-working but congenial atmosphere of a Beaux-Arts atelier prevailed, was also a training ground for a new generation of important designers and Ecole professors, such as Henri-Paul Nénot (1853–1934), Jean-Louis Pascal (1837–1920), and Julien Guadet (1834–1908). The international legacy of the Opéra Garnier is considerable. It is evidenced in Garnier's own Casino in Monte Carlo (1879), and an amusing pastiche is Rio's Municipal Theater, the design of which originated in 1903 in a competition won by Albert-Désiré Guilbert (1866–1949), a Parisian architect trained at the Ecole des Beaux-Arts.

Today, these buildings are considered to be "in the Beaux-Arts style." In Paris, architects were taught how to prepare meticulous ink washes and decorate walls and ceilings. Most importantly, they learned how to adopt a problem-solving mindset and conceptualize a set of functional and symbolic requirements dictated by a program. Through Ecole assignments and travel sketches, students gained an intimate knowledge of French historical styles up to 1750. However, Ecole competitions did not coerce students into adopting a dedicated style. Tenets pertaining to its peak years of influence around 1900 find their clearest expression in Guadet's *Eléments et Théorie de l'Architecture* (*Elements and Theory of Architecture*; 1901–04). His four-volume manual restated time-honored principles: the subservience of construction to design; the pre-eminence of two-dimensional drawings over "distorted" perspectives; the precedence of studies in plan; and the preference for symmetrical and axial composition and distrust of the picturesque. The notion of "character" was defined as "the connection between the architectural [design] content and the moral [cultural] content of the program." Trusting informed intuition, Guadet stressed the freedom that atelier heads had to adopt a personal teaching style and that students had to interpret a program, to select historic precedents best suited to the problem at hand and to manipulate "non-finite" proportions. His exposé of "elements" comprising a building started with walls, not antique orders. Guadet's major contribution was his distinction between rooms at the core of each program (lecture halls, courtrooms, etc.) and their ancillary spaces. This concept could be used regardless of style.

Guadet's book gave a nod to new commercial and residential programs and technologies, but did not embrace them. After World War I, the gap between academic teaching and real-life practice in France continued to widen. Many talented students were lost to the war and the Ecole attracted fewer foreigners, especially Americans who could follow its competition regimen at home, under the aegis of the Beaux-Arts Institute of Design. A willingness to tackle grandeur, however, emboldened a brilliant interwar generation of international urban designers, such as Léon Jaussely (1875–1932) and Jacques Gréber (1882–1962), and U.S. skyscraper architects Harvey Wiley Corbett (1873–1954), Raymond Hood (1881–1934), and William Van Alen (1883–1954). **IG**

Opéra House 1860–75
CHARLES GARNIER 1825–98

Opéra House,
Paris, France

◈ NAVIGATOR

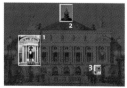

When Charles Garnier won the two-stage, fast-track competition for Paris's new opera house, a pet project of Emperor Napoleon III and his wife Eugenie, it rekindled the architect's sluggish career. As befitted an Ecole pupil, Garnier masterfully composed his plan to ease traffic flow and maximize pleasure among operagoers. The Opéra was the greatest construction site associated with Second Empire Paris after the New Louvre (1852–57), to which it is linked by a grand avenue and esplanade lined with dignified and unified apartment buildings. The antithesis of stale Neoclassicism, the Opéra was an aesthetic and societal turning point in French architecture. In it, Garnier expressed what he called a *style actuel*, which complied with the spirit of the time and reflected the designer's personal taste. Massing is very expressive: the grand gable above the stage is surrounded by a cascade of roofs, and that of the auditorium is echoed by rotundas topping two lateral pavilions, providing separate entries and amenities for the emperor and for subscribers. Garnier was also in full command of the complex decorative program, which he entrusted to painters and sculptors with a Beaux-Arts pedigree, many of whom were Rome Prize winners. **IG**

◉ FOCAL POINTS

1 DECOR

Despite its extravagant appearance, the decor is kept under control by underlying compositional axes. The juxtaposition of columns and pilasters of different heights, and the insertion of a bust in a hollowed oculus depart from the Neoclassical tradition.

2 APOLLO, POETRY, AND MUSIC

At the very top, 154 feet (47 m) above ground level, stands the group of Apollo, Poetry, and Music by French sculptor Aimé Millet. Profiling allegorical sculpture against the sky as a way to end key compositional axes became a favorite motif among Beaux-Arts architects.

3 *LA DANSE*

The enchanting *La Danse* by Jean-Baptiste Carpeaux features a lively group of dancers intertwined. The sculpture stirred a scandal at the time it was unveiled because the nudity of the dancers was seen as an affront to common decency.

◄ The central staircase brilliantly catered to the showmanship of its high-society users. It connects a frontal bar (superimposing the main entrance lobby and foyer) with a relatively modest horseshoe-shaped auditorium with fewer than 1,200 seats.

GARNIER'S SKETCHES

Charles Garnier was admitted to the Ecole des Beaux-Arts at the age of seventeen and studied under the ultra-classical Louis-Hippolyte Lebas (1782–1867), winning the Rome Prize when he was only twenty-three. Garnier's tenure at the French Academy in Rome was extended by travels to Greece and Turkey, where sketching unleashed his artistic talents and broadened his interest in applied decoration, especially with polychrome marble. A direct inspiration for the strictly composed but profusely decorated front elevation of the Opéra is the Library of St. Mark, Venice (1537–88), by Jacopo Sansovino (1486–1570), which Garnier recorded in a measured drawing (right) given by his widow to the Ecole des Beaux-Arts.

Organization of American States 1910
PAUL CRET 1876–1945,   ALBERT KELSEY 1870–1950

Organization of
American States,
Washington, D.C., USA

 NAVIGATOR

The United States government intended this building to be a symbol of its "civilizing" impact on Central and South America, and only United States architects were allowed to submit designs (which explains the partnership between French-born Paul Cret and United States architect Albert Kelsey). According to writer Elizabeth Grossman, the program opposed two visions of Classicism: Charles McKim, who headed the jury, equated Roman imperial grandeur with efficient government and put a premium on expressive elevations; Cret aimed to translate in plan the democratic and domestic character of a house for the American Republics. The tile roof above the entrance is a character nod to Latin civilization. Here, Cret distanced himself from the excesses of the modern French style and combined the compositional tenets that he learned in Paris with a pared-down modern Classicism. Cret's scheme is a textbook illustration of the Beaux-Arts rule of thumb that first-time visitors must find their way without verbal orientation, thanks to variations in heights, illumination, and decoration. Instead of the fixed-seating auditorium that most competitors devised, Cret envisioned the assembly room as a multipurpose space, reminiscent of the *salle des fêtes* (reception room) found in grand French city halls. **IG**

1 IRONWORK
The ironwork on the lamps echoes that seen on the three entrance doors and illustrates Cret's decorative skills, honed at the Ecole des Beaux-Arts in Lyon. Flights of steps extend the horizontal composition. Posts and lamps generate a secondary vertical axis.

2 PYLON
The counterpoint to the entrance motif is a sparingly adorned pylon, with seated female figures. This contrast between smooth unadorned stone surfaces and figural representations recalls Charles Garnier's Paris Opéra House (1860–75; see p.296).

3 MOTIFS
The main facade is centered on an inviting triple-arch motif, framed by higher walls placed behind the main vertical circulation. Triple arcades were a favorite Beaux-Arts motif, which Charles McKim had already used at the Boston Public Library (1895).

◄ Cret's bold move was to superimpose the two major spaces—the assembly room and library—instead of placing them across a court of honor, as did most other competitors. Access to both spaces is through an enclosed Mediterranean-looking patio centered on an Aztec-style fountain.

🕐 ARCHITECT PROFILE

1876–1903
Born in Lyon to a lower-middle-class family, Paul Cret was admitted to the Ecole des Beaux-Arts, Lyon, at the age of twenty-one, ranking first among nearly 300 candidates. He then chose to join the atelier of Jean-Louis Pascal (1837–1920), where many Americans studied. He garnered medals for his swift *esquisses* (sketches) and was awarded the Prix Rougevin in 1901. After his *diplôme*, Cret moved to Philadelphia in 1903.

1904–30
Adapting the teachings of Julien Guadet (1834–1908) and Auguste Choisy (1841–1909) to the needs of United States's students and society, Cret taught advanced design at the University of Pennsylvania for nearly thirty-five years. His best-known student was Louis Kahn (1901–74), who worked in the architect's studio from 1929 to 1930. The Ecole des

Beaux-Arts had prepared Cret for design competitions and he won his first commission: the Organization of American States Building. He also became consulting architect for the American Battle Monuments Commission, designing a stunning memorial above Château-Thierry, France (1930).

1931–45
Cret enjoyed great success as an architect of grand civic structures and his designs range from the Delaware River Bridge to train cars, and include the development plan for the University of Texas at Austin (1931). All his buildings were dignified, with highly legible organization in plan and elevation, which won him the Gold Medal of the American Institute of Architects in 1938. Cret was in France at the outbreak of World War II and served in the French army throughout the conflict.

REGIONAL VERNACULAR

1 **Cathedral of St. Michael (1848)**
Architect unknown
Sitka, Alaska, USA

2 **Holy Trinity Chapel (1825)**
Architect unknown
Fort Ross, California, USA

3 **Tabby Cabin (c.1800)**
Architect unknown
Kingsley Plantation, Fort George Island,
Jacksonville, Florida, USA

International trade by sea accelerated during the eighteenth and nineteenth centuries. Building materials became ballast and trade goods. Fired bricks, coral blocks, timber, clapboards, pickets, palings, battens, door and window frames, blinds and sashes, and "houses, complete or nearly so" were frequent shipments. In 1849 a bowling alley was listed as an export from the port of Honolulu, similar no doubt, to the indoor bowling alley at Roseland Cottage, Woodstock, Connecticut (c.1846). International cargo was more than building materials, however. Churches in Alaska, California, Hawaii, and Chile represent local vernacular merged with religion brought by commerce and missionaries. Coastal forts evidence human slave cargo in Africa and "tabby" cabins (see image 3) in the United States are where many slaves lived.

Fort Vancouver (1824) in Washington state was a trading station of the Hudson's Bay Company. Its infrastructure includes salvaged Roman bricks imported from Britain (similar to Greek and Roman *spolia*), and mortared with coral harvested from the company station in Hawaii. The Russian Orthodox Cathedral of St. Michael (see image 1) in New Archangel (Sitka), Alaska, was built in the wake of the commercial interests of the Russian American Company whose territory included California and Hawaii. A contemporary account describes their presidio at Ross, north of San Francisco as a fort with a large square, towers "at two angles," and a gated entrance. The fort's Russian Orthodox Holy Trinity Chapel (see image 2) was built by colonists and crews from Russian ships, which may explain the porthole on the truncated second tower.

KEY EVENTS

18th century	18th century	1727	1755	1780	1793
Johann Wolfgang von Goethe and Marc-Antoine Laugier use the vernacular hut as a contrast to Baroque architecture.	The Cuban *bohio campesino* (a peasant house thatched with Cuban royal palm) and tiled-roof wooden houses define Cuban vernacular architecture.	The city of Goiás Velho, Brazil, is founded. Its modestly scaled Colonial Vernacular influenced Brazilian Modernists such as Lúcio Costa (1902–98).	Laugier publishes the second edition of his *Essay on Architecture* with what would become an influential illustration of a primitive hut.	Goethe writes a poem on the wall of a hunting cabin in Thuringian Forest, Germany. It becomes a pilgrimage spot and fuels a "cult" of vernacular huts.	The facades of the Baroque Casa de los Azulejos, Mexico City, are covered in *talavera* tiles, a vernacular addition by Countess del Valle de Orizaba.

Hawaii was a common center for the three principal Pacific whaling grounds, and its relative proximity to the growing populations of California and Oregon made it an essential trade nexus for multiple commercial interests. Sir George Simpson, Governor of the Hudson's Bay Company (1820–60), described early nineteenth-century Honolulu houses as "built in the native fashion, but there are also many substantial wooden edifices, some of them of two storys, of wood, adobe, coral, and stone, with tinned roofs, which generally speaking, are finished with balconies, verandahs, and jalousies" (adjustable or fixed horizontal window slats, common in tropical and subtropical zones). Kawaiahao Church (1836–42; see p.304) in Honolulu, was built of coral block and designed by the leader of the New England missionaries Reverend Hiram Bingham (1789–1869). Like Bingham, the Reverend Richards (1793–1847) designed a similarly dated church at Lahaina, Maui, but his failure to allow for structural settlement meant the steeple was held "fast by iron clamps and chains."

Bunce Island off the coast of Sierra Leone, West Africa, was one of the main eighteenth-century trafficking points for slaves to colonial North America, particularly South Carolina and Georgia rice plantations. When Britain banned slavery in 1807, Bunce Island's trafficking role ended, but the area became a flashpoint for Britain's Africa Squadron, which patroled the seas for slave traffickers. Bunce's buildings are in ruins, but shell mounds for lime mortar remain, and were a link to "tabby" shell construction in United States slave states. The slave cabin (1805) at Retreat Plantation, Georgia, was built of tabby: a mix of equal parts of sand, lime, oyster shell, and water with burned oyster shell mortar. Although raw tabby walls with visible shells exist in Georgia and elsewhere in the South, tabby was usually stuccoed, and the cabin's restoration returned the original stucco and faux stone scored finish. The etymology of the word "tabby" is African/Arabic, and the method was brought to North America by the Spanish in Florida. Coquina quarry (shell rock) superseded tabby in Florida, but tabby use in Georgia continued to the 1890s.

Although remote, the Chiloé archipelago off the coast of Chile was important to Spain's Pacific possessions and international trade. The Jesuits' Circular Mission in the seventeenth century was continued by the Franciscans, and introduced the Chilota School of distinctive wooden churches that dot the area (see p.302). A mix of European and native building traditions, the churches were built by the community, similar to how the Russian Orthodox Chapel at Ross Presidio was raised. During the second voyage of HMS *Beagle*, Charles Darwin admired Castro's eighteenth-century Chilota church built of coigüe and cypress trees from island forests, and geographer Alexander Findlay deemed it handsome. Findlay, who devoted a chapter to Chiloé in his book on Pacific navigation in 1851, noted Chiloan timber was a major export, and in the same year Reverend Henry Cheever recorded Chile as the sixth country in value of imports to Hawaii, underscoring the breadth and diversity of global trade. **DJ**

1849	1850	1851	1854	19th century	19th century
The British Crown grants Vancouver Island, Canada, to the Hudson's Bay Company. It takes on the role of "urban planner" for the new community.	Honolulu is a major import, export, and re-export hub for global trade, including timber house parts and house "kits."	Alexander Findlay's *A Directory for Navigation of the Pacific* details trade routes and ports, and devotes a large section to the Chiloé archipelago.	*Walden; or, Life in the Woods* by Henry David Thoreau is published. It reflects on "simple life" in a self-built cabin on land owned by Ralph Waldo Emerson.	In Bassari Country, Senegal, round mud houses are built with multi-tiered thatch roofs, held in place with a radial cap of vertical saplings.	Hallstatt-Dachstein, Austria, is seen as quintessential village architecture by the Chinese, who build a replica town in the twenty-first century.

Santa María de Loreta de Achoa c.1735

ARCHITECT UNKNOWN

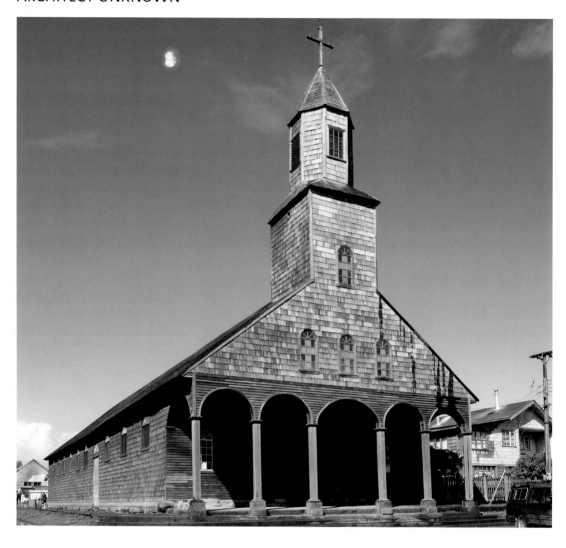

Santa María de Loreta de
Achoa, Achoa, Chiloé, Chile

NAVIGATOR

Forts and churches were among the first buildings erected by the colonizers of new territories. The Chiloé archipelago off the coast of Chile was part of Jesuit missionary expansion in South America in the seventeenth century. Spanish and Portuguese *mudéjar* architecture was adapted to local conditions, culture, techniques, and materials in dozens of wooden churches in a style that became known as the Chilota School. One of three permanent Jesuit missions in the archipelago, Santa María was built by a native workforce, possibly under the supervision of an Austrian cabinetmaker and a Spanish carpenter. The three-aisled church is timber framed (mortise and tenon) from native alerce (cypress), has a clapboard roof, and is decorated inside with moldings and a carved *artesonado* (coffered) ceiling. A central door on one aisle interrupts the row of nine arched windows on each side. Chilota churches were positioned on hills to be visible to ships and often became navigational landmarks if they were situated near harbors. The esplanades in front of churches acted as gathering places for the community and passing sea traffic. By the nineteenth century, the archipelago was well known on the Atlantic–Pacific trade route and visitors included HMS *Beagle* during its second voyage with Charles Darwin. **DJ**

◉ FOCAL POINTS

1 TOWER

Above the portico rises a square tower with an octagonal lantern and short spire in a tiered progression called *cañas*. Aside from one rebuilt after a fire, the sixteen Chilota wooden churches all have similar distinctive porticoes and tiered towers, a typology atypical of similarly dated mainland Colonial construction.

2 SHINGLES

The wooden shingled exterior is made of alerce (cypress), its value reflected in the trade of shingles as the monetary substitute "Real de Alerce." In the nineteenth century, the Jesuits failed to establish missions in Hawaii, which by then was a trade partner with Chile, whose major export was alerce.

3 PORTICO

The left and right pairs of the six square columns of the hexastyle arched prostyle (projecting) portico are balanced at either end to allow increased width for the central pair, which frame the recessed entrance. The horizontal wood clapboards above the column capitals delineate the portico from the shingled pediment.

▲ A tiered *cañas* cornice supports a five-arch, ribbed barrel vault with a three-dimensional *artesonado* ceiling. This *mudéjar* feature was influenced by the Islamic *muqarnas* (honeycomb vault).

PREFABRICATED BUILDINGS

Trade, colonies, and commerce increasingly required portable architecture. Steam-powered mills made it easier to saw parts for prefabricated buildings, and the invention of corrugated galvanized iron in the 1820s led to a prefabrication unit that became ubiquitous. The prefabricated house of New South Wales Governor Arthur Phillip in Australia was a timber infill frame with canvas walls. The infill system was perfected in the 1830s as the Manning Portable Colonial Cottage; this allowed for interchangeable panels to be slotted into grooved posts. Each piece was designed to be carried by one person if necessary. Prefabricated cottages built in Port Stanley, Falkland Islands, in 1849 (right) were brought by London Chelsea Pensioners to form a garrison and colonize the islands.

Kawaiahao Church 1836–42
REVEREND HIRAM BINGHAM 1789–1869

Kawaiahao Church, Honolulu, Oahu, Hawaii, USA

Described in 1851 as "the first object of art the eye rests upon in coming into port," Kawaiahao Church was "conspicuous through the spy-glass far out to sea." Also known as Honolulu First Church, Kawaiahao replaced a thatched chapel that had been set alight by a firebug, after which native royalty agreed that a new and larger church be built. The new church was planned by Reverend Hiram Bingham, building materials were paid for by the chiefs and people, and the church was built by its members. Blocks of coral were cut by divers from the reef on the leeward side of the island of Oahu and then shaped like bricks. Coral was also burned in kilns to produce lime mortar. The building's style references Federal Church architecture in Bingham's native New England, and may be based on the Center Church on the Green (1814) at New Haven. The lime and sand render applied to the columns, entablature, windows, and gable ends was presumably intended to emulate the carpentry detailing of buildings such as Center Church. The interior features an atypical door at the east apse and a balcony in the style of English and New England churches. Pews for the royal family on either side of the entrance feature native Koa wood. The nave's roof trusses and purlins are exposed. After Bingham was recalled to New England in 1840, Reverend Armstrong completed Kawaiahao. **DJ**

✛ NAVIGATOR

◉ FOCAL POINTS

1 TOWER

A short pyramid spire was removed from the tower in 1885. Its shape may have been intended to link Honolulu's First Church to the First Temple of Solomon in the Old Testament. The tower was subsequently redesigned and the new plan encased the twin lancet windows in single arched reveals.

2 CLOCK

Made by Howard & Davis, Boston, and installed in 1850, the Kauikeaouli clock was donated by King Kamehameha III. Removed in 1885, the railed gallery above the clocktower was a common feature for nineteenth-century Honolulu buildings, the tops of which were equipped with lookouts for spying approaching vessels.

3 PORTICO

The paired, engaged Doric columns on the shallow portico are highlighted with render. They support a minimal entablature under which a window jalousie (originally a sash window) sits over the arched door. The gable roof end is a broken pediment from which the truncated clock and bell tower rises.

MODEL CHURCHES

New England missionaries sailed from New Haven, Connecticut, and arrived in Hawaii in 1823. They followed the inaugural group led by Reverend Hiram Bingham in 1820. Ithiel Town (1784–1844), like other early U.S. architects, began his profession in the building trade. Builders relied on practical handbooks and pattern books for ideas, but often copied existing buildings. Town's contract to build the Trinity Church on the Green (1815) cites existing churches in Providence, New York, and New Haven as models for architectural elements of the new church. Town's brick and timber Center Church on the Green (1814; below) in New Haven would have been known to many of the missionaries and probably influenced the design of Kawaiahao Church. In Honolulu, a render highlights the portico, windows, entablature, and pediment in a similar fashion to related areas of Town's church in New Haven.

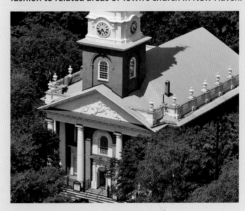

◀ Horizontal wooden louvres for ventilation in the arched and square windows resemble traditional sash windows. The natural spring that provided the name for the church is commemorated with a fountain on the church grounds.

5 | 1870–1950

FUNCTIONALISM: SKYSCRAPERS

When questioned about the relationship of function to design, Ludwig Mies van der Rohe (1886–1969) replied dismissively "Function[alism] is sweeping dirt!" This may be a reaction to simplified dicta from an earlier era, such as "form ever follows function" by Louis Sullivan (1856–1924) and "form and function are one" by Frank Lloyd Wright (1867–1959). However, Mies and his European architectural colleagues all acknowledged the importance of those early functionalist skyscrapers from the first "Chicago School" of commercial architecture. These high-rises of the 1880s and 1890s, which often projected freshness, simplicity, and rationality—eliciting the admiration of European Modernists after World War I—owe their creation to a confluence of events in the 1870s and early 1880s.

The first of these involves disaster: the Great Chicago Fire of October 8 to 10, 1871, a firestorm that decimated more than 2,000 acres (809 ha) of the city center. This calamity during a national recession spurred a movement of architectural talent from across the nation to help rebuild the city, including Sullivan, John Wellborn Root (1850–91), and Peter Wight (1838–1925). The latter hired Root and Daniel Burnham (1846–1912) and patented a system of fireproofed construction. Alongside the development of effective fireproofing and wind-bracing for iron and (later) steel structures, the safety passenger elevator—first

KEY EVENTS

1871	1874	1882	1885	1885	1888
The Great Chicago Fire of October 8–10, kills hundreds and destroys 2,000 acres (809 ha) of the city center.	Peter Wight patents his "fireproof columns" and later establishes the Wight Fireproofing Company producing Fire Clay Tile Ceilings.	Daniel Burnham and John Wellborn Root design the ten-story Montauk Block, one of the first buildings to include two hydraulic elevators.	William Le Baron Jenney creates the first skyscraper: the Home Insurance Building.	The Chicago window is used by Solon Spencer Beman at the Romanesque First Studebaker Building.	Burnham and Root create the Rookery, complete with a commercial atrium based on French department stores.

installed in 1857 in New York, with the first electric model demonstrated in 1880—helped spark further development of early high-rises to a height of some ten stories, dubbed "sky-scrapers" in the contemporary press. The 138-foot-high (42 m) Home Insurance Building (1885, since demolished), designed by William Le Baron Jenney (1832–1907), is often considered to have been the first elevator-serviced skyscraper of fireproofed, masonry-braced iron construction. Others, in a variety of eclectic styles, filled out the gridded lots and streets of U.S. cities in the later 1880s and early 1890s—ten- to eighteen-story blocks that consumed the site so as to maximize rentable space within. The eleven-story Romanesque-style Rookery Building (see image 1), by Burnham and Root, features a retail atrium based on French department stores such as Bon Marché (c.1869) and Printemps (remodeled in 1881), its Eiffel Tower–like structure and staircase topped by a lacy iron-and-glass roof. Above this, four rectangular office wings surround the court, allowing light and air to penetrate into offices planned off double-loaded corridors, to make the most of the available space on each floor. This became standard in many of Burnham's later commercial buildings, such as the Railway Exchange Building (1904; later the Santa Fe Building).

The 1890s saw the introduction of glazed terracotta as a decorative protective cladding for the fireproofed steel frame, and the increased popularity of the Chicago window—a large fixed center pane with double-hung side panels. Glazed terracotta provided durability, resistance to urban soot, and a lightweight cost-effective material for cladding steel structures. The Chicago window was probably seen first in large, lower-floor retail display windows of early high-rises such as the Romanesque First Studebaker Building (1885; later Fine Arts Building) by Solon Spencer Beman (1853–1914). Soon these large-scale fenestrations could be seen throughout the city: examples include the Reliance Building (see image 2) and Fisher Building (1896), both by Burnham's firms; the Second Studebaker Building (1896) by Beman; and the Gage Group and McClurg Building (1899) by Holabird & Roche. Although Chicago buildings of this era tend to look as if they are stacked floors, Louis Sullivan, writing in *The Tall Office Building Artistically Reconsidered* (1896), expressed the idea that buildings should look tall and have a rational design appearance in the manner of a column: a substantial base, a vertically expressed shaft, and an elaborately ornamented top, as in his Wainwright Building (1892) in St. Louis.

The coordinated architectural ensemble overseen by Burnham at the World's Columbian Exposition (1893) in Chicago helped to promote the popularity of French Beaux-Arts Classicism and the classicist City Beautiful movement throughout the United States. This increasingly found expression in the steel high-rises of the next generation, such as Burnham's own Flatiron Building (1902) in New York. Its limestone, brick, and terracotta-covered floors stacked 285 feet (87 m) high fill out the little triangular site, while its distinctive form has been a source of inspiration to many artists and photographers. **JZ**

1 **Rookery Building (1888)**
Burnham and Root, remodeled by Frank Lloyd Wright (1905)
Chicago, Illinois, USA

2 **Reliance Building (1895)**
Burnham and Root/D. H. Burnham & Co.
Chicago, Illinois, USA

1889	1890s	1893	1899	1902	1909
In Chicago, Dankmar Adler (1844–1900) and Louis Sullivan create the Auditorium hotel, theater, and office building, an early multi-use building.	Glazed terracotta becomes popular as a decorative cladding for steel frames.	Burnham is master planner of the World's Columbian Exposition in Chicago, an event that has a huge impact on his career and city planning.	Sullivan is hired to design the prominent Schlesinger and Mayer Store (1899; 1904; see p.310) on State Street, Chicago.	Burnham's Flatiron Building is built on a difficult site. The same year, Marshall Field hires him to build a huge flagship store (1902–14; see p.312).	Burnham's career is at its zenith with buildings across the United States and in London, too, with the opening of Selfridge's department store.

Schlesinger and Mayer Store 1899; 1904

LOUIS SULLIVAN 1856–1924

Schlesinger and Mayer Store
(now Sullivan Center),
Chicago, Illinois, USA

⚙ NAVIGATOR

Louis Sullivan's Schlesinger and Mayer Store both relates to his own design theories and provides an excellent example of the simple facade style of the Chicago School of Architecture. The intersection where the building was located was said to have been the busiest in the world; the street itself was immortalized in the song "Chicago (That Toddlin' Town)" (1922) as "State Street that great street." Sullivan created a vertically accentuated turret at the corner entry located at the center of a string of department stores. The facade features horizontally stacked floors with Chicago windows that allowed light to penetrate the loft floors above, as well as showcasing the store's wares at the lower level. A highly ornamented cast-iron facade wraps around the building. Today, the Schlesinger and Mayer Store (now the Sullivan Center) incorporates retail at the two lower levels but above houses offices, as well as studio spaces for the School of the Art Institute of Chicago. Additions were made to the store in the twentieth century by several firms, including Sullivan's, who in 1903 to 1904 made the first changes in just fourteen weeks. **JZ**

👁 FOCAL POINTS

1 ENTRY TURRET
The turreted facade faces an important intersection and marks the entry point to the store. It bears the name of Carson Pirie Scott & Co., the retail chain that bought the store from Schlesinger and Mayer in 1904, after Sullivan had completed his expansion of the building. Carson's flagship store remained here until 2007, when it closed for good.

2 SHOW WINDOWS
The spectacular show windows at the pedestrian level of the building invite potential shoppers into an exciting retail world beyond. These windows were intended to display the store's merchandise within an exotic foliage frame of cast-iron vegetation, which was originally painted green to look as if it had an aged bronze patina.

3 CHICAGO WINDOWS
The simply detailed, glazed terracotta facade projects an image of severity. It features Chicago windows, a style that originated in the Chicago School. Consisting of a large center panel flanked by two smaller, double-hung sash windows, these windows offered both light and ventilation. They create the effect of a grid pattern on the facade.

🕐 ARCHITECT PROFILE

1856–78
Born in Boston, Louis Henry Sullivan studied at the Massachusetts Institute of Technology before working for Philadelphia architect Frank Furness (1839–1912). During the recession, he moved to Chicago in 1873 to work with William Le Baron Jenney and then studied briefly in Paris at the Ecole des Beaux-Arts in 1874, before returning to Chicago.

1879–95
Dankmar Adler employed Sullivan as a draftsman/designer in 1879, making him a partner in 1883. With Adler, Sullivan created some of the most important works in Chicago, including the Auditorium Building (1889), the Schiller Building (1891), and the Chicago Stock Exchange Building (1894).

1896–1924
Sullivan's last large solo work was the Schlesinger and Mayer Store. Apart from a series of small, jewelbox–like banks in the Midwest, Sullivan's commissions dwindled. He spent the last years before his death writing *A System of Architectural Ornament* and *The Autobiography of an Idea* (both 1924).

▲ In the lush ornamentation around the entry, the corner's original address of "4" is interwoven into the scheme, part of an underlying geometry that Sullivan felt was integral to all things natural.

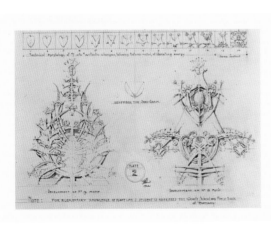

SULLIVAN'S SYSTEM

The original drawings for Louis Sullivan's *A System of Architectural Ornament According with a Philosophy of Man's Powers* (1924) survive as his masterpiece of ornamental design (left). Their subtlety is not at all conveyed in the reproductions in the book of the same title published by the American Institute of Architects shortly after his death. The drawings demonstrate his idea that a rational geometry underlies all things natural, despite the irrational appearance of his lettuce-leaf ornamentation. The drawings were in part commissioned by the Art Institute of Chicago, one of several efforts locally to help the penniless Sullivan in his later years.

Marshall Field Building 1902–14

DANIEL BURNHAM 1846–1912

👁 FOCAL POINTS

1 ENTRY

The building features a simple Classical entry with Ionic columns in the center flanked by large display windows to showcase the store's goods, their design simplicity deferring to the exuberant Classical details within.

2 CLASSICAL DESIGN

The two units of the store along State Street (built 1902 and 1907) were constructed according to a simple yet strong Classical design, with large Chicago windows throughout its massive twelve-story facade.

3 FACADE

The store's simple granite facade compares with the robust severity of the Marshall Field's Wholesale Store (1885–87) by Henry Hobson Richardson (1838–86), which prefigured the blocklike mass of this State Street complex.

4 CLOCK

The corner clock is one of the few extravagant details on the building's exterior. The clock itself is a symbol of Chicago; it appeared on a *Saturday Evening Post* cover in 1945 in a Norman Rockwell painting entitled *The Clock Mender*.

The flagship store that Daniel Burnham created for Marshall Field was built in multiple stages on four sites of the entire block on State Street. It features elaborately detailed classical interiors, including two courts, one of which has a mosaic ceiling designed by Louis Comfort Tiffany. A classically detailed, wood-paneled restaurant on the seventh floor, the Walnut Room, evokes the fine dining that existed in department-store restaurants of this period. When the store opened in 1907, even before completion of all the spaces, it was claimed to be the largest retail store in the world, employing more than 7,000 staff. Burnham's use of atria within buildings such as this derive from those within French department stores of the era. Marshall Field appointed Harry Gordon Selfridge to head his retail division in 1887, and Selfridge was a key player in Burnham's architectural developments for Marshall Field, although Selfridge abruptly resigned in 1904 and very briefly owned the Schlesinger and Mayer Store down the street. In 1906, he moved to London where he ran his own highly successful store based on his retail experiences in Chicago, Selfridge's on Oxford Street, which opened in 1909 and was also designed by Burnham. **JZ**

⬟ NAVIGATOR

Marshall Field Building (now Macy's), Chicago, Illinois, USA

⏱ ARCHITECT PROFILE

1846–74
Born in upstate New York and raised in Chicago, Daniel Hudson Burnham graduated from high school in 1865 and tried several jobs before apprenticeship with William Le Baron Jenney. After the fire of 1871, he was hired in 1872 by Peter Wight of Carter, Drake and Wight. There he met John Wellborn Root and together they formed Burnham and Root.

1875–91
The partners made their initial mark with a house for John Sherman, who was cofounder of the Union Stock Yards. This led them to eventually create hundreds of projects from the Midwest to the West Coast. Chicago buildings included the Insurance Exchange (1885) and Monadnock Building (1884–91).

1892–1912
After Root's death, Burnham reorganized the firm as D. H. Burnham & Co. In 1909, the *Plan of Chicago*, created with Edward H. Bennett (1874–1954), was published, the culmination of their planning efforts in San Francisco and Manila (1905).

▲ The large open spaces of Marshall Field's store are reminiscent of French department stores. The beautifully detailed acanthus capitals on classical columns evoke the elegance of the era.

FLATIRON BUILDING

On April 30, 1902, Charles McKim (1847–1909) wrote to Burnham about his Flatiron Building (above) in New York: "The only building higher. . .is the Tower of Babel." Indeed, Burnham, with associate Frederick P. Dinkelberg (1858–1935), created a New York landmark to rival that biblical one in the popular imagination. Its tall, triangular form within the open space around 23rd Street may have inspired the slang expression "23 skidoo." Down-drafts caused women's skirts to swirl upward, prompting nearby policemen to shout their disapproval at girl watchers and tell them to move on.

ARTS AND CRAFTS

1 **Debenham House (1907)**
Halsey Ricardo
Holland Park, London, UK

2 **Hvitträsk (1903)**
Herman Gesellius, Armas Lindgren,
and Eliel Saarinen
Helsinki, Finland

3 **Thorsen House (1910)**
Henry and Charles Greene
Berkeley, California, USA

W illiam Morris laid the foundation of the Arts and Crafts Movement
when he declared "production by machinery is altogether an evil."
The movement advocated the primacy of "truthful" works of solid
construction, made by hand with "honest" materials and "simple" ornament,
and suited to their sites. The style emerged in Britain in the 1880s and spread
internationally, including to the United States, where its chief adherent, Gustav
Stickley (1858–1942), praised not just the pleasure of making with one's hands,
but that doing so increased the "pleasure in possessing them." Historian Nikolaus
Pevsner recognized the Morris Movement as a bridge from the pursuit of
architectural truth in the Gothic Revival (see p.284) and the Modern Movement.
His shorthand reference refers to the main promoter of the style, Morris, who
was inspired initially by critic John Ruskin's *The Stones of Venice* (1851–53).

At times paralleling international Art Nouveau (see p.320), which was seen
in Britain as a style for aesthetes, Arts and Crafts architecture was not intended
as a style, but as materials and function orchestrated by the architect. The
L-shaped Red House (1859) in Bexleyheath, Kent, designed by Philip Webb
(1831–1915), was intended as a square courtyard complex for the families of
Morris and Edward Burne Jones, but remains incomplete. While practitioners
valued vernacular architecture and decoration in moderation, the definition of
moderation varied. U.S. architect Louis Sullivan (1856–1924) deemed ornament

KEY EVENTS

1880s	1882	1887	1893	1896	1897
Led by John Ruskin and William Morris, the Arts and Crafts Movement flourishes in Britain and quickly spreads across Europe and the United States.	The Art Workers' Guild is founded in London, a cross-disciplinary forum for its diverse membership, which includes craftsmen, artists, and architects.	Bookbinder T. J. Cobden-Sanderson coins the term "Arts and Crafts" when names are considered for the Arts and Crafts Exhibition Society.	*The Studio* magazine is launched in London. Subsequent influential magazines include *Country Life*, *Dekorative Kunst* (Germany), and *The Craftsman* (USA).	London County Council Central School of Arts and Crafts is established, with architect W. R. Lethaby (1857–1931) as joint principal.	The Boston Society of Arts and Crafts, the movement's first U.S. society, is founded. Others follow in the Midwest and California.

a 'luxury', although he advocated 'organic ornament'. Debenham House in London (see image 1) by Halsey Ricardo (1854–1928) is an understated and yet exuberant three-storey, three-bay arcade and pilaster faience confection of green, turquoise and white-glazed brick under a green, glazed pantile roof.

Although British Arts and Crafts originated in London, Manchester, Birmingham and Glasgow, it became associated with escapism from the city to the countryside. Scottish artist Mary Fraser Tytler Watts and her artist husband G. F. Watts founded the Compton Potters Art Guild in Surrey for the preservation of rural handicrafts. Apprentice potters were housed in a mass concrete, brick and rough render hostel and gallery (1904) designed by Christopher Hatton Turnor (1873–1940), who trained under Edwin Landseer Lutyens (1869–1944). Guild output under Mary's guidance included her wheel-shaped brick and terracotta Watts Mortuary Chapel in Compton (1898).

Journals such as *The Studio*, published from 1893, promoted architects including Charles Francis Annesley Voysey (1857–1941) and Mackay Hugh Baillie Scott (1865–1945), who received commissions in Germany and Switzerland. *Country Life*, first published in 1897, also promoted Arts and Crafts architecture, particularly houses designed by Lutyens. Social responsibility was inherent in the Arts and Crafts Movement. Lutyens's Goddards (1900) in Abinger Common, Surrey, was a philanthropic commission for two cottages with a central common room, where 'ladies of small means' could enjoy summer holidays. Its two-bedroom wings were splayed on either side of a garden court, similar to the way the two hostel blocks frame the central Watts Gallery in Compton.

In Nordic countries the style was associated with National Romanticism. Hvitträsk (see image 2), near Helsinki, designed by Herman Gesellius (1874–1916), Armas Lindgren (1874–1929) and Eliel Saarinen (1873–1950), was their studio and multi-family home, and incorporated Arts and Crafts features. In the United States, Frank Lloyd Wright (1867–1959), Robert Spencer Jr (1864–1953), Myron Hunt (1868–1952) and Dwight Perkins (1867–1941) were inspired by the Arts and Crafts Movement and Louis Sullivan, for whom Wright had worked, in creating the Prairie School of architecture. In 1908, Wright identified its characteristics as 'sloping roofs, low proportions, quiet sky lines, suppressed heavy-set chimneys, and sheltering overhangs, low terraces and out-reaching walls'. In California, Arts and Crafts houses by Charles Sumner Greene (1868–1957) and Henry Mather Greene (1870–1954) include David B. Gamble House (1909; see p.318), Pasadena, and Thorsen House (see image 3), Berkeley, which since 1942 has had the university's Sigma Phi fraternity as custodians of its exquisite joinery, stained glass windows, deep eave overhangs and clinker brick walls.

In 1930, architectural critic John Betjeman described Arts and Crafts as 'now a term of abuse'. Its legacy is its emphasis on well-sited houses and garden suburbs, such as Hampstead Garden Suburb in London (1907), the design for Canberra (1912) and Radburn in New Jersey (1929).

1904	1904–05	1905	1908	1914–18	1936
Harold Desbrowe-Annear (1865–1963), a leading exponent of the Arts and Crafts style in Australia, designs Chadwick House, Melbourne.	Hermann Muthesius (1861–1927) publishes his three-volume book *Das Englische Haus*, which popularizes Arts and Crafts architecture in Europe.	Voewood (see p.316), Holt, Norfolk, is completed. Designed by Edward Schroeder Prior, it utilizes a butterfly plan.	Ramsay Traquair (1874–1952) designs Skirling House in the Scottish Borders. It has Arts and Crafts details, as well as wrought-iron applied decoration.	World War I halts the building of large country houses; however, the movement's legacy endures in smaller suburban houses.	Critic Nikolaus Pevsner cites the movement's contribution to modernism in *Pioneers of Modern Design: From William Morris to Walter Gropius*.

Voewood 1905

EDWARD SCHROEDER PRIOR 1852–1932

Voewood, Holt,
Norfolk, UK

C lients commissioning houses near the north Norfolk coast at the turn of the
nineteenth century wanted sunshine, fresh air, and access to sea bathing. In 1903,
the Reverend P. R. Lloyd commissioned Edward Schroeder Prior to design a family
house near Holt. Prior designed an extreme example of Arts and Crafts architecture for
his client—possibly too extreme, as Lloyd's family never lived at Voewood. Initially rented
to another cleric, then used for institutional purposes, it is now a private home. Prior's
first country house, The Barn at Exmouth (1897), Devon, had a "suntrap" plan, its two
wings angled at 90 degrees; this butterfly layout was also used by Prior for Voewood.
However, the patterning used in local vernacular building, which Prior created by facing
its reinforced concrete construction with various materials, subverts the formality of his
plan. He learned about concrete while working with Richard Norman Shaw (1831–1912).
Here, it is faced with bricks made from clay excavated from the site (which created a
sunken garden facing the front elevation), pebbles that were found on site, and zigzagged
patterns formed by thin tiles placed on edge, with cut sandstone quarried locally at the
corners. Prior's use of building materials from the immediate vicinity reflected the Arts
and Crafts ideal of houses growing organically from their sites. Nikolaus Pevsner
described the entrance and front yard facades as "inventive and daring" although some
other writers have been less enthusiastic. **CM**

◆ NAVIGATOR

FOCAL POINTS

1 GREEN SETTING
The front lawn is arranged axially. The terrace walls extend the diagonal lines of the house's butterfly wings, which enfold the sunken yard. This was created after the house's building materials were excavated and it protects plants from the wind.

2 FACINGS
Different colored facings are used to create patterns. The gray facing of unbroken flints contrasts with the yellow sandstone dressings and their wide white joints. These in turn contrast with the yellow-red tiles, which are arranged in a herringbone design.

3 SOLAR ORIENTATION
The two wings on the south-facing front elevation are oriented at 120 degrees to the central range. This means that seven of the house's ten main faces catch the summer sun as it moves from east to west, with some rooms being lit from several sides.

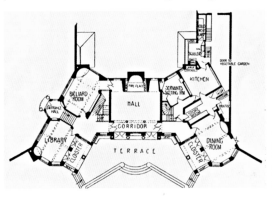

◀ Prior's butterfly plan for Voewood resembles a truncated "H." The house is symmetrical at its front and back, and also on its entrance side.

ARCHITECT PROFILE

1852–79
Edward Schroeder Prior was born in London in 1852 and attended school at Harrow. After graduating from Cambridge University, Prior was articled to leading architect Richard Norman Shaw. Shaw, for whom he worked from 1875 until 1879, considered him "perhaps the most gifted pupil of them all." As Clerk of Works for Shaw's St. Margaret's Church (1879) in Ilkley, Yorkshire, he gained practical experience of construction and exposure to craftsmen's expertise.

1880–94
Prior established his own London practice in 1880, securing commissions such as High Grove (1881) in Eastcote, Harrow, and a terrace of lodgings in West Bay (1885), near Bridport, Dorset. In 1882, he became a founding member of the Art Workers' Guild, which brought together craftsmen, artists, and architects in a cross-disciplinary forum. Prior wrote the Guild's first prospectus and was later elected to its governing committee in 1889.

1895–1905
In 1895, Prior designed his first butterfly-plan house for an exhibition at the Royal Academy. The following year he was commissioned to build The Barn in Exmouth (1897), which allowed him to put his butterfly design into practice. The Barn was built using local materials and construction methods, providing a forerunner to Voewood. Around this time, Prior became increasingly interested in Gothic art and architecture, and in 1900 he published *A History of Gothic Art in England*.

1906–32
After the construction of St. Andrew's Church (1907) in Roker, Sundeland, Prior built very little. In 1912, he was appointed Slade Professor at Cambridge University, with the task of establishing the new School of Architecture. There, he played a major role in the development of the school's syllabus and the instigation of a research program. He remained as Slade Professor until his death from cancer in 1932.

David B. Gamble House 1909

CHARLES S. GREENE 1868–1957, HENRY M. GREENE 1870–1954

David B. Gamble House,
Pasadena, California, USA

NAVIGATOR

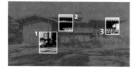

The David B. Gamble House was the last of a series of houses designed between 1903 and 1909 by Charles Sumner Greene and Henry Mather Greene in Pasadena, California. It is their only intact *Gesamtkunstwerk* (total work of art), which expresses their complete concept for a home. They designed its external and interior architecture, including fixtures and furnishings, such as metalwork, stained-glass windows, furniture, and rugs, as well as landscaping its yard. The basic plan and construction of the house are thoroughly Californian. Its four-square, two-story massing, typical of a Swiss chalet, was constructed using standard western framing clad with U.S. colonial-style shingles. Their design also incorporated elements of Japanese domestic architecture, such as the use of mortise-and-tenon joints. However, the most progressive aspect of the design is the Greenes' adroit fusion of U.S. and Japanese cultures. The Gamble House was positioned so that it was cooled by prevailing afternoon breezes descending from the nearby mountains. Deep overhangs protect the terraces and the sleeping porches from extreme weather. These outdoor rooms, furnished with benches, willow furniture, and oriental rugs, integrate the house with its surroundings, blurring the distinction between indoors and outdoors. Visiting the Gamble House in 1909, British designer Charles Robert Ashbee recognized that, in working with the master craftsmen and contractor, the Greenes had successfully fulfilled William Morris's Arts and Crafts' intentions. **CM**

1 LAWN

The gently rising lawn hides the brick-paved driveway from public view, creating the illusion that the grass continues uninterrupted to the steps leading up to the entrance. The gnarled oak tree branches depicted in iridescent glass panels at the teak-framed entrance also unite the house and yard.

2 ELEVATION

Two disparate design elements, a traditional gabled elevation (on the left) and a heavily timbered sleeping porch (on the right), are unified by the shared horizontal line of deep eaves and exposed rafters and beams. The mass of the first and second floors is heightened and balanced by a single attic room.

3 PORCHES

The second floor sleeping porches at the front and the rear of the house are sheltered from the heat of the sun and inclement weather by deep eaves. In turn, these porches shelter the recesses of the first-floor terraces. Intended for outdoor living, they create a connection between house and nature.

⏱ ARCHITECTS' PROFILE

1868–1894

Charles Sumner Greene was born in 1868 and his brother Henry Mather Greene in 1870. Educated at the Manual Training School of Washington University in St. Louis, Missouri, the brothers studied architecture at the Massachusetts Institute of Technology. In 1894, they established Greene & Greene, an architectural and design practice in Pasadena, California.

1895–1922

Over the course of their partnership, the brothers designed approximately 140 houses. They produced their finest work from 1903 to 1909, in particular five houses for wealthy clients built between 1907 and 1909. Their use of exotic hardwoods and inlays differentiated them from their contemporaries, as did their incorporation of elements of Asian design, which they had encountered at the World's Columbian Exposition in Chicago in 1893. The practice's fortunes declined after 1911, and in 1916 Charles moved to Carmel to pursue other creative interests. The brothers dissolved the firm in 1922.

▲ Sunshine transmitted through the iridescent glass panels illuminates the main staircase, which is constructed from intersecting horizontal and vertical lengths of Burmese teak.

INTERNATIONAL ART NOUVEAU

A rt Nouveau was less a style and more of an international movement
that was popular from 1890 to 1914. It expressed the diversity and
ambiguity of the complex sociopolitical investigations that took place
in architecture and design. Whiplash curves and sinuous organic lines are its
most familiar hallmarks; however, Art Nouveau forms are much more varied
and complex. Arising from mid-nineteenth-century design reform
movements—especially Arts and Crafts (see p.314) and Aestheticism in the
United Kingdom—Art Nouveau came at a time of increasing
internationalization in the arts, largely through the spread of periodicals, such
as *The Studio*, and international exhibitions in Europe and the United States.

Although Art Nouveau was referred to in French and Belgian artistic
journals from the late 1870s, the term was not popularized until 1895, when
German art dealer Siegfried Bing opened his gallery Maison de l'Art Nouveau
in Paris. Bing had been an importer of Japanese and other Asian decorative
arts since 1875, and launched the highly influential monthly journal *Le Japon
Artistique* in 1888. Much like his British counterpart, Arthur Lasenby Liberty,
Bing was key in introducing the fashion of collecting Asian objets d'art. He

KEY EVENTS

1889	1893	1896	1897	1898	1899
At the Paris Exposition, a wrought-iron tower by Gustav Eiffel (1832–1923) shows the strength, economy, and versatility of new technology.	U.S. architect Louis Sullivan (1856–1924) designs the colorful Transportation Building for the World's Columbian Exposition in Chicago.	The Guaranty Building in Buffalo, New York, by Sullivan and Dankmar Adler (1844–1900), includes terracotta ornament.	The Brussels International Exposition features pavilions by Henry van de Velde and Paul Hankar.	Otto Wagner begins Majolica House, Vienna. Victor Horta designs his home and studio in Brussels (now the Horta Museum).	Horta's Maison du Peuple is built for the Belgian Workers' Party; it includes an office and meeting space, a cafe, and a concert hall that seats more than 2,000.

offered his imports alongside works in the new style by leading European artists in an interior designed by Belgian architect Henry van de Velde (1863–1957), and with stained glass by U.S. artist and designer Louis Comfort Tiffany. Van de Velde was one of the leading figures associated with Art Nouveau, who worked not only as an architect, but also as a designer of print advertisements, furniture, interiors, and even clothing. His practice is exemplary of the way in which many architects approached their work holistically, not limiting themselves to the mere design of a structure, but preferring to craft a *Gesamtkunstwerk*—a total work of art.

This approach is illustrated in two of the earliest Art Nouveau buildings—Hôtel Tassel (see image 2) by Victor Horta (1861–1947) and Hôtel Hankar (1894; see p.324), the home and studio of Horta's close friend Paul Hankar (1859–1901). Both townhouses are situated on narrow, deep plots—typical of Belgian town planning at the time—in St.-Gilles, the dense area of central Brussels now renowned for its numerous Art Nouveau masterpieces. Such plots require a tall, constricted orientation, but Horta suggested an innovative solution for this: rather than adhering to the typical plan of dividing the townhouse into two asymmetrical zones, he arranged a radical open-plan configuration based on the cruciform, so that the house is divided into four broader areas across the depth of the plot. This lack of bilateral division is expressed in the facade of Hôtel Tassel, which is graced with a broad, symmetrical bow window that alleviates the strict vertical impression of similar townhouses. From a distance, the facade seems somewhat Beaux Arts (see p.292) in its symmetrical composition and pale stone palette. However, the detail is pure Art Nouveau, from the capitals and bases of the columnlike mullions that wrap plantlike onto their braces, to the wrought-iron balustrade and stained-glass windows from the United States.

The interest in abstracted organic forms of ornamentation originated in the mid-nineteenth century, when it was promoted in *The Grammar of Ornament* (1854), a pattern book by British architect Owen Jones (1809–74), and subsequently appeared in the work of designers such as the Scottish-born Christopher Dresser (1834–1904) and in the schemes of Morris and Company. Art Nouveau architect-designers embraced this organicism because it was particularly suited to the new materials they preferred, especially ironwork, which was lauded by the French Gothic Revival (see p.284) architect Eugène Viollet-le-Duc (1814–79) in 1877 for both its economy and longevity: "The judicious use of iron, cast and wrought, would not unfrequently enable us to build very economically, and with an assured prospect of stability for a certain period, a hundred years, e.g., which is quite sufficient."

Hankar was influenced by Viollet-le-Duc, as was Hector Guimard (1867–1942) in France. The Paris Metro entrance at Porte Dauphine (see image 1) is one of the best surviving examples of Guimard's works, together with the

1 **Porte Dauphine Metro Station (c. 1900)**
Hector Guimard
Paris, France

2 **Hôtel Tassel (1894)**
Victor Horta
Brussels, Belgium

1900	1901	1904	1904	1910	1914
Paris Metro entrances are designed by Hector Guimard. Charles Rennie Mackintosh shows work to acclaim at the eighth Vienna Secession exhibition.	The first exhibition of the Darmstadt Artists' Colony (exemplary of Jugenstil/Secession style) is held in Ernst Ludwig House (1900) by Joseph Maria Olbrich.	Charles Rennie Mackintosh and his artist wife, Margaret MacDonald, design their finest public work, the Willow Tea Rooms in Glasgow.	Russian architect Mikhail Eisenstein (1867–1921) builds several important works on Albert Street in Riga, Latvia, now a World Heritage Site.	In his lecture "Ornament and Crime" Adolf Loos (1870–1933) argues that ornamentation is wasted labor and makes architecture obsolete before its time.	The outbreak of World War I effectively ends Art Nouveau as a viable style due to its perceived decadence and expense.

entrances (or edicules) at Abbesses and Châtelet (reconstructed). The cast-iron and glass canopies are as much sculpture as they are architecture, and demonstrate an engagement with Belgian architects, whom Guimard visited and studied, but also with his French contemporaries in the decorative arts, such as René Lalique and Emile Gallé. In Paris, Art Nouveau was even called Le Style Métro by some.

These organic forms of Art Nouveau developed a popular (if somewhat brief) new approach to architecture and design across Europe. It would be erroneous to credit any one particular place, such as Brussels, as the "genesis" of this style, as it seems to have arisen in many locations during this cultural moment, and for a variety of different reasons. Places such as Riga, Prague, Kraków, and even Moscow began to embrace the style for the (mis)perception that it was not based on any historical precedent, an idea that was appealing to those who were searching for their own sense of identity, whether it be artistic or national. It is even perhaps questionable to label similar manifestations as Art Nouveau. In Germany, for example, Jugendstil (young style), which was inspired by the art journal *Die Jugend* (established in 1896), was the preferred term; whereas in Italy it was known as Stile Liberty in direct reference to designs produced by Liberty of London. Perhaps the most complex form of this organic approach was that of *Modernisme* in Catalonia, as practiced by Antoni Gaudí (1852–1926). The Spanish architect combined a close study of nature with inspiration from regional vernacular and the Gothic Revival to create a unique syncretic architecture as seen in Casa Batlló (see image 3) in Barcelona, which Gaudí was commissioned to redesign in 1904, and in the ongoing construction of the epic Sagrada Familia cathedral, which began in 1882.

In the area of the Austro-Hungarian Empire, Art Nouveau was expressed in a more revolutionary manner, under the banner of Secession. For Vienna, this meant a break from conservative academic systems to establish a unified approach to creative production that was wholly inspired by the Arts and Crafts Movement, particularly approaches promoted by the Glasgow School of Art (1896–1909; see p.328) in Scotland. Artists, architects and designers, including

Josef Hoffman (1870–1956), Koloman Moser (1868–1918), Gustav Klimt, and Joseph Maria Olbrich (1867–1908), established the Vienna Secession on April 3, 1897. Olbrich designed its exhibition hall as an architectural manifesto for the cause. The building represents a complete break from traditional Viennese styles, and it was criticized for looking like anything from a mausoleum to a warehouse with a head of cabbage on top. The ground plan is simple and open, and allows for flexible use within. The facade (see image 4) consists of unbroken planes of white, and symbolic ornamentation in cast concrete, and gold-painted metalwork, notably the spherical dome of gold laurel leaves mounted high above the entrance, beneath which is written the motto of the group: *Der Zeit ihre Kunst. Der Kunst ihre Freiheit* (To every age its art, to every art its freedom).

Another Austrian Secessionist, Otto Wagner (1841–1918) was a talented architect and city planner, who also showed a keen interest in a more historicist approach early in his career. In 1872, he designed the Rumbach Street synagogue in Budapest in the Moorish Revival style. In the heart of the Jewish quarter in Pest, this early work inspired a similar rebellion among a number of young Hungarian architects, such as Ödön Lechner (1845–1914) and Károly Kós (1883–1977), who called the style *szecesszió*. Responding to the new European influences, they, like Gaudí, also looked to regional sources of inspiration, particularly Magyar and Transylvanian vernacular, to create a style that was particular to Hungary. Lechner worked with Gyula Pártos (1845–1916) on one of his most characteristic Art Nouveau buildings, the Museum of Applied Arts (1896; see p.326) in Budapest.

This search for a sense of national identity appears across many examples of Art Nouveau to the extent that some scholars have considered whether "National Romanticism" might be a more appropriate term. The National Romantic nominally refers to the architectural style of Scandinavian countries during this period, which looked again to vernacular tradition as a way of expressing progressive sociopolitical ideals, particularly in Finland as it became independent of Russian rule in 1917. This is illustrated in the National Museum of Finland, designed in 1904 by Herman Gesellius (1874–1916), Armas Lindgren (1874–1929), and Eliel Saarinen (1873–1950), father of the Modernist architect Eero Saarinen. It is an eclectic building, meant to represent several periods of Finnish architecture; it includes natural and symbolic decorative elements, such as frescoes, on themes from the epic poem the "Kalevala." Although the building looks revivalist, it was the political situation of the country that transformed the design into something radical.

A similar tension was expressed in places such as Glasgow, Scotland, which is part of the United Kingdom, but retained a strong sense of its own history and identity. The Glasgow Style is a fusion of Arts and Crafts and Art Nouveau ideals which, in the work of Charles Rennie Mackintosh (1868–1928), responds as much to Scots baronial architecture as it does to the more modern Symbolist interests that also influenced the Belgian and Viennese artists. This multifaceted approach reflects the international character of Art Nouveau, seen in examples as widespread as the United States, where Louis Sullivan incorporated a diversity of folk ornamentation onto his tall office buildings and "jewel box" banks (see image 5), crafted in terracotta and wrought iron alike.

While the increasing interest in stripped-down modern design brought about the demise of Art Nouveau, its true death knell was the outbreak of World War I in 1914. The style was perceived as too decadent, perhaps even too hopeful, for it represented an ambitious spirit—a reverence for the old alongside a quest for the new. Furthermore, it channeled a desire to reconcile the tension between these opposing ideas, expressed in organic forms and symbolic ornamentation, and wrought in materials of the modern age. **RC**

3 **Casa Batlló (1906)**
Antoni Gaudí
Barcelona, Spain

4 **Secession Building (1897)**
Joseph Maria Olbrich
Vienna, Austria

5 **Merchants' National Bank (1914)**
Louis Sullivan
Grinnell, Iowa, USA

Hôtel Hankar 1894
PAUL HANKAR 1859–1901

Hôtel Hankar,
St.-Gilles, Belgium

Having founded a successful practice in the late 1880s, Paul Hankar designed for himself a combined home and atelier that would represent his style at a glance. He chose to build at 71 Rue Defacqz, St.-Gilles, not far from where his friend Victor Horta was building his first masterpiece, Hôtel Tassel. Although perhaps less well known, Hôtel Hankar is important for the way it exemplifies the influence of the Arts and Crafts Movement and Aestheticism on early Art Nouveau. Although Hankar's plan follows the traditional scheme for Belgian townhouses, it is rendered in an entirely different aesthetic on the facade. About two-thirds of the plan is given over to his studio and atelier at the front and some living space toward the rear; while the remaining third accommodates circulation, services and additional residential requirements. The atelier is framed by an oriel window over two floors, surmounted by a loggia; while the narrower circulation space is signaled by a modified lancet window inspired by Romanesque architecture. The Arts and Crafts (see p.314) influence can be seen in the decorative brickwork, especially on the division in the contrasting red and yellow brick framing the right-hand windows. On the left, the influence of Japonisme presides, particularly in hidden details such as bees and insects on the corbels, and the painted decoration under the oriel window. **RC**

◉ FOCAL POINTS

1 WROUGHT IRON

In addition to using it for the frames of the oriel window, Hankar used decorative wrought iron on the loggia to create a light, airy balcony. Likewise, it is found over the windows at basement level, at the entrance, and in the struts that support the overhang. The green patina complements the red brick facade.

2 ORIEL WINDOW

The wide expanses of glass allow significant amounts of light into the studio. The window is set within a stone frame in a traditional Italian style, yet the painted and iron decoration is more modern, inspired by Japanese prints. The charming scheme depicts three cats lounging and hunting butterflies.

3 RUSTICATION

The rusticated ashlar across the first floor adds weight to the lower left facade, making the oriel window seem lighter. Hankar also included it at the lower right around the entrance to bring a sense of unity at ground level. The effect is reminiscent of revival styles, such as Richardsonian Romanesque.

SGRAFFITO

From the Italian *graffiare* (to scratch), this decorative technique involves applying layers of color to a surface and scratching through the upper layers to reveal the lower. The color will be bound in different materials depending on the media; for example, in ceramics it might be carried out with colored clays or glazes. In architecture, the technique is done in layers of plaster and has been practiced since antiquity. It was a method promoted in the Renaissance and as such had a revival in the nineteenth century. Sgraffito was the preferred method for applying wall decoration in Belgian Art Nouveau, perhaps for the rich texture it imparts. The material lends itself to linear decoration, as well as the kind of Symbolist motifs architects wished to represent. Hankar collaborated with Adolphe Crespin at Hôtel Hankar, and again in realizing designs of the Symbolist painter Albert Ciamberlani as a narrative on the facade of the studio-home he built for him on Rue de Turin (below). These monumental works influenced future architect-designers, such as Paul Cauchie (1875–1952), most notably on the facade of his own home.

Museum of Applied Arts 1896
ODÖN LECHNER 1845–1914

Museum of Applied Arts,
Budapest, Hungary

NAVIGATOR

Although similar in spirit to the Vienna Secession, the Hungarian *szecesszió* is different in being rooted in regional vernacular traditions that resist Austrian associations. In fact, in Budapest, buildings in a more typical "whiplash curve" style are often called Jugendstil, while *szecesszió* is represented by works such as Odön Lechner's Museum of Applied Arts. Lechner studied in Paris and London, where Arts and Crafts and burgeoning Art Nouveau principles transformed his style; however, he is one of the key architects whose works have been reconsidered under the auspice of National Romanticism for its distinct Hungarian character. Lechner was the son of a tile manufacturer, an influence that appears throughout his work in his use of Zsolnay tiles and the colorful patterns that are his hallmark. He has often been compared to Gaudí for the way in which he grafted local influences into unique organic schemes. Lechner's design for the new museum—modeled in theory on the South Kensington Museum (now the Victoria & Albert Museum) in London—reflects this in the bold patterns throughout that reference the Hungarian (Magyar) vernacular as well as more Eastern roots in Mughal and Islamic motifs. The building's purpose is reflected in its materials and decorative scheme, which resembles textile patterns particular to Magyar folk art. The interior is painted all in white, a stark contrast to the colorful exterior. It is a fusion of the old and new: Eastern ogee arches flank a central court topped with a glass and steel roof, and the overall curvilinear aspect of the interior was meant to evoke the tents of Mughal tribes, the ancestors of the Magyar. **RC**

◉ FOCAL POINTS

1 POLYCHROME ROOF
The roofline is reminiscent of the Gothic, but is idiosyncratic in the color and patterning that is distinctly Eastern. Rich green and saffron tiles evoke Hungarian folk embroidery. The lantern perched above the cupola allows light to pass through a colorful stained-glass skylight at its base to the white hall within.

2 EASTERN INFLUENCE
Across the facade, ogee windows and parapets reflect a fusion of Gothic and Arabesque architecture. The East-meets-West motif is apparent on the facade and main entrance to the museum, both of which use majolica and Zsolnay tiles in floral motifs that are reminiscent of Magyar folk embroidery.

3 CAST CONCRETE
The columns at the entrance of the building were cast and polychromed for decorative effect. Although his buildings referenced historical motifs, Lechner used modern technologies, such as pyrogranite and cast iron, to achieve his desired look. Reinforced concrete was also found to be highly useful.

▲ The completely white interior of the museum is colored by a stained-glass skylight, which, together with the curvilinear scheme, suggests a Magyar tent.

ZSOLNAY TILES

Lechner used tiles from the Hungarian manufacturer Zsolnay (right) in all his buildings, such as the iridescent eosin tiles of the Museum of Applied Arts entrance, with elaborate saffron yellow handrails on the stairs cast in pyrogranite ceramic. Vilmos Zsolnay was a pioneer in developing glazing technology. Pyrogranite, so-called for its high-temperature firing and durability, was developed in the 1880s. It is highly resistant to temperature variation and even performs well with contemporary pollution, including acid rain. For this reason, it makes an excellent material for exterior tiles, especially roofs. Eosin, developed later in the 1890s, was first produced in a rich red tone before a range of colors was created. Its iridescence and luster make it suitable for both exterior tiling and decorative objects. The process for making eosin glaze remains a trade secret today.

Glasgow School of Art 1896–1909
CHARLES RENNIE MACKINTOSH 1868–1928

Glasgow School of Art,
Glasgow, Scotland

 NAVIGATOR

Charles Rennie Mackintosh won the competition to design the new permanent building for the Glasgow School of Art in 1896. Although his original plan conceived of the building as a whole, the budget was exhausted on the east and central portions. As a result, completion was put on hold for eight years until further funds were raised. This was to the benefit of the building: Mackintosh redesigned the west side, making a subtle shift in style from a historical Scots baronial influence to a more modern look. Inside the building there are a multitude of influences, from the heavy timber beams of the Arts and Crafts–inspired museum to the Symbolist decorative details found throughout. The interior also shows Japanese influence, particularly in the way in which spaces transform from dark to light. Students and staff agree that the scheme allows for plenty of light, even on a typical gray Glaswegian day. Until it was severely damaged by fire in May 2014, the Mackintosh building had retained most of its original features and undergone very little intervention, testifying to the strength of its design. **RC**

👁 FOCAL POINTS

1 WROUGHT IRON

The organic motif is most pronounced in the ironwork, which suggests the sprouting and growing of plant life in the rails and especially in the brackets across the front windows. A sweeping arch frames the entrance, topped with a stylized Glasgow city coat of arms, featuring a bird, tree, bell, and fish.

2 WINDOWS

While large windows are expected in a studio environment, Mackintosh thoughtfully oriented the largest north, to allow even light throughout the year. Their clever arrangement hides the fact that the balanced facade is asymmetrical, with three windows to the east of the entrance, and four to the west.

3 STONE CARVINGS

The modeling of stone is one of the building's most beguiling features. Over the entrance two stylized female figures picking roses are symbolic of beauty and art. The organic theme is carried out more ambiguously in the architraves, cornices, and pediments that emerge from the flat surface of the building.

▲ Rendered in dark timber and lit by elegant bay windows, the double-height library was a feat of engineering. Sadly it was destroyed in the fire of 2014.

REID BUILDING

The rebuilt School of Design (now the Reid Building, named after the first female director, Dame Seona Reid; right) opened across the street in early 2014, replacing a former Brutalist complex that the school had outgrown. Architect Steven Holl (b.1947) took inspiration from Charles Rennie Mackintosh's mastery at manipulating light into the depths of the building, similarly orienting much of the studio space to the north to take advantage of diffused Scottish light, while also bringing illumination to its depths through "driven voids"—light shafts meant to add vertical circulation. Holl's design has met with mixed reviews, with some seeing it as a bold response, and others feeling the plan lacks sympathy with Mackintosh's. In time, when the building has been tested, it will be interesting to hear the opinion of the school's most valuable critics: its students.

MODERN COLONIAL

In the decades from 1890 to 1950, vast portions of the globe became
entangled in a complex web of capitalist colonialism. During this time
significant exchanges of resources, people and ideas resulted in both
sociocultural transplantations and modern hybridity. Although not the first
phase of imperialist expansion—Spain and Portugal had claimed much of the
New World during the seventeenth and eighteenth centuries—these years saw
unprecedented power consolidation in just a few European states. In this
second wave of European imperialism, France and the United Kingdom (which
came to rule almost a quarter of the world's population and nearly a quarter of
its territory by 1938), and to a far lesser extent Italy, Portugal, Germany, and
Belgium, conquered and occupied extensively.

Colonialists exhibited their perceived superiority by building environments
familiar to European outsiders, but also by acting as self-declared conveyors of
modernity in a so-called "civilizing mission." To these ends, imposing Neoclassical
(see p.272) works were intended to dominate, differentiate, and eventually
assimilate local populations in what historian François Béguin has called the
"conqueror's style." Algeria and Vietnam (French Indochina) remain scattered
with such commanding edifices. For example, the mansard roofs of the

KEY EVENTS

1892	1906	1912	1917	1919	1921
François Hennebique patents his reinforced concrete (*béton armé*) system. By 1906, it has been used in more than 14,300 projects worldwide.	Marseilles hosts France's first Colonial Exposition, showcasing its colonial dominions. Jean-Emile Resplandy (1866–1928) wins the Grand Prize.	France declares Morocco a protectorate, alongside Algeria and Tunisia, thus consolidating its dominance of North Africa.	French architect Albert Laprade (1883–1978) publishes plans for his Habous District, a "new indigenous city" for Moroccans in a booming Casablanca.	The Treaty of Versailles formally concludes World War I, and France's Cornudet Law requires formal town plans for municipalities of 10,000 or more inhabitants.	Exemplary of the popular colonial style, the Indo-Saracenic Victoria Memorial Hall by Sir William Emerson (1843–1924) opens in Calcutta (Kolkata).

330   1870–1950

Municipal Theatre, Algiers, and the city halls of Bône (Annaba) and Oran refer directly to metropolitan models. Farther afield, Dakar's Palace of the Republic (Palais du Gouvernement Général; 1907) and the Municipal Theatre/Opera House in Hanoi (1911; see p.336) also demonstrate this aesthetic through similar architectural paraphrasing of Parisian models. As in North Africa, the Hanoi theater's arcade, roofline, and general Neoclassical appearance make clear connections to contemporary styles popular in France, in this case Paris's iconic Opéra (1860–75; see p.296). The resulting urban ambience successfully recalled home for many colonists and visitors, such as English historian Douglas Sladen, who in 1906 saw in Tunis's *ville nouvelle* (new town) "a little bit of Paris abroad." Similarly, the neo-Baroque Town Hall (see image 2) in British-run Durban by Stanley Hudson (1877–1928) dressed city administration in majestic Edwardian grandeur designed to project the prosperity and solidity of the London-based empire. Its tall dome and pedimented temple fronts were inspired by Belfast's City Hall, further demonstrating the complexity of imperial networks and the extent of colonial ambitions in southern Africa.

As empires stabilized and conquest became sustained occupation, it became necessary to at least appear less imposing. As political and sociocultural sensitivities came to favor association with locals over their supposed assimilation, architecture remained an important tool, but it changed, too. Subtlety and the paternalistic borrowing of local forms became architectural motifs and inspired new locally flavored colonial styles. The popularity of these new aesthetics was demonstrated by their common use in some form or another in French, British, and Italian imperial contexts. Although labels differed—"Arabisant" or "Arabesque," "Indo-Saracenic," "Mediterranean"—the message and intent were usually similar. Designers sought to create a sense of indigenous place in part to assuage growing discontent among locals, but also to further legitimize colonialism, while demonstrating a mastery of native tradition through modernization. As director of the Public Works Department in Tunisia, Raphaël Guy (1869–1918) was the champion of the resulting Arabesque style there. Like his Tunis Agricultural Ministry and Law Courts (Palais de Justice) in Sousse, his crenellated City Hall (Hôtel de Ville) in Sfax (1905; see p.334) exemplifies the phenomenon and is essentially European in plan and program, although clad in locally inspired decorative elements. Employed by Morocco's French Resident General Hubert Lyautey, Adrien Laforgue (1871–1952) designed the Central Post Office (Hôtel des Postes) in Casablanca (see image 1), which remains another exemplar of the colonialist interpretation of traditional local architecture. Its simple facade and loggia were praised when completed for their contextual propriety and successful masking of the city's modern communication nexus. The rich green tile (*zellij*) frieze and blue panels framing the recessed entry, typical of traditional Moroccan buildings, added a celebrated splash of local color to the whitewashed mass.

1 **Central Post Office (1920)**
Adrien Laforgue
Casablanca, Morocco

2 **Durban Town Hall (1910)**
Stanley Hudson
Durban, South Africa

1933	1936	1943	1945	1946	1947
French-Swiss architect Le Corbusier (1887–1965) publishes his radical *Plan Obus*, a daring proposal for the future of the growing city of Algiers.	Benito Mussolini ushers Italy into the competitive European colonial network by invading and occupying Abyssinia (now Ethiopia).	Le Corbusier's "Athens Charter" is published; architects and planners around the globe quickly embrace its modern, rational planning principles.	World War II ends and reconstruction begins throughout Europe, North Africa, and East Asia amid growing discontent among colonized peoples.	The First Indochina War begins in Vietnam, which will, after more than seven-and-a-half years of fighting, result in independence from France.	The United Kingdom acquiesces to India's demands for independence and concludes a century and a half of colonialist involvement there.

This appropriation of local aesthetics was not unique to France, however. The so-called Indo-Saracenic style became popular in the late nineteenth century and reflected an interest in marrying local Indian architecture with that of Victorian England. Bombay's Victoria Terminus (1888) by F. W. Stevens (1847–1900) is among the best-known examples of this hybrid style, but the practice persisted into the early decades of the twentieth century. Edwin Lutyens (1869–1944) blended traditional Indian forms with monumental Neoclassicism in the stunning Viceroy's House, New Delhi (1929; see p.338), while in British-ruled Cyprus, architect Maurice Webb (1880–1939) continued the trend at Government House (see image 3) in Nicosia. Home of the colonial governor, this building plays on the island's Orthodox Christian identity through its vaguely Byzantine dome and monastic arcades. It also recalls Cyprus's brief administration by the English king Richard the Lionheart (1191) and the subsequent Crusader era in its use of pointed arches and gargoyles. With its Ottoman-inspired elements as well, its synchronistic pastiche produced an effect intended to be comprehensively Cypriot.

Italy, a latecomer to the modern imperial process, also developed colonial regionalisms in its limited possessions in Africa and the Mediterranean. Italian architects Carlo Enrico Rava (1903–86) and Florestano di Fausto (1890–1965) debated the essential nature of regional architecture and saw value in both site context and climate. The latter's bold National Insurance Institute (see image 4) in Tripoli, with its tripartite, archlike passageway and framing stacked towers, references classical Roman forms, as well as local ones, thus supposedly rendering the building as Italian as Libyan. The resulting work appears to be the natural distillation of the Mediterranean region, which the proud architect described as the "cradle and crucible of the highest human civilization."

Over time colonial cities were increasingly viewed by many architects and urbanists as living laboratories for modernist experimentation. French Resident-General Lyautey, for example, viewed Morocco to be "what the Far West is for America: an excellent testing ground for creating new energy, rejuvenation, and fecundity." Many architects and projects were successful there, where lessons learned in Algeria, Indochina, and elsewhere were put into practice. Indeed, in many ways Casablanca (in terms of zoned planning and urban infrastructure) was more "modern" than cities in France during the early 1900s. To a considerable extent much of this creativity was inspired by persistent urban housing crises caused by the growing numbers of indigenous

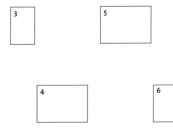

peoples migrating toward cities and, in places, considerable war damage. Many Modernists became involved, Bernard Zehrfuss (1911–96), Olivier-Clément Cacoub (1920–2008), and Le Corbusier (1887–1965) among them, from the North African context. Grand urban master plans, taller buildings, and zoned residential and industrial districts were among their common tools.

The needs of the colonized were not identical to those of the colonists. As early as 1916, French architect Albert Laprade began designing the Habous District in Casablanca, developing what he called a "new indigenous city" of rationalized traditional typologies with picturesque appeal. The Cité Musulmane El Omrane (see image 5) in Tunis took the modernizing process even further in the wake of World War II's destruction. Single-story, whitewashed courtyard homes, narrow streets, markets, and a neighborhood mosque were intended to replicate, and even improve upon, the living situation experienced in historic North African city cores (medinas) that had long since been neglected and engulfed by sprawling colonial cities. The ATBAT-Afrique towers, including the "Nid d'abeille" (honeycomb) building (1953; see p.340) in Casablanca, were also designed to respect local customs. Like the Climat de France (1959) complex by Fernand Pouillon (1912–86) in Algiers, it was intended to "modernize" the lives of locals. Architectural gestures and infrastructure improvements failed to mitigate anticolonial resentment, however. It was all too little, too late. Despite piecemeal promises for increased regional autonomy and housing projects, a wave of independence movements swept the postwar colonial world.

Within the former colonies inhabitants of colonial-era built environments have negotiated complicated relationships with inherited legacies. Building demolition and modification, such as the repurposing of ATBAT-Afrique's distinctive balconies by space-seeking residents, as well as heritage preservation have been undertaken in many places. Further contributing to the complexities of the postcolonial condition, architecture, planning, and preservation in many ex-colonies remain mostly in their original colonial-era forms, with language, pedagogies, and practices remaining largely unchanged. Sited in an open square amid a forest of Parisian-style lamp posts, the Town Hall (see image 6) in Tunis by Tunisian architect W. Ben Mahmoud (b.1942), was completed in 1998. Its pastiche of regional architectural references and its monumental facade recall Guy's work in Sfax. This compelling postcolonial landmark suggests that colonial-era legacies often remain relevant in today's globalizing world. **DC**

3 **Government House (1937)**
Maurice Webb
Nicosia, Cyprus

4 **National Insurance Institute (1938)**
Florestano di Fausto
Tripoli, Libya

5 **Cité Musulmane El Omrane (1944)**
G. Glorieux and L. Glorieux-Monfred
Tunis, Tunisia

6 **Town Hall (1998)**
W. Ben Mahmoud
Tunis, Tunisia

City Hall 1905
RAPHAËL GUY 1869–1918

City Hall (Hôtel de Ville),
Sfax, Tunisia

T he City Hall (Hôtel de Ville) in Sfax was designed by Tunisia's chief proponent of the
regionally inspired Arabesque style, Raphaël Guy, who was said to work skillfully
"with the valiance of a Gothic master" by writer Charles Géniaux. The building
sits on a landscaped square at the heart of the coastal city's gridded European district;
it anchors the busy Rue de la République at the opposite end of which lies one of the
walled medina's major gateways. The City Hall's imposing facade dominates in a manner
befitting modern municipal governance and its homage to Tunisia's historic indigenous
architecture was praised as a reflection of the conciliation and tolerance espoused by a
more sensitive colonial administration. The overall project was intended to be, as the
architect himself described in an essay posthumously published in 1920, like precolonial
buildings had been—"living expression[s] of local customs."

   The building's stately facade, praised by Géniaux for its stylistic purity and logical
utility, is divided by its projecting horseshoe-arched portal. On each side, recessed arch
windows create the effect of an elevated arcade framed in pinkish masonry panels.
Rectangular windows at street level create a visually solid foundation. The structure's
boxlike appearance is punctuated by its central dome and slender clock tower, the latter
taking the fanciful form of a mosque's minaret. The grandiose air and amalgam of elements
bring to mind the imaginative architecture so often used to represent European colonies at
many of the continent's world's fairs and expos of the early 1900s. Although the structure's
original "L"-shape plan was later made rectangular to enclose a central courtyard, the
building remains Sfax's city hall and also houses the city's archaeological museum. **DC**

✪ NAVIGATOR

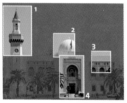

⊙ FOCAL POINTS

1 CLOCK TOWER

The 115-foot (35 m) high clock tower is the structure's most striking feature. Together with the adjacent building's corner tower, it picturesquely frames a principal avenue and punctuates the skyline. By repurposing the minaret form, Guy reorganized and secularized the day—marking the passing of time not by the five daily calls to prayer, but by the systematic passing of hours.

2 DOME

The ribbed dome, a feature common to regional funerary and religious structures, accentuates the main entrance, while balancing the building's corner tower. Erected using the Hennebique reinforced concrete system, and whitewashed, it holds aloft a spherical finial as many domes traditionally did.

3 CRENELLATION

Sawtooth rooflines were common in Guy's Arabesque architecture in Tunisia. Although they were defensive elements in the old city's fortifications, to which it was claiming strategic association, here and elsewhere in regional vernacular architecture they function decoratively.

4 PORTAL

Beneath a horseshoe arch, which was generally considered to have been the definitive element of traditional local architecture, stylized free-standing stone columns and a spindle-screened window border the building's central doorway. Spanning two stories, the portal dominates visually in a manner that is atypical of local precolonial architecture, which largely reserved decoration for interior spaces.

▼ The lofty council chamber, with its wooden ceiling, upper registers of geometrically carved plasterwork, and patterned stone paneling, is an exemplary Arabesque interior. Hanging pendant lamps add to the space's natural light, which is filtered by the replicated *mashrabiya* (carved wooden latticework) window screens.

⏲ ARCHITECT PROFILE

1869–98

Raphaël Guy was born in Rennes, France, in 1869. He received his architecture degree from the prestigious Ecole des Beaux-Arts in Paris in December 1898 under the direction of Gaston Redon, with a successful final project for a men's night asylum.

1899–1902

Having relocated to Tunisia he was appointed the principal architect for the General Directorate of Public Works there. Following his commissioning in 1900, he began designing prodigiously for the growing colonial capital and the Protectorate's other major cities.

1903–05

In 1903, Guy completed Sfax's Municipal Theatre on a site adjacent to the later City Hall in a complementary Arabesque style for which he was to become renowned. The theater was later destroyed during World War II bombing raids that devastated much of the coastal city.

1906–18

During 1906, a particularly busy year at the Public Works Department, Guy completed many structures for Tunis, including the crenellated Directorate of Finances building, the Civil Hospital's maternity ward, a city prison guardhouse, and a post office in the capital's Bab Souika neighborhood. In both the guardhouse and post office, he again repurposed the minaret form—in the former as a patrol platform and in the latter, like Sfax, as a clock tower. His Law Courts in Sousse were finished in 1907 and his imposing Tunis Directorate of Agriculture building was completed the following year. Guy died in 1918 in the northern suburb of La Marsa. In 1920, *L'Architecture Moderne de Style Arabe* was published; an extensive catalogue of Guy's work in Tunisia, it included an essay by the architect on the significance of the style.

Municipal Theatre/Opera House 1911

FRANÇOIS LAGISQUET 1864–1936

Municipal Theatre/Opera
House, Hanoi, Vietnam

Opened in 1911, after decades of planning, financial difficulty, and the involvement of several architects and engineers, Hanoi's Municipal Theatre/Opera House was designed to reflect the grand Neoclassical, Baroque, and Second Empire appearance of the colonial metropole in the so-called "Paris of the East." The architectural paraphrasing of the Paris Opéra designed by Charles Garnier (1825–98; see p.296) is unmistakable here. The facade's broad Ionic colonnade framed by domed corner pavilions, stepped approach, and pitched slate roof make this building a simplified rendition of its Parisian model. Overlooking the city's main avenue, which it anchors, the shaded loggia opens onto a mirrored salon. The adjacent grand stairway provided the opportunity for the city's European elite to see and be seen. Originally with seating on three levels, the semicircular auditorium addresses a typical proscenium-style stage. Colossal Corinthian columns hold aloft a frescoed shallow dome ceiling on squat pendentives trimmed in gold, while the stage is crowned with a gilded arch and winged figure with lyre. The decadent theater was the scene of violence and political activity during the independence era and Vietnam War, but it was largely restored in 1997 and now hosts opera and ballet performances. **DC**

✷ NAVIGATOR

👁 FOCAL POINTS

1 LOGGIA

A colonnaded loggia dominates the facade. Although far simpler than the ornate series of paired composite capitals at Garnier's Paris opera house, this space addresses an open square below and a grand interior gallery. It provides a covered space for conspicuous socializing.

2 ROOF

Steeply pitched roof elements clad in slate recall the mansard roofs popular in France during the reign of Emperor Napoleon III from 1852 to 1870. Sculpted round windows, stone balustrades, and finials further contribute to the structure's simplified Second Empire style.

3 *PORTE-COCHERE*

The theater includes an Art Nouveau–styled *porte-cochère*, or coach gate, on either side of the building. As in many late-eighteenth- and nineteenth-century buildings, these secondary entrances provided cover for privileged guests arriving by carriage or car.

◄ The focal point of the Art Nouveau auditorium space is the stage and proscenium arch. Here, three seating levels fill the semicircular hall that when constructed could accommodate most of the city's adult European population. Restoration in 1997 revived the grandeur of the hall's lavish red velvet, gold trim, and sky-blue frescoed ceilings.

ENTERTAINMENT ARCHITECTURE

Theaters and casinos were not uncommon alongside the administrative architecture of colonial cities. They reinforced ideas of civility and sophistication, while demonstrating colonialist conceptions of culture to locals. As elsewhere, theaters in Algiers, Bône, and Saigon (Ho Chi Minh City) were local landmarks that reflected metropolitan aesthetics. In Tunis, Jean-Emile Resplandy (1866–1928) created a confectionerylike theater facade (1902; right) that included the typical arcaded entrance and loggia, as well as classically inspired decorative elements. The theater was linked to a casino complex that incorporated an indoor winter garden, music hall, and cafe. A relatively modest colonial city, Tunis had at least eight cinemas and performance venues by 1930.

Viceroy's House 1929
EDWIN LUTYENS 1869–1944

👁 FOCAL POINTS

1 DOME
Said by Lutyens to have been inspired by Rome's Pantheon, the copper-clad, concrete dome rests on a tall drum wrapped in a stone latticework pattern taken from Sanchi's iconic stupa. Taller than initially planned, it looms over the city below.

2 COLONNADE
The columns' capitals are of Lutyens's ribbed "Delhi Order" and incorporate symbolic bell pendentives drawn from Hindu-Jain contexts. Shaded by a *chhajja*-like cornice, the recessed patio is similar to the classical temple front or Greek stoa.

3 *CHATRIS*
Symbols of high social status, these dome-shaped pavilions add to the air of traditional architecture endorsed by Viceroy Hardinge. With larger fountain basins nearby, the *chatris* punctuate the broad roofline.

4 FORECOURT
Framed by the eastern facade's two wings, the vast forecourt serves as a suitably grandiose ceremonial entrance to the palace. Gravel-covered and open, it and the palace are the terminus of the King's Way axis.

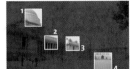

H aving relocated several villages and railway lines to make space just south of Old Delhi, British architects Edwin Lutyens and Herbert Baker (1862–1946) planned a series of Beaux Arts and City Beautiful–inspired radially intersecting boulevards, green spaces, and imposing structures for New Delhi. The former Mughal center had been declared the new capital of colonial India in 1911 and the primary motivation in its aesthetic development was the expression of ordered imperial grandeur. Built by 29,000, mostly Indian, laborers, the 350-room Viceroy's House and immense Mughal Garden are larger than Versailles, France. Despite Lutyens's well-documented disdain for what he considered to be inferior Indian architecture, Viceroy Charles Hardinge insisted on a hybrid style—"plain classic with a touch of Orientalism"—representing the intended permanence of British rule in India, but with an acknowledgment of the local context. The subtly incorporated elements of local Hindu, Buddhist, and Islamic cultural aesthetics nonetheless fail to obscure the geometric purity of Lutyens's Palladian Neoclassicism (see p.272). Indian historian Aman Nath identifies in the building a "thrusting exhibitionistic posturing" that epitomized an aloof imperialism. The palace's hallmark feature, its huge hemispherical dome, breaks the complex's generally horizontally massed series of wings and courtyards. Shaded colonnades, wide stairs, and a tall foundational podium dwarf visitors. The overall composition complements Baker's adjacent Secretariat buildings along the ceremonial King's Way, the slope of which obscured the distant view of the residence's broad red and buff sandstone facade, thereby causing a sensational row between the architects. Now the Rashtrapati Bhavan, home of India's president, the building has been restored twice since the 1980s. **DC**

Viceroy's House (now Rashtrapati Bhavan), New Delhi, India

▲ Beneath the double dome is the palace's Durbar Room, which houses a pair of honorific thrones for the former Viceroy and Vicereine. The austerely appointed interior is classically inspired and largely undecorated. Coffered apses, "Delhi Order" columns, and a two-ton chandelier make the space appropriately imposing.

◷ ARCHITECT PROFILE

1869–1911
Edwin Lutyens was born on March 29, 1869 in London, UK. He studied architecture at London's Royal College of Art. In 1888, he established his own firm and designed private residences in the Arts and Crafts style (see p.314). From 1896, with garden designer Gertrude Jekyll, he began to establish his own personal style in a series of country houses.

1912–23
When India's colonial administration elected to relocate the seat of government to Delhi, it commissioned Lutyens, together with Herbert Baker, to design a quarter there to house the new Indian capital. Lutyens was knighted in 1918, and in 1919 his original Whitehall Cenotaph was unveiled as a memorial to British veterans from World War I. The monument eventually became the country's primary war commemorative site.

1924–44
Lutyens's popular "Queen Mary's Dolls' House" went on display at the British Empire Exhibition in Wembley, Middlesex, in 1924; it represented some of the finest small-scale craftsmanship of the time. The same year he was appointed a member of the Royal Fine Art Commission. In 1930, King George V made Lutyens a Knight Commander of the Order of the Indian Empire. Lutyens died in 1944.

ATBAT-Afrique, "Nid d'abeille" 1953

GEORGES CANDILIS 1913–95,   SHADRACH WOODS 1923–73

ATBAT-Afrique, "Nid d'abeille"
Carrières Centrales,
Casablanca, Morocco

NAVIGATOR

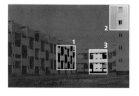

West of Casablanca is the Carrières Centrales site, with its expansive grid of rationalized courtyard houses and its culturally specific, balcony-clad towers. Built by a progressive group of architects, planners, and technicians (collectively known as ATBAT-Afrique), the project was intended to respect local customs and provide cost-efficient and densely arranged housing for the city's growing Muslim population. Having studied unplanned settlements and mountain villages, the group hoped that its work would be welcomed by residents—a comprehensive "habitat" rather than unsympathetic Modernist "machines for living." The so-called "Nid d'abeille" (honeycomb) units included two rooms and hallmark stacked patios. British architects Alison Smithson (1928–93) and Peter Smithson (1923–2003), critics of universalizing Modernism, appreciated the concern shown by ATBAT-Afrique for local context and viewed its work here to be the greatest architectural achievement since Le Corbusier's Marseilles Unité d'Habitation housing block (1947–52). Residents pierced walls to create windows and enclosed balconies to suit their needs after Morocco gained independence. As elsewhere in the postcolonial world, acts such as these humanized modernity through processes of appropriation and change. **DC**

◉ FOCAL POINTS

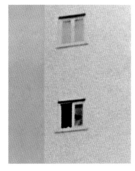

1 BALCONIES

The building's balconies render its sun-drenched south facade a series of solids and voids. In making the traditional interior courtyard into an appended exterior space, architects used high walls to ensure privacy. Each patio contained the unit's hearth and sanitary facilities.

2 WHITEWASHING

Whitewashing is a typical North African surface finish. It reflects the region's harsh sunlight, thereby helping to keep interiors cool. Many twentieth-century architects were attracted to its stark simplicity, making it a hallmark feature of Modernism.

3 COLOR PANELS

An otherwise blank facade is rhythmically animated by panels of primary colors. Recalling the art of the De Stijl movement and the architecture of Le Corbusier, the bold palette is particularly striking on an elevation with neither windows nor visible people.

◄ With two towers at the site's edge, the "Nid d'abeille" stands out amid the sea of single-story houses. Built according to tradition with enclosed courtyards at their center, this housing could not provide the needed density, thus inspiring the experimental pseudo-European "vertical city."

URBAN MASTER PLANS

Increased professionalization of urban planning practice during the early 1900s and changing city growth challenges inspired more comprehensive thinking about urban development. Following much debate in Paris, the Cornudet Law of 1919 required French cities with 10,000 or more residents to prepare plans for urban extension and embellishment. Henri Prost's iconic plan of 1915 for Casablanca (right) predates the Cornudet Law, but reflected many of the era's utopian and technocratic perspectives. It illustrates a series of intersecting boulevards ringing the precolonial city, as well as separate industrial zones and business districts, a new port, parks, and social centers. This master plan, like most, approached the city as a universal problem to be solved rationally.

CASABLANCA

JAPAN: MODERNIZATION

1 **Bank of Japan (1896)**
Tatsuno Kingo
Tokyo, Japan

2 **Koide Family House (1930s)**
Horiguchi Sutemi
Tokyo, Japan

3 **Governor-General's Office Building (1919)**
Uheiji Nagano
Taipei, Taiwan

For Japan, the period from 1895 to 1945 began with victory in the First Sino-Japanese War and ended with defeat in World War II, demarcating five decades bookended by the formation and dissolution of the Japanese empire. The new government, established in 1868 under Emperor Meiji, had inaugurated a program of rapid modernization following European and U.S. precedents, placing architecture and engineering at the forefront of Japan's transformation into an industrialized nation. It supported the development of European-style architectural education, design, and practice, and one primary aim was the production of stately buildings in Classical and Gothic Revivalist styles, equal to those of major Western countries. Yet, the mastery of foreign methods also kindled debates over how best to incorporate indigenous building traditions into modern design and construction. Japanese imperialist expansion overseas further complicated the role of architecture in nation and empire building. Not only did designers face an eclectic array of technological and stylistic options, they were also presented with an expanding geopolitical arena.

Major architectural projects were concentrated in Tokyo, which served as a showcase for Japan's progress. The 1890s witnessed a new generation of university-trained Japanese architects, who began to replace experts from Britain, France, and Germany. They faced the challenge of giving form and expression to unprecedented building types for governance, education, culture

KEY EVENTS

1893	1895	1897	1909	1910	1923
The Japanese pavilion at the World's Columbian Exposition in Chicago replicates the Phoenix Hall (11th century) of Byodoin Temple in Uji.	Japan gains Taiwan as its first overseas colony after victory in the First Sino-Japanese War.	The Ancient Shrines and Temples Preservation Law is established to protect historical buildings and the objects housed inside them.	The Maruzen Bookstore in Tokyo, by Sano Riki (1880–1956), debuts as Japan's first steel-frame structure with a non-load-bearing facade.	The Architectural Institute, Japan's primary association of architects, sponsors two debates on "The Future of our National Architectural Style."	The Great Kanto earthquake hits Tokyo and Yokohama; nearly all timber structures are burned and more than half of brick structures toppled.

and commerce. The Bank of Japan (see image 1) by Tatsuno Kingo (1854–1919) and the Akasaka Palace (1909) by Katayama Tokuma (1854–1917) demonstrate a thorough engagement with European academicism: both structures are of monumental proportions and feature quintessential Classical elements such as columns, pediments, and balustrades. The use of structural steel also indicates the drive for state-of-the-art construction practice.

Official initiatives to survey and document premodern temples and shrines resulted in recognition of the visual and symbolic impact of invoking tradition in new design. The most demonstrable sites for heralding national identity through traditional styles and materials were commemorative imperial shrines and Japanese pavilions at world's fairs. The replication of specific historical styles involved traditional, new, and emerging expertise: master carpenters, architects, and architectural historians. Yet, the majority of projects from the 1890s to the 1930s that appropriated premodern architectural forms did so in fragmentary fashion. The most common technique of expressing a uniquely indigenous style involved capping a structure with prominent hip-and-gable and gable roofs. Applied to offices, banks, hotels, stations, and museums (see p.344), this "Imperial Crown" style (*teikan yoshiki*) embodied cultural hybridity by also featuring reinforced concrete for the remainder of the building.

One of the repercussions of the Great Kanto earthquake of 1923 was the accelerated adoption of reinforced concrete construction, and experimentations with the fire- and earthquake-resistant material paralleled rising Modernist movements. The Imperial Hotel (1923) by Frank Lloyd Wright (1867–1959) is best remembered for its innovative use of structural concrete, but it is also noted for consciously styling a Japanese design without East Asian or European decorative motifs. Whereas projects by renowned foreign architects became a rarity in early twentieth-century Japan, information about avant-garde architecture developing abroad was accessible through periodicals and firsthand travel. Seeing the past through a new lens, Japanese Modernists drew upon principles of traditional architecture. The 1930s residences (see image 2) by Horiguchi Sutemi (1895–1984) were distinguished by their asymmetric, geometric, and planar composition as well as by their organic integration of house and garden.

Japanese-controlled territories and colonies provided additional prospects for large-scale planning and building. The imposition of new urban grids, infrastructure, and administrative zones visibly asserted imperialist authority. The Governor-General's Office Building in Taiwan (see image 3), a red and white masonry pile designed by Uheiji Nagano (1867–1937), occupied an entire city block. However, more than a decade of armed conflict in the Asia-Pacific region, ending with Japan's surrender to the Allies in 1945, greatly restricted building activity in the home islands. In an environment of limited design opportunities, architectural competitions—even those for monuments to war and empire— attracted architects of diverse political and stylistic inclinations. **AYT**

1933	1936	1937	1940	1945	1946
Bruno Taut (1880–1938) visits Katsura Imperial Villa (17th century) in Kyoto and praises it as an exemplar of functionalist architecture.	After almost five decades of operating in successive temporary structures, the Imperial Diet opens its session in a permanent building in Tokyo.	Exchange of gunfire near Marco Polo Bridge outside Beijing incites fully fledged war between Japan and China.	Plans for holding the Summer Olympic Games in Tokyo and a world's fair in the same year are canceled due to the escalation of war.	Japan surrenders after U.S. firebombing of its major cities and the atomic bombings of Hiroshima and Nagasaki.	In response to the housing shortage, the first two Premos units, prefabricated structures by Maekawa Kunio (1905–86), are completed.

Tokyo Imperial Household Museum 1937

JIN WATANABE 1887–1973

Tokyo Imperial Household
Museum (now Tokyo National
Museum), Tokyo, Japan

The competition for the Tokyo Imperial Household Museum (now the Tokyo National Museum) in 1930 attracted 273 entries and was won by Jin Watanabe. His design required quake- and fire-resistant construction as it was replacing the museum's original brick structure that had partially collapsed during the earthquake in 1923. Furthermore, the competition guidelines requested a building "based on Japanese taste" to reflect the collection of East Asian art to be held inside it. A further stylistic consideration was harmonization with the adjacent French Beaux-Arts–style exhibition hall and the traditional Japanese garden at the rear. Watanabe met these requirements by fusing a modern, ferro-concrete body clad in stone and tiles with a retro tiled-and-gabled roof. A *porte cochère* (large porch) in matching tile and concrete accentuated the stark material and color contrast, and the bilateral symmetry of the building. Modernists such as Maekawa Kunio (1905–86), together with members of the Japan International Architectural Association, protested against the eclectic pairing of materials and forms from such different cultures and times, yet more than half of the competition entries met the call for a Japanese style through a visually prominent sloping tiled roof. Watanabe's expansive two-story structure enabled the integration of spaces for exhibition, storage, and administration, and it also assumed a physical monumentality appropriate to the museum's stature as the nation's most significant cultural institution. **AYT**

✿ NAVIGATOR

1 GABLE

The *porte cochère* attached to the central bay of the museum is capped by a decorative triangular gable, called a *chidori hafu*, a common roof ornamentation typically found in multiples on castle turrets and Shinto shrines. The single gable here establishes a strong central, frontal emphasis.

2 BALCONY

The shallow, balconylike protrusion above the *porte cochère* deliberately resembles timber post and lintel construction, as suggested by the articulation of horizontal and vertical members, bracket sets, and jewel-shaped finials, which mimic those found in temple and shrine architecture.

3 WINDOWS

The huge tall windows of the building were originally designed with the intention that the twenty-five exhibition rooms located on both floors would receive ample natural lighting. Changing exhibition and conservation practices have since required the permanent shuttering of the windows.

⏱ ARCHITECT PROFILE

1887–1920

Jin Watanabe graduated from the architecture program at Tokyo Imperial University, after submitting a final design project titled "A Memorial Art Gallery." After working in the Ministry of Communications and Transportation, he opened his own architectural practice at the age of thirty-three.

1921–73

Having already taken part in several high-profile architectural competitions, including those for the Meiji Shrine Treasure Hall and the Soldier's Hall, Watanabe won first prize to design the Tokyo Imperial Household Museum in 1930. In contrast to the museum's Imperial Crown style, two buildings completed a year later in Tokyo achieved vastly different forms with reinforced concrete. The Daiichi Seimei Building is an example of stripped Classicism, while the Hara Residence (now Hara Museum) is an example of Bauhaus Modernism. Watanabe's work slowed down considerably in the postwar period and no known buildings of his survive from this time.

▲ The most luxurious details of the building are in the grand entry hall, which features a central staircase, marble flooring and walls, coffered ceilings, sculpted cornices, and bronze door panels.

EARLY MODERN

E nglish architect Peter Smithson (1923–2003) expressed the long-awaited fulfillment of the idea of Modernism in terms of "a building that is so different from those which preceded it as to establish a new architecture as a fact, not as a possibility." Influences came from an older generation of architects, often by direct contact, including Auguste Perret (1874–1954) with his rationalist use of concrete in France, the stripping down of Classical decoration in Austria by Otto Wagner (1841–1918), the concept of architecture as a form of product design by Peter Behrens (1868–1940) in Germany, and probably most important of all, the inventive compositions and plan forms— playing old games with new counters—of Frank Lloyd Wright (1867–1959) in the United States. These and others paved the way for further advances. In the Fagus Factory in Germany (see image 1), by Walter Gropius (1883–1969), all the characteristics of Modernism were made plain. The reduction of the corner to a junction of glass panes, the suppression of the brick-clad steel frame behind the plane of the windows, and the heady sense of pure form thus created mark the shift to a much-anticipated land of promise. After World War I, attempts at recovery and the desire for radical change brought urgency to the movement.

KEY EVENTS

1910	1914	1919	1922	1923	1927
Frank Lloyd Wright's designs are published as lithographs by Ernst Wasmuth in the "Wasmuth Portfolio." They provide inspiration for European designers.	Cologne's Werkbund Exhibition includes Proto-Modernist buildings by Walter Gropius, Adolf Meyer (1881–1929), and Bruno Taut (1880–1938).	Walter Gropius founds the Bauhaus school in Weimar. There is no formal architectural teaching before 1928, although architecture pervades the syllabus.	The *Chicago Tribune* competition attracts European Modernists, but a Gothic Revival (see p.284) project by Raymond Hood (1881–1934) is chosen.	Le Corbusier publishes *Vers une Architecture* (*Toward a New Architecture*), the leading polemic of Modernist architecture.	*The Victory of the New Building Style* by Walter Curt Behrendt, a leading supporter of Modernism, is published.

In order to emphasize the difference of outlook, Early Modernist buildings had distinctive formal properties: flat surfaces, brightly colored or dazzling white, assembled into cubic forms that avoided the compositional symmetry or hierarchies of the past. Materials—concrete, glass, and steel, above all— came out of hiding and contributed to the possibility of defying the disciplines of weight and mass that previously ruled European architecture. Science contributed to the engineering, while production methods attempted to emulate Henry Ford's assembly line. F. W. Taylor's time and motion studies represented an ideal of efficient functional planning. Advocates of Modernism were convinced that it represented more than just a style or an advance in cheapness or efficiency, however. Its rapid international diffusion was proof that it embodied, as Walter Curt Behrendt wrote, "the will to return to basic principles and elementary rules of building," and thus to reconnect with the deeper meaning of past architecture.

Preoccupations with hygienic living in the early twentieth century shaped Modernism's transformative mission. Sanatorium buildings, such as the Zonnestraal (see image 2) at Hilversum in the Netherlands by Bernard Bijvoet (1889–1979) and Johannes Duiker (1890–1935), and the Paimio Sanatorium (1929) in Finland by Alvar Aalto (1898–1976), used concrete construction to open up the rooms to health-giving light and air. Duiker designed partially open-air schools in Amsterdam, and in the town of Suresnes in the western suburbs of Paris, the Ecole en Plein Air (1934) by Eugène Beaudoin (1898–1983) and Marcel Lods (1891–1978) missed no opportunities for giving its sickly pupils the benefits of shower baths and heated classrooms with walls that folded away to admit fresh air, all in a leafy hilltop setting. Open-air bathing establishments in Switzerland and Czechoslovakia carried these ideals to the masses, and in south London a revolutionary experiment in public health was carried out within the practical concrete floors and columns of the Pioneer Health Centre, Peckham, by Sir Owen Williams (1890–1969) in 1935.

Separate national artistic movements, such as De Stijl, Constructivism, and Futurism (see p.368), merged into a collective effort that spread into the Baltic States, Greece, and Turkey. In France, Le Corbusier (1887–1965) was a leading figure, initially as much through his writings and planning proposals, such as the Plan Voisin for Paris of 1925, as through completed buildings. His formal inventiveness made him a powerful inspiration, and his romantic temperament contradicted hard-edged slogans such as "a house is a machine for living in." In his interiors, such as the Pavillon de l'Esprit Nouveau (Pavilion of the New Spirit) at the Art Deco (see p.358) exhibition, Paris, in 1925, storage furniture and late Cubist paintings demonstrated the connection between art and daily living. In his houses for a workers' colony at Pessac, near Bordeaux, Le Corbusier first experimented with luminous colors on different wall surfaces to enliven the geometric forms.

1 **Fagus Factory (1911)**
Walter Gropius
Alfeld, Germany

2 **Zonnestraal (1927)**
Bernard Bijvoet and Johannes Duiker
Hilversum, the Netherlands

1927	1928	1929	1930	1930	1932
The competition for the League of Nations building in Geneva is held. Le Corbusier claims the final plans are plagiarized from his submission.	The first meeting of Congrès International d'Architecture Moderne (CIAM) in Switzerland creates a network of leading Modernists.	*Befreites Wohnung* (*Liberated Living*), by critic and secretary of CIAM Sigfried Giedion, extolls the health-giving aims of Modernism.	The Stockholm Exhibition marks Sweden's adoption of Modernism by former Classicists, such as Gunnar Asplund (1885–1940).	Le Corbusier and his cousin, Pierre Jeanneret (1896–1967), complete Villa Savoye (see p.350), a Modernist villa in Poissy, France.	The "International Exhibition of Modern Architecture" takes place at the Museum of Modern Art in New York.

In Germany, unbuilt projects by Ludwig Mies van der Rohe (1886–1969) assumed great importance owing to their clarity of constructional concept, involving extensive glass walls. At Mies's German Pavilion at the Barcelona Exhibition of 1929, architecture was reimagined through fundamental relationships of planes and spaces, beautifully detailed and crafted, and at the Tugendhat House at Brno (see image 3), he turned them into a rethinking of daily living without separate rooms.

In most countries, some of the key Early Modern buildings were private middle-class villas, owing to the willingness of a small number of patrons to experiment, such as at Le Corbusier's Villa Savoye (1930; see p.350) in France. The classical idea of simple elegant living in a rural setting referred to Renaissance precedent, now endowed with roof terraces for exercise and sunbathing. A more complex interpretation of modern living was offered at the Maison de Verre (Glass House; 1932), concealed behind a conventional street frontage on the Left Bank in Paris, by Bijvoet and the furniture designer Pierre Chareau. With a structure reduced to steel and glass bricks, this building went beyond functional elegance and achieved Surrealist poetry.

For many modern architects, mass housing was the principal ambition. The published plan for an industrial city by Tony Garnier (1869–1948) in 1904 — with its zoned, rational layout and buildings enveloped among trees — was an influential model for a transition from the picturesque suburb to a rationally planned version with taller apartments in Lyon (1920–34) that broke away from urban courtyard forms to admit more air and light. In the early 1920s, developments by J. J. P. Oud (1890–1963) as municipal housing architect for Rotterdam (Hook of Holland, 1924; Kiefhoek, 1929) attracted attention for their realization of pure white streamlined row houses. City housing authorities developed standardized plan types for economy and speed of construction. Often placed on greenfield sites beyond the existing city, the layouts emphasized individual gardens for growing food as a persisting legacy from wartime shortages, offering health and self-sufficiency, often fertilized by the composting toilets included in the suburban Törten Estate, Dessau (1928), by Gropius, with low-rise, concrete row houses.

3 **Tugendhat House (1930)**
Ludwig Mies van der Rohe
Brno, Czech Republic

4 **Bergpolder Apartments (1935)**
W. van Tijen, Johannes Brinkman,
and Leendert van der Vlugt
Rotterdam, the Netherlands

5 **Stuyvesant Town–Peter Cooper Village (1947)**
Irwin Clavan and Gilmore Clarke
New York, New York, USA

Bruno Taut's (1880–1938) Berlin estates for the GEHAG housing association mixed low-rise houses with medium-rise apartments, including the photogenic horseshoe of apartments at Britz Siedlung (1927) that enclosed a public garden. As city architect and planner in Frankfurt, Ernst May (1886–1970) was responsible for creating 15,000 housing units, each with an individual character. At Römerstadt (1928), May created long curved retaining walls with yards on the flood plain of the River Nidda and streets of two-story houses behind, minimal but carefully planned and fitted with the compact and ergonomically efficient "Frankfurt kitchen" developed by Grete Schütte-Lihotzky (1897–2000).

Proximity to nature and equal access to sunlight shaped the Zeilenbau pattern of parallel four- or five-story slab blocks of apartments aligned north and south with swathes of grass and trees between them, seen in the Siemensstadt (1931) in Berlin, where Walter Gropius and Hans Scharoun (1893–1972) contributed different sections. In France, lightweight steel framing was used by Beaudoin and Lods at the Cité de la Muette, Drancy (1934), with courtyard formations of apartments filled with greenery and punctuated by five slender tower blocks that prefigure the skyline of much postwar housing. The same "Mopin" construction was adopted at Quarry Hill (1938), Leeds, by R. A. H. Livett (1898–1959) in the most visually spectacular of a small number of British Modernist residential developments prior to 1945. In the long term, a more influential block was Bergpolder (see image 4), Rotterdam, by W. van Tijen (1894–1974), Johannes Brinkman (1902–49), and Leendert van der Vlugt (1894–1936). Consisting of a slender nine-story slab block with one face composed of access galleries, the other a grid of individual balconies, it went beyond the appearance of masonry walls of the 1920s to present a building assembled from dry-mounted industrial components.

In the United States, radical new town planning, such as at Radburn, New Jersey, in 1929, did not generate radical-looking buildings. The original Zeilenbau design for the Carl Mackley Houses (1935), Philadelphia, by German émigré Oskar Stonorov (1905–70) with Albert Kastner (1900–75), was modified in plan form and materials to take on a more picturesque local character. The smooth tiled exteriors, without balconies, are similar to the large-scale housing for postwar veterans on Manhattan's Lower East Side, Stuyvesant Town–Peter Cooper Village (see image 5). Here the Corbusian vision of housing in a park was realized with gaunt brick housing blocks offset by car-free pathways, formal public spaces, and many trees.

While these housing projects met a direct social need, they also contributed to the polemics of Early Modernism, feeding into the discussions of the Congrès International d'Architecture Moderne (CIAM), which first met in 1928, and setting the agenda for collaborative research and public presentation. The Deutsche Werkbund was founded more in relation to product design in 1907 and took on a promotional role for architecture with the Weissenhof Siedlung in 1927, and its lesser-known successors at Breslau (1929) and Vienna (1932). These were live housing exhibitions, open to the public for a season, which then became full-time dwellings. As media events, these were precursors of demonstration projects, such as the Hansaviertel (1958), Berlin, to which famous Modernists contributed free-standing blocks of flats amid grass and trees, and the Internationale Bauausstellung (IBA), which took place in Berlin from 1979 to 1987, signaling a turnaround of ideology and a return to the tradition of the medium-rise urban courtyard block. However, if the planning forms and stylistic constraints of Modernism were reversed at the IBA, the desire to teach the world how to build better cities was retained.

The Early Modern Movement has had a worldwide influence for the last hundred years, and although modified by time and place, its aesthetic has prevailed, if not always its social mission. **AP**

Villa Savoye 1930

LE CORBUSIER 1887–1965,   PIERRE JEANNERET 1896–1967

Villa Savoye,
Poissy, France

NAVIGATOR

I n the 1920s, Le Corbusier used his private house commissions to develop his architectural ideas, among them "Five Points of a New Architecture." Villa Savoye's requirement for a weekend retreat was interpreted by the architects as a symbolic enactment of modern man linked by car to the metropolis, returning to the health-giving, spiritually restorative effects of nature. Thus the car circles beneath the pilotis (the first of the five points)—the concrete columns that raise the main rooms above the ground—dropping its passengers at the door. They enter an austere vestibule and, ascending a ramp, they catch the cinematic perspectives of the raised terrace roof garden (second point), which has its own concrete table, and the main living room, overlooking the landscape through a long ribbon window (fifth point). The ramp continues up to a roof-terrace solarium, with a curved suntrap wall, softening the facade (fourth point). Le Corbusier called this sequence the "promenade architecturale." The Villa Savoye was the culmination of a series of designs, resolving formal geometry and the arabesque lines of walls that reinforced concrete allowed (third point). It was also the most explicit Modernist reworking of the idea of the classical retreat, exemplified by Palladio's sixteenth-century Veneto villas. **AP**

1 RIBBON WINDOWS
For Le Corbusier *fenêtres en longeur* (ribbon windows) provided optimum daylight in a room. While internal partitions might separate the rooms within, the outside appearance was of a continuous band, allowing for future reconfiguration of the plan.

2 SOLARIUM
The incongruous curved screen walls are the ghostly remnants of an extra bedroom story that was eliminated from the design to reduce costs. Their outside shell was retained, however, as a rooftop solarium, reinforcing the ambiguity of inside and outside spaces.

3 PILOTIS
Le Corbusier reinvented columns as an architectural principle, raising the building and allowing the garden to pass beneath it. He may have been inspired by the excavation of prehistoric lake dwellings on stilts, as well as by the potential of the concrete frame.

◀ A large roof terrace fills the space between the arms of the L-shaped arrangement of the rooms, its outer wall ambiguously windowlike. Sheltered with a roof at one end, it is easily accessed from the ramp, or from the sliding floor-to-ceiling glass wall of the salon.

⏱ ARCHITECT PROFILE

1887–1917
Charles-Edouard Jeanneret was born in the Swiss watchmaking town of La Chaux de Fonds. He initially studied to become an engraver of watch cases, but was lured into architecture. He built houses locally from an early age, and after periods working with Auguste Perret and Peter Behrens absorbed the latest European Proto-Modernist thinking. Settling in Paris in 1917, he created a new persona as Le Corbusier—polemicist, painter, planner, and architect. In Le Corbusier, science and creative intuition are continuously in dynamic dialogue.

1918–28
From 1922 to 1927, Le Corbusier and his cousin Pierre Jeanneret designed many private houses for clients around the outskirts of Paris, including Villa Savoye, Maison Cook (1924), Maison Planeix (1928), and Maison La Roche (1925), which houses the Fondation Le Corbusier. He published a collection of essays, *Vers une Architecture*, exploring the concept of modern architecture in 1923 (*Toward a New Architecture*, 1927). In 1928, Le Corbusier was one of the founding members of the Congrès International d'Architecture Moderne (CIAM), and he proved to be particularly influential in urban planning.

1929–65
Le Corbusier was comparable to Picasso in his dominance and unpredictability, shifting from one version of Modernism to another. His self-belief was not shared by many clients, and large buildings came to him mainly after 1945, when he reinvented his style with *béton brut* (raw concrete) at the Unité d'Habitation housing, Marseilles (1947–52), and in the government buildings at Chandigarh, the new capital of the Punjab, India, which he worked on from 1951 until his death.

REGIONAL REVIVAL

1 **Royal Hawaiian Hotel (1927)**
Warren and Wetmore
Waikiki, Honolulu, Hawaii

2 **Monk's Hill Terrace (1930s)**
Architect unknown
Newton, Singapore

3 **Coloane Library (1917)**
Swan & Maclaren
Coloane, Macau, China

A s the Eclecticism of the nineteenth century awoke in an era of Modernism, the revival styles that were once considered luxuries, often atypical of their surroundings, became necessities that were increasingly representative of new regional vernacular vocabularies. Supported by theorists still seeking a modern style suitable to local climates and building methods, regional adaptations followed ecological and evolutionary analogies. Ecological buildings adapted to their environment, such as the "black and whites" of tropical Singapore. Evolutionary buildings emerged from successive replications or variations, as seen in the 1930s library in Coloane, Macau. Hybrids include the New England Colonial Cape Cod cottage, which became a universal style across the United States. However, the Proto-Modern Mission and Spanish Revival styles associated with early twentieth-century boomtown Florida, and with population expansion in the southwestern states and California, were those that went native and became Modern. Irving Gill (1870–1936) reduced Mission to its minimalist essence, thereby creating a new California Modernism supported by new building technologies, such as tilt-wall construction.

The 1930s "black and whites" in Monk's Hill Terrace, Singapore (see image 2), are not imitations of English Tudor Revival cottages, but local interpretations adapted to the tropics. Deep eave rooflines shade facades. Horizontal and vertical louvers work in tandem to direct cool air. Shutters admit or block sunlight, and second-floor verandas have pull-down sunshades.

KEY EVENTS

1913	1927	1932	1940	1947	1948
Alice Lee and Katherine Teats commission Irving Gill to build Teats House (see p.354).	An extravagant gala event is held in Waikiki, Hawaii, to celebrate the opening of the luxury Royal Hawaiian Hotel.	*Woman's Home Companion* publishes a Cape Cod design in its journal and receives a record number of requests for its plan.	*The Modern House in America* by James Ford and Katherine Morrow Ford categorizes U.S. Modernism as regional, counting seven areas of regional styles.	Architectural critic Lewis Mumford's suggestion of a Bay Region Style, in an article for *The New Yorker*, ignites lengthy debate.	New York's Museum of Modern Art rebuffs Mumford's Bay Region Style with the symposium "What is Happening to Modern Architecture?"

Nominal half timbering connects the terrace to British antecedents. In *The Evolution of Designs* (1979), Philip Steadman noted the likelihood of "strange and wonderful reinterpretations and elaborations" as a result of accidental variations. He could have been referring to the one-story library in Coloane (see image 3). Unreflective of obvious Portuguese influence from Macau's lengthy foreign administration, the library's six Ionic columns on the deep portico are classical in origin. Lightly fluted chubby shafts sit atop bold square bases. The volutes of the capitals are deconstructed and disengaged, their twin spirals segmented into four proportionally undersized circles and reattached at four equidistant points beneath each column's flat tablet abacus. The effect is unintentionally Postmodern.

Although U.S. journals and architectural competitions in the 1930s were the domain of flat-roofed Modernism, the general public preferred the comfort of its nascent history. In 1932, Herbert Hoover, President of the United States from 1929 to 1933, awarded the grand prize in a national small house competition to the architect of a Cape Cod cottage. Sparked by enthusiasm for Colonial Williamsburg (a living history museum opened in 1932) and the popularity of historic city quarters such as St. Augustine, Florida, and Albuquerque, New Mexico, living history continued to grow with the widespread distribution of New England Colonial styles and the assimilation of Mission and Spanish Revival styles as "native" architecture. When the French government had commissioned Alexis de Tocqueville to visit the United States in 1831 to 1832 to report on its penal system, the historian wrote of his joy at sailing into New York City and seeing "a multitude of small, artfully embellished candy-box houses." Whether those houses included the seventeenth-century Colonial Cape Cod is not known, but the Cape Cod evolved into an evergreen national vernacular style (see p.356).

In 1980, U.S. critic Paul Goldberger wondered whether there was such a thing as a national residential style, and decided that if there were it might be the Cape Cod or southern California's version of Spanish Revival styles. Spare Spanish styles had become de facto vernacular in several southwestern U.S. states, in Florida and, surprisingly perhaps, in Hawaii, where examples include the Royal Hawaiian Hotel (see image 1). U.S. architect Bertram Goodhue (1869–1924) won the commission to design the Panama-California Exposition (1915–17) in San Diego, assisted by Irving Gill. However, Goodhue favored the flamboyant Churrigueresque Spanish Baroque Revival at the expense of the indigenous Mission style. Gill resigned and continued to influence the modern style of southern California with his development of Mission architecture, in parallel with George Washington Smith (1876–1930). The excess of foreign Baroque style did not suit the United States's pioneer spirit, but the redefined candy-box Cape Cod and the inherent Modernism of Mission and Spanish Revival styles captured the diversity and desires of a new nation. **DJ**

1958	1959	1963	1981	1983	1996
The Velasca Tower in Milan, by architectural firm BBPR, is criticized for its cantilevered upper stories and medieval atmosphere.	Editor of *Casabella* magazine Ernesto Rogers calls for "tolerant" modernism that includes the "historicism" of regional architecture.	*Design with Climate: A Basic Approach to Architectural Regionalism* by Victor Olgyay prioritizes local climates and materials.	Robert Davis develops Seaside, Florida, with design codes for a harmonious cottage style, reflecting nonspecific regional architecture.	Kenneth Frampton's *Toward a Critical Regionalism* calls for modern architecture tempered by geographical context.	The Congress for New Urbanism issues the Charter of the New Urbanism for metropolitan and regional planning.

Teats House 1913

IRVING GILL 1870–1936,   WILLIAM HEBBARD 1863–1930

Teats House
San Diego, California, USA

⚙ NAVIGATOR

An important early southern California developer, Alice Lee purchased plots on Seventh Avenue in Hillcrest, near Balboa Park, San Diego, and in 1905 commissioned architects William Hebbard and Irving Gill to design three houses with a communal garden. Gill was already building experimental houses in the Hillcrest area, such as his bungalow of 1903 with a curvilinear Mission parapet on Albatross Street and his cube house of 1909. Together with Katherine Teats, Lee developed a Hillcrest subdivision (1913) and commissioned Gill. Teats House was one of two pairs of cube houses proposed for the site; it was reduced to basics—the straight line, the arch, the cube—by Gill's "passion for elimination." The facade is a geometric positive–negative monumental volume; the stucco surface finish of Mission architecture is translated with poured concrete. The recessed doorway sits within an arched flat-roof box porch terminating in short elbow bends, and quadrilateral frameless casement windows offset the void and solids of the "J-shaped" fireplace and chimney. The interior void follows the seamless flow of the recessed fireplaces, flush baseboards, and moldings of Gill's Lewis Court (Bell Vista Terrace) cottages in Sierra Madre (1910). California-based architect Richard Neutra (1892–1970) awarded Gill's architecture the accolade "indigenous modernism." **DJ**

◉ FOCAL POINTS

1 PORCH

Repeating forms in the design of the house include the shaft and "foot" of the J-shaped fireplace, which are borrowed, turned and repeated for each half of the arched porch. The porch arch is repeated in the recessed arched front door, and is repeated again in the arched entry of the Gill house next door.

2 ROOF

Terracotta barrel roof tiles are limited by Gill to the four ridges of the low-profile hipped roof, "punctured" by the facade chimney. Deep roof eaves reveal Mission-style exposed square roof beams (*vigas*), a style popularized from the 1880s by the Santa Fe and Southern Pacific railways who adopted it for their stations.

3 WINDOWS

Although a style dating back centuries, the vertical side-hinged, single or double pane casement window was a modern alternative to the double hung sash window with its multiple panes. The Chicago windows on the side elevation have top-hinged transom windows above the side casements.

CONCRETE HOUSES

Irving Gill used "tilt slab" concrete construction for La Jolla Woman's Club (1914), California, and Dodge House (1916), Los Angeles. In a technique invented by Robert Aiken, concrete walls were poured in flat forms and when dry were tilted up onto the foundation. Rudolf Schindler (1887–1953) and Clyde Chace used Gill's concrete equipment to make tapered tilt-up walls for the Schindler-Chace House, West Hollywood (above), in 1922. Cured in forms lined with soap, paper, and burlap to allow smooth separation, several elevations feature vertical channels of glass between the concrete sections. Inventor Thomas Edison released his patent for concrete houses cast in iron formwork, which Charles Ingersoll improved using cheaper wooden formwork for concrete houses in Union, New Jersey, in 1917. In 1918, the Ingersoll-Rand Company commissioned concrete houses in Phillipsburg, New Jersey, built with Portland cement from Edison's cement company.

◄ On the side elevation, Louis Sullivan–style Chicago windows are paired with Mediterranean-style balconies and French windows. Gill and Frank Lloyd Wright worked at Adler & Sullivan in Chicago, but Gill's principles are more Mission and Modern than Prairie House.

Cape Cod Houses Early twentieth century
ARCHITECT UNKNOWN

Cape Cod Houses,
Chatham, Chicago,
Illinois, USA

The seventeenth-century colonial Cape Cod house—a pitched-roof shingle or clapboard rectangular timber-framed house—was both a regional and a national style by the twentieth century. It achieved this distinction because Capes fell outside the sphere of Modernism that writer Carlos Eduardo Días Comas described as a "fetishist cult of the original uncorrupted by diffusion." Here the three Cape houses on a suburban street near Chicago are joyfully corrupt and deliberately diffuse, and defy the narrowness of Modernism. They exemplify regional adaptation set by climate, materials, and taste. The proliferation of suburban "tract" or developer housing in the United States during the twentieth century was sparked by the Levittown, Long Island, development of standard Cape-style houses. Developer houses could not be classed as vernacular, observed J. B. Jackson in "The Domestication of the Garage" (1976), because they were "the creation of the housing industry." He did, however, identify adapted use by the homeowner, particularly the incorporation of the garage as a living area, as "an authentic example" of vernacular. The trio of Chatham Capes incorporate the asymmetry (off-center doors and windows) of the original "half Cape" and "three-quarter Cape," plus the steep pitched roof and snug single-story profile, while adding non-original awnings, quoins, and Gothic and Tudor details. The houses honor Cape Cod colonial revival more in the breach than in the observance, and in doing so create a unique version of a quintessential American home. **DJ**

✦ **NAVIGATOR**

1 RED HOUSE, LEFT

Colonial-era Capes in New England and Canada's Atlantic seaboard were built from wood, not brick, and clad with wood clapboard or shingles. Bay windows are not original features, nor are the faux stone quoins at the bay's corners, which combined with the "battlement"-style red garden edging create a "Gothic" Cape.

2 YELLOW HOUSE

Colonial Capes often had an idiosyncratic number and arrangement of windows on the gable ends. Sash windows with jaunty yellow awnings sit beneath the steep pitched gable roof, which like Colonial Capes is designed to shed snow quickly. The asymmetrical elevated gable porch sits above a raised basement.

3 RED HOUSE, RIGHT

Colonial revivals in the twentieth century usually retain the small footprint of their namesakes. Although nominally one story like the originals, this trio have raised basements and living space tucked into the attic. Roof dormers help increase usable space. The white half timbering is a nod to Tudor style.

SALTBOXES

Saltboxes are a colonial New England house style dating to the mid-17th century. The saltbox shape—two stories with a central chimney on a pitched roof sloping sharply to one story at the back (right)—became ubiquitous largely due to its flexibility. The termination of the slope functions as a lean-to addition to the main house, a feature that could be added after the main house was built. Timber-frame construction was the main building method in 17th- and 18th-century America, before balloon-frame construction superseded it in the 19th century. Timber framing joins large pieces of wood with mortise-and-tenon joints using wooden pegs instead of nails or glue. Log houses and timber framing are now regaining popularity, partly because of their inherent green credentials and an emerging mindset of self-sufficiency and resilience against rapidly evolving and unpredictable climate change.

ART DECO

I t is a paradox of the architectural history of the twentieth century that some of the most popular buildings, such as New York's Chrysler Building (see image 1) by William Van Alen (1883–1954) or great cinema interiors, such as Louxor Palais du Cinéma in Paris (see image 2), often fail to find a place. The dominance of Modernism and its concern with policing its boundaries has ensured that a large tranche of the actual production is excluded or relegated to appendices. Partly as a result of this segregation, there is no commonly accepted term to cover all the alternatives to Modernism after 1900, although certain subcategories, such as Art Deco, are named and defined.

A description only widely used after 1968, Art Deco was a colloquialism arising from the title of the Exposition Internationale des Arts Décoratifs et Industriels Modernes in Paris in 1925. French architects had developed a recognizable style that was not overtly historical, yet which, in most cases, observed the compositional rules of Classicism. Simplified floral or geometric ornament, derived from contemporary textile patterns and other decorative objects, which in turn were often taken from "primitive" historical styles, such as Egyptian, Aztec, and Asiatic, augmented classical elements. This was the high period of Robert Mallet-Stevens (1886–1945) in Paris, with villas and apartments luxuriously furnished in styles emanating from the Vienna

KEY EVENTS

1913	1922	1923	1924	1925	1925
Théâtre des Champs-Elysées opens, with designs by Auguste Perret (1874–1954), sculpture by Antoine Bourdelle and paintings by Maurice Denis.	Raymond Hood wins the Tribune Tower competition with John Mead Howells.	The first Gothenburg Tricentennial Jubilee Exhibition is held as a launch pad for Swedish Classicism and decorative arts, as well as urban planning.	The British Empire Exhibition opens at Wembley, London, with displays influenced by Gothenburg, such as murals and a concrete Classical stadium.	Pierre Patout (1879–1965) designs a sumptuous Art Deco pavilion (Pavillon de Collectionneur) for the Paris International Exhibition.	Le Corbusier publishes *The Decorative Art of Today*, a polemic condemning the content of the Paris International Exhibition of 1925.

Secession and the work of Scottish architect Charles Rennie Mackintosh (1868–1928). The interpenetrating horizontal planes and 45-degree angles of Frank Lloyd Wright (1867–1959) also became favorite decorative devices. Cubist painting, from which a "Cubist House" was derived in 1912 and a style known as Czech Cubism, provided a further origin for faceted forms.

Although austere at times, Art Deco was a style of feminine elegance and emancipation, deliberately recalling the great French styles of the past. The Salon d'Automne in Paris was the showcase for novel interiors in which the *ensemblier*, acting as architect and decorator, brought together the luxury work of artists and craftsmen. The Paris International Exhibition of 1937 did not differ substantially in its overall presentation from the exhibition in 1925. Ornament was less in evidence and the buildings, such as the Palais de Chaillot by Boileau, Carlu & Azéma, tended to be grander and more columnar.

The Paris exhibition in 1925 helped to spread the style worldwide, and its influence lasted until 1939. Architects in the United States, where European Modernism was slow to take hold, substituted Art Deco when not selecting Classical, Gothic, or other historical styles, such as Spanish Colonial. The top of the Chrysler Building is a good example of the upward directional, similar forms also seen in jewelry and furniture. These forms are found in the Bullocks Wilshire store (1929), Los Angeles, by John (1861–1935) and Donald (1895–1945) Parkinson, and in the blockier forms of New York skyscrapers by Raymond Hood (1881–1934), such as the Daily News (1929) and Rockefeller Center (1937), for which Hood was the chief designer. Hood launched his career in Chicago by winning the Tribune Tower competition (with John Mead Howells, 1868–1959) in 1922 against a distinguished international field. One of the leading architects in the 1920s was James Gamble Rogers (1867–1947). His Stirling Library (1930) at

1 **Chrysler Building (1930)**
William Van Alen
New York, New York, USA

2 **Louxour Palais du Cinéma (1921)**
Henri Zipcy
Paris, France

1930	1931	1933	1935	1937	1939
Construction of the Rockefeller Center, fourteen buildings in the Art Deco style, begins in New York City, with Raymond Hood as principal architect.	The International Colonial Exhibition, a celebration of the exotic, takes place in Paris. The Palais de la Porte Dorée exhibit hall still remains today.	The Century of Progress World's Fair is held in Chicago—a "Rainbow City" of colored lights and Streamline Moderne forms.	SS *Normandie* enters service. A technical marvel, it features streamlined interiors by French architect Roger-Henri Expert (1882–1955) and others.	The Palais de Tokyo (1937; see p.362) is one of the few surviving structures from the Paris International Exhibition. It is now an art museum.	The New York World's Fair provides the last moment for Art Deco before European Modernism leads to different styles.

3 **Rodin Museum (1929)**
Paul Cret
Philadelphia, Pennsylvania, USA

4 **Stockholm Concert Hall (1926)**
Ivar Tengbom
Stockholm, Sweden

5 **Duveen Galleries (1937)**
John Russell Pope
Tate Britain, London, UK

6 **Musée de la Mer (1933)**
Hiriart, Lafaye, and Lacoureyre
Biarritz, Aquitaine, France

Yale University uses many Art Deco compositional devices. Bertram Grosvenor Goodhue (1869–1924) made the transition from Gothic and Romanesque to a clearly identifiable Art Deco with buildings completed after his death in 1924, such as Los Angeles Public Library and Nebraska State Capitol.

After 1930, some Modernist aspects, such as the streamlining associated with Erich Mendelsohn (1887–1953), ushered in a second phase of Art Deco, sometimes called "Streamline Moderne." Many buildings in Miami Beach were designed in this style, which continued until the New York World's Fair in 1939. Little ornament appeared in Streamline Moderne, but Modernists believed the efforts to be superficial copies of serious works, lacking a coherent relationship between form, structure, and purpose, and designed to be self-consciously eye-catching. The distinctions between Art Deco and Streamline Moderne are sometimes hard to distinguish, and the former was sometimes condemned merely for being a perceived out-of-date form of Modernism.

Alongside Art Deco lies a substantial corpus of buildings that were less modern without being fully historical. Their modes could vary between the Classical and Gothic, and they were often the successors of the National Romantic styles of the late nineteenth century. "Stripped Classicism" is a term sometimes applied to them, denoting the reduction of ornament. This was a process begun in Austria and Germany before 1914 by architects such as Otto Wagner (1841–1918), and by Auguste Perret (1874–1954) in France. Stockholm City Hall (1923) by Ragnar Ostberg (1866–1945) is a notable and influential example, more Romantic than Classical. Arrays of simplified columns were revived from Neoclassicism (see p.272) by Peter Behrens (1868–1940) in the German Embassy in St. Petersburg (1913) and by Ivar Tengbom (1878–1968) in the Stockholm Concert Hall (see image 4) in a style called "Swedish Grace" that dominated the Nordic countries in the 1920s. Figure sculpture by Carl Milles was the normal accompaniment to Swedish buildings of this kind (see image 4).

Students at the Ecole des Beaux-Arts, Paris (see p.292), similarly followed their masters by retaining the underlying plan and elevation strategies of their teaching but responding to Modernism in the simplification of detail and ornament. Art Deco thus emerged from several sources, often revealing its ancestry. Beaux-Arts graduate Paul Cret (1876–1945), who was summoned to teach in Philadelphia, gave the city a range of finely planned monumental buildings, such as the Rodin Museum (see image 3) and influenced his student Louis Kahn (1901–74). The Beaux-Arts tradition of involving mural painters and sculptors in the finished building was adopted in the interwar period.

Stripped Classicism was almost universal in the 1930s, from United States post offices built during the Depression to the Moscow Metro and the headquarters of the Royal Institute of British Architects in London. Italy was perhaps the most prolific producer of such buildings, constructing massive post offices in Naples and elsewhere, transforming city centers in Rome, Bergamo, and Milan, and building new settlements, such as Sabaudia, south of Rome, as Mussolini's patronage was steered toward a more conservative Classicism manifested in the unfinished Esposizione Universale Roma (EUR Rome).

Not all architects abandoned the purity of their Classical principles. U.S. architect John Russell Pope (1874–1937) remained true to the pure classical orders, as seen in the Jefferson Memorial (1940) in Washington, D.C., and the Duveen Galleries at London's Tate Britain (see image 5). Perhaps the grandest project of all, the Viceroy's House at New Delhi (1929; see p.338) by Sir Edwin Lutyens (1869–1944), has touches of originality and humor, but remains a demonstration of the symbolic power of the basic Classical forms.

Art Deco influenced nearly all types of architecture in most countries between the wars, especially countries under colonial rule where buildings reflected the styles of the colonizers, but often with more freedom and vernacular influences. It was particularly suited to new building types, such as cinemas, gas stations, hydroelectric dams, and power stations, and to places of entertainment, where a touch of chrome in jagged shapes brought a trace of metropolitan glamour. Art Deco designs were also favored in the bright light and shadow of the seaside, where they were used for private villas and hotels, such as the Musée de la Mer (see image 6) in Biarritz, France. These styles persisted in reduced form after World War II. Despite the rise of Modernism, the decorative impulse remained but it turned toward a version of organic modernist patterning and color schemes, already prefigured in the 1930s in the work of Josef Frank (1885–1967), and taken further in South America during the war and supplemented by the postwar collage aesthetic of Giò Ponti (1891–1979) in Italy. Modernism continued to be shadowed by a new escape route into fantasy and frivolity that was needed for the interiors of bars, restaurants, and even churches, and satisfied human weaknesses for kitsch and exaggeration that Modernism affected to disdain. Art Deco was revived by collectors, film buffs, and graphic designers in the late 1960s, and elements from the style were also apparent in Postmodernism (see p.502) during the 1970s and 1980s. **AP**

Palais de Tokyo 1937
PAUL VIARD 1880–1943,   MARCEL DASTUGUE 1881–1970

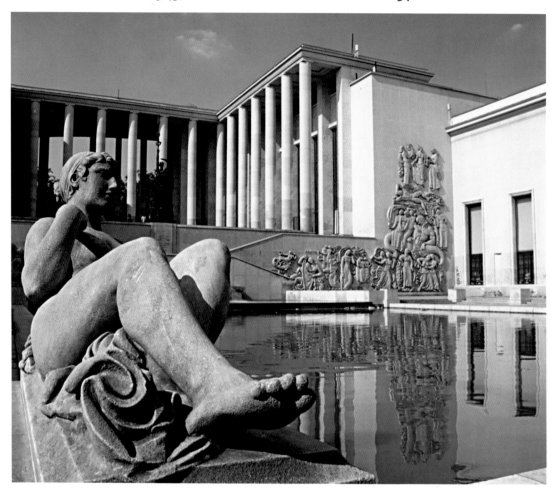

Palais de Tokyo (Museum of Modern Art of the City of Paris), Paris, France

The Palais de Tokyo represents the State Neoclassicism of the interwar period and is one of the surviving structures from the Paris International Exhibition of 1937. The plan by Paul Viard and Marcel Dastugue was described as "an extraordinarily graceful and sensitive production on modern academic lines." During the exhibition, the buildings displayed the glories of French art and design, but the peculiar architectural form of this pair of independent museum buildings originates from the longer term intention to build a new national museum of modern art to replace the Palais du Luxembourg. Funds were limited, but the project expanded when the City of Paris bought the old Polish Embassy and enlarged the site, adding its own separate museum as a twin structure of almost identical design (Museum of Modern Art of the City of Paris; opened 1961). The colonnade forms a gateway, with steps down to a viewing terrace and reflecting pool, and access to the river. The concrete-framed structures with brick infill are clad in two tons of Fontainebleau stone. Contemporary sculpture flanked the pool, with a central bronze figure by Antoine Bourdelle. The blank walls toward the river feature relief sculptures by Alfred Janniot; there are also decorative glass and bronze relief doors. The Museum of Modern Art collection moved to the Centre Pompidou in 1977, and in 2002 its former galleries (in the west wing) were stripped out to form the Site for Contemporary Creation. The Museum of Modern Art of the City of Paris continues to occupy the east wing. **AP**

✪ NAVIGATOR

👁 FOCAL POINTS

1 COLUMNS

The slender gray stone columns, massed together as a three-sided open portico, resemble the Pergamon Altar (excavated in the 1880s from Asia Minor), but on the scale of the grand hall at Persepolis. Too elongated to allow for the use of conventional Classical forms, these pillars have a simple abacus capital and no base.

2 SCULPTURE

Alfred Janniot created the twin reliefs depicting "The Legend of the Earth" and "The Legend of the Sea." He wrote that "sculpture must be decorative before conveying an idea or expressing feelings." A veteran of the 1925 exhibition in Paris, he also worked on the decor of the Normandie ocean liner and New York's Rockefeller Center.

3 WALLS

Sheer stone punctuated by simple openings, with a coping at the top to deflect rainwater, was typical of the Stripped Classical style. The upper section, concealing the top-lit galleries, has square reliefs between every third window opening and the wings curve back to reveal the view of the River Seine.

▲ The transformation of the old museum reveals the elegant reinforced concrete construction of the stairs. Dropping down from the corners of the wings to the service spaces at basement level, they represent a hidden Modernism within the outwardly more conventional building.

🕐 ARCHITECTS' PROFILE

1880–1970

Paul Viard was born in 1880 and Marcel Dastugue in 1881. They were the senior members of the four architects who won the competition for the Palais de Tokyo in 1935, all of whom had previous official commissions in Paris. Jean-Claude Dondel (1904–89) and André Aubert (1905–87) were just starting their careers in 1937, and went on to work on public buildings after the war. Viard died in 1943 and Dastugue in 1970.

1971–89

Dondel's work included housing, schools, and the water sports complex at Massy en Ligne (1971). In addition to working for the Ministries of Education and Post and Telecommunications, Aubert directed the postwar reconstruction of Vendôme and Blois, including work on the *secteur sauvegardé* (protected historic quarter) in the latter. He also designed a celebrated school at Sceaux-Bagneux and the headquarters for the St.-Gobain glass company at Neuilly-sur-Seine in 1962. Aubert died in 1987 and Dondel in 1989.

PARIS INTERNATIONAL EXHIBITION 1937

The "opposite but equal" nature of the Soviet and Nazi régimes was nowhere so clearly demonstrated as in the confrontation between their pavilions across the main axis of the exhibition site. Albert Speer (1905–81), brought in by Hitler at a late stage to design the German Pavilion (below left), had a preview of the Soviet Pavilion (below right) by Boris Iofan (1891–1976) and made his taller, "checking this onslaught, while from the cornice of my tower an eagle with a swastika in its claws looked down on the Russian sculptures."

EARLY ORGANIC

1 **Einstein Tower (1921)**
Erich Mendelsohn
Potsdam, Germany

2 **Lovell Health House (1929)**
Richard Neutra
Los Angeles, California, USA

O rganic modern architecture has been viewed conventionally as a reaction to mainstream Modernism. However, as shown by one of the main Organic protagonists, Hugo Häring (1882–1958)—who shared an office with one of the defining Modernists, Ludwig Mies van der Rohe (1886–1969) in 1920s Berlin—they were more closely related than this suggests. Like the Bauhaus, the organic grew out of the tensions of the earlier Arts and Crafts (see p.314) and Art Nouveau (see p.320) movements. It sprang from a desire to convey a new human spirit through freely expressive forms, and a determination to use the new materials of the industrial era to build an architecture capable of meeting the needs of the twentieth century.

The expressively restrained, Japanese-influenced work of U.S. architect Frank Lloyd Wright (1867–1959) proved that the Organic and the Modernist could be successfully combined, and his influence runs through European Modernism. The tendency, however, was to emphasize one style more than the other. At the Deutscher Werkbund Exhibition in Cologne in 1914, for example, the emotive lines of the theater by Henry van de Velde (1863–1957) confronted the ordered assemblage of the Model Factory by Walter Gropius (1883–1969) and Adolf Meyer (1881–1929). More important than either of these, however, was the Glass Pavilion (1914) designed by Bruno Taut (1880–1938), a building of sublime

KEY EVENTS

1914	1914	1914	1917	1917	1921
The Deutscher Werkbund Exhibition, held in Cologne, Germany, sets out the tensions between the expressive and the rational.	Rudolph Schindler (1887–1953) emigrates from Vienna to California via Chicago, working for Frank Lloyd Wright before setting up his own practice.	Bruno Taut designs the Glass Pavilion for the Deutscher Werkbund Exhibition. It demonstrates the ways in which glass can be used in buildings.	Taut publishes his utopian *Alpine Architecture*, which envisions purely cosmic cities of glass and organic forms.	Construction begins of the De Dageraad housing block in Amsterdam by Michel de Klerk (1884–1923) and Piet Kramer (1881–1961).	Ludwig Mies van der Rohe submits his designs for a free-form, all-glass skyscraper to the competition for a building on Friedrichstrasse, Berlin.

effects made possible through transparent, obscured, and colored glass, and brilliant illumination. Glass subsequently became the defining material of the twentieth century, and its possibilities dominated Mies's work—from the expressive mass of his curvilinear Berlin Friedrichstrasse skyscraper design in 1921 to the sublimely mute Seagram Building, New York (1958; see p.418).

After World War I, Organic architects challenged the Cartesian approach to design. They sought out expressive combinations of different, often traditional, materials to create a weighty, earthy architecture with a markedly northern sensibility. Designed by Erich Mendelsohn (1884–1953) to house a solar telescope, the Einstein Tower (see image 1) at Potsdam, which was derived from Taut's Expressionist forms, linked the new era of science to a sensuous form entirely molded by human will. In Switzerland, the anthroposophist Rudolf Steiner (1861–1925) built two versions of his Goetheaneum (1919–28) at Dornach, firstly in timber, and then in shuttered, board-marked concrete. The Amsterdam School similarly manipulated traditional brick to construct a visionary architecture that at the same time served the pragmatic needs of social housing.

By the 1920s, the wilder forms of what some called "Onomatopoeic Expressionism" were not suited to the larger volume of building activity, and a number of architects sought to combine the attention to users and emotive effects that distinguished the Organic with more conventionally buildable structures. Mendelsohn's sequence of department stores from 1927 to 1931 maintained the sweeping lines, variety of materials, and dramatic lighting effects of his earlier work, but on a larger urban scale, as did Taut's Berlin housing schemes. This restraint was always evident in the "bio-regional" architecture of Richard Neutra (1892–1970) in Los Angeles; a benign, climate-responsive strain of Modernism that grew out of the mesa, coast, and hills. Lovell Health House (see image 2) formulated the California lifestyle of sun and exercise in a building that seemingly hangs from the hillside, along with a bright, fluid interior that integrates natural and artificial lighting effects using blinds, translucent glass and reflected light sources.

As Modernism was reformulated into the conventions of the International Style (see p.416) during the 1930s, the Organic concern with building expressively in response to people, place, and materials became increasingly attractive to Modernists. In a very different climate to California, Alvar Aalto (1898–1976) conceived perhaps the most complete Organic synthesis yet in Villa Mairea (1939) in Finland. The house explicitly links the international and modern with the rustic and local, with inspiration taken from traditional Finnish farmhouses and Japanese houses and gardens, as much as his earlier Modernist work. Even Le Corbusier (1887–1965) evolved his own expressive construction and embraced the use of local and traditional materials, while Wright's Fallingwater, Bear Run, Pennsylvania (1939), showed a renewed genius infusing his original Organic architecture with the dynamism of his later contemporaries. **HC**

1923	1926	1927	1928	1930	1939
Richard Neutra emigrates to California from Berlin after working for Erich Mendelsohn, then briefly works with Rudolph Schindler in Los Angeles.	Hugo Häring completes the Gut Garkau (see p.366) complex of farm buildings near Lübeck in Germany.	Willem Dudok (1884–1974) completes a series of public buildings in Hilversum, the Netherlands, renowned for their use of brick and asymmetry.	Häring is sidelined by Le Corbusier at the inaugural meeting of the Congrès International d'Architecture Moderne (CIAM) in Switzerland.	Finns Aino and Alvar Aalto begin making bentwood furniture with Otto Korhonen. It combines international techniques and ideas with local resources.	Frank Lloyd Wright completes the house at Fallingwater in western Pennsylvania and the Johnson Wax Building at Racine in Wisconsin.

Gut Garkau Farm 1926

HUGO HÄRING 1882–1958

Gut Garkau Farm
near Lübeck, Germany

⚙ NAVIGATOR

Gut Garkau is the singular masterpiece of Hugo Häring's attempt to design in response to the unpredictable nature of society—in this case, a society of forty-two cows. Commissioned by progressive farmer Otto Birtner, only the barn, cowshed, and toolshed were completed from the original plan for an entire farm. The barn is a single large covered space that makes incredible use of materials and structure; the cowshed is more complex, and is articulated by Häring's critical response to the needs of caring for and feeding the cows. Its plan reflects the natural feeding pattern of cattle—a circle squashed into an oval to save space, which is then squeezed at one end to form a teardrop with the single bull placed at its tip, expressing its role as father of the herd. The section is equally specific; the hayloft has a sloping floor to ease pushing feed to the cows below, and the resultant sloping soffit to the ceiling below encourages the natural convection of hot air from the cows out of a high-level slot. Häring expresses these programmatic details directly on the exterior, rather than suppressing them into an overarching geometrical order, generating a remarkable three-dimensional collage of form. Largely forgotten at the height of Modernism, the farm was rediscovered in the late 1950s by the New Brutalist architects of Team X who opposed the same determinist axioms as Häring had before them. **HC**

⏱ ARCHITECT PROFILE

1882–1920
Hugo Häring was born in Biberach an der Riss in southern Germany. Häring was a pupil of the National Romantic architect Theodor Fischer (1862–1938) at the Technical High School (Stuttgart), together with Erich Mendelsohn and Ernst May (1886–1970).

1921–27
In 1921, he moved to Berlin, where he met Ludwig Mies van der Rohe, with whom he founded "the Ring" group of Modernist architects. Häring was a great influence on Hans Scharoun (1893–1972), who joined the Ring in 1926. Häring participated in the Werkbundsiedlung building exhibition of the Deutscher Werkbund in Stuttgart in 1927. The ensemble of buildings created there included work by many of the future key members of the Modernism movement in architecture.

1928–31
In 1928, he was one of the twenty-eight founding members of the Congrès International d'Architecture Moderne (CIAM),

organized by Le Corbusier in Switzerland. Although few of his architectural projects were realized, those that were include the Gut Garkau farm complex, the Sausage Factory at Neustadt (1926), and the apartment blocks he created for the Siemensstadt housing project in Berlin (1931).

1932–58
Häring was a central figure in the architectural debates of 1930s Berlin. He sought an architecture that reflected people's nature and the way they behaved, which was expressed in plan, section, and elevation, as well as in the choice of materials. He determined to create architectural "organisms" (*Organwerk*), and developed a methodology that stressed the individuality of each project, not the individuality of the artist, calling the outcome a "performance form" (*Leistungsform*). This was in clear distinction to many of his Modernist colleagues' generalized solutions, and led to him becoming increasingly ostracized from organizations such as the CIAM. He died in Göppingen in 1958.

👁 FOCAL POINTS

1 CONSTITUENT PARTS
Each element is allowed to find its own form, and the resulting overall form is an expressive collage of these individual functions, which Häring sculpts into an *Organwerk*. The shapes are further reinforced by changes to the horizontal or vertical coursing of the brickwork and timber cladding.

2 IRREGULAR SHAPES
The cowshed has a concrete frame that is expressed externally to emphasize the floor levels. The frame allows for curves and sweeping corners, with the voids in the frame infilled with non-load-bearing materials and openings sited wherever they are required. Different brick coursing emphasizes the shapes.

3 ROUGH MATERIALS
The concrete frame, brick walls, and timber cladding are left untreated, bar wood stain. Robust brickwork accentuates the heavy use of the lower parts of the building and the timber boards at the upper level include gaps for ventilation. Häring saw his rough, untreated materials as appropriate to a new farm vernacular.

▲ The lower heavyweight concrete frame acts as a table on which the lightweight timber roof sits. The roof is a lamellar construction made from readily available short lengths of timber bolted together, and the curvature of the roof is an organic expression of the construction.

EUROPE: ART INTO ARCHITECTURE

1 **Gosprom (1928)**
Sergei Serafimov, Samuel Kravets,
and Mark Felger
Kharkov, Ukraine

2 **Monument to the Third International (1928)**
Louis Lozowick, after Vladimir Tatlin's model

3 **Narkomfin Apartments (1932)**
Moisei Ginsburg
Moscow, Russia

After World War I ended in 1918, pent-up energy exploded into new forms of architecture, painting, and sculpture, which operated in conjunction with utopian aspirations as agents for a cleansed and perfected world. Constructivism emerged in postrevolutionary Russia with a Marxist belief in scientific method and a mission to find new forms for a new society. "Construction" is a translation of several Russian words with overlapping meanings, ranging from the physical to the social and linguistic, making the designer's subjectivity secondary to objective concerns with a new social order. With its heightened sense of the potential for change, Constructivism involved a systematic, ground-up rethinking of design methods. In the early revolutionary years, when building opportunities were scarce, teaching and visionary projects played a major role. Constructivism offered a coherent and radical definition of modern architecture for a wider world (even when later caricatured as extreme functionalism and politicization of design, and even if the reality showed deep origins in Russian beliefs and thought) and was assimilated into a wider and more continuous stream of architectural thought.

The unbuilt Monument to the Third International (see image 2), a red Eiffel Tower wrapped around suspended rotating geometric solids, by Vladimir Tatlin (1885–1953) represents the grandeur of scale, political symbolism, and disdain for physical constraints typical of early Constructivism. More practically,

KEY EVENTS

1914	1917	1917	1918	1918	1919
In Milan, Antonio Sant'Elia (1888–1916) exhibits Città Nuova (New City) drawings with the *Messaggio* text that becomes the Futurist manifesto.	The October Revolution in Russia gives the impulse to artistic forms for modern architecture and abstract art.	Hamburg-based architect Fritz Schumacher (1869–1947) publishes an influential manifesto for brick building.	The Arbeitsrat für Kunst (Work Council for Art), an important discussion group for Expressionist architecture, is formed in Berlin.	*Wendingen* magazine is founded by H. T. Wijdeveld (1885–1977) in Amsterdam and becomes a major outlet for Dutch Expressionism.	Walter Gropius (1883–1969) refounds the Weimar Kunstgewerbeschule (School of Applied Art) as the Bauhaus.

workers' clubs offered sports facilities and entertainment in prominent buildings, where the volumes of space gave character to the external form in place of the trimmings of academic tradition. At the Paris International Exhibition in 1925, Konstantin Melnikov (1890–1974) showed a specimen interior in his ingenious timber Soviet Pavilion and at his Moscow Rusakov Workers' Club (1928) the shapes of internal spaces project to create the external character.

Most representative of the opposite strand—meeting social needs with ingenious new spatial and structural forms—were the Narkomfin Apartments (see image 3) for civil servants in Moscow designed by Moisei Ginsburg (1892–1946). The apartments span between the two faces of the long ribbon block, and their stepped internal cross section allows access corridors to be less wasteful of space. Communal kitchens, nurseries, and laundry facilities were provided. Constructivist buildings and projects were largely found in Moscow, although the Gosprom (see image 1) at Kharkov in Ukraine, by Sergei Serafimov (1878–1939), Samuel Kravets (1891–1966), and Mark Felger (1881–1962), is a notable exception: a government center for the Ukrainian capital that temporarily replaced the more reactionary city of Kiev. The architects were more opportunists mimicking the Constructivist style than dedicated believers, yet they gave physical reality to the kind of scheme often left on paper: a series of skyscraper towers of U.S. origin linked by eighth-story walkways in the sky, a partial fulfillment of the Constructivist desire to conquer gravity.

Through the tersely titled magazines *ABC* and *G*, the latter founded by the visionary artist and designer El Lissitzky in 1922, Constructivist projects and ideas were circulated with similar designs from the avant-garde in Germany and the Netherlands. They entered the mainstream of Modernism, as seen in the statements and unbuilt projects by the formerly more conservative Ludwig Mies van der Rohe (1886–1969), thus emphasizing the primacy of construction over form. After the rise of Stalin in the Soviet Union, Constructivism was increasingly derided and replaced by traditional styles, which despite their bourgeois associations were deemed to be more in tune with the tastes of the workers. The major monuments of the style that survived until the fall of Communism in the 1990s have been widely celebrated, but many are still at risk from lack of investment and possible demolition.

Expressionism was primarily a movement in painting and graphics that originated before 1914 and was mainly associated with Germany. It was anti-classical, socially engaged, and interested in primitive and peasant art, as seen in the work of the Berlin group Die Brücke (The Bridge) in 1905, and its Munich counterpart, Der Blaue Reiter (The Blue Rider) in 1911. Architecture responded slightly later to these impulses, but Expressionist tendencies appear in the crystalline dome and fantastical colored glass interior of the Glass Pavilion by Bruno Taut (1880–1938) at the Deustcher Werkbund Exhibition, Cologne, in 1914, inspired by transcendental poet-novelist Paul Scheerbart's evocations of

1920	1924	1926	1929	1932	1938
VKHUTEMAS state art and technical school is founded in Moscow to prepare master artists for industry and builders/managers for technical education.	Moisei Ginsburg publishes the major Constructivist text, *Style and Epoch* in response to *Toward a New Architecture* by Le Corbusier (1887–1965).	Critic Adolf Behne distinguishes between Functionalism and Rationalism, giving credit to Expressionism, a term he coined in 1913.	The Van Nelle Factory (see p.372) in Rotterdam, the Netherlands, is completed. Its design shows the influence of Russian Constructivism.	Stalin selects a monumental, Stripped Classical design by Boris Iofan (1891–1976) for Moscow's Palace of the Soviets, ending the Constructivist era.	The Futurist-style Fiat Tagliero Building (see p.376) in Asmara, Eritrea, is completed.

an immaterial future of glass and color. In the work of Peter Behrens (1868–1940) and others, elements of organic form and exaggerated scale carried over from Art Nouveau (see p.320) re-emerged after a phase of Classical purification, emphasizing repetitive geometric patterning rather than sinuous curves, such as the Hoescht Headquarters in Frankfurt (1924).

As a temporary response to the extremities of hope and despair in Germany at the end of World War I, the style drew many leading figures into Die Gläserne Kette (The Glass Chain), a group writing project (1919–20) that defined the German core of the movement. Many were pupils of Theodor Fischer (1862–1938). It included Walter Gropius, whose Sommerfeld House, Berlin-Lichterfelde (1921, now destroyed), was a log cabin with chevron-patterned paneling and irregular abstract windows, in line with the early Arts and Crafts (see p.314) ethos of the Bauhaus School. For Gropius and others, Expressionism was a phase, and some later historians and critics almost succeeded in eliminating it from the record as a shameful and reactionary display of emotion. Since the 1960s, however, Expressionism has been celebrated as a romantic and humanistic counterweight to excessive technocratic rationalism.

For Erich Mendelsohn (1887–1953) the search for form through a dynamic sculptural expression of a building's use and program was most extreme in the Einstein Tower at Potsdam (1919). In later projects, smoother surfaces created a calmer effect, while retaining a strong sense of directional form through extended horizontal lines. Fritz Höger (1877–1949), a builder by origin, produced the trademark image of the movement in the Chilehaus office building (see image 4) in Hamburg. His sublime and historically evocative use of brick was widely adopted in church architecture by Dominikus Böhm (1880–1955), for example at Cologne's St. Engelbert (1930; see p.374), and Rudolf Schwarz (1897–1961), who ensured Germany was at the forefront of religious building between the wars. Expressionist forms spread widely but were usually diluted or vulgarized, which contributed to National Romanticism in northern Europe and Art Deco (see p.358) throughout the world. In the 1920s, the Amsterdam School was a cognate movement with its own roots in the reformist brick architecture of H. P. Berlage (1856–1934), and its notable manifestation the Eigen Haard (Our Hearth; 1919) housing in Amsterdam by Michel de Klerk (1884–1923), where playfulness of brickwork reached a climax.

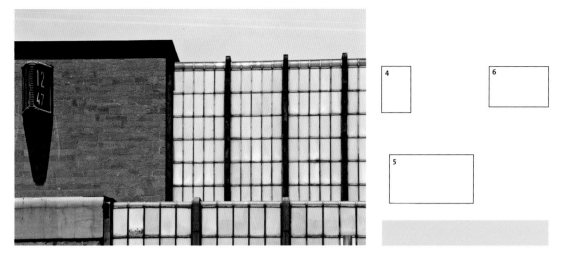

Like Expressionism and Constructivism, Futurism was also an art movement that crossed over into architecture, where its foothold was more tenuous. Futurism was Italy's contribution to the international avant-garde, noisily projected by its founder, the poet F. T. Marinetti. As its name indicates, it rejected the past in favor of an exciting world of machines, warfare, and danger. The painter Gino Severini saw Futurist art as the visualization of the modern world to come, typified by "moving tram or car + avenue + man going somewhere." In this respect, the outcome lay as much in the domain of urban planning, for example in Le Corbusier's free-flowing urban highways, as in the domain of architecture. However, the principal exponent of Futurist architecture on paper, Antonio Sant'Elia, created a science-fiction, Piranesian projection of soaring towers and stepped-back cross sections, envisaged for railroad or power stations, straddling railroad tracks and roads. The vision of transitoriness was further explored by Virgilio Marchi (1895–1960), who imagined cities of the future filled by luxurious caravans in marshalling yards.

Sant'Elia's manifesto of Futurist architecture, published in July 1914, was a synthesis of many precursory themes that reached a wider audience. Mario Chiattone (1891–1957) exhibited similar evocative drawings of massive imaginary buildings the same year, and later, but took the movement no further. In 1928, the first and last exhibition of Futurist architecture took place, but by then the main trends in Italy were a more austere Rationalism and a revival of monumental Classicism. Between these positions, however, there was a body of Italian architecture produced under the Fascist regime that, while not directly connected to Futurism, translated some of its concepts into built form. Giacomo Matté Trucco (1869–1934) was given the ideal Futurist commission by the Fiat car company in Turin—to design the largest car plant in the world with a production line that delivered completed vehicles at rooftop level, where they could career around the test track (see image 5). Railroad stations never achieved Sant'Elia's soaring lines (and it was never clear what function these superstructures might perform), but the long horizontals of Santa Maria Novella Station (see image 6) by Giovanni Michelucci (1891–1990) in Florence are an example of the expression of speed that still respected its historical setting.

The historical and theoretical map of Modernism is complex. The three movements described fed into a central pool and in the process lost their individual edge. All were rediscovered in later years when the resolution of the contradictory trends of Early Modernism began to feel like an entropic loss of energy and creativity. **AP**

4 **Chilehaus (1924)**
Fritz Höger
Hamburg, Germany

5 **Fiat Lingotto Factory (1923)**
Giacomo Matté Trucco
Lingotto, Turin, Italy

6 **Santa Maria Novella Station (1932)**
Giovanni Michelucci
Florence, Italy

Van Nelle Factory 1929
LEENDERT VAN DER VLUGT 1894–1936

Van Nelle Factory,
Rotterdam, the Netherlands

T ime and motion studies showed industrialists in the 1920s how economy and efficiency were beneficial for owners and workers alike. Van Nelle was an established firm producing tea, coffee, chocolate, and tobacco, imported as raw materials, processed, and sold in pioneering, sealed, branded packages that replaced the old system of loose goods weighed and sold over the counter. One of the owners, Kees van der Leeuw, was an enlightened employer who chose young architects for the massive new factory outside Rotterdam. In a lecture at the Dutch Institute of Efficiency in 1930, he showed his understanding of building technology when he argued for the economic and space benefits of continuous glazing, along with the human element in design and the importance of high-quality finishes. The design is based on a repetitive sequence of elements and it was one of the first buildings in Europe to use concrete columns with "mushroom" heads connecting to the floor slab, with no beams beneath the ceiling, thus maximizing light within. The windows are vertical sheets of glass giving an unobstructed view, and the steel window frames form an integral unit with the spandrel panels beneath, instead of the brick upstands originally intended. The Van Nelle Factory became a classic of Modernism and was carefully restored in 2000. **AP**

✦ NAVIGATOR

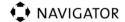

FOCAL POINTS

1 CURTAIN WALL

An early use of this feature, in which the window units mask the masonry structure and create a sheer facade. These units were built off-site, with four panes of standard-size greenhouse glass and a steel spandrel with an internal insulation layer. They were fixed from inside, avoiding the need for scaffolding.

2 ROOFTOP PAVILION

The circular glazed reception pavilion on the rooftop was a late addition, following the completion of the main building. It took advantage of the views over the surrounding flat landscape between Rotterdam and the sea. Later known as "the chocolate box," it has been used as a tea room and restaurant.

3 OFFICE BLOCK

Completed after the main factory, the curved building reconciles the different angles of the site and approach road, making the building highly photogenic. Management occupied the middle level of the block, with glazed offices and surveillance of the factory interior and surroundings. Other spaces housed accounts, marketing, advertising, and design.

▼ Inside, the mushroom-headed columns were cheap and relatively thin. The flared heads removed the need for light-obstructing beams on the underside of the floor slab—a bold innovation.

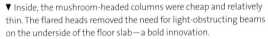

ARCHITECT PROFILE

1894–1928

Leendert van der Vlugt was born in Rotterdam, the Netherlands. After the death of architect Michiel Brinckman (1873–1925) his engineer son, Johannes (1902–49), took over the practice and invited van der Vlugt to become his partner. Van der Vlugt designed a School for Trades and Industry at Groningen (1922) and Theosophical Association buildings (1926) in Amsterdam.

1929–36

Van der Vlugt was wholly responsible for the design and construction of the Van Nelle Factory, despite the titular partnership and claims made by Mart Stam (1899–1986), who worked on the project. He also designed a house in Rotterdam (1929) for his Van Nelle patron, Kees van der Leeuw. He worked with W. van Tijen (1894–1974) on the influential Bergpolder, Rotterdam (1935), a nine-story block with a new glassy look in contrast to the earlier dominance of concrete wall surface.

St. Engelbert 1930
DOMINIKUS BÖHM 1880–1955

St. Engelbert,
Cologne, Germany

NAVIGATOR

K nown locally as the "lemon squeezer," owing to its ring of convex segments, this church marked a breakthrough for Dominikus Böhm. His desire to adapt architectural tradition to a form of worship centered on participation in the Mass with an unobstructed view of the altar was shaped by religious thinkers in the industrial Rhineland, where Catholicism retained its following after 1900. To the Catholic belief in the emotional power of design, Böhm added a Modernist perspective that the planning of a unified space, with minimal decoration, was key to re-creating the fervor of the early Church and appeal to the working class. At St. Engelbert, Böhm used inverted parabolic vaults in reinforced concrete, although these were plastered inside, and walled externally with brick. The altar is housed in a choir attached to the east segment, and a tall bell tower stands to the north, overlooking the steps up to the entrance. Historian Kathleen James Chakraborty has compared the placing of the church next to the beltway as a sacred version of Bruno Taut's secular idea of the Stadtkröne (symbolic city crown). Internally, the diffused light from the high windows creates a sense of mystery in the circular space, while the altar area is brightly lit from one side. Böhm avoided the angularity associated with Expressionism but related strongly to its aim of challenging architectural and social convention with a mixture of elements from the past and present, and using architecture as a means of curing the alienation of modern man and restoring a sense of community. **AP**

👁 FOCAL POINTS

1 BELL TOWER
The slender brick bell tower features blank walls punctuated by high-level arched openings to spread the sound. It serves as a marker for the church in its suburban setting. It is one of many similar towers designed by a range of German church architects in a style that was imitated in the UK.

2 ROOF
The eight segments of the church roof rise from the ground, using thin reinforced concrete (known as "shell concrete"), which corresponds to the interior space. The church appears exceptionally Modern in its construction as well as its liturgical planning, although the mix of concrete and brick softens the effect.

3 STEPS
Although smaller than many of Böhm's churches, St. Engelbert's gains a sense of majesty from the width of the approach. German Catholic churches were often raised on a crypt with monumental steps leading up to the west doors, which marked out the role of the church in the local community.

⏱ ARCHITECT PROFILE

1880–1919
Dominikus Böhm was born in Jettingen, Bavaria, in Germany. He graduated from Augsburg University of Applied Sciences in 1900, and went on to become a teacher in 1908 at the School of Design (Hochschule für Gestaltung), Offenbach, where he taught until 1926. He shared a joint workshop there with architect Rudolf Schwarz (1897–1961). During this time Böhm also attended lectures on architecture by Theodor Fischer (1862–1938) at the University of Stuttgart, eventually setting up his own practice in 1903.

1920–38
Böhm created a new tradition of Modern church architecture characterized by a simple monumentality. Many of his buildings are examples of the brick Expressionist style developed in Germany. His design for St. Paul, Dettinghen (1920), was recognized as the first Modern church in Germany, although like St. John the Baptist, New Ulm (1926), it uses a mixture of materials in horizontal layers, suggesting its endurance through time. Böhm moved into using brick at Christ the King, Mainz-Bishofsheim (1926), with a tall and deeply recessed Gothic entrance arch. His range of materials developed, and Our Lady Star of the Sea, Norderney (1932), uses the smooth white walls of international Modernism but without its strict shapes. His thinking about liturgy and planning continued to develop from one project to another, as did his use of concrete and other modern building materials and techniques.

1939–55
Although he effectively became a member of the National Socialist German Workers' Party during World War II, Böhm did not carry out construction work for the government. He subsequently lost his position as Professor of Christian Art at Cologne but was reinstated after the war and built eight more churches in the badly damaged city. He was awarded the Federal Cross of Merit in 1950 and the Order of St. Sylvester in 1952. His son, architect Gottfried Böhm (b.1920), is the only German architect to be a Pritzker Prize laureate.

◄ The altar space brings complexity to the plain interior through the theatrical play of perspective in the triple arches and the way their shapes are revealed by the light flooding from the great window on the north side.

Fiat Tagliero Building 1938

GIUSEPPE PETTAZZI

Fiat Tagliero Building,
Asmara, Eritrea

NAVIGATOR

Asmara is a Modernist city frozen in time and painted in pastel colors beneath a blazing sun. The city has ancient roots; it attracted Italian colonists in the late nineteenth century and became the capital of Eritrea. After the construction of a railroad to the coast, Asmara grew in importance and after the Italo-Abyssinian War in 1935 was almost wholly transformed by Italian architects for its mainly colonial population. The result is one of the most complete ensembles of Modern architecture of its time. The designs are not all the most up-to-date of their period, but without the constraints of Italian heritage around them, the architects often recalled aspects of Futurism twenty years after the movement's peak. No building in Asmara fits the Futurist label better than the Fiat Tagliero, an ordinary gas service station made extraordinary by its cantilevered wings. The airplane analogy is enhanced by the cockpit-like, wraparound window of the central tower. Above this rises an ornamental upper stage carrying the Fiat name in elongated letters and a downward pointing arrow. The cantilevers were bold examples of engineering, and as a precaution, Pettazzi showed supporting columns on the application drawings. These were built as wooden posts so that they could be struck away in a dramatic gesture after completion. When the moment came at the opening ceremony, Pettazzi reputedly put a gun to the head of the timorous builder, but his calculations have been vindicated for seventy-five years. **AP**

FOCAL POINTS

1 STREAMLINING

The central window above the canopy expresses speed through its resemblance to the bridge of a ship or the control tower of an airport, offering uninterrupted panoramic vision. Breaking forward around the central bow and wrapping around the sides, the window itself appears in motion, poised for take off.

2 LETTERING

Commercial buildings with smooth white surfaces provided an ideal background for the display of brand names. Sans-serif typefaces were developed in Germany in the 1920s, but Art Deco created its own variant styles, seen here in the elongated word "FIAT" and the low slung cross bars of the word "TAGLIERO."

3 CANTILEVER

Reinforced concrete has great tensile strength suitable for deep unsupported projections. Inside these canopies there is a mesh of steel rods, calculated to give the necessary support, and tied to the central structure. A wet climate causes rusting of the reinforcement, but in Asmara this has not been a problem.

GAS STATION MODERN

Architecturally significant gas stations are rare, as these relatively ephemeral structures are prone to disappear. The Skovshoved Gas Station (1937; right) by Arne Jacobsen (1902–71) is an outstanding example. Located at a beach resort north of Copenhagen in Denmark, it features a thin circular disk canopy on a single pole support. Shell concrete roofs in the form of hyperbolic paraboloids were briefly popular, including one by Sam Scorer (1923–2003) on the A1 road at Markham Moor, Nottinghamshire (1961), designated a historic building in 2012. Frank Lloyd Wright (1867–1959) made several designs, one of which, from 1958, survives at Cloquet, Minnesota, while Ludwig Mies van der Rohe and colleagues built one with two glass volumes of equal size and overhanging roofs in 1962 to serve a housing complex at Nun's Island, Montreal. Closed in 2008, it was given heritage status the following year.

TROPICAL MODERNISM

1 Girls' College Library Building (1954)
Maxwell Fry and Jane Drew
Chandigarh, India

2 Plans and sections of Vaughan-Richards
House (early 1960s)
Alan Vaughan-Richards
Alagbon, Ikoyi, Lagos, Nigeria

3 Los Eucaliptus Apartments (1941)
Juan Kurchan and Jorge Ferrari Hardoy
Belgrano, Buenos Aires, Argentina

The term "Tropical Modernism" describes a particular type of architecture that was built largely in the geographic area between the tropics of Capricorn and Cancer from the mid-1930s. The modification of hot and humid climatic conditions to create cool, well-ventilated interiors is at the core of Tropical Modernism. Modernist lines and geometric forms combine with open-plan arrangements to exploit natural settings, oriented at 45 degrees to the prevailing wind in order to expose at least two facades to cool winds and to minimize heat gain. The south facade is particularly vulnerable climatically, so many architects reduced its surface area and openings (in the southern hemisphere, the north-facing facade is minimized). A house built by Enrique Yáñez de la Fuente (1908–90) on Calle Suchil (1957), in the lava field of Jardines del Pedregal, Mexico City, incorporates this methodology. The southern entrance of the low-slung basalt house is fortresslike, with a deep, angular, shaded entrance. It also demonstrates a Modernist incorporation of national history, seen in its syncopated cornice inspired by Maya glyphs. Tropical Modernists began to measure and calculate rudimentary climate devices, which led to developments in building physics and construction technology.

However, the style should not be viewed only as one of technological advances. Tropical Modernism was the perfect remedy for building in newly independent countries that desired an architecture free from colonial

2 Plans and sections (see p.382)

KEY EVENTS

1931	1935	1941	1942	1947	1949
A congress on colonial urbanism is held in Paris, with extensive discussion on developing building techniques for hot and humid climates.	Work starts on the Golconde Dormitory, Pondicherry (see p.382), designed by Antonin Raymond and built by the congregation of Sri Aurobindo Ashram.	Juan Kurchan and Jorge Ferrari Hardoy design the *jalousie*-clad Los Eucaliptus Apartments, Buenos Aires, around existing eucalyptus trees.	Robert Gardner-Medwin, Leo De Syllas, and Gordon Cullen (1914–94) conduct research into Tropical Modernism building techniques in the West Indies.	Maxwell Fry and Jane Drew publish the tropical building manual *Village Housing in the Tropics: With Special Reference to West Africa*.	University College, Ibadan, Nigeria, is designed by Fry and Drew. Its library features a concrete latticelike sun breaker.

connotations. Its scientifically calibrated Modernism was presented as politically inert and ahistorical, while simultaneously being at the forefront of architectural advances. The style was embraced across Africa, the West Indies, India, and Southeast Asia, taking various guises and being tailored to local demands. Leo De Syllas (1917–64) developed an important approach to school design at Bishop's High School, Georgetown, Guiana (1944), taking the old colonial veranda and loggia concept to form external corridors supplemented with a hardwood grid structure and slender roof profile. His collaborator, Robert Gardner-Medwin (1907–95), acknowledged, "We soon learnt not to depend on finesse of detail, but rather on direct structural simplicity." Raised on piloti, or piers, their designs were one room deep to benefit from cross-ventilation. Maxwell Fry (1899–1987) and Jane Drew (1911–96) formed part of a cohort of British architects employed in Ghana and Nigeria on various development and welfare projects from the late 1940s. Their work often incorporated more overt reference to local African decoration cast into concrete balustrades.

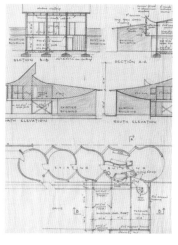

James Cubitt (1914–83) designed several buildings at Kwame Nkrumah University of Science and Technology, Kumasi, Ghana, which demonstrate a more expressive and playful approach to tropical architecture. The engineering laboratory (1954) is defined by bold, formal, concrete extrusions that bring light into the deep plan and also provide shade. In Lagos, Nigeria, John Godwin (b.1928) and Gillian Hopwood (b.1927) used projecting concrete sun shields, hoods, and lattices for numerous projects, as well as fixed exterior louvers at the Australian High Commissioner's residence. Alan Vaughan-Richards (1925–89), originally part of the Architects Co-Partnership established by De Syllas, developed highly experimental projects, such as his own house in Lagos (see image 2). It was built over a thirty-year period and incorporated local crafts, a careful use of materials, playful lighting, and a geodesic dome added in the 1970s. Local materials and building techniques were prioritized, too. The Japanese-inspired Modernist Jack House in Wahroonga, Australia (1957), by Russell (b.1925) and Pamela Jack, works with, rather than against, its steep site and incorporates a small creek. The open plan has louvered and full-height glass walls on the non-public side, with floor and roof planes extending beyond the house perimeter to connect with the bush and to provide shade.

Asian *jaalis*, or perforated screens, accentuate airflow and provide shade and privacy without preventing views. Perforated screens are used globally in a climate context, including in Mexican *cancelas* (interior gates) and Cobogó hollow-brick screens in Brazil. The louver, or *jalousie*, is arguably the feature that unites all Tropical Modernism. It comprises a mechanical system of adjustable fenestration and partition, and the slats are often made of wood, but also glass or concrete. It permits indirect light to enter the interior and also directs ventilation. Tropical Modernists used the *jalousie* extensively, sometimes for an entire facade, as seen at Los Eucaliptus Apartments (see image 3) in

1950	1952	1953	1955	1967	1978
Fry and Drew design new buildings for Wesley Girls' School in Cape Coast, Ghana (see p.384).	The XXI International Congress for Housing and Town Planning on housing in tropical climates is held in Lisbon.	The conference on tropical architecture, held at University College London, is organized by Nigerian Adedokun A. Adeyemi.	The tropical architecture course starts at the Architectural Association, London, led by Maxwell Fry and James Cubitt.	Designed around summer and winter compartments, Parekh House Ahmedabad, by Charles Correa, exploits the extreme climates of each season.	Alfred Brown Parker (1916–2011) completes Woodsong, Florida. Three pods for living, eating, and sleeping are connected by a covered walkway and pool.

4 **Bird-Cage House (1949)**
Igor Polevitzky
Miami, Florida, USA

5 **Cocoon House (1951)**
Paul Rudolph and Ralph Twitchell
Sarasota, Florida, USA

6 **Carmen Gunasekera House (1959)**
Geoffrey Bawa
Colombo, Sri Lanka

Buenos Aires, designed by Juan Kurchan and Jorge Ferrari Hardoy. Their design prioritized the incorporation of three eucalyptus trees into the orthogonal concrete facade grid; the trees serve as an organic foil to vertical, full-height, louverlike wooden solar devices in each of the grid's apartment balconies.

A hybrid of the *jalousie* and *jaalis* is the *brise soleil*, or sun shade. A second skin to a building, it sits proud of the exposed facade to provide a thermal break from the sun's rays. Frequently constructed from concrete in finlike or egg-box forms, the *brise soleil* faces the sun, permitting light to enter through the shaded openings. Fry and Drew collaborated with Le Corbusier (1887–1965) and Pierre Jeanneret (1896–1967) in Chandigarh, India, where they developed the concrete sun breaker for housing, college, and school projects, as seen at the Girls' College Library building (see image 1), which is also raised on piloti to encourage cross-ventilation. Fry's Government Printing Press factory (1954) in Chandigarh used glazed *jalousie* across its entire north-facing facade. This approach was influenced by Czech-American architect Antonin Raymond (1888–1976), who designed the Golconde Dormitory in Pondicherry, India (1935; see p.382), with adjustable concrete louvers. The *brise soleil* became a stylistic device and was even used on north-facing facades, where it served no climatic function. Le Corbusier used the *brise soleil* for his Carpenter Center for the Visual Arts (1963), Harvard University, where it is glazed to shut out severe Massachusetts winters.

In Hawaii, Vladimir Ossipoff (1907–98) exemplified the Tropical Modernism style through projects such as Liljestrand House (1948), Honolulu. In Florida, outstanding examples of one-off housing, educational and commercial designs were also completed during the same period. Some of the houses were weekend residences or starter homes and, as a result, they were built frugally and stripped back to bare essentials. However, the priority was always the view and the outside space. Other residences incorporated internal patios, or the structural column and beam extended out into the yard, blurring the distinction between home, shelter, yard, and wilderness. Igor Polevitzky (1911–78) designed numerous houses in Florida, but the most influential was

Bird-Cage House (see image 4), which screened the space rather than enclosing defined volumes. Paul Rudolph (1918–97), the most internationally well-known architect from this period, designed several houses in south Florida with Ralph Twitchell (1890–1978). Projecting over Siesta Key in Sarasota like an outrigger canoe, their steel and timber Cocoon House (see image 5) has an exposed, timber-structure, *jalousie* facade on a concrete base, with a flexible spray-on roof that used technology that had been developed to mothball (retire) airplanes after World War II. Rudolph taught Norman Foster (b.1935) and Richard Rogers (b.1933) at Yale School of Architecture, New Haven, Connecticut, and their subsequent High Tech approach (see p.484) was influenced by the exposed columns, tensioned steel rods, and catenary (a perfect curve formed when a cord hangs freely from two suspended ends) roof of Cocoon House. Rudolph's later builds continued his climatic solutions. The high-rise Dharmala Building (1982) in Jakarta, Indonesia, has a breezeway atrium entrance and deep overhangs on each floor, reminiscent of local vernacular roofs that provide shade and catch breezes.

The work of Charles Correa (b.1930) in India consistently looks to create "open-to-sky" environments and "empty centers," such as Gandhi Smarak Sangrahalaya museum in Ahmedabad (1963) and Koramangala House in Bangalore (1988), both based around courtyards and interconnected clusters. In Sri Lanka, Geoffrey Bawa (1919–2003) began with a stark approach, reminiscent of Fry and Drew's work in Africa, but developed a more regional style with the Carmen Gunasekera House in Colombo (see image 6), while incorporating bold concrete frames that supported roof terraces and enclosed courtyards. The De Silva House in Galle (1959) cleverly exploited a sloping site with a single flowing roof uniting a series of rooms. The result is an interior journey of contrasting volumes and light as visitors move through the dwelling.

Tropical Modernism not only offered an alternative to today's penchant for air conditioning, but also, beyond its green credentials, highly crafted and innovative spaces, supplemented with careful detailing and materials. The style looked to break down the stark and often blunt divisions between inside and outside, and to create enclosures that flowed and merged while ensuring privacy and security. Universally applicable designs were not desired by Tropical Modernists; instead, they pursued highly tailored solutions that complemented the beautiful settings in which they worked. **IJ**

Golconde Dormitory 1935

ANTONIN RAYMOND   1888–1976

Golconde Dormitory,
Sri Aurobindo Ashram,
Pondicherry, India

NAVIGATOR

Antonin Raymond was offered the commission to design a dormitory for the Sri Aurobindo Ashram in Pondicherry, India, in 1935. A former employee of Frank Lloyd Wright with a practice in Japan, Raymond was a pioneer in the use of reinforced concrete. He had been taken with the ashram while spending time in India, and by 1935 a preliminary design for the Golconde Dormitory had been developed, with Raymond's associates George Nakashima (1905–90) and Francois Sammer (1907–73) acting as site architects. Sri Aurobindo, co-founder of the ashram with Mirra Alfassa, was concerned about construction noise disrupting the tranquillity of the ashram and decreed that the devotees should build the structure. A full-scale prototype house was constructed to help train the workforce and they set about building the dormitory. It took around six years to construct (Raymond had hoped to complete the construction in six months). The quality of the work is extremely high and the building is still used by the ashram today. The architecture is dominated by a concrete *jalousie* that occupants can adjust to suit the changing seasons and weather. As a result, the facade is in constant flux and, despite the repetitive arrangement of the design, monotony is eluded and the eye kept in motion. **IJ**

1 *JALOUSIE*

A *jalousie* made from asbestos-concrete clads the entire south-facing facade. It is fully adjustable from the interior and shelters the semi-exterior walkways. No other ornament or decoration is found on the building, bar a small lotus that is carved into the overscaled teak front door.

2 **SCALLOPED ROOF**

A series of parasol-like scalloped structures form the roof, which insulates the dormitories below. They are clad in broken ceramic to help repel the sun's rays. This vaulted roof idea was utilized by other Modernists working in the tropics, and was perhaps a precursor for Le Corbusier's 1950s High Court Palace at Chandigarh, India.

3 **LAWN**

On the south side of the building is a lush shade lawn, contrasting with an exposed plane on the north side. This arrangement creates a temperature differential that drives breezes through the building. Evaporation from ornamental ponds in the yard also helps to cool the air.

◀ The sliding interior partitions are made from woven teak and permit further ventilation while ensuring privacy. All the *jalousie* brass hardware, balustrades, and hinges were cast on the site.

TROPICAL BUILDING GUIDES

The British Military Engineers and Public Works departments of the 19th century frequently published their ideas for tropical construction and left a rich heritage for the 20th century. Bringing some of these ideas up to date with a greater focus on improving conditions for the indigenous populations, several tropical building guides were produced in the mid-20th century. A well-known example is Maxwell Fry and Jane Drew's booklet, *Village Housing in the Tropics* (1947), but A. E. S. Alcock's manuals *How to Plan Your Village* (1953) and *How to Build for Climate* (1960; right), which he produced with Helga Richards, were also used extensively. These building guides were more practical and more easily interpreted than those of Fry and Drew. However, Fry and Drew went on to write two further guides—*Tropical Architecture in the Humid Zone* (1956) and *Tropical Architecture in the Dry and Humid Zones* (1964)—and Otto Koenigsberger's *Manual of Tropical Housing and Building* (1974) became an instant classic for designers working in hot climates.

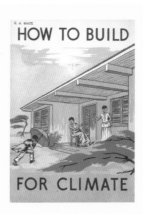

Wesley Girls' School 1951

MAXWELL FRY 1899–1987, JANE DREW 1911–96

Wesley Girls' School,
Cape Coast, Ghana

✪ NAVIGATOR

Wesley Girls' School was one of around twenty schools and teacher-training colleges that Maxwell Fry and Jane Drew designed in Ghana from 1947 to 1955. None of the schools are identical, but they have a family resemblance and similar planning arrangement, each being tailored to its site and the precise requirements of the school. The schools were intended to help prepare and train the future leaders of Ghana, and as such they adopted what was considered a radical modernity, breaking away from the old colonial architectural style while creating a solution that tempered the climate. The general arrangement includes an administrative block entrance portal or gateway, beyond which a series of courtyards or quads contain teaching and residential buildings set about an axis leading to the chapel. A concrete frame structure is used on all the schools, with precast concrete block infill adopting a variety of patterns. Wesley Girls' School is arranged around a dominant central pedestrian walkway focused upon the assembly hall and the cylindrical campanile-water tower. The two wings flanking the walkway are used as residences, with gallery access that offers shade to the walkway and rooms below. **IJ**

👁 FOCAL POINTS

1 LOGGIA AND VERANDA
The loggia and veranda give external circulation as well as offering shade to the story below. Timber louvers are used to create shade and prevent unwanted glare and solar gain. The holes in the concrete balustrade permit ventilation and reduce costs and weight.

2 "EGG CRATE" GRID
The "egg crate" concrete grid suggests *brise soleil*, but is more of a screening device to enclose a large space with minimal material, while recessed louvers cut out direct sunlight. Fry was fond of using strong geometric patterns in his facade arrangements.

3 EAVES
Large overhanging eaves that completely cover the walkway below are used to provide shelter from both sun and heavy rainfall. Although this school has hipped roofs, it was more common for Fry and Drew to use monopitched roofs that were easier to build.

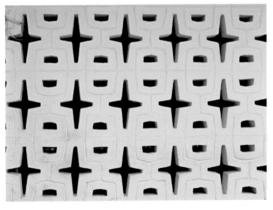

◀ Precast concrete blocks in a variety of patterns are used extensively. They permit light and ventilation while offering some shade. They were also used to represent African decorative patterns in abstract that Fry and Drew observed on cloth, pots, and dwellings.

🕐 ARCHITECT PROFILE

1911–44
Jane Drew was born in Thornton Heath, Surrey, in 1911. She studied at the Architectural Association School of Architecture, London, and, following workplace discrimination after graduation, she established her own women-only practice designing small factories and a yacht works. In 1942, Drew married fellow architect Maxwell Fry, whom she met through the Modern Architectural Research Group.

1945–50
Following the end of World War II, Drew spent eighteen months working with Fry on development and welfare planning projects in West Africa. This led to numerous architectural commissions there, including hospitals and schools in Ghana and the Ivory Coast and the University of Ibadan in Nigeria.

1951–60
In 1951, Drew invited Le Corbusier to join her and Fry on the design of Chandigarh, the new capital city of the state of Punjab, India. Drew spent three years living on site at Chandigarh, designing housing projects, schools, clinics, and hospitals following extensive consultation with the end users. Drew and Fry went on to complete further works in the tropics, including banks in Nigeria, oil offices in Singapore and Kolkata, and Tema Manhean fishing village in Ghana.

1961–96
Drew continued to practice, lecture, and write, designing several buildings in London, including the Institute of Contemporary Arts (1964), the School for the Deaf (1968), and Carlton House Terrace Art Gallery (1970). She was made a Dame in 1996, and died that same year.

REGIONAL VERNACULAR

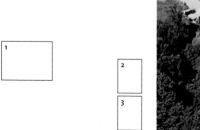

1 Defence Line of Amsterdam (1883–1920)
Architect unknown
Amsterdam, the Netherlands

2 Nikka Distillery (1934)
Masataka Taketsuru
Yoichi, Hokkaido, Japan

3 Murphy Windmill (1905)
Alpheus Bull, Jr.
San Francisco, California, USA

W
ater is both boon and bane. For the whisky industry on Speyside in the Scottish Highlands, water is a critical boon to the distillery process that creates "the water of life." For the Netherlands, "water of life" means something quite different. The sea, canals, rivers, and waterways are bulwark against attack, but water itself must be managed to drain and prevent flooding. The Defence Line of Amsterdam (or Stelling van Amsterdam, see image 1) is the only system of multiple fortifications intended to control water for military defence. It sits in counterpoint to the less dramatic, but no less important water functions of windmills, such as Onrust Mill, which manages the water supply of the Naardermeer marshes east of Amsterdam.

The now redundant Defence Line of Amsterdam encircles the city in an 83-mile (135 km) network of forty-five fortifications. Built before airplanes changed the strategy of warfare, it was intended to repel ground attack. The system allowed the lowlands to be flooded to about 14 inches (30 cm), too shallow for boats, too deep for vehicles, a strategy first used by the Dutch in the sixteenth century when the polder system was used as a defensive flood system. In an early use of the material, non-reinforced concrete was one of the building materials used for the forts, which were sited at the mouths of waterways. Regulations ensured buildings within about a half-mile (1 km) radius were built of wood, so that they could be intentionally torched to further repel enemies. The Defence Line of Amsterdam is an outstanding hydraulic engineering and military strategic achievement. It highlights the limitations of coastal defence,

KEY EVENTS

1883	1890s–1900s	1906	1910	1920s–30s	1921–54
Construction begins on the Defence Line of Amsterdam to protect the city from attack by water.	In Port-au-Prince, Haiti, wooden gingerbread houses display expert carpentry skills in latticework, shiplap siding, and fretwork patterns.	Tom Kelly builds an adobe and glass-bottle house in Rhyolite, Nevada. It eventually becomes a pilgrimage point for self-build enthusiasts.	Walter Gropius (1883–1969) proposes standard industrialized house assembly lines, three years before Henry Ford achieves the same for cars.	The multistory concrete tower fortifications in Diaolou, Kaiping, China, demonstrate a fusion of Chinese and Western architecture.	Simon Rodia (1879–1965) constructs Watts Towers in Los Angeles. The seventeen structures are built using scrap metal and found objects.

such as at Deal Castle (1540) on the English coast, where the enemy could choose to sail by and land at an undefended area of the coastline.

The design of the pagoda ventilation hoods for malthouse chimneys by Charles Chree Doig (1855–1918), as seen at Strathisla Distillery in Speyside (eighteenth–nineteenth century; see p.388), improved chimney efficiency by providing a stronger draw for the furnace peat fires for dozens of distilleries that adopted Doig's design during the distillery building boom. Malthouses generally have a distinctive typology with a long, low building for growing and storage, ventilated with multiple adjustable louvered windows, and anchored by the malthouse kiln with furnace on first level, kiln on the second floor and chimney above. Until the 1950s, malting, fermenting, and distilling were all carried out on site. Only a few distilleries retained on-site maltings after 1950. Although Doig's pagoda design outlived its function when malting was moved off-site, it nevertheless became the enduring "logo" for Speyside distilleries.

The rooflines of the Nikka (Yoichi) Distillery (see image 2) near Sapporo, Japan, resemble a red forest of medieval castle donjons, with Doig's pagoda roofs seemingly referenced, but without the characteristic corner upturns. Founder Masataka Taketsuru was apprenticed in Scottish distilleries from 1919 to 1920 and became a major influence in the nascent Japanese whisky industry. He chose the Sapporo location for its temperature and terrain similarities to the Scottish Highlands. Whether the design of Doig's pagoda was influenced by the late nineteenth-century fashion for Japonisme and exhibitions such as the "Japanese Village" (1885–87) in London is not known, but the export of a pagoda motif from East to West, and its reintroduction to Japan via Taketsuru and his Scottish wife, is a design trail of interest. Pagoda roofs became synonymous with the design of Japanese whisky distilleries.

Distillery windmills in the Netherlands, such as Dirkzwager (built in phases from the seventeenth to the twentieth century) in Schiedam, are symbolic like Doig's pagoda, but retained their functional purpose beyond this period. Other distilleries, such as the Nolet Mill (2006), also in Schiedam, use the traditional windmill shape with Dekker wings (airfoil-shaped improved sails) to cloak an automated wind turbine, which provides electricity to the distillery. Dekker wings represent one of many sail designs that followed a nineteenth- and twentieth-century surge among Dutch millwrights to improve sail performance.

The Commissioners at the Golden Gate Park in San Francisco noted the role of Dutch windmills such as Onrust Mill in the critical role of water management. They built the Dutch Windmill (1903) and the Murphy Windmill (see image 3)—the sails of which turn clockwise like a wind turbine rather than counterclockwise like a traditional windmill—to provide irrigation for the sand-dune–based park, but also to circumvent the purchase of water from commercial sources. Motorized pumps eventually made the sails redundant and the windmills became a decorative feature. **DJ**

1922	1926	1928	1930s	1940s	1947
The shipbuilder's yard in Whitstable, Kent, UK, is converted into terraced houses, united by a ship's mast as the collective roof ridgepole.	Sears, Roebuck and Company sells the Wellington model kit house via its mail order "Modern Homes" initiative.	The prefabricated town of Fordlandia is established by Henry Ford in the Brazilian Amazon as a source of rubber for car tires.	Soviet Russia, and later Cuba, chooses prefabricated concrete panel systems over counter-revolutionary, labor-intensive, brick and tile construction.	Polychromatic houses are built in Tamil Nadu, India. They inspire the 1980s Memphis style of Ettore Sottsass (1917–2007), who visits Tiruvannamalai in 1961.	Lustron Corporation manufactures affordable, prefabricated houses. Despite the popularity of the houses, the business is declared bankrupt in 1950.

Strathisla Distillery Eighteenth–nineteenth century
KILN ATTRIBUTED TO JOHN ALCOCK 1861–1909

Strathisla Distillery,
Keith, Speyside, Scotland

⚙ NAVIGATOR

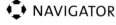

When Alfred Barnard toured British whisky distilleries for *Harper's Weekly* in the late 1880s, his description of Strathisla (then Milton) Distillery listed the production steps that required main buildings: malting, fermentation, distilling, filling, and cask maturation. Ancillary buildings included cooperage, cart sheds, and stables. The distillery's courtyard paving stones were sourced from its original namesake, sixteenth-century Milntown (Milton) Castle. At the waterside, Barnard noted offices for the clerks, excise, and partners. The number of buildings and their distinct use, reflected in their design, underscore the complexity of whisky distilling. Water is essential to whisky production as is a dram of magic. Strathisla is the oldest, continuously operating Highland distillery since 1786, and its distinctive pagoda chimneys create a focal point for the eighteenth- and early nineteenth-century architecture. Yet Strathisla's "magic" is its recipe and the source of its distillation water, Broomhill Spring. Kelpies (supernatural water horses) were said to roam the spring. It was renamed Fons Bulliens after the Chivas Brothers took over, perhaps to link it with European "medicinal" springs. Malt kilns draw hot air from the furnace through the malt by way of an updraft chimney effect encouraged by the characteristic steep roofs and Doig-style pagoda heads. The pagoda design proliferated throughout the distillery industry and influenced whisky distillery design in Japan. **DJ**

⊚ FOCAL POINTS

1 STILL HOUSE

Still houses are often described as "cathedral-like"—the result of economy of design. The triangular still house accommodates the height of the stills without wasted space. Designed for two copper stills, it houses four in a tight fit that requires removal of part of the roof for major repair work to the stills.

2 PAGODA CHIMNEY

The malthouse kiln pagoda chimney is a Doig ventilator named after its inventor. It is highly symbolic of Scottish whisky distilleries despite its wide-scale redundancy. Only a handful of distilleries maintain in-house maltings, but the famous Doig pagoda is inevitably added to the design of new distilleries.

3 WATERWHEEL

The distillery's hydropower was once supplied by the 1881 undershot waterwheel—one of the oldest (and least efficient) designs—whose water source was the River Isla. Kinetic energy is produced when water flows over paddles attached to the wheel rim. The tight water channel prevents overspill water loss.

DOIG VENTILATORS

Charles Chree Doig was a Scottish engineer and architect who specialized in whisky distilleries. He designed between fifty-six and one hundred distilleries, but also remodeled or extended many others. Although there is debate as to whether Doig designed Strathisla's twin chimneys, it is generally agreed that John Alcock (1861–1909) later designed Glentauchers Distillery in Speyside under Doig's supervision. Doig's pagodalike ventilator was designed for Daluaine Distillery after a fire in 1889. Sketches reveal that the design evolved through serial iteration. The design improved chimney efficiency and despite the shift to off-site maltings, which made the chimneys and hoods redundant, Doig's pagoda remains a distillery motif. The visitor center of Glenfarclas Distillery (right) in the Highlands incorporates a Doig ventilator into the entrance portico. The ventilator remains a unique example of adaptive vernacular design.

6 | 1950–PRESENT

MATERIALS MODERNISM

Modernism in architecture is often associated with steel-and-glass rectilinear boxes, and poured concrete used as a steel substitute. Yet this denies the most important aspect of concrete: its huge potential for plasticity and its ability to create new, exciting spatial experiences. Although the use of concrete (or stone and lime mortar aggregate) can be traced back to antiquity, applications as we know them today date from the Industrial Revolution. The ancestor of modern concrete is essentially Portland cement, which was invented in 1824 by British mason Joseph Aspdin; concrete reinforced with metal rods was patented by Frenchman Joseph Monier in 1867. What is known as reinforced concrete today was patented by François Hennebique in 1892, but there is evidence that the William E. Ward House in Port Chester, New York (1875), was among the first, at least in the United States, to be built from that material.

By the early twentieth century, concrete buildings were becoming as common as steel ones. The structurally expressive use of this building material in more dynamic shapes, especially for religious buildings that evoke spiritual experiences, dates back to the Sagrada Família in Barcelona (begun in 1882), by Antoni Gaudí (1852–1926), and the Bahá'í Temple in Wilmette, Illinois (begun in 1912), by Louis Bourgeois (1856–1930). The use of concrete in places of worship reached a peak during the decades between the world wars, particularly in the work of German Expressionist architects, who took advantage of the plasticity of concrete in curved, arched, and angular forms—as seen in the projected

KEY EVENTS

1950	1953	1955	1955–57	1959	1962
Structural engineer Anton Tedesko introduces a ribless, thin-shell concrete structure in a scale model test in Harvey, Illinois, USA.	The term "Brutalism" (see p.422) is coined to describe a holistic design approach to architectural and mechanical systems.	Le Corbusier designs the Notre Dame du Haut chapel in Ronchamp, France. Some observers liken its swooping roof to a giant nun's hat.	Alburquerque Civic Auditorium in New Mexico is built, with a poured-in-place concrete dome. It was demolished in 1987.	Metabolism (see p.454) emerges at the Congrès International d'Architecture Moderne (CIAM) in anticipation of the Tokyo World Design Conference.	The wing-shaped TWA Terminal (see p.396) at New York's John F. Kennedy International Airport is completed. It is dubbed "the Grand Central of the jet age."

Star Church (Sternkirche; 1922) by Otto Bartning (1883–1959) or the work of Dominikus Böhm (1880–1955), especially his St. Johann Baptist in Neu-Ulm (1922) and St. Engelbert in Cologne (1930; see p.374). Other early dreams for exciting curvilinear buildings were expressed in the sketches of Erich Mendelsohn (1887–1953), which showed a variety of sweeping curved structures, the most dynamic being the Einstein Tower (Einsteinturm) in Potsdam (1921).

German structural developments in thin-shell concrete roof construction led to its widespread use within commercial and industrial buildings. The first thin-shell reinforced-concrete roof is regarded as that created in 1922 for the Zeiss optical company in Jena, Germany, by construction firm Dyckerhoff & Widmann. Their techniques were further developed by structural engineer Anton Tedesko (1903–94), who designed what is often taken to be the first large-span thin-shell roof for a sports arena in Hershey, Pennsylvania (1936), although some authorities have suggested that earlier U.S. examples of thin-shell roofs were present in the Travel and Transport Pavilion and the Brook Hill Dairy Farm Exhibit of the Century of Progress Exposition (1933–34). Other early examples of curved concrete roofs range from the arched roofs created by French architect Auguste Perret (1874–1954) in his church at Le Raincy (1923) to the ribbed air-force hangars at Orvieto (1942) by Italian architect-engineer Pier Luigi Nervi (1891–1979). Likewise, the Swiss engineer Robert Maillart (1872–1940) created beautiful bridges and structures using curved and parabolic shapes, most notably in his reinforced-concrete Salginatobel Bridge (1930).

The postwar era benefited from these early twentieth-century experiments in design, which encouraged even greater creativity with the plasticity and texture of concrete. Sometimes these buildings were a continuation or evolution of prewar work. For instance, Tedesko's thin-shell vaults in the terminal at Lambert–St. Louis International Airport (see image 2) by Minoru Yamasaki (1912–86) are a development of his prewar work in this technique. Spanish-born architect Félix Candela (1910–97) developed comparable thin-shell structures in Mexico during the postwar era. Nervi's Sports Palace (1957), built for the Rome Olympic Games in 1960, is an evolution of his earlier ribbed-concrete designs. The bold ecclesiastical work of Dominikus Böhm found continued expression in the work of his son Gottfried Böhm (b.1920), in the stretched flying buttresses of St. Albert's Church (1953) in Saarbrücken and the dramatic angular shapes and spaces of the Pilgrimage Church of Mary, Queen of Peace (Wallfahrtskirche Maria Königen des Friedens, 1972; see p.400), at Neviges. Finally, Le Corbusier (1887–1965) is known for the beauty of his poured concrete, which showed the striking patterns of wooden formwork. Examples can be found in Villa Savoye (1930; see p.350) and the postwar Unité d'Habitation housing blocks in Marseilles (1952) and Berlin (1957). His increasing use of bold design forms combined with sprayed concrete or Gunnite over rough-cast walls can best be seen in the Notre Dame du Haut chapel in Ronchamp, France (see image 1).

1 Notre Dame du Haut (1955)
Le Corbusier
Ronchamp, France

2 Lambert–St. Louis International Airport Terminal (1954)
Minoru Yamasaki
St. Louis, Missouri, USA

1963	1972	1977	1979	1986	1995
The University of Illinois Assembly Hall in Champaign, Illinois—designed by Max Abramowitz—becomes the first concrete-domed arena.	Gottfried Böhm witnesses the completion of his design for the pilgrimage church at Neviges, Germany (see p.400).	John Portman creates otherworldly concrete interiors within the Renaissance Center in Detroit and Westin Bonaventure Hotel in Los Angeles.	A strikingly organic design by Günther Domenig for the Central Savings Bank in Vienna uses a mixture of materials, including concrete.	Reyner Banham's book *A Concrete Atlantis* documents concrete's widespread industrial use in the United States, especially in grain elevators.	Tadao Ando receives the Pritzker Architecture Prize. The jury citation applauds his "smooth-as-silk" concrete buildings.

The textural feature of wood formwork patterns within concrete is often associated with Brutalism (see p.422) , an architectural phrase created in 1953 by British architects Alison (1928–93) and Peter Smithson (1923–2003) from the French term *béton brut* (raw concrete), and further popularized by author Reyner Banham in *The New Brutalism* (1955). As the Smithsons envisioned, the new style also meant making visible the workings of a building, highlighting the industrial engineering aspects, such as HVAC systems (heating, ventilation, and air conditioning), as much as the design surfaces and structure. This attitude is well demonstrated in their work, such as Hunstanton Secondary Modern School (1954) in Norfolk and the Economist Building (1964) in London, although neither of these structures used poured concrete to project an image of bold rawness.

In the Endo Pharmaceuticals Building (see image 3) in Garden City, New York, U.S. architect Paul Rudolph (1918–97) further exploited the textural quality of concrete surfaces. In this building a poured-concrete foundation supports a steel framework that is clad in concrete panels. These have a highly textural surface created by manipulating the concrete after casting to give it a corduroylike appearance, which became a trademark of Rudolph's work. About the same time in Chicago, another U.S. architect, Bertrand Goldberg (1913–97), began to industrialize the process of creating curved concrete shapes in his Marina City (1967; see p.398) and the public housing of the Hilliard Homes (1967) by replacing wood formwork with fiberglass molds, thereby creating a smooth rather than a wood-textured surface. For Goldberg, this seemed more appropriate for the contemporary image of the building as a mass-produced industrial object.

During the 1960s, Japanese Metabolist architects created dreams of modularized city structures that could organically expand, giving concrete another boost in terms of design. Notable among these is Yoyogi Gymnasium (1964; see p.498) by Kenzo Tange (1913–2005), which was built for the Tokyo Olympics in 1964. Poured-concrete curvilinear walls and ramps along with the sweeping tensile-steel roofline, and correspondingly curved interior space, all evoke Japanese temples and castles in a dynamic, futuristic way. Perhaps the most expressive forms in poured concrete from the 1960s are the TWA Terminal (1962; see p.396) in New York's John F. Kennedy International Airport and the main terminal of Washington Dulles International Airport (1962) in Virginia, designed by Eero Saarinen (1910–61). The late 1950s and early 1960s were a golden era for flight, during which architects and designers worked on new terminals, aircraft interiors and corporate imagery, with air carriers striving to distinguish themselves. Many observers have described Saarinen's terminals as

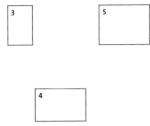

allegories of flight that visually demonstrate the drama of air travel, and they became iconic buildings of the early jet age.

The works of John Portman (b.1924) in the 1970s—particularly the Renaissance Center (1977) in Detroit and the slightly earlier Westin Bonaventure Hotel and Suites (1976) in Los Angeles—provided curvilinear concrete urban environments housed within steel-and-glass towers. Their interiors are open, multilevel mazes of concrete core, ramps and balconies, all of which project the image of a futuristic city. New Mexico–born architect Bart Prince (b.1947), a follower of Bruce Goff (1904–82), creates individualistic organic designs that emerge out of the landscape, often using concrete for supporting structures together with a mélange of wood, steel, and other materials, as did his mentor. Goff himself was a disciple of Frank Lloyd Wright (1867–1959), as was Italian-American architect Paolo Soleri (1919–2013), whose dream for Arcosanti (1970), the self-sufficient city constructed in the Arizona desert, can be included here as well, with this architect's practice of cast-in-situ concrete structures of highly primitive forms.

Although expressive concrete forms are usually associated with the 1960s and 1970s, concrete construction and the search for plasticity continues today. Austrian architect Günther Domenig (1934–2012) was probably best known for his creative manipulation of materials and structure to create anthropomorphic forms of steel, glass, and concrete in the Central Savings Bank (Zentralsparkasse) on Favoritenstrasse in Vienna (1979). His angularly expressionistic concrete Stone House, or Steinhaus (see image 4), near Klagenfurt, which he started building in 1980, has rugged forms that blend into the landscape. Tadao Ando (b.1941) has been crafting meticulously detailed poured-in-place concrete homes since the 1970s, and used reinforced concrete for Ibaraki's Church of the Light (see image 5) in Osaka, Japan, in 1989. The Jubilee Church in Rome (2003) by Richard Meier (b.1934) features three curved, sail-like forms in white concrete that is self-cleaning, the design an homage to similar concrete shell forms used in the monumental Sydney Opera House (1973) by Jørn Utzon (1918–2008). Similarly, the undulating, "whipped-cream-topped" shell-roofs for the renovated Hauptbahnhof railroad station in Stuttgart (2013) by Christoph Ingenhoven (b. 1960) are a tribute to the curvilinear Expressionism of Erich Mendelsohn's dreams as well as the thin-shell concrete roofs developed in his native Germany almost a century ago. **JZ**

3 **Endo Pharmaceuticals Building (1969)**
Paul Rudolph
Garden City, Long Island, New York, USA

4 **Stone House (2008)**
Günther Domenig
Lake Ossiach, near Klagenfurt, Austria

5 **Church of the Light (1989)**
Tadao Ando
Ibaraki, Osaka, Japan

TWA Terminal 1962

EERO SAARINEN 1910−61

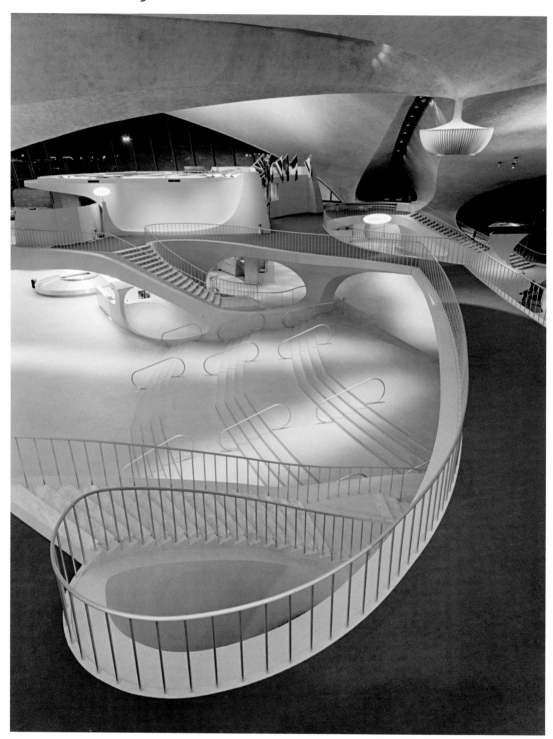

TWA Terminal, John F. Kennedy
International Airport, New York, USA

When the new terminal for Trans World Airlines (TWA) opened at what was then Idlewild International Airport, it was one of a series of distinctive, decentralized terminals on a beltway, designed by a variety of architects. This plan was popular in early jet age airport planning, in part so that airlines would have a way to expand their own facilities, and successfully compete with one another. This was the context for Eero Saarinen's strikingly individualistic design in poured concrete, which, understandably, became the new centerpiece at the airport for years to come.

His masterpiece received rave reviews in the architectural and popular press as expressing the excitement of air travel, which was Saarinen's intention. In 1959, he stated that he wanted it to be "a place of movement" within a concrete shell of "four intersecting barrel vaults. . .which makes a huge umbrella over all the passenger areas." A year later, he likened his work here to that of Baroque architects who "were trying to see how far they could go into a non-static architecture." Recent authors have linked this building with his theater design background. In the words of a taxi driver quoted in 1963, "This is not just a building, Mac. It's a feeling. You get inside and you feel like you're floating." **JZ**

🧭 NAVIGATOR

👁 FOCAL POINTS

1 SCULPTURAL INTERIORS
The sculptural interiors were intended to be an immersional experience, or as Saarinen said, "a total environment," where curvilinear forms could be seen in the Saarinen plastic furniture throughout as well as in the signage, countertops, and tables, all belonging to the "same form world."

2 DYNAMIC SHAPE
Airlines like TWA strove to create exciting environments for their passengers in the early jet age. The shapes of the vaults and other architectural forms throughout the space were intended to visually create an uplifting experience and a compatible shelter for the similarly curved furnishings within this immersional stage set—the travelers all being actors in this dynamic panorama of air transportation.

3 CURVILINEAR JOURNEY
The numerous curvilinear ramps and landings throughout the building, as well as the sweeping, slightly arched tubular arrival and departure corridors, were intended to reinforce the experience of journey for the passengers. Rugs within the concrete spaces were all branded TWA red.

🕐 ARCHITECT PROFILE

1910–45
Eero Saarinen was born in 1910, the son of Finnish architect Eliel Saarinen (1873–1950). The family moved to the United States in 1923, where Eero attended Cranbrook Academy of Art and met future design leaders Charles and Ray Eames and Florence Knoll. He studied in Paris, then at Yale (graduating in 1934) and worked on Crow Island School in Winnetka, Illinois (1940), with Perkins and Will. During World War II, he designed projects for the Office of Strategic Services (OSS).

1946–61
He won the competition for the Jefferson Arch in St. Louis in 1948 (built 1965), and created the molded Tulip Chair in 1955. Other works include the Chapel and Kresge Auditorium at Massachusetts Institute of Technology and the General Motors Technical Center in Warren, Michigan (both 1955). The 1950s also saw the design beginnings of the TWA and Dulles (1962) airport terminals.

▲ Although some said the design of the building resembled a bird in flight, Saarinen stated this impression had not been intentional, although people had the right to see it that way if they wanted.

Marina City 1967

BERTRAND GOLDBERG 1913–97

Marina City,
Chicago, Illinois, USA

M arina City, affectionately called the "Corn Cobs," is arguably Chicago's most distinctive ensemble. This multiuse project is built on 3 acres (1.2 ha) and originally contained housing, parking, offices, theater, supermarket, restaurants, a bowling alley, and a boat marina; it was originally touted as a "City within a City." Commissioned by the Service Employees International Union, the two towers cost $36 million to construct and house 900 apartments.

The towers and complex were built by an industrialized process using fiberglass forms to create uniform surfaces for the concrete. The architect, Bauhaus-trained Bertrand Goldberg, stated that "we can build a far better concrete by having the smoothest forms we can achieve," and argued that Marina City was a contemporary "monument of rationality, ecology, and industrialization. . .the forms themselves create the monument." They create great balcony spaces as well as somewhat strange trapezoidal rooms. The complex has been altered at various times: offices were replaced with the Sax Hotel and the House of Blues concert venue has taken the place of the original cinema. **JZ**

✪ NAVIGATOR

👁 FOCAL POINTS

1 MULTIPLE USE

The complex sits atop a large plinth that has parking ramps as well as a marina for eighty pleasure boats. Parking extends to the twentieth floor of the towers, each of which were intended to house 450 cars. The Marina City parking lot was notably featured in the film *The Hunter* (1980), in a scene in which a villain's car becomes airborne after crashing out of the parking lot, before catapulting into the Chicago River.

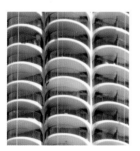

2 BALCONIES

The design of the complex featured spacious balconies but with Chicago's blustery weather most of the year, the balconies are not ultimately that functional. The pie-shaped apartments begin on the twenty-first floor and all featured state of the art appliances when first built.

3 HEIGHT

The sixty-five-story apartment towers were the tallest reinforced-concrete buildings in the world when they were constructed; they stand 587 feet (179 m) tall. The towers of Marina City use a central reinforced-concrete core to brace the surrounding structure.

▲ The adjacent balconies and floor-to-ceiling glazing of each apartment provide unobstructed views of the urban landscape.

CHICAGO LIFESTYLE

Goldberg's plans for the apartments at Marina City radiated from a central elevator core (below), the units themselves having trapezoidal rooms that culminated in generously curved balconies. This may seem like a commodious arrangement, however, Chicago's harsh winters and short summers are not receptive to year-long balcony use, and trapezoidal rooms present the unit's occupants with difficulties of furniture layout.

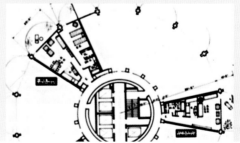

Pilgrimage Church of Mary, Queen of Peace 1972
GOTTFRIED BÖHM b.1920

Pilgrimage Church of Mary,
Queen of Peace,
Neviges, Germany

◆ NAVIGATOR

Gottfried Böhm is the son of an architect and three of his four sons also took up the profession. His father, Dominikus Böhm, created powerfully expressive churches in the 1920s and Gottfried acknowledges this heritage. When he received the Pritzker Architecture Prize (1986) he stated that his father "was my guide." Indeed, the bold angular mountain-peak shapes of the church's exterior and the resultant cavelike interior spaces intended to accommodate 7,000 pilgrims, illuminated only by a few windows and roof lights, hark back to his father's works as well as those of German Expressionists in the 1920s, particularly the brothers Bruno (1880–1938) and Max (1884–1967) Taut. In Böhm's Pritzker acceptance statement he further claimed that "new buildings should fit naturally into their surroundings, both architecturally and historically." This implies the connections to Taut and Gottfried's father, and confirms the overall historic and environmental context of this building. Although considered Böhm's masterpiece of Expressionism, he also used bold angular forms in other buildings, from the Rathaus (City Hall; 1969) in Bensburg to the Peek and Cloppenburg store in Berlin (1995). **JZ**

1 PILGRIMAGE SPACE

The original program for the church was to seat 900 with additional standing space for up to 3,000, but Böhm's design called for 800 seats with room for 2,200 standing. The consecration and dedication of the church on May 22–23, 1968 saw 7,000 pilgrims visiting the church over the course of the ceremonies. The new church continued to attract so many visitors that heating systems were added after construction, and the resultant temperature and humidity changes have impacted on the resilience of the concrete structure.

2 BOLD CONCRETE PEAKS

The bold peaks of the poured-concrete shapes provide a landmark appearance that also relates to the surrounding townscape and landscape. The exterior has few windows and skylights. Visitors approach the church up gently terraced steps in a plaza with curved hostel rooms for pilgrims, all looking somewhat regularized compared with the perceived irregularity of these dramatic angular forms. The concrete vaults within create strong shadows and are almost a reminder of giant fabric folds.

3 ANGULAR FORMS

The angled, folded concrete forms inside the church are visible expressions of exterior shapes. The dramatic sculptural pulpit recalls the tradition of monumental Gothic and Baroque architecture, combined with the Expressionist set design of films such as *The Cabinet of Dr. Caligari* (1920) and *Metropolis* (1927). Because of budgetary constraints, the church was originally built only for summer use, without heat and insulation, but the new facility experienced year-round attendance by pilgrims.

▲ Böhm intended that this concrete, asymmetric structure should complement its environment, for example, by planning its angles to match those of nearby residential roofs.

ALPINE ARCHITECTURE

Bruno Taut's drawings for his book *Alpine Architecture* (1917–19; below) probably served as a literal inspiration for Gottfried Böhm's church at Neviges. As some have articulated, the peaks of Böhm's church become an Alpine architecture in concrete. In his book, Taut's proposals project a utopian city in the Alps designed during World War I as a city of peace, much as Erich Mendelsohn's fantasy sketches of the same era attempted to transcend the horrors of that war-to-end-all-wars with an idealistic, dynamic architecture for the postwar future.

REGIONAL MODERNISM

1 **Brasília (1956–70)**
Oscar Niemeyer
Brasília, Brazil

2 **Sports Palace (1957)**
Pier Luigi Nervi
Piazza Apollodoro, Rome, Italy

3 **Nordic Pavilion (1962)**
Sverre Fehn
Venice Biennale Campus, Venice, Italy

Despite the tendency of Modernism toward universalizing forms, the idea of Regional Modernist architecture is as old as Modernism itself. Although capitalism and industrialization continued to shape the aesthetics and purpose of buildings in the second half of the twentieth century, architects increasingly strayed from purely utilitarian forms. The new generation of architects found the utopian promise of a new, homogenous, and universal architecture increasingly implausible. Instead, they hybridized the Modernist zeitgeist with vernacular tradition to express regional difference.

In the late 1890s, German theorist Richard Streiter recommended a form of Modernism that adapted to geographical conditions and building traditions. The Prairie Style Winslow House in River Forest, Illinois (1893), by Frank Lloyd Wright (1867–1959) is a prototypical example of this idea and site-specific modern building in the United States never abated. In the 1920s, regional ideas were championed by the Regional Planning Association of America, but it was only in the late 1940s that they intensified in the United States and Britain. Sigfried Giedion's manifesto "The Need for a New Monumentality" in 1943 stressed the importance of buildings being more than merely functional. In his article "Bay Region Style" in *The New Yorker* (1947), Lewis Mumford anticipated the deluge of critics who condemned Modernism as sterile and disregarding of building traditions.

The next generation of architects challenged the "form ever follows function" rationale of Louis Sullivan (1856–1924) and sought more sensitive and lyrical modes of expression. Historian Nikolaus Pevsner acknowledged that for

KEY EVENTS

1950	1951	1956	1957	1960	1965
A History of Modern Architecture by Bruno Zevi (1918–2000) is published. Juan O'Gorman begins Ciudad Universitaria (UNAM), Mexico City.	Spanish engineer Félix Candela constructs the Cosmic Rays Pavilion in Mexico City, using his invention of thin-shell reinforced concrete.	Brazil's President Kubitschek orders the building of Brasília. He commissions urban planner Lúcio Costa and Oscar Niemeyer to build the new capital.	Pier Luigi Nervi uses his technological innovations in reinforced concrete to construct the Sports Palace for the 1960 Olympics in Rome.	After an earthquake devastates Agadir in Morocco, Jean-François Zevaco (1916–2003) is commissioned to rebuild the city (1965; see p.404).	Joseph Philippe Karam (1923–76) is chosen to redesign Beirut's City Center. His egg-shaped design shows inventiveness and idiosyncrasy.

many, the pilgrimage chapel of Notre Dame du Haut at Ronchamp (1955) by
Le Corbusier (1887–1965) emblematized the emergence of a new, non-historicist
and anti-rational monumentality. Developments in Mexico City by Luis Barragán
(1902–88) and Juan O'Gorman (1905–82), which syncretized Mexican muralism
with the International Style (see p.416), set precedents for adapting Modernism
to the idiosyncrasies of sociocultural and geographical locales. Technological
advances in the middle of the century also facilitated greater architectural
experimentation. Spanish engineer Félix Candela (1910–97) created a thin-shell
reinforced concrete that allowed for the creation of parabolic structures, and the
Italian Pier Luigi Nervi (1891–1979) patented a lighter form of reinforced concrete
(*ferro cemento*), which enabled the construction of the ribbed dome of the
Sports Palace building (see image 2) for the Rome Olympic Games in 1960.

Commissioned by President Juscelino Kubitschek de Oliveira, Brasília (see
image 1) was considered the iconic example of Modern monumentality by
Giedion. Oscar Niemeyer (1907–2012) was the chief architect responsible for
transforming the barren central plateau of the country into a new capital.
Competitive with the scale and socioideological drive behind Le Corbusier's
development of Chandigarh (1951–63) as the regional capital of Haryana and
Punjab, Brasília presents a dramatic statement of confidence in the future of
Brazil. Rather than adhere to the geometric confines of Rationalism, Niemeyer
injected Brazilian sensuality and playfulness into Modernist rhetoric. He created
"floating" concrete basins and embraced the world of curves.

In Scandinavia, where there was a direct transition from Neoclassicism
(see p.272) to the New Objectivity, architects returned to the landscape for
inspiration. The intimate, yet open, Nordic Pavilion (see image 3) in Venice by
Norwegian architect Sverre Fehn (1924–2009) combines clean lines of purist
International Style Modernism with a concern for vernacular authenticity
signified by three plane trees reaching through the open unsupported central
space. The trees underscore the ascendancy of nature and a move away from
the rationalist model. In this respect, both Fehn and Alvar Aalto (1868–1976)
share affinities with Frank Lloyd Wright. Elsewhere, similar projects established
regional interpretations of Modernism: the Bunker House, Sardinia (1967; see
p.406), by Cini Boeri (b.1924) successfully integrates Modernist architectural
design with the landscape and the Institute of Management in Bangalore (1972)
by Balkrishna Vithaldas Doshi (b.1927) combines instruction learned from
Le Corbusier with native Indian philosophy.

By the 1960s, Modernist architecture seemed incapable of dealing with the
complexities of late capitalism. The grand ideals of implementing social change
by imposing a universal environmental order had failed. So too had the notion
that technological innovation would lead to humankind's salvation. Modernism
was to survive, but only after realizing its totalizing ambitions could not be
sustained. Its evolution depended on adapting to new circumstances. **CH**

1968	1970	1972	1986	2001	2013
Luis Barragán integrates Le Corbusier's clean lines with traditional vernacular in the Cuadra San Cristóbal equestrian estate in Mexico City.	Augustin Hernández (b.1924) builds Casa Hernández, Mexico; it fuses the Modernist lexicon with the nation's pre-Columbian heritage.	Balkrishna Vithaldas Doshi founds the Center for Environmental Planning and Technology in Ahmedabad, India.	Charles Correa (b.1930) designs the Jawahar Kala Kendra arts complex in Jaipur, India, in which he marries Old and New World traditions.	Vittorio Gregotti (b.1927) melds a spare Modernist vocabulary with Italianate vernacular for the design of Pujiang Town in China.	The National Library of Latvia, designed by Gunnar Birkert (b.1925), references Riga's church spire.

Courtyard Houses 1965
JEAN-FRANÇOIS ZEVACO 1916–2003

Courtyard Houses,
Agadir, Morocco

 NAVIGATOR

As part of a huge reconstruction effort that followed the Agadir earthquake in 1960, the Ministry of the Interior commissioned Jean-François Zevaco to design and build economical, easily maintained urban dwellings appropriate for middle-income Muslim families. He responded by modernizing the typology of the ancient courtyard settlement. His residential development communicates important aspects of his avant-garde design theories and is a superlative example of Moroccan Modernism. The idea of a courtyard as a domiciliary space goes back to the Neolithic period. Its distinctive form occurs in many world regions, but it is traditionally associated with hot, arid landscapes and forms the urban pattern in Islamic medinas. Apart from the climatic and functional efficiencies of this type of housing, the sociocultural practices of the local people helped to shape its design. Zevaco used his experience with the Mediterranean patio house to design seventeen interlocking single-story row dwellings. Each house has five patios and a service court. Living and sleeping rooms enjoy light and air from two directions. The whitewashed concrete residences interact with the sun, while fine openings and recesses project a progressive expression of Moroccan architecture. **CH**

👁 FOCAL POINTS

1 BENT ENTRANCE

The "bent entrance" principle facilitates the privacy of female household members. In Islam, guests are welcome, but often with a separation of genders. Zevaco placed a thick wall to the left side of the L-shaped entrance to prevent visitors viewing activity on the patio.

2 DOUBLE ORIENTATION

In traditional houses, courtyards perform an important task as a climate modifier. Zevaco designed rooms to have two openings. Winter sun entered all residential spaces, while summer heat was moderated by cross ventilation.

3 HIGH WALLS

In North African culture, religion defined the formation of residential units. The need for privacy led Zevaco to make the surrounding walls a similar height to that of the house, so that families could enjoy the indoor and outdoor spaces in private.

◀ An important aspect of the comfort of a courtyard is a monumental tree or a calm and cool pond. Zevaco continues this tradition by planning outdoor spaces to be planted with trees and flowers, offering homeowners a place to commune with nature.

⏱ ARCHITECT PROFILE

1916–47

French architect Jean-François Zevaco was born in Casablanca, Morocco. He studied at the Ecole des Beaux-Arts in Paris under Emmanuel Pontremoli (1865–1956) and Eugène Beaudoin (1898–1983), and in 1945 received his diploma (DPLG) in architecture. In 1947, he returned to Morocco, where he set up his own architectural practice.

1948–60

As a member of the Union of Modern Artists (UAM) and a founder member of the Modern Moroccan Architects' Group (GAMMA), Zevaco brought principles of international modernity to North Africa. He developed elegant modern houses, such as Craig Villa (1949), Casablanca, and larger-scale buildings, including the airport terminal, Tit Mellil (1951), Georges Bizet School, Casablanca (1958), and a thermal bath complex, Sidi Harazem (1960). He was awarded the Grand Prize at the Salon d'Automne, Casablanca (1956), for his collaboration with sculptor Oliver Seguin.

1961–80

Commissioned to reconstruct Adagir after the earthquake, Zevaco designed the Central Post Office (1963) and Fire Station (1963). Other notable projects included Yasmina Hotel, Cabo Negro (1968), Villa Zniber, Rabat (1970), and Villa Zevaco, Casablanca (1975). In 1980, he received the Aga Khan Award for Architecture for his affordable housing in Agadir.

1981–2003

With the exception of Villa Zniber, Casablanca (1988), and Villa Zniber, Marrakech (1998), Zevaco's opportunities dwindled in his later career. He died in 2003, leaving behind some 165 buildings, mostly in Morocco but also in Chad and Sudan.

Bunker House 1967

CINI BOERI b.1924

Bunker House,
La Maddalena, Sardinia, Italy

NAVIGATOR

When utopian aspirations of a complete synthesis of the arts were dwindling, Italian designer and architect Cini Boeri embarked upon her Bunker House. Built into the granite coast of the archipelago of La Maddalena, Sardinia, the house integrates Modernist architectural design with the landscape, demonstrating a mature understanding of both the functionality of space and the psychological relationship between humans and the environment. The understated project masterfully renovates a dialogue between form and function. Boeri has made a career of exploring expandability and pliability across several disciplines. Suitability of materials, consideration of cost, accessibility, and a concern for methods of production unify her experimentation within industrial design, and interior and exterior architecture. Bunker House, pertaining to laws of design efficiency promulgated by Le Corbusier (1887–1965), brings together programmatic ideas for economical design on a macro and a micro level: double-thickness, reinforced-concrete walls, slit windows and a glazed central living area. More than improving serviceability, Boeri's design focuses on the human relationship with surroundings, optimizing flexibility, welfare, and well-being. The low-lying structure hunkers on the shoreline, providing a formal analogy with the military forts found all over the archipelago. Invocations to a Brutalist aesthetic (see p.422) are manifest. **CH**

⊙ FOCAL POINTS

1 PROTECTIVE DOUBLE WALLS

Built on the wind-swept tip of the island of La Maddalena, and nestled down into the hillside, the house is configured from trapezoidal reinforced-concrete buttresses and double walls. The air cavities within the walls provide extra insulation and protection against the extreme coastal weather conditions.

2 SLIT WINDOWS

Boeri uses non-reciprocal viewing to increase inhabitants' privacy. The view from the inside of the building to the outside is cinematic, but from the outside looking in, only dark slits are visible. The interior is designed to be intimate and safe in contradistinction to the inhospitable environment.

3 WOODEN SHUTTER FRAMES

Always seeking innovative ideas that could improve quality of life, Boeri designed wooden shutters to provide seclusion from intense light and protection from wind. The retractable shutters border the door windows, which are cut directly into the cement. These large glazed doors are recessed back from the external walls.

⊙ ARCHITECT PROFILE

1924–63

Born in Milan, Cini Boeri graduated from Milan Polytechnic in 1951, and worked with Giò Ponti (1891–1979) before collaborating with Marco Zanuso (1916–2001). Her independent professional career in civil architecture and industrial design began in 1963.

1964–71

Boeri's notable early designs included the Burgundy chair (1964) and a single-mothers' nursery, Milan. She also developed a number of holiday homes in La Maddalena, such as Punta Cannone (1966), Bunker House (1967), and Villa La Rotonda (1969). In 1967, she produced the Monoblock chair for Artflex and a suitcase design for Franzi, and later designed the Lunario Table and Gradual Lounge for Knoll (1970). Her breakthrough came in 1971 when she created the Snake chair.

1972–89

In 1979, Boeri received the Compasso d'Oro award for her Strips sofa system, designed in 1972 and manufactured by Artflex. She was also responsible for the restoration of Palazzo Forti, Verona (1976). Boeri gave lectures all over the world and, from 1981 to 1983, taught architectural design and industrial design and decoration at Milan Polytechnic. Her work was recognized by a number of prizes, including the Saiedue Prize (1983), the Bio 10 Gold Medal Ljubljana (1984), the Roscoe Prize, New York (1978 and 1984), and the Stuttgart Prize (1985). In 1986, she designed a project for the 17th Milan Triennial Exhibition of Decorative Arts and Modern Architecture, which was followed by Trump Tower, New York, in 1988.

1990–present

Boeri's later career featured architectural projects such as the designs for a country house in Piacenza (1990) and for office buildings in Rome (1997). More recently, she designed Museo e Tesoro del Duomo di Monza (Museum and Treasury of the Cathedral of Monza; 2007). Further accolades include the Gold Medal, Milan (2003), and Silver Lady, Milan (2006). In 2008, she was awarded the Lifetime Achievement Award, Los Angeles, and Good Design Award, Chicago.

◄ The house has a symmetrical layout. Four single rooms with bathrooms are at each corner of the bunker. The communal area or sitting room is in the center of the house, where spectacular views of the natural world outside are enjoyed through glazed windows with ample natural light.

NEW ORGANIC

F ollowing World War II, Organic architecture was less a distinct grouping, as it had been after World War I, than a sensibility within mainstream Modernism. In 1947, the once hostile Congrès International d'Architecture Moderne (CIAM) declared it sought a "physical environment that will satisfy man's emotional and material needs." Many of the clients commissioning postwar reconstruction were not so accepting. They saw a concern with the specifics of individual users, place, and craft as an unaffordable luxury. Significantly, the leading postwar Organic architect, Alvar Aalto (1898–1976), worked in Finland, where a specific climate, small-scale building industry, and the commissioning of public buildings by architectural competitions encouraged these same values.

Yet it was in the affluent United States that the first distinctly "new organic" trait emerged, a practice that Harwell Harris (1903–90) called the "Regionalism of Liberation," which aimed to take advantage of local conditions to explore architectural possibilities more freely. In California, architects such as Richard Neutra (1892–1970), John Lautner (1911–94), and the Bay School developed the "bio-climatic" architecture of the 1930s, while in New England a tradition of site-responsive private houses was established, which informed the later work of architects such as Charles Moore (1925–93) at Sea Ranch (1965; see p.414). Outside the United States, a crucial aspect of regional expression was the readmission of tradition as a source of creativity. Luis Barragán (1902–88) mixed Modernist spatiality with the Mexican pueblo vernacular, integrating abstract planes and pigment colors into a landscape of watercourses, subtropical planting, and rocks in works such as Cuadra San Cristóbal (see image 1). In Sri Lanka, Geoffrey Bawa (1919–2003) built a remarkable variety of buildings and landscapes, sometimes marking out the projects at 1:1 scale on site.

In Europe, at least on the periphery of the main industrialized countries, the Organic developed through engaging Modernism with local materials, forms, typologies, and building methods. The Porto School in Portugal, led by Alvaro Siza (b.1933) and Fernando Távora (1923–2005), merged a Modernist aesthetic with a free interpretation of the local; similar resonances are found in the work of Barcelona architect José Coderch de Sentmenat (1913–84). An emphasis on craft was strong in Scandinavia, for example in the Louisiana Museum in Denmark by Jørgen Bo (1919–99) and Vilhelm Wohlert (1920–2007). In Britain, architects such as James Stirling (1926–92) looked less to the vernacular and more to the anonymous "Functional Tradition" of nineteenth-century industrial brick structures. Nowhere is the presence of the past and a Ruskinian concern with the particular skills of a region as clear, however, as in the almost Byzantine work of Carlo Scarpa (1906–78), with its use of local techniques and materials and exquisite detailing. Scarpa's work also grew from a call to restore what his compatriot Ernesto Rogers (1909–69) called "the heart of the city," famously represented by the postwar Warsaw plan of Helena (1900–82) and Syzmon Syrkus (1893–1964). Architects such as Aalto saw the medieval and Renaissance city as a datum of naturalness, and sought to create buildings as seamless parts of their urban context, as in the Rautatalo Building in Helsinki (1955).

International group Team X sought a "place form" sourced from the vitality of urban life; Aldo Van Eyck (1918–99) spoke of the "labyrinthine clarity" of the traditional city. The Economist Building (1959–64) in London by Alison (1928–93) and Peter (1923–2003) Smithson, and Byker Wall (1969–82), Newcastle upon Tyne, by Ralph Erskine (1914–2005), reflect this Organic ideal. The group's most remarkable legacy, however, is the forty-year development by Giancarlo de Carlo (1919–2005) of his Urbino master plan (1958), which treated the city and its landscape as a body onto which he grafted sensitive insertions and organic extensions, such as at Il Magistero, Urbino University (see image 2).

Implicit to the engagement with locality, craft, and history was a concern with users and their experience of architecture as an organic part of life. It is this that links architects as disparate as Hans Scharoun (1893–1972) with later ones such as Enric Miralles (1955–2000) and Carme Pinós (b.1954). Built forty years apart, Scharoun's Lünen and Marl schools in Germany, with their attention to the nuances of schoolchildren and learning—from coat hook to concert hall—are entirely in sympathy with the metaphors and ritualized cultural landscape of Miralles's and Pinós's Igualada Cemetery (1985–94) in Spain. **HC**

1 **Cuadra San Cristóbal (1968)**
Luis Barragán
Los Clubes, Mexico City, Mexico
© DACS / Barragan Foundation, Switzerland

2 **Il Magistero (1976)**
Giancarlo de Carlo
School of Education, Urbino University, Italy

1962–63	1963	1963	1969	1982	1991
Hans Scharoun completes the Lünen School and the Berlin Philharmonic Concert Hall.	Alvaro Siza completes the Boa Nova Tea House (see p.412) on the cliffs of the Matosinhos seashore in Portugal.	Lawrence Halprin (1916–2009), with Moore, Lyndon, Turnbull, Whitaker Architects, begins work on Sea Ranch, California (see p.414).	Giancarlo de Carlo publishes *Architecture's Public*, concerning the need for the participation of users in the design process.	Ralph Erskine's Byker Wall Estate in Newcastle upon Tyne is completed after a thirteen-year, phased design process involving residents.	Enric Miralles and Carme Pinós complete the Archery Range for the Barcelona Olympics, beginning a New Organic aesthetic and dynamism.

Säynätsalo Town Hall 1951

ALVAR AALTO 1898–1976

👁 FOCAL POINTS

1 BRICKWORK

The brickwork is deliberately variegated. Differing hues to the bricks, together with carefully irregularly laying, raked pointing, and the use of Monk bond brickwork, break up the surface into a faceted texture of light and shade.

2 TOWER

The place of democracy is put at the highest point, with an exaggeratedly tall form to denote its importance in the community. The roofline is asymmetrically composed for dynamism and to suggest a ruinous, ancient appearance.

3 ENTRANCE

The entrance to the Town Hall is modest, but—mediated by a pergola and planting, changes in floor surface, and a leather-bound door handle— undemonstratively welcoming. It also begins the spiral that leads up to the council chamber.

4 GRASS STEPS

From the forested side of the complex, a series of planks hold back turf steps that, in purposeful contrast to the more rigid granite steps of the town side, flow down from the upper garden court and its surrounding features.

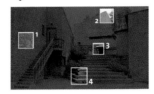

⬡ NAVIGATOR

A lvar Aalto won the commission for Säynätsalo in a competition for a building to serve
as the heart of a forestry company town in central Finland. Aalto had the freedom
to build what is, in effect, a miniature version of his organic ideal of restoring both
the natural world and the humanist city to modern times. In place of a single Modernist
object, the project is experienced as a journey through a sequence of fragments. Discrete
masses and volumes containing civic activities delineate a raised courtyard approached by
two staircases that extend from their respective milieus: a chiseled granite flight from the
town side and a set of grass steps leading from the forest. From the court, the citizen is
directed to the library, the health center, an internal cloister off which the council offices
open, and finally, a spiraling, brick-lined staircase that emerges into the 36-foot (11 m) tall
council chamber. These moments are all tied together with a tactile treatment of surfaces
and a painterly attention to detail, landscape, and materials. The building's concrete frame
allows Aalto to dispose elements as he sees fit, and to give fluidity to the apparently massive
form. Floors change from rough to smooth, granite to turf; battered brickwork is set off by
sculpted handrails and door handles. **HC**

Säynätsalo Town Hall,
Säynätsalo, Finland

🕐 ARCHITECT PROFILE

1898–1933
Alvar Aalto was born in Kuortane, Finland. After graduating
from Helsinki Institute of Technology, he set up his own
architecture practice in Jyväskylä in 1923. In 1925, he married
architect Aino Marsio and they traveled in Europe where they
were influenced by Modernism and the International Style.
His functional design for the Paimio Sanatorium (1929–33)
led to his international breakthrough.

1934–51
Aalto treated a building's design as a "total work of art," from
furniture to light fittings. In 1935, he and Aino formed the
furniture company Artek. In the 1940s, Aalto's buildings were
characterized by the use of organic forms and natural materials.
After Aino's death, Aalto married another architect, Elissa,
with whom he also collaborated. From the 1950s, Aalto worked
mainly on public buildings, such as at Säynätsalo.

1952–76
Aalto also worked on urban master plans, including Seinäjoki
(1965) and Rovaniemi (1976) city centers. He died in Helsinki.

▲ Aalto celebrates local woodworking in the roof, with two splayed
structures high above the almost sepulchral gloom of the chamber,
which is dimly lit by louvered windows and pendant lamps.

Boa Nova Tea House 1963
ALVARO SIZA b.1933

Boa Nova Tea House,
Leça da Palmeira,
Matosinhos, Portugal

NAVIGATOR

Situated in Alvaro Siza's home town, the Boa Nova Tea House pays homage to Siza's near namesake, Alvar Aalto, in particular his Muuratsalo Summer House (1953), with which it shares an approach, as well as formal and material attributes. In 1967, Siza described his aim to design the house as a complete environment: the project not only "builds the site," but acts as a framework that enhances the experience of it. The visitor approaches from the road across the grass swathe on a stone path that steps and drops, revealing and obscuring views of the rocky shore. Up close, the building presents a sweeping tiled roof above a closed frontage of white-rendered walls that hide half-buried kitchens and storerooms. Entering the building at the highest point of the site, the visitor drops down into the west-facing tea room through a top-lit, double-height hall that provides glimpses of sky and sea. Externally, the untreated concrete of the seaward walls merge with the rocky outcrop, a reversal of the white walls of the landward elevations that stand in contrast to their green surroundings. However, the complex, tile-clad, timber roof unites the two faces to form a coherent whole—sheltering the house and casting its walls into shadow, and closely tying the form of the building to the lay of the land. **HC**

◉ FOCAL POINTS

1 WHITE WALLS
The building's white walls are another common feature of the locality, but they also reflect the abstract forms of early Modernism. However, unlike in those works, here the white forms are used in a highly particular manner to denote plinth, steps, chimneys and the entrance.

2 LANDSCAPE
The white concrete acts as a foil to the contours and colors of the rocky landscape, with the planting deliberately allowed to grow over it. The form of the building responds to the site, with visitors being raised up and dropped down as they move toward, and through, the building.

3 TILED ROOF
The Roman roof tiles are typical of houses in the region and they immediately connect the building to the local vernacular. The tiles are treated freely as individual planes that are tilted and broken up—sweeping down to the ground or reaching up to admit light through clerestories or roof lights.

▲ The interior is lined throughout in timber, with polished Afizelia wood setting off the white walls. A ribbon window, framed by the overhanging copper eaves and rocks of the foreshore, gives the room a panorama to the sea and the horizon.

🕐 ARCHITECT PROFILE

1933–55
Alvaro Siza Vieira was born in Matosinhos, a small coastal town near Porto in Portugal. His career as an architect can be divided into two halves: one of isolation and one of international celebrity. He was educated at the University of Porto and immediately began working in the Porto region during the Estado Novo dictatorship (1933–74). He opened his own practice in 1954, a year before he graduated.

1956–73
The architect's early work consists of houses and small-scale public commissions, in which he merged the local vernacular with a Modernist sensibility. During the same period, he established the Porto School of Architecture—with colleagues including Fernando Távora (1923–2005)—as one of the most consistent schools in Europe.

1974–92
Following the Carnation Revolution in 1974, Siza's work gained recognition for its austere regionalism and contextual urbanism. In 1977, he was commissioned to build a collection of 1,200 low-cost housing units for a social housing project in Evora. In 1988, after fire destroyed Chiado, a historic square in Lisbon, Siza led a team of architects to renovate the site. It took more than ten years to complete and Siza was awarded the renowned Pritzker Architecture Prize in 1992.

1993–present
The architect has also attracted increasing numbers of international commissions. His first work in South America was the Southern Municipal District Center, Rosario, Argentina, in 2002. In 2005, he was commissioned to build the temporary summer pavilion at the Serpentine Gallery, Hyde Park, London.

Sea Ranch 1965
VARIOUS ARCHITECTS

Sea Ranch,
Sonoma County, California, USA

Architect and planner Al Boeke (1922–2011) conceived Sea Ranch in 1963 as an intentional community of like-minded inhabitants living on the Sonoma coast clifftops north of San Francisco. Sea Ranch's character was shaped by landscape architect Lawrence Halprin; he led a small team of architects who were sensitive to the locale to acknowledge the structure, appearance, and placement of the ranch's existing barns. Halprin undertook an ecological survey, marking out natural and man-made major features—the lay of the land, hedges, watercourses, and farm tracks—and planned the layout of the dwellings and shared facilities in accordance. The outcome was tight clusters of buildings set back from the shoreline against the existing landscape. Linked around a semi-enclosed courtyard, the condominium by MLTW is sited as a dynamic emphasis of the contours of the clifftops, whereas the "hedgerow houses" by Joseph Esherick (1914–98) merge effortlessly with the Monterey cypresses. The dominant form is the simple monopitch block, assembled into fragmented compositions or elongated into sweeping slopes that follow the land. Internally, buildings are multilevel and open-plan with large bay windows emphasizing the connection to the coast. **HC**

⬡ NAVIGATOR

👁 FOCAL POINTS

1 SLOPING ROOF

The dominant feature of what has become known as "Sea Ranch style," the "shed" roof follows or counters the contours of the coastal site. It deflects wind and, with no overhanging eaves, avoids uplift. The roof is covered in shingles, and seen from afar it merges with the tone and color of the walls.

2 COURTYARD

Approaching the condominium from the highway, residents enter through a stepped grass court, which provides framed views of the clifftops. From there, they enter their individual dwellings. This communal space is an important element of the social lifestyle that Sea Ranch continues to promote.

3 BAY WINDOW

While roof lights brightly illuminate the spaces, bay windows are punched out through the flat redwood cladding to allow the inhabitants to enter into the space of the commons and the coast. Where possible, the bay windows are sited on the corners of units, emphasizing the projections.

⏱ ARCHITECT PROFILE

1962–65

MLTW was a relatively short-lived architectural practice established in 1962 by Charles Moore (1925–93), Donlyn Lyndon (b.1936), William Turnbull (1935–97), and Richard Whitaker (b.1929). Moore, Lyndon, and Turnbull had been classmates at Princeton University, and Whitaker was a colleague of Moore's at the University of California in Berkeley. The Sea Ranch Condominium was their first major commission and brought the firm to public prominence.

1966–70

MLTW went on to design several other Californian buildings, including Kresge College of the University of California at Santa Cruz (1965–74) and the Faculty Club of the University of California at Santa Barbara (1967–68), but disbanded in 1970. Moore and Turnbull went on to establish their own successful practices, while Lyndon turned his focus to writing and teaching.

▲ A series of aedicules (frames) delineate the space of a sleeping loft or a seating area, combining the open plan with the specific qualities of individual rooms.

LATE INTERNATIONAL STYLE

1 **860–880 Lake Shore Drive (1951)**
Ludwig Mies van der Rohe
Chicago, Illinois, USA

2 **Lever House (1952)**
Skidmore, Owings and Merrill
New York, New York, USA

3 **Time-Life Building (1968)**
Harry Weese
Chicago, Illinois, USA

World War II brought about numerous changes in society but the immediate postwar era saw a struggle between those who wanted to return to prewar life versus those who wished to build on wartime social progress. The same contest can be found in architecture. High rises built in the United States at the time did occasionally push the limits, but also reverted to a more conservative, prewar Modernism, as witnessed in Chicago's granite-clad Prudential Building (1955) by Naess & Murphy. When reviewed by *Architectural Forum* in 1952, it was likened to New York's Rockefeller Center (1939) rather than to the new skeletal, steel-and-glass Lever House (see image 2) by Skidmore, Owings and Merrill (SOM). Developments in postwar West Germany also paralleled this conflict. Blocky, masonry-clad buildings, such as the Kempinski Hotel (1952) by Paul Schwebes (1902–78) in Berlin, gave way to steel-and-glass constructions of the later 1950s, such as Berlin's Europa-Center (1965) by Hubert Petschnigg (1913–97) and Helmut Hentrich (1905–2001).

Modernists, such as Arne Jacobsen (1902–71) in Denmark, Egon Eiermann (1904–70) in West Germany, Jean Prouvé (1901–84) in France, and Kenzo Tange

(1913–2005) in Japan, all began transforming their native landscapes around the globe with their own versions of the International Style. Even in the Soviet Union, Josef Stalin's death in 1953 and the rise of Nikita Khrushchev changed the nation's architecture overnight and led to the outlawing of Stalinist-style classicism in 1955.

After the war, New York's Museum of Modern Art's exhibition "Built in USA: 1932–44" toured Europe to showcase the diversity of U.S. modern architecture. The International Style in a variety of steel-and-glass expressions within the United States was slowly taking hold as the symbol of corporate America. This was seen especially in the works of SOM after Lever House and can also be glimpsed in the U.S. television series "Mad Men" (2007–15). This rather pluralistic context for International Style architecture in the United States is reflected in the work of Ludwig Mies van der Rohe (1886–1969) and SOM. Mies moved from Berlin to Chicago in 1938 to head the school of architecture at Armour Institute of Technology, later the Illinois Institute of Technology. He and fellow German immigrants changed the school's direction toward steel-and-glass International Style structures, first exemplified in his strikingly minimal twin towers of 860–880 Lake Shore Drive (see image 1), which historian Carl Condit likened to a second School of Chicago Architecture related to the functional skyscrapers of the 1890s. Although the towers were lampooned by Frank Lloyd Wright (1867–1959) as "flat-chested architecture," these twenty-six-story steel buildings set the tone for most of Mies's work to come, through to Chicago's IBM building (1971), his last.

Architectural and engineering firm SOM was founded in Chicago in 1936 after Louis Skidmore (1897–1962) and Nathaniel Owings (1903–84) worked together on the Century of Progress Exposition in Chicago in 1933. The first branch opened in 1937 in New York City, and John O. Merrill (1896–1975) joined the partnership in 1939. The firm stressed comprehensive design and engineering, along with teamwork, to create buildings, rather than making a consistently repetitive, branded appearance as was often the case with Mies. SOM design partners who came to prominence in the Chicago office during the 1950s included Myron Goldsmith (1918–96), Bruce J. Graham (1925–2010), and Walter Netsch (1920–2008), each with his own "look." These are exemplified by Goldsmith's Brunswick Building (1965), Graham's Equitable Building (1965), and Netsch's Harris Trust and Savings Bank (1960), all in Chicago. Ironically, this pluralistic approach helped to break the Miesian hold on architecture. Some steel-and-glass high rises, such as Harry Weese's Time-Life Building (see image 3), are very different designs executed in strikingly textured Corten steel. This expanding pluralistic approach to the International Style paralleled a greater appreciation of history as the nation celebrated its bicentennial in 1976. This opened the door further to an appreciation of historic architectural context and a rejection of the International Style. **JZ**

1960	1963	1964	1965	1974	1978
Arne Jacobsen's SAS Hotel opens in Copenhagen; it is one of the first Modernist boutique hotels.	The United States Air Force Academy Chapel (1963; see p.420) in Colorado is completed at a cost substantially more than the initial $126 million budget.	Corten steel, with its protective rust coating, is first used for the John Deere Headquarters designed by Eero Saarinen (1910–61).	The Chicago Civic Center (now the Daley Center), designed by Mies follower Jacques Brownson (1923–2012), is completed.	Carl Condit, one of the pioneers of the architectural history of the skyscraper, publishes his last book on Chicago architecture.	Stanley Tigerman's photomontage, *The Titanic*, depicts Crown Hall—Mies's temple of the International Style—sinking into Lake Michigan.

Seagram Building 1958

LUDWIG MIES VAN DER ROHE 1886–1969

Seagram Building,
New York, New York,
USA

Two factors secured Mies van der Rohe this commission. Firstly, he had created the prominent 860–880 Lake Shore Drive high-rise apartments (1951) in Chicago, buildings that were set apart distinctly in an open space and had made their mark in the global design community. More importantly, he had the support of Phyllis Lambert, daughter of Samuel Bronfman, Seagram's CEO. Lambert's book *Building Seagram* (2013) recounts the story of how a number of architects were shortlisted in 1954 for this prominent job. When her father asked her advice, she became involved in the selection process, striving to elevate the building and its role within New York. She picked Mies and eventually went on to become a student of his at the Illinois Institute of Technology (IIT). Philip Johnson also worked on the project, notably on the interiors. The result is spectacular. Seagram is 516 feet (157 m) high, its steel structure and concrete core clad in bronze, and the interiors display lavish use of travertine and marble—all expensive high-level surfaces. It cost $45 per square foot, supposedly the most expensive office built in Manhattan at the time (860–880 Lake Shore Drive had cost a mere $10 per square foot). After Seagram, Mies went on to build major towers in Toronto, Montreal, and Chicago. **JZ**

◆ NAVIGATOR

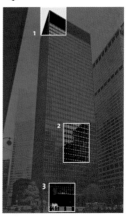

◉ FOCAL POINTS

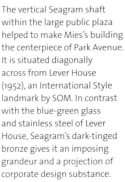

1 PROPORTION

The phrase "God is in the details" has been attributed to Mies, and there is every reason to think that he believed it. The detail and proportion of the building's windows recall school exercises that the architect instituted, in which his students carefully designed every brick in a brick wall.

2 COLOR

The vertical Seagram shaft within the large public plaza helped to make Mies's building the centerpiece of Park Avenue. It is situated diagonally across from Lever House (1952), an International Style landmark by SOM. In contrast with the blue-green glass and stainless steel of Lever House, Seagram's dark-tinged bronze gives it an imposing grandeur and a projection of corporate design substance.

3 PLAZA

Phyllis Lambert worked with Mies on the plaza in a conscious effort to bring open, publicly accessible space to midtown Manhattan. In many ways this bold move set the tone for other International Style slabs that were built in public plazas on Manhattan avenues in the mid to late 1960s.

◷ ARCHITECT PROFILE

1886–1951

Ludwig Mies van der Rohe was born in Aachen, Germany. He was apprenticed as a stone mason and worked for Berlin architect Bruno Paul (1874–1968) in the early 1900s. His key early works included the German Pavilion at the Barcelona World's Fair (1929) and the Tugendhat House in Brno, Czech Republic (1930). With the rise of National Socialism, he realized that he would have few design opportunities for International Style buildings. He moved to Chicago in 1938 to the Armour Institute of Technology, where he shaped the curriculum and built steel-and-glass structures, such as Farnsworth House (1951).

1952–69

His masterpieces include IIT's Crown Hall (1956) and the Seagram Building. Before his death in 1969, Mies witnessed construction of most of the Federal Center in Chicago, which served as a model for large complexes in Montreal and Toronto. He received the Presidential Medal of Freedom in 1963.

▲ Philip Johnson designed much of Seagram's interior, including the Four Seasons restaurant (1959). The interior was designated a landmark by the New York City Landmarks Commission in 1989.

United States Air Force Academy Chapel 1963

WALTER NETSCH 1920–2008

United States Air Force Academy Chapel, near Colorado Springs, Colorado, USA

NAVIGATOR

Since public monies in excess of $126 million were involved, numerous individuals wanted a say in this project (particularly with regard to the chapel)—from official design consultants such as Eero Saarinen (1910–61) and Pietro Belluschi (1899–1994) to Frank Lloyd Wright, who dismissed the initial design as a "factory." When SOM received the commission for the U.S. Air Force Academy (USAFA), the firm was at its peak. Walter Netsch was the chapel's design partner at SOM. The original design from 1955 featured a roof of folded concrete plates, which immediately drew the ire of politicians and the public because of its perceived secular appearance. Further design developments led to an A-frame aluminum, steel-and-glass solution with seventeen spires creating an interior space almost 100 feet (30.5 m) high. Trucked in and assembled on site, the tetrahedrons in some ways related to the prefabricated industrial design of some Air Force hangars. The final result was a chapel touted as "Air Age Gothic." The chapel's two-level plan was hall-like rather than cruciform, to reflect interfaith worship. Space was allocated according to the cadet population's demographics: the larger main level for Protestant services, the lower levels for Catholic, Jewish, and Buddhist worshippers. **JZ**

1 TETRAHEDRONS

The chapel distinguishes itself from other campus buildings by its steel-tubed tetrahedrons— more prominent than the folded-plate roofs in the initial concept from 1955. There are one hundred tetrahedrons in every spire, each one filled with clear aluminum panels.

2 SPIRES

The repetition of these immense peaks serves to underline their epic presence. Netsch's original plans called for nineteen spires, but financial limitations—the budget was over-running by a projected $1 million—reduced this figure by two.

3 GEOMETRIC FORMS

These tetrahedrons set between the spires are filled with stained glass. Their shape hints at Netsch's fascination with strong geometric forms in his designs, a characteristic that shaped his own design principles, which became known as the Field Theory.

◀ The stained-glass interior of the main space evokes the Gothic La Sainte-Chappelle in Paris but in angular, futuristic forms. The chancel includes a huge aluminum cross over 46 feet (14 m) high and 12 feet (3.5 m) wide and weighing 1,200 pounds.

🕑 ARCHITECT PROFILE

1920–47

Walter Netsch studied at the Massachusetts Institute of Technology and served in the United States Army Corps of Engineers during World War II. After military service he worked with suburban house architect L. Morgan Yost (1946–47).

1948–63

Netsch began what was to be a thirty-year career with SOM, which focused mostly on institutional buildings, particularly universities. He was made a general partner in 1955 and was designing the Inland Steel Building in Chicago when he was shifted to work on the Air Force Academy Chapel.

1964–79

After the Air Force Academy, Netsch developed his own design process called the Field Theory, in which rotational geometry determines what appears initially to be irregularly placed walls and spaces. This was used first in the student center at Grinnell College, Iowa (1965), and continued in jobs such as the campus buildings of the University of Illinois in Chicago in the 1960s and the School of the Art Institute of Chicago in the 1970s. Although his earlier Field Theory buildings received mixed reviews from their occupants, often leading to major design modifications by clients, his last building before retirement was arguably his best—the Miami University Art Museum (1979) in Oxford, Ohio.

1980–2008

After taking an early medical retirement from SOM in 1979, Netsch taught and practiced architecture and served on a variety of public service boards, including the United States Commission of Fine Arts (1980–85). In 1981, he started up his own architecture practice.

BRUTALISM

The term itself seems pejorative: Brutalism—harsh, aggressive, lacking delicacy or restraint. However, the roots of Brutalist architecture are, in fact, sensitive and sensible. Early Brutalism was largely a product of post–World War II rebuilding efforts. For cities such as London, pockmarked with ruins, Brutalism became shorthand for rapidly built, high-density structures, whose aesthetic—characterized by many critics and passers-by as ugly—is symbolically strong (undressed concrete), literal (ornamented with exposed building mechanisms or conduits), and pragmatic (contingent upon simple geometric shapes, such as squares and rectangles).

Often regarded as an outgrowth of Modernism, the Congrès International d'Architecture Moderne (CIAM) proposed European postwar urban plans in 1953, considered by some as doctrinaire. Implementation often met with resistance from citizens, such as those in Dresden who declared the plans an attack on the city. In turn, the congress led to the formation of the group Team X, whose members included adherents of the style that would become known as Brutalism. A negation of the past, Brutalism was intended to mobilize users into the postwar era by wiping cities clean of nostalgic or disheartening reminders of buildings and streets lost to rubble. Its deliberate lack of historical cues resulted in buildings that are now well known as being

KEY EVENTS

1952	1953	1954	1955	1964	1966
Le Corbusier's housing unit in Marseille is perhaps the first example of Brutalism for its aesthetic, materials and social philosophies.	Alison Smithson coins the term"New Brutalism," capturing postwar architectural progressions in a single phrase.	Chamberlin, Powell, and Bon are asked to produce a design for the Barbican site in London, to include housing for 5,000 residents.	Critic Reyner Banham's article "The New Brutalism" for The Architectural Review signifies Brutalism as a new architectural language.	Ieoh Ming Pei's poured-concrete Society Hill Towers open their doors in Philadelphia. The design is a successful example of high-density Brutalism.	Clorindo Testa's Brutalist headquarters for the Bank of London and South America opens in Buenos Aires.

representative of the style, such as London's Southbank Centre (1951–68). As the style evolved, structures such as the Garden Building for St. Hilda's College, Oxford (1970), by English architects Alison (1928–93) and Peter (1923–2003) Smithson cloaked the pragmatic Brutalist ethos with, in this case, an expressive oak floating frame, reminiscent of an English half-timbered Tudor house.

Although sometimes characterized as "cold" in appearance, Brutalism is "warm" in its fundamental ideals: a vast capsule for the communities designed to flourish within it, a reinforced structure for cohesive microsocieties in otherwise broken worlds. No architect was more vocal about parting from forms and expenses not befitting the times than Le Corbusier (1887–1965), who is often cited as the forefather of Brutalism. His postwar works—made of frugal *béton brut* (raw concrete)—are proto-Brutalist in appearance, material and function. Chief among them is the rectilinear, ferro-concrete housing unit in Marseilles (Unité d'Habitation; 1952)—a mass-housing triumph or a nightmare, depending on which critic is asked. It was designed to promote rich interior public life for its inhabitants, aided by indoor "streets" or corridors, communal centers, and a small hotel. Art historians Marvin Trachtenberg and Isabelle Hyman cite the building as giving "the impression of a massive ship of humanity, carrying an entire village across the suburban greenery of Marseille." The metaphor can be applied to later examples of Brutalism, such as the National Library of the Argentine Republic (see image 2), designed by Clorindo Testa (1923–2013). A concrete geometric craft, the library visually hovers above Buenos Aires, as if riding waves of monumental social change.

Peter and Alison Smithson were outspoken leaders of the New Brutalism style, a term coined by Alison to describe their unbuilt house (1952) in a bombed area of Fitzrovia, London. They further defined the term in 1957 as "rough poetry," dragged from "confused and powerful forces." The "forces" were not only mass production, but also the patchwork of postwar urban bomb sites, such as those described by Graham Greene in *The Ministry of Fear* (1943). These sites were not merely flat canvases, but were integral to a new architecture. Critic Reyner Banham delved into the etymology of Brutalism in his seminal article "The New Brutalism" for *The Architectural Review* (1955). He asserted that "what moves a New Brutalist is the thing itself, in its totality, and with all its overtones of human association." The Smithsons' first major project, the Hunstanton Secondary Modern School in Norfolk, UK (1954), merged earlier Modernism (Miesian glass), with their brand of Brutalism (an exposed structural frame, for example) and the ability to turn faults (a functional water tank) into features (a tower). Its designation as Brutalist, however, was debated in 1987 in an interview by Charles Jencks with Jack Zunz of Ove Arup, the school's engineers. Widely acclaimed upon opening, Hunstanton became a template for school design, despite classrooms that were akin to caldariums in summer and frigidariums in winter due to its generous strips of windows.

1 The Egg (1978)
Harrison & Abramovitz
Albany, New York, USA

2 National Library of the Argentine Republic (1992)
Clorindo Testa
Buenos Aires, Argentina

1969	1969	1972	1976	1978	1982
John M. Johansen (1916–2012) uses Brutalist principles to joyful ends in the L. Frances Smith Elementary School, Columbus, Indiana.	William L. Pereira (1909–85) submits his design report for the Geisel Library in San Diego (see p.426).	Construction of the Trellick Tower in London ends. Its architect, Erno Goldfinger (1902–87), housed his office there until 1977.	Freeway Park (see p.428), a terraced park designed by Lawrence Halprin (1916–2009) to sit above a freeway in Seattle, is completed.	Harrison & Abramovitz unveil The Egg in Albany, New York, breaking with Brutalism's straight lines, but not its symbolism.	Lina Bo Bardi completes Sesc Pompéia in São Paulo: a visionary, multiuse community center, or "Brutalism with a heart."

Brutalism was not exclusively the result of postwar rebuilding. The main material of Brutalism—concrete—was not only a practical budgetary option, but also it represented the future. In the West, it reflected left-of-center political thinking, which, in turn, produced high-density U.K. public-housing estates, Paris's *périphérique banlieues* (peripheral suburbs), and public housing projects in the United States. Although it is easy to blame Brutalism for the social failure of buildings, the Society Hill Towers in Philadelphia (1964) by Ieoh Ming Pei (b.1917) demonstrate that high-density Brutalism does not in itself beget social disorder. The triplex of poured-concrete, thirty-one-story towers was built as social housing, but now comprises sought-after private condominiums.

Similarly, Brutalist public buildings, such as Yale University Art and Architecture Building (see image 4) in New Haven, Connecticut, by Paul Rudolph (1918–97), often went from hero to zero in a short space of time. A cast-in-place, ribbed-concrete statement, the structure was welcomed with acclaim, but subsequently drew so much criticism that a fire in the building in 1969 was deemed by sharp tongues to have been set by ire. In 1971, *The New York Times* architecture critic Ada Louise Huxtable called it "the building you love to hate," whereas others referred to it as an architect's ego trip—a common, if unfair, insult leveled at many Brutalist structures because of their forceful, "can't miss it" presence that rarely communicates humility. Often sculptural and eye-catching, Brutalism can be a showcase and a showboat for a different way of living. It is a style that produces beloved icons, as evidenced by New York's whimsical The Egg (see image 1), an "oval" performance art center by Wallace Harrison (1895–1981) and Max Abramovitz (1908–2004), which breaks with Brutalism's straight lines but not its function as an easily read symbol.

The Sesc Pompéia in the city of São Paulo (see image 3) by Lina Bo Bardi (1914–92) is among the finest examples of visionary Brutalism with a heart. Inaugurated in 1982, the development—a community and recreation center, learning facility, library, exhibition space, theater, and eating areas—was designed to engage diverse members of the community. The project began with a disused 1930s factory bought by the Social Services for Commerce (Sesc), who selected Bardi as architect based on her renovation of an old sugar mill (Solar do Unhão) in Salvador. The red-brick original buildings and their "city in a city" streetscape were preserved. Structural iron trusses allowed the demolition of walls to create open spaces. Three new reinforced-concrete towers are linked with multiple enclosed footbridges, criss-crossing above a stream. The

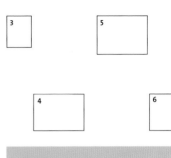

towers address the site's industrial past, disrupt its scale and reinvigorate the neighborhood. Sesc Pompéia cuts to the very psychology of a Brutalist building: connected, connecting, and forward-looking.

By contrast, Heroic Military College (1976), the military institute building designed by Mexican architect and sculptor Agustín Hernandez (b.1924) and located south of Mexico City, meets all the philosophical requirements of Brutalism. However, the internal community meant to thrive within its walls is not the gardening microcosm of Le Corbusier's daydreams, but a national army. Hernandez's monolith of exposed concrete is a striking sculptural representation of nation and identity. In *Constructing Identity in Contemporary Architecture: Case Studies from the South* (2009), Peter Herrle and Stephanus Schmitz argue that Hernandez "channels the art of the ancient cultures of Mexico" by evoking, in the main building's facade, "the [abstracted] mask of the rain god of the Mayas. . .in monumental proportions."

Brutalism's monolithic spare forms also became a trademark for Socialist architecture during the Cold War era (c.1947–91). Bold, geometric structures were meant to foster collective productivity and were an understandable progression of Constructivism (see p.368). Many of the most exemplary futuristic Brutalist structures are found in former Soviet republics. However, the House of Soviets in Kaliningrad (see image 5) is also an example of the most absurd. Built after World War II in place of the severely damaged Prussian Königsberg Castle (1255) to symbolize a new order in town, the rectilinear concrete administration building was never completed or occupied. It remains an ambitious relic of unrealized clout.

As Brutalist architecture has aged and global contexts have shifted, the style has a vanguard of fans and defenders. Brutalist philosophies breathe with new relevance in times of global recession; a renaissance of interest and nostalgia has emerged since the onset of the financial crisis in 2007. The popular blog F*ck Yeah Brutalism, established in 2011 by Michael Abrahamson, champions Brutalist structures such as the triangular Mathers & Haldenby Architects' Robarts Library, in Toronto (see image 6). Using few words, the site presents Brutalism as worthwhile and an exquisite vision of the future. Lending itself to very modern conversations about how ideas from "back then" can shape what is coming, Brutalism is a language still widely spoken. As a philosophy and aesthetic, it has proven elastic, despite its rigid forms. **KT**

3 **Sesc Pompéia (1982)**
  Lina Bo Bardi
  São Paulo, Brazil

4 **Yale University Art
  and Architecture Building (1963)**
  Paul Rudolph
  New Haven, Connecticut, USA

5 **House of Soviets (begun 1960)**
  Architect unknown
  Kaliningrad, Russia

6 **Robarts Library (1973)**
  Mathers & Haldenby Architects
  Toronto, Canada

Geisel Library 1970
WILLIAM L. PEREIRA 1909–85

Geisel Library,
University of San Diego,
La Jolla Campus, San Diego,
California, USA

NAVIGATOR

Dedicated to author Theodor Geisel, better known as "Dr. Seuss," the library was described by its architect as "powerful and permanent hands that are holding aloft knowledge itself." However, the strong physical shape of the library has encouraged equally strong metaphors: a central beacon, a concrete-and-glass eucalyptus tree, a spaceship. Sited at the head of a small sloping canyon, the Geisel Library (originally the Central University Library) opened two years after breaking ground. Balanced atop a two-story concrete trunk, the glass and reinforced-concrete tower hovers above the plaza. The original design resembled a sphere, but the architect later turned it inside out, revealing sixteen concrete brackets on the exterior to maximize interior space and to cut costs. The solution further underscores Brutalism's principle of architectural transparency. Not only are the building's materials revealed, but also their structural functions. Geisel Library breaks with this tradition by visually defying gravity, resembling a levitating mass but also lifting the seriousness associated with libraries. An addition in 1993 by Gunnar Birkerts and Associates, described as "deliberately subordinated" to Pereira's original, added underground wings without changing the library's silhouette. **KT**

⊙ FOCAL POINTS

1 EXPOSED BENTS
The building was originally designed to be constructed of steel, with cantilevered floors taking the shape of a tiered sphere. However, the support system was moved to the building's exterior and made of concrete, evocative of Brutalism's structural candor.

2 WINDOWS
Floor-to-ceiling windows provide 360-degree views of the campus from upper stories, linking those studying inside the library with the surrounding nature and community. Plate glass gives the building's exterior a complex, otherworldly quality.

3 SLOPE BEAM COLUMNS
On each side of the building, four cast-in-place columns, or bents, angled upward toward the sixth floor, bear the stress and weight of the cantilevered building. Steel rods attach each column to its partnering column on the opposite side of the building.

◄ The library's resemblance to a spaceship becomes even more pronounced when the building is lit up at night. This similarity has led to persistent rumors that the library appears as an alien craft in Stephen Spielberg's *Close Encounters of the Third Kind* (1977), but they are not true.

⏲ ARCHITECT PROFILE

1909–33
William L. Pereira was born in Chicago, Illinois. He studied in his home town and graduated with a degree in architecture from the School of Architecture, University of Illinois. He began his architectural career in 1930 working in Chicago for Holabird & Root, but before long set up his own practice. Early commissions included a chain of cinemas and a health center. At the Chicago World's Fair in 1933, he won twenty-two out of twenty-five industrial design competitions.

1934–48
Pereira married actress Margaret McConnell in 1934 and moved to Los Angeles four years later. He quickly found work in Hollywood and was employed to design the Motion Picture Country House in Woodland Hills, California (1942). In addition to his architectural projects, Pereira worked as an art director,

production designer and producer, winning an Academy Award for Best Special Effects for *Reap the Wild Wind* (1942).

1949–63
In 1949, Pereira was appointed professor of architecture at the University of Southern California, where he met Charles Luckman (1909–99). The two architects worked in partnership until 1959; perhaps their best-known work is the Theme Building at Los Angeles International Airport (1961). Pereira then formed William L. Pereira & Associates and entered his most prolific stage. In 1962, his expansive Brutalist master plan for the University of California Irvine campus was approved.

1964–85
In his later career, Pereira completed two of his most iconic works: the Geisel Library and the TransAmerica Pyramid skyscraper in San Francisco (1972).

Freeway Park 1976
LAWRENCE HALPRIN 1916–2009

Freeway Park,
Seattle, Washington, USA

NAVIGATOR

I n his book *Freeways* (1966), Modernist landscape architect Lawrence Halprin encouraged readers to accept the increasingly prevalent "freeway as part of the cityscape and [to] tame it, rather than complain about it." His Seattle solution demonstrated this by reuniting neighborhoods divided by the construction of Interstate 5 during the 1960s. The precedent-setting result is a powerful example of a distinctively humanized form of Brutalist Modernism that is neither cold nor alienating. Irregularly shaped, the terraced lawns by Halprin and lead designer Angela Danadjieva (b.1931) are a "lid" atop the sunken freeway and extend into adjacent neighborhoods. Diverse vegetation functions as a comforting backdrop and screens views of the city, while water features mask the roadway's roar. Sheltered spaces delineated by "tree island" buffers, concrete planters, berms, and winding pathways facilitate meandering and the descent into downtown. As suggested in a brochure from 1976, the park "possesses the kind of grandeur one usually associates with natural wonders" and "balances the extremes of dynamic motion and peaceful reflection." Evoking the region's rich environmental identity, its clifflike concrete outcroppings, verdant landscaping, and rugged terrain were thoughtfully restored in 2006. **DC**

⊙ FOCAL POINTS

1 CONCRETE FINISH
Timber shuttering formwork for the raw concrete pour left impressions of the wood's natural grain in the concrete, a textural homage to both manual craftsmanship and Seattle's lumber industry. The effect is one of exposed cliff faces or a petrified forest.

2 CANYON WATER FEATURE
During the warm months, 28,000 gallons (105,000 l) of recirculated water tumble over the Canyon fountain's 30-foot (9 m) face. Visitors are invited to climb and explore the canyon, and to view the muffled freeway below through an opening in the wall.

3 LANDSCAPING
Vegetation was not intended to be strictly indigenous or particularly pretty, but to create muted, sheltered spaces for human activity. Peripheral plantings were densely arranged to shield users from pollution, wind, and noise from the city and freeway beyond.

◀ Resting on two separate precast bridges—its girders ranging from 34 to 133 feet (10–40 m) in length—the park covers the deep channel of the interstate. The image of the park from below is designed to match the speed and scale of the freeway approach.

⊕ ARCHITECT PROFILE

1916–48
Born in Brooklyn, New York, Lawrence Halprin was inspired to become an architect in 1939 during a visit to the Taliesin estate in Wisconsin, home of Frank Lloyd Wright (1867–1959). While he was at Harvard Graduate School of Design during the early 1940s, his professors included Walter Gropius (1883–1969) and Marcel Breuer (1902–81).

1949–80
Following service in the U.S. Navy, Halprin founded a firm in 1949 in San Francisco. In 1958, he began working on the master landscape plan for Seattle's 1962 World's Fair. Back in San Francisco he set a standard for successful urban renewal projects by renovating the iconic Ghirardelli Square in 1968. Two years later, renowned architecture critic Ada Louise Huxtable declared his Forecourt Fountain Plaza (now Keller Fountain Park) in Portland, Oregon, "one of the most important urban spaces since the Renaissance." Among Halprin's many successful urban street pedestrianization projects, his Downtown Mall in Charlottesville, Virginia, opened in 1976. Similar works revitalized spaces in Denver, Minneapolis, Portland, and Los Angeles during the decade.

1981–2009
Twenty-one years after Halprin won the commission for the Franklin Delano Roosevelt Memorial, Washington, D.C., the park was dedicated in 1997. One of his favorite works, it earned him a Presidential Design Award in 2000. Upon his death, Halprin was hailed by The New York Times as "the tribal elder of American landscape architecture," and in 2010 his Heritage Park Plaza (1980) in Fort Worth, Texas, was added to the United States National Register of Historic Places.

CONTEMPORARY ISLAMIC

1 **Al-Sulaiman Palace (1979)**
Abdel-Wahed El-Wakil
Jeddah, Saudi Arabia

2 **Quba Mosque (622–rebuilt 1986)**
Abdel-Wahed El-Wakil
Medina, Saudi Arabia

ontemporary Islamic architecture begins with Egyptian architect Hassan Fathy (1900–89), who started documenting medieval Cairene houses in 1937. He discovered consistent typologies derived from a common set of socioreligious and environmental constraints. The typologies are now the lingua franca for those reviving Islamic architecture; because of this, they require brief explanation. One typology is the *magaz*, or indirect entrance, a primary paved forecourt paired with a second, landscaped one, joined by a breezeway, or *taktaboosh*, which allows cool night air trapped in vegetation to move by convection to the front court as the morning sun heats the paving. A *maqaad*, or covered porch, on the first floor of the forecourt also catches the cooler prevailing breeze at sunset. Fathy's spatial ensemble is completed by a *qaa*, or reception room, with a vertical projection, or *malkaf*, above it to introduce cool air, and a wind tower, or *shuksheika*, to expel heated air.

Fathy then sought more diverse sources of national heritage in the Nubian vernacular architecture of southern Egypt and northern Sudan. Here, he found an ingenious system of construction using mud bricks but without scaffolding, due to a shortage of wood in this barren region. Fathy first used this integrated system at New Gourna, relocating villagers from Old Gourna in the Valley of the Kings and Queens to the west bank of the Nile. But villagers were reluctant to leave the tombs, which provided income through tourism, so only part of the village was completed. Including a mosque, it was a synthesis of Cairene typologies and Nubian building traditions.

KEY EVENTS

1952	1969	1980	1980	1981	1989
Hassan Fathy's New Gourna project in Luxor comes to an end.	Fathy publishes *Architecture Pour La Peuple.* University of Chicago Press releases it in English in 1973 with a new title, *Architecture for the Poor.*	Fathy receives the Chairman's Award from the Aga Khan.	Abdel-Wahed El-Wakil receives an Aga Khan Award for the Halawa House in Agamy, Egypt.	Fathy designs Dar al-Islam in Abiquiu, New Mexico.	Fathy dies on November 30 at Beit Labib, Cairo.

Abdel-Wahed El-Wakil (b.1943) was apprenticed to Fathy and was the first to perpetuate his ideas, although he deliberately sought patronage, believing that this would more effectively disseminate his principles. An Aga Khan Award in 1980 for the Halawa House, in Agamy, Egypt, brought him international recognition. He relocated to Saudi Arabia and found important patrons in Jeddah: Mayor Muhammed Said al-Farsi and Sheikh Abdel Aziz al-Sulaiman. El-Wakil's Al-Sulaiman Palace (see image 1) eloquently elaborates on the Fathy lexicon, with a soaring *qaa*, a *taktaboosh*, and *maqaad*, but it is also a critical commentary on the prevalence of the free-standing villa throughout the Kingdom today, since it turns the traditional tower house of old Jeddah on its side. El-Wakil was then commissioned to design a mosque (*masjid*) for Al-Sulaiman, and he continued his exploration of the wealth of the Islamic heritage, reinvigorating and perpetuating a body of knowledge that was threatened with extinction. Using Fathy as his starting point, El-Wakil recorded building techniques involving complex, sacred Islamic geometries, focusing on specific aspects of the most prominent surviving examples of the Classic period of Islamic architecture. These include the geometric complexities of decorative plaster corbels, or *muqarnas*, which he replicated by writing a computer program. He even purchased salvaged examples and stored them for further study.

The Al-Sulaiman Palace and Mosque brought El-Wakil to the attention of powerful people within Saudi Arabia, including the future king, Prince Fahd ibn Abdul-Aziz. El-Wakil was addressing the loss of national heritage and searching for a progressive architectural language that would reflect Islamic traditions and their core importance in the Muslim world. El-Wakil creatively extrapolated the synthesis first formulated by Fathy to achieve these goals. To encourage a return to traditional values, Mayor Al-Farsi commissioned El-Wakil to design four mosques—Island, Ruwais, Abraj, and Corniche—on prominently visible sites on the Jeddah coast. Four more commissions for larger mosques followed. El-Wakil then achieved the highest level of national recognition by being asked to renovate the Quba Mosque (see image 2), near Medina, one of the most significant religious institutions in the Islamic world, after the Mosque of al-Haram and Kaaba in Mecca (see p.98) and the Prophet's Mosque in Medina (see p.96), because it was established by the Prophet Muhammad. Khalifa Uthman ibn Affran first extended Quba and Khalifa al-Walid ibn Abd al-Malik, the builder of the Great Mosque of Damascus, altered it. El-Wakil's Quba design was completed in 1986, and the al-Qiblatain and Miqat mosques the following year. Realizing these projects in such a short period of time—and at such a high level of artistic and technical skill—was a remarkable achievement, especially when El-Wakil's painstaking investigation into Islamic architecture is also taken into account.

Although he never worked with Fathy, as El-Wakil did, Jordanian architect Rasem Badran (b.1945) is also an important disciple of the master. His extensive research into the history and context of each of his projects is prompted by

what he calls "narratives" to produce a concept based on relevant typological precedents. This is most obvious in his design of the Qasr al Hokm Palace of Justice and Mosque (1992; see p.434) in Riyadh, Saudi Arabia.

Cairo-based Abdelhalim Ibrahim is a third notable Fathy disciple. His largest project to date is the master plan for the American University in Cairo's new campus in Qattameya (see image 4). Relocation from the middle of Cairo was a difficult, but retrospectively prescient, decision for the university. Its reputation as an urban institution serving a diverse student body, tempered by growth beyond its strict boundaries, had made it necessary to move to an open site near the new airport. Abdelhalim and his Community Design Collaborative conceived the idea of the campus as an oasis in the desert. They sought to determine the essence of the University in Cairo, beginning with its dense urban setting and its history of strong social and communal ties. The conclusion was that this character would be best preserved and re-created in the form of a new urban canyon or street set in the expanse of desert.

Abdelhalim used the courtyard as an organizational device to implement this overall concept. It enabled the university to be divided into built, unbuilt and landscaped areas that would maximize the environmental benefits of a challenging microclimate. Following Fathy's lead, the architect divided the 2.7-million-square-foot (250,000 sq m) site into a hierarchical sequence of internal courtyards that, like those in medieval Cairo, act as reservoirs for cool night air. This approach also inspired his design of the individual departments of the university, which were conceived as *dar*, or houses, and provided with the formal equivalent of a *qaa*, as well as a courtyard garden court and a *maqaad* on the first floor for receiving visitors and guests. Abdelhalim also used the Al-Azhar Mosque in Cairo as a precedent, as it is regarded throughout the Islamic world as a model of scholastic excellence and moral authority.

The last of the most influential Fathy disciples is Jaafar Touqan (b.1938), the son of renowned Palestinian poet Ibrahim Touqan. When the architect moved from Beirut to Amman in 1976, he found a critical shortage of quality building materials and products, few good construction companies, and no tradition of quality building procedures. This encouraged him to build with the local stone, and to investigate ways to detail it. The result was a series of masterful houses that reinvented the typologies introduced by Fathy.

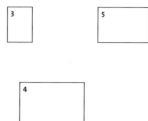

Touqan revealed his Rationalist preferences in his design of the Sheikha Salama Mosque (see image 3) in Abu Dhabi, where a pair of powerful, monumentally scaled minarets at the edge of the street announce the *sahn*, or forecourt that separates them from the more protected, main worship space at the back of the site. Touqan skillfully used the square as the geometrical generator of the project. To the public walking or driving by on the main street, the square first appears at the top of the two minarets, and is mirrored in their square forms. It then proliferates in the main worship space. The architect's original intention, of using the square opening as an architectural motif to link the foreground visually with the background, is clearly shown in earlier plans. However, in the version that was actually built, high walls screen both the *sahn* and the worship space from a side street, so the intended crescendo of rectilinear openings from front to back is relatively subdued.

Fathy's legacy, and the imageability that El-Wakil achieved by adapting it, is evident in the Sheikh Zayed Grand Mosque in Abu Dhabi (see image 5) by Mohammed Ali al-Ameri. Inspired by the Hassan II Mosque in Casablanca, Morocco, and the Badshahi Mosque in Lahore, Pakistan, it has a prayer hall for up to 40,000 worshippers, a 180,000-square-foot (16,800 sq m) courtyard and minarets that are 377 feet (115 m) high at each of its four corners. Most distinctive are the fifty-seven domes of various sizes that serrate the desert skyline, conjuring visions of Mughal and Moorish glory that are as equally unrelated to local history as that of Egypt to Saudi Arabia.

The U.K.'s Oxford Centre for Islamic Studies (2012), sponsored by the Prince of Wales and designed by El-Wakil, and the first phase of Masdar City (2012), Abu Dhabi, planned by Norman Foster (b.1935), both use the principles first codified by Fathy. They demonstrate that the master's ideas are now mainstream. Each of the second generation of pioneers who promote these ideals now has large firms employing hundreds of committed young followers. These, along with smaller offshoots, include Jamal R. Badran of Badran Design Studio, Abdelhalim Ibrahim Abdelhalim's Community Design Collaborative, Jaafar Touqan's Consolidated Consultants, and Rami Dahan and Soheir Farid, whose Ismaili Center (2008), Dubai, defines the thrust of the movement. The original Egyptian-influenced successes have enabled other directions within the genre, too, such as the impressive Campus for Innovation and Sport (2011; see p.436) in Beirut, by 109 Architects and Youssef Tohmé (b.1969). All of this activity demonstrates the remarkable diversity of Islamic architecture, and shows that the Muslim diaspora is once more on the ascendant. **JMS**

3 **Sheikha Salama Mosque (2011)**
   Jaafar Touqan
   Al Ain, Abu Dhabi, United Arab Emirates

4 **American University in Cairo (2008)**
   Abdelhalim Ibrahim
   Qattameya, New Cairo, Egypt

5 **Sheikh Zayed Grand Mosque (2007)**
   Mohammed Ali al-Ameri
   Abu Dhabi, United Arab Emirates

Qasr al Hokm Palace of Justice and Mosque 1992

RASEM BADRAN b.1945

Qasr al Hokm Palace
of Justice and Mosque,
Riyadh, Saudi Arabia

Centrally located in the old district of Riyadh, birthplace of the nation of Saudi Arabia, the Qasr al Hokm site is layered with memories. Rasem Badran researched traditional Najdi architecture of the Riyadh region in order to uncover and express the site's layers of symbolic meaning. Referring to prototypes such as the mosque at Darriyah, above the Wadi Hanifah (ancestral home of the ruling Saud family), he replaced the vernacular mud brick with locally produced brick of a similar appearance. Badran's design revolved around a series of *midans*, or courtyards, starting with the 120,560-square-foot (11,200 sq m) Mohammad Ibn-Saud Plaza in front of his new Palace of Justice, followed by the smaller Al-Safa Plaza, which leads to the Imam Turki Ibn Abdullah Mosque. The architect's plan included a triangular commercial zone that mitigates between this linear sequence and the street. It is significant because it reintroduces the historical connection between secular and sacred uses without compromising the spiritual and temporal authority of the Qasr al Hokm Palace of Justice and Mosque. In his design, Badran preserved precious cultural memories, balancing tradition with modernity. **JMS**

✦ NAVIGATOR

👁 FOCAL POINTS

1 PLAZA

The large plaza that joins the Palace of Justice and the mosque replicates an historic public space. Badran uncovered rare photographs of the area taken in the 1920s, and these guided him in determining the plaza's scale and proportion.

2 MOSQUE

The Imam Turki Ibn Abdullah Mosque accommodates 17,000 worshippers within its enclosed prayer hall, with space for more in the forecourt, or *sahn*. The mosque has two traditional square minarets, 165 feet (50 m) high, located at the ends of the prayer hall.

3 ARCADE

The arcade provides shade during the day, and there are also retail outlets inside it. In the past, mosques were typically connected to commercial and residential interests, but in recent years they have become increasingly isolated from them.

◀ The new Imam Turki Ibn Abdullah Mosque has a hypostyle (column-supported roof) prayer area. Attempting to combine tradition and technology, Badran took advantage of the uniform distribution of the columns by locating air-conditioning units inside them, making them less obtrusive and more efficient.

🕑 ARCHITECT PROFILE

1945–69

Rasem Badran was born in Jerusalem to a prominent Palestinian family of artisans, artists, and intellectuals. His father, Jamal Badran, and uncle, Abdel Razak, championed the preservation of traditional Islamic decorative arts and crafts in their Badran Studio for the Arts in Jerusalem. Jamal Badran opened his own atelier in Ramallah in 1962, gaining fame with his restoration of the twelfth-century Minbar of Saladin, a historic wooden pulpit that stood in the Al-Aqsa Mosque in Jerusalem until it was burned down by a tourist in 1969. Rasem assisted his father, before leaving to attend the Technical University of Darmstadt, Germany.

1970–95

After graduating in 1970, Badran researched the old city of Jerusalem, going on to co-found Shubeilat Badran Associates,

later Dar al-Omran, in Amman in 1973. After achieving considerable success in several high-profile competitions, Badran was commissioned to participate in the redevelopment of the Old City Center of Riyadh, and, in particular, to design a completely new replacement for the city's historic Qasr al Hokm complex. He won an Aga Khan Award for Architecture for that project in 1995.

1996–present

Badran won the development competition for Sidon Sea Front, Lebanon, in 1996. The following year he won the international competition for the Islamic Arts Museum in Doha, Qatar. Badran's approach is heuristic, involving an assimilative process of background research, extensive sketching, and contextual absorption, resulting in a synthesis of traditional typologies and technological innovation.

Campus for Innovation and Sports 2011
109 ARCHITECTS WITH YOUSSEF TOHMÉ b.1969

Campus for Innovation and
Sports, Université Saint-Joseph,
Beirut, Lebanon

NAVIGATOR

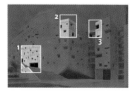

Youssef Tohmé, with a project team including Ibrahim Berberi, Nada Assaf, Rani Boustani, Etienne Nassar, Emile Khayat, Naja Chidiac, and Richard Kassab, conceived this complex inside the Université Saint-Joseph (USJ) campus as a city within a city. This particular university department is located on Damascus Street, with passageways and courtyards of various sizes seemingly carved out of one monolithic mass of concrete, creating six building blocks of various sizes across a large, triangular site. These *siqs*, or gorges, are strategically aligned to frame memorable, signature views of the city beyond. They also modulate the heat and mitigate the amount of natural light, which can be extreme in this location, thus serving as a monumental means of passive climate control. Inside, the inert concrete building skins are sculpted into a delicate abstract rendition of the classic Arab latticework window, or *mashrabiya*.

The overall solidity of the cluster is offset by the architectural equivalent of a hillside, a huge stairway that unifies all the buildings' levels. When considered along with the interlocking courtyards, Tohmé's overall planning approach clearly acknowledges other contemporary Islamic projects, even though its language and provenance differ. **JMS**

⊙ FOCAL POINTS

1 PASSAGEWAYS

By varying the sizes of the passageways, the architect has controlled the amount of light penetrating the interior space. Close to the Mediterranean, Beirut has a relatively benign climate, but this strategy helps to offset extreme seasonal temperatures when they occur.

2 WINDOWS

By cutting windows of various sizes into the massive walls of each of the six major blocks and smaller circulation towers, Tohmé created a powerful visual relationship between solid and void. This tension offsets what could have been overwhelming monumentality.

3 VISUAL EXCITEMENT

Changes of level, grand stairways, hidden corridors, and open courtyards all contribute to the visual excitement of this project. The corners of some of the buildings are lifted off the ground, giving a sense of adventure.

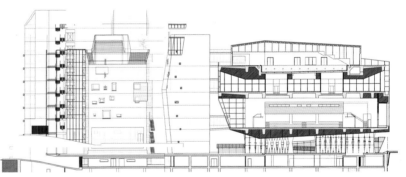

▲ The Campus for Innovation and Sports is a city in microcosm. The roofs of each of the building blocks are linked together to create one large, interconnected garden.

◄ Visual surprises continue inside, especially on the internal walls of buildings facing into courtyards, where the fragility and transparency of glass replace the ubiquitous mass and texture of concrete.

NEO-RATIONALISM

1 **Museum of Modern Literature** (2006)
David Chipperfield Architects
Marbach, Germany

2 **Banque de Luxembourg** (1994)
Arquitectonica
Boulevard Royal, Luxembourg

3 **Schützenstrasse Quarter** (1997)
Aldo Rossi
Berlin, Germany

The foundation of Neo-Rationalism in the mid-twentieth century began in Italy with the formation of Gruppo 7 in 1926. "We do not intend to break with tradition," their manifesto stated. Inspired by articles Le Corbusier wrote for the journal *L'Esprit Nouveau* (1920–25), their tenets were based on logic, rationality, Functionalism, and Classicism. A return to Classical Greek and Roman art and architecture had been prompted by the aftermath of World War I, and was advocated by Italian artist Giorgio de Chirico in his influential essay "The Return to Craft" (1919). For de Chirico and many of his artist and architect contemporaries, the road to redemption was lined with the Cleansing purity of classical statuary and architecture.

The purest examples of Gruppo 7's Italian Rationalism were built in the area of Rome known as E42 (renamed EUR after World War II to downplay fascist associations), designed between 1937 and 1938. Construction halted during World War II and although many of the buildings were completed in the 1950s, the war signaled the end of the Rationalist movement. Its classical legacy, however, re-emerged in the 1960s to the 1990s, and in some cases into the twenty-first century, as Neo-Rationalism.

The association of Rationalism with fascism and authoritarianism proved difficult to suppress. Neo-Rationalist buildings are often described as sparse, rigorous, stringent, powerful, and obsessive, both as accolades and as code for Rationalism's continued association with the ultra-classicism of authority.

KEY EVENTS

1954	1957	1961	1971	1977–84	1978
Carlo di Carli (1910–99) and Antonio Carminati (1894–1970) evolve postwar Rationalism with their four-story house on Milan's Via dei Giardini.	Luigi Moretti argues for mathematical, rational design methods to address architectural complexity and reject aesthetic and moral modernism.	La Rinascente in Rome, designed by Franco Albini (1905–77) and Franca Helg (1929–89), is completed. It features a steel frame with red masonry infill.	The Olivetti Residence Hall in Ivrea, Italy, designed by Roberto Gabetti and Aimaro Isola, is completed (see p.440).	British architect David Wild designs and builds fraternal twin Neo-Rationalist houses in north London, one of which is his home.	Bruno Zevi publishes "The Italian Rationalists" in *The Rationalists: Theory and Design in the Modern Movement*, edited by Dennis Sharp.

The view of Rationalism as a "disease" was promoted by Italian architect and historian Bruno Zevi (1918–2000), for whom columns, symmetry, order, and clarity ceased to be hallmarks of a backlash to World War I, but rather had evolved into symbols of the evils of the European Axis powers.

As youthful members of Gruppo 7 became senior members of the architecture community they adapted and modified the severity of Rationalism, as seen in buildings designed by Luigi Figini (1903–84) and Gino Pollini (1903–91) at the Olivetti campus (Officine ICO) in Ivrea, Italy. Neo-Rationalist counters to these works included the Olivetti Residence Hall (1971; see p.440) by Roberto Gabetti (1925–2000) and Aimaro Isola (b.1928), better known by its nickname, "Talponia," for its circular, "molelike" skylights in its earth berm roof. It was representative of Gabetti's Neo-Liberty movement, founded in the 1950s in Italy as a reaction to Rationalist architecture and dismissed by critic Reyner Banham as a retreat from the Modern Movement. However, the hall of residence seems to signify not a retreat, but an acknowledgment that salvation had not been found in Classical architecture.

The Neo-Rationalist design by Luigi Moretti (1907–73) for a theater in Piazza Imperiale at E42 was remarkably similar to David Chipperfield Architects' Museum of Modern Literature, Marbach, Germany (see image 1), which is perhaps why Pamela Buxton, in *RIBA Journal* (2009), deemed it "just the right side of the fine line between stripped back classicism and fascistic allusion." Banks that associated their headquarters with Neo-Rationalism often attracted criticism. Arquitectonica's Banque de Luxembourg (see image 2) was described by critic Johann Meiers as a "curved glass tower, sharp as a knife, slic[ing] violently through a rectangular Rationalist volume" before "aggressively bursting into the Boulevard Royale." The "noble attempts," wrote Meiers, of Rationalism and Modernism in the twentieth century to bridge the past and the future were translated by Arquitectonica into "an advertisement for international capitalism at its most aggressive and heartless."

Similarities with isolated Classical elements are evident in Il Palazzo Hotel (1989), Fukuoka, Japan, by Aldo Rossi (1931–97). The staircase, with its Egyptian pylon-like entrance, introduces the red travertine pillars and green copper lintels of the monumental blind facade. The hotel faces a square and is flanked by two low buildings; windows are restricted to side walls. Like Structuralism, Rossi's style of Neo-Rationalism was a reaction to Functionalism as well as to fascism. The urban renewal objectives of Rationalism re-emerged in Berlin in the 1980s, in an international building project (IBA), to which Rossi later contributed the Schützenstrasse Quarter (see image 3). In Belgium, the main building of the SWIFT headquarters in La Hulpe (1989; see p.442), by Ricardo Bofill (b.1939) and Constantin Brodzki (b.1924), reinterprets Andrea Palladio's Villa Emo (1559), Veneto, Italy, as a sorting house for the guardians of international banking codes rather than for the guardians of the grain harvest. **DJ**

1980	1987	1994	2003	2010	2014
Diener + Diener Architects is founded. The Swiss-based firm's spare designs are described as "stringently Neo-Rationalist."	The Kochstrasse building (part of the IBA building program in Berlin) is described as Rationalist by *The Architectural Review*.	Critics suggest that the Neo-Rationalist style of Banque de Luxembourg reflects "international capitalism at its most aggressive."	Peter Eisenman (b.1932) publishes his homage to Italian Rationalist architect Giuseppe Terragni (1904–43).	The concrete rational grid of Kaufhaus Tyrol, Innsbruck, Austria, by David Chipperfield Architects, is inserted seamlessly in the urban retail street.	*The Rationalist Reader* by Andrew Peckham and Torsten Schmiedeknecht divides Rationalist architecture into two periods: 1920 to 1940 and 1960 to 1990.

Olivetti Residence Hall (Talponia) 1971
ROBERTO GABETTI 1925–2000, AIMARO ISOLA b.1928

Olivetti Residence
Hall (Talponia),
Ivrea, Piedmont, Italy

🔘 NAVIGATOR

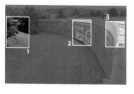

Talponia is one of the final schemes of Adriano Olivetti's utopian vision for Olivetti's factory campus in Ivrea. The Italian engineer and industrialist's interest in architecture created a campus of factories, workshops, residences, canteens, and a hotel, designed by various Italian architects—although the master plan had been designed in 1940 by Luigi Piccinato (1899–1983). With its 230-foot (70 m) radius, the semicircular Talponia was commissioned as an employee residence. The curved facade and entrance are a matrix of clear and stained glass, facing woodlands and opposite a housing area. Single rooms were 860 square feet (80 sq m) and duplexes housing three to four people were 1,290 square feet (120 sq m). It compares to other Italian employee residences that were built after World War II, such as BBPR's Sempione Estate in Milan (1946) and Borsalino in Alessandria (1951) by Ignazio Gardella (1905–99). The earlier architectural achievements of these buildings are reflected in Talponia, including truth to materials, modulation of volumes, and the cut and rhythm of apertures. Like Borsalino, Talponia's structure and plan combine to "naturalize it both inside and outside, relative to the sun and the air, the landscape, and the whole of nature." The demise of the Olivetti Company's fortunes resulted in the partial abandonment of its campus buildings, including Talponia, thereby creating less of a vibrant utopia and more of an open-air museum of Italian architecture. **DJ**

⊚ FOCAL POINTS

1 TERRAIN

Although earth-sheltered, Talponia was not built within the ground. It has a purposely built lawn and pedestrian railing, overlooking the lawn in front of the semicircular building. The structure mimics berm architecture, inserted into natural terrain, and its cloaking lawn provides a level of natural insulation.

2 WINDOWS

The steel-and-glass facade recalls the lead cames of Gothic stained-glass windows. Its network hides tall, narrow glass doors with simple metal hoods and double-height glass above. Doors are surrounded by a matrix of windows and small metal ventilation panels. Rectangular four-pane windows mimic sash windows.

3 PEDESTRIAN WALKWAY

The design was part of a research report by Roberto Gabetti and Aimaro Isola on architecture and nature, which led them to bury the residence under a pedestrian walkway. The steel matrix facade is vertically extended above the roof to create a guardrail for pedestrians on the upper surface.

▲ The name Talponia was inspired by the mole mounds (*talpa* is Italian for "mole")—concrete-based, plastic-domed, porthole skylights—on the roof lawn. The renovation of Stadel Museum, Frankfurt in 2013 included a gallery beneath a lawn dotted with structural glass portholes.

EARTH ARCHITECTURE

A resurgent interest in designing sustainable holistic environments fostered the rise of Landscape Urbanists in the 21st century. Their thesis describing "living processes," "flow," and "ecological infrastructure" prioritizes the landscape over the arrangement of buildings on the urban grid. However, before the boundary between architecture and landscape architecture became blurred, and the output labeled by some as "earth-itecture," architects were designing houses in which retention of the landscape was a priority. For example, the cast-in-place concrete walls of Hilltop House (1975; right) in Brooksville, Florida, by William Morgan (b.1930) cant upward to create a pyramid structure that sits within an earth berm. His curvaceous Dune House (1975), also in Florida, is berthed like a submarine within a sand dune, its porthole windows arranged like eyes.

SWIFT II 1989

RICARDO BOFILL b. 1939,   CONSTANTIN BRODZKI b. 1924

SWIFT II (Gulliver II),
La Hulpe, Belgium

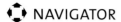
NAVIGATOR

The contrast between void and solid is a feature of Classical and Neoclassical architecture, including twentieth-century Italian Rationalism, which borrowed from the monumental architecture of imperial Rome. These forms were translated into Modernism by architects such as Luigi Moretti, whose Watergate complex (1962–72), Washington, D.C., displays strong contrasts between its ribbonlike levels. This classical idiom evolved with Ricardo Bofill's design for the second building of the SWIFT (Society for Worldwide Interbank Financial Telecommunications) headquarters. The success of Constantin Brodzki's precast concrete double-facade system for the first building in 1984 encouraged SWIFT to make the material's use a condition for Bofill's building. Sited on a hill at the periphery of parkland near Brussels, the monumental pyramid staircase of SWIFT II rises to the "temple" atrium. The clear glass atrium offsets the formalism of the pediments and dark glass of the colonnade wings. Sophisticated joints between concrete sections were, says Brodzki, the result of "thinking like a carpenter." Bofill's United Continental Airlines headquarters (1992) in Chicago, Illinois, furthered this exploration of masonry and glass. **DJ**

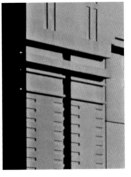

1 PILASTERS

Double T steel beams are hidden in pocket voids in the precast concrete skin. Concrete cast joints are hidden as well as highlighted by decorative horizontal shaft rings on pilasters. Bofill cites Frank Lloyd Wright (1867–1959) as inspiration for the arrangement of the pilasters.

2 CONCRETE

The facade is precast in Brodzki's SWIFT I double-skin sectional system. Concrete surfaces were treated with acid to mimic the texture of stone. Black steel glazing bars in the atrium were finished with an industrial texture that contrasts with the classic chiseled surface of the concrete.

3 PROPORTIONS

The ordered facade is based on the classical proportions of the golden ratio (approximately equal to 1.618). The building's setting in a country park near Chateau de La Hulpe (1840), the former seat of the Solvay family, underscores the classical symbolism.

◄ The building is composed of an atrium, two wings, and a satellite restaurant, connected by a covered walkway. Bofill's SWIFT II sits across the park from Brodzki's SWIFT I.

SWIFT I

The two SWIFT buildings are named Gulliver I and Gulliver II: a play on the company's acronym and on Jonathan Swift's novel *Gulliver's Travels* (1726). Brodzki's proprietary castconcrete system for SWIFT I, developed after research in the United States and with Belgium cement company CBR, for whom he designed similar precast offices, features a double-skin concrete facade (right). Sectional oval windows sit behind the curvilinear columnar sections. Cavity insulation is sandwiched between facades. Perhaps in a nod to the fantasy size references in Swift's book, the entrance is not immediately visible. Although the window proportions are conventional outside, the floor height inside makes them intentionally disproportionate.

PARALLEL MODERNISMS

Even before World War II, the freedoms that Modernism had initially promised seemed increasingly hidebound by an emerging architectural establishment—the Modern Movement and its International Style (see p.416)—that laid claim to universal aesthetics and technical solutions. With the massive scale of postwar reconstruction and the emergence of a consumer society, the mass production of "one-size-fits-all" structures that on the one hand ignored traditions, context, and climate, and on the other eschewed genuine innovation and alternative technologies, was swiftly recognized as much a problem as a solution. As Alvar Aalto (1898–1976) said in 1957: "Like all revolutions: it starts off with enthusiasm and stops with some kind of dictatorship." However, whereas architects such as Aalto sought to evolve an organic Modernism within the limits of industrial society, others broke away to work and explore architecture beyond it.

This was particularly the case in the United States, where postwar wealth, coupled with enduring pioneer myths—and a legacy of transcendentalism with its credo of individualism and self-reliance as defined by Henry David Thoreau and Ralph Waldo Emerson—offered a unique environment for experimentation, and indulgence. Frank Lloyd Wright (1867–1959), an architect

KEY EVENTS

1955	1956	1959	1961	1965	1966
Bruce Goff completes the Bavinger House in Norman, Oklahoma, which combines structural daring with space age taste.	Paolo Soleri conceives of "arcology" as a unity of architecture and ecology.	Frank Lloyd Wright dies, leaving Taliesins West and East, as well as his Usonian Houses, as models for an alternative tradition of American life.	Cedric Price collaborates with the theater director Joan Littlewood on the design of the Fun Palace in east London.	Ricardo Porro, Roberto Gottardi, and Vittorio Garatti's National Arts Schools in Cuba, commissioned by Fidel Castro in 1961, are abandoned.	John Entenza and *Arts and Architecture* magazine complete the last of their Case Study Houses, exemplars of a new Californian lifestyle.

who never saw himself as a Modernist, inherited both these traditions, and from 1910 onward lived his life in self-conscious defiance of convention. Thirty years later, he had completed a built, drawn, and written manifesto of what he saw as a natural, democratic American life. It included a paternalistic model factory and office for the Johnson Wax Company in Racine, Wisconsin, the extraordinary wilderness retreat at Fallingwater, Pennsylvania, and various "Usonian" Houses—a brilliantly conceived home for everyman that he hoped would populate Broadacre City, his vision to abolish the city and replace it with 1-acre (0.4 ha) self-sufficient smallholdings linked by super highways.

While recognizably suburban, Broadacre presented a beguilingly romantic mixture of ecological and technological thinking—a libertarian vision of modernity quite at odds with the collective views that dominated Modernism. Moreover, as Wright aged he threw convention to the wind in a seemingly endless mixture of geometries, colors, and materials, and while his projects for self-contained city centers remained largely unbuilt, hundreds of his houses were erected. The influence of this "genius without taste" set the scene for an idiosyncratic group of architects in the western states, including Bruce Goff (1904–82). The brilliant spiraling Bavinger House (see image 1) in Oklahoma is suspended from a central pole, from which circular platforms of sponge-backed, deep-pile carpet are suspended—a marked contrast with the enclosing rubble walls. Goff's assistant Bart Prince (b.1929) and pupil Herb Greene (b.1947) also worked in a similar vein. The most portentous envisioning of this posturban transcendentalism was the "arcology" (architecture-ecology) of Paolo Soleri (1919–2013), whose Arcosanti project (see image 2) in Arizona lies as an unfinished, Ozymandian proto-ruin just north of Taliesin West (1959; see p.448), while the most joyous are the works of the Ant Farm collective from 1968.

Another group of U.S. designers found inspiration in the potential of the country's advanced industry and materials, which they felt were barely being touched upon by aesthetically led Modernists. Foremost among these were three polymaths who had not trained conventionally as architects, and who brought a freer material approach. Charles Eames (1907–78) and his wife, Ray (1912–88), observed their environment with an untrammeled enthusiasm for facts and the potential of an artistry grounded in them. The Eames House and Studio at Pacific Palisades (Case Study House No. 8, 1949), California, were sourced from catalogues and "off-the-shelf" materials, all assembled with a Japanese sensibility to frame and screen, and a De Stijl use of color.

Emigrés from the Bauhaus, Josef (1888–1976) and Anni (1899–1994) Albers arrived in Asheville, North Carolina, in 1933 to teach at the new counterculture Black Mountain College (BMC), founded by Theodore Dreier and John Andrew Rice. They brought the vigor of the original Weimar Bauhaus and encouraged a brief flowering of truly modern, interdisciplinary invention that transcended the ever more deracinated Modern Movement. It was while teaching at BMC

1 **Bavinger House (1955)**
Bruce Goff
Norman, Oklahoma, USA

2 **Arcosanti (1970–present)**
Paolo Soleri
Arizona, USA

1967	1973	1973	1975	1976	1982
Richard Buckminster Fuller designs the United States Pavilion (now the Biosphère) for the 1967 World's Fair (Expo '67) in Montreal.	Hassan Fathy's *Architecture for the Poor* is published in English, spreading his ideas about using appropriate technology for building.	The Centre for Alternative Technology (CAT) opens in Machynlleth, Wales, setting out alternatives for sustainable living and construction.	Christopher Alexander publishes *The Oregon Experiment*, leading to the later *Pattern Language* (1979), delineating a "timeless way of building."	Lucien Kroll completes his Medical Faculty Housing at the University of Louvain in Belgium.	The Bangladesh National Assembly in Dhaka, by Louis Kahn (1901–74), is completed (see p.452).

that Richard Buckminster Fuller (1895–1983) built his first geodesic dome, a genuinely radical structural advance. That geo-domes are lightweight and easily assembled from a minimal amount of almost any material has recommended them for countless uses, from cane and bamboo versions in the developing world to the vast Eden Project (2000) in Cornwall.

Buckminster Fuller conceived design as a laboratory process aimed at deducting the best solutions to human survival on "Spaceship Earth." While he offered his services to NASA, his greatest influence was arguably in the United Kingdom, especially on Cedric Price (1934–2003), with whom he collaborated on the Claverton Dome project (1962) in Bath. Price brought a Pop Art sensibility to combinations of ready-made industrial products teamed with service technologies to provide realizable non-hierarchical infrastructures for new democratic urban activities, such as the Inter-Action Centre (1971) in London. Even more tightly bound to a Pop Art approach, Archigram rendered a series of apparently free-for-all images of highly stylized and serviced structures capable of indeterminate manipulation, and continual extension. Their ideas, premised on endless resources, had a profound influence on British High Tech (see p.484).

Matching those whose belief in the liberating possibilities of technology would culminate in the moon landings of 1969 was an equally fervent anti-technological movement reflected in the anti-capitalist demonstrations of 1968, whose desire for a "lighter way of living" on the planet was given meaning by the oil crisis of 1973. As with that of the technologists, this movement took the form of those architects exploring a genuinely sustainable architecture, and those who simply wanted the appearance of doing so. The most enduring and effective consequence of this has been the (glacially slow) adaptation and tightening of building regulations worldwide, led by individuals and legislators pushing against the dead hand of the building industry. However, there were those who undertook a more holistic view, researching and building a new ecological approach to design, and the use of appropriate, intermediate technologies. Of these, the most robust and determined is the Centre for Alternative Technology (CAT) in Machynlleth, Wales, which since 1973 has pioneered a sustainable approach to almost every aspect of the built environment, from energy conservation to "cradle-to-cradle" construction.

In part, such early green architects were following on from dissenting architects and builders in developing countries who, in the face of official development strategies that favored the aping or importing of the

International Style, instead developed their own appropriate architecture. From the 1940s, Hassan Fathy (1900–89) demonstrated the possibilities of traditional Egyptian adobe construction, with its formwork-free, Nubian-vault, climate-responsive thermal mass and windcatchers, in projects such as New Gourna (1947). In India, Laurie Baker (1917–2007) revived indigenous forms of design and construction, culminating in the Centre for Development Studies in Thiruvananthapuram (1971; see p.450). His architecture reinvigorated the vernacular as a basis for future innovation, with sweeping, free-form, perforated brick *jaali* walls and found materials integrated with the landscape.

In the Communist "Second World," a few architects challenged the normative aesthetics of doctrinaire systems building. In Cuba, Ricardo Porro (b.1925), Roberto Gottardi (b.1927), and Vittorio Garatti (b.1927) built the astonishing National Art Schools in Havana (see image 3), extending the traditional Catalan vault with an architectural lyricism of flowing spaces merging building and landscape form into a field of artistic potential and expression. In Eastern Europe, Hungarian Imre Mackowecz (1935–2011) constructed a series of organic timber structures seemingly merging animal forms with folklore, such as at the Farkasréti Cemetery Mortuary Hall (1975), before veering toward a National Romantic revival.

For many of these architects, a building should not just be an expression of an architect's artistic authority; they believed that allowing the users of a project to instigate its procurement, and contribute to its design and even its construction, could produce a radically inclusive, communal architecture. Architect and theorist Christopher Alexander (b.1936) developed an entire methodology, *The Oregon Experiment*, for consultation and participation with users at every stage. In Belgium, Lucien Kroll (b.1927) developed a Situationist approach to design itself, with projects reflecting the forces that shaped them and the people who inhabited them. His Medical Faculty Housing at the University of Leuven (see image 4) and various schemes for the radical rebuilding of seemingly intractable, large-scale housing schemes, such as the ZUP Perseigne rehabilitation (1975) in Alençon, France, give up the idea of individual authorship and replace it with a collectivist bricolage of desire and possibilities. **HC**

3 *National Art Schools* (1965)
Ricardo Porro, Roberto Gottardi,
and Vittorio Garatti
Havana, Cuba

4 Medical Faculty Housing, University
of Leuven (1976)
Lucien Kroll
Leuven, Belgium

Taliesin West 1959

FRANK LLOYD WRIGHT 1867–1959

Taliesin West,
Scottsdale, Arizona, USA

NAVIGATOR

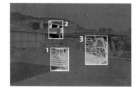

Begun some twenty-five years after the original Taliesin homestead in Wisconsin, Taliesin West echoes Henry David Thoreau's hut on Walden Pond in its intention to construct an alternative way of life. Site specific, climate responsive, and built of materials sourced from the desert, Taliesin West was the winter base for Frank Lloyd Wright and his "Fellowship" of apprentices, who migrated from Taliesin Wisconsin each autumn to the Sonoran desert. Wright conceived Taliesin West as an ongoing experiment. Under his direction, the Fellowship designed the buildings, beginning with the great drafting room (a glorified tent of great timber trusses and canvas), a common dining room, and private quarters for Wright and his family. Wright added the social spaces he saw as integral to the Fellowship, including a theater and lecture hall. Breezeways incorporating level changes encourage cross-ventilation, as does the tilted roof plane, while stone and concrete floors act as a thermal flywheel, absorbing heat in the day and releasing it at night. Inspiration for the decorative geometric forms and the pigment colors are taken from the Hohokam Native American Indian culture, as well as the desert fauna and flora. **HC**

⊚ FOCAL POINTS

1 DESERT STONE CONCRETE
In contrast to the light timber roofs, the walls were made from a concrete in which large, variously colored boulders from the desert were cast as "aggregate" into cement. Like the roof, the walls were built by members of the Fellowship.

2 NATIVE COLOR
Wright turned, as he had at Taliesin East, to the local cultures and landscape for his colors. The timber is "Cherokee Red": linseed oil mixed with iron oxide; walls are painted with desert "mud," applied just after the formwork was struck.

3 ANGLES
The compound is characterized by a 45-degree angle shift in plan between the main building and the landscaping. The tension created by this is exploited in the stepped-pyramid steps. In section, a similar contrast is made between the pitched roof and low horizontal walls.

▲ A low ceiling, careful variation in lighting and the location of windows, together with the use of varying angles and finishes, mean the intimacy of the space belies its size.

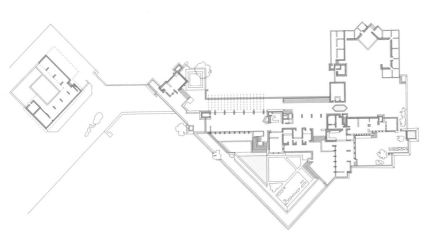

◄ The building began as a more or less temporary camp that could be reassembled each year in various forms. The permanent form used motifs and shapes taken from the surroundings, and did not require footings because it sat on a bed of calcium carbonate.

Centre for Development Studies 1971

LAURIE BAKER 1917–2007

Centre for Development
Studies, Thiruvananthapuram,
Kerala, India

NAVIGATOR

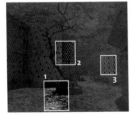

The Centre for Development Studies in Thiruvananthapuram was set up in 1971 as an interdisciplinary social science research institute. Laurie Baker was a natural choice for the project; he was invited to lay out a self-contained campus with all the traditional facilities on a sloping, heavily forested, 12-acre (5 ha) site. Baker's plan centers on a major complex at the highest point of the site, culminating in a spiraling, six-story library that dominates the center. This is surrounded by faculty and learning spaces with the residential quarters pushed to the edges of the campus. The sloping site and the position and shelter of the forest direct the design, with walls that curve around existing mature trees and respond to natural contours. Baker eschewed wasteful energy-intensive materials and methods, and evolved a strikingly innovative, witty, and enduring set of spaces and structures. Landscape and built form merge imperceptibly with patios nestling within dwarf "crinkle crankle" walls with vegetation blurring inside and outside. Latticed *jaali* walls of varying patterns of perforated brickwork are the most distinctive architectural feature and are arranged to allow air to enter evenly through the spaces. The air is then drawn up through chimneylike shafts at the top of the structure or through tilted roofs. Illuminated with patterns of dappled light and shade, the walls create intermediate zones at the edge of the buildings between the darker interiors and the exposed exteriors. **HC**

1 COURTYARD

Courtyards modulate the climate and provide shaded, informal areas for social gatherings. They bring planting into the midst of the center, which is sometimes retained in planters but in other areas grows over the building itself. The canopy of trees also provides further cooling of the environment.

2 CONSTRUCTION

Locally sourced brickwork is bonded with lime mortar, which eliminates the need for expansion joints. The center's walls either interlock or are curved in plan to reduce the amount of material required for a rigid structure. Concrete floors allow for the easy construction of large spans.

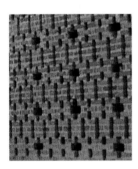

3 VENTILATION

Jaali walls with varying shaped openings allow passive ventilation throughout the building. Facing walls enable the even cross ventilation of air through the interior spaces. The walls are coupled with a roof-level shaft, which, as hot air rises, creates a stack ventilation system.

1917–47

Laurie Baker was born in Birmingham, UK. He grew up as a Methodist and became a Quaker in his teens. He studied at the Birmingham School of Architecture and became an associate of the Royal Institute of British Architects (ARIBA) in 1938. During World War II he provided medical assistance through the Quakers' Friends Ambulance Unit. In 1941, he went on a mission to help at a medical camp at Kutsing in inland China, and subsequently went to work at a leper colony. Following a chance meeting with Mahatma Gandhi, he went to India in 1945 as chief architect of the Mission to Lepers.

1948–68

In 1948, he married a doctor, Elizabeth Jacob, and they moved to Pithoragarh, where they set up a clinic. After fifteen years there, the Bakers moved in 1963 to Vagamon, Kerala, where they started a hospital and several schools. There, he had opportunities to build and develop his skills in the extreme climatic conditions. He dedicated himself to making design simpler and more inclusive, which he refined into a set of principles, including: "No innovative architect can hope to proceed in work without having gained an understanding of the local wisdom of a place." He took familiar (if ignored) indigenous techniques and advanced them to meet high standards of environmental comfort and a dynamic new aesthetic. Displaying an innovative frugality, Baker constructed all kinds and scales of buildings from entire villages to bespoke houses; his buildings not only made use of local traditions, but also salvaged local materials and components that others considered waste.

1969–2007

In 1969, the Baker family settled in Thiruvananthapuram; there, Baker built more than 1,000 residences and more than forty churches, chapels, and other buildings. In 1983, Baker was appointed a Member of the Order of the British Empire (MBE). He became an Indian citizen in 1988. In 2006, he was nominated for the Pritzker Architecture Prize. The Laurie Baker Centre for Habitat Studies was established after his death in 2007 to continue his philosophy and work.

◀ The walls act as visual screens, creating an intermediate zone at the edge of the building. Their curvature allows differing glimpses out as one moves past the wall. The glare of the bright sun is mediated to become a playful, moving pattern of light and shade.

Bangladesh National Assembly 1982
LOUIS KAHN 1901–74

Bangladesh National Assembly,
Sher-e-Bangla Nagar,
Dhaka, Bangladesh

◆ NAVIGATOR

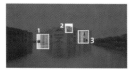

Perhaps as famed for his opaque, metaphysical writings as for the few buildings he realized, Louis Kahn is one of the great twentieth-century U.S. architects. Schooled in the Beaux-Arts tradition (see p.292), Kahn was dissatisfied with the stark, inhuman Functionalism of the emerging Modernist Movement, and sought a synthesis of the two schools of thought: a new monumentality that was as accomplished spiritually as buildings derived from classical antiquity, yet that embraced the materials and techniques of the modern age. Nowhere is Kahn's vision for a third way better embodied than in the Bangladesh National Assembly: here is a building of an entirely different order. Appearing to float weightlessly on the artificial lake, its great mass can resemble an ancient citadel, a timeless ruin immortalizing the ambition of some proud, now-forgotten civilization. Mandalalike in plan, eight centrifugally arranged blocks express their subservience to the parliamentary grand chamber and, in turn, the building forms the centerpiece of the wider Kahn-designed complex. Yet, despite an almost cosmic, transcendent geometry, Kahn avoids the context-free Modernism of his contemporaries by drawing on vernacular and monumental tropes from Bangladeshi architecture. A great building, for Kahn, must "go through measurable means" to be designed and built, but "in the end must be immeasurable." The quiet majesty of this structure and its subtle play of silence and light stand as an achievement beyond measure. **TH**

FOCAL POINTS

1 MATERIALS

An advocate of the authentic, direct use of materials without artifice, Kahn here employed poured-in-place concrete with inlaid marble strips, and local red brick throughout the complex. The dramatic setting of the artificial lake suggests the wetlands of Bangladesh, while providing a natural cooling and insulation system.

2 ROOF

Multiple variations were explored for the way the roof brought light into the parliamentary grand chamber, yet the designs proved too heavy for the structure below and had to be reduced to a single story. Within the chamber, artificial lighting is carefully concealed to allow daylight to enter unobstructed.

3 GEOMETRIC OPENINGS

Sheer concrete walls control the temperature and protect rooms from direct sunlight and heavy rain, while bringing a single-story unity to the exterior. The large geometric openings, abstractions of forms taken from Bangla art and architecture, allow light to enter the interior spaces in a subtle and changeable way.

▼ Louis Kahn had a near-mystical devotion to light as the "giver of presences": as the substance underlying all things and the basic material of the architect. In the sculptural interior spaces, he carefully controlled the play of light as it changed through the day.

ARCHITECT PROFILE

1901–43

Born Louis Isadore Kahn on the island of Osel, off the coast of Estonia, he emigrated to Philadelphia, Pennsylvania, as a child, going on to study architecture under Paul Cret (1876–1945) at the School of Fine Arts, University of Pennsylvania. After a tour of Europe in his late twenties, he struggled to find work.

1944–61

Kahn's first major solo essay was published in 1944, titled "Monumentality." In 1947, he began teaching at Yale University, and in 1951 designed the Yale Art Gallery extension. In 1955, he became professor of architecture at University of Pennsylvania and designed the Medical Research Building there.

1962–74

In 1962, work began on the Indian Institute of Management and the Bangladesh National Assembly. Commissions followed for the Philips Exeter Academy library and dining hall, the Kimbell Art Museum, and the Yale Center for British Art. In 1969, he gave his famous "Silence and Light" lecture.

METABOLISM

1 **Model of Marine City (1958)**
Kiyonori Kikutake

2 **Izumo Shrine Administration Building (1963)**
Kiyonori Kikutake
Izumo, Shimane prefecture, Japan

There are times when anything seems possible, no matter how audacious. The 1960s was one of those periods. Implausible advances in science and technology fired optimistic expectations that society's problems could be solved and the Metabolists reflected this idealistic era. The group's name was written in Japanese with four characters—new, state, replace, apologies—in other words, "out with the old, in with the new—sorry!" It sounded scientific and vaguely Buddhist. The Metabolists were young men who came of age as Japan was being rebuilt rapidly after widespread ruin in World War II. The original group was limited to the handful of contributors to a slim, ninety-page pamphlet called "Metabolism/1960" that sold for 500 yen at Tokyo's World Design Conference (WoDeCo) in 1960, and became the group's manifesto. The event attracted industrial and graphic designers, architects, and landscape architects from around the world. Roughly a third of the 227 participants came from overseas, which created a cosmopolitan ambience at a time when international travel was still rare. For Japan, the year 1960 also marked the beginning of a decade of aggressive internationalization.

Four of the original group were architects: Masato Otaka (1923–2010), Kiyonori Kikutake (1928–2012), Fumihiko Maki (b.1928), and Noriaki (Kisho) Kurokawa (1934–2007). Noboru Kawagoe (b.1926), formerly editor of one of Japan's leading architecture magazines, guided the group and is listed in the pamphlet as an inaugural member. Still unknown, these men stood shoulder-to-shoulder with global leaders in design. Kikutake spoke on a panel with Ralph

KEY EVENTS

1955	1959	1960	1961	1962	1966
German architect Konrad Wachsmann (1901–80) gives a seminar in Tokyo where he introduces prefabricated space frame structures.	Congrès International d'Architecture Moderne meets in Otterlo, the Netherlands; Kenzo Tange (1913–2005) presents Kikutake's Sky House and Marine City.	The World Design Conference is held in Tokyo. It is partially funded by the Japanese government.	Tange presents his "Plan for Tokyo 1960" on Japan's public TV network, NHK. Prime Minister Hayato Ikeda announces his "Income Doubling Plan."	"This Will be Your City" exhibition is curated at the Seibu Department Store, Tokyo, by Kikutake and Kawagoe.	Tange is appointed master planner for Expo '70 with Marxist architect Uzo Nishiyama (1911–94), whom he ultimately pushes aside.

Erskine (1914–2005), Otaka with Jean Prouvé (1901–84), and Kurokawa with industrial designers Carl Auböck and Erik Herløw. One evening, Louis Kahn (1901–74) joined a group visiting the only built work featured in the pamphlet, Kikutake's Sky House in Tokyo (1958); with Maki translating, he expostulated on architecture there until dawn. Paul Rudolph (1918–87) returned home and recommended that two other proposals from the pamphlet—Kikutake's Marine City (see image 1) and Kurokawa's Agricultural City (1960)—be exhibited at New York's Museum of Modern Art later in the year, hanging alongside schemes by Le Corbusier (1887–1965) and Frank Lloyd Wright (1867–1959). Offering inspiring, bold ideas illustrated in little more than sketches or models produced from ridiculously modest materials, the Metabolists were acknowledged as global leaders almost overnight.

In their manifesto, Maki and Otaka outlined an idea of clustered "group forms" in architecture, rendered in stacked sugar cubes. Kurokawa's proposals were diverse in scale and sensibility, ranging from the massive, gridded Agricultural City to sweeping curves on a raised house's roof. Kikutake's work dominated, however, filling more than a third of the pamphlet's pages. He took a particularly dim view of the landscape of Japan: "our society and our life are being suffocated. . .congestion of traffic causes arterial sclerosis. . .cities are turning into a graveyard." He proposed state-of-the-art replacements rising directly from the waters of Tokyo Bay or the ocean beyond, built of steel, concrete, and plastic. Illustrations of his own home presented a monumental concrete structure thrusting upward from a leafy slope, but not the elegant calligraphy and *shoji* screens within. Although Metabolism would be later seen as a uniquely Japanese movement that embraced the nation's traditions, the manifesto was infused only with a passion for scientific pioneering.

Metabolist architecture became known for its distinctive vocabulary: disdain of the existing city in favor of an "artificial ground" of virginal platforms floating over land or sea, thick concrete skeletons incorporating utilities and structural support, and dainty prefabricated residential units that could be easily replaceable. (Housing shortages were estimated in the millions in Tokyo alone.) Unseen at the time, but clearer in retrospect, the Metabolists represented the beginning of an important social shift from collective communities to isolated individuals. The seeds are evident in Kikutake's tiny "movenet" bedrooms and Kurokawa's cloistered capsules—and in the way the Metabolists themselves would ultimately move on, each one more interested in personal ambitions than in the ideals they once shared.

Maki and Otaka began to distance themselves from the group soon after the conference, being more concerned with space than structure and with rehabilitating cities than in a tabula rasa. Others who had been active in the movement were acknowledged after the pamphlet had been printed: industrial designer Kenji Ekuan (b.1929) was inclined to operate behind the

1968	1970	1973	1976	2007	2011
Japan's GDP is the second highest in the world, a rank it will hold for almost forty years.	Expo '70 costs almost $3 billion and draws over 60 million visitors. Kikutake's Expo Tower receives an Architectural Institute of Japan Prize.	Middle Eastern countries embargo oil, severely slowing the global economy. Japan's miraculous economic expansion halts abruptly.	Kurokawa's Sony Tower, sporting colorful mechanical and movement systems is completed in Osaka. It is the last Metabolist building.	The youngest Metabolist, Kisho Kurokawa, dies, galvanizing others to chronicle the movement and collect its artifacts.	"Metabolism: The City of the Future" opens in Tokyo. Organized by Hajime Yatsuka (b.1948), Tange's last student, it redefines Metabolism in Japan.

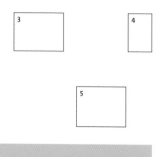

scenes, and the pamphlet's graphic designer, Kiyoshi Awazu (1929–2009), was named honorary chairman of the group shortly after WoDeCo ended.

Kawagoe and Awazu offered the media savvy that was just starting to be important in architectural practice. The Metabolists became publicity darlings, who exhibited in department-store galleries, on television, and in popular magazines, where their faces were as likely to be on the cover as their work. Ironically, they became so busy they never produced the promised second volume, "Metabolism/1965." This might explain why the group was considered dormant abroad; in the late 1960s, one British journal featured an article on "Whatever Happened to the Metabolists?" Distance, language, and cultural differences made it hard for outsiders to follow Metabolism's standard-bearers, but they had already become productive architects, unlike their European counterparts Archigram or Superstudio.

Kikutake's work in the decade following 1960 enjoys particularly enduring appreciation, especially the Izumo Shrine Administration Building (see image 2), Toku'unji Columbarium (1965), and Miyakonojo Civic Center (1966). He also produced a number of resort hotels that hewed closely to the Metabolist aesthetic, such as Hotel Tokoen (see image 3). Kurokawa, too, in spite of being the youngest of the group, was busy designing the Nitto Food Cannery (1964), the $20-million Yamagata Dreamland (1967), and Odakyu Drive-in (1969). Maki was still teaching in the United States in the early 1960s, but he began the iconic Hillside Terrace in Tokyo in 1967 and completed the first phase in 1970. Otaka's Sakaide Artificial Ground (1967) was an exquisitely clear evocation of the movement's intentions. In 1969, Maki, Kikutake, and Kurokawa came together once more, with a proposal for low-cost housing in Lima, Peru, one of three winning solutions in a competition organized by the United Nations.

Two other architects are so closely associated with the Metabolists that they are often mistakenly described as part of the group: Kenzo Tange (1913–2005) and Arata Isozaki (b.1931). Isozaki is best thought of as a "shadow" Metabolist: his graphic work used a similar vocabulary, although darkly expressed, such as his unbuilt design Incubation Process (see image 4). It would be more accurate to call Tange the movement's father; he was active in bringing WoDeCo to Tokyo and, when it became clear that he would be in the United States when it was being planned, he arranged for his assistant at the University of Tokyo, Takashi Asada, to organize and guide the group. Tange would adopt their vocabulary in his proposal for Tokyo Bay (1961)—which Kurokawa and Isozaki contributed to as students—and those for the Yamanashi Culture Center and Shizuoka Broadcasting Center, both completed in 1967.

Tange brought the Metabolists and Isozaki together one final time at Expo '70 in Osaka. He delegated master planning and a signature 393-foot (120 m) tall tower with barnaclelike pods to Kikutake, as well as a broad entrance platform soaring over the highway to Otaka; Ekuan designed a monorail, street furniture, and signage. Kurokawa gained commissions for two daring steel pavilions: the Takara Beautillion (assembled in only six days), designed with Ekuan, and the Toshiba IHI Pavilion, for which Kurokawa used computers in design for the first time. Tange himself designed the Festival Plaza (see image 5); its roof—a 354 ⅜ by 958 foot (108 x 292 m) space frame—the largest in the world—lifted lightly on just six pylons. The structure was an architectural expression of his relationship to the younger architects; capsules by Awazu, Maki, and Kurokawa were tucked into its open lattice and 65-foot (20 m) tall robots designed by Isozaki orbited below. Kawagoe also curated many of the Festival Plaza's events and installations. Expo '70 was the movement's climax and is often seen today as its dramatic finale.

Two other important Metabolist buildings were completed afterward— the Nakagin Capsule Building (1972; see p.458) by Kurokawa, and Kikutake's Aquapolis for the Okinawa Exposition in 1975. Ironically, both outlasted their usefulness, poignantly rusting yet remaining unchanged. The optimistic and progressive era that launched the Metabolists into international acclaim came to an abrupt end with the oil crisis of 1973, and with it Japan's booming economic expansion. The individuals that made up the Metabolists, however, continued to influence design both at home and overseas for decades to come. Abroad, the Metabolists are best remembered for their enthralling images of cities on the sea and their ability to build when others like them in Europe had not. Japanese architects felt differently; for more than half a century they recalled only the movement's later flirtation with technocratic and overscaled megastructures. However, a comprehensive exhibition curated by Hajime Yatsuka (b.1948) in 2011 rekindled the recognition in Tokyo that the Metabolists' greatest legacy was their amazing ambition inspired by an exciting time in history, and their success in expressing it architecturally. **DB**

Nakagin Capsule Tower Building 1972

KISHO KUROKAWA 1934–2007

Nakagin Capsule
Tower Building,
Shinbashi, Tokyo, Japan

⟡ NAVIGATOR

Kisho Kurokawa's Nakagin Capsule Tower Building proved it was possible to construct a prototype that rigorously reflected Metabolism's ambitious ideas, and to do so quickly. Thanks to prefabrication, it went up in about a year. Two concrete towers house elevators, stairs, and utility shafts. As the towers were being poured on site, a factory off site fabricated tiny capsules (7½ x 12½ x 6⅞ feet / 2.3 x 3.8 x 2.1 m). Plastic bathrooms built at another location were installed in the capsules, a pod within a pod. All 140 capsules took forty days to attach, each clipped to the towers with four precisely located bolts. The abiding affection for this structure—rusting and almost abandoned, but with fans around the world fighting for its survival—also owes much to the elegant external organization of the parts. Capsules gently step up around the perimeter, irregularly rotated in a pattern of long and short facades. Portholes, some with futuristic "privacy hoods," play out a secondary rhythm. The two towers—one eleven stories high, the other thirteen—thrust well beyond the capsules, sliced at a sharp angle that reflects Kurokawa's artful attention to detail. **DB**

⊙ FOCAL POINTS

1 CENTRAL CORES
Two cores at the heart of the building act as both a load-bearing infrastructure and a framework for services such as elevators, evacuation stairs, and utilities. The cores are connected by open bridges on every third floor. Flexible utility jacks link each capsule to its supportive core.

2 CAPSULES
Capsules built like shipping containers were produced in four models and flipped for further variation; there are twelve of one type and fifty-five of another, adding to the variety. Employing the same approach to structured variation developed in the automotive industry, each unit cost about the same as a small car.

3 ARTIFICIAL GROUND
The Metabolists proposed raised platforms, with architecture above, creating an "artificial ground." The capsules thus start several floors above street level. Kurokawa's design for his Agricultural City (1960) envisioned a whole community built on top of an elevated concrete slab.

⊙ ARCHITECT PROFILE

1934–69
Kisho Kurokawa was born near Nagoya, Japan. He graduated from Kyoto University in 1957, and in 1959 he completed his Master's degree at the University of Tokyo, where he studied in Kenzo Tange's Laboratory and contributed to the Tokyo Bay Plan. In 1960, he was one of the founders of Metabolism and also founded a think tank in 1969.

1970–2007
In the 1970s, Kurokawa produced a number of grandiose but unbuilt proposals in Africa and the Middle East, including the Tanzania parliament (1972) and the Baghdad free trade zone (1975). He was appointed a professor at Tsinghua University, Beijing, in 1986. He wrote several books, including *Philosophy of Symbiosis* (1987). He designed the Chinese–Japanese Youth Center (1990), and his design for Zhengdong New Town (2001), to house two million people, is still under development.

▲ Each capsule was white and furnished with up-to-date apparatus, including air conditioning, refrigerator, reel-to-reel tape player, and even a bed, unusual in a nation where the futon was the norm.

BUILT-IN OBSOLESCENCE
Kurokawa believed buildings should adapt over time, with a fixed program for replacement. The Nakagin Capsule's towers were expected to last sixty years; the capsules clipped to them were to change after only twenty-five or thirty-five years. In 1996, Kurokawa proposed a Capsule Renewal Plan. However, the unique design and the fact that many of the capsules were rented made adaptation difficult. Perceived inefficient use of air space remains a temptation to developers to make better use of the expensive land beneath the building. Kurokawa spent the last year of his life defending the structure from destruction. Maki, too, has spoken out against the scrap-and-build strategies the Metabolists once embraced. The exciting ideas of the Metabolists may well outlast the era's architecture.

PETITE ARCHITECTURE

1 **Final Wooden House (2006–08)**
Sou Fujimoto
Kumamoto, Japan

2 **Pao I (1985)**
Toyo Ito, Kazuyo Sejima,
and Kazumichi Iimura
Tokyo, Japan

3 **Small House (2000)**
Kazuyo Sejima
Tokyo, Japan

At the beginning of the 1920s, Le Corbusier (1887–1965) proposed a revolution in the design of domestic space: "dwelling machines" and "equipment" instead of homes and furniture. The chaise longue (1928), designed by Charlotte Perriand (1903–99), Le Corbusier, and Pierre Jeanneret (1896–1967) was a critical icon from this period. Its technical precision, luxurious materials, and approach to relaxation suggested a playful, modern nomadism, anticipating the tendency in France at the end of the 1930s to enjoy weekend excursions in prefabricated small mobile dwellings. By 1938, Perriand had produced mountain shelters reflecting this experimental approach to form and materials, blended with an eroticism that caused her demountable architecture to stand out from the work of her cohorts.

Perriand's Bivouac shelter (1938)—designed with careful selection and control in collaboration with engineer André Tournon—was a lightweight prototype for a holiday retreat for a six-member family. The elegance of the aluminum detail parallel to the entrance door, and the fine structure that lifted the construction from the ground, transformed the concept of emergency shelter into an object for pleasure. Two decades later, Perriand and Jean Prouvé (1901–84) collaborated on the Maison du Sahara (1958), a prototypical Petite transportable residence for a nomadic existence. The Maison du Sahara combined a superb technical display, designed to counter extreme weather, with an exquisite design that accommodated body movement.

KEY EVENTS

1956	1958	1967	1969	1973	1985
Jean Prouvé designs A House for Better Days (Maison des Jours Meilleurs) in response to an appeal for emergency housing for homeless people.	Charlotte Perriand and Prouvé collaborate on the design of the Maison du Sahara, a modern prototype of a house built for extreme climate conditions.	Peter Cook (b.1936) publishes *Architecture, Action and Plan*; he announces that "architecture will become infinite and transient."	Kisho Kurokawa (1934–2007) publishes *Homo Movens*, in which he envisions a mobile society where people time-share among five or six environments.	In his book of essays, *Small is Beautiful*, economic thinker E. F. Schumacher reasoned that, "Man is small, and, therefore, small is beautiful."	Toyo Ito builds Pao I: Dwellings for a Tokyo Nomad Woman, a response to the nomadic lifestyle of people in Japanese cities in the 1980s.

Half a century after the emergence of Petite in France, Toyo Ito (b.1941) proposed a new architecture for the era of liberation. He developed Pao I: A Dwelling for Tokyo Nomad Women (see image 2). Designed by Ito, Kazuyo Sejima (b.1956), and Kazumichi Iimura, Pao I was the embryonic capsule of a new wave of Petite architecture in Japan. The search for pleasure—associated with consumerism—led form and materials to be seen as a playful system, and Pao I became a foretaste of a nomadic urban tendency in contemporary Japan.

In 1988, Sejima designed the first of her Platform Houses. These early residential works integrated furniture, dwelling, and technology, and their designs were based on the relationship of the moving body to the architecture that surrounds it. Sejima incorporated a refinement and luxury that was unusual in the design of this type of temporary dwelling. Her Platform II (1990) can be seen as technological furniture set under a light cover. In its design, Sejima introduced circles and sinuous curves, using new lightweight industrial materials and products. Later, she designed the Small House, Tokyo (see image 3), a technological furniture dwelling, where sheet metal patterns provided a jewel-shaped home for the temporary enjoyment of an urban family. The playfully wiggling form, the sensibility of details, and the sensual gestures of its stairs make it Petite Architecture. From the anthropomorphic character of the Small House, Sejima moved over to the abstract forms of the House in a Plum Grove, Tokyo (2003; see p.462). This experimental style, in which a bed turns into a bedroom and a desk turns into an office, is in reality a piece of furniture that has expanded to become inhabitable.

Following Sejima's approach, other young Japanese architects have also designed paradigmatic Petite Architecture projects; among them, Sou Fujimoto (b.1971) stands out. His Final Wooden House, Kumamoto (see image 1), is a hybrid between architecture, furniture, and the body. This project shows that when designers stand up for spontaneity and casual freedom, without forgetting efficiency and comfort, the result is Petite Architecture. Parallel to this, projects by Junya Ishigami (b.1974) introduced a new ingredient in the definition of petite: the use of nature as construction material. His concern for defining a different scale for architecture based on nature is manifest in Row House, Tokyo (2005), where architecture is diluted in a magma of furniture and vegetation.

Nowadays, the global environmental and financial crisis challenges professionals to think about efficient, environmentally friendly buildings and construction processes. It also challenges architects to turn their attention to industrial and technological development. Petite Architecture is an option that addresses our contemporary concerns. It takes advantage of the most advanced methods of construction in order to provide a new and immediate architecture that is adapted to the needs of the modern economy. It acknowledges sustainability as today's overriding imperative and sensibility. **MR**

1988	2003	2003	2004	2004	2010
Kazuyo Sejima's Platform I Vacation House has a main room or platform set at a half level between the sleeping (first) floor and the upper kitchen.	Terunobu Fujimori (b.1946) completes his Ku-an Teahouse (Right-Angle Teahouse) in Kyoto, Japan (see p.464).	Sejima builds the House in a Plum Grove, in Tokyo (see p.462) as a "temporary perch" for a family rather than a cosy place that would lead to nostalgia.	The earthquake-resistant "Cell Brick" living space by Yasuhiro Yamashita (b.1960) is constructed by bolting stacked steel boxes into a stable structure.	Fujimori builds the Takasugi-an (Too-High Teahouse), a teahouse precariously atop two trees and accessible only by ladder.	The Small House in Tokyo by Unemori Architects occupies a plot of only 43 square feet (4 sq m). A spiral stairway connects its three floors.

House in a Plum Grove 2003
KAZUYO SEJIMA b.1956

House in a Plum Grove,
Tokyo, Japan

 NAVIGATOR

azuyo Sejima starts her designs in plan, establishing a strict budget of boxes that outline minimally necessary programmatic areas. For House in a Plum Grove, this yielded fourteen rooms, some two stories tall, others only a meter wide, all interlocking like puzzle pieces in just 839 ½ square feet (78 sq m) of space. The result: a quintessentially Tokyo house, addressing the city's congestion with lean, compact, functionally flexible architecture. The paper-thin walls, made from ⅝ inch (16 mm) structural steel plates, only incompletely slice off each area from the whole; large cutouts in each preclude a sense of enclosure or privacy. A family of five inhabits the house independently of one another, separated by the unusually small spaces, yet connected by sight and sound. The house highlights the individual over the nuclear family; there is no hearth, no hierarchy, no heart. Nonetheless, House in a Plum Grove's critical success at home and overseas is surely due not only to the methods, but also to the ingeniously minimal use of material, later the basis for project architect Junya Ishigami's own work. **DB**

👁 FOCAL POINTS

1 STEEL AND GYPSUM

The building's abstract exterior expression is intensified by sharp steel corners and a crisply cut parapet. The exterior walls—made up of gypsum board glued to steel slabs—are just 2 inches (50 mm) thick; a paint developed by NASA provides insulation and resists weathering. Eschewing ornament and erasing any marks of construction, these white walls are less concerned with the conventions of residential design than those of the world of art.

2 SQUARE SHAPES

The cubic form of the building and the scrupulously square window shapes underscore Sejima's inclination to avoid hierarchy. The exterior is entirely uninflected, avoiding the horizontality of mid-century Modernism. The loose window layout also conceals any awareness of interior spatial quality.

3 ENIGMATIC ENTRANCE

The Japanese do not entertain at home, so there was little need for the entry door to be welcoming. Instead, it very clearly cuts off this private home from its surroundings. Puny plum trees fringe the house's skimpy setback, giving it its name. A tiny sheltering canopy is the only accommodating gesture in Tokyo's sometimes rainy climate. Overall, the house is coolly imperturbable.

4 WINDOWS

A stingy approach to space only informs the plan, its restraint released in sections. Large, square panes of glass prevent the small spaces from feeling claustrophobic, introducing bright light to the interior from all sides and simultaneously putting it on display. Most glass is fixed in place, requiring only minimal frames.

🕐 ARCHITECT PROFILE

1956–80

Kazuyo Sejima was born in 1956. She graduated in architecture from the Japan Women's University in 1979 and completed a Master's degree at the same school in 1981. One of her chief subjects was housing.

1981–2000

From 1981 to 1987, she worked for Toyo Ito and was project architect for his Pao II, a tentlike installation designed for the needs of Tokyo's nomadic female consumer. She started her own office in 1987 and hired Ryue Nishizawa (b.1966) in 1990. Early works included the Saishunkan Seiyaku Women's Dormitory (1991) and many private houses. Other important residential work includes S-House (1996), Gifu Kitagata Apartments (1998/2000), and Small House (2000).

2001–present

Sejima also designed exhibition installations, furniture, and small objects. She was the first female curator and director for the architectural biennale in Venice in 2010. Her strong ties to the arts community are evidenced by awards received from the American Academy of Arts and the Swedish Academy of Fine Art, and by her support for young European artists using compatibly flat, cool approaches to architectural photography. In 1995, Sejima and Nishizawa established three independent yet loosely associated practices: hers, his, and SANAA (Sejima and Nishizawa and Associates), which handles larger projects. The partners won the Pritzker Architecture Prize in 2010.

▲ A tiny room, only big enough for a bed, is typical of the cellular spaces. Two openings on opposite walls connect the child within to others nearby.

Ku-an Teahouse 2003
TERUNOBU FUJIMORI b.1946

◉ FOCAL POINTS

1 STAINED GLASS

The window is made of hand-blown glass imported from France, set in a patchwork of lead lines. Hitoshi Akino built the most ornamental features of the teahouse, such as this window and the carefully crafted copper roof.

2 MUD AND STRAW WALLS

Fujimori cooks up unique plaster finishes for each building. This exterior wall is plywood and mortar with a coating of mud and straw. As in many of his buildings, it is applied straight from hand. The interior wall features lime from oyster shells.

3 BARKED BRANCHES

The architect and his clients cut down the chestnut tree for the base from a hill above his childhood home. It was barked, shaped with a chain saw, and lightly charred. Deeply charred finishes became a signature element in Fujimori's work.

4 PLANTS USED ODDLY

Fujimori's designs often utilize living plants, from dandelions to pine trees. The grass arch refers to Le Corbusier's Palace of the Soviets; the undulating grass belt to Salvador Dalí. The arch acts as a gate on the garden path.

In the last few decades, teahouses have become opportunities for experimentation in Japan, midway between object and architecture. Ku-an, begun in 2002, was Fujimori's first effort to design a free-standing teahouse. It was completed almost simultaneously with One-Night Teahouse (Ichiya-Tei), where prefabrication and other shortcuts were used to meet an accelerated schedule. Ku-an sits in the rear garden of a Kyoto temple. An outhouse was once located in the corner of the damp plot, inspiring Fujimori to lift the teahouse up above whatever waste remained (real or remembered), balancing it on three spreading branches. Entrance is up a crooked, handmade ladder and through a tiny door in the floor. These devices are seen in later teahouses, notably his successful Too-High Teahouse (2004).

Ku-an's client, artist and chief priest Hitoshi Akino, came to know Fujimori during the construction of a museum for his mother's paintings, a building from 1997 that remains among Fujimori's largest works. Akino built much of the teahouse himself, with assistance from an artist-builder collective that often completed Fujimori's work. Amusingly, this tearoom lacks the two widely recognized tea adornments Fujimori incorporated into his own home: there is no *tokonoma* (built-in recessed space) and no sunken hearth. **DB**

Ku-an Teahouse,
Kyoto, Japan

⏲ ARCHITECT PROFILE

1946–86

Terunobu Fujimori was born in a remote area of Nagano prefecture, Japan. He graduated from Tohoku University in 1965 and was awarded a PhD from the University of Tokyo in 1980. In 1981, he was hired as an instructor and remained on faculty until his retirement in 2010. He carried out noteworthy research as an architectural historian, which involved extensive fieldwork discovering the lost architectural legacy of the Meiji era (1868–1912). His findings were published in the best-selling *Adventures of an Architectural Detective: Tokyo* (1986).

1987–present

Fujimori launched a second career as a designer with Jinchokan Moriya Historical Museum (1991). After receiving a major award in 2001 for his largest work, a student dorm, Fujimori resolved to confine his future efforts to the most intimate scale, primarily private homes and teahouses. He had his first one-man show at Tokyo's Gallery Ma in 1998. He exhibited at the Venice Biennale in 2006, where he built a small cave for viewing videos and photographs. This led to his first free-standing teahouse, built in Australia (2009). He has since built another in London (now relocated to California) and three in Taiwan.

▲ The Japanese tea ceremony is tightly choreographed against the grid of a *tatami* floor. However, Fujimori's informal spaces are set on smooth floors, which makes the scripting less rigid.

ADDITIONS

1 **Neues Museum (1855/2009)**
David Chipperfield and Julian Harrap
Berlin, Germany

2 **Embassy of Mexico (1796/1986)**
Peter Vercelli
Washington, D.C., USA

3 **Castelvecchio (Twelfth–
fourteenth centuries/1958–64)**
Carlo Scarpa
Verona, Italy

nterplay between old and new architecture has happened for centuries. Change often occurs as part of routine multigenerational maintenance of religious and secular shrines, or as anastylosis, the archaeological reassembly of ruins. The architecture of additions in the twentieth and twenty-first centuries has been a way to save and reuse historic buildings, and occasionally, achieve synergy when the sum of the whole is greater than the sum of its parts.

The Early Modern addition (1937) by Erik Gunnar Asplund (1885–1940) to the nineteenth-century Göteborg Law Courts, Sweden, stands shoulder to shoulder with its Neoclassical elder. Asplund's addition is tempered circumspection on the exterior, but his interior, a warm embrace of honey-colored timber with ample daylight and open stairwells, seems to promise justice for all. In the twenty-first century, synergistic success includes the retained facades and new building by Eric Parry (b.1952) at the Crown Estate's development (2013; see p.476) in Piccadilly in London. One well-loved, synergistic addition was by Carlo Scarpa (1906–78) to the medieval Castelvecchio fortress (see image 3).

When Castelvecchio became a museum in the early twentieth century, architect Ferdinando Forlati (1882–1975) pursued both speculative reconstruction and purposeful fantasy not dissimilar to the methodology of nineteenth-century restorations in France by Eugène Viollet-le-Duc (1814–79). Scarpa's program of rehabilitation let the castle speak rather than be spoken to.

KEY EVENTS

1958	1959	1977	1980	1988	1997
Carlo Scarpa begins a six-year program of additions to the medieval Castelvecchio fortress in Verona.	Steen Eiler Rasmussen publishes *Experiencing Architecture*, in which he asserts that ancient ruins have dignity and should not be tampered with.	Taft Architects of Galveston, Texas, win award for adaptive reuse of Hendley Building. Old and new architectural elements are distinguished.	J. B. Jackson, in *The Necessity for Ruins*, describes the architecture of ruins and its relationship to "manufactured" historical environments.	Tadao Ando proposes an "Urban Egg" ovoid auditorium to be inserted within a historic building in the Nakanoshima area of Osaka, Japan.	Daniel Libeskind's proposed addition to London's V&A Museum is criticized as the Guggenheim Bilbao "beaten senseless with a hammer."

His redactions and additions include the roof, where series of raised-profile red clay tiles are truncated; the roof drops a level to continue with Scarpa's gently pleated turquoise replacement material. Likened to a stage set, Forlati's program is akin to what landscape writer J. B. Jackson described as a sixteenth-century spectacle of "dramatic production with a well-defined space," whereas Scarpa's approach relies on understated "drama and the analysis of problem."

Paul Spencer Byard, author of *The Architecture of Additions* (1998), coined the word "additions" (as well as "facadomy" as a substitute for facadism) to identify "combined works"; his examples included Scarpa's Castelvecchio and the Queen's House (1619) in London by Inigo Jones (1573–1652), which was incorporated into the Royal Hospital, Greenwich (begun 1692). The Greenwich ensemble is an early example of the additions controversy; plans to block the Queen's House river view with the hospital were altered to allow the central focus to be the Queen's House and the landscape of Greenwich Park.

The 1980s were characterized in the United States by a battle between those who wanted to preserve the historical, cultural, and environmental assets of historic buildings, and those who preferred to exploit the economic return on investment of a historic building and its site. "Facadism" was the nominal compromise: retention of a veneerlike facade, demolition of the rest, and erection of a building behind that was usually much larger and often visually incompatible. The jarring anomaly of two Federal townhouse facades of 1796 attached like fridge magnets to the nine-story Embassy of Mexico (see image 2) in Washington, D.C., is exemplary facadism.

International written standards for preservation, restoration, and additions to historical buildings began with artist and writer William Morris and the manifesto of the Society for the Protection of Ancient Buildings (1877) in Britain, which denounced "feeble and lifeless forgery." Protection and maintenance, not restoration, were the objectives, and accretions were to be respected as part of a building's history. Repairs, where necessary, were to look new. Conventions, charters, memorandums, and proposals proliferated in the twentieth century, beginning with the Athens Charter for the Restoration of Historic Monuments (1931), and continue apace in the twenty-first. The "View from Rome" blog of Professor Steven Semes discusses the implications of various charters, including the fascist Italian government's Charter of Restoration (1942), which instituted a ban on historical styles for both restoration and new construction. Contemporary traditional buildings were decreed a "double falsification of history." The idea that aping traditional architecture enhances neither history nor contemporary architecture was incorporated into the Venice Charter (1964), and the Italian Charter for Restoration (1972).

Ruins created by World War II further complicated this issue, resulting in the Convention for the Protection of Cultural Property in the Event of Armed Conflict (1956). The sympathetic six-year restoration, redesign, and repair

1998	1999	1999	2006	2012	2012
Paul Spencer Byard, in *The Architecture of Additions*, coins the terms "additions" and "facadomy" to identify "combined works."	The reconstruction of the Reichstag, by Foster & Partners, is completed (see p.470). The Bundestag meets there for the first time on April 19.	The Peroni brewery in Rome is converted for use by the Museum of Contemporary Art with a dynamic addition by Odile Decq.	The MVRDV architectural practice creates an instant landmark with its electric-blue "village" atop a three-story Rotterdam building.	Amanda Levete Architects win the V&A addition commission with what is described as "a coiled, Alienlike form partly embedded in Boilerhouse Yard."	An addition to the Stedelijk Museum (1895) in Amsterdam, designed by Benthem Crouwel Architects, is nicknamed "the bathtub."

4 CaixaForum (1899/2003–08)
   Herzog & de Meuron
   Madrid, Spain

5 Gasometer Apartments (1896–99/
   1999–2001)
   Moss and Coop Himmelb(l)au
   Vienna, Austria

6 Ballet Valet Parking Garage (1996)
   Arquitectonica
   Miami Beach, Florida, USA

(see image 1) of the war-damaged Neues Museum, Berlin (1855) by David Chipperfield (b.1953) and conservation architect Julian Harrap (b.1942), reflects the objectives of the international agreements. Bullet-strafed walls and fire-damaged columns were accepted into Chipperfield's ecumenical outcome. The Museum of Natural History, also in Berlin and damaged by war, was renovated and enlarged with an east wing by Diener + Diener Architekten (2010). Owing homage to artist Rachel Whiteread's *House* (1993), the architects took molds of existing elevations, which were cast in concrete and fitted into gaps.

The Vienna Memorandum (2005) elaborates on the Nara Document on Authenticity (1994), which in turn is built on the Venice Charter. The ultimate expression of the three goes beyond material retention of a building to include retention of a building's "cultural diversity." Sutton House (1535), in Hackney, east London, was built by Sir Ralph Sadleir, a courtier of King Henry VIII. Its subsequent history includes occupation by merchants and refugee Huguenot silk weavers, culminating in squatters who lived in the house during the 1980s. Sutton House's new guardian, The National Trust, controversially decided to preserve and display not only sixteenth-century Tudor graffiti, but the squatters' wall art as well. More controversial is whether interior furnishings of historic buildings such as Sutton House adequately avoid "all forms of pseudo-historic design." The confused corollary, as highlighted by François Barré, former Director of the French Department of Architecture and Heritage, is that we "condemn facadism but [we] only have laws that protect exterior[s]." The Georgian–Palladian Drayton Hall (1742) near Charleston, South Carolina, avoids pseudo-historic interiors with its purposely empty rooms; contrary to expectation, they project a strong feeling of inhabitation.

Frank Lloyd Wright (1867–1959), dismissing nineteenth-century houses as mostly "a bedevilled box with a fussy lid," captured the essential quality of twenty-first-century additions, where a new building sits atop the old like a lid on a box. At a 2007 debate, Steven Semes asked, "How do you have a dialogue between two [buildings] that don't have a common language?" He referred to Herzog & de Meuron's Elbphilharmonie, Frankfurt (2017), berthed like a tankship atop a nineteenth-century harbor warehouse, but equally his example could have been Herzog & de Meuron's CaixaForum (see image 4) in Madrid. Here, the primitive splicing of facadism is gone, replaced by what

the architects describe as a "surgical" and "sculptural" process. The rusticated granite foundation of Madrid's decommissioned Mediodía Power Station (1899) was removed to make the whole appear to float above Herzog & de Meuron's subterranean addition. The levitation motif is mirrored in the roof addition, which slots into the power station's gable roofline like a sculptural expression of the levitating rock in René Magritte's painting *Clear Ideas* (1958).

Although technically facadism, Arquitectonica's Ballet Valet Parking Garage retail block (see image 6) in Miami transcends the pejorative. A terraced row of heterogeneous but harmonious small Art Deco store fronts is topped by a cascade of luxurious, tropical plants in a manner similar to the living green wall of artist-botanist Patric Blanc that sits at right angles to the CaixaForum plaza. But the addition nonpareil is the Palazzo Chupi (2008; see p.474) in Manhattan, by artist Julian Schnabel (b.1951). Described by some as eccentric "folly," and by a reporter for *The New York Times* as "float[ing] like Citizen Kane's Xanadu," the eleven-story pink Venetian-style palace is atop an unremarkable, low-rise, skylighted 1930s brick industrial building.

Additions that drop inside the original include the Vienna Gasometer Apartments (see image 5) of Eric Owen Moss (b.1943); four redundant, drum-shaped gasometers (1896–99) were adapted to include apartments designed by Moss and Coop Himmelb(l)au. Conservation restrictions prohibited alteration of the gasometers' external appearance, or buildings supported on the brick carcasses. Moss inserted stacked wedges with viewing gaps aligned with the shell's original openings, while a Himmelb(l)au addition looms and leans ladderlike toward its gasometer shell. Moss described his outcome as one of "reciprocity in favor of the new."

Outcry over proposals by Mario Botta (b.1943) for Milan's Teatro alla Scala, "venerated as a sacred relic of Piermarini Neoclassicism," was rebuffed if not ridiculed by *Abitare* magazine in 2002. Botta's realized plans include a highly visible, drum-shaped, rooftop addition. "The truth is," the editorial declared, "[La Scala is] as hybrid and phoney as any building can be. Its history from 1778 to the 1950s was a neverending story of restoration and reconstruction .... So La Scala may seem fetishistically untouchable, but in reality it's the posh-looking door to a cumbersome wardrobe crammed with assorted junk." This description offers tacit, if unintended, acknowledgment that facadism exists in forms additional to the crude guise popularized in the 1980s. **DJ**

The Reichstag 1999
FOSTER & PARTNERS

The Reichstag,
Berlin, Germany

⬟ NAVIGATOR

Burned, bombed, resurrected, then reconstructed (1961–64), only the carcass of the Neo-Baroque Reichstag (1894) by Paul Wallot (1841–1912) remained when Germany was reunified in 1989. The Bundestag (German Parliament) voted to move from Bonn to the Reichstag in 1990, to be followed by the government's upper chamber, the Federal Bundesrat, in 1996. City planners pressed for the widespread reuse of existing buildings. Reconciliation with history, says historian Michael Imhof, makes Berlin's post-reunification architecture notable, but success is also measured by how effectively new and old are combined, particularly when an older building is "given up for the sake of the new one." The competition to transform the Reichstag was a joint win between Norman Foster, Santiago Calatrava (b.1951), and Pi de Bruijn (b.1942) in the first round. The second-round brief restricted designs to the Reichstag's footprint, and Foster's design encased the building in a High-Tech framework. However, the Bundestag insisted that a dome be built, inspired by the design for a glass cupola with spiral walkway submitted by Gottfried Böhm (b.1920) in 1988. Foster capitulated and designed an environmentally friendly dome with a mirrored cone that directs sunlight into the debating chamber below. **DJ**

FOCAL POINTS

1 NEO-BAROQUE FACADE

Too early be a representation of what U.S. architecture theorist Charles Jencks describes as "Hitlerian Classicism," Wallot's Neo-Baroque design includes an overscaled raised basement supporting four monumental facades. After the war, these required extensive restoration.

2 SKYLIGHT

Described as a "democratic lightbulb" by Jencks, Foster's skylight replaced Wallot's lantern dome. Mitigating the bombast of Wallot's building, its profile creates a visual effect similar to that of the classical dome of the Bank of Scotland, Edinburgh (1806).

3 CORINTHIAN COLUMNS

A large, wide staircase creates a dramatic approach to the second-floor, six-columned (hexastyle) portico. The Corinthian-capital columns frame the glass walls of the parliament's main chamber. The open effect is deliberate, signifying open government.

◄ A mirrored funnel inside the dome reflects daylight through the center of a round glass floor, ringed by railing to allow the public to watch the government at work beneath. Passive use of daylight is one of multiple sustainable features designed to reduce the Reichstag's energy consumption.

OBERBAUM BRIDGE

The Oberbaum Bridge (1896) in Berlin was designed in Germanic Gothic Revival style by Otto Stahn (1859–1930) to span the River Spree. The towers were inspired by Middle Gate Tower in Prenzlau, Germany. In 1945, at the end of World War II, the Wehrmacht blew up the double-decker central span in a bid to stop the advancing Soviet army. During the succeeding Cold War period, the bridge was one of the division points between East and West Germany. Reunification after the fall of the Berlin Wall led to Santiago Calatrava being commissioned to rebuild the central span. Rather than restore what had been before, he rebuilt it as a steel section (1995); its distinctive profile serves as a permanent, mute reminder of war and peace.

Scottish Parliament Building 2004
ENRIC MIRALLES 1955–2000

**Scottish Parliament Building,
Holyrood, Edinburgh, Scotland**

Scotland's first parliament since 1707 is not the monumental, context-free spectacle common to many major new public buildings. Catalan architect Enric Miralles, working with local firm RMJM, envisioned a subtle, democratic addition to the Scottish landscape and culture that should "arise from the sloping base of Arthur's Seat and arrive into the city almost surging out of the rock." Conceived as a series of modest, low-lying buildings, and with most of the site given over to a new landscaped public space, a parliament-for-the-people symbolism runs throughout. Complex interior spaces feature Scottish saltires impressed into concrete vaults. Exquisite detailing in the Arts and Crafts tradition (see p.314) utilize locally sourced woods. Nooks and crannies facilitate informal conversation, recalling conspiratorial corridors from dark Scottish castles, then lead up into the light of the main debating chamber, where an elliptical arrangement marks a democratic turn away from the opposing two-party benches of Westminster. Rising up above the hall is the imposing backdrop of Arthur's Seat, as if to remind members that it is the land that presides over the government, and not the other way around. On the Canongate Wall, an inscription reads: "If a man were permitted to make all the ballads, he need not care who should make the laws of a nation." The poetry of Miralles' masterwork is set to influence the course of Scotland for centuries to come. **TH**

✪ NAVIGATOR

⊙ FOCAL POINTS

1 CONTEMPLATION SPACES
Distinctive *mashrabiya*like window seats protrude from the northern side of the Members' offices, providing places of quiet reflection. Their shape has been compared to the subject of Henry Raeburn's iconic painting *The Skating Minister* (1790s).

2 VISUAL METAPHOR
It is said that at the first design meeting Miralles placed a cluster of twigs on the table and proclaimed, "This is the Scottish Parliament." Such poetry finds form in the shape of leaflike skylights and, here, a roofline resembling upturned fishing boats on the shore.

3 FACADE
Next to the rich finery of the interior, the public face of the building can, in places, appear rather ordinary. This, plus spiraling construction costs, caused many locals to question whether the Scottish Parliament Building met its own democratic aims.

◀ The debating chamber is a spectacular mix of the high-tech and the hand-crafted. The roof's complex structure of steel-reinforced oak beams, inspired by the hammer beam roof of its 1639 predecessor, rests amid a cacophony of technical apparatus. Desks are bespoke creations in oak and sycamore.

ANTI-TERROR ARCHITECTURE

The events of 9/11 are defined by an extraordinary failure of architecture: the collapse of the Twin Towers in New York. The half-built Scottish Parliament Building found itself already in need of expensive adaptation to new security requirements. Changes included closing off the glazed ground-level facade to visitors, and with it sacrificing the democratic openness envisaged for the site. Due to similar concerns, the UK Embassy in Warsaw (right) by Tony Fratton (b.1945) was moved mid-project to an out-of-town site. But the restrained Modernist elegance of the main block was retained, by hiding defensive walls behind a sacrificial glass facade. With a smoke-and-mirrors subtlety, this suggested the confidence in democracy that the United Kingdom wanted to communicate to foreign cultures and, indeed, to terrorists.

Palazzo Chupi 2008

JULIAN SCHNABEL b.1951

Palazzo Chupi,
West 11th Street,
New York, New
York, USA

I n a city not short of idiosyncrasy, artist Julian Schnabel's five-unit condominium is both loved and loathed for its audacity. To critics, it embodies Oscar Wilde's "a peacock in everything but beauty," and the artist's supposed blind eye to height restrictions; to fans, it is a fantasy folly of setbacks atop a three-story brick industrial building (c.1915). Shortly after its completion, architecture critic Nicolai Ouroussof called it "crudely cobbled together" and a "bright pink stucco box adorned with Venetian-style arched windows . . . plopped atop an existing warehouse." He conceded, however, that "the overblown scale and collision of styles have a refreshing bluntness; in some ways it's closer in spirit to the vernacular architecture of the Far East, an atavistic approach that is a nice counterpoint to the hyper-modernity of so much contemporary work."

Chupi's color, though known as "Pompeiian Red," is the faded pink of the once red first-floor doors, whose brick piers host white, hand-painted warnings: "no parking" and "your car will be towed." The lettering is akin to Schnabel's "Recognition" paintings, featuring similar writing on recycled boxing-ring tarpaulin, a material "with a history," says Schnabel. Historian J. B. Jackson deemed the popularity of "historical, theatrical, make-believe" architecture as a "state of innocence" where "history ceases to exist." **DJ**

⊙ FOCAL POINTS

▲ Chupi's setback structure conforms to regulations designed to avoid the lightless street "canyons" caused by vertical buildings.

1 WINDOWS

Venetian Gothic windows are a luxurious counterpoint to interiors said to exude "the character of Stanford White's cottage architecture." The comment is ironic, as White's late nineteenth-century cottages were the mansions of the first U.S. gilded age, whose economic disparities reflect those of the current gilded age.

2 BALCONY

The minimalist, double-box balcony is a vernacular rendition of examples such as Emperor Maximilian I's "Golden Roof" in Innsbruck, Austria (c.1500). There, the city-center double-height oriel balcony, intended as a royal box for viewing life below, has an awning roof covered in gilded copper fishscale tiles.

3 GALLERY

The double height "Venetian" gallery, with its round, Renaissance-style arches, is a setback from the vertical elevation, described as a "new so-called" style in 1927. Setback introduces illumination into streets otherwise denied light by buildings with flat "cliff faces." Steel frames allowed steeper ranks of setbacks.

BOROS SAMMLUNG

Palazzo Chupi is one of many art-related additions. Inspired by the concrete buildings of Tadao Ando (b.1941) and the New National Gallery in Berlin (1968), the owners of a five-story bunker in Berlin commissioned a glass penthouse for the roof. First built in 1943 to shelter war-time evacuees, it is now used as the Boros Sammlung art gallery (below).

212–214 Piccadilly 2013
ERIC PARRY b.1952

212–214 Piccadilly, One Eagle Place,
London, England

E ric Parry used the term "urban dentistry" to describe his complex redevelopment of the Crown Estate fronting London's Piccadilly. The project included retention of a Grade II-listed (historic) building, preserved Victorian and Edwardian facades on Piccadilly and Jermyn Street, and new facades and structure by Parry. The adjacent building at 210–211 Piccadilly was mnemonic and a "stabilizing element" in urban terms, and was conserved through contemporary anastylosis—dismantled, stored, and reassembled in the same location, but raised 6 feet (1.8 m) to unify with the floors of 212–214. The redevelopment conforms to horizons set by the master plan of Richard Norman Shaw (1831–1912), an achievement Parry likens to a "kind of collage." The double-ordered bays and suppressed attic of Parry's ceramic faience facade include black window frames on the north face, with deckle reveals intended as "red cheeks." Subtly linked to Blomfield's mitered-corner corbeling, the thirty-nine polychromatic blocks of the subattic cornice were designed by Richard Deacon (b.1949) with fourteen faceted profiles. The blocks were cast by Shaws of Darwen and the silkscreen designs fired in Stoke-on-Trent. Parry linked the corbels and glazed facade to the "animation" and "artificiality" of nearby Piccadilly Circus; the feature was "absolutely to do with artifice beyond craft." **DJ**

FOCAL POINTS

1 ORIEL WINDOWS
While the oriels of Parry's 50 Bond Street, London, sit proud of the ceramic facade, the black-framed oriels on Piccadilly are recessed within double-height red deckle frames. The plastic qualities of architectural ceramic faience made it possible to produce a subtle downward bow in the cills.

2 CORBEL BLOCKS
The surfaces of thirty-nine corbel blocks are bonded with up to eight silk screen transfers by an initial high firing of up to 2,200 °F (1,200 °C). The firing makes the corbels water resistant. A second, lower firing burns off the transfer material to allow the ceramic glaze of the designs to bond into the corbel surfaces.

3 PERFECTION OF JOINTS
Perfection of joints between blocks is a Parry signature. Known for his scrupulous use of materials, Parry says he had "endless battles about joints" for his stone block office building in Finsbury Square, London. Free of a steel frame and cladding, it boasts a 1-mm tolerance, much less than the 6-mm industry standard.

THE QUEEN'S CHAPEL

Parry cites as inspiration the "articulated rhythm" of the Vitruvian–Palladian classicism of the Queen's Chapel at St. James's Palace, London, by Inigo Jones. It is a Roman temple *cella* with corbeled cornice and the horizontal breaks of a Palladian villa. The chapel's faux stone rustication is evidence of Jones's inheritance of the sleight of hand of Andrea Palladio (1508–80). Architectural historian Vaughan Hart claims that Jones's use of classicism was symbolic of Stuart court policy, which makes it paradoxically "consistent with the Puritan artistic sensitivities of Stuart England." Is it too great a leap to suggest that the classical designs of Jones, the consummate courtier, were one of the causal factors for the execution in 1649 of King Charles I in a country besotted with Tudor–Gothic style, and which wanted no part of classical foreignness? Jones was known for his theatrical masque balls, and perhaps his classicism was, as his adversaries claimed, Catholicism boldly cloaked in a classical mask.

STRUCTURALISM

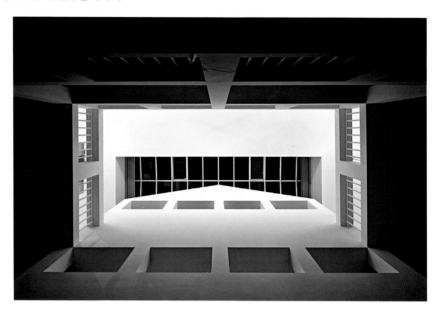

1 **German Architecture Museum (1984)**
Oswald Mathias Ungers
Frankfurt, Germany

2 **Kasbah Housing (1973)**
Piet Blom
Hengelo, the Netherlands

3 **"Beehive" Apartments (c.1967–80)**
Zvi Hecker
Ramot Polin, Jerusalem

S tructuralism was a reaction to the perceived rigid Functionalist rationalism of post–World War II urban planning and architecture, in which the car was king and high-rise corporate hierarchy meant light-filled perimeter offices for management and central open-plan cubicles for the rank and file. The Netherlands proved central to a building scale shift in about 1970, which architectural historian Michelle Provoost described as "not more human [but] more individual." Aldo Van Eyck (1918–99) used Dutch magazine *Forum* to promote the Structuralism of Team X, an offshoot of the Congrès International d'Architecture Moderne (CIAM) whose members in the Netherlands were known as the Forum Group. The family home or "cell" was their baseline, and its form was repeated to express buildings as "villages." Repetitions were often based on cubes, which, unlike finite "slab and tower" Functionalism (see p.308), could be "infinite" and added to or altered as required.

The concept of "living cells" was based on Van Eyck's spatial system of "aesthetics of numbers," formed in 1959, which interpreted buildings as a system of cells. Each addition was complete in itself, creating Van Eyck's "labyrinthian clarity." He underscored the drive for symbiosis between two apparently competing objectives: "One cannot be together with others in a space if one cannot be alone there in the midst of others." Prefabricated or modular elements were not chosen for large-scale repetition out of necessity, but as a consequence of the aim to make each element individual. Forum

KEY EVENTS

1959	1959	1959	1960	1961	1965
Team X begins to be disenchanted by Rationalism and the CIAM approach to urbanism, led by Le Corbusier (1887–1965).	Dutch members of Team X, including Jaap Bakema (1914–81) and Aldo Van Eyck, are known as the Forum Group.	Van Eyck creates "aesthetics of numbers," also known as spatial systems architecture, which views buildings as replicable living cells.	Van Eyck designs his "small city," Amsterdam Orphanage, a critical example of Structuralism.	John Habraken (b.1928) promotes "architecture of chance," which relies on the participation of a building's users.	Jan Verhoeven (1926–94) designs his home in Hoevelaken, employing geometrical forms to reconcile the duality of light-dark, closed-open, big-small.

members have been called single minded and individualist because of their pursuit of replicating units, but their reaction to the postwar surge of U.S.-style functional and technocratic reconstruction—epitomized in the Netherlands by the buildings of Hugh Maaskant (1907–77), and in the United States by any number of high-rise buildings—chimed with changing times. The monumental expression of hierarchical corporate or government power was under fire.

Although Van Eyck's Amsterdam Orphanage (1960) is often cited as the critical example of Structuralism, the Lin Mij factory extension in Amsterdam (1964) by Herman Hertzberger (b.1932) demonstrated the patterned growth potential of Structuralism. The original twentieth-century factory was viewed as dark and cheerless by some, but Hertzberger considered it redeemable, and he responded to the company's growth prediction by treating the factory as an artificial rock formation, where his thematically related prefabricated cube units could reproduce like an artificial reef on a scuttled ship. The cube islands of Hertzberger's Centraal Beheer insurance company building in Apeldoorn, the Netherlands (1972; see p.480), were subdivided into four corner units by cruciform circulation. Cantilevered corners and connecting bridges allowed employees vertical and diagonal contact. Team X member Ralph Erskine (1914–2005) sought a similar village outcome with his layout for The Ark in London (1991), in which he "tried to infiltrate [the office] with common social ideals."

The cubes designed by Joop van Stigt (1934–2011) for the refectory at Twente Technical College in Enschede, the Netherlands (1965), were each subdivided into four living rooms by cruciform conjugate roof beams. The Kasbah Housing (see image 2) in Hengelo by Piet Blom (1934–99) comprised cubes of four units sharing a communal terrace. German adherent Oswald Mathias Ungers (1926–2007) interpreted Structuralism metaphorically with his redesign of a nineteenth-century villa for the German Architecture Museum (see image 1) in Frankfurt. His interior focal point is a cube house. Its four corners create pillars to demarcate the floor above, where they emerge to create a baldachinlike canopy offering the symbolic promise and protection of home.

The human-centered goals of Structuralism were not limited to Europe. Donlyn Lyndon (b.1936)—well known for Condominium 1 with MLTW at Sea Ranch, California (1965; see p.414), part of a compound centered on a communal courtyard—edited a selection of U.S. architecture in 1966, in which importance was no longer solely "the complex context into which people and objects are placed [but the context] which people and objects also form." In Jerusalem, the "Beehive" Apartments (see image 3) by Zvi Hecker (b.1931) are based on the repetitions of dodecahedron walls and pentagonal faces. They appear as though a prototype for Blom's cubic houses (1977): a "forest village" on hexagonal pylons in Helmond and Rotterdam. Evolutions of Centraal Beheer's influential office design include the Advanced Technology Centre (1987; see p.482), Edmonton, Canada, designed by Barry Johns (b.1947). **DJ**

1967	1970s	1977	1981	1983	2012
Herman Hertzberger cites the influence of Metabolism, including Habitat 67 housing complex, Montreal, Canada, by Moshe Safdie (b.1938).	The non-hierarchical community spaces of Hertzberger's Centraal Beheer (1972; see p.480) influence the design of creative businesses such as Apple.	The cubic houses in Rotterdam, designed by Piet Blom, are symbolic of the port city's architecture.	Work begins on Zvi Hecker's Spiral Apartment House in Ramat Gan, Tel Aviv.	Arts center De Kubus in Lelystad, the Netherlands, by Wim Davidse, reflects the Structuralist concept of replicable cells.	Hertzberger is awarded the Royal Gold Medal by the Royal Institute of British Architects.

Centraal Beheer 1972
HERMAN HERTZBERGER b.1932

Centraal Beheer,
Apeldoorn, the Netherlands

NAVIGATOR

Emancipation from hierarchies, power, and dictated form was Herman Hertzberger's goal for Centraal Beheer. Rejecting sculptural expression and the primacy of the exterior, he designed a humanist building. A field of stacked two-, three-, and four-level cubes, with multiple entrances on all sides, the building is a city with streetscapes and towers reminiscent of medieval towns. Space is equally developed in vertical and horizontal directions. The core of each level is a social space with coffee shop, restaurant, and relaxation areas. A crisscross arrangement of escalators supports the liveliness of the first-level "streetscape," whose axial "streets" were described by Hertzberger as "kebab skewers." Despite the predominance of masonry blocks, the architect created a beloved, cosy, unique "workshop," where employees were encouraged to personalize their space with posters, plants, and furniture from home. Cubes are island units based on a square-on-cross plan, divided by cruciform circulation into four corner work areas. Cube tower junctures create roof grid voids to allow additional daylight to permeate. Original ceiling light tubes mimicked the module grid, and restaurant seating mirrored the eight T-beam islands with its square wooden tables and eight chairs. **DJ**

⊙ FOCAL POINTS

1 GLAZING

Hertzberger believes that buildings should be easily transformed. His once-open cubes were glazed decades later for acoustic baffle. Retrofit designs suggested in 2003 (not by Hertzberger) create a Panopticonlike environment, a sad evolution for Hertzberger's democratic space.

2 "BALCONIES"

The perimeter "balconies" of four-person cubes have wood and glass corner shelving. Beneath the shelf bench top, these glass cases were once home to eclectic employee displays, which were visible to others vertically and diagonally and to the "street."

3 T-BEAMS

Based on kitlike components, plates are underpinned by central columns and support eight vertical T-beams for each cube tower. The portholes of the horizontal T-beams are left visible and the beams slot together with eight vertical beams within the framed floor of each cube.

◄ Sixty towerlike cubes create the horizontal plan of Centraal Beheer, built on an isolated reservation, hemmed by a highway and a railroad line. Hertzberger intended to link Centraal Beheer to town by a tunnel lined with public stores.

FORTIFIED VILLAGE

Members of the Dutch Forum Group of architects used analogies to describe their democratic social spaces: Hertzberger cited the amphitheater and Piet Blom the kasbah. Aït Benhaddou (17th century; right) in Souss-Massa-Draâ, Morocco, is a Berber adobe *ksar*, a fortified village within which are small and large (kasbah) houses and collective structures, such as a granary, mosque, shrine, and hammam as well as stables, meeting rooms, stores, and two cemeteries, Muslim and Jewish. Winter and summer living areas sit above the business-based first floors. Centraal Beheer's plan was criticized by some observers, but, like the *ksar*, its layout and nuances were loved by employees—a fortified village for the Centraal Beheer "family."

Advanced Technology Centre 1987

BARRY JOHNS b.1947

Advanced Technology Centre,
Edmonton Research Park,
Edmonton, Canada

✦ NAVIGATOR

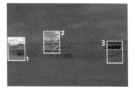

A high-tech business center embedded into the landscape of the Alberta plains, the Advanced Technology Centre today seems ahead of its time, anticipating some key concerns of the twenty-first century: how to encourage technological innovation and enterprise, while displaying a keen sensitivity to the environment. Commissioned to help stimulate the local economy by creating a flexible business hub for nascent tech giants, the project has the capacity to alter individual layouts easily and allow companies to grow (and shrink) quickly, without the need to relocate. Skylit underground corridors, like streets under the soil, provide a clear, comprehensible circulation and encourage a communal atmosphere, with shared meeting rooms, support resources, and library. The immediate landscape was integral to the design process, with architect Barry Johns seeking to "explore the space between earth and big sky in a quest for prairie authenticity." By creating a ravinelike hollow and piling up the earth around the building, the landform shapes the nature of the building, and vice versa. Intimately connected with its prairie heritage, the Advanced Technology Centre is a building that takes a bold step toward a bright future, while treading lightly on the earth. **TH**

1 BUILDING AS LANDSCAPE

A vocal advocate of sustainable architecture, Barry Johns paid careful attention to the local environment and its landscaping, weather formations, and culture, making a building that respects and reflects its ancient prairie heritage and, in his words, "becomes one with its site."

2 SKYLIGHTS

A lack of windows in the subterranean sections of the building is offset by extensive north-facing glazing that floods communal areas with light. A light sculpture by artist Michael Hayden uses holographic panels to diffract the sun's rays, illuminating the public space.

3 BERMING

The berm-like nature of the building makes it naturally insulating, and allows it to manage the wide temperature fluctuations of the Edmonton climate. As a result, the heating requirements are greatly reduced for a business building of this size, to those that might be expected for a large house.

◄ Tenant areas on both sides look onto a skylit communal "street" that runs the length of the building and provides a social focus. Exposed mechanical and electrical systems throughout allow for straightforward installation and repair.

THE NORTH AMERICAN PIT-HOUSE

As an energy-efficient, semi-subterranean building, the Advanced Technology Centre stands within a tradition of Canadian prairie architecture stretching back more than 3,000 years. Thought to be North America's oldest house type, the pit-house (right) was the permanent winter home of the peoples of the prairie, providing protection from the extreme climate. It consisted of a log-framed structure over an excavated floor, with a concentric circle of webbed rafters leading to a smoke hole at the apex. The roof was completed with a tight layer of wooden poles, thickly padded with pine needles or grass to protect against the rain. The excavated earth would be spread over the roof, and the house became part of the prairie landscape. A central hearth kept the house warm, and, when covered by snow, the dwelling was so well insulated that only a small fire was needed.

HIGH TECH

During the 1980s, the architecture press debated whether High Tech was a style or an evolution of Modernism. In 1992, an editorial in *World Architecture* voiced a "consensus": "High-Tech architecture dramatizes structure while Modern architecture expressed function." Such dramatized structure included a notable feature: mechanical services were often on the outside of buildings, as in the Centre Pompidou (1978), Paris, by Renzo Piano (b.1937) and Richard Rogers (b.1933). The "consensus" divided into historicists, who believed Crystal Palace, London (1851), by Sir Joseph Paxton (1803–65) was High Tech's ancestor, and those who saw it first expressed in the Reliance Controls Factory (1967) in Swindon, Wiltshire, by British firm Team 4—Su Brumwell, Wendy Cheeseman (d.1989), Norman Foster (b.1935), and Richard Rogers.

Critic Reyner Banham suggested that the California Case Study Houses in the mid-twentieth century provided inspiration for the prophets of High Tech, Foster, Rogers, and Piano. While the prefabricated materials of the single-story Reliance are similarly pragmatic, a likelier candidate for the first British High-Tech building is the eleven-story Park Road Apartments (1968) in London by the Farrell Grimshaw Partnership. The building has a central load-bearing core and sinusoidal-wave aluminum cladding enabled round corners and curved ribbon windows.

KEY EVENTS

1960	1961	1963	1963	1964	1970
British architectural critic Reyner Banham publishes *Theory and Design in the First Machine Age*.	The experimental architecture collective Archigram is founded by six young London architects.	British architecture graduates Richard Rogers, Su Brumwell, Norman Foster, and Wendy Cheeseman form Team 4.	James Stirling (1926–92) and James Gowan (b.1923) finish Leicester University's Engineering Building, paving the way for the highly expressed structures of High Tech.	Archigram's Peter Cook (b.1936) and Ron Herron (1930–94) come up with the hypothetical projects of the Plug-In City and the Walking City, with living pods.	Barton Myers (b.1934) employs industrial characteristics in the design of his home, Myers Residence, in Toronto (see p.488).

Influences on High Tech range from the construction toy set Meccano to the roof-lit workshops of the Department of Engineering at the University of Leicester and Archigram's "visionary" cities. However, a significant influence was the oil embargo and global energy crisis of 1973, which motivated a rethink of how to reduce energy use in buildings. Instead of traditional separate floors for mechanical services, they began to appear on the outside of buildings. The Federal Reserve Building (see image 1), Minneapolis, by Gunnar Birkerts (b.1925) "turned the structure on the surface" so it became a service, says Birkerts, The architect told *The New York Times* in 1978 that he did not believe in "hiding such paraphernalia." Manhattan developers Melvyn and Robert Kaufman "advertised" the mechanical floor of their 127 John Street (Emery, Roth & Sons; 1971) with lighting and brightly painted equipment. Critic Paul Goldberger described Emery, Roth & Sons's building at 17 State Street, New York (see image 2), as a "high-tech celebration" of machinery and technology and a new kind of "commercial vernacular," comparing it to the "almost handmade" look and "Baroque elaboration" of Foster's HSBC (Hong Kong) building and the Centre Pompidou.

Archigram's theoretical Plug-In City (1964) included crane-mounted pods. Farrell Grimshaw Partnership's International Student Service Tower (London, 1968) "plugged" a prefabricated tower of glass-reinforced plastic bathrooms, cantilevered from a steel spine, into the back of six row houses converted to a student dorm. Derided by some as "plug-in idealizers," Rogers used plug-ins in the Lloyd's Building (1986; see p.486), where external mechanical elements facilitated repairs and gave rise to its "Inside Out" nickname. Stainless steel lavatory modules were meant to be "unplugged" for servicing. The modular steel plug-in hotel rooms of the Contemporary Resort tower (1971) by Welton Becket (1902–69) at Florida's Walt Disney World were designed to be craned in and out for refurbishment, but the steel expanded and the units stayed put.

A forgotten triumph of British High Tech is the Farnborough College of Technology redevelopment (1986) by Colin Stansfield Smith (1932–2013), which Marcus Binney cites as the British equivalent of Illinois Institute of Technology by Ludwig Mies van der Rohe (1886–1969). The historian described it as combining "high-tech construction with the elegant pedestrian courts of a traditional university." In Germany, High Tech includes University Hospital Aachen by Weber Brand & Partner (1985) and Munich's Hypo-Haus (see image 3) by Walther (1929–2010) and Bea (b.1928) Betz, which has floors five to nine cantilevered from a central frame. Simple and flexible were Foster's imperatives for his HSBC Bank, Hong Kong (1985). Robert Hughes described its lack of a solid central core as "a reverse of dogma." The "glass underbelly" allows "banking to be seen as a dynamic activity . . . a showcase to be viewed from the plaza below." These were different approaches to "inside out" functionality, and signaled that the days of dramatizing services as external features were in decline. Mechanical services in Foster's Stansted Airport, Essex (1991), are hidden from public view. **DJ**

1976	1978	1983	1986	1991	2013
Michael Hopkins builds his steel prefabricated High-Tech home in an historic conservation area of Hampstead, London.	Renzo Piano and Richard Rogers's Centre Pompidou in Paris transforms the public's perception of museums and their use.	Weber Brand & Partner completes University Hospital Aachen (Klinikum Aachen) at the Technical University of Aachen, Germany.	Rogers's Lloyd's Building, London (see p.486), and Foster's HSBC Bank headquarters, Hong Kong, are completed.	Stansted Airport is completed. The design turns the terminal "upside down"; it gives passengers spatial clarity and has services under the concourse.	The "Richard Rogers RA: Inside Out" exhibition at the Royal Academy in London has a Meccano model of an uncompleted project and a Lego model of the Centre Pompidou.

Lloyd's Building 1986
RICHARD ROGERS b.1933

Lloyd's Building,
London, England

I t is said that a true work of art shows the means by which it is made. Rembrandt did not disguise his brushstrokes. Rodin did not paint his sculptures to resemble flesh. Whereas nineteenth-century bridges and steam trains explored forms that embodied new technologies, architecture of the time often disguised, decorated, or screened off the unpalatable truth of their construction. The Lloyd's building is the apotheosis of the Modernist truth-to-materials mantra, revealing not just the naked structure but turning things inside-out to bring inner organs out into the open: ducts, toilets, stairs, and elevators are all expressed with fetishistic zeal. Such exoskeletal architecture sought an authentic visual richness to parallel the medieval flying buttress: a steampunk gothic that glorified the machine age. Sadly it proved that exposing all to the elements brought complications that belied Modernist pragmatism. Directly opposite Lloyd's is a newer Rogers-designed skyscraper where, tellingly, structure and services are clothed within a curtain wall of glazing. Now Grade I–listed, the Lloyd's building and its intellectual bravado stand as a monument to a vision of the future that has since passed. **TH**

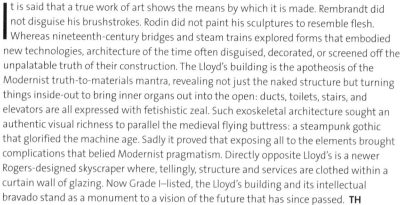

FOCAL POINTS

1 SERVICE TOWERS
At the heart of the client's brief was a need for flexibility: having relocated twice in a short space of time, Lloyd's wanted a building that could adapt to technological and market changes. Taking advantage of the irregular site, Rogers dispersed circulation and utilities into structurally independent towers at the margins, freeing up the center for the creation of an open-plan rectangular space that could be altered easily.

▲ The cathedral-like atrium lends a serenity to the busy underwriters' trading floor, known simply as "The Room."

2 LAVATORY MODULES
With the plug-in aesthetic of an Archigram drawing, toilets were prefabricated offsite before being assembled in parallel with the structure. The addition of marble worktops, mirrors, and ceramic tiles to the rudimentary initial design proved too heavy for cranes and were fitted in situ.

2001: A SPACE ODYSSEY

An extraordinary quirk of the Lloyd's Building is the Adam Room, an opulent classical interior designed by Robert Adam in 1763, which twice relocated with the company. The clash of epochs is startling, creating a change of scene reminiscent of Stanley Kubrick's *2001: A Space Odyssey* (1968; below). Adam's bright Neoclassical elegance amid Rogers' dark hypermodern Gothic questions, like Kubrick, the influence of technological advances on the way we live.

3 ELEVATORS
Like the escalators at Rogers's Centre Pompidou, the external elevators add dynamism to the composition and reinforce the Meccano playset look. With few windows in the building, high-speed panoramic views set among the elements offer invigorating contact with the outside world.

Myers Residence 1970
BARTON MYERS b. 1934

Myers Residence,
Toronto, Canada

NAVIGATOR

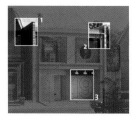

Set among rows of Victorian workers' cottages, the house that Barton Myers designed for his own family brings iconic High-Tech architecture into residential Toronto, while showing a polite respect to the form and scale of its more well-established neighbors. Continuing his exploration into steel, Myers transposed factorylike elements into a private house, and although steel never became established as a common material for residential housing, the experiments here found their way into later projects. Reflecting Myers's interest in the relationship between a building's structure and natural light, the choice of a steel frame made large spans possible, allowing interior spaces to be bathed in light through a translucent fiberglass barrel-vaulted roof. The hub of the house is a double-story courtyard that connects the entranceway and garage with living areas toward the rear of the house, which are linked on the upper level by a steel bridge. This central courtyard was conceived of in the manner of a traditional Roman "atrium": as both the social nexus of the house for living, dining, and entertaining, and as the physical center with the different rooms radiating outward. A feature of many Myers buildings is the close relationship between interior and exterior, and here the main living area opens directly out into a garden to the rear. South-facing, with bountiful plantings and the sounds of running water emanating from a small pool, the yard provides a contrasting retreat into nature from the High-Tech experimentation of the house. **TH**

FOCAL POINTS

1 CONTEXT
Local planning rules decreed that the building must be more than a meter from each adjacent house, and must not exceed the existing front edge. Myers also chose to align his house to the existing roofline, creating a coherence to the street that belies the stylistic contrasts between buildings.

2 MATERIALS
In keeping with Myers's forward-looking, industrial approach to techniques and components, the front facade does not shy away from a direct, honest use of modern materials. Walls of bare concrete are left exposed and untreated, and the steel frame structure remains naked for all to see.

3 HUMAN TOUCH
Despite the stark, functionalist use of materials, a warm, human touch is given to the public face of the building through the use of large blocks of bright color, oversize contemporary typography for the house number, and a gently curved entranceway that welcomes visitors to the front door.

▲ Polished concrete floors, ceilings made of ribbed steel decking, exposed ductwork, and a monochromatic color scheme reinforce a functionalist aesthetic. The space is softened with plants, rugs, antique furniture, and sail-like canvas panels that can be hoisted across the ceiling to keep out light or cold.

ROGERS HOUSE

Another rare example of High-Tech domestic architecture is the steel-framed house (1968; right) in Wimbledon, London, designed by Richard and Su Rogers for his parents. Like the Myers house, it offers an intimate relationship between inside and outside, but with more English reserve. The yard conceals the house from neighbors, and at the street, little can be seen besides a screen of bamboo, a parking space, and a small door. The project was a family affair, with son Ab going on to design a building on the site, and Richard's mother, Dada, designing the landscape and conceiving the vibrant color scheme of the interior. With its flexible interior space, use of prefabricated elements, and innovative approach to structure and utilities, the building anticipates the High-Tech experiments of Rogers's later Centre Pompidou and Lloyd's Building (see p.486).

ENGINEERED MODERNISM

1 **U.S. Pavilion for World's Fair (Expo '67)**
(1967, renovated in 1995)
Richard Buckminster Fuller
Montreal, Canada

2 **Centre Pompidou (1971–77)**
Renzo Piano and Richard Rogers
Paris, France

3 **Sony Center (2000)**
Helmut Jahn
Potsdamer Platz, Berlin, Germany

It is possible to argue that civil and structural engineering date back to the pyramids of ancient Egypt (see p.24), although engineering as a specialized profession goes back only as far as the eighteenth century. Engineers often create practical applications for scientific principles, or use scientific discoveries to solve practical problems. Structural engineers combine pragmatism with artistic solutions. The mid to late nineteenth century saw the emergence of engineers who made an impact on their landscape. Prominent examples include Isambard Kingdom Brunel (1806–59), builder of the Clifton Suspension Bridge, Bristol, and the Great Western Railway; John A. Roebling (1806–69), creator of the Brooklyn Bridge, New York; and Gustave Eiffel (1832–1923), engineer for the Statue of Liberty, New York, and creator of the Eiffel Tower, Paris. These structures are not necessarily visually attractive, however. Robert Maillart (1872–1940) probably best exemplifies an early example of an aesthetically inclined civil engineer whose solutions are both practical and beautiful—such as the Salginatobel Bridge (1929–30) in Switzerland.

After World War II desperately needed infrastructure reconstruction drove the expansion of civil engineering firms into massive design-build companies. One of the largest is Bechtel. This San Francisco-based firm has built such well-known projects as the Channel Tunnel (1994), between France and England, and King Fahd International Airport in Saudi Arabia (1990). Its jobs

KEY EVENTS

1964	1967	1970	1977	1986	1994
Frei Otto establishes the Institute for Lightweight Structures in Stuttgart, Germany.	Expo '67 takes place in Montreal: it features Buckminster Fuller's geodesic dome of the U.S. Pavilion and Otto's tensile-roof structure of the German Pavilion.	SOM's John Hancock Center is built of braced tube construction, an engineering solution by Fazlur Khan that enables SOM to design ever taller skyscrapers.	The Centre Pompidou, Paris, by Renzo Piano and Richard Rogers with Arup, opens, incorporating revolutionary exterior experiential elements.	The Lloyd's Building, London, is completed. All of the skyscraper's engineering services are located outside the building, as in Rogers's earlier Centre Pompidou.	Working on an enormous scale, as was often the case, Bechtel completes the Channel Tunnel between France an England.

are not uncontroversial, however: witness the spiraling costs and construction setbacks of Boston's "Big Dig" tunnel. In many ways, civil engineers at companies such as Bechtel are the inheritors of the traditions of Brunel and Roebling, although their designs are often more utilitarian than aesthetic.

Structural engineering firms often have a symbiotic design relationship with architects, who visually articulate an engineer's solutions and may go on to create their own aesthetically engineered experiences. This blurs the lines of professional demarcation yet, in the end, provides a more interesting result. For example, consider some of the buildings created between the 1960s and the 1980s that highlight artistic engineering: the geodesic domes of Futurist Richard Buckminster Fuller (1895–1983), particularly the U.S. Pavilion for Montreal's Expo '67 (see image 1); the Centre Pompidou, Paris (see image 2), by Renzo Piano (b.1937) and Richard Rogers (b.1933)—and, even more so, Rogers's later work, such as the Lloyd's Building, London (1986; see p.486); and many of the strongly designed buildings by Norman Foster (b.1935) such as the HSBC Bank in Hong Kong (1983–86) and 30 St. Mary Axe, London (2001–04).

Anglo-Danish structural engineer Ove Arup (1895–1988) was something of a silent partner in the visibly engineered, High-Tech, structurally expressive buildings by Rogers and Foster. Although the John Hancock Center in Chicago (1970; see p.492) by designer Bruce J. Graham (1925–2010) and engineer Fazlur Khan (1929–82), both of Skidmore, Owings and Merrill (SOM), also fits into this category, it is clearly not as overtly expressive as works by Rogers and Foster. The work of architect turned engineer Frei Otto (b.1925) in developing tensile steel tentlike structures is more subtle and focused in that genre than works by his High-Tech colleagues, particularly in the evolutionary relationship between the roof structure of his German Pavilion at Montreal's Expo '67 and that of the Olympic Stadium in Munich (1972; see p.494).

This relationship continues in more recent works such as those of German-born Chicago architect Helmut Jahn (b.1940), nicknamed "Baron von High Tech" in the 1970s and 1980s. Jahn's work has become more skeletally sophisticated by his associations with Arup and structural engineer Werner Sobek (b.1953). Both Arup and then Sobek worked with him on design aspects of the Sony Center in Berlin (see image 3), while Jahn and Sobek have expressed their philosophies together in a book titled *Archi-Neering* (1999). At the time Sobek was the engineer for Jahn's massive Suvarnabhumi Airport, Bangkok (2005), which became their collaborative masterpiece. Zürich-based Spanish architect, engineer, and sculptor Santiago Calatrava (b.1951) is fascinated by structure as well as human and animal motion, and combined both in his Quadracci Pavilion for the Milwaukee Art Museum (2001). There, a moveable sunscreen with a 217-foot (66 m) steel span is programmed to open and close at various times of the day and, when the wind exceeds a sustained 23 miles per hour (37 kph), shuts automatically. **JZ**

1995	2001	2004	2005	2010	2011
Having been destroyed by fire in 1976, the U.S. Pavilion for Expo '67 is renovated and opens as a water museum.	Santiago Calatrava's Milwaukee Art Museum is completed, with a giant *brise soleil* (sun shade) an architectural and engineered experiential feature.	Norman Foster's 30 St. Mary Axe, a twisting steel-and-glass skyscraper nicknamed the "Gherkin," becomes a contemporary symbol of London.	Suvarnabhumi Airport in Bangkok opens, its massive terminal vaults the work of architect Helmut Jahn and engineer Werner Sobek.	The world's tallest skyscraper, Burj Khalifa, Dubai, opens at 2,717 feet (828 m) high—made possible by Fazlur Khan's work in tube construction.	Rogers's Lloyd's Building, a symbol of the affluent 1980s in London, becomes the newest building on Britain's historic buildings registry.

John Hancock Center 1970
SKIDMORE, OWINGS AND MERRILL (SOM)

John Hancock Center,
Chicago, Illinois, USA

☼ NAVIGATOR

The John Hancock Center was designed by architect Bruce J. Graham and structural engineer Fazlur Khan for SOM. Khan's great invention was the framed tube system in which four outside load-bearing walls create a tube whereby each wall braces the next. He refined this further in conjunction with an X-braced high-rise thesis project by Mikio Sasaki in 1964. Khan later created the Hancock's braced or trussed tube system, the X-braces clearly evident on the exterior of the John Hancock Center as well as some interior spaces. When completed the Hancock was Chicago's tallest building at 100 stories and 1,145 feet (349 m) high. The completion of the building sparked the creation of other multiuse commercial buildings nearby, notably Water Tower Place (1976). In the Hancock, a recessed plaza and first five floors contain retail space with six floors of parking above. Further above are twenty-seven floors of office space and the Skylobby. Apartments are situated on floors 45–92, with floors 93–100 for building services and additional income-generating functions. At the top, there is an observatory, restaurant, and bar. **JZ**

◉ FOCAL POINTS

1 ANTENNAE

Broadcasting antennae are another means of income for tall buildings, as are restaurants and observatories immediately below the tops of such structures. The Council on Tall Buildings and Urban Habitat in Chicago, the arbiter of the world's tallest buildings, keeps a record of skyscraper heights, with and without antennae.

2 X-BRACED TUBE

The key constructional feature of the John Hancock Center is the trussed or X-braced tube, the sides of which brace one another with the cross braces providing additional support for a mega-high-rise such as this. Angling the walls adds even more support and creates a distinctive urban monument in the Chicago skyline.

3 SKYLOBBY

On the forty-fourth floor of the building is the Skylobby, which was invented by Fazlur Khan. A sky lobby is an interchange floor, where people can swap from an express elevator that stops only at the Skylobby to one that stops at every floor within a portion of the building. This Skylobby serves only the residential part of the building.

▲ The Hancock's architect Bruce J. Graham stated that it was akin to the Eiffel Tower in structural expression, reinforcing the "honesty of structure" that was a Chicago tradition.

EXPRESSIVE ENGINEERING

Some may think of the John Hancock Center's X-braced trussed tube structural system as a one-off design, but its expressive engineering established the groundwork for future spectacular architectural structures and spaces. Perhaps the most renowned of these were created by British architect Norman Foster, whose designs for the HSBC Bank headquarters in Hong Kong (1983–86; right) and the Century Tower in Tokyo (1991) demonstrate similarly engineered expressions. By contrast with the earlier John Hancock Center by SOM, which essentially has stacked loft floors within, Foster made maximum use of the X-braces to create a visual impact in the exciting interior spaces of these structures. Striking exteriors and dramatic interiors have since become trademarks of his firm's work today.

Olympic Stadium 1972

GÜNTHER BEHNISCH 1922–2010,   FREI OTTO b.1925

Olympic Stadium,
Munich, Germany

NAVIGATOR

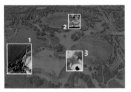

Günter Behnisch and Frei Otto shared a formative experience while serving in Germany's armed forces during World War II. Otto, a Luftwaffe pilot, spent time in a French prison camp where he made tentlike shelters. After forming his practice in 1952, he made his mark designing such structures for garden exhibits. Behnisch was a U-boat commander who, while imprisoned by the British at the war's end, studied architecture and apprenticed as a bricklayer. After graduating from Stuttgart's Technical High School, he opened his practice in 1967. The pair came together in the competition for Munich's Olympic Stadium. Their design met the brief for a site with short walking distances between events in spaces that were connected to greenery and enclosed under one umbrella. Various buildings were scattered across the parkland, with Behnisch's stadium as the centerpiece, and the swimming area and smaller sports hall under an undulating tensile roof designed by Otto. Otto had devised a similar roof for the German Pavilion at Montreal's Expo '67; he recycled the full-scale mock-up of one section for that pavilion into the Institute for Lightweight Structures in Stuttgart (1964). He used these experiences as the basis for creating the spectacular open roof that visually encompasses the stadium. JZ

1 CABLE-STAYED TOWERS

The cable-stayed towers—the tallest of which is some 262 feet (80 m) high—support a tensile roof of approximately 18.48 acres (74,800 m²), the largest ever constructed. There are eight towers for the stadium roof alone, which covers an area of approximately 8.5 acres (34,550 m²).

2 STADIUM

The stadium Behnisch designed originally held 88,000 people but later alterations lowered the capacity to fewer than 70,000 with contemporary figures at about 58,000. Since the Olympics in 1972, it has held soccer matches and rock concerts, among other events.

3 ORGANIC UMBRELLA

The view from above the Olympic Park reveals the organic tensile structure, which appears to float above the landscape. It is a reminder of Otto's aviator beginnings and his continued interest in the geometry of natural forms in relation to tents, the first simple man-made structures.

◄ Otto's tensile roof consists of steel cables stretched to hold acrylic glazing, which allows light to penetrate through, creating an amazing anthropomorphic, diaphanous tent.

EXPO ARCHITECTURE

The German Pavilion that Frei Otto created for Expo '67 in Montreal acted as a smaller-scale model for his later design at the Munich Olympics. The Expo pavilion had a steel-mesh and plastic-lined tensile roof of some 100,000 square feet (9290.5 sq m) that was supported by eight steel masts, the tallest of which stood 120 feet (36.5 m) high. Exhibits within the exposition space ranged from an operational Gutenberg printing press and a U.S. astronaut's camera to Berlin-style restaurants. Together with architect Rolf Gutbrod (1910–99), Otto created an imaginative sequence of exhibition terraces that blended with the natural surroundings, of which the Expo pavilion, with its striking curvaceous silhouette, was the architectural highlight.

JAPAN: MODERNISM

S ymbolized by the Yoyogi Olympic Pool and Gymnasium (see p.498), the Olympic Games of 1964 announced the end of Japan's World War II recovery and ushered in an era of rapid architectural and urban growth that lasted until the country's "bubble" economy burst in the 1990s. Fueled by monetary strength and technological advances, opportunities for designers proliferated and the scope of architectural expression broadened, turning Japan into a land of architectural innovation.

Once its postwar reconstruction was complete, Japan flexed its muscles by hosting the Olympics in Tokyo in 1964, Expo '70 in Osaka, and embarking on large-scale developments in major cities. Preparing to welcome the world's athletes to Tokyo, the government built sports facilities and upgraded infrastructure. The Shinkansen bullet train, new expressways, and subway-line extensions improved circulation and paved the way for urban expansion. While "bedtowns" (planned residential communities) began cropping up at city edges, office buildings began popping up in city centers. Tokyo's Kasumigaseki Building (see image 2), Japan's first high rise, laid the groundwork for Japan's changing cityscapes.

By the mid-1970s the country was promoting an array of architectural agendas. Monuments to the new wealth, a cluster of skyscrapers emerged near Tokyo's Shinjuku Station, each one the product of an established firm or

1 **Sendai Mediatheque (2001)**
Toyo Ito
Sendai, Miyagi prefecture, Japan

2 **Kasumigaseki Building (1968)**
T. Yamashita Architects & Engineers
Kasumigaseki, Chiyoda-ku, Tokyo, Japan

3 **Row House (1976)**
Tadao Ando
Sumiyoshi, Osaka, Japan

KEY EVENTS

1964	1967	1968	1968	1970	1973
The summer Olympic Games open in Tokyo; Japan becomes the first Asian country to host the Games.	Takamitsu Azuma (b.1933) completes Tower House on a tiny, triangular plot left over after road widening in preparation for the Olympics.	The thirty-six-story Kasumigaseki Building, Japan's first high rise, opens, a joint venture by Mitsui Fudosan, Kajima Construction, and Yamashita Sekkei.	The Imperial Hotel in Tokyo, designed by Frank Lloyd Wright (1867–1959), is demolished to make room for a high-rise version.	Overseen by Kenzo Tange (1913–2005), Expo '70 opens in Osaka with pavilions by Kisho Kurokawa, Kiyonori Kikutake, and other Metabolists.	The Organization of Arab Petroleum Exporting Countries (OAPEC) introduces an oil embargo, causing a worldwide energy crisis.

construction company with the technical know-how needed to build tall in earthquake-prone Japan. While big firms tended to land the large commissions, avant-garde ateliers, such as those headed by Toyo Ito (b.1941), Itsuko Hasegawa (b.1941), and Hiroshi Hara (b.1936), pushed conceptual boundaries with small jobs.

The pace of construction slowed during the energy crisis of 1973, but Japanese cities continued to grow and evolve into visually chaotic environments, devoid of street grids, greenbelts, or other urban organizational elements present in many Western cities. Buildings did not form a unified streetscape but instead vied for attention. Some architects responded with objectlike buildings that ignored their neighbors; others simply shut out the surroundings. Fronting the street with a blank concrete wall, the Row House in Sumiyoshi (see image 3) by Osaka's self-taught designer Tadao Ando (b.1941), jolted Japan's architectural establishment and had a profound impact on young designers. For many emerging talents, the building frenzy during the "Bubble Era" was a chance to shortcut a lock-step career path and realize their ideas immediately. It also opened the country to a flood of foreign architects. Teamed with local collaborators, some set up branch offices in the country but most supplied drawings from home. As property values soared, landowners hoped to maximize their holdings by hiring these and other architects. Promoted by the burgeoning Internet and a spate of new design publications targeting Japanese consumers, their unique, attention-grabbing buildings garnered instant popularity—and commercial success.

Previously beyond the reach of many firms, public projects became accessible thanks to a rise in competitions and government initiatives such as Kumamoto prefecture's Artpolis program. Launched in 1988 under architect Arata Isozaki (b.1931), Artpolis opened the market to a broad spectrum of specialists who turned an agricultural backwater into an architectural destination. Separating vehicles and pedestrians, the double-decker Mamihara Bridge (1995) put a tiny town and a newly minted architect, Jun Aoki (b.1956), on the proverbial map.

Not all Bubble Era projects succeeded, but collectively they raised design awareness among Japan's public. There was no going back. Even after the economy collapsed, the government used construction projects to kick-start it again, hiring architects in droves. In some locales, their justification was the replacement of outmoded facilities; elsewhere, the goal was to raise the quality of life by adding cultural amenities. Among the most influential works was Ito's Sendai Mediatheque (see image 1), a civic center for the exchange of visual, digital, and print information. Supporting this unprecedented function was an extraordinary physical feature: thirteen hollow columns, each structural as well as space-defining, ringed with steel pipes. Morphing as they ascend, the see-through tubes tilt side to side, shrink and expand. The project required collaboration with a structural engineer and a shipbuilder skilled in steel fabrication. This inextricable relationship between architect and engineer yielded an entirely new form of tectonic expression befitting the start of a new millennium. **NP**

1975	1988	1991	1992	1995	1996
Moving away from Modernism's pure, rectilinear forms, Arata Isozaki finishes the barrel-vaulted Kitakyushu Municipal Library.	Initiated by the Kumamoto prefectural governor, Morihiro Hosokawa, and architect Arata Isozaki, Artpolis asks architects to create public works.	Land prices in Japan peak, then begin to decline dramatically, triggering the collapse of the country's Bubble Era economy.	Fumihiko Maki (b.1928) completes Hillside Terrace I–VI, a phased, mixed-use complex serving as an antidote to Tokyo's chaotic, urban context.	Measuring 6.9 on the Richter scale, the Great Hanshin Earthquake shakes Kobe, causing $132 billion worth of damage.	Commissioned through an international competition, the Tokyo Forum, by Rafael Viñoly (b.1944), opens on the former site of Kenzo Tange's City Hall.

Yoyogi Olympic Pool and Gymnasium 1964
KENZO TANGE 1913–2005

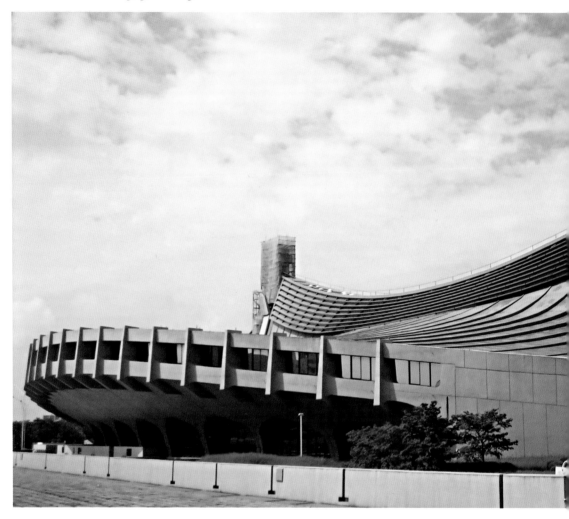

Yoyogi Olympic Pool and
Gymnasium, Yoyogi Park,
Tokyo, Japan

By 1961, Kenzo Tange's portfolio included the Peace Memorial Park at Hiroshima and public offices throughout Japan. He was an obvious choice for one of the country's most internationally important projects: the complex for the first Olympics in Asia. Most "master" architects called attention to their singular artistry, but Tange emphasized managerial successes, fully crediting his chief collaborator, engineer Yoshikatsu Tsuboi (1907–90); his professional staff at URTEC (founded to maintain control of the working drawings); and the contractor, Shimizu. The complex was designed in twelve months and built in eighteen. The main arena, for a swimming pool and 15,000 spectators, had the world's largest cable-supported roof. While designers elsewhere were content to express straightforward catenaries (arches) in cables, Tange, emphasizing ties to Japanese architectural traditions, exaggerated their sweep by unevenly weighting them during construction, adding to the complexity involved. (A cast-steel saddle that rotated as loads shifted the cables outward was required.) The roofs evoke Buddhist temples and tall rural farmhouses, giving the sophisticated structures a distinctly Japanese character.

The work established Tange and Tsuboi as global pioneers in the design of lightweight structures and international icons of a third, "plastic" period in modern architecture. **DB**

NAVIGATOR

FOCAL POINTS

1 CONCRETE RING

The concrete ring of the main area and the massive base housing more mundane functions act as visual foils emphasizing the daintiness of the cables and pylons. These areas are less sculpted and rendered repetitively, but the ring rises gracefully in response to the dip at the center of the cables' span.

2 ROOF

Twenty-eight unusual ribs draw the two central cables apart, creating space for a spinal skylight: steel plates are welded to smaller cables to form the evocative concave curve seen at each pylon. At mid-span, the roof loses its concavity, becoming a hyperbolic paraboloid shape more resistant to strong winds.

3 CABLES

The larger roof hangs from paired high-tension cables that are drawn up over 137 foot (42 m) tall pylons spaced almost 410⅛ feet (125 m) apart; the weight is countered by enormous concrete anchors. The cables are exposed at the entrances, between pylon and anchor, introducing a delicate line, and they also serve to frame skylights that dramatically light each interior.

▼ The elegant curve of each roof is picked out on its underside in supple steel struts, painted to stand out visually—dark steel against aluminum in the main arena.

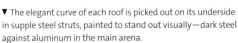

ARCHITECT PROFILE

1913–61

Kenzo Tange was born on Shikoku Island but spent some of his childhood in Hankow and Shanghai. He graduated from the University of Tokyo in 1938 and joined Kunio Maekawa's office. He returned to the university as a graduate student in 1942 and became a professor in 1946. In 1949, he won the competition for a memorial in Hiroshima. In 1961, he established URTEC (later Kenzo Tange Associates). Tange became unrivaled as "state architect," designing major civic structures throughout Japan.

1962–2005

Tange did some of his greatest work for Expo '70 in Osaka, which he designed with protégés, including many Metabolists. Tange worked mostly in the Middle East, Africa, and Singapore, and his architecture grew overscaled. He completed three large structures in Tokyo: a city hall replacing his 1957 structure, United Nations University (1992), and Shinjuku Park Tower (1994).

Silver Hut 1984
TOYO ITO b.1941

Silver Hut,
Omishima Island, Japan

NAVIGATOR

Toyo Ito built Silver Hut for his three-generation family—his widowed mother, wife, and young daughter. Naked concrete supported steel vaults comprised of equilateral triangles; the perforated aluminum skin would soon be adopted around the world. Industrial materials were the only ornament: car-window cranks, tiny trusses, and three-sided skylights in primary colors, bolts, tie-rods, and over-large rain gutters. The architecture was cheerfully casual and ad hoc, lacking the purpose-built precision of High Tech (see p.484). Inside, assertively simple, soaring spaces were loosely wrapped around three sides of an airy central courtyard. It was built in 1984, in Tokyo's densely built-up Nakano Honmachi district; Ito's sister lived on an adjacent plot in his masterpiece the concrete "White U" (1976). In 2010, Silver Hut was relocated to an island on Japan's Inland Sea, where it serves as archives and office for the Toyo Ito Museum of Architecture. What was once the rear wall is now its entry, enclosed in flat, meticulously mounted aluminum panels. Walls on the waterside of the rebuilt residence are no longer sheltering, but open to the sea. The living/dining area, his mother's tatami-floored bedroom, and the adjacent water closet are now part of a sprawling central space, covered to accommodate events. **DB**

👁 FOCAL POINTS

1 TRIANGULATED STEEL VAULTS
The steel structural vaults are an early expression of Ito's efforts to avoid the right angle, sometimes with arcs, sometimes acute angles— here, both. The faceted curve and simple bolted connections were expressed with unusual frankness for the times.

2 OPEN TO THE AIR
Influenced by Le Corbusier's Maison Domino (1914–15), Ito used unbounded edges, suggesting that walls and thresholds were unimportant. The open vault-ends anticipated the way large glass walls would be whisked open at his Sendai Mediatheque (2001).

3 "PUNCHED" ALUMINUM SKIN
Perforated aluminum appeared often in Ito's work in the late 1980s and early 1990s. It offered an ambiguous surface— reflecting, concealing, or revealing, depending on the way light struck. Aluminum has remained an obsession in his work.

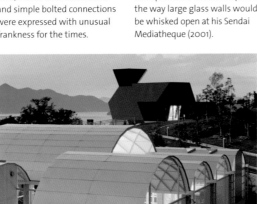

◀ Silver Hut in its scenic new setting. While a solid roof now spans its central space, it remains open and airy. Steel Hut (2011) is its antithesis, dark and enigmatically enclosed, an aggregation of oddly proportioned polyhedrons.

🕐 ARCHITECT PROFILE

1941–69
Toyo Ito was born in Keijo, Seoul, in 1941. His family originally came from an area of Japan that declined economically in the early twentieth century and they moved to Korea, then a colony of Japan. Ito returned to Japan in 1943. After graduating from the University of Tokyo, Ito worked for Kiyonori Kikutake, the eldest and most experienced of the Metabolist architects (see p.454), from 1965 to 1969.

1970–2001
Ito established his first firm, named URBOT ("Urban Robot"), in 1971; in 1979, it became known as Toyo Ito & Associates. At the time, oil shortages were slowing down Japan's economic growth, and much of his early architectural work was residential, sometimes for families. As Japan's economy began to expand again in the 1980s, Ito was awarded public commissions. He began to build his reputation abroad through inventive installations and writings. He was one of the first architects to appreciate that digital technology would change architecture and society; his two best-known essays from the 1990s are "A Garden of Microchips" (1993) and "Tarzans in the Media Forest" (1997). The era ended with his highly acclaimed Sendai Mediatheque, which was completed in 2001.

2002–present
Ito worked on projects in Europe, South America, and parts of Asia beyond Japan. In 2002, he designed the temporary pavilion of the Serpentine Gallery, London. He has been awarded the Royal Institute of British Architects Royal Gold Medal (2006), the Praemium Imperiale (2010), and the Pritzker Architecture Prize (2013), among many other accolades.

POSTMODERNISM

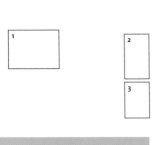

In 1981, a trio of architects, Michael Graves (b.1934), Rem Koolhaas (b.1944), and George Baird (b.1939), traveled from Europe and North America to a conference in Sydney, Australia, where the organizers of "The Pleasures of Architecture" hoped to ignite debate on the "crisis of modernity." Postmodern architecture was near its apogee, but the style had simmered for twenty years. The man who codified Postmodernism was Yale University student Robert A. M. Stern (b.1939); in 1965, he edited the architecture department's *Perspecta 9/10*, which prophetically identified many who would become leading Postmodern architects, such as Charles Moore (1925–93), whose essay "Creating of Place" (1966) championed the "ordinary." *Perspecta 9/10* included the opening chapter of what later became *Complexity and Contradiction in Architecture* (1966) by Robert Venturi (b.1925). Equally importantly, *Perspecta* staked the flag for style, decoration (as opposed to Modernism's "design"), populist architecture, and the public realm. Disneyland (1955) in Anaheim, California, was declared "the most important single piece of construction in the West in the past several decades." Central to the diversity of Postmodernism and its rejection of the purity and "pseudo primitive simplicity" of Modernism, Stern described himself as an "adaptor," "informed eclectic," and one who designs from what exists. His description can be read as a definition of Postmodern architecture.

As an adjunct to the conference, seventeen Australian architects responded to a brief to resolve a "mutilated" Regency villa from the 1830s in Sydney. Daryl Jackson (b.1937) added a floor and replaced the lost facade with the front of an archetypal Australian house enclosed in a timber lattice. At the exhibition "Speaking a New Classicism: American Architecture Now" at Smith College Museum of Art, Massachusetts, in 1981, which identified many of the nascent qualities of Postmodernism, architectural historian Helen Searing identified "burgeoning popular support for historical preservation" as a contributing factor to "the new classicism" in architecture, including Postmodernism. While the conference and its brief were popular, it provoked an attack from Modernist architect Harry Seidler (1923–2006) who warned of youth who take too seriously "reversion to licentious decorative caprice."

Postmodernism's celebration of Disneyland was offset by social concerns, including, for example, Stern's reference to the housing advocacy of people's champion Jane Jacobs in his winning entry for the Roosevelt Island, New York, housing competition (1975). Venturi's seminar "Learning from Levittown" (1970) looked at the mass prefabricated housing suburb (1947–55) for lessons architects could bring to the public realm. The public's identification with Postmodern architecture was captured not by mass housing, however, but by unique buildings praised, pummeled, or parodied by the media, and by publicly accessible Postmodernism. The broken pediment of the AT&T Headquarters (see image 2) in Manhattan (now the Sony Tower) became a media staple, and featured as a giant telephone cradle in a cartoon cover of *The New Yorker* (1989), while Charles Moore's Piazza d'Italia, New Orleans (1978; see p.508), and the Best Products showrooms were examples of popular public Postmodernism.

The decorative and eclectic aspects of Postmodernism reached a wider public in the United States with the "highway architecture" of catalogue retailer Best Products, whose seventy-four "big box" showrooms were distributed across ten states. In 1972, they commissioned SITE architectural group to manipulate the "generic identity" of their showrooms. Best Products directly commissioned the punchy, floral porcelain-enameled, steel-paneled facade of their Pennsylvania showroom (see image 1) from Venturi, Rauch, and Scott Brown, but it was SITE who interpreted vernacular United States novelty architecture, and combined it with expressive Postmodern tropes for the showrooms. Contrary to expectations, SITE's artistic facades exemplified the "duck" and "decorated shed" concepts introduced in *Learning from Las Vegas: The Forgotten Symbolism of Architectural Form* (1977) by Venturi, Denise Scott Brown (b.1931), and Steven Izenour (1940–2001). A concrete duck-shaped building erected in 1931 to sell ducks and their eggs inspired the metaphor. A duck expressed function through its form, and a decorated shed used applied symbols to convey the building's message.

The exhibition of unbuilt designs for Best Products showrooms in 1979 at New York's Museum of Modern Art (MoMA) included one by Robert Stern that referenced the restoration (1829) of the twin temples to Hera at Paestum because "household goods" had become "household gods." Moore's fragmented mirror reflected an elephant motif borrowed from the New York

1984	1988	1990	1990	2003	2009
James Stirling (1926–92) completes the Neue Staatsgalerie in Stuttgart, Germany. Its influence can still be seen in contemporary public spaces.	The Office of Metropolitan Architecture (Rem Koolhaas) builds a "decorated shed"— The Netherlands Dance Theater, The Hague.	Hans Hollein's Haas House in Vienna references historical context while breaking free from it.	Team Disney Building Orlando (see p.510), by Japanese architect Arata Isozaki (b.1931), opens in Lake Buena Vista, Florida.	Michael Graves teams with Lindal Homes and Target Corporation to sell a range of "Pavilions"—small house kits costing $10,000 to $26,000.	Venturi & Rauch Lieb House (1969) is preserved by sailing it on a barge from New Jersey to its new home in New York.

World's Fair of 1939 augmented by "sculptures depicting Babylonian or Persian triumphs." Allan Greenberg and Michael Graves used classical references—Greenberg with a Tuscan column portico, and Graves with a colossal stoa. The artistry of the Best Products facades is echoed by the design for the Jewelry Store Schullin I in Vienna (1974; see p.506) by Hans Hollein (1934–2014). Wedged in a row of urban retail, the site demanded Hollein focus fully on the facade.

In his foreword for the Best Products exhibition catalogue, architect Philip Johnson (1906–2005) declared "The Modern Movement seems really gone from the scene . . . architects today are more inclusive, more permissive, more popular-oriented, indeed more popular, than the Modern Movement allowed." Unlike in the United States, it was the popularity factor that marked the card for Postmodernism in the United Kingdom where it was viewed by many in the media as vulgar. In Italy, *Domus* magazine, founded by architect Giò Ponti (1891–1975), took a different view, and commissioned Studi Nizzoli to design the Editoriale Domus headquarters near Milan (1980). Its monumental white stucco facade with bulls-eye volutes is countered by the triple setback, red brick rear elevation centrally cleaved by glass rooflights and topped by a roof garden.

Postmodern triumphs include El Gouna Resort Hotel in Egypt (1995; see p.512) and the Portland Public Service Building (see image 3) in Portland, Oregon, both by Michael Graves. Helen Searing saw the latter building's small roof structure as a reference to theorist Abbé Laugier's "primitive hut" of 1753, but equally it recalls the temples atop Mesoamerican stepped pyramids. The pointillist punctuation of windows, giant plinth, and colossal fenestrated pilasters beneath a keystone became an archetype of Postmodernism. The repetition of small square windows was widely copied and adapted for advertising and product design. In New York, Philip Johnson's Lipstick Building (see image 4) (its twin setbacks resemble a retractable lipstick tube), features a "flame-finished" banded red granite and reflective glass telescoping tower. An oval building in a square environment, it is Postmodern more for its attitude and shape than for the historical elements it lacks. Johnson loosely modeled the granite-clad tower's monumental plinth on the colonnade of the Pazzi Chapel, Florence (attributed to Filippo Brunelleschi; 1443); its fenestrated floors rise to a Postmodern pinnacle—a monumental classical broken pediment, which together with the Portland Public Service Building, came to symbolize the

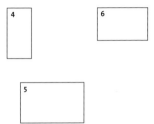

architecture of the decade and underscored that Postmodernism was not only a style, but one, Stern said, that defied the "nihilism" of Modernism's glass boxes.

Exuberant praise and hyperbolic contempt accompanied the debut of the National Gallery Extension (The Sainsbury Wing; see image 5). Venturi and Scott Brown borrowed the material (Portland stone) and height from the main gallery of 1838, but added a purposely idiosyncratic rhythm of classical pilasters, square entrances, and glass and steel to create what Venturi likened to "jazz." Vociferous opinions were published in various media including *The Architectural Review*. The accusation "trahison des clercs" (intellectual, artistic, or moral betrayal), penned by one reader, revealed an undercurrent of British elitism toward Postmodernism's populism, ridiculed by Prince Charles and others. It is not overly speculative to see this derision as a simmering continuation of the "U and non-U" class debate stoked by Professor Alan Ross and writer Nancy Mitford in the 1950s. Postmodernism was, and still is for some, both too popular (non-upper class) and too allied to commercial clients (anathema at the time to European Marxists). In a nod to Ludwig Mies van der Rohe (1886–1969), the extension's east facade is mainly glass and steel. From across a walkway it reflects the main gallery, a Postmodernism trope where architecture reflects its context. The grand staircase parallels the glass wall, and allows views of the original gallery, establishing the relationship between interior and exterior. Charles Moore achieved these types of relationships earlier with his own house (1961) in Orinda, California. Unlike Venturi's house for his mother, Vanna Venturi House (see image 6), Moore's house used salvaged columns to introduce his "simple" exterior to his "complex" interior. Venturi, however, merged classical and vernacular features to create a complex interior that at times becomes surreal. Critic Vincent Scully noted Venturi's adaptation of Lutyens' trope of hidden doors. The deep-set entrance—equal in depth to the broken pediment above—conceals double entrance doors.

In a theatrical gesture that itself can be seen as Postmodern, critic Charles Jencks dated the "death" of Modernism to July 15, 1972 in his book *The Language of Post-Modern Architecture* (1977). However, when *The Architectural Review* declared the death of Postmodernism in its August 1986 issue, sneering it was a "painted corpse" championed by "pasticheurs" and adopted by "rampant capitalism," Jencks paid no mind. Although Postmodernism was past its peak, late exemplars such as the National Gallery Extension were built. In the seventh edition of his book in 1991, Jencks held electrodes to the "painted corpse" and galvanized it into an afterlife where Postmodernism lives in blithe happiness as derivative and diminished architecture. **DJ**

4 **Lipstick Building (1986)**
Philip Johnson
New York, New York, USA

5 **National Gallery Extension (1991)**
Robert Venturi and Denise Scott Brown
London, UK

6 **Vanna Venturi House (1964)**
Robert Venturi
Chestnut Hill, Philadelphia,
Pennsylvania, USA

Jewelry Store Schullin I 1974

HANS HOLLEIN b.1934

Jewelry Store Schullin I,
Vienna, Austria

Schullin jewelry store is clad in shiny square tiles of Baltic Brown granite cleaved by a giant fissure, as though a gemmologist has split the granite to reveal a mysterious geode cavity in its igneous rock host. A gradient of golden metal edges the fissure's black vug, fills the fissure's tail, and spills in free form over the shop's door frame, partially encasing the mirrored door and traveling around the square window. Stainless-steel tube ends peek through the fissure, suggestive of the pipes of an organ or of metallic finger rings. At odds with the fantasy facade, they are prosaically functional and serve as intakes for the building's air conditioning. Hollein's visual alchemy calls into question any presumed hierarchy of materials deemed precious and valuable. The "naked" section of the door reflects the viewer and the city street, allowing reality and fantasy to collide. A window displays some of the treasures hidden inside and rests on a recessed faux plinth of black granite tiles, which echo the black vug. The original narrow interior is made warm and intimate by wood walls and ceilings, burgundy fabrics, and lighting that is reminiscent of a movie star's dressing-room mirror. As an example of Postmodernism, the shop negates any aesthetic stereotypes: the exterior might allude to Gustav Klimt and Art Nouveau, but it is simply architecture's version of controlled improvisation. **KT**

👁 FOCAL POINTS

1 WINDOW

Whereas the fractured granite is a figurative peek "inside," the window—bare in its geometries and an unornamented, square contrast to the adjacent door—is quite literal in its function. The window allows a glimpse into the store itself, speaking a dual language of reality and aspiration.

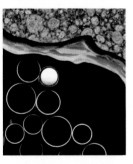

2 FRACTURED SURFACE

Hollein's "crack" in his shiny granite facade is a moment of meta-architecture, in which the architect pulls back the curtain of an exterior only to reveal another curtain made of layered golden bronze. As playful as it is beautiful, the technique is transparent about the use of a sophisticated, decorative system.

3 "VOID" AS SUBSTANCE

From the street, a visitor steps under a granite awning and bronze arch. The door's golden layers roughly outline the shape of a standing human—a Postmodernist use of "void" as material. Turning the doorknob, the visitor fills the door's decorative vacancy, becoming part of the architectural expression.

🕐 ARCHITECT PROFILE

1934–63

Born into a family of mining engineers, Hans Hollein studied at the Academy of Fine Arts, Vienna, under Clemens Holzmeister (1886–1983). Diploma and scholarship in hand, Hollein moved to the United States, where he earned his Master's degree at the University of California, Berkeley, in 1960. Ludwig Mies van der Rohe, Frank Lloyd Wright (1867–1959), and Richard Neutra (1892–1970) shaped his American experience.

1964–2014

Hollein began working independently in 1964, while serving as editor of a design magazine. His teaching career was also extensive. The architect designed a second, bigger shop for Dr. Herbert Schullin in 1982, and the same year realized the much-acclaimed Museum Abteiberg, near Dusseldorf. In 1985, Hollein won the Pritzker Architecture Prize. More recently, in 2010, Hollein partnered with Ulf Kotz and Christoph Monschein to form Hans Hollein & Partner, based in Vienna. Many of Hollein's artworks can be found in collections worldwide.

▲ Working within a narrow structure, Hollein creates an intimate grotto of mostly wood furnishing and walls.

Piazza d'Italia 1978

CHARLES W. MOORE 1925–93

Piazza d'Italia,
New Orleans, Louisiana, USA

NAVIGATOR

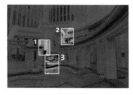

Realized in collaboration with Perez & Associates, Charles Moore's Piazza d'Italia in downtown New Orleans was conceived as a community space to honor the city's Italian-American community. Practicing the architect's philosophy of "inclusion," the Piazza envelops the viewer in symbolism and architectural reference: Tuscan, Doric, Ionic, Corinthian, and Composite classical orders fan around the circular space. Composed of Pompeian reds and yellows, stainless steel and neon lighting, the arched frames evoke a spirit of the past in their representation of the present. They read as composite segments of shared memory. A representation of the geographic boot of Italy protrudes from the floor, surrounded by water (St. Joseph's Fountain). Moore symbolically brought the Adriatic and Tyrrhenian seas to New Orleans, where they are fed from waterspout heads depicting the architect. The project attempted to revitalize a largely abandoned strip of downtown, so Moore's approach included classical cues calling for social engagement. Although the Piazza is among the most important examples of Postmodernism, critics heavily debated the design. Recent revitalization efforts in New Orleans have breathed new life (and funding) into the Piazza and it lives on as a significant public space. **KT**

👁 FOCAL POINTS

1 COLORS
Moore's yellows, reds, and blues coincide with colors typically associated with ancient Italian architecture. However, the neon illuminating the Piazza at night speaks a colloquial language of attraction, advertisement, and brightly lit modern life.

2 MIXED REFERENCES
In mixing Tuscan, Doric, Ionic, Corinthian, and Composite orders, a Postmodern order emerges, in which relationships between architectural conversations are examined. Moore's references prompt certain collective memories drawn from architecture.

3 MAP OF ITALY "SCULPTURE"
In a response to the Modernists preceding him, Moore moved away from pure "abstraction," achieving radical results by turning to literal representation, like that of the Italian "boot" or sculptural map outline protruding from the Piazza's fountain.

◄ Moore's dramatic entrance, allowing visitors access through a triumphal arch, calls for a suspension of disbelief upon entering. In order to serve as a "natural" gathering space, the Piazza must first be experienced as one.

🕐 ARCHITECT PROFILE

1925–47
Charles Willard Moore was born in Benton Harbor, Michigan, and graduated in architecture in 1947 from the University of Michigan, where he was influenced by Dean Roger Bailey.

1948–61
After graduation, Moore worked in San Francisco, before traveling on a fellowship to Europe and Egypt between 1949 and 1950. He later served in Korea and, upon his return, enrolled as a graduate student of architecture at Princeton University, New Jersey, receiving his doctorate in 1957.

1962–74
In 1962, Moore became chair of the University of California, Berkeley architectural program. He also founded the architectural firm MLTW (Moore/Lyndon/Turnbull/Whitaker), which realized the spectacular Sea Ranch resort just north of

San Francisco in 1965 (see p.414). From 1965, Moore lived and worked in New Haven, serving as chair and later dean of the architectural department at Yale University. At Yale, he founded the Yale Building Project with professor and author Kent Bloomer, which aims to demystify social responsibility and the construction process for first-year students.

1975–93
Moore joined the faculty of the University of California, Los Angeles in 1975, and continued to design, teach, and write prolifically. In 1984, he became the O'Neil Ford Chair in Architecture at the University of Texas. In Austin he joined forces with Arthur Andersson (b.1957), with whom he collaborated on the Louisiana World Exposition in New Orleans (1984). Moore received the Gold Medal from the American Institute of Architects in 1991.

Team Disney Building 1990
ARATA ISOZAKI b.1931

HEIGH-HO, HEIGH-HO, IT'S OFF TO WORK WE GO

Team Disney Building,
Orlando, Florida, USA

According to Paul Goldberger in his review for *The New York Times*, "Disney has now made its contribution to the history of architecture." Despite a complex aesthetic, Arata Isozaki's concept can be expressed in a single word: time. Poetic in the crests and crashes of its colorful cubic forms, including a red cube that tops a pink rectangle serving as its skylight, Team Disney culminates in a circular centerpiece. Like a concrete exclamation point, an eight-story tower interjects the rectangular office wings below. As visitors enter, the tower walls unfurl to reveal a hollow atrium, exposed to the elements from above. Built into the tower's rim is a yellow pointer, which is, in fact and function, a large sundial. Within the atrium, loose rocks form a dry pond around the visitor, who can cross via a set stone bridge, engraved with quotes about time. The quotes are perhaps the only literal element of this space. In all other ways, it addresses only those concepts of time that words cannot: the atrium's primary function is to call into question spirit, cosmos, and existence. It is possible that the building's users might see the space as nothing more than a passageway from one wing to another—a fact that raises its own questions about time's value in the modern world. Perhaps Isozaki shaped the archway to resemble Mickey Mouse ears in order to alleviate the anxiety caused by such built-in allegorical doubts. However, Goldberger notes that within the context of Isozaki's amalgamated design, even a well-known logo becomes an abstract symbol worthy of pause. **KT**

❖ NAVIGATOR

◉ FOCAL POINTS

1 COLOR

Intricate clashing patterns and colors are essential to Isozaki's design. Differentiated by colors, the building's shape emerges as a collection of disparate boulders rather than a single mass. In contrast, the office wing interiors are more monochrome, signaling a change of intended use and atmosphere.

2 ASYMMETRY

Despite its geometric appearance, Isozaki's composition is asymmetrical. Cubic repetition on either side of the sundial is subverted with details or movements that purposefully throw off an even balance. The sundial itself is asymmetrical in order to properly function, further compounding aesthetic fluidity.

3 "EAR" ARCHWAYS

Mickey Mouse ears shape archways leading up to and into the building. Recognizable symbols are important to any conversation about Postmodernism, but in this design the instantly legible logo also functions as an abstracted, fluid geometric shape, in harmony with the rest of the building.

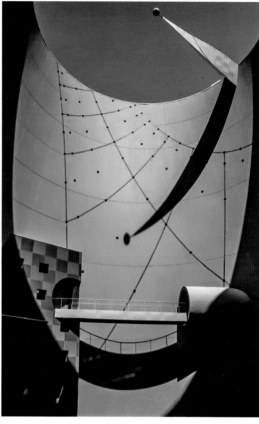

▲ The sundial atrium is arguably the building's most vital organ. Intrinsic to Postmodernist design is the ambiguity and negative space. This atrium has no prescribed use; its meaning and function, beyond telling time, transform according to the individual.

🕐 ARCHITECT PROFILE

1931–62

Born in Oita City, Japan, Arata Isozaki graduated from the University of Tokyo Department of Architecture in 1954. While there, he was taught and influenced by Kenzo Tange (1913–2005). After graduation, Isozaki began his architectural career working for Tange and design team Urtec. He began to work independently in 1960 and realized Oita Medical Center in the same year.

1963–79

In 1963, Isozaki established his own practice, Arata Isozaki & Associates, in Tokyo, but continued to design for Tange into the 1970s. One of Isozaki's early commissions was the Oita Prefectural Library, which he completed in 1966. It remains one of his best-known works. Isozaki's range as an architect cannot be described by any one style, as evidenced by the experimentation that has marked his career. This is exemplified even in relatively early works, such as the Museum of Modern Art, Gunma, Japan (1974).

1980–89

During the 1980s, Isozaki's designs began to demonstrate the influences of Italian painters and architects Giulio Romano (1492/99–1546) and Michelangelo (1475–1564). His development of Tsukuba city center, Japan (1983), recalls Michelangelo's Capitoline Square (1546) in Rome. Other notable works include Los Angeles County Museum of Contemporary Art (1985), which remains one of the best-known works in the United States by a Japanese architect. In 1986, Isozaki was awarded the Royal Institute of British Architects Gold Medal.

1990–present

In 1992, he completed Saint George's Palace for the Barcelona Olympic Games. That same year, he won the National Honor Award from the American Institute of Architects for Team Disney. Isozaki continues his practice, but also works as a critic, curator, and jury member. Among his recent projects is Ark Nova (2013), an inflatable mobile concert hall created with sculptor Anish Kapoor.

El Gouna Resort Hotel 1995

MICHAEL GRAVES b.1934

El Gouna Resort Hotel,
El Gouna, Egypt

⬧ NAVIGATOR

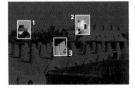

The single letter difference between the name of the resort hotel and the village of New Gourna, near Luxor, is an unlikely accident. According to Michael Graves, the hotel's context is Egyptian rural buildings, and New Gourna (1952)—a project designed by Hassan Fathy (1900–89) to rehouse unofficial tomb excavators—was a likely inspiration. Graves's complex of cycloid, funnel, dome, and chimney roofs reflects Fathy's belief that no two homes should be identical. Both architects used local materials and traditional techniques, but while Fathy hated "the precision of the T-square" and stopped workers when wall heights seemed "about right," the hotel's construction adheres to international codes. The colored rendered concrete references not only the alluvial Nile mud that enabled local masonry techniques, but also the silhouettes and block colors typical of Postmodern architecture. The guestrooms and public areas include catenary arches (modeled on the inversion of the drape of a chain hanging from its ends) and domes, and the cupolas—brick domes on polygonal bases—that Fathy favored at New Gourna. Bounded by shoreline, canals, and lagoons, the site plan mixes circles and squares, arches and vaults, straight and sinusoidal lines, achieving an apparently idiosyncratic but highly controlled outcome. **DJ**

1 VAULTS

Dome sail vaults on polygonal bases create recessed vaults between the pendentives for beds or seating areas in some of the 400 guestrooms. Similar in design, Hassan Fathy's New Gourna cupolas were measured with a stick compass to determine radius.

2 ROOFS

The hotel features domed roofs with closed, round, chimneylike projections from which internal light fittings hang. They resemble the multiple stupalike domes at Husain-Doshi Gufa, Ahmedabad (1995), by Balkrishna Doshi (b.1927).

3 GEOMETRY

Graves repeats simple geometric shapes in multiple formats. Vaults include catenary and cycloid. Architects known for cycloid vaults—a curve traced by a point on a circle's circumference as it rolls on a straight line—include Louis Kahn (1901–74).

◀ Graves uses functional catenary arches—widespread in classical and vernacular Islamic architecture—throughout El Gouna Resort Hotel. The merging of classical and vernacular, often as motifs and without the implied utility of the vernacular forms, is a feature of Postmodern architecture.

ARTS CENTER, HARRANIA

Ramses Wissa Wassef (1911–74) founded and designed the mud-brick arts center (right) in 1951 to teach Egyptian weaving to children. Trained at the Ecole des Beaux-Arts, Paris, and a one-time associate of Hassan Fathy, Wassef viewed the arch, vault, and dome as quintessential Egyptian vernacular, evidenced by the Nubian architecture of Lower Egypt and Northern Sudan, and typified by buildings on Sehel Island, southern Egypt. Aspects of Nubian architecture are reflected at El Gouna Hotel. Similar to the layout of Nubian homes, all the rooms and function areas of the hotel face water. El Gouna's courtyards, roof terraces, and seemingly non-replicating forms are inspired by the Egyptian vernacular promoted by Fathy and Wassef.

RESILIENCY

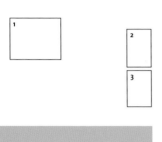

1 **Torre Cube (2005)**
Carme Pinós
Jalisco, Guadalajara, Mexico

2 **Al Bahar Towers (2012)**
Aedas
Abu Dhabi, United Arab Emirates

3 **Copan Apartment Building (1957)**
Oscar Niemeyer
São Paulo, Brazil

Natural disasters are traditionally the antagonists of architecture, but advocates of twenty-first-century Resilient architecture and infrastructure seek to work with nature as both protagonist and ally. Resiliency also describes the speed at which utilities, transportation, businesses, and households recover from natural disasters. Crucial to its success is learning from passive precedents, such as Islamic *mashrabiya* screens, and from nonindustrialized countries such as Bangladesh, where adapting to climate change is an unavoidable rule, not an exception.

Resilient architecture includes concepts such as passive solar, in which the climate of the building is maintained without the use of mechanical devices. This is seen in the design of Daylight Research Residence (1957), Ann Arbor, Michigan, with its directional clerestory glass and prismatic glass skylights; the *mashrabiya*-influenced Al Bahar Towers in Abu Dhabi (see image 2); the "eco hats" at Oxley Woods (2006), Milton Keynes, UK, which mimic ancient Islamic wind towers; the fire-break roof pools of the Toro Canyon House in California (1999; see p.520); and development shifts in the Netherlands from defensive dykes to artificial archipelagos for floating habitation. Resilient architecture increasingly includes incrementally affordable, expandable, and demountable housing as advocated by the Mississippi Renewal Forum after Hurricane Katrina in 2005. Forerunners include Barbadian Chattel houses (see p.518) and incremental models include

KEY EVENTS

1970	1979	1999	2000	2002	2003
The Myth of the Machine Vol II: The Pentagon of Power, by architecture critic Lewis Mumford, criticizes the wastefulness of planned obsolescence.	Anti-professional architecture books such as *The Integral Urban House* (1979) refute the idea that progress is reliant on technology.	Barton Myers completes the Toro Canyon House in California (see p.520). It features steel shutters and reservoirs that act as firebreaks.	Herzog & de Meuron complete the RIVP Social Housing project in Paris (see p.522). Parts of the building can be adapted by its users to suit their needs.	*Cradle to Cradle* by Michael Braungart and William McDonough champions abundance through the continual renewal of resources.	Jonathan Zimmerman uses materials with five times the robustness required by FEMA for his Florida Dome Home after hurricanes destroy his previous homes.

the low-cost, low-rise Elemental Iquique housing (2003) by Alejandro Aravena (b.1967) in Chile, where homes can be expanded into intentional gaps.

Houses and small mosques on Bangladesh's barrier islands and floodplains are by necessity basic and designed to be dismantled quickly and moved. Longevity between moves can be extended by mounding earth at least 6 feet (1.8 m) for an elevated foundation. The artificially elevated grade beneath a New Orleans house designed by Barry Fox Associates contributed to its survival of Hurricane Katrina, as did its steel infrastructure, whereas dozens of neighboring stilt houses built to Federal Emergency Management Agency code were washed away. Fragile footings are also prone to earthquake collapse, as seen in Kobe, Japan, in 1995. Increased earthquake resiliency can include footings up to 65 feet (20 m) deep for commercial buildings, and concrete foundations and lighter roofs for houses. In Peru, adobe houses are built with earthquake technology developed by Lima's Catholic University. In Jalisco, Guadalajara, Carme Pinós (b.1954) designed Torre Cube (see image 1) with less dead weight for its high seismic activity location. Its double-skin *brise soleil* (sunshade) facade manages solar gain and aids the building's natural ventilation system.

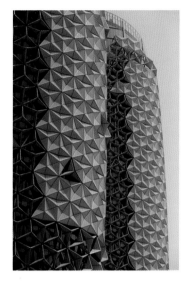

Passive heating, cooling, and solar shading includes *cobogó* and *mashrabiya* screens, louvers, *jalousies* (blinds or shutters), and wind towers. *Mashrabiya*—pierced wooden screens often enclosing a raised profile window seat—reduce solar gain and redistribute cool air. Contemporary *mashrabiya* can be combined with kinetic properties: the facade of the Institut du Monde Arabe (1987), Paris, by Jean Nouvel (b.1945), has once-functional kinetic circular shutters. The Al Bahar twin towers have a dynamic, *mashrabiya*-inspired external skin, modeled by Gehry Technologies Digital Project software. Teflon-coated steel, aluminum and fiberglass triangles array on the south, east, and west facades. Controlled naturally (light, wind, and water sensors) and by computer, the facade reacts to climatic change, and the umbrellalike clusters open like a harmonious but heterogeneous field of flowers.

Solar gain is greatest on north facades in the Southern Hemisphere and south facades in the Northern Hemisphere, leading to radically different architectural climate solutions on each facade, as seen in the Copan Apartment Building in São Paulo (see image 3) by Oscar Niemeyer (1907–2012), which pairs *brises soleil* on the north with balconies on the south. In 2011, in *The Architectural Review*, Christopher Mackenzie argued that Le Corbusier (1887–1965), credited as the inventor of *brise soleil* (the design of which originates in Islamic architecture), incorrectly oriented his Unité d'Habitation, Marseilles (1952), and several subsequent buildings, making his fin and slab *brise soleil* less effective. MBM Arquitectes designed the glazed ceramic and concrete Avinguda Meridiana Apartments, Barcelona (1964), with *mashrabiya*-inspired windows. The site's pre-selected east–west orientation was improved by projecting triangular oriels, open to the south and closed to north. The prismatic angles

2004	2011	2013	2013	2014	2014
"Resiliency" becomes the watchword for defensive and predictive architecture in the wake of natural disasters such as the tsunami in Southeast Asia.	The National Trust for Historic Preservation reports that the gains of sustainable building are negated when buildings suitable for rehab are demolished.	The *Midcentury (Un)Modern: The 1958–73 Manhattan Office Building* report compares retrofit with replacement.	Resilient Idaho architect Macy Miller self-builds a tiny house with reclaimed materials, following a divorce and foreclosure.	Bjarke Ingels Group promotes "hedonistic sustainability" with its design of Copenhagen power station as an urban "mountain" with ski slopes.	Ijburg floating village, Amsterdam, works with floods and water using the same resilient mindset that built the polder dyke system and Dutch defence lines.

of the oriel glass reflect more light, with greater diffusion to the interior, than conventionally glazed windows. This passive but nontraditional *mashrabiya* iteration may have inspired Barcelona-born Enric Miralles (1955–2000), whose west-facing "dreaming windows" for the private Members' offices at the Scottish Parliament (2004; see p.472) are modern *mashrabiyas*.

Louvers (called *persianas* in Brazil referencing Islamic origin), *jalousies*, and shutters have been used since the nineteenth century in tropical and subtropical climates. In the 1940s, Australian architects designed the D and C series of elevated, narrow houses flanked by banks of louvers. These designs influenced the resilient and passive cooling designs of architects Glenn Murcutt (b.1936) and Richard Leplastier (b.1939). The horizontal louvers in plantation shutters open and close via an interior central vertical bar. In the twentieth century, the shutters were updated with a side crank handle to allow minute adjustment of what were usually glass, not wooden, slats. An adherent of louvers was Florida Modernist architect Alfred Browning Parker (1916–2011), who placed banks of louvers on multiple levels in his buildings to direct air circulation. The conference "Weather and the Building Industry" (1950), in which Parker participated, advocated the merger of climatology and building technology to create resilient contemporary architecture. The Hayloft House in Texas (2004) by Max Levy (b.1947) includes a corrugated-metal roof where the sinusoidal wave edge encourages natural air exchange between inside and outside, enough, Levy says, "to make your hair stand on end" when in the house's attic. Herzog & de Meuron's social housing (2000; see p.522) in Paris's 14th district includes two blocks with folding shutter facades and a third with vertical rolling tambour doors.

Cobogó perforated block walls are privacy and solar screens, and represent an element of Brazil's Muxarabi style, a mix of Portuguese colonial and vernacular architecture. An early expression of Muxarabi is Rio de Janeiro's Parque Guinle (see image 4) by Lúcio Costa (1902–98). The orthogonal facade's squares of *cobogó* and vertical louvers are reminiscent of door treatments in Diamantina, an eighteenth-century colonial diamond-prospecting village that was a known source of inspiration for Costa. Brasil Arquitetura's *cobogó* facade for Museu Luiz Gonzaga, Recife (2014), borrows branchiate forms, including the indigenous drought-resistant juazeiro tree for the design of each *cobogó* block. In São Paulo, Cobogó House (see image 5) by Marcio Kogan (b.1952) features

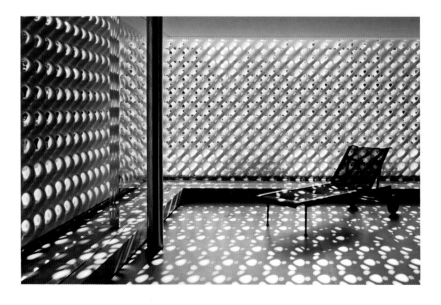

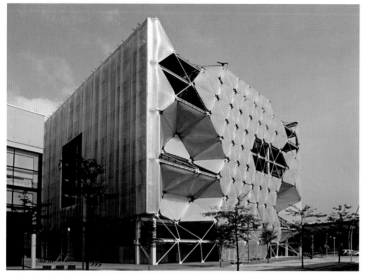

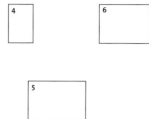

artist Erwin Hauer's updated *cobogó* screens. In the mid-twentieth century, the Superlite Builders Supply in Phoenix, Arizona, produced similar blocks. They combined locally mined, lightweight, strong, and high thermal mass volcanic scoria with cement and sand to create structural "lace curtain" blocks. The shift to "romantic" Modernism by U.S. architect Edward Durrell Stone (1902–78) was attributed to his Italian–Spanish wife, and perhaps she introduced him to *cobogó* and Iberian *mashrabiya*. Stone designed *cobogó* facades at the U.S. Embassy, New Delhi (1954), at his New York townhouse (1956), and at Celanese House, New Canaan, Connecticut (1959). The last includes twelve prismatic glass pyramid skylights, and its white wood *cobogó* facade appears to mimic molecular cell structure.

Media-Tic in Barcelona (see image 6) is Cloud 9 Architecture's first completed project. Computer-controlled, multiple-membrane "pillows" of clear and fritted ETFE—a recyclable plastic polymer—are sunscreens on the southwest and southeast facades. The southwest pillows inflate with nitrogen gas to further diffuse sunlight. "Strip away the whiz bang technology," said *Australian Design Review*, "and what you are left with really isn't such a radical departure from the traditional modernist office block." The building's reliance on Cloud 9's in-house-designed computer systems makes it a questionably resilient building.

Don Belt reported for *National Geographic* in 2011 on the resilient mindset of those living in southern Bangladesh flood zones. A network of dykes was built in the 1960s with advice from Dutch engineers to protect fields and villages. Similar to coastal engineering on the eastern seaboard of the United States, where seawalls repel wave energy so violently that sand beaches are sucked out to sea, floods in Bangladesh broke through dykes, leaving fields waterlogged. Desperate farmers breached the dykes to allow water to flow and drain naturally. Sediment deposits increased and field levels were naturally raised. The dyke breach is not a new innovation but a centuries-old technique, and it is still being used in the Netherlands in the twenty-first century. Although the technique is improving natural land management in Bangladesh, climate change flooding still occurs. One of Don Belt's interviewees in Bangladesh gestured to his flooded land. "Tell [your readers] it's a preview of what South Florida will look like in forty years." Technology-driven architecture is only part of the solution. Passive low-tech systems, land-focused infrastructure and resilient mindsets are key to twenty-first-century architecture. **DJ**

4 **Parque Guinle (1954)**
Lúcio Costa
Rio de Janeiro, Brazil

5 **Cobogó House (2011)**
Marcio Kogan
São Paulo, Brazil

6 **Media-Tic (2010)**
Cloud 9 Architecture
Barcelona, Spain

Chattel house Date unknown
ARCHITECT UNKNOWN

Chattel house,
Chapel Street, Speightstown,
St. Peter, Barbados

Chattel houses first appeared in Barbados after the Master and Servants Act (1840), which introduced the "located labor" system for slaves. In exchange for labor, they were allowed to build Chattel houses on land they did not own. Designed for disassembly, the small, timber-framed, one-story, two-room Chattels were moored temporarily on stacked coral or cinder blocks. Sequential additions and solid foundations indicate that tenancies became more secure in the twentieth century, and increased dramatically after 1980, when tenantry legislation created Chattel owner-occupiers. However, native lumber supplies were depleted in the nineteenth century, and North American pine was imported for Chattels. Symmetrical plans reflect colonial Georgian architecture. Vented gable roofs replaced hipped roofs, and sash windows were paired with louvered half-shutters to allow different combinations of ventilation. Exterior wood cladding covered a standard stud frame, which was left visible on the interior. Gable additions were built at the back, slightly wider than the original and with louvered windows in the overwidth. Although threatened by luxury developments, Chattels remain viable. In 2012, Barbadian senator and proponent of Chattels Henry Fraser spoke of the houses' "renaissance," exemplified by a couple who moved their Chattel house from St. Philip to Christ Church, bequeathed it to their son, who in turn bequeathed it to his daughter. Her Chattel is a combination of home and hair salon. **DJ**

NAVIGATOR

FOCAL POINTS

1 JALOUSIE

The door of the atypical side extension to the Chattel house has a twentieth-century glass *jalousie*. The design of the *jalousie* was updated when an interior side crank handle replaced the central wooden bar that was used previously to raise and lower the wooden slats of the original.

2 ROOF

The triple-gable roofline indicates two rear additions have been made to the original Chattel. All three roofs are covered in corrosion-resistant, corrugated, galvanized iron or steel, but joins between the additions are vulnerable to leaks. A sizeable V-shape metal valley gutter extends over the side.

3 IMPROVEMENTS

A short flight of masonry steps leading to the entrance and a permanent foundation indicate that the Chattel house is less likely to be moved. The typical incremental enlargement of Chattel houses tends to protect owners from improvement loans that have punitive interest rates.

DEMOUNTABLE HOUSES

In 1952, *Science and Mechanics* magazine declared portable, or demountable, homes superior to mobile homes because the latter are not designed for frequent moves. In the late 1960s, Finnish architect Matti Suuronen (b.1933) designed a futuristic portable home, known as the Futuro (right). Businessman Stan Grau purchased one of twenty Futuro homes created and took it to San Diego, California, with the intention of marketing it. Zoning conflicts forced him to move the house six times in the 1970s, until the neighborhood of Hillcrest eventually offered it sanctuary. In 2002, architect Milford Wayne Donaldson (b.1943) bought the house, restored it and moved it to Idyllwild in the San Jacinto Mountains, California. The move revealed the irony of portables: mobility is a flaw, not a feature. Permits, measurements, route planning (including tree trimming), and prayers were required to make it "roadable."

Toro Canyon House 1999
BARTON MYERS ASSOCIATES

Toro Canyon House,
Montecito, California, USA

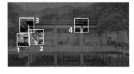
♦ NAVIGATOR

In the Santa Ynez Mountains near Santa Barbara, the Mediterraneanlike paradise of Montecito is at high risk of wild fires fueled by sundowner winds, and hundreds of homes have been incinerated. However, the design of Toro Canyon House means that fire has little chance to claim it. The one-story complex reflects the architect's relationship with the landscape and climate, and also the pragmatic realization of the adage "the best defence is a good offence." In order to avoid felling old-growth trees, the architect separated buildings on terraces: the garage and guesthouse on the lower terrace; the main residence in the middle, with bedrooms in a rear "caboose"; and a studio on the upper terrace. The exposed steel frame and concrete buildings open with sliding, pivoted, and glass-paneled doors, which roll up and slide away parallel to the ceiling. Doors work in tandem with clerestory windows to exchange air without recourse to artificial air units, and the steel shutters can enclose the house like a cocoon. Water reservoirs on the flat roofs are not only contemplative pools but also firebreaks that cascade water from roof to roof, and into emergency reservoirs and back again via a pump. Barton Myers (b.1943) cites as inspiration the work of Southern California architects, such as Charles (1907–78) and Ray (1912–88) Eames and their Case Study House (1949). Their influence is evident in his exploration of new uses for industrial materials, but the extent of his welcome and challenge to Mother Nature exceeds the architects who came before. **DJ**

FIREPROOF HOUSING

In 1907, Frank Lloyd Wright (1867–1959) published his design for a fireproof house (above) in an article for *Ladies' Home Journal* titled "A Fireproof House for $5000." He was probably inspired not only by historical conflagrations, including the Great Chicago Fire of 1871, which was fueled by the wooden city, but also by the increasing use of steel-reinforced concrete. Wright recommended a monolithic, steel-reinforced concrete cube cast in identical formwork for all four sides of his house. Although the material was believed to be fireproof, his design—somewhere between his Prairie and Usonian styles—did not have inherent fireproof features or inflammable innovations. Inventor Thomas Edison was another advocate of the fireproof qualities of concrete for housing. However, in 1914 fire destroyed a significant part of his West Orange, New Jersey, laboratory complex. The extent of the damage exceeded $2 million, but Edison had undervalued replacement costs to a fraction—$238,000—because the concrete buildings were believed to be fireproof. Edison saw value in disaster, and the ruins fueled him to start anew and build better.

👁 FOCAL POINTS

1 BEDROOMS
Three bedrooms align perpendicular to the rear of the main residence. Two bedrooms have rolling doors and are kept cosy in winter with chimney-based heat pumps and fireplaces.

2 USE OF STEEL
Steel can span wide distances without support, which allows greater opportunity for the house to open to nature. Horizontal steel cylinders above wide doors hold the roll-down fire shutters.

3 TEMPERATURE CONTROL
Overhanging roofs and the correct site orientation, with main elevations facing west to the Pacific Ocean, ensure that summer sun is mitigated and winter sun permeates.

4 DOORS
Myers pioneered the domestic use of industrial steel-and-glass garage doors. Counterbalances allow the motor-free doors to open easily for a seamless flow to the building's rooftop pool.

DIGITAL ARCHITECTURE

The term "digital architecture" does not refer to an architectural style; it describes the relationship between architecture and technology. The emergence of digital architecture is often dated to the early 1980s, when desk-based CAD (computer-aided design) software became a reality for most architects, but its history reaches back to the first networked computers in the late 1960s. Closely linked with advances in computing, software, and digital networks, digital architecture has evolved from the digitally inspired, through the digitally formed—where digital tools allow the creation of a new formal vocabulary, as seen in buildings such as UN Studio's Living Tomorrow Pavilion in Amsterdam (2000)—into twenty-first-century digital networks, which transform the architectural process and change the role of the architect.

In the 1960s, architecture was disrupted by the cybernetics revolution that evolved from pre–World War II United States engineering institutions, whose projects synthesized control, communications, and computing. Norbert Wiener articulated the concept of cybernetics in his book *Cybernetics: Or the Control and Communication in the Animal and the Machine* (1948). While teaching at the Architectural Association in London, prominent cybernetic thinker Gordon

KEY EVENTS

1970	1985	1991	1992	1994	1995
Architecture Machine Group and Nicholas Negroponte (b.1943), exhibit a responsive digital architecture model, Seek, inhabited by rodents.	Frank Gehry begins his Lewis Residence project in Lyndhurst, Ohio. It is one of the first structures that Gehry designs with the aid of Catia software.	Shoei Yoh (b.1940) designs a gymnasium for Odawara, Japan, using digital structural analysis to create a minimal, non-uniform structural frame.	Gehry completes the Peix (Catalan for "fish"), an enormous digitally designed sculpture for the Barcelona Olympic Games.	Architect Greg Lynn (b.1964) and others start "paperless studios" at Columbia University in New York.	Pioneer John Frazer exhibits a digital machine that evolves as people interact with it at the Architectural Association, London.

Pask, with contemporaries including Cedric Price (1934–2003) and the avant-garde architectural group Archigram, influenced the incorporation of cybernetics into architecture. One notable project was a proposal for a London "Fun Palace" (1961), an enormous structure inspired by the British tradition of pleasure gardens, conflated with the latest cybernetic theories. Pask acted as cybernetic consultant on the project, helping Price to design a building that responded technologically to the desires and needs of users. The Fun Palace and its inventors were influential in changing the idea of architecture from a static environment to a responsive, adaptable one, which had precedents in eighteenth- and nineteenth-century responsive scientific architecture such as Crystal Palace, London (1851), by Joseph Paxton (1803–65). Although the Fun Palace was unrealized, a prototype—the Interaction Centre (1976)—was built as a small, adaptable community center in Kentish Town, London.

Peter Eisenman (b.1932) is one architect whose work was inspired by the digital. He rose to prominence as part of the "New York Five," a group of late twentieth-century Modernists. Both practitioner and theorist, Eisenman called for the absorption of digital culture into architectural practice. Drawing on the work of philosophers such as Gilles Deleuze, and technologies including fluid-dynamics simulation software, Eisenman developed an architecture that sought to describe the complex digital contemporary world. One of his early experiments in the development of this language was the Aronoff Center for Design and Art in Cincinnati (see image 2): a stack of awkward geometries creating a labyrinthine interior that architect Frank Gehry (b.1929) described as "insane spaces." Although there is a digital precision to the complexity of the Aronoff Center, the building retains elements of Eisenman's earlier Deconstructivist (see p.530) fragmentation. The type of digital architecture typified by the Aronoff peaked and separated from its Deconstructivist influences with the competition to redesign Osanbashi Pier as the Yokohama International Port (now ferry) Terminal in Japan (1995; see p.526). The winners, Foreign Office Architects, rarely describe their submission in digital terms, but its curvaceous form could have been created only with the assistance of digital software.

In the early 1990s, the changing intellectual context informing the nonlinear architecture of Eisenman and Foreign Office Architects was mirrored by improvements in architectural software, which were often co-opted from other professions. Gehry was a notable early adopter. His practice adapted aeronautical industry software to design a fish-shaped sculpture for the Barcelona Olympic Games in 1992. The software, Catia, allowed the complex mathematics required to model three-dimensional curved surfaces. Gehry and his practice went on to employ Catia in the creation of one of the most influential digitally designed buildings: the Guggenheim Museum Bilbao, Spain (see image 1). Originally a sculptural exercise, the museum's initial form did not come from digital methods but from Gehry's appraisal of the landscape and context.

1 **Guggenheim Museum Bilbao (1997)**
Frank Gehry
Abando, Bilbao, Spain

2 **Aronoff Center for Design and Art (1996)**
Peter Eisenman
University of Cincinnati,
Cincinnati, Ohio, USA

1997	1997	1998	2003	2008	2011
Gehry's Guggenheim Museum Bilbao opens, bringing digitally designed architecture into the global consciousness.	Peter Eisenman designs a ferry terminal for Staten Island, inspired by digital models of fluid dynamics.	Zaha Hadid Architects wins the competition to design the MAXXI Museum (see p.528) and builds a concrete manifesto of parametric ideas.	Lynn designs an edition of tea and coffee sets for Alessi; it comprises ninety-nine digitally generated variations on a single theme.	Italian inventor Enrico Dini creates a prototype of a three-dimensional printer, which he claims will be capable of printing buildings.	Patrik Schumacher publishes his manifesto, "The Autopoiesis of Architecture," claiming parametric, digital architecture as the successor to Modernism.

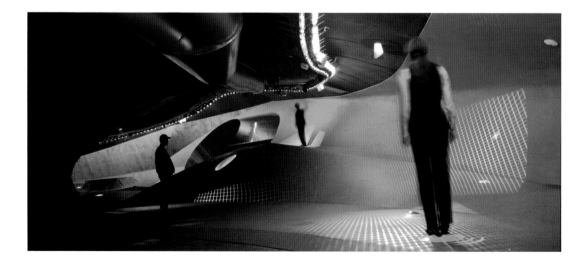

3 HtwoOexpo Pavilion (1997)
Lars Spuybroek and NOX
Vrouwenpolder, the Netherlands

4 Villa Nurbs (2009)
Enric Ruiz-Geli
Empuriabrava, Spain

5 Gantenbein Vineyard Facade (2006)
Gramazio & Kohler in cooperation with
Bearth & Deplazes Architekten
Fläsch, Switzerland

As the design progressed, Gehry was increasingly impressed by the ability of digital software to generate form. The prosaic, curvaceous boxes of his previous museum, Vitra Design Museum in Weil am Rhein, Germany (1989), became much more organic with the improved digital techniques available in the design for Bilbao. Although previously architects had made curved forms without digital design tools, Gehry achieved it at Bilbao on a grand and complex scale, and within budget. The digital processes not only allowed him to give the construction team accurate instructions, but also enabled the builders to be dimensionally efficient with the titanium and limestone. Although this economic efficiency is rarely discussed in terms of digital architecture, it is a critical factor in the success of a landmark public building, such as the Guggenheim Museum Bilbao, which became symbolic of both the digital shift in architects' vocabularies and the beginning of a period of commissioning expressive buildings as a tool for the regeneration of cities.

Designers increasingly rejected the uniform linearity of Modernism in favor of distorted and "blobby" forms. Lars Spuybroek (b.1959) and NOX, a Dutch architecture practice, developed projects that explored the new formal potential of digital software. As with Gehry and Eisenman, their inspiration came from organic forms, such as flowing water, but instead of mimicking these forms, Spuybroek and NOX aspired to generate a "liquid architecture" in their HtwoOexpo Pavilion in the Netherlands (see image 3).

One of the principal achievements of digital modeling programs is the employment of NURBS (non-uniform rational B-Splines), which allow designers to manipulate curved surfaces. The ability to create these forms easily has generated buildings that have been dubbed "blobitecture," but the model also gave Villa Nurbs in Spain (see image 4) its name. Designed by Enric Ruiz-Geli (b.1968) and his practice, Cloud 9, the villa looks like a purely theoretical project—too strange to be a domestic house—which is perhaps why it remains incomplete. Although its design is courageous, Villa Nurbs has come to embody the difficulties that can emerge during attempts to realize formally complex digital architecture. Unlike Bilbao, digitality increased the cost and complexity of Villa Nurbs by necessitating bespoke design in large areas of the house.

As computer modeling has evolved, it has transformed from a tool that enables architects to model their formal intentions to one that can help generate designs. Chief among these approaches is parametric design: the use of variable digital inputs (such as daylight, site constraints, or material costs) to inform design output (such as form, scale, or window size). One of

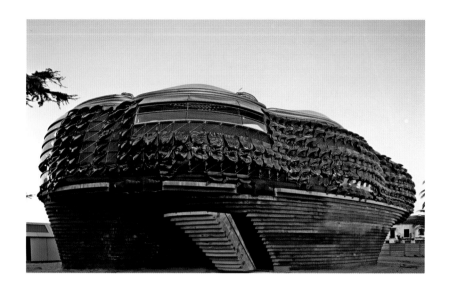

parametric design's key proponents is the co-director of Zaha Hadid Architects, Patrik Schumacher (b.1961). He goes beyond discussing parametric design as a technique and claims that Parametricism is a style, and the natural successor to Modernism. In 1998, Zaha Hadid (b.1950) won the competition to design the MAXXI Museum in Rome (2010; see p.528), prior to the established use of generative digital design within her practice. However, Schumacher describes MAXXI as a "built manifesto demonstrating the capacity of Parametricism." The architecture of Hadid's practice increasingly employs parametric techniques in order to find form and to enable its realization. The architects frequently create digital models that parametrically link the smallest details, such as cladding panels or formwork for casting concrete, to the overall form of the building, so that the model is responsive and adaptable to the slightest design change.

The interconnectivity of what previously had been separate parts of the design process is for many the most interesting aspect of contemporary digital culture. Historian of digital architecture Mario Carpo believes that BIM (building information modeling), a type of networked design system, will be the next direction for twenty-first-century digital architecture. The more formal era of digital architecture appears to be over, and, in the era of the social web, digital architecture is more about communication than form.

One example of the technologies that might enable this more communicative, participatory digital architecture is the robotic architecture that is being developed by Swiss architects Fabio Gramazio (b.1970) and Matthias Kohler (b.1968). Their digital architecture aspires toward an architecture that is not built allographically by builders but autographically by a direct connection of digital design and fabrication processes. Another possibility that would allow this is three-dimensional printed buildings, which are frequently discussed but not yet practical. Gramazio & Kohler's robots are closer to reality. For the Gantenbein Vineyard facade in Switzerland (see image 5), the robots acted as bricklayers, developing a non-standard brick facade with a high degree of precision and articulation. This allowed the design to be re-created faithfully in the construction of the building. From the start of digital architecture, the desire has been to make a responsive building, as demonstrated in the Fun Palace, and one that is highly expressive and accurate, as epitomized by the Guggenheim Museum Bilbao. With technologies such as robotic bricklayers, the adaptive and networked architecture of those early cyberneticians might be within the grasp of the current generation of digital architects. **GS**

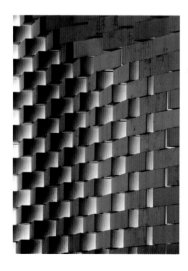

Yokohama International Port Terminal 1995

FOREIGN OFFICE ARCHITECTS 1993–2011

Yokohama International
Port (now Ferry) Terminal,
Yokohama Bay, Japan

NAVIGATOR

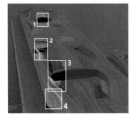

In 1994, an international competition was announced to redesign the Osanbashi Pier as a modern infrastructural gateway for Japan—the Yokohama International Port (now Ferry) Terminal. Foreign Office Architects (FOA)—Farshid Moussavi and Alejandro Zaera-Polo—won with their design for a multifunctioning landscape that fused the typologies of harbor and garden. The formal concept of the building was to unify the wholeness of Modernism and the fragmentation of Deconstructivism in a new continuous structure that FOA characterized as "coherent differentiations." This was achieved by the sinuous timber cladding—curving and folding to form a landscape—that incorporates all major elements of the building and creates the effect of it hardly seeming like a building at all; there are few positions where the viewer is able to read it as such. To the pedestrian it is a landscape garden, and to the seaborne passenger a pier, whereas to the inhabitant it is a continuous infrastructural shed. FOA's descriptions of the building are notable for the absence of references to the digital, yet digital modeling allowed the architects to achieve the complexity required to form all elements of the building into one continuous surface. The Yokohama International Ferry Terminal is one of the most successful examples of early digital architecture and its formal attributes pointed toward the possibilities for the digital "blobs" that were to follow. **GS**

👁 FOCAL POINTS

1 FLOOR/DOOR/WINDOW

The floor is cut and folded to form what the architects call "bifurcations" that are used as windows and doors to the lower level. Critic Charles Jencks described these as providing a continuity to the experience of moving around the building "like the way origami folds unite a complex pattern into a single sheet of paper."

2 SLOPING TIMBER FLOOR

Foreign Office Architects used its sloping timber floor to achieve vertical circulation across the building: the "continuous floor" forms a large, "global" unified landscape with moments of "local" differentiation. The technique was memorably employed by Frank Lloyd Wright (1867–1959) in the Solomon R. Guggenheim Museum in New York to create "one great space on a single continuous floor."

3 CONTINUOUS STRUCTURE

The structure of the terminal is conceived as a system of arched elements that span across the width of the building. They demonstrate the move away from individual elements, such as walls and columns, toward what FOA referred to as "singularities within a material continuum." This structural strategy dovetails the formal ambitions of early curvilinear digital architecture with an intelligent defense against earthquakes.

4 "CONFETTI" FURNITURE

The positioning of the rooftop furniture is used to accentuate the complexity of the landscape and make it feel like a naturally inhabited field. "Confetti" was a term used by FOA's mentor Rem Koolhaas (b.1944) to describe the compositionally chaotic arrangement of amenities in his competition entry for the Parc de la Villette, Paris, in 1982.

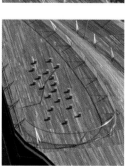

▲ The main interior spaces of the building are housed in long, undulating, column-free shallow halls created by a structure of spanning steel ribs.

DIGITAL NATURE

The Surrealists proposed "organic flexibility" in the 1920s, and it appeared in embryonic form in the work of Antoni Gaudí (1852–1926), at Casa Milà in Barcelona (below), for example. Yet, it was with the advent of digital tools that natural forms truly became part of an architect's vocabulary. Frank Gehry repeatedly employs organic forms, such as fish. Lars Spuybroek and Peter Eisenman were inspired by the fluidity of water, just as Leonardo da Vinci had been 500 years previously. Enric Ruiz-Geli's design for the Villa Nurbs began with the form of melting ice nodules. In his writing on nonlinear architecture in the 1990s, critic Charles Jencks was keen to link the possibilities of digital design to the re-creation of natural complexity. He saw the Yokohama terminal as mimicry of a natural landscape, but one that is artificially manipulated in order to bend it to the needs of the building, thereby taking our impulse toward the re-creation of nature to its apotheosis.

MAXXI Museum 2010

ZAHA HADID b.1950

MAXXI Museum,
Rome, Italy

The MAXXI Museum in Rome was completed in 2010 as a new home for contemporary art and architecture. It was built in the Flaminio neighborhood, which until that point was best known as the host of the 1960 Olympic Games. Inspired by two differing grid plans of its urban context, the building's pattern draws the grids into the site and distorts them to create a series of complex spaces and vistas. The effect is less a compartmentalized gallery, rather a field of continuous gallery experience throughout the interwoven volumes. This knotted geometry of the overall form can be most clearly read by the visitor in the form of ribbonlike concrete ribs that weave through the galleries, opening up views to the Roman sky. The in-situ cast concrete is the dominant material and Zaha Hadid perfected a detailed construction that gives the powerful appearance of a single concrete exoskeleton, but in reality conceals thermal insulation breaks. The MAXXI could be described as one of the purest manifestations of Hadid's Deconstructivism. It could also be seen as a work that clearly shows the nonlinearity of early digital architecture. Although it does not share the bloblike forms of more digitally formal architecture, it can be read as a manifesto of parametric design. **GS**

◆ NAVIGATOR

👁 FOCAL POINTS

1 IN-SITU CAST CONCRETE
The huge concrete exterior walls were cast on site with a self-compacting mix to achieve their complex geometries. Hadid perfected this method in the digital design of the BMW factory in Leipzig (2005) and the Phaeno Science Center in Wolfsburg (2005).

2 PILOTI
These columns were favorites of Le Corbusier (1887–1965) and one of the totems of the Modernist Movement. Hadid uses them as she does compositional lines in her paintings: to achieve a "field of buildings by intertwining exterior and interior spaces."

3 CANTILEVERS
In order to achieve the sinuous form of Hadid's concept, the building arrives at some extraordinary structural moments. Most notable is the emphatic top floor gallery with its view over Rome, its enormous concrete shear walls allowing this acrobatic feat.

◄ The deep concrete ribs of the main internal spaces inside the gallery are partly formal (they accentuate the curvilinearity of the building) and partly environmental (they filter the light coming into the gallery). Their slender concrete forms give them an elegance and demonstrate Hadid's mastery of her material.

🕐 ARCHITECT PROFILE

1950–80
Zaha Hadid was born in Baghdad, Iraq. She left in the 1970s and went to study at the Architectural Association in London in 1972; she was awarded the Diploma Prize in 1977. After graduating, she took up a partnership with her former tutor Rem Koolhaas at his practice, the Office for Metropolitan Architecture (OMA). She also taught with him at the Architectural Association. She left OMA in 1980 to set up her own practice.

1981–84
Hadid entered a competition to design the Irish Taoiseach's (Head of the Irish Government) Residence. The beautiful, fragmentary paintings she produced of this and subsequent projects, such as the Peak Leisure Club in Hong Kong in 1983, became typical of her early Deconstructivist approach.

1985–93
Zaha Hadid Architects began to build its radical ideas with the construction of Vitra Fire Station in Weil am Rhein, Germany (1990–93). The first of Hadid's major projects, the building captured the 'frozen movement' of her early unbuilt work.

1994–present
Hadid and her practice increasingly digitized their design methods as their commissions began to increase in size and complexity. They have since transformed themselves into established leaders of digital architecture. Hadid's practice designed the Rosenthal Center for Contemporary Art in Cincinnati, which opened in 2003. In 2004, Hadid was the first woman to be awarded the prestigious Pritzker Architecture Prize. She won the Stirling Prize for the MAXXI Museum in 2010.

DECONSTRUCTIVISM

In 1988, the annus mirabilis for Deconstruction, a symposium at the Tate Gallery, London, and exhibitions at the Museum of Modern Art, New York, and the Institute of Contemporary Arts, London, independently introduced the tenets and the architects of the movement that became known as Deconstructivism. At the International Symposium on Deconstruction, architect Bernard Tschumi (b.1944) declared: "We inhabit a fractured space of accidents." His words summarized the impetus behind the nascent movement. A development of Postmodern architecture (known as Deconstructionism in Europe and Deconstructivism in the United States), the movement emerged within architectural theory and practice in the 1980s, in opposition to the ordered reasoning of Modernism and to what many saw as the nostalgic historicism of Postmodernism. Calling into question "the very values of harmony, unity, and stability," Deconstructivism interrogates and manipulates built form to present a chaotic, dislocated and predictable architecture that disturbs tradition by being deliberately unfamiliar, alienating, and unsettling.

Deconstructionism and Deconstructivism allude to different sources of influence. A key point of departure for the former was French philosopher Jacques Derrida, founder of Deconstruction theory. It was through his involvement in the design of Tschumi's Parc de la Villette (1998; see p.534),

(1998; see p.534),

KEY EVENTS

1976	1978	1982	1983	1988	1988
Jacques Derrida's text "Of Grammatology," within which he first introduces his Deconstruction theory, is translated into English.	Frank Gehry begins the first phase of alterations to the Gehry Residence, Santa Monica, one of the earliest Deconstructivist buildings.	Zaha Hadid gains prominence with her design for The Peak, a leisure club overlooking Hong Kong. It was never built.	Bernard Tschumi wins a competition to design the Parc de la Villette, having consulted Derrida on the development of his design proposal.	The International Symposium on Deconstruction is held at the Tate Gallery, London on March 26.	Deyan Sudjic curates "Metropolis: New British Architecture and the City" at the Institute of Contemporary Arts, London. It runs from August 4 to October 1.

the first architectural work to investigate Deconstructionist concepts of disassociation, that Deconstructionism gained prominence. Pivotal in the development of the latter was the "Deconstructivist Architecture" exhibition at New York's Museum of Modern Art in 1988. Curated by architects Philip Johnson (1906–2005) and Mark Wigley (b.1956), the exhibition of models and drawings by seven international architects—Tschumi, Coop Himmelb(l)au (est. 1968), Peter Eisenman (b.1932), Frank Gehry (b.1929), Zaha Hadid (b.1950), Daniel Libeskind (b.1946), and Rem Koolhaas (b.1944)—marked what the curators called "the emergence of a new sensibility in architecture."

The exhibition was located within a historical context: it introduced the Deconstructivists through a selection of Russian Constructivist art from the museum's collection, inferring that the art movement was central to the development of the architecture. However, in the preface to the exhibition catalogue, Johnson acknowledged that several of the younger architects were unaware of the similarities to Constructivism, and therefore of any formal comparisons that could be made. Of the seven, only Hadid was known to have clearly referenced the work of the Constructivists (particularly El Lissitzky, Kazimir Malevich, and Alexander Rodchenko). Other key influences, such as the impact of Cubism on Gehry, of Expressionism on Coop Himmelb(l)au, and of Lebbeus Woods (1940–2012) on Hadid, were not acknowledged.

Johnson emphasized in the preface that, unlike the museum's "Modern Architecture: International Exhibition," which he co-curated in 1932, the purpose of "Deconstructivist Architecture" was not to proclaim a new style or movement; instead, he described the exhibition as "a confluence of a few important architects' work of the years since 1980 that shows a similar approach with very similar forms as an outcome." Other architects who were not included in the exhibition but who are sometimes associated with Deconstructivism include Thom Mayne (b.1944) of Morphosis (also influenced by Woods), Eric Owen Moss (b.1943). and Hajime Yatsuka (b.1948).

It is difficult to identify common ground in the supposed roles of Deconstruction theory and Russian Constructivism, and although the architects exhibiting at the Museum of Modern Art have apparent commonalities in the appearance of their designs, their influences and theoretical groundings vary. However, like Tschumi, Eisenman was influenced by Derrida, and the pair collaborated on an entry for the Parc de la Villette competition. Eisenman's first major public building, the Wexner Center for the Arts (see image 1) in Columbus, Ohio, was directly informed by the city's street grids and the campus of the Ohio State University. Situated on the boundary between these conflicting urban geometries, the building alternates between the grids, with inevitable conflict highlighted by Eisenman's inclusion of a white scaffoldlike structure, intended as a challenge to the symbolism of shelter. Like many of his Deconstructivist contemporaries, Eisenman is often accused of overlooking the

1 **Wexner Center for the Arts (1989)**
Peter Eisenman
Ohio State University,
Columbus, Ohio, USA

2 **UFA Cinema Center (1998)**
Coop Himmelb(l)au
Dresden, Germany

1988	1989	1994	1997	1998	2001
"Deconstructivist Architecture" is curated by Mark Wigley and Philip Johnson at the Museum of Modern Art. It runs from June 23 to August 30.	Peter Eisenman's Wexner Center for the Arts is considered to be the first major piece of Deconstructivist architecture built in the United States.	Tschumi's *Architecture and Disjunction* is published. It is a collection of his essays, including key texts on Parc de la Villette and Deconstructive theory.	Eisenman and Derrida publish *Chora L Works*, documenting their Parc de la Villette project through text and drawings.	Coop Himmelb(l)au's UFA Cinema Center in Dresden is completed, challenging the monofunctional public building types found in European cities.	The Libeskind Building at the Jewish Museum, Berlin opens, after being designed in 1988 and completed in 1999. It is Libeskind's first international success.

need for functionality in favor of what *The Architectural Review* (1994) deemed "fatuous arbitrariness." But that which is fatuous to some can be interpreted by others as a delightful, functional, faux-folly building. Although the Wexner closed from 2002 to 2005 for extensive repairs (as did Eisenman's Aronoff Center for Design and Art (1996) in Cincinnati, Ohio, which was reported by writer Lawrence Biemiller in 2010 to be "deconstructing itself"), building robustness is not a problem unique to Deconstructivism.

Coop Himmelb(l)au's UFA Cinema Center (see image 2) in Dresden, Germany, addresses the issue of public space and the manner in which it is threatened within European cities. Drawing on an urban design concept defined by employing diagonals and tangents to generate a 'dynamic spatial sequence', the angular building is presented as a public space that maintains a visual conversation with the surrounding city through its visible circulation system and public passageways. Conversely, the public areas of the Libeskind Building of the Jewish Museum (see image 3) in Berlin are derived from a dislocated Star of David aligned on axes. Interior circulation routes express Libeskind's aim to evoke powerful and unsettling experiences of invisibility, emptiness, and absence through slivers of light, dead ends, and empty spaces.

Hadid's Vitra Fire Station (1993) in Weil am Rhein, Germany, draws on geometries found in its surrounding landscape. Conceived as an "alert" structure, it is representative of a freeze-frame of movement, evoking both a constant state of tension and a sense of instability, with its program elements contained between the elongated, sloping, and curved walls of its linear form. In more recent years, Hadid's forms have not only become larger, but also more daring, owing to continuous developments in engineering, technology and digital modeling, and her reliance on the parametric capabilities of Building Information Modeling software.

Before the declaration of a Deconstructivist movement in 1988, Gehry developed a unique and idiosyncratic approach to architectural design that prefigured Deconstructivism, and he did so using his family's 1920s bungalow in Santa Monica, California, as his prototype. Extended and redesigned by Gehry in 1978 and 1991, the Gehry Residence (see image 4) has a multitude of subtractions and additions, deconstructions and constructions. Experimenting with cheap, off-the-shelf materials, Gehry prioritized sheet metal, plywood, and chain-link fencing. The extension wraps the exterior of the original house, purposefully creating tension and demarcation between construction phases.

Gehry's house can be seen as a foil to 708 House (see image 5), a one-story Case Study House (designed by James H. Caughey in 1948) in Pacific Palisades, California, which Moss remodeled for his family. Its angles and unexpected juxtapositions are deemed by the Los Angeles Conservancy to be "an exuberant testament to the lighter side of the Deconstructivist style," and both houses create a compulsive typology of "subversive suburbanism."

In an interview in 1980, Gehry stated, "I don't believe you can jump out of your time," a declaration that explains in part the architect's early preference for prosaic material and his later pursuit of metal-clad digital form, such as the Guggenheim Museum (1997) in Bilbao and the Walt Disney Concert Hall (2003) in Los Angeles. The success of the Guggenheim (dubbed the "metallic flower" by Gehry) spurred a copycat global public architecture building boom, called the "irritable Bilbao Syndrome" by those who realized that the boom was often a bust in terms of architectural quality. Coop Himmelb(l)au's Deconstructivist John S. and James L. Knight Building (2007) at Akron Art Museum, Ohio, was critiqued by Martin Filler as "formally chaotic, haphazardly detailed, instantly dated-looking," with "strenuously flamboyant yet oddly inhospitable" interior spaces. "Provincial," he wrote, and far from being "the next Bilbao."

Many question the premise that linguistic philosophy can be applied to architecture. Others view Deconstructivism's dismissal of history and aggressive treatment of the senses as being destructive to the discipline of architecture. It is no surprise, then, that several of the architects associated with the exhibition of 1988 have distanced themselves from the Deconstructivist label. Even Tschumi aired his misgivings, and Gehry, too, denies that he is a Deconstructivist. Although Deconstructivism has been subject to extensive criticism, the movement has produced significant architecture. It is speculative to assume that the Museum of Modern Art exhibition alone galvanized the careers of its architects, yet several of the seven (in particular Gehry, Hadid, and Koolhaas) became household names and were referred to as "starchitects"—a term that later became a pejorative. Koolhaas told *Der Spiegel* in 2008, "[Starchitect] gives the impression of referring to people with no heart, egomaniacs who are constantly doing their thing, completely divorced from any context." The snide observer might hear unintended irony, but others will celebrate starchitects such as Gehry, who showed that, in the right hands, suburbia and urbia could become deconstructed wonderlands. **KS**

3 **Libeskind Building (1999)**
Daniel Libeskind
Jewish Museum, Berlin, Germany

4 **Gehry Residence (1978/1991)**
Frank Gehry
Santa Monica, California, USA

5 **708 House (1982)**
Eric Owen Moss
Pacific Palisades,
Los Angeles, California, USA

Parc de la Villette 1998

BERNARD TSCHUMI b.1944

Parc de la Villette,
Paris, France

⬖ NAVIGATOR

Having participated in the original and unrealized Parc de la Villette design competition in 1976, Bernard Tschumi revised his proposal for the second competition in 1983, and won. Constructed between 1984 and 1998, Parc de la Villette was part of a large-scale architectural program—initiated by François Mitterrand, French president from 1981 to 1995—to provide Paris with modern monuments that were symbolic of France's leadership in economy, politics, and art. Parc de la Villette was designed to be an "urban park for the twenty-first century," housing workshops, playgrounds, museums, a gymnasium, bathing facilities, and spaces for exhibitions and concerts. Influenced by Jacques Derrida's literary Deconstruction theory, Tschumi aimed to create a park that had no coherent meaning. There was to be "no rhythm, no synthesis, no order," stated Tschumi. Each visitor's experience would be unique. Largely ignoring existing structures, the nonhierarchical scheme overlays a series of theoretical lines (avenues), surfaces (planting and paving), and points (marked by thirty-five red follies) on the site, with a strong emphasis on the lack of resolution of these three systems and their intersections. The programmatic requirements for the project are located at the junctions, with a series of themed "cinematic" gardens linked by a snaking path and two covered galleries at perpendicular angles to each other. Alongside the landscape, Tschumi also designed a number of the follies. **KS**

Although they are supposed to be empty of meaning, the abstracted red follies, "with their gridded frames, geometric shapes, disdain for conventions of wall and roof, and objectlike detachment" are reminiscent of 1920s Modernism and, in terms of composition, the paintings of De Stijl.

2 WALKWAY

The walkway is one of several key paths across La Villette. The intersections of these paths provide links to other parts of the park and "unexpected encounters with unusual aspects of domesticated or 'programmed' nature." In contrast to the follies, the paths do not follow a set organizational structure.

⏱ ARCHITECT PROFILE

1944–82

Bernard Tschumi, son of well-known Swiss architect Jean Tschumi (1904–62), was born in Lausanne, Switzerland, and studied architecture in Zürich, graduating in 1969. Throughout the 1970s, he worked at the Architectural Association in London, alongside Rem Koolhaas and Elia Zenghelis (b.1937), with Zaha Hadid as one of his students. Between 1976 and 1981, he exhibited and published *The Manhattan Transcripts*, a series of architectural drawings that "aimed to offer a different reading of architecture."

1983–present

Tschumi established an office in Paris in 1983, the same year that he won the prestigious Parc de la Villette design competition. In 1994, he published a collection of theoretical essays, *Architecture and Disjunction,* which included seminal texts on topics such as Deconstructive theory. Parc de la Villette reached completion in 1998, two years after Tschumi was awarded France's Grand Prix National de l'Architecture.

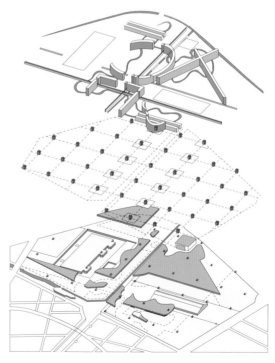

▲ Areas of deliberate conflict arise between the main north–south axis, which references the orientation of the former cattle market Grand Halle, and several of the follies, which are positioned on a differently aligned grid. The unstructured character of Parc de la Villette is one of its central features.

GREEN TOWERS

1 **Organic Building (1993)**
Gaetano Pesce
Osaka, Japan

2 **Solaris Building (2008)**
Ken Yeang
Fusionopolis, 1–North, Singapore

Many buildings are becoming distinctly shaggier. Whereas tall buildings were once characterized by sleek, smooth lines, an increasing number are becoming less defined, with hairy roofs and plants climbing up their sides. Some have "sky gardens," with shrubs, trees and even crops growing on every available horizontal surface. This movement developed particularly in Europe and started with green roofs. The idea was pioneered in Switzerland, where the city of Basel has the world's highest concentration of green roofs, thanks in part to financial incentive schemes introduced in 1996 and 2005. However, some of the largest green roofs are found in the United States, for example, on the Ford Motor Company's River Rouge Plant in Dearborn, Michigan, and the 24-acre (9.9 ha) Millennium Park, built on top of the Millennium Garage in Chicago.

The advantages of green roofs are manifold. They provide biodiversity in built-up areas; they reduce the rate of water run-off in storms; they protect roof membranes; and they help reduce temperature extremes in buildings, as well as the urban heat-island effect. Yet buildings, especially tall ones, have limited roof area relative to their overall surface. Attention has therefore turned to vegetating the walls. "Living walls" were initially controversial, not only because they require intensive maintenance and watering, but also because failures were often the result of living walls being treated as building elements

KEY EVENTS

1985	1988	1993	1995	2001	2004
Ken Yeang completes one of his early experimental bioclimatic buildings, the Roof-Roof house in Kuala Lumpur, Malaysia.	Patrick Blanc, the modern innovator of the green wall, creates his first wall at the Museum of Science and Industry in Paris.	The Consorcio Building in Santiago, Chile, by Enrique Browne and Associates, has a "double vegetal facade" on the west side that cuts heat gain.	Ken Yeang wins the Aga Khan Award for Architecture for his work on the Menara Mesiniaga (IBM headquarters) in Malaysia.	Chicago City Hall's green roof heralds the mayor's city-wide green initiative program.	Edouard François completes the nine-story Flower Tower, Paris. Plant pots, inspired by Parisian window planters, make up the main facade.

rather than as landscape. At least one infamous, costly failure is documented in London, but it is offset by successes, such as botanist Patrick Blanc's lush living wall on the Athenaeum Hotel, Piccadilly, London. There were earlier precursors to living walls, however. Architect-designed green buildings were pioneered by Edouard François (b.1958); for example, his innovative rock face-like Chateau le Lez, Montpellier, France (2000), with its seed-studded, stone-filled gabion cages. The vivid orange Organic Building in Osaka, Japan (see image 1), by Gaetano Pesce (b.1939), with its modular, plant-filled "wall pockets," is emblematic of a more decorative strand of green walls.

If the greening of buildings in temperate climates can be seen as a gradualist approach, in the tropics and Asia in particular, greening began as a treatment of the total building. Malaysian architect Ken Yeang (b.1948) pioneered this approach as the outcome of his doctoral thesis, which looked at the relationship of architecture and the biosphere. His firm, T. R. Hamzah & Yeang, designed "bioclimatic skyscrapers" using shading, form, and vegetation as strategic ventilation. Menara Boustead (1986) in Kuala Lumpur City—Yeang's first "hairy" tower—incorporated transitional spaces as a precursor to the sun-path building, Menara Mesiniaga (1992), Malaysia. Their "urban park in the sky," with vegetation running throughout the building, reached its culmination in the fifteen-story Solaris Building (see image 2), part of Fusionopolis, Singapore (Phase 1 designed by Kisho Kurokawa, 1994–2007), with continuously spiraling roof gardens, culminating in a green roof.

A city-state with a growing population and an aspiration to increase the proportion of green space, Singapore is addressing seemingly conflicting needs through densification of housing and the creation of parks both between and within its buildings. With a tropical climate that encourages rapid plant growth, it is an ideal laboratory for such experimental buildings. Projects such as Oasia Downtown (2014), a mixed-use tower designed by WOHA, have a living green facade and a series of sky gardens. Designed with large openings to facilitate vegetation, the building has a "green plot ratio" of 750 percent. The public spaces have high-volume, low-speed fans to enhance comfort in the sky gardens. In a city where most people prefer to be in air-conditioned spaces whenever possible, these designs make being outside in a tropical environment cool again.

Other cities are also going green to address densification and to create biological habitats. Milan's twin residential towers, Bosco Verticale (2014; see p.540) by Stefano Boeri (b.1956), is a defiant act of urban reforestation, with tree balconies and outposts reminiscent of "tree tenants" on Lucca's medieval towers. The online magazine *Leaf Review* pegs construction costs at just 5 percent in excess of traditional tower builds, and described Bosco Verticale in 2013 as representing the future—no longer a green facade or wall, but "nature entering the built environment." **RSI**

Flower Tower 2004
EDOUARD FRANÇOIS b.1958

Flower Tower,
Paris, France

The notion of using a window box or potted plants to enhance the view from a summer window is a common one. With his Flower Tower, French architect and urban planner Edouard François seized on the concept and turned it into an extraordinary architectural statement. The Flower Tower is one of a number of residential blocks that surround a park in the urban regeneration zone of Hauts Malesherbes, Paris, masterplanned by Christian Portzamparc (b.1944). Three of its sides are covered with balconies that have large white "flowerpots" set into them, planted with bamboo. The bamboo both filters the light and provides a constant rustling sound, disguising the noise from nearby rail lines and roads.

The overall effect is far more coherent than a random collection of window boxes would be, although perhaps a little less disciplined than the architect had hoped, as the bamboo often grows beyond story height and overlaps the balcony above. Internally the building is also unusual in that there are no structural dividing walls, so the social housing residents can arrange their space in any way that they wish. Whether or not they feel, as is the intention, that their homes are a vertical extension of the park, they are certainly living in an unusual and intriguing home. **RSI**

⊕ NAVIGATOR

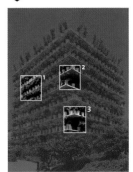

👁 FOCAL POINTS

1 BAMBOO

The 380 concrete "flowerpots" that adorn the balconies are planted with bamboo. It is not a regularly flowering plant, but when bamboo does flower, the plants tend to bloom all together and the effect is quite dramatic. Flowering can weaken the clumps and it is common for bamboo plants to die after flowering.

2 DUCTAL

Ductal is an ultra-high performance concrete developed by the cement manufacturer Lafarge. The material's great ductility allows it to be used in slender sections, most often without any reinforcement. Its use in the construction of the Flower Tower balconies was one of its earliest applications.

3 WATERING SYSTEM

The bamboo plants are fertilized and watered automatically by artificial stems that run inside the metal balustrades of each story. The system uses recycled rain water, and its automated design means that minimal care for the plants is required from residents of the building.

🕐 ARCHITECT PROFILE

1958–98

Edouard François trained at the Ecole Nationale des Beaux-Arts in Paris and the Ecole Nationale des Ponts et Chaussées, and has been an architect and urban planner since 1986. He set up his own practice in 1998, which today has offices in France, India, and New Zealand.

1999–2008

François established his committment to sustainability and a particular interest in incorporating nature in his buildings. One of his first projects was The Building that Grows in Montpellier (2000), an apartment building with gabion walls in which vegetation was encouraged to establish. In 2004, he completed the Ventilation Chimney in Paris's high-rise business district La Defense, where he clad an unsightly ventilation shaft in patinated copper and trained morning glory plants to climb up it each summer.

2009–10

In 2009, François designed the 262-foot (80 m) Planted Tower of Nantes, which, in contrast to the monoculture of the Flower Tower, is wrapped in plants from around the globe, gathered by the Botanical Gardens of Nantes. However, vegetation is not the only means that the architect has used to make the exteriors of his buildings unusual. For the Coming Out housing project in Grenoble (2010), he placed the insulation on the outside of the building, covered only by a lightweight waterproof skin. Despite not being a specifically vegetated building, Coming Out also features trees planted within its footprint, space for window boxes, and mesh on which climbers are encouraged to grow.

2011–present

François continues to explore the possibilities of green vegetal facades with projects such as the M6B2 Tower of Biodiversity in Paris (2015) and the residential towers for Gurgaon in India (commissioned 2013), both of which incorporate wild plants. On France's northern coast, his Hills of Honfleur (2015) is a sustainable retail center that is largely hidden under landscaped strips.

Bosco Verticale 2014
STEFANO BOERI b.1956

Bosco Verticale,
Milan, Italy

The Bosco Verticale is intended to be a vertical forest. Two forests, in fact, as there are two towers—360 feet (110 m) and 246 feet (75 m) high. Hundreds of trees and thousands of shrubs create the "forests" that are planted on the balconies. However high up the building, people have shade from the Mediterranean sun. Part of the architect's plan to increase urban green space, the trees filter microparticles, absorb carbon dioxide, and provide cooling and acoustic shielding. How the trees will fare over time is problematic, though; large trees are difficult to transplant and replacement will be labor intensive. However, there is a successful precedent, albeit one where crown growth is not restricted by a balcony above. Vancouver in Canada has a 37 foot (11 m) Pin Oak in a giant bowl cantilevered from the nineteenth story of a waterside building. Planted in 1987, it commemorates the 200-foot (61 m) crown height achieved by the city's old-growth forests. The oak has weathered extreme storms, but the real issues are maintenance, access, and longevity. Its pot limits growth and it will never achieve its 100 foot (30.5 m) potential; these are salient points to consider for the caretakers of the trees of Bosco Verticale. **RSI**

⬡ NAVIGATOR

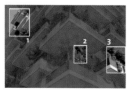

◉ FOCAL POINTS

1 TERRACES

Terraces on the apartments vary in size and measure up to 9 ⅞ feet (3 m) deep. The planting, which includes more than 1,000 species in total, will not only provide a pleasing environment, but will also ensure that there is no overlook between terraces.

2 GLAZING

The employment of full-height glazing in the two buildings gives a feeling of lightness and transparency. It also maximizes the views across the city and to the balconies. For residents, the result is a sense of floating in an airborne vertical forest.

3 "FOREST" OF TREES

Each apartment features a balcony planted with trees. Collectively, these will envelop the entire building's perimeter in a "forest" (of 900 trees and thousands of shrubs and flowering plants), covering an area equivalent to 107,639 square feet (10,000 sq m).

◀ The towers are wrapped in irregular reinforced-concrete, cantilevered balconies that extend 11 feet (3.5 m) outward. The number of trees in each vertical forest is equivalent to 75,347 square feet (7,000 sq m) of forest on flat land.

ALGAE CLADDING PANELS

Engineers Arup have designed the world's first building that will derive all its power from algae. Growing in glass louvers, the micro-algae contained within specially designed transparent cladding panels generate electricity. Constructed around the BIQ building (right) in Hamburg, the facade formed part of an international building show in 2013. Sunny weather encouraged the algae to grow, providing shade when needed. At regular intervals, the algae were "harvested" and fermented to fuel a biogas plant that generated electricity for the building from a special technical room. The bioreactor facade was also used to heat hot water for the building. Algae may be less attractive than trees, but they have great "green" potential.

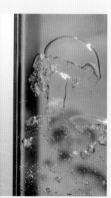

TALL TOWERS

1 **Burj Khalifa (2010)**
Skidmore, Owings and Merrill
Dubai, United Arab Emirates

2 **Taipei 101 (2004)**
C. Y. Lee & Partners
Taipei, Taiwan, China

S upertall buildings are some of the most complex engineering structures
that exist, yet in terms of purpose they could not be simpler. Their role is
merely to be taller than their neighbors. In no other form of building is
the superlative so important—who cares about the building with the largest
area, the deepest basement, or the thinnest cladding? With tall buildings, height
is everything, which is why the Council on Tall Buildings and Urban Habitats, an
international organization based at the Illinois Institute of Technology, Chicago,
maintains a competitive league table of tallness with various tall categories.
The supertall category starts at 984 feet (300 m) in height, and the term
"megatall" was coined by the council for those that exceed 1,967 feet (600 m).

One of the tallest buildings in the world, the Burj Khalifa (see image 1)
in Dubai, was completed in 2010. Some 2,717 feet (828 m) high, with 163
floors, it contains the popular mixed-use model for extremely tall buildings:
office, residential, and hotel. The same pattern was used for the 1,004-foot
(306 m) high Shard (see p.546) in London, designed by Renzo Piano (b.1937)
and completed in 2012, becoming Western Europe's tallest building (until
Foster + Partner's twin towers at Hermitage Plaza in Paris is completed by the
projected date of 2016). The mixed-use template means that offices occupy

KEY EVENTS

1989	1997	1998	2001	2004	2005
The U.S. Bank Tower in Los Angeles, by Henry N. Cobb (b.1926), becomes the tallest building in the world to have a helipad on its roof.	Commerzbank Tower is completed in Frankfurt's central business district. Designed by Foster + Partners, it is Germany's tallest building.	The Petronas Twin Towers in Kuala Lumpur, Malaysia, designed by Cesar Pelli & Associates, reach 1,483 feet (452m).	The terrorist attack on buildings One and Two at the World Trade Center in New York makes them the tallest buildings ever destroyed.	Taipei 101, by C. Y. Lee & Partners, opens in Taiwan, with a height of 1,667 feet (508 m).	Q1 Tower, Gold Coast, Australia, designed by Atelier SDG for Sunland Group, becomes one of the world's tallest residential towers at 1,058 feet (322 m).

the lower floors, with prestige views at higher floors usually reserved for hotels. Residential apartments at the pinnacle are a superior use of the smaller footprint (since most towers taper), and reflect the decreased residential demands on internal transport versus commercial.

Elevators are one of the elements that make the construction of towers difficult. Because the cost of construction is high, developers need to maximize usable floor area. Yet they find themselves filling their towers with essential infrastructure that consumes footprint. Structures need to be strong enough to withstand weight and to not buckle. They must also resist wind loadings, fire, and, in some parts of the world, earthquakes. Taipei 101 (see image 2) in Taiwan, for example, features a huge suspended ball designed to act as a damper in an earthquake. Structures also need to be rigid enough to prevent excessive sway at the top. Even when sway is safe, people are unlikely to pay millions of dollars for a penthouse apartment that makes them feel seasick during storms.

Moving people is an additional challenge. Tenants, hotel guests, and owners of apartments do not want to wait for elevators. While the invention of the elevator was the driving force behind the construction of the first really tall buildings in New York and Chicago, the technology has developed greatly since Elisha Otis developed the elevator brake in 1853. Elevators are faster and there are better management techniques, with dedicated elevators to serve banks of floors swiftly. The heavy weight of steel cable is, however, self-limiting, making it necessary to use more than one elevator to reach the top of tall towers. Elevator manufacturers are developing carbon-fiber core ropes, with high-friction coatings that greatly reduce cable weight, which will allow up to double the current length of a steel cable. Implementation will reduce the need for elevator banks and will increase speed, although speed limitations to avoid adverse impact on the human ear will still need to be taken into consideration. Buildings also transport electricity and water. Water usually requires breaks and pumping at intermediate levels, because the pressure of a single column of water is immense. And all this must be achieved in a way that not only takes up minimal space, but also does not interfere with views. For buildings in whole or part used as offices, it is necessary to create column-free spaces for open-plan working, resulting in a range of structural solutions as well as sculptural forms.

Can tall towers be green, too? In 2013, Skidmore, Owings and Merrill (SOM)—an engineering firm responsible for many of the world's most advanced skyscrapers—announced its Timber Tower Research Project, to investigate the viability of a forty-two-story mass timber-framed building. Its benchmark for the project is the forty-two-story concrete Dewitt Chestnut Apartments (1965) in Chicago, designed for SOM by Fazlur Khan (1929–82), using his revolutionary "framed-tube" design. SOM's timber prototype is a hybrid system of mass timber, concrete, and steel that is intended to reduce the design's carbon footprint by 60 to 75 percent. **RSI**

2010	2010	2012	2012	2013	2013
The mixed-use Burj Khalifa in Dubai, by Skidmore, Owings and Merrill, becomes the world's tallest building with a height of 2,717 feet (828 m).	Singapore's Marina Bay Sands complex opens. An ensemble of three towers, each 636 feet (194 m) tall, it is topped by the world's highest infinity pool.	The Makkah Clock Royal Tower (see p.544) in Mecca is completed. Designed by Dar al-Handasah Shair and Partners, its final height is 2,000 feet (610 m).	The Shard in London (see p.546), designed by Renzo Piano, becomes the tallest building in Western Europe at 1,004 feet (306 m).	One World Trade Center, New York, is topped out. Its spire is 1,776 feet (541 m) high, a symbolic reference to the year of the U.S. Declaration of Independence.	Construction begins on Kingdom Tower, Jeddah, Saudi Arabia. Designed by Adrian Smith + Gordon Gill Architecture, its estimated height is 3,281 feet (1,000 m).

Makkah Clock Royal Tower 2012
DAR AL-HANDASAH SHAIR AND PARTNERS

Makkah Clock Royal Tower,
Mecca, Saudi Arabia

The Abraj Al-Bait is a complex of nineteen high-rise towers of luxury hotels in Mecca. The tallest of these is the Makkah Clock Royal Tower, at completion the second-tallest building in the world. Topped with four giant clocks, its size and eclectic references were described by *Building Magazine* as "a dystopian joint venture between Madame Tussauds and Batman." The 2,000-foot (610 m) tall Makkah tower houses a five-star hotel, but the most noticeable feature is the four-sided clock, which has a light display above it announcing the five daily calls to prayer. The clock faces are the largest in the world and have to withstand the desert's extreme temperature variations. German company SL Rasch designed the entire upper part of the tower housing the clock to adhere to strict weight limits. The strict weight restriction was imposed on the superstructure because the lower part of the building was already under construction when the decision was made to top it with the clocks. The tower is as much a symbol as a building. It houses the highest hotel rooms in the world, and for those with the best rooms, a direct view of Islam's holiest place, the Kaaba. **RSI**

👁 FOCAL POINTS

1 CRESCENT

A gold crescent tops the pinnacle of the tower. The building has a prayer room, capable of accommodating 10,000 people, for pilgrims undertaking the Hajj. However, for those wanting something more exclusive, the crescent, also the largest ever built, houses the world's tallest prayer room.

▲ The view from the crescent located on the top of the clock tower offers a panorama of the city of Mecca, including the Great Mosque.

2 CLOCK

The 130-foot (40 m) clock is said to be visible from 10½ miles (17 km) away. Swabian clockmaker Perrot built up the hands of the clock from layers of carbon fiber, up to 150 in some parts. The hands weigh a total of 12 tons and the drive that powers them weighs 21 tons. It is the tallest clock drive in the world.

3 OTHER TOWERS

The Makkah Clock Royal Tower has 120 floors. The other towers in the Abraj Al-Bait complex—with heights ranging from 787 feet (240 m) to 853 feet (260 m)—have between forty-two and forty-eight floors. In most cities, the shorter towers would be sizeable structures in their own right. The other towers house residences, hotels, and a shopping mall.

ICONOCLASM

Mecca's twenty-first-century transformation has included changes to accommodate an increase in the number of pilgrims. Wahhabism, the Saudi state religion, rejects icon and idol worship, a view that enables developers to raze historic sites, but iconoclasm is global. In China, loss of historic architecture is allied to commercial development. The Galaxy Soho development (below) in Beijing dwarfs nearby historic hutongs and was described by a local conservation center as a "typical unfortunate example [of] the destruction of Beijing old town." **DJ**

The Shard 2012
RENZO PIANO b.1937

The Shard, London Bridge,
London, England

The Shard was, for a brief period, the tallest building in Europe at 1,004 feet (306 m). It sits above London Bridge station, but on the "wrong" side of the River Thames to be considered in the City of London. The tower was the brainchild of developer Irvine Sellar, who was determined to kick-start a development now known as the London Bridge City Quarter. Italian architect Renzo Piano compared the tapering glass-clad structure to a glass spire, and the name "Shard" came from derogatory comments from conservation group English Heritage, which said it would be "a shard of glass through the heart of London." The tower contains a mixture of uses. Starting from the bottom they are: retail, offices, restaurants, hotel, apartments, viewing gallery, and the uninhabited spire itself. Occupying the equivalent of fourteen floors, the spire has been described as a splintered crown and as a cake-icing nozzle. Initially intended to house an eco-cooling device, its role is now purely visual. Although the height of the Shard was reduced because of the concerns of air-traffic controllers, the structure is a major presence in London; its height is emphasized by its distance from the cluster of towers across the river. As intended by Piano, the glazing helps the Shard to disappear on gray days, but its bulk tends to become intrusive at ground level, where its circumference is daunting to navigate. **RSI**

◆ NAVIGATOR

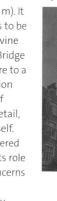

👁 FOCAL POINTS

1 SPIRE
The spire was prefabricated from 800 pieces of steel, weighing nearly 500 tons. One hundred crane lifts were needed to lift all the elements into position. A dry run was done near the fabricator's works to ensure that it all fitted together and to avoid any nasty surprises when working at height.

2 CLADDING
Designed to be as transparent as possible, but also to perform well thermally, the cladding is of low-iron laminated glass, with a colorless low-emissivity coating to reduce the reflection of infra-red light back into the building. The panes oversail the glazing beads and butt up against each other for a flush finish.

3 WINTER GARDENS
Occupants have access to fresh air through the winter gardens that are on every floor. Placed where the angles of the Shard meet, these areas have windows that open. They are separated from the rest of the floor plate by single-glazed partitions so as not to impair the efficiency of the air conditioning.

⏱ ARCHITECT PROFILE

1937–71
Born in Genoa in northern Italy to a family of builders, which gave him a lifelong interest in the technology of building, Renzo Piano studied at Milan Polytechnic, graduating in 1964. After early years spent working with architects such as Louis Kahn (1901–74), Piano formed an association with Richard Rogers (b.1933). Together they designed what is still probably the best-known building by either: the Centre Pompidou in Paris, which opened in 1971.

1972–present
In his diverse portfolio, Piano has always explored a fascination with materials and making, as well as with technology. He has built all over the world, and designed most types of buildings, ranging from Kansai Airport in Japan (1994) to the Jean-Marie Tjibaou Cultural Center in New Caledonia (1998). Piano is one of the most admired architects in the world, recognized by awards such as the Royal Institute of British Architects Gold Medal in 1989 and the Pritzker Architecture Prize in 1998.

▲ Occupying the sixty-eighth to the seventy-second floors, the viewing platform is so high that it tends to flatten out London.

NEW VERNACULAR

The words "kitsch," "flamboyant," "vulgar," and "farce" appear regularly in publications of the late twentieth and twenty-first centuries as code for architecture that relies heavily on motifs and ideas from the local landscape and history. These buildings are not vernacular (local materials, local labor, highly functional, suitable to location, built by "amateurs"). However, local references—an all but mandatory requirement of many Western planners and local governments keen to prove that their new builds have meaningful links to their landscape and history—has accelerated the vernacular meme.

In order to win commissions, architects often pursue the vernacular meme, in which surface ciphers prevail like hobo code in the Great Depression of the 1930s, when down-and-outs chalked runiclike symbols as directories for fellow migrants: "safe to camp here" or "homeowner has gun!" The grillework "lace" cipher at Nottingham Contemporary (see image 2) by Caruso St. John references the all-but-extinct local lace industry. High-profile architects avoid the obvious and prioritize concepts that are relayed to clients and the public in what author and journalist Tom Wolfe called "theoryspeak." The Petronas Towers, Kuala Lumpur (1996), by César Pelli (b.1926) were mocked by *The Architectural Review* in 1997 for representing "a certain kind of Western architect, who, when working [in places other than their own locale] attempts to foster regionalism (so often ignored by insensitive locals) by copying the

KEY EVENTS

1952	1961–79	1963	1966	1972	1975
Concrete champion Le Corbusier builds his one-room log *cabanon* (hut) in Roquebrune, France.	Park Chung Hee's "New Village Movement" in South Korea calls for the nationwide replacement of thatched roofs with metal ones.	Sea Ranch housing (see p.414), designed by Charles Moore (1925–93) in California, prioritizes vernacular.	The geodesic dome community Drop City, Colorado, USA, uses scraps and recycled materials following ideas by Buckminster Fuller (1895–1983).	The *Limits to Growth* report issued by the Club of Rome spreads the message of finite world natural resources.	*Garbage Housing* by Martin Pawley champions inexpensive architecture using post-industrial and consumer wastes and by-products.

most obvious traditional forms and liberally smearing them about." The problems with the vernacular meme treble when tourism underpins the local economy. There are few twenty-first-century architects who avoid the meme but build in what can be described as "new vernacular." Fewer still do it well. However, Peter Lorenz (b.1950) and Gion Caminada (b.1957) have been successful in Innsbruck, Austria, and Vrin, Switzerland, respectively, despite the expectations of their local tourism industries, which seek to elevate kitsch to vernacular.

Tourism is a key industry in Austria and Switzerland. Exploiting the local vernacular of timber chalets, Fraktur, and traditional dress is common. Occasionally, it results in the apotheosis of vernacular: an isolated and idyllic *hameau* (hamlet) similar to Marie Antoinette's eighteenth-century "farm" on the grounds of Versailles, France. The Grand Hotel Alpina in Gstaad, Switzerland (2012), which *Forbes* magazine called the "Billionaire's Hotel in a Billionaire's Swiss playground," can be described as a vernacular *haute hameau*. It was designed by Jaggi and Partner AG, with interiors by HBA London, and its weathered timber envelope and Ringgenberg limestone embrace legend, location and Swiss provenance. Ceilings and walls were reclaimed from vernacular Swiss chalets, and faux-naive paintings hang on reclaimed fir-plank walls. Farm buildings from the Saanenland region influenced the slatted wooden screens.

The vernacular of the Grand Hotel Alpina is akin to the Musheireb mixed-use, high-density development in "old town" Doha, Qatar. An architect in the Western team of the main developers explained the concept to *The Architects' Journal* in 2012. Beyond the site boundaries were "tired, rag-tag buildings and unloved streetscapes." The development is a catalyst for their renewal as this is "the Darwinian way in which cities evolve: quality breeds quality, value breeds value." The site chosen for "mock-ups" was a pile of rubble, and was the site of one of the oldest houses in Doha: the homestead of the British Consulate farm. It became a touchstone and a "tangible manifestation of memory," with its courtyard, classic Qatari rooms, liwan portico, and roof terrace. The house is "consistent with the Musheireb vision to be home grown and rooted in tradition." The description climaxes to portray "the enchanting simplicity and robust timelessness . . . reborn within a language of contemporary Qatari vernacular," or what locals describe as "new old." Similar to developments in the West, new old vernacular in Qatar proceeds apace, not least because real vernacular, such as the semi-ghost town village of Al Wakrah, 12 miles (20 km) south of Doha, cannot be moved feasibly—which is just as well. Artist Donald Judd fulminated against the faux: "The best [of art and architecture] is that which remains where it was painted, placed or built."

Peter Lorenz rejects these ideas of vernacular. He insists that modern architecture must undermine the comforting security of traditional buildings. Born and based in the tourist heart of the Alps, the federal state of Tyrol, he

1990	1993	2004	2011	21st century	21st century
Rick Lowe rescues twenty-two shotgun African American houses in Houston, Texas, and founds Project Row Houses.	The globally influential Rural Studio, Alabama, is founded by Samuel Mockbee and D. K. Ruth.	As interest in vernacular accelerates, Stein Halvorsen Arkitekter uses the "leaning wall" of the Sami people in the design of Tana Courthouse, Norway.	The facade of Liyuan Library, Beijing, China, features vertical kindling sticks. It wraps the structure, creating an effect similar to a palisade fortress.	Resurgent interest in vernacular includes South Korean thatched mud-wall houses, seen as curative for chronic illnesses such as asthma and eczema.	Landscape urbanists from Harvard University vie with the vernacular approach of New Urbanists led by Andrés Duany (b.1949) for control of urban planning theory.

says locals are "addicted to kitsch" because tourists expect to see "regional charm." He rhetorically asks if tourism requires architecture, implying that aggregates of timber and Fraktur are anything but architecture. Lorenz's Konigsrainer House in Austria (see image 1), with its floating pavilion roof that is common to the region, represents "critical regionalism," he says, fulfilling the requirement of British architect Kenneth Frampton (b.1930) for "marginal practice within a modern architectural legacy." Unlike in Modernism, the house is not meant to be a sculptural object, but a building embedded on the site and in its surroundings. Lorenz's buildings know their history but firmly reject Tyrolean kitsch. They are secondarily a stand against the resurgence of political extremism, which often allies demagoguery with traditional values and architecture.

Gion Caminada is a native of the village of Vrin, Switzerland, and sees himself as a member of the village who works in the same way in which the baker makes bread. In 2003, he was interviewed by students from the Architectural Association School of Architecture in London. He explained that he is interested in typology, and although *Strickbau* (local log construction) is plentiful in his work, "vernacular" means "How can I transform it?" and "What can I let go?" This is the essence of new vernacular. It is not the "pattern language" of fellow Austrian architect Christopher Alexander (b.1936), who lamented in 2008 that amateurs using his language often build something fairly drastically wrong, but rather the "editing" of vernacular. Unconcerned with regional issues, Caminada wants his buildings to reflect the local, as seen in his butcher's building and two cowsheds (1999; see p.552). "Most architects are only concerned with aesthetics and form," he says. However, his buildings are built only after ad hoc public consultation, and Caminada asks his neighbors to debate each sketch casually. If the sketch is too clear, people will quickly come to the conclusion that the architect is talking to himself. His Totenstube mortuary reflects aspects of Vrin's Baroque church, but his concern is not style but performance: how people use it. During bereavement the

mortuary belongs to the family, but otherwise it belongs to the community, who he says, rearranged his idea of how the body should be displayed. Caminada did not mind the changes because he believes that "one has to create a form in which experiences can happen."

Vrin faces similar tourism issues to the Tyrol. Caminada recalled how the annual South Tyrol cattle drive was made a weekly event in order to satisfy tourist demand. "If you think like that," he says, "then culture is degraded to pure stupidity." He and Vrin are too stubborn to make the same mistake. The familiar must not exclude the strange. The idea of huge picture windows, like those designed by Peter Zumthor (b.1943) for his thermal baths in Vals (see image 3), is wrong, Caminada says. A good room uses nature but when the weather is really wild he argues that a retreat is needed. His views echo those of Swiss architect Luigi Snozzi (b.1932). When a client wanted a Ticino-style, red-tiled house, he convinced her using a relaxed Caminada-style approach. The result was a new vernacular house covered with a pavilion roof, but not in Ticino style. Panoramic windows were avoided because Snozzi believes that they make "you feel as though you are neither indoors nor outdoors." The owner agreed. "In the summer I feel as though I'm in a tent," she said, "and in the winter I feel as well protected as though I were in a castle."

However, despite the continued efforts of architects such as Caminada, Lorenz, and Snozzi, vernacular kitsch seems unavoidable. MVRDV's Glass Farm (see image 4) in the Netherlands is a mixed-use building in the village square. Skinned in a fritted semitranslucent glass collage, photographs of local traditional farms are enlarged to create an illusion of height (a technique that was pioneered in 1955 by Disneyland's Main Street, where first level is 3:4 scale, the second floor 5:8 scale, and the third floor 1:2 scale). The forced perspective allows adults to experience being child size again. Kitsch? Probably. At the Venice Biennale of Architecture in 2008, architecture critic Aaron Betsky declared: "Most buildings are not designed by architects . . . for that reason most buildings are ugly, useless, and wasteful." Vernacular meme represents kitsch, while renegade locals such as Caminada and Lorenz champion New Vernacular. However, maybe the best is neither kitsch nor New Vernacular, but "original" vernacular by amateurs and the self-taught. One such example is the Skylight Inn in Ayden, North Carolina (see image 5). It is the home of the best barbecue in the world, served up under a metal scale replica of the Capitol dome (1793) in Washington, D.C., designed by self-taught architect William Thornton (1759–1828). **DJ**

3 **Therme Vals (2009)**
Peter Zumthor
Vals, Switzerland

4 **Glass Farm (2012)**
MVRDV
Schijndel, the Netherlands

5 **Skylight Inn (c.1979)**
Pete Jones
Ayden, North Carolina, USA

Butcher's Building and Two Cowsheds 1999

GION CAMINADA b.1957

Butcher's Building
and Two Cowsheds,
Vrin, Switzerland

Gion Caminada is the architect of the Alpine farming village of Vrin in Switzerland. He describes *Strickbau*, the local vernacular log-building style that he adapts for his buildings in Vrin, as "knitted" architecture, most notable in stacked "knit" corners. Shunning the fixation of most architects with aesthetics and form, Caminada avoids copying *Strickbau* construction techniques, and instead figuratively dismantles the style to rebuild it in ways that are related to the end use. At the edge of the village, his ensemble of a butcher's building and cowsheds is evidence of how contemporary architecture can be more than pure form; it can knit buildings into the service of the human and animal cycle of life. Calves live with their mothers throughout their lives and herds spend summer on the mountain. In the 1980s, the village collectively purchased land to prevent land speculation, to stem outward migration, and to harmonize the village's historic and new buildings. A by-law requires those who purchase village land to live in Vrin as their primary residence for a minimum of twenty-five years. As a native of Vrin, Caminada was hired to design new buildings, including the village hall, bakery, sawmill, and a wooden telephone kiosk. In 1998, the village won the Wakker Prize for its unification of old and new architecture. There is no kitsch Heidi culture in Vrin, only the rare courage to build beautiful dignified architecture for human and animal needs. **DJ**

✦ **NAVIGATOR**

FOCAL POINTS

1 VENTILATION

Spaced rows of horizontal narrow rip-cut flat planks face the cowshed with wide wooden rip-cut planks placed on the diagonal behind them, creating ventilation. Sheet-metal panels cover the cowshed's wooden roof and deep eaves reveal the square roof beams.

2 BUTCHER'S BUILDING

The drystone and wood butcher's building sits above a basement where farmers can slaughter their animals. The second-floor meat curing area is rip-cut wood planks backed with an internal ventilated wood wall. The ensemble of buildings reflects Vrin's concern with cradle-to-grave animal welfare.

3 RIP-CUT WOOD

Rip-cut wood is a traditional feature of vernacular *Strickbau* architecture and timber beam construction in other countries. A cut is made parallel to (in the same direction as) the grain of the wood. Caminada designed the interior with generous space for each animal in the first-floor stalls.

LOG HOUSES

Abundant timber in northern Europe encouraged log-based vernacular styles, including Russian *isba*, German *blockhaus*, and numerous Scandinavian designs (right). Immigrants to North America introduced log houses, including the Illinois-Indiana-Iowa 'I' house where adjacent additions required a second front door rather than a connecting interior door because of the depth of the log walls. Despite regional differences, techniques were similar. Log stacks interlocked under log pole roofs. Carpentry joins were used in lieu of nails or glue. Design evolution moved to logs with corner posts and combinations of wood frames and logs with minimal masonry. Contemporary Swiss law requires existing *Strickbau* buildings to be demolished when a new barn or house is built in order to preserve the landscape. Villages like Vrin elect not to demolish *Strickbau* architecture, but to refurbish it for new generations.

GLOSSARY

adytum (Greek) / adyton (Latin)
A small sanctuary or deity space located in the inner chamber of a temple, an area restricted to priests and other religious celebrants.

all'antica
A style of the Italian Renaissance, in which architects borrowed from ancient (*antica*) Rome. However, opportunities, innovation, or constraints, such as the narrow city plot awarded to Vincenzo Scamozzi (1552–1616) for his Teatro all'antica (1590), resulted in a reflective, not a copyist, style.

ambo
An early predecessor of the Christian church pulpit, comprising a small, mobile, stepped platform, often railed, on which the Gospel or Epistle was read to a congregation.

apadana
A columned audience hall particular to the Achaemenid (Persian) Empire, with open triple porticos on the north, east, and west sides, monumental entrance staircases, stone columns, and wooden ceiling beams.

arch
A curved, open construction, whose lateral thrust on its two sides is contained by abutments. Open arches such as bridges require inward thrust to keep the ends from spreading, with anchorage provided by either natural (riverbanks, canyons) or artificial (buttresses) sources. Used in Western and Islamic architecture, types common to both include the pointed arch. Those more specific to Islamic architecture include the horseshoe and poly-lobed arches, while those particular to the West include the lancet, trefoil, and Tudor.

bad gir
A traditional Persian wind tower that "catches" and redistributes air currents into a building. Known in Arabic as *malqaf*, the basic square tower design is used in multiple countries, but vents (and vent designs) can differ regionally and nationally.

baldachin
An interior canopy placed over a secular throne or religious altar. It can be suspended, free standing, or projected from a wall.

ballcourt
A narrow, open-air playing field found in Mesoamerica, walled on its two long sides. Originally open-ended, later designs enclosed the end zones to create an I-shaped structure.

Beaux-Arts (adj)
An eclectic style of the late 19th and early 20th century that borrowed and adapted the monumentality and rich decorative detail of French architecture from the 16th to 19th centuries. The term is often used as a pejorative to indicate florid, ostentatious style or a lack of relevant theory.

berm
A raised earth barrier or earth parapet. Medieval military engineers used berms between a parapet or defensive wall and a walled ditch or moat. Contemporary use includes earth-sheltered architecture for high insulation value.

boiserie
A French term for wood paneling or wainscot (paneling on the lower part of a wall only), used primarily in reference to elaborate shallow-relief carved interior paneling of the 17th and 18th centuries.

brise-soleil
A permanent sun-break feature used to shade windows (often vertical or horizontal fins, but also including open-patterned masonry blocks), particularly in hot climates. It was popularized by Le Corbusier, but has roots in vernacular Islamic architecture.

buttress
A masonry or brickwork mass that supports a wall. Buttress types include "clasping," which creates a flush embrace to a building angle, and "flying," which is an arch or half-arch brace that repels the building's outward thrust. More basic buttresses include

timber planks wedged at 45-degree angles against walls.

charbagh
A Persian-derived quadrilateral garden with four axial paths or water courses. The design strongly influenced Mughal garden plans.

chhatri
A dome-shaped pavilion on the roof of a building. It is commonly associated with Indian architecture, particularly the Rajput architecture of Rajasthan.

Chicago window
A three-part window composed of a fixed sash (non-opening) window in the center, framed on either side by narrow moveable sash windows. It is associated with the Chicago School of architecture of the late 19th and early 20th century. Iterations include casement windows on either side of the fixed central window.

chinoiserie
A style of architecture imitative of Chinese models, particularly pagodas. It was popular in Europe during the 17th and 18th centuries.

ciborium
An interior canopy over a Christian altar that is supported on columns. It is similar to the baldachin.

clerestory
A windowed area in the upper part of a church nave, above the aisle roofs. Its unimpeded location enables light to infiltrate the interior. The term is also used to describe similar arrangements that are found in secular buildings and domestic architecture.

Coade stone
A fired ceramic "stone" produced from a white pottery clay, to which is added sand, powdered flint, quartz (to vitrify), and "grog" (waste ceramic). It was marketed in 18th century England by Eleanor Coade, who called it *Lithodipyra* (stone fired twice). The material remained popular into the early 19th century for monuments, sculpture, and architectural decoration.

Cor-ten
Known generically as "weathering steel," Cor-Ten is the trademark name of a steel alloy that forms an intentional protective rust skin. It has perceived decorative properties that differ in outcome depending on the environment, location, and level of exposure to the elements.

crenellated
Describes a building with battlements, in particular the symmetrical, alternating vertical pattern of low points (embrasures) and high points (merlons) on the top of a parapet.

feng shui
The Chinese art of orientating and arranging objects and structures to harmonize with the spiritual forces of Yin and Yang and enable the appropriate flow of energies.

ferro cemento
The Italian term for ferrocement, a Portland cement and sand mix with plaster-like fluidity. When placed over a reinforced steel framework, it can be used to create structures that are light, thin, and plastic. Material failure is generally limited to deformation or spider cracks. Round ferrocement water tanks are renowned for their longevity and low maintenance.

formwork
Also known as "shuttering," formwork is a temporary or permanent timber, metal, fibreglass, or plastic mold that holds and shapes poured concrete until it cures to create precast concrete. The formwork's texture, particularly timber, will imprint on the concrete. Intentional textures and raised-profile finishes are created with bespoke formliners placed inside the mold.

gopura
Often one in a series, the *gopura* is a rectangular entrance gateway with a barrel vault roof that is found in southern Indian Hindu temple enclosures. *Gopuras* steadily increased in size from the mid-12th century to become colossal gateways dominating temple complexes.

High-Tech (adj)
A style of architecture inspired by the materials and techniques associated with engineering and other technologies. The term was adopted from the interior design book *High Tech: The Industrial Style Sourcebook for the Home* (1978) by Joan Kron and Suzanne Slesin, and replaced the "Industrial Style" label that was used to describe such architecure in the 1970s.

International Style
An architectural style that emphasized form over social context, as first defined by Henry Russell Hitchcock and Philip Johnson in 1932. Lasting from approximately 1925 to 1965, the style emerged from the European Modernist movement and the Bauhaus. Focus then shifted to the United States, from where the style was exported globally. Influential typologies include the corporate skyscraper.

iwan
A rectangular hall or room located near the entrance of a mosque, usually vaulted with one end open. Also known as liwan, they are sometimes used in domestic Islamic architecture.

jaali
A pierced screen carved in an open calligraphic or geometric pattern, which allows air exchange and permits semi-concealed views. It is used in Islamic and Indian architecture.

jalousie windows
Also known as louvres, jalousie windows are lapped, horizontal glass or wood panels held in twin vertical tracks, which allow the plates to open outward in unison via a mechanical crank handle or central wooden rod. They are common to semi-tropical and tropical climates and are often paired with external shutters. The plates can be angled to allow them to be open during rainstorms without rain ingress.

keystone
A wedge-shaped stone in the apex of an arch or vault that locks the other stones in place by allowing lateral forces to "lean" into it.

Lady Chapel
A Christian chapel dedicated to the Virgin Mary, typically built as a projecting satellite east of the high altar in a cathedral and south of the high altar in a church. It is generally rectangular in plan.

loggia
A long gallery open on one or more sides, supported by columns. The main open side is usually orientated toward a specific view, such as a public square or a garden.

mansard roof
A double slope roof where the lower slope on each of its four sides is taller and more acutely angled than the smaller four-sided upper slope, whose lower pitch can conceal it from casual observation. The design is characteristic of the French Renaissance and was a common feature of 19th century Second Empire architecture in France.

mashrabiya
A window or projecting enclosure shielded by intricately carved wooden latticework. An element of traditional Arabic architecture since the Middle Ages, it enables the occupants of a building to survey the outside without being seen, in addition to providing shade and natural ventilation. Highly skilled carpenters dovetailed each piece of the screen to allow for natural expansion and contraction of the wood under the duress of extreme heat.

mestizo
An 18th and 19th century vernacular interpretation of European Baroque architecture, found in provincial areas of Spain's colonial territories in South America. Its chief characteristic is intentional deep shadows created by undercut carving.

muqarnas
A decorative transitional feature used in Islamic architecture, such as between a squinch arch and a dome. Corbel-like projections are intricately tiled in mathematical patterns, of which three geographically diverse core designs have been idenfitied.

narthex

A general term for the antechurch (porch) at the entrance of a medieval Christian church. Two types of narthex are found in Byzantine churches: the esonarthex, which precedes the nave and aisles, and the exonarthex, which precedes the facade. For both types, the division is made clear by columns, rails, or a wall between the zones.

ogee arch

A pointed arch with an S-shaped curve on both sides.

pendentive

A concave triangular space that acts as a transition between a circular dome and the square or polygonal base on which the dome is set.

peripteros

An Ancient Greek or Roman temple cell that is enclosed by a continuous wall, surrounded at a proportionate distance by a gallery of columns creating a portico.

piano nobile

The main floor of a grand house, containing public reception rooms. Generally it is located on a raised ground floor and has higher ceilings than the storys above.

piloti

Pillars, columns, or stilts that support the raised floor of a building, leaving open circulation beneath. Popularized by Le Corbusier, their origins lie in vernacular architecture. Variations include Oscar Niemeyer's V-shaped and W-shaped piloti.

pisé de terre

The French term for rammed (compressed) earth wall construction. An ancient and natural building method, it has high thermal efficiency and uses sustainable materials such as earth, chalk, lime, or gravel.

pishtaq

A prominent projecting gateway or portal of a mosque, often an arched doorway set within a flat rectangular "frame" that leads to the *iwan*.

porte-cochère

A covered entrance to a building that provides shelter for passengers entering and leaving carriages or cars. Generally it is open on all four sides, with a driveway running through its center.

reinforced concrete

A type of concrete in which metal bars or wire are embedded to increase its tensile strength.

stack ventilation

A natural form of ventilation that exploits the phenomenon of hot air rising above cool air in an enclosed space (stack effect). Providing an exit for the hot air creates a partial vacuum, which draws in cooler air from the outside atmosphere to replace the hot air in a cyclical fashion. The system works best in climates with marked differentials between exterior and interior temperatures.

stupa

A domed or beehive-shaped Buddhist commemorative monument.

synthronon

A series of clerical benches in early Christian and Byzantine churches that were placed in a semi-circle in the apse or in rows on either side of the bema (a raised area in the apse).

talud-tablero

A pre-Columbian Mesoamerican style, also known as slope-and-panel, which is commonly associated with the pyramids at Teotihuacán in Mexico. It consists of an inward-sloping wall (the *talud*), atop which rests a platform (the *tablero*) that generally protrudes slightly from the lower section.

tatami

A traditional rice straw and rush Japanese floor mat. It is made according to a standard aspect ratio of 2:1. This gave rise to the "jo" unit of measurement for real estate area, whereby one jo corresponds to the size of one tatami mat. Measurements vary regionally and older buildings may differ in jo measurements from newer builds.

tholos

Refers to the dome of a circular building; the round domed building itself; or a stone, corbel-vaulted, pointed dome Mycenean tomb.

timber framing

A carpentry-based construction method also known as post and beam, which connects large pieces of timber with woodworking joints such as the mortise and tenon (whereby a hole is made to receive a projection of similar dimension, creating a "male-female" joint). Areas between the open wood frame are infilled with a material such as plaster, brick, wood siding, or straw bale.

trabeated

A basic construction method also known as the post-and-lintel system, where two upright posts support a bridging horizontal lintel across their top surfaces.

trumeau

The central vertical post support in a trabeated doorway, often used to support a half-circle tympanum in Christian churches and cathedrals.

tympanum

The semi-circular or triangular area above a doorway, bounded by a lintel and arch. It is often decorated with relief sculpture.

X-brace

An X-shaped brace that allows a building's lateral load to be reduced by transferring it to the exterior. It was developed by engineer Fazlur Khan. His application of a hinged flexible X-frame stiffened with diagonal supports to the exterior of the John Hancock Center (1970) in Chicago revolutionized skyscrapers in terms of achievable heights and and reductions in the total weight of steel required.

zenana

The zoned quarters, apartments, or areas that are reserved for women in Islamic architecture. They can range from elaborately designed rooms in royal complexes to simple screened or curtained areas.

CONTRIBUTORS

Dr. Lindsay Allen (LA)
is Lecturer in Greek and Near Eastern History at King's College London. She specializes in the history of the Achaemenid Empire and its reception in later scholarship. She has also held research posts at the Warburg Institute, the Institute for the Study of the Ancient World, NYU, Wolfson College Oxford, and the British Museum in London.

Ektoras Arkomanis (EA)
teaches History and Theory of Architecture in the CASS, London Metropolitan University. He recently completed his first feature film, *Another London* (2014), a documentary about architecture and urban space in London, with emphasis on places and spaces that are peripheral geographically, as well as in the city's consciousness.

Dana Buntrock (DB)
is a professor at the University of California, Berkeley. Her research focuses on cross-disciplinary professional practices and the innovations that result. Since 2011, her primary interest has been the ways that Japan is addressing changing energy supply caused by the Fukushima nuclear accident.

Cammy Brothers (CB)
is the Valmarana Associate Professor at the University of Virginia and Director of the Venice Program. She is the author of *Michelangelo, Drawing, and the Invention of Architecture* (Yale University Press, 2008), which won the Charles Rufus Morey Prize of the College Art Association, 2010, and the Alice Davis Hitchcock Prize of the Society of Architectural Historians, 2010. She is currently working on a book about architectural exchange between Italy and Andalusia.

Robyne Erica Calvert (RC)
(PhD, MLitt, MA) is a lecturer in the history of architecture and design at the Glasgow School of Art. Her research focuses on 19th and early 20th century visual culture, emphasizing collaborative practice and sartorial expression.

Harry Charrington (HC)
is an architect and Principal Lecturer in Architecture at the University of Westminster. He studied architecture at Cambridge University, where he was the founding editor of *Scroope: Cambridge Architectural Journal*, and later obtained his PhD from the LSE. He has combined academia and practice in England and Finland, lecturing at the Universities of Bath, UWE Bristol, and Helsinki, as well as working for Elissa Aalto and developing the UK's first new-build CoHousing scheme. His most recent book, an oral history of the Aalto atelier, *Alvar Aalto: the Mark of the Hand* (Rakennustieto Publishing, 2011), won the RIBA President's Award for Research 2012.

Daniel E. Coslett (DC)
is a doctoral candidate at the University of Washington's interdisciplinary Built Environment PhD program in Seattle. He studies colonial, postcolonial, and revolutionary North Africa, focusing specifically on intersections among architecture, urban planning, historic preservation, and tourism development.

Dr. Soledad Garcia Ferrari (SGF)
is Senior Lecturer at Edinburgh University. Professionally qualified in Architecture and Urbanism in Uruguay, her research focuses on urban regeneration in Latin America and Europe. She has taught Architecture in Montevideo and Spain. She is Director of Quality and Enhancement at Edinburgh and Coordinator of Research and Development for the University's Centre for Contemporary Latin American Studies.

Prof. Bill Finlayson (BF)
is Director of the Council for British Research in the Levant (the British Academy's institute for advanced research in the region), and has directed several excavations at Mesolithic and Neolithic settlements. His current research examines the origins of agriculture and village life in the Near East, and the role of communal architecture in organizing Neolithic societies.

Shirin Fozi (SF)
(PhD Harvard University, 2010) is Assistant Professor of the History of Art and Architecture at the University of Pittsburgh, where she is currently writing a book on Romanesque tomb effigies. Fozi's research has been supported by grants from the Mellon and Kress foundations, among others, and she was the 2011 recipient of the annual dissertation prize of the Europäisches Romanik Zentrum in Merseburg, Germany.

Jana Gajdošová (JG)
studied art history and history at Rutgers University in New Jersey and obtained her MA from the Courtauld Institute of Art. She is currently in the last year of her PhD research under the supervision of Dr. Zoë Opačić at Birkbeck College, University of London, which focuses on the Charles Bridge in Prague.

Isabelle J. Gournay (IJG)
(Architecte DPLG, PhD) teaches at the University of Maryland. She specializes in cross-currents between France and the United States. With Marie-Laure Crosnier Leconte, she is completing a book on the Parisian studies of architects officially registered at the Ecole des Beaux-Arts who were active in the United States.

Peter Guillery (PG)
is an architectural historian and editor for the Survey of London in the Bartlett School of Architecture, University College London. Publications include *The Small House in Eighteenth-Century London* (Yale University Press, 2004), *Behind the Façade, London House Plans 1660–1840* (Spire Books Ltd, 2006, with Neil Burton), and, as editor, *Built from Below: British Architecture and the Vernacular* (Routledge, 2011).

Junko Habu (JH)
is a professor at the University of California, Berkeley. Her research interests include hunter-gatherer subsistence and settlement, prehistoric Jomon hunter-gatherers in Japan, East Asian archaeology, ceramic analysis, and historical archaeology in Japan.

Dr. Clare Heath (CH)
is an independent curator and art advisor who is specialized in the field of Italian and British 20th-century art and architecture. She graduated from the Courtauld Institute of Art, London, and has worked for Sotheby's and for the British Council. She lectures widely and is a contributor to *The Burlington Magazine*, *Artforum*, and *The Art Newspaper*.

John S. Henderson (JSH)
is Professor of Anthropology at Cornell University. He has taught anthropology and archaeology at Cornell since 1971, and has served as Director of Cornell's Archaeology and Latin American Studies Programs. His interests center on identity and early complex societies, especially how distinctions in status, wealth, and authority develop. He has written extensively about these issues in the context of ancient Mexico and Central America. He has written or edited seven books, including *The World of the Ancient Maya* (Cornell University Press, 1981/1997), a popular introduction to ancient Maya civilization. He has also written many articles for professional books and journals, and for popular magazines.

Puay-peng Ho (PPH)
is Professor of Architecture at the School of Architecture, The Chinese University of Hong Kong. He is a qualified architect and received his PhD in the art and architecture history of China from SOAS, University of London. His research interests and publications are in the fields of Chinese art and architectural history, Buddhist art and architecture, and architectural conservation.

Tom Howey (TH)
studied theory of architecture at the University of Sheffield, with a special focus on the phenomenology of architecture. His MA at London College of Communication looked at the relationship between poetry and typography. He works as a book designer for publishers including Thames & Hudson and Prestel.

Kathryn Marie Hudson (KMH)
received an Associate of Arts degree in Foreign Languages from Georgia Perimeter College and then attended Georgia State University, where she graduated *magna cum laude* with research honors and received Bachelor of Arts degrees in both Anthropology and History. She holds a Master's degree in Archaeology from Cornell University and is currently a doctoral student at the University at Buffalo. She can be reached at khudson@buffalo.edu.

Iain Jackson (IJ)
is an architect and senior lecturer at the Liverpool School of Architecture. He is currently finishing a monograph on the work of Maxwell Fry and Jane Drew and has a broader interest in tropical and colonial architecture.

Denna Jones (DJ)
is a US-born, London-based architecture and design writer and consultant. She has collaborated on multiple major UK urban regeneration projects, including an Urban Homesteading scheme in Devonport, Plymouth. A Creative Futures Fellow of Creative Scotland, she also developed the "Your New Home" building project for North Edinburgh Arts. She has twice been a judge for Zurich International's New Homes Awards. In 2014 she began a project that reintroduces the 18th-century concept of small, urban vernacular artisan housing to London. She holds an MA from the Courtauld Institute of Art.

Thomas Kaffenberger (TK)
studied Art History, Byzantine Art History, Christian Archaeology, and Comparative Literature in Mainz and Famagusta. He is currently working on his PhD, which focuses on the architecture of late medieval Cyprus, in Mainz and at the King's College London. He has held teaching appointments at the Universities of Mainz and Heidelberg and has published numerous articles on the architectural history of Cyprus, on early 20th century art in Germany and on issues of virtual heritage.

Dr. Nikolaos Karydis (NK)
is a Lecturer in Architecture at the University of Kent. He graduated as an architect from the National Technical University of Athens and holds a MSc (Conservation of Historic Buildings) and a PhD from the University of Bath. From 2010 to 2012, he taught in the Rome Studies Program of the University of Notre Dame.

Colin Martin (CM)
writes widely on architecture, art, and design. His academic qualifications encompass the arts and sciences: BA, BSc (Hons) and M App Sc (University of Melbourne).

Naomi Pollock (NP)
is an American architect who lives in Tokyo, where she writes about Japanese design. In addition to magazine articles, she is the author of several books including *Modern Japanese House* (Phaidon Press Ltd, 2005) and *Made in Japan: 100 New Products* (Merrell Publishers, 2012).

Dr. Alan Powers (AP)
writes widely on 20th century architecture, art, and design. He has a long association with the Twentieth Century Society, the statutory amenity society in England for buildings after 1914, and is one of the editors of its journal, *Twentieth Century Architecture*, and its series of monographs, *Twentieth Century Architects*. He teaches for NYU London and his most recent book was *Eric Ravilious: Artist and Designer* (Lund Humphries Pub Ltd, 2013).

Marta Rodriguez (MR)
is an Assistant Professor of Architecture at the University of Houston. She was previously a visiting fellow at CEE (Sciences Po, Paris), visiting scholar at CJS (UC Berkeley), a researcher for the Spanish Ministry of Innovation and Science, and an employee of OMA (Rotterdam).

Dr. Henrik Schoenefeldt (HS)
is currently Lecturer at the University of Kent School of Architecture. His research is in sustainable design, with

a particular interest in the history of environmental design. During his PhD in Cambridge he studied the development of 19th-century glass structures, including case studies on the Crystal Palace from a technical and environmental perspective. His current research includes projects on the adoption of the PassivHaus standard in the UK, the Victorian stack ventilation system at the Houses of Parliament, and environmental design education.

Roger Simmons (RS)

is a retired architect who has spent the last thirty years working on the repair and conservation of historic buildings, latterly as a conservation manager for the Churches Conservation Trust. He has lived in Islington for over forty years and current interests include travel and travel writing.

Ruth Slavid (RSl)

is a freelance writer and editor specializing in architecture, landscape, and lighting. She is the author of six books on architecture. For fifteen years she worked for *The Architects' Journal* in a variety of senior roles. She currently edits *Landscape*, the journal of the Landscape Institute.

Giles Smith (GS)

is a designer and writer based in London. His interest in digital architecture dates from his studies at the Royal College of Art, where he explored the architectural consequences of contemporary digital culture. He is also a co-founder of Assemble, a participatory architecture practice.

James M. Steele (JMS)

is an architect, professor, and writer whose focus has primarily been on the Middle East and on both the vernacular and contemporary architecture of that region. He has also written about sustainability.

David B. Stewart (DBS)

is a US architectural historian and a former student of Sir Nikolaus Pevsner. He has been Professor of Architecture

at Tokyo Tech since 1976 and is author of *The Making of a Modern Japanese Architecture* (Kodansha America, 2003/1987).

Margaret Stewart (MS)

is a lecturer in architectural history at the Edinburgh School of Architecture and Landscape Architecture at the University of Edinburgh. She has published on Neoclassicism, the history of architectural education, and the Art Nouveau period in Scotland. Her book about the architectural plans of the 6th Earl of Mar (1675–1732) will be published in the spring of 2015.

Dr. Karlyn Sutherland (KS)

is a recent graduate who has studied and taught architecture at both Edinburgh College of Art and the University of Edinburgh. With a focus on addressing the human need for a sense of place and attachment, her research explores the translation of key place-related theories from within the discipline of environmental psychology into a replicable strategy for architectural design and practice.

Dr. Edmund V. Thomas (EVT)

teaches Greek and Roman art and architecture at Durham University. He is the author of *Monumentality and the Roman Empire: Architecture in the Antonine Age* (Oxford University Press, 2007) and is presently completing a book on the history of the keystone in Greek, Roman, and later architecture.

Doria Tichit (DT)

is an art historian specializing in the art and architecture of South Asia. She studied Archaeology and Art History at the University Paris-IV Sorbonne and holds a PhD from the Welsh School of Architecture, Cardiff University. Her research has focused on the art and architecture of northern and central India, especially Madhya Pradesh and Maharashtra in the 10th and 12th centuries. She regularly lectures on South Asian art at the School of Oriental and African Studies, Sotheby's Institute of Art, and Birkbeck College, London.

Alice Y. Tseng (AYT)

is Associate Professor of Japanese Art and Architecture at Boston University. Her research interests include the history of institutional buildings, collections, exhibitions, and transnational and transcultural connections between Japan and Euro-America. She is the author of *The Imperial Museums of Meiji Japan: Architecture and the Art of the Nation* (University of Washington Press, 2008).

Katya Tylevich (KT)

is Editor-at-Large for *Elephant Magazine*, Contributing Editor for *Mark Magazine* and *White Zinfandel*, and frequent contributor to other international magazines like *Domus*, *Pin-up*, and *Frame*. In November 2013, she was artist-in-residence at The Storefront for Art and Architecture in New York. Her writing appears in books on art and architecture, and she is currently working on a book on contemporary art to be published in 2015. Katya is co-founder of Friend & Colleague, a company producing original content and art projects. For more information please visit www. katyatylevich.com.

Lorenzo Vigotti (LV)

trained as an architect in Florence, Italy, and is currently writing his PhD dissertation on early Renaissance domestic architecture at Columbia University. His interests include early modern urban planning, cultural exchanges between Europe and the Islamic world during the Renaissance, and structural problems and preservation issues in medieval and Renaissance architecture.

John Zukowsky (JZ)

earned a PhD in art and architectural history from Binghamton University. He was Curator of Architecture at the Art Institute of Chicago from 1978 to 2004, where he created a number of award-winning exhibitions and books on architecture and design. Since then he has held several executive positions at institutions in Chicago, New York, and Ohio. He is currently a museum consultant.

SOURCES OF QUOTATIONS

INTRODUCTION

p.9 "Simplify! Simplify!" *Simplify: Selected Writings from Henry David Thoreau: Walden, Civil Disobedience, Life Without Principle, and Reforms and Reformers*, Lenny Flank (ed), Red and Black Publishers, 2010

p.10 "magnificent mutiny," *Terminal Architecture*, Martin Pawley, Reaktion Books, 1998

p.10 "eternal hourglass of existence," *The Gay Science*, Friedrich Nietzsche, 1887

p.12 "would have the feeling of being part of a working community without being lost in the crowd," http://www.carusostjohn.com/media/artscouncil/history/structuralist/index.html

p.12 "barely readable academic jargon," *Architects' Journal*, 19 April 2013

p.15 "low road," *How Buildings Learn: What Happens After They're Built*, Stewart Brand, Viking Press, 1994

CHAPTER 1

p.48 "Roman architectural revolution," *Gardner's Art Through the Ages: The Western Perspective, Volume 1*, Fred Kleiner, Clark Baxter, 2014

CHAPTER 3

p.165 "static, spatial and decorative potential," *The Story of Gothic Architecture*, Francesca Prina, Prestel, 2011

p.196 "largely imagined by me, since very little can be understood from the ruins." https://archive.org/details/trattatodiarchioomartgoog

p.233 "an edge. . .ordinary thatching," *Voyage of HMS Blonde to the Sandwich Islands, in the years 1825–1825*, Captain the Right Hon Lord Byron, Commander, Cambridge University Press, 2013

p.233 "small Iron Sluggs. . .Thatcht-House," *The Destruction of Urban Property in the English Civil Wars, 1642–1651*, Stephen Porter, PhD thesis, King's College, University of London

CHAPTER 4

p.238 "artificial parallax" and "not enclosing walls, but a series of open arcades. . .beyond the confines of the room," *Changing Ideals in Modern Architecture, 1750–1950*, Peter Collins, McGill-Queen's University Press, 1998

p.239 "ridiculous jumble of shells, dragons, reeds, palm trees and plants," Jacques-François Blondel quoted in *Architecture in France in the Eighteenth Century, Volume 38*, Wend von Kalnein, Yale University Press, 1995

p.250 "House!. . .hang on one's watch," *The Georgian Era: Political and Rural Economists. Painters, Sculptors, Architects and Engravers. Composers. Vocal, Instrumental and Dramatic Performers*, Clarke, Nabu Press/BiblioBazaar, 2010

p.262 "antidote to unreflective revivalism, and not an example of it." *Mapping St. Petersburg: Imperial Text and Cityshape*, Julie A. Buckler, Princeton University Press, 2007

p.263 "advertising," "vulgar," "ornament," "purity of outline" and "elegance of proportion," *Changing Ideals in Modern Architecture*, Peter Collins, Faber and Faber Limited, 1965

p.265 "its high drum. . .topped by a lantern and the neoclassical portico" and "because it looked convincingly genuine." *Turquerie and the Politics of Representation, 1728–1876*, Nebahat Avcioglu, Ashgate Publishing, 2011

p.300 "houses, complete or nearly so," *Life in the Sandwich Islands: or, The Heart of the Pacific, as it was and is*, Henry T. Cheever, A S Barnes & Co, 1851

p.301 "built in the native fashion. . .verandahs, and jalousies," *Narrative of a Journey Around the World During the Years 1841 and 1842*, Sir George Simpson, H. Colburn, 1847

p.301 "fast by iron clamps and chains," *Life in the Sandwich Islands*, Henry T. Cheever, Barnes & Co, 1856

p.304 "the first object of art the eye rests upon in coming into port" and "conspicuous through the spy-glass far out to sea," *The Island World of the Pacific: Being Travel Through the Sandwich or Hawai'ian Islands and Other Parts of Polynesia*, Henry T. Cheever, 1851

CHAPTER 5

p.308 "Function[alism] is sweeping dirt!" Mies van der Rohe, Art Institute of Chicago oral history of Mies student Werner Buch

p.314 "production by machinery is altogether an evil," *Pioneers of Modern Design: From William Morris to Walter Gropius*, Nikolaus Pevsner, Yale University Press, 2005

p.314 "pleasure in possessing them," Gustav Stickley, *The Craftsman*, March 1905

p.315 "ladies of small means," *Goddards: Sir Edwin Lutyens*, Brian Edwards, Phaidon Press Ltd, 1996

p.315 "sloping roofs, low proportions. . .low terraces and outreaching walls," *Frank Lloyd Wright's Robie House: The Illustrated Story of an Architectural Masterpiece*, Donald Hoffman, Pan America, 1984

p.315 "now a term of abuse," "Kelmscott Manor," Nicholas Cooper, *Country Life*, 25 November 2005

p.321 "The judicious use of iron. . .quite sufficient." Lecture XVIII "Domestic Architecture (cont'd.)," *Discourses on Architecture, Vol. II*, Eugène-Emmanuel Viollet-le-Duc, Benjamin Bucknall (trans), Grove Press, 1959

p.330 "conqueror's style," *Arabisances*, Francois Beguin, Dunoud, 1983

p.331 "a little bit of Paris," *Carthage and Tunis: The Old and New Gates of the Orient Vol. II*, Douglas Sladen, Hutchinson, 1906

p.332 "cradle and crucible of the highest human civilization," "Visione mediterranea della mia architectura," Florestano Di Fausto, 1937, quoted in *Architecture and Tourism: Perception, Performance and Place*, D. Medina Lasansky, Brian McLaren (eds), Berg, 2004

p.332 "what the Far West. . .and fecundity," *The Politics of Design in French Colonial Urbanism*, Gwendolyn Wright, Chicago University Press, 1991

p.334 "with the valiance of a Gothic master," "L'oeuvre artistique du gouvernement tunisien," Charles Géniaux, *Revue bleue*, 29 April 1911

p.334 "living expression[s] of local customs," "L'Architecture moderne de style arabe," R. Guy, *La Construction Moderne*, 16 May 1920

p.339 "plain classic with a touch of Orientalism," Viceroy Charles Hardinge quoted in "The Making of New Delhi," M. Juneja, *Modernity's Classics*, Sarah C. Humphreys, Rudolf G. Wagner (eds), Springer, 2013

p.339 "thrusting exhibitionistic posturing," *Dome Over India: Rashtrapati Bhavan*, Aman Nath, India Book House, 2002

p.346 "a building which is so different. . . not as a possibility," *The Heroic Period of Modern Architecture*, Alison and Peter Smithson, Rizzoli, 1981

p.347 "the will to return to basic principles and elementary rules of building," *The Victory of the New Building Style*, Walter Curt Behrendt, Harry Francis Mallgrave (trans), Los Angeles, Getty Research Institute, 2000

p.354 "passion for elimination," "Irving Gill and Rediscovery of Concrete in California: The Marie and Chauncey Clarke House 1919–22," Sean Scensor, MA Thesis, Massachusetts Institute of Technology, Department of Architecture, 1995

p.356 "fetishist cult. . .by diffusion," Carlos Eduardo Días Comas cited in *Transculturation: Cities, Spaces and Architectures in Latin America*, Felipe Hernández et al (ed), Editions Rodopi B.V., 2005

p.356 "entirely. . .industry" and "an authentic example of vernacular," *The Necessity for Ruins, And Other Topics*, J. B. Jackson, University of Massachusetts Press, Amherst, 1980

p.362 "an extraordinarily graceful and sensitive production on modern academic lines," *Architect and Building News*, 25 June 1937

CHAPTER 6

p.392 "the Grand Central of the jet age," Robert A. M. Stern quoted in "Stay of Execution for a Dazzling Airline Terminal," Herbert Muschamp, *The New York Times*, 6 November 1994

p.408 "physical environment. . .man's emotional and materials needs," http://www.rudi.net/books/10548

p.408 "Regionalism of Liberation," Harwell Harris quoted in *Harwell Hamilton Harris*, Lisa Germany, University of California Press, 2000

p.409 "the heart of the city," cited in *Il cuore della città: per una città più umana delle comunità* (The Heart of the City: Towards the Humanisation of Urban Life), E.N. Rogers, J.L. Sert, J. Tyrwhitt, Hoepli, 1955

p.409 "labyrinthine clarity," Aldo Van Eyck quoted in *The Situationist City*, Simon Sadler, MIT Press 1999

p.417 "flat-chested architecture," Frank Lloyd Wright quoted in *The Sky's the Limit: A Century of Chicago Skyscrapers*, Jane Clarke, Pauline Saliga, Rizzoli, 1990

p.439 "noble attempts" and "an advertisement. . .heartless," "Outrage," Johann Meiers, *The Architectural Review*, November 1994

p.439 "stringently Neo-Rationalist," Christian Brensing, *The Architectural Review*, November 2004

p.439 "international capitalism at its most aggressive," "Outrage," Johann Meiers, *The Architectural Review*, November 1994

p.440 "naturalize it. . .whole of nature," *Position of Architecture* (film), Angelo Mangiarotti, Carlo Bassi, 1953

p.444 "Like all revolutions. . .kind of dictatorship," *Alvar Aalto*, Nicholas Ray, Yale University Press, 2005

p.478 "not more human," but "more individual," *Hugh Maaskant: Architect of Progress*, Michelle Provoost, NAI Publishers, 2013

p.478 "One cannot be. . .midst of others," "Labyrinthian Clarity," Aldo van Eyck, *World Architecture 3: Art and Technology: towards a third culture in architecture*, John Donat (ed), Studio Vista London, 1966

p.479 "tried to infiltrate [the office] with common social ideals," Ralph Erskine quoted in "Home from Home," Elain Harwood, *Crafts Magazine*, November/ December 2004

p.479 "the complex context into which people and objects are placed [but the context] which people and objects also

form," "USA essay (1)," Donlyn Lyndon, *World Architecture 3: Art and Technology: towards a third culture in architecture*, John Donat (ed), Studio Vista London, 1966

p.485 "high-tech celebration," "commercial vernacular," "almost handmade" and "Baroque elaboration," "Architecture View," Paul Goldberger, *The New York Times*, 17 July 1988

p.485 "high-tech construction. . .courts of a traditional university," http://www.worldandischool.com/public/1993/february/school-resource10384.asp

p.485 "a reverse of dogma," "glass underbelly" and "banking to be seen. . .the plaza below," "Norman Foster: Lifting the Spirit," Robert Hughes, *TIME*, 19 April 1999

p.502 "the most important. . .several decades," *The Everything Family Guide to the Disneyland Resort*, Betsy Malloy, F&W Publications, 2002

p.503 "burgeoning popular support. . . preservation," *Speaking a New Classicism: American Architecture Now*, Helen Searing et al, Smith College Museum of Art, 1981

p.503 "reversion to licentious decorative caprice," http://seidler.net.au/index.php?id=100

p.504 "sculptures depicting Babylonian or Persian triumphs," http://www.moma.org/pdfs/docs/press_archives/5790/releases/

p.530 "the very values of harmony, unity and stability," "Deconstructivist Architecture," Mark Wigley, *Deconstruction: Omnibus Volume*, Andreas Papadakis (ed), Rizzoli, 1989

p.533 "formally chaotic. . .dated-looking," "strenuously flamboyant yet oddly inhospitable," "Provincial" and "the next Bilbao," *New museums: The good, the bad, and the horribly misguided*, Martin Filler, 2008, quoted in *Architectural Record*, June 2008

p.535 "with their gridded frames. . .object-like detachment," http://dspace.bracu.ac.bd/bitstream/

p.545 "typical unfortunate example [of] the destruction of Beijing old town," Adam Sherwin, *The Independent*, 1 August 2013

INDEX

Page numbers in **bold** refer
to illustrations

PICTURE CREDITS

The publishers would like to thank the architects, museums, galleries, archives, and photographers for their kind permission to reproduce the works featured in this book. Every effort has been made to trace all copyright owners but if any have been inadvertently overlooked, the publishers would be pleased to make the necessary arrangements at the first opportunity.
(Key: top = t; bottom = b; left = l; right = r; center = c)

2 © Chicago Historical Society / Hedrich Blessing / VIEW 8 © Dave Zubraski / Alamy 9 © The Protected Art Archive / Alamy 10t duncid/ Wikimedia Commons/CC-BY-SA-2.0 10b Patrick.charpiat/Wikimedia Commons/CC-BY-SA 3.0 11 © age fotostock / Alamy 12 Willem Diepraam 13 Hélène Binet 14 Abdullah Aljassar/Flickr 15 Courtesy of MIT Museum 16 anshar/Shutterstock 18 Klaus-Peter Simon/Wikimedia Commons/ CC-BY-SA 3.0 19t Bill Finlayson 19b Rowan Flad/Flickr 20 Bill Finlayson 21c Bill Finlayson 21b © Nathan Benn / Alamy 22 © David Lyons / Alamy 23c Tony Sherratt 23b Copyright Aberdeenshire Council Archaeology Service 24 w:es:Usuario:Barcex/http://commons.wikimedia.org/wiki/ File:Great_Pyramid_of_Giza_-_20080716a.jpg 25 © Jochen Schlenker/Robert Harding World Imagery/Corbis 26t Glen Scarborough 26b Marc Ryckaert (MJJR)/http://commons.wikimedia.org/wiki/File:Karnak_Khonsu_Temple_R01.jpg 27t © Richard Bryant/Arcaid 27b Werner Forman Archive / The Bridgeman Art Library 28 © David Parker / Alamy 29c Glowimages 29b DEA / G. DAGLI ORTI 30 © age fotostock / Alamy 31tl Julian Love 31c © George Steinmetz/Corbis 31b Isadora Pamplona 32 Antonio Abrignani 33t Khirman Vladimir 34t © Ron Watts/Corbis 35t © Ladislav Janicek/Corbis 35b Anastasios71 36 Edmund V. Thomas 37ct Edmund V. Thomas 37cb Edmund V. Thomas 37b Edmund V. Thomas 38 Dmitri Ometsinsky 39tc Edmund V. Thomas 39tr Edmund V. Thomas 39c © National Geographic Image Collection / Alamy 39b lornet 40 TakB 41b © Richard Einzig/Arcaid/Corbis 42 Pedram Veisi 43t Darafsh Kaviyani/Wikimedia Commons/CC-BY-SA 3.0 43b © Peter Horree / Alamy 44 © INTERFOTO / Alamy 45c Tigergallery 45b Ahura21/Wikimedia Commons/CC-BY-SA 3.0 46 Laurence Delderfield 47b Vincenzo Lerro 48b © Giuseppe Giglia/epa/Corbis 49t SF photo 49b Michelle McMahon 50 GiuliaL./Flickr 51tl De Agostini/Getty Images 51cl De Agostini/Getty Images 51cb De Agostini/Getty Images 51tr Edmund V. Thomas 51b Edmund V. Thomas 52 De Agostini/Getty Images 53cr Gianluca Figliola Fantini 53br © Mirek Weichsel/First Light/Corbis 54 Courtesy of the Center for the Art of East Asia, Department of Art History, University of Chicago 55 Photo Bruce M. White.© 2014. Princeton University Art Museum/Art Resource NY/Scala, Florence 56 livepine/http://www.flickr.com/ photos/75275041@N00/8323508479/in/photolist-dFwa5T-dFRkqM/CC-BY-2.0 57 © TAO Images Limited / Alamy 58 © China Images / Alamy 59br © LOOK Die Bildagentur der Fotografen GmbH / Alamy 60 Lui TAM 61c livepine/http://www.flickr.com/photos/75275041@N00/8327250401/ in/photolist-dFRkqM/CC-BY-2.0 61b © UNESCO/Liu Hao 62 © JTB MEDIA CREATION, Inc. / Alamy 63t © Chris Willson / Alamy 63b 663highland/ Wikimedia Commons/CC-BY-SA-3.0 64 © JTB MEDIA CREATION, Inc. / Alamy 65c Goshono Jomon Hakubutsukan 65b © Robert Gilhooly / Alamy 66t Marcus Cook/Flickr 67 © The Art Archive / Alamy 68t © imagebroker / Alamy 68b © Danièle Schneider/Photononstop/Corbis 69 De Agostini/Getty Images 70 © Rebecca Lennon Photography 2014 71tc © Rebecca Lennon Photography 2014 71tr © Rebecca Lennon Photography 2014 71c © Yann Arthus-Bertrand/Corbis 71b John S Henderson 72 Ross Burns 73 © Elio Ciol/Corbis 74t © age fotostock / Alamy 74b © Angelo Hornak / Alamy 75t George M. Groutas/Wikimedia Commons/CC-BY-2.0 75b © José F. Poblete/CORBIS 76 Bernard Gagnon/ Wikimedia Commons/CC-BY-SA-3.0 77t Edmund V. Thomas 77c Edmund V. Thomas 77b © The National Trust Photolibrary / Alamy 78 Mike Gadd 79b © Liquid Light / Alamy 80 De Agostini/Getty Images 81cr Edmund V. Thomas 81br anshar/Shutterstock 82 © jozef sedmak / Alamy 83 Daniel Mouton 84t © Melvyn Longhurst / Alamy 84b © Gaertner / Alamy 85 © Hemis / Alamy 86 Nikolaos Karydis 87tr Nikolaos Karydis 87b Nikolaos Karydis 88 Berthold Werner/Wikimedia Commons 89c Nikolaos Karydis 89b User:Orjen/Wikimedia Commons 90 Nikolaos Karydis 91b Nikolaos Karydis 92 Mark Daffey 93 Isaac Torrontera 94t © Robert O›Dea/Arcaid/Corbis 94b Mohammed Mashkour 95 David Collection, Copenhagen/Hans Munk Hansen 96 © Ahmad Faizal Yahya / Alamy 97br National Geographic/Getty Images 98 © Images & Stories / Alamy 99c © Photosindia / Alamy 100 JM Travel Photography/Shutterstock 101t Lukas Hlavac/Shutterstock 101b Chetan/Wikimedia Commons/CC-BY-SA-3.0 102 Benjamin Pautrot 103c Stephen M. Bunting - Lewes, DE US 103b © vdbvsl / Alamy 104 © Robert Harding Picture Library Ltd / Alamy 105tr © Nik Wheeler/Corbis 105b The J. Paul Getty Museum 106 © Simon Batley / Alamy 108 Leandro Neumann Ciuffo from Rio de Janeiro, Brazil/ Wikimedia Commons/CC-BY-2.0 109 © The Art Archive / Alamy 110t © The Art Archive / Alamy 111t © Larry Larsen / Alamy 111b Gus MacLeod/ Flickr 112 © Robert Harding/Robert Harding World Imagery/Corbis 113c John S. Henderson 113b John S. Henderson 114 Rudra Narayan Mitra/ Shutterstock 115t Adam Hardy 115b © Paul Strawson / Alamy 116t Stuart Forster 116b Doria Tichit 117 Martin Gray 118 © Robert Harding Picture Library Ltd / Alamy 119c Doria Tichit 119b Doria Tichit 120 © Bernard O'Kane / Alamy 121t © Tibor Bognar/Corbis 121b Roman Sigaev/Shutterstock 122t Jana Gajdošová 122b Arturo Ortiz 123t Matthew Collingwood/Shutterstock 123b mountainpix/Shutterstock 124 James Gordon 125c Matej Kastelic/Shutterstock 125b Sean Pavone/Shutterstock 126 hakuna_jina/Shutterstock 127b © Peter Horree / Alamy 128 Isabel Eeles 129 © CpC Photo / Alamy 130 © Asia Images Group Pte Ltd / Alamy 131br © B.O'Kane / Alamy 132 VisitBritain/Rod Edwards 133 © Julia Waterlow/Eye Ubiquitous/Corbis 134 Jim Forest 135t Nicolas Thibaut 135b © Simon Batley / Alamy 136 H & D Zielske 137br Dom-Museum Hildesheim 138 © Stéphane Lemaire/Hemis/Corbis 139cr © The Art Gallery Collection / Alamy 139b © Michael Busselle/CORBIS 140 Lui TAM 141 © Henry Westheim Photography / Alamy 142 Photo by and (c)2007 David Chen/Wikimedia Commons/CC-BY-3.0 143c © TAO Images Limited / Alamy 143b Li Jie 144 © Miguel A. Muñoz Pellicer / Alamy 145 © Robert Harding Picture Library Ltd / Alamy 146 Kenneth Dedeu/Shutterstock 147b © Steven Vidler/Eurasia Press/Corbis 148 © ian woolcock / Alamy 149 © B Lawrence / Alamy 150 Stuart Whatling 151t Jana Gajdošová 151b © Danita Delimont / Alamy 152 © funkyfood London - Paul Williams / Alamy 153br RIEGER Bertrand 154 © Sylvain Sonnet/Corbis 155cr steve Monti 155br Facsimile copy of Ms Fr 19093 fol.31v Exterior and Interior Elevation of the Lateral Walls of Reims Cathedral (pen & ink on paper) (b/w photo), Villard de Honnecourt (fl.1190-1235) / Bibliotheque Nationale, Paris, France / Giraudon / The Bridgeman Art Library 156 © Andriy Kravchenko / Alamy 157br Jana Gajdošová 158 Alexander Newman 159t © Pep Roig / Alamy 159b © Martina Katz/imagebroker/ Corbis 160 Daniel Fernandez 161c Pastaitaken/Wikimedia Commons/CC-BY-SA-3.0 161b My beautiful Iran- Saeed Massoudi Farid/Flickr 162 Dennis van de Water/Shutterstock 164 © CTK / Alamy 165t Thomas Kaffenberger 165b Thomas Kaffenberger 166 Dennis van de Water/ Shutterstock 167br Maurice Alexandre F.P. 168 Thomas Kaffenberger 169tr Thomas Kaffenberger 169b Prof. Richard T. Mortel, Prince Naif Institute for Research and Consulting Services, Al-Imam University, Riyadh, Saudi Arabia 170 Thomas Kaffenberger 171br Thomas Kaffenberger 172 pio3/ Shutterstock 173 © M.Flynn / Alamy 174t UIG via Getty Images 174b © raphael salzedo / Alamy 175 amst/Shutterstock 176 © Mondadori Electa/ Arcaid 177b Julian Elliott/Arcaid 178 © Best View Stock / Alamy 179t British Library/Robana via Getty Images 179b Fotosearch 180 TAO Images Limited 181c TAO Images Limited 181b Takashi Usui/Shutterstock 182 © Robert Preston Photography / Alamy 183 © age fotostock / Alamy

DACS, London 2014. / © ADAGP, Paris and DACS, London 2014 351c © Bildarchiv Monheim GmbH / Alamy 352 © Douglas Peebles Photography / Alamy 353ta a leaf of.../Flickr 353b Trevor To 354 Adam Janeiro 355tr © VIEW Pictures Ltd / Alamy 355b Johnson & Johnson Architecture, San Diego 356 Eric Allix Rogers 357b © Erin Paul Donovan / Alamy 358 © Robert Harding Picture Library Ltd / Alamy 359 © Davide Del Giudice/ Demotix/Corbis 360t © Philip Scalia / Alamy 360b © PAUL MARSHALL / Alamy 361t Evan Faught 361b © Eye Ubiquitous / Alamy 362 © Michael Jenner / Alamy 363tr myyorgda/Flickr/CC BY 2.0 363br AFP/Getty Images 364 Astrophysikalisches Institut Potsdam 365 Harry Charrington 366 seier+seier/Flickr 367r seier+seier/Flickr 368 Phant/Shutterstock 369t Monument to the Third International after a photography of Tatlin's model, after Vladimir Efgrafovich Tatlin, 1920-1925 (pen & ink on laid paper), Lozowick, Louis (1892-1973) / Mead Art Museum, Amherst College, MA, USA / Gift of Thomas P. Whitney (Class of 1937) / The Bridgeman Art Library 369b Richard Bryant/arcaid.co.uk 370t © imagebroker / Alamy 370b © Paul Raftery/Corbis 371 Michael Hinsch 372 © VIEW Pictures Ltd / Alamy 373b Alan Powers 374 Christine Hohpe 375b © Bildarchiv Monheim GmbH / Alamy 376 © Edward Denison 2014 377b © Niels Quist / Alamy 378 Iain Jackson 379t Remi Vaughan-Richards/Edinburgh College of Art 379b 380 © Ezra Stoller/Esto 381t © Ezra Stoller/Esto 381b Geoffrey Bawa Trust 382 VIRMUELLER ARCHITECTS PVT. LTD. 383c VIRMUELLER ARCHITECTS PVT. LTD. 383br Iain Jackson 384 Iain Jackson 385c Iain Jackson 386 © frans lemmens / Alamy 387t Alexandre Vingtier 387b Allie_Caulfield/Wikimedia Commons/CC-BY-2.0 388 © Cephas Picture Library / Alamy 389b Glenfarclas Distillery 390 © Brian Jannsen / Alamy 392 mediacolor's / Alamy; © FLC/ ADAGP, Paris and DACS, London 2014. 393 Wampa-One 394t Kelvin Dickinson/Flickr 394b © mediacolor's / Alamy 395 © LOOK Die Bildagentur der Fotografen GmbH / Alamy 396 Library of Congress, Prints & Photographs Division, LC-DIG-krb-00609 397br Library of Congress, Prints & Photographs Division, LC-DIG-krb-00599 398 © Nikreates / Alamy 399cr © Martin Adolfsson/Galeries/Corbis 399br UIG via Getty Images 400 © LOOK Die Bildagentur der Fotografen GmbH / Alamy 401tr © dpa picture alliance archive / Alamy 401bt Bruno Taut, Alpine Architektur. Hagen, Germany: Folkwang Verlag Publishing, 1919, plate 7, Ryerson and Burnham Libraries, Art Institute of Chicago 402 © Gregg Newton/Corbis 403t Saverio Sassano/Flickr 403b Jonas Aarre Sommarset 404 Christopher Little/Aga Khan Trust for Culture 404c Christopher Little/Aga Khan Trust for Culture 406 Gabriele Basilico 407b Gabriele Basilico 408 Armando Salas Portugal; © 2014 Barragan Foundation / DACS. 409 © DigitalGlobe 410 Jonathan Rieke 411b Ryan Theodore 412 UIG via Getty Images 413c Jonathan Chanca 414 Library of Congress, Prints & Photographs Division, LC-DIG-highsm-16081 415br 416 John Zukowsky 417t Henry Fok 417b Getty Images 418 © Angelo Hornak / Alamy 419br © Bettmann/CORBIS 420 © Blaine Harrington III / Alamy 421c © Jim West / Alamy 422 © Alan Schein Photography/Corbis 423 Ignacio Sanz/Flickr/CC BY-SA 2.0 424t JanManu/Wikimedia Commons/CC-BY-SA-3.0 424b © Thomas A. Heinz/ CORBIS 425t Maarten Dirkse 425b © Oleksiy Maksymenko Photography / Alamy 426 © Richard Cummins/Corbis 427c Alexander Kurz 428 Evan Chakroff 429c Brian Paquette 430 (c) Aga Khan Award for Architecture 431 Nabeel Turner 432t © Robert Harding World Imagery / Alamy 432b © Shawn Baldwin/Corbis 433 © G. Bowater/Corbis 434 Mehmet Karakurt/AKTC 435c Rasem Badran Architects/AKTC 436 Albert Saikaly 437c Albert Saikaly 438 © Caro / Alamy 439t © Arcaid Images / Alamy 439b Christian Beirle González 440 Giovanni Mello 441c Andrea Mazzola 441br William Morgan Architects, Courtesy of the University of Florida Architecture Archives 442 RICARDO BOFILL TALLER DE ARQUITECTURA 443c RICARDO BOFILL TALLER DE ARQUITECTURA 443b Atelier Antex 444 Lynne Rostochil 445 © Number 7 / Alamy 446 Corbin Keech/Flickr 447 Xavier de Jauréguiberry; © DACS 2014 448 © Stephen Saks Photography / Alamy 449c Harry Charrington 451b © Dinodia Photos / Alamy 452 Raymond Meier / Trunk Archive 453b Arnout Fonck/Flickr 454 Photo by Paul Prudence (www.paulprudence.com) 455 Osamu Murai 456 Bigjap/ Wikimedia Commons/CC-BY-SA 3.0 457t Isozaki, Arata (b. 1931): Incubation Process, Perspective, 1990. New York, Museum of Modern Art (MoMA). Silkscreen of 1962 drawing, 41 X 34 3/8 (104.1 X 87.3cm). Gift of the architect in honor of Philip Johnson. Acc. n.: 358.1996.© 2014. Digital image, The Museum of Modern Art, New York/Scala, Florence 457b © Tomio Ohashi 458 © Tomio Ohashi and courtesy of Kisho Kurokawa Architects 459cr © Tomio Ohashi and courtesy of Kisho Kurokawa Architects 459br Noritaka Minami 460 © VIEW Pictures Ltd / Alamy 461t © Tomio Ohashi 461b Takashi Homma 462 © Louise Grønlund 463br Kazuyo Sejima & Associates 464 Michael Freeman 465br Michael Freeman 466 © Dennis Gilbert/VIEW/Corbis 467t Kevin Baird 467b Matthew Gilbert 468 © Jeremy Pembrey / Alamy 469t G.Pfi/Flickr 469b Phillip Pessar 470 © Rod McLean / Alamy 471c pisaphotography/Shutterstock 471b © Kuttig - Travel - 2 / Alamy 472 Karl Blackwell 473c © Toddlerstock / Alamy 473b © VIEW Pictures Ltd / Alamy 474 Tony Cenicola/The New York Times/Redux / eyevine 475cr Jim Coyle 475br Karl Johaentges 476 Dirk Linder/Eric Parry Architects 477r © Simon Weinstock / Alamy 478 Christian Zacke/Flickr 479t Lourens Huizinga 479b © Israel images / Alamy 480 Herman van Doorn 481c Herman Hertzberger 481b Loïc Brohard - www.facebook.com/LoicBrohardPhotography 482 Edmonton Economic Development 483c Edmonton Economic Development 483b © Lee Foster / Alamy 484 © WorldFoto 485t Baxter Tocher 485b © Angelo Hornak/Corbis 486 © Pixel Youth movement / Alamy 487cr © RichardBakerWork / Alamy 487br REX/Moviestore Collection 488 Barton Myers Architecture 489tr Barton Myers Architecture 489br © Arcaid Images / Alamy 490 UIG via Getty Images 491t © Brian Jannsen / Alamy 491b Ben124/Flickr/CC BY 2.0 492 John Zukowsky 493tr John Zukowsky 493br © xPACIFICA / Alamy 494 © imagebroker / Alamy 495c © Pxel / Alamy 495b Getty Images 496 © Arcaid Images / Alamy 497t © amana images inc. / Alamy 497b Hiromitsu Morimoto/ Flickr/CC BY-SA 2.0 498 Jamie Barras 499b Osamu Murai 500 © Iwan Baan 501c © Iwan Baan 502 Photographer: Tom Bernard, Courtesy of Venturi, Scott Brown and Associates, Inc. 503t © Mathias Beinling / Alamy 503b © Nikreates / Alamy 504t © Patrick Batchelder / Alamy 504b © Alan Gallery / Alamy 505 Carol Highsmith 506 © Bildarchiv Monheim GmbH / Alamy 507br Franz Hubmann 508 © James Quine / Alamy 509c © Philip Scalia / Alamy 510 Jill Travis 511r Dan Freund 512 John Rae 513c Mo Elnadi 513b Hassan El Ghayesh/Flickr 514 Rodrigo García/Flickr 515t © STRINGER/Reuters/Corbis 515b © Stefano Paterna Photography / Alamy 516t Emiliano Homrich 516b Architecture: studio mk27 - marcio kogan + carolina castroviejo, Photographs nelson kon 517 EditorUOC/Wikimedia Commons/CC-BY-3.0 518 Chaloos 519br REX/OKSANEN 520 ©2001 Russ Widstrand - Portland, OR 521tr Frank Lloyd Wright 522 © Markus Bassler /Arcaid 523 Darko Glazer 524 NOX/Lars Spuybroek 525t Cloud 9 Architecture 525b © Ralph Feiner 526 © Satoru Mishima and courtesy of Farshid Moussavi Architecture 527tr © VIEW Pictures Ltd / Alamy 527br © Ben Pipe/Robert Harding World Imagery/Corbis 528 © Iwan Baan 529c © Iwan Baan 530 OZinOH 531 © PHOTOBYTE / Alamy 532t Studio Daniel Libeskind (Architecture New Building); Guenter Schneider (photography)/Wikimedia Commons/ CC-BY-3.0 532b © Kenneth Johansson/Corbis 533 Eric Owen Moss Architects 534 © Universal Images Group / DeAgostini / Alamy 536 Hiromitsu Morimoto 537 © T. R. Hamzah & Yeang Sdn. Bhd. (2013) 538 © Alexandre Tabaste / Artedia / VIEW 540 Stefano Boeri Architetti 541c Barcroft Media via Getty Images 541b © Axel Schmies/NA/Novarc/Corbis 542 © Tim Griffith/arcaid/Arcaid 543 © FORRAY Didier/SAGAPHOTO.COM / Alamy 544 © HO/Reuters/Corbis 545cr Wurzelgnohm/Wikimedia Commons/CC-Zero 545br © VIEW Pictures Ltd / Alamy 546 Paul Daniels/ Shutterstock 547br Tim E White 548 Studio Utimpergher 549 © Richard Brine/VIEW/Corbis 550 Scott Schultz 551t Daria Scagliola 551b David R. Ross 552 Erblin Bucaliu 553br Diana Höhlig

Quintessence would like to thank Caroline Eley for the index and Helen Jones for the illustrations.